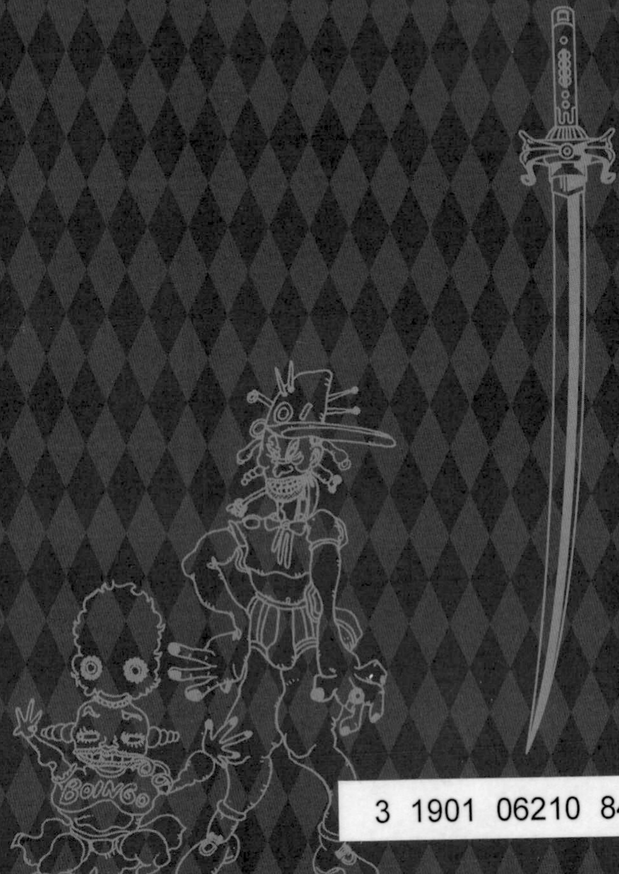
BOINGO

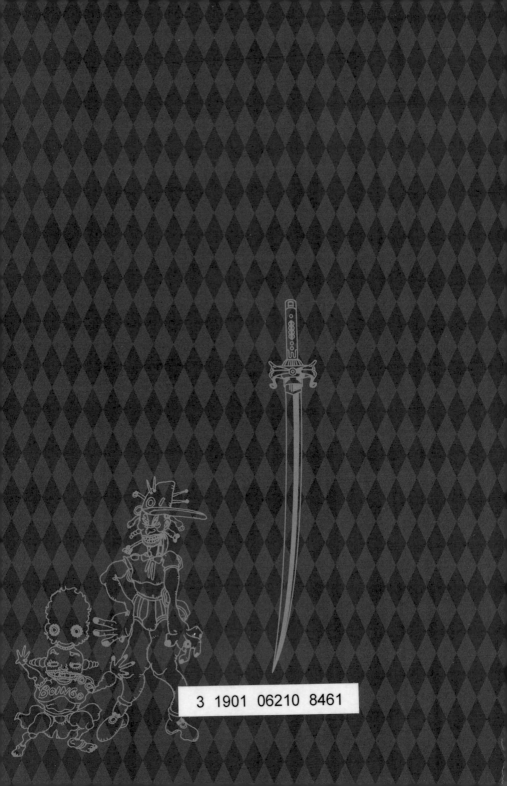

06

JoJo's
BIZARRE ADVENTURE

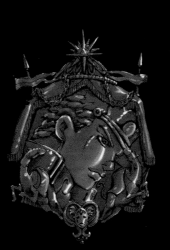

PART 3
STARDUST CRUSADERS

HIROHIKO ARAKI

JoJo's BIZARRE ADVENTURE
PART 3 STARDUST CRUSADERS

06

CONTENTS

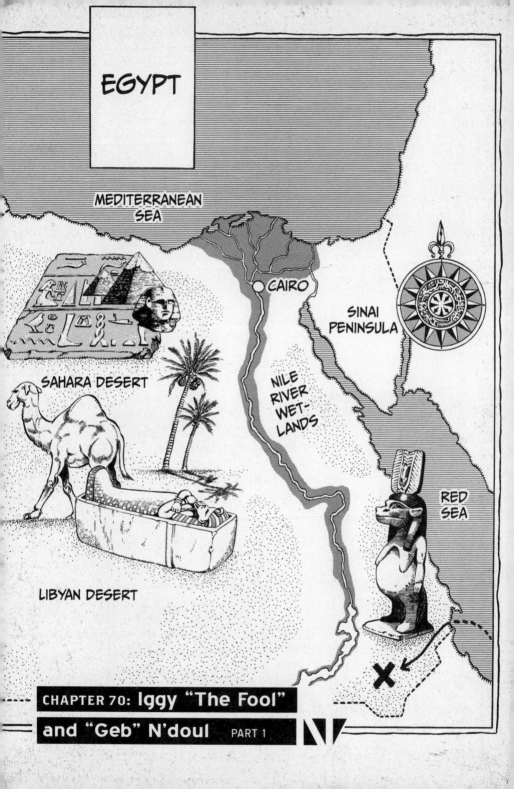

EGYPT

MEDITERRANEAN
SEA

CAIRO

SINAI
PENINSULA

SAHARA DESERT

NILE
RIVER
WET-
LANDS

RED
SEA

LIBYAN DESERT

**CHAPTER 70: Iggy "The Fool"
and "Geb" N'doul** PART 1

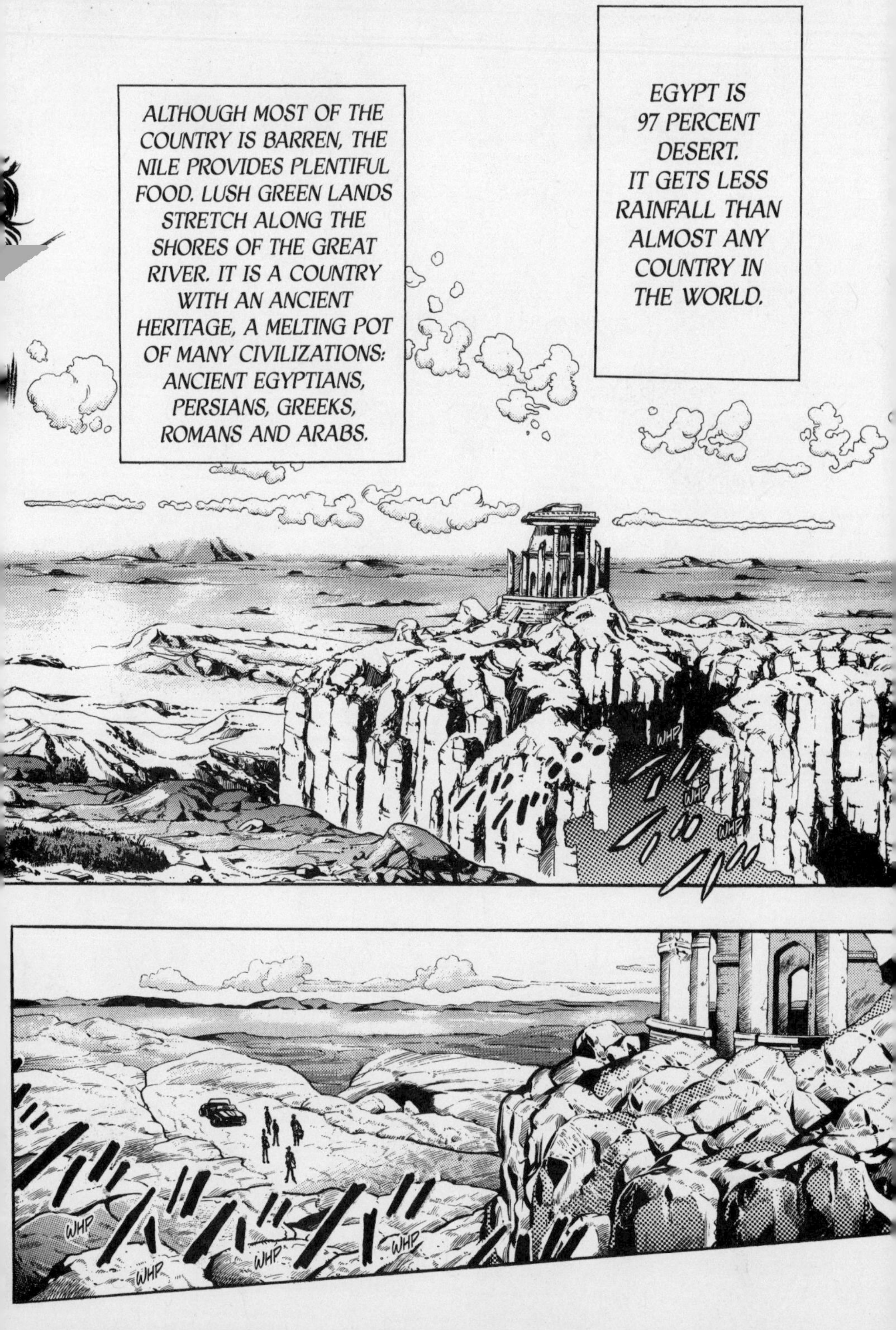
EGYPT IS 97 PERCENT DESERT. IT GETS LESS RAINFALL THAN ALMOST ANY COUNTRY IN THE WORLD.
ALTHOUGH MOST OF THE COUNTRY IS BARREN, THE NILE PROVIDES PLENTIFUL FOOD. LUSH GREEN LANDS STRETCH ALONG THE SHORES OF THE GREAT RIVER. IT IS A COUNTRY WITH AN ANCIENT HERITAGE, A MELTING POT OF MANY CIVILIZATIONS: ANCIENT EGYPTIANS, PERSIANS, GREEKS, ROMANS AND ARABS.
WHP
WHP
WHP
WHP
WHP
WHP
WHP

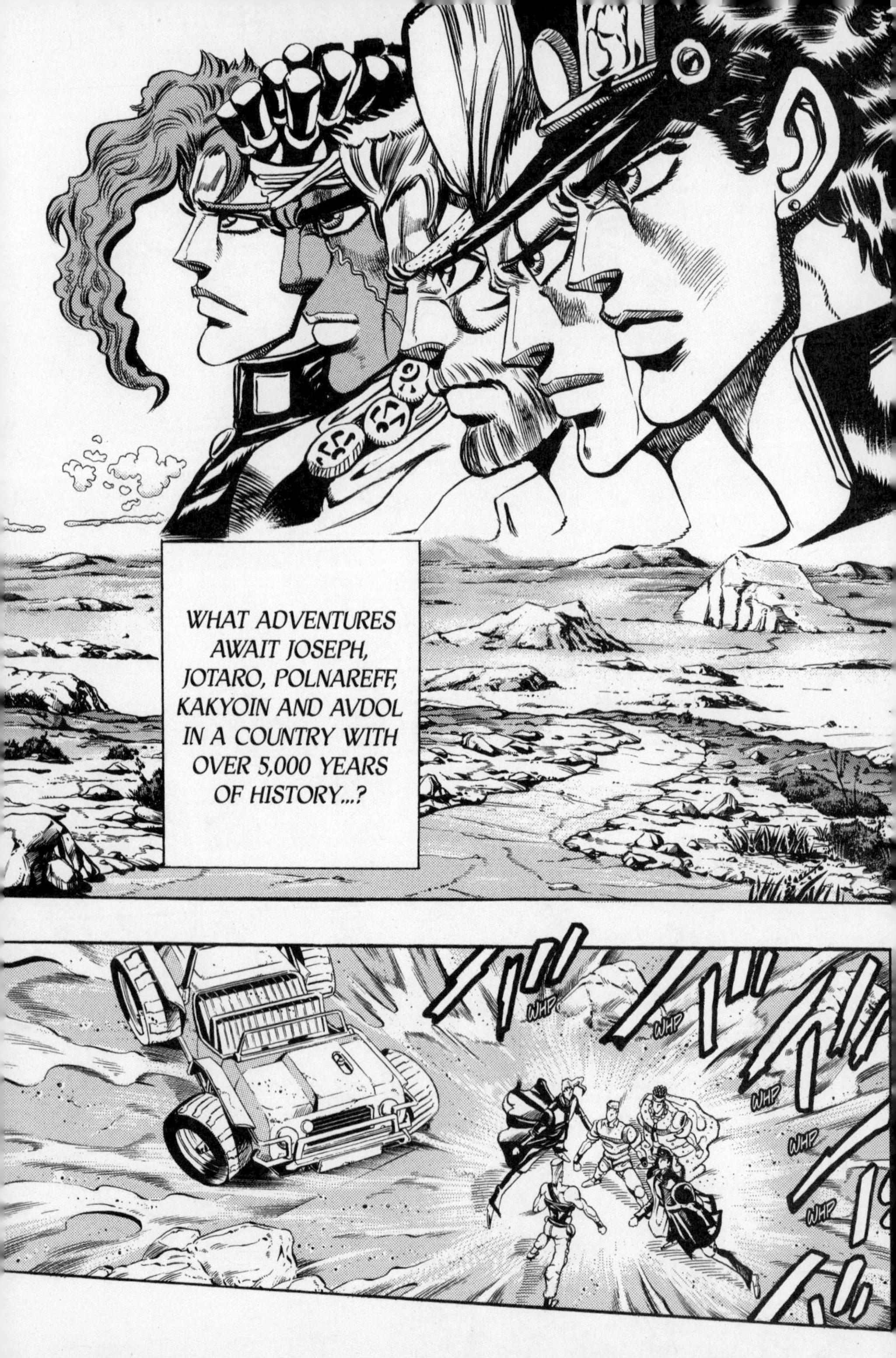
WHAT ADVENTURES AWAIT JOSEPH, JOTARO, POLNAREFF, KAKYOIN AND AVDOL IN A COUNTRY WITH OVER 5,000 YEARS OF HISTORY...?
WHP
WHP
WHP
WHP
WHP

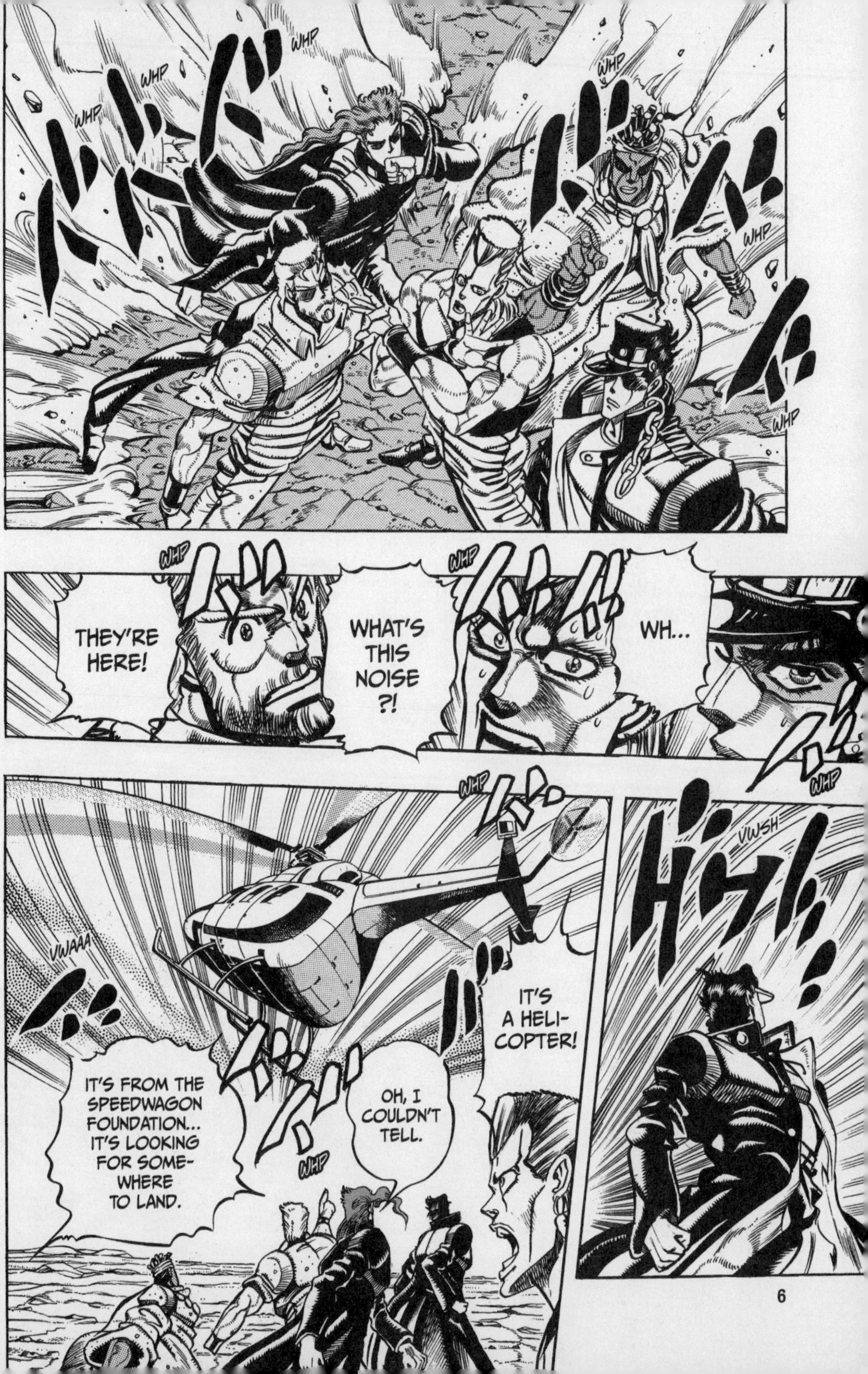
WHP
WHP
WHP
WHP
WHP
WHP
WH...
WHP
WHAT'S THIS NOISE?!
WHP
THEY'RE HERE!
WHP
VWSH
WHP
IT'S A HELI-COPTER!
VWAAA
OH, I COULDN'T TELL.
IT'S FROM THE SPEEDWAGON FOUNDATION... IT'S LOOKING FOR SOME-WHERE TO LAND.
WHP

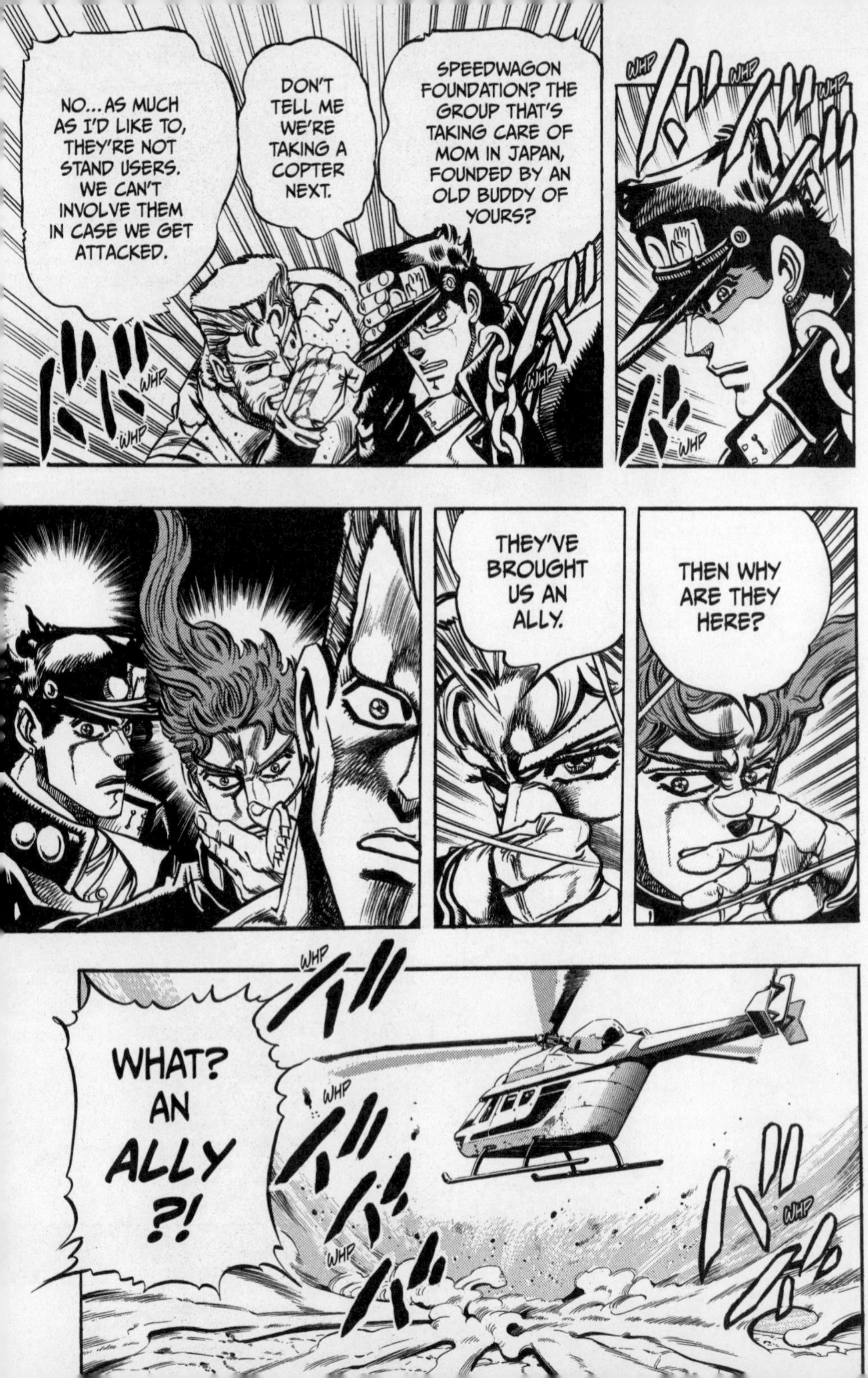
WHP
WHP
WHP
WHP
SPEEDWAGON FOUNDATION? THE GROUP THAT'S TAKING CARE OF MOM IN JAPAN, FOUNDED BY AN OLD BUDDY OF YOURS?
DON'T TELL ME WE'RE TAKING A COPTER NEXT.
NO...AS MUCH AS I'D LIKE TO, THEY'RE NOT STAND USERS. WE CAN'T INVOLVE THEM IN CASE WE GET ATTACKED.
WHP
WHP
WHP
THEN WHY ARE THEY HERE?
THEY'VE BROUGHT US AN ALLY.
WHP
WHP
WHP
WHP
WHAT? AN ALLY?!

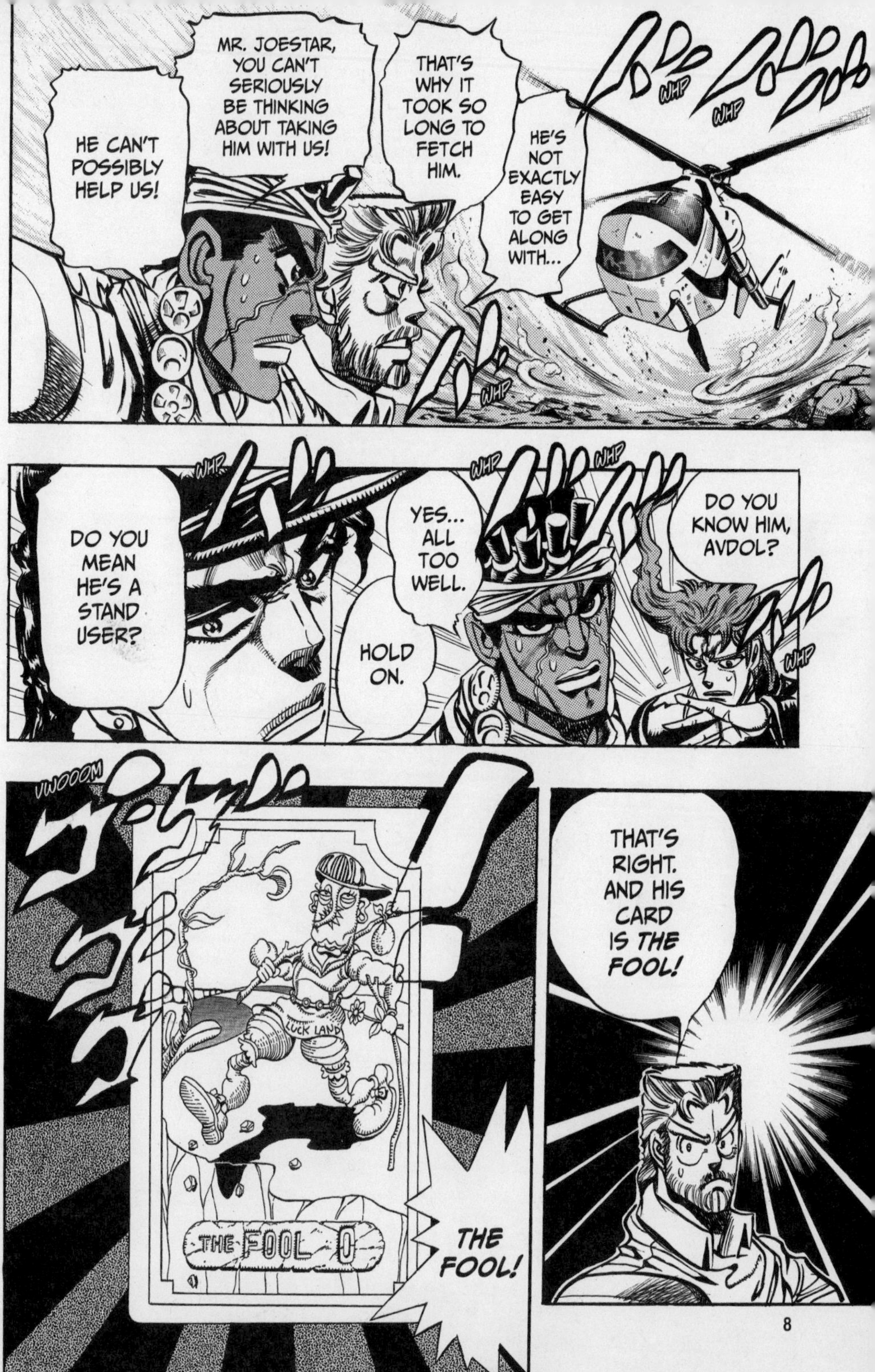
WHP
WHP
THAT'S WHY IT TOOK SO LONG TO FETCH HIM.
HE'S NOT EXACTLY EASY TO GET ALONG WITH...
MR. JOESTAR, YOU CAN'T SERIOUSLY BE THINKING ABOUT TAKING HIM WITH US!
HE CAN'T POSSIBLY HELP US!
WHP
WHP
DO YOU KNOW HIM, AVDOL?
WHP
WHP
YES... ALL TOO WELL.
HOLD ON.
WHP
DO YOU MEAN HE'S A STAND USER?
THAT'S RIGHT. AND HIS CARD IS THE FOOL!
VWOOOM
LUCK LAND
THE FOOL 0
THE FOOL!

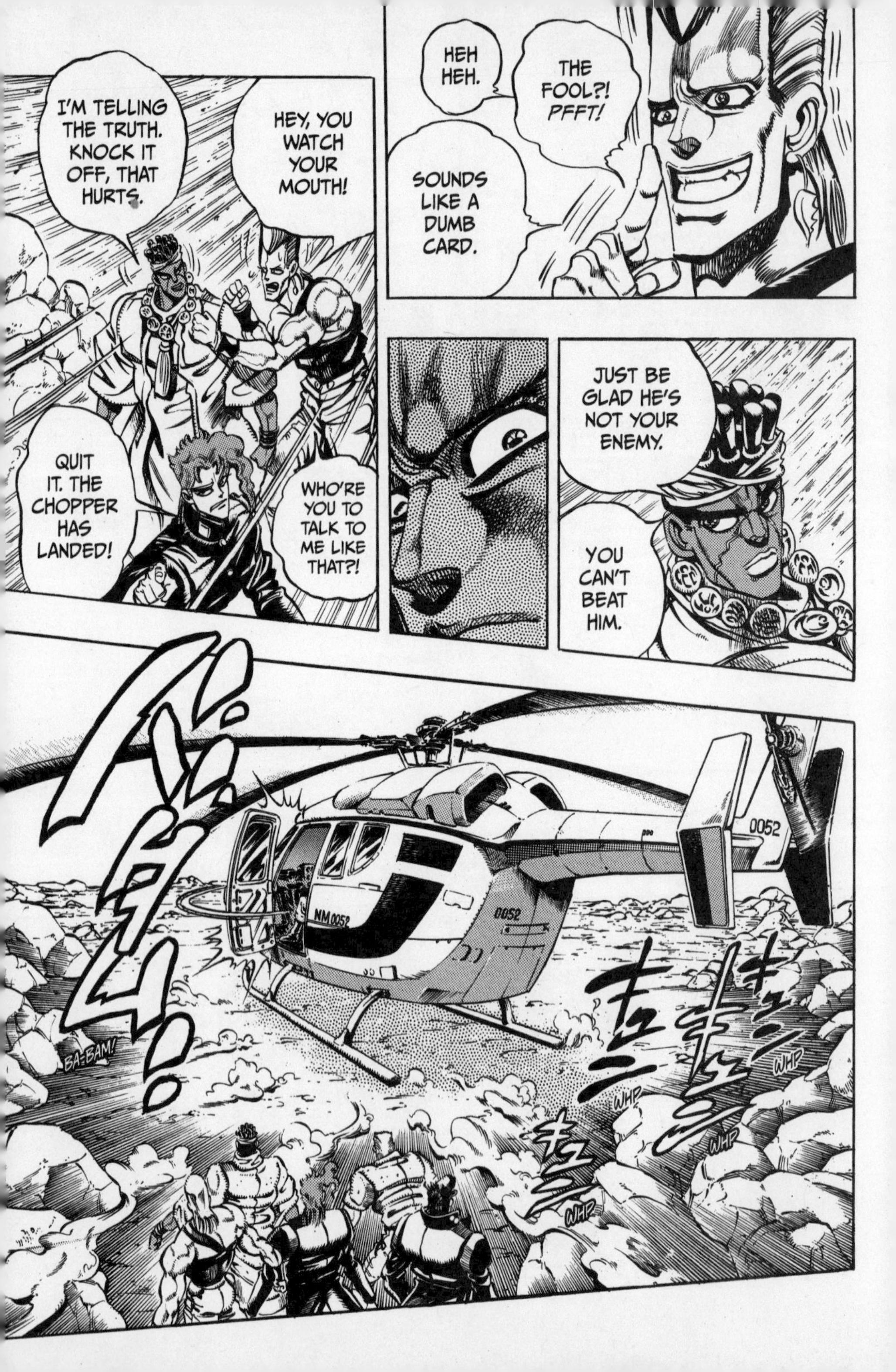

THE FOOL?! PFFT!
HEH HEH.
SOUNDS LIKE A DUMB CARD.
JUST BE GLAD HE'S NOT YOUR ENEMY.
YOU CAN'T BEAT HIM.
HEY, YOU WATCH YOUR MOUTH!
I'M TELLING THE TRUTH. KNOCK IT OFF, THAT HURTS.
WHO'RE YOU TO TALK TO ME LIKE THAT?!
QUIT IT. THE CHOPPER HAS LANDED!
0052
NM 0052
0052
WHP
WHP
WHP
WHP
BA-BAM!

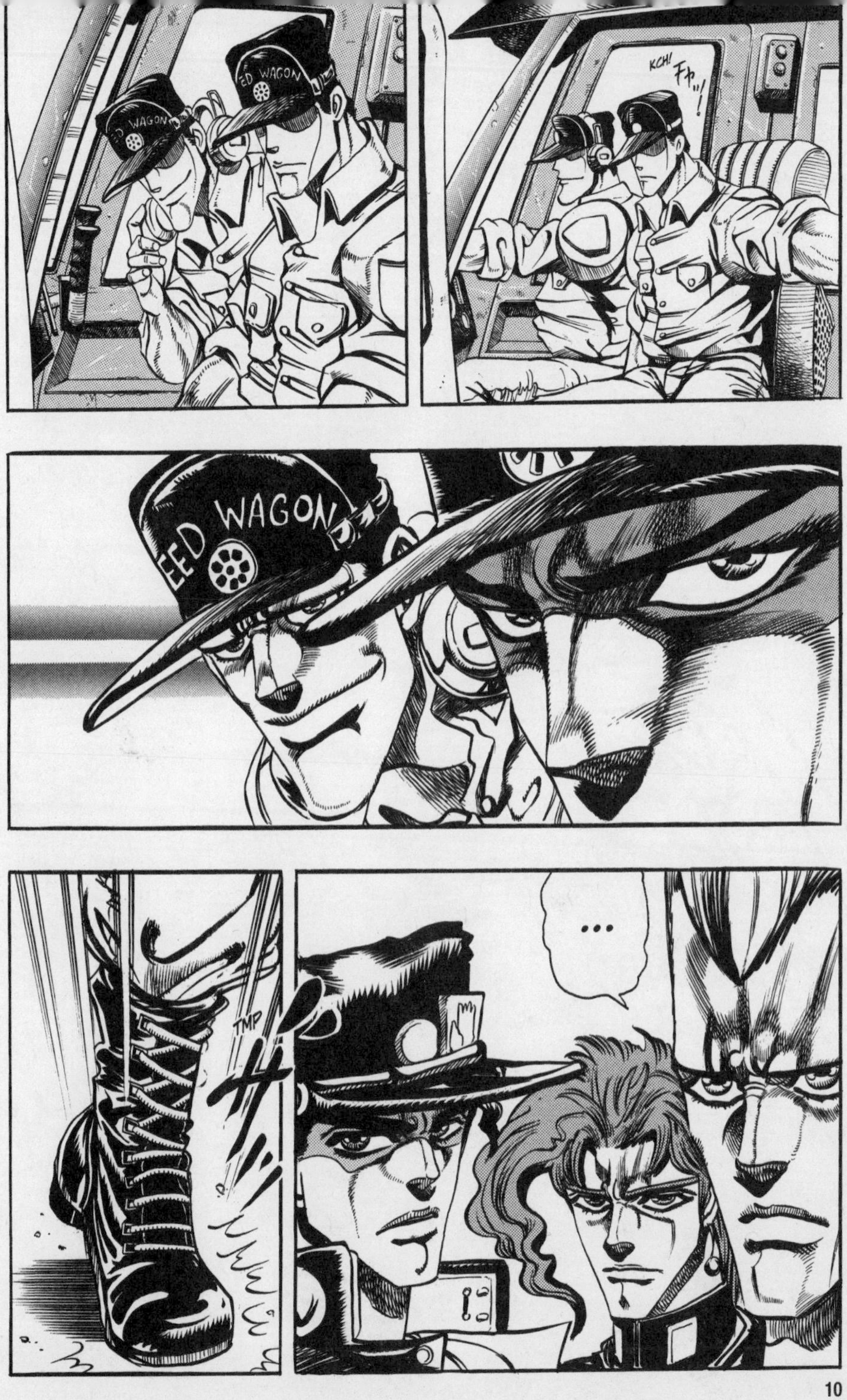
KCH!
チャッ!
...
TMP

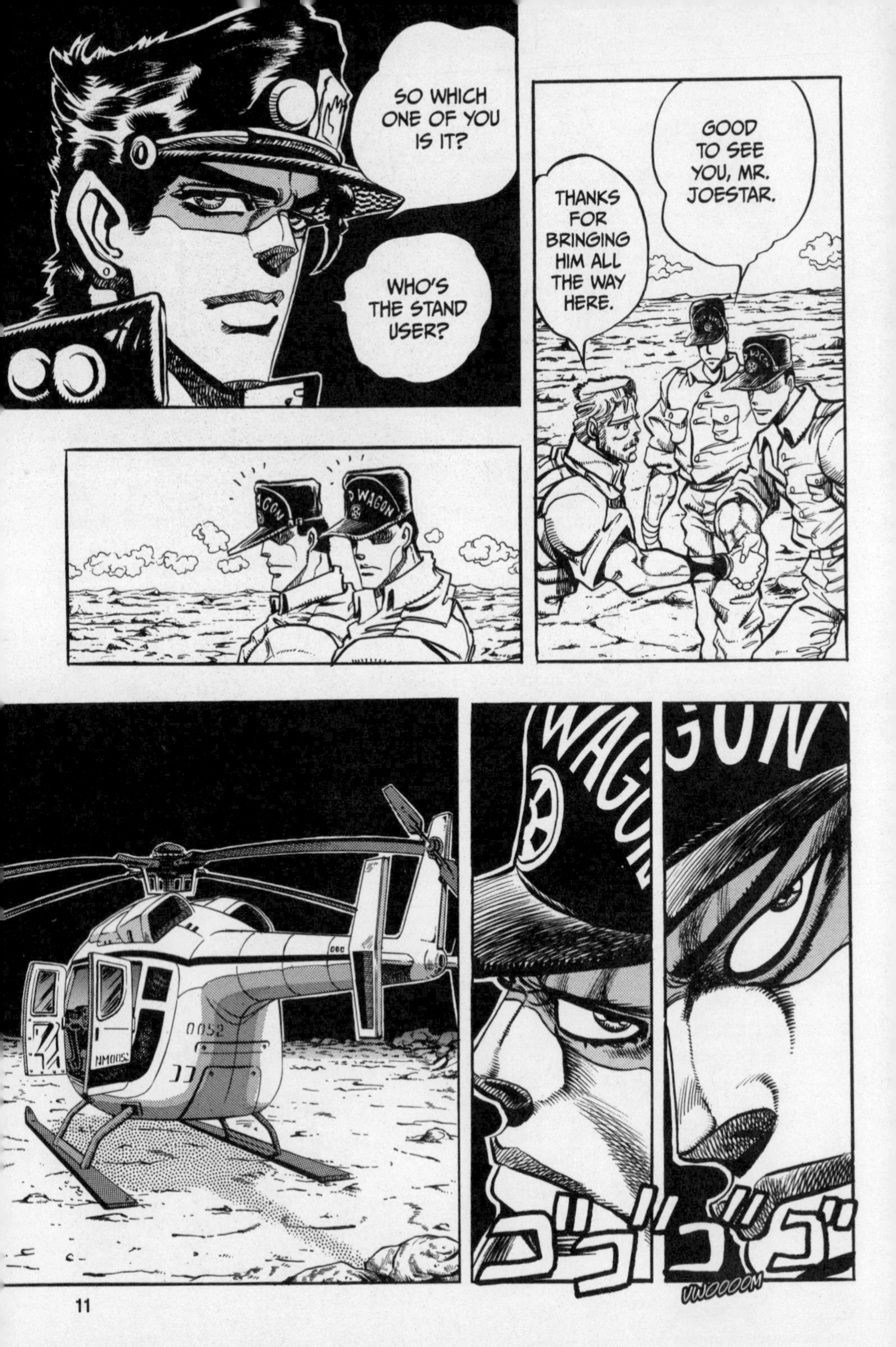
GOOD TO SEE YOU, MR. JOESTAR.
THANKS FOR BRINGING HIM ALL THE WAY HERE.
SO WHICH ONE OF YOU IS IT?
WHO'S THE STAND USER?
ゴゴゴゴ
VWOOOOM

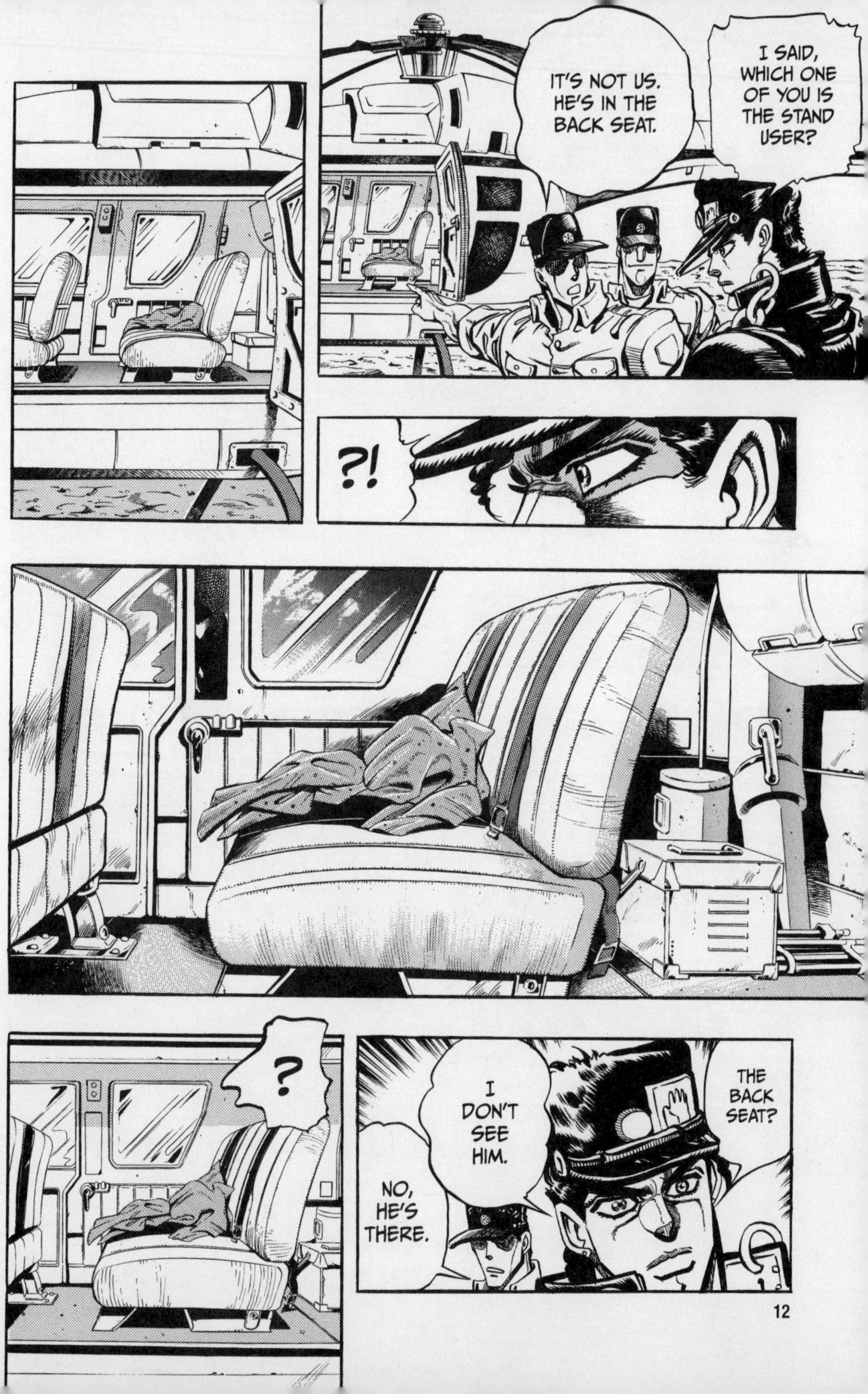
I SAID, WHICH ONE OF YOU IS THE STAND USER?
IT'S NOT US. HE'S IN THE BACK SEAT.
?!
THE BACK SEAT?
I DON'T SEE HIM.
NO, HE'S THERE.
?

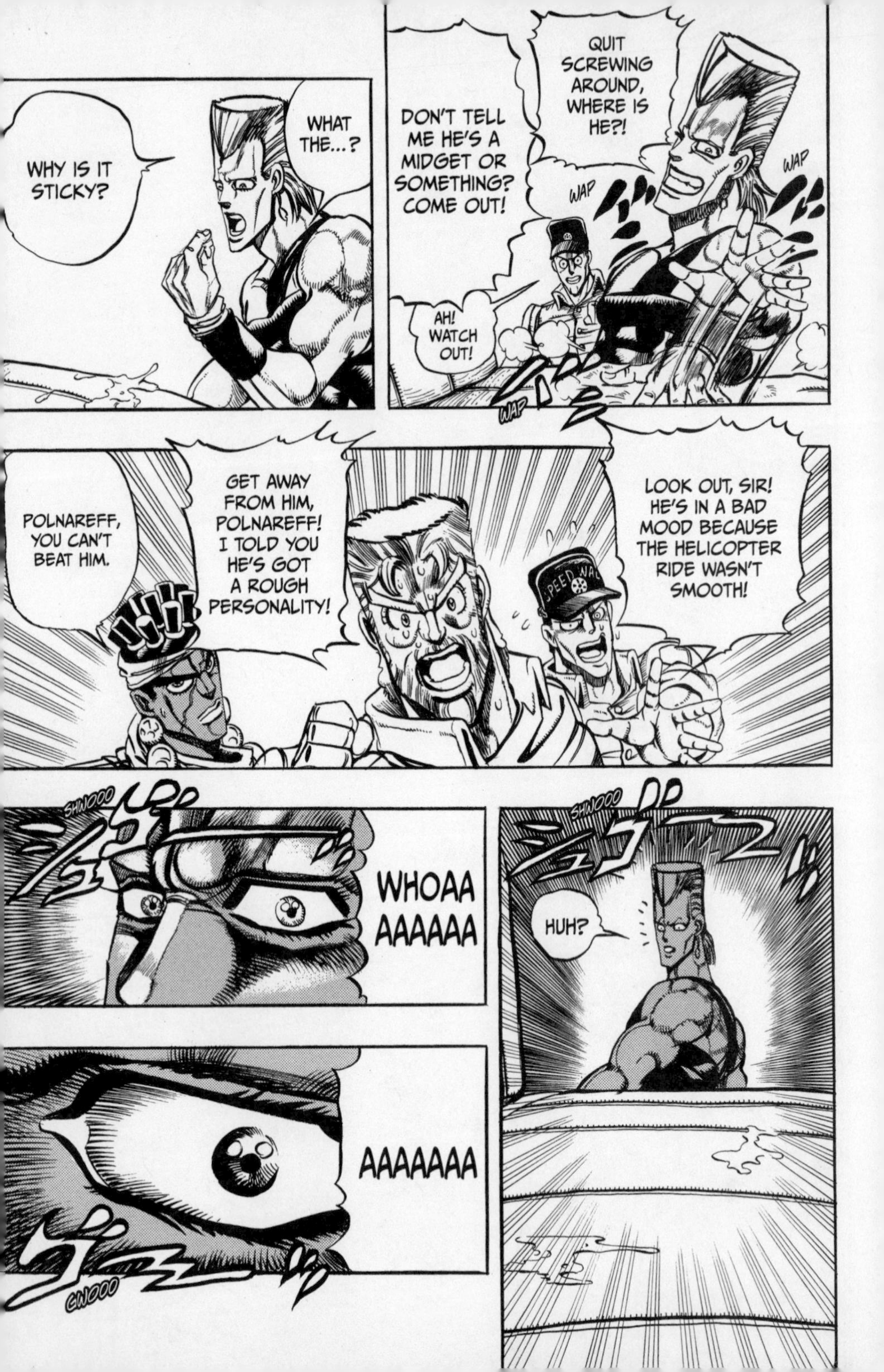
QUIT SCREWING AROUND, WHERE IS HE?!
DON'T TELL ME HE'S A MIDGET OR SOMETHING? COME OUT!
WAP
WAP
AH! WATCH OUT!
WAP
WHAT THE...?
WHY IS IT STICKY?
LOOK OUT, SIR! HE'S IN A BAD MOOD BECAUSE THE HELICOPTER RIDE WASN'T SMOOTH!
GET AWAY FROM HIM, POLNAREFF! I TOLD YOU HE'S GOT A ROUGH PERSONALITY!
POLNAREFF, YOU CAN'T BEAT HIM.
SHWOOO
HUH?
SHWOOO
WHOAA AAAAAA
AAAAAAA
GWOOO

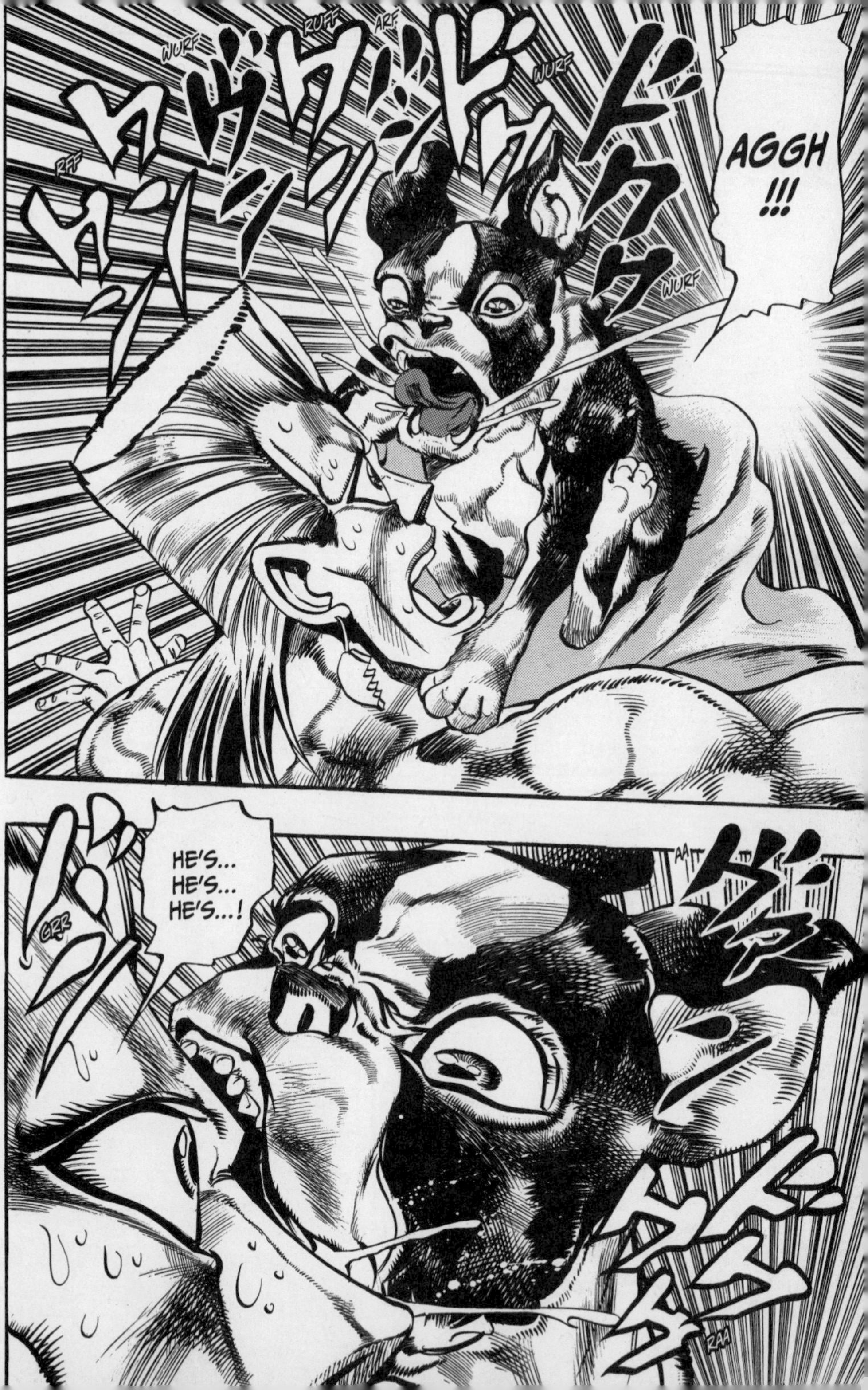
AGGH!!!
WURF
WURF
ARF
RUFF
WURF
RFF
AA
RAA
HE'S... HE'S... HE'S...!
GRR

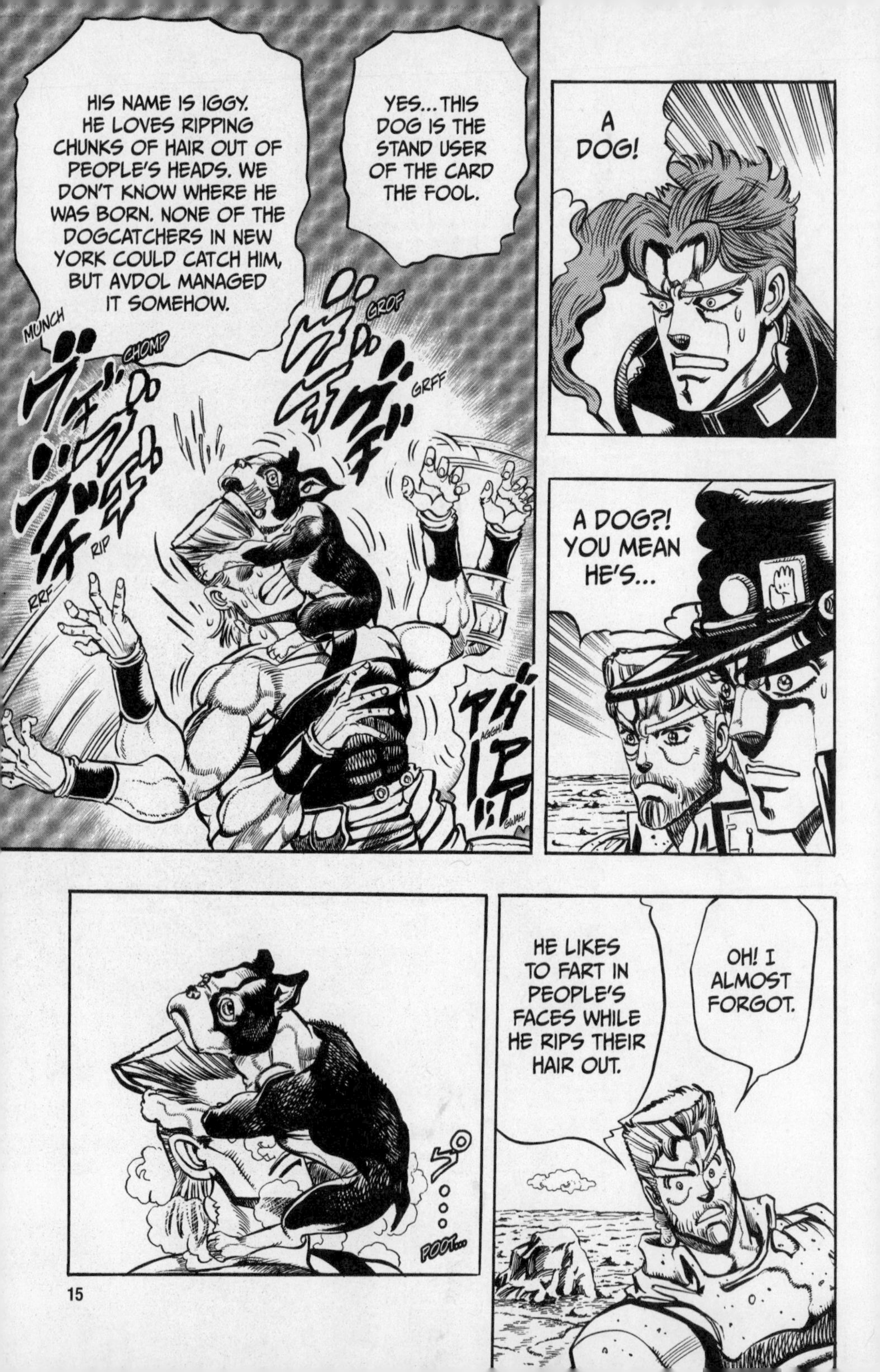
A DOG!
A DOG?! YOU MEAN HE'S...
YES...THIS DOG IS THE STAND USER OF THE CARD THE FOOL.
HIS NAME IS IGGY. HE LOVES RIPPING CHUNKS OF HAIR OUT OF PEOPLE'S HEADS. WE DON'T KNOW WHERE HE WAS BORN. NONE OF THE DOGCATCHERS IN NEW YORK COULD CATCH HIM, BUT AVDOL MANAGED IT SOMEHOW.
GROF
GRFF
MUNCH
CHOMP
RIP
RRF
AGGH!
GWAH!
OH! I ALMOST FORGOT.
HE LIKES TO FART IN PEOPLE'S FACES WHILE HE RIPS THEIR HAIR OUT.
POOT...

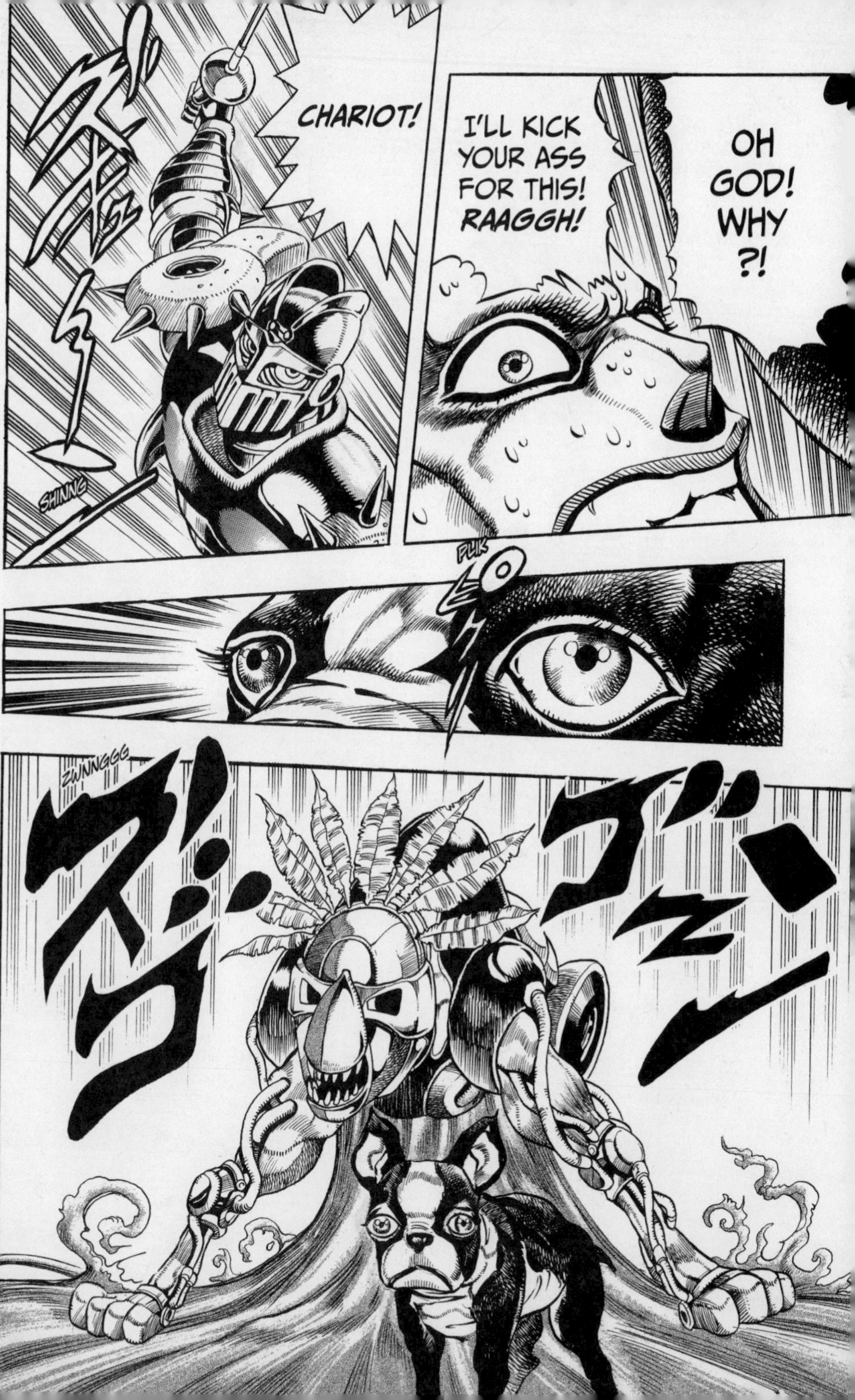
OH GOD! WHY ?!
I'LL KICK YOUR ASS FOR THIS! RAAGGH!
CHARIOT!
SHINNG
PUK
ZWNNGGG

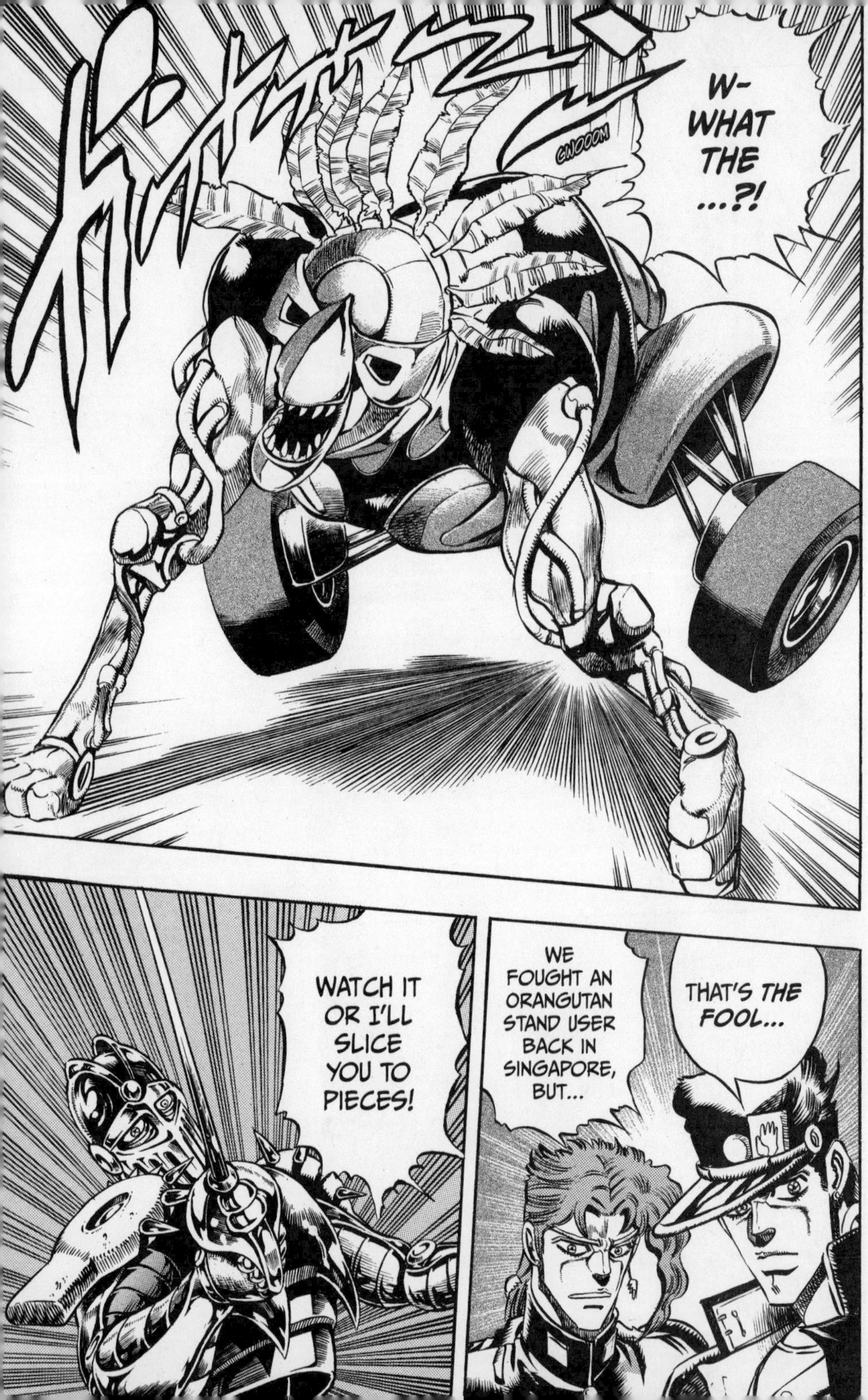
CWOOOM
W-WHAT THE ...?!
THAT'S THE FOOL...
WE FOUGHT AN ORANGUTAN STAND USER BACK IN SINGAPORE, BUT...
WATCH IT OR I'LL SLICE YOU TO PIECES!

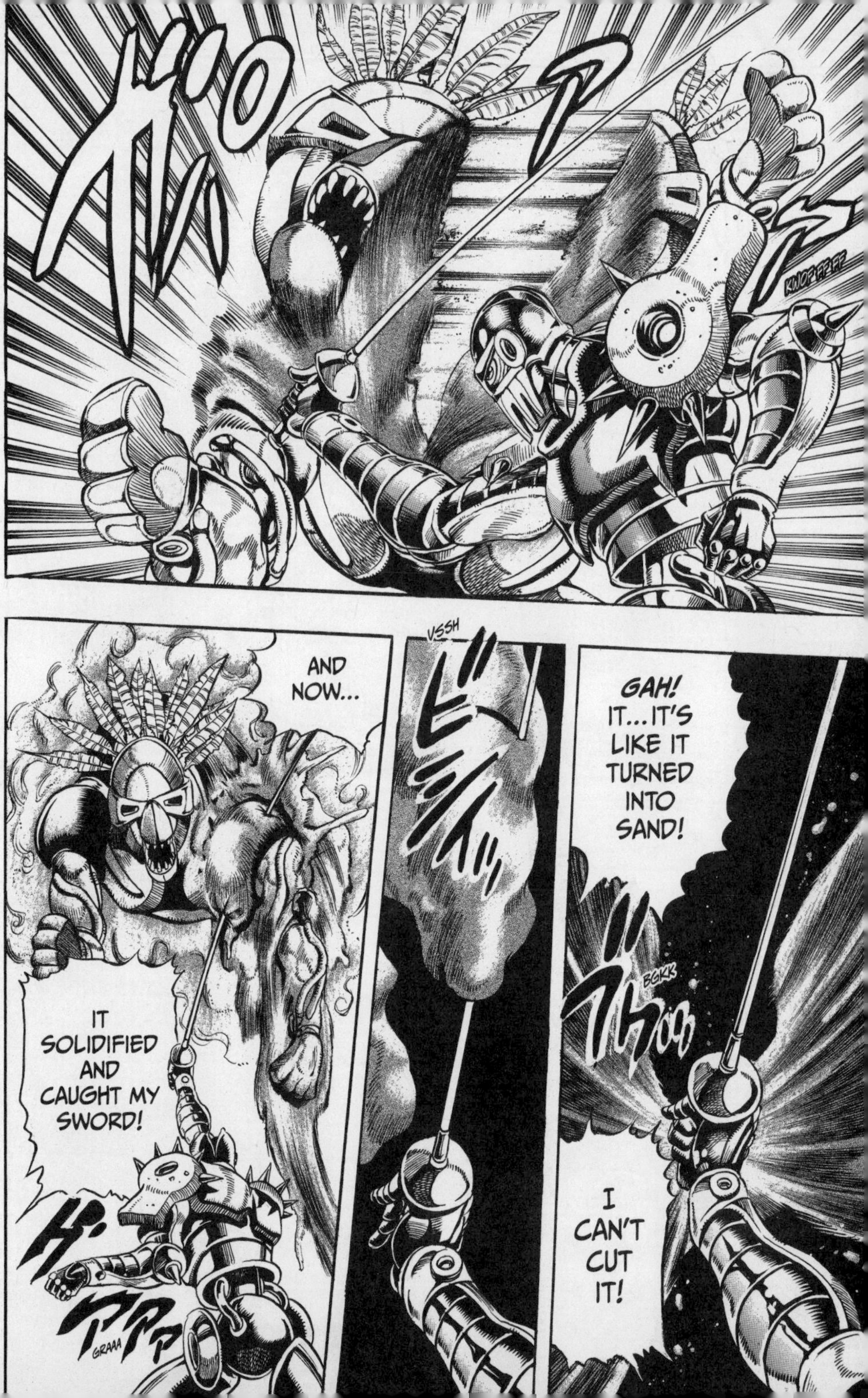
KWOOFFFFF
GAH! IT...IT'S LIKE IT TURNED INTO SAND!
BGKK
I CAN'T CUT IT!
VSSH
AND NOW...
IT SOLIDIFIED AND CAUGHT MY SWORD!
GRAAA

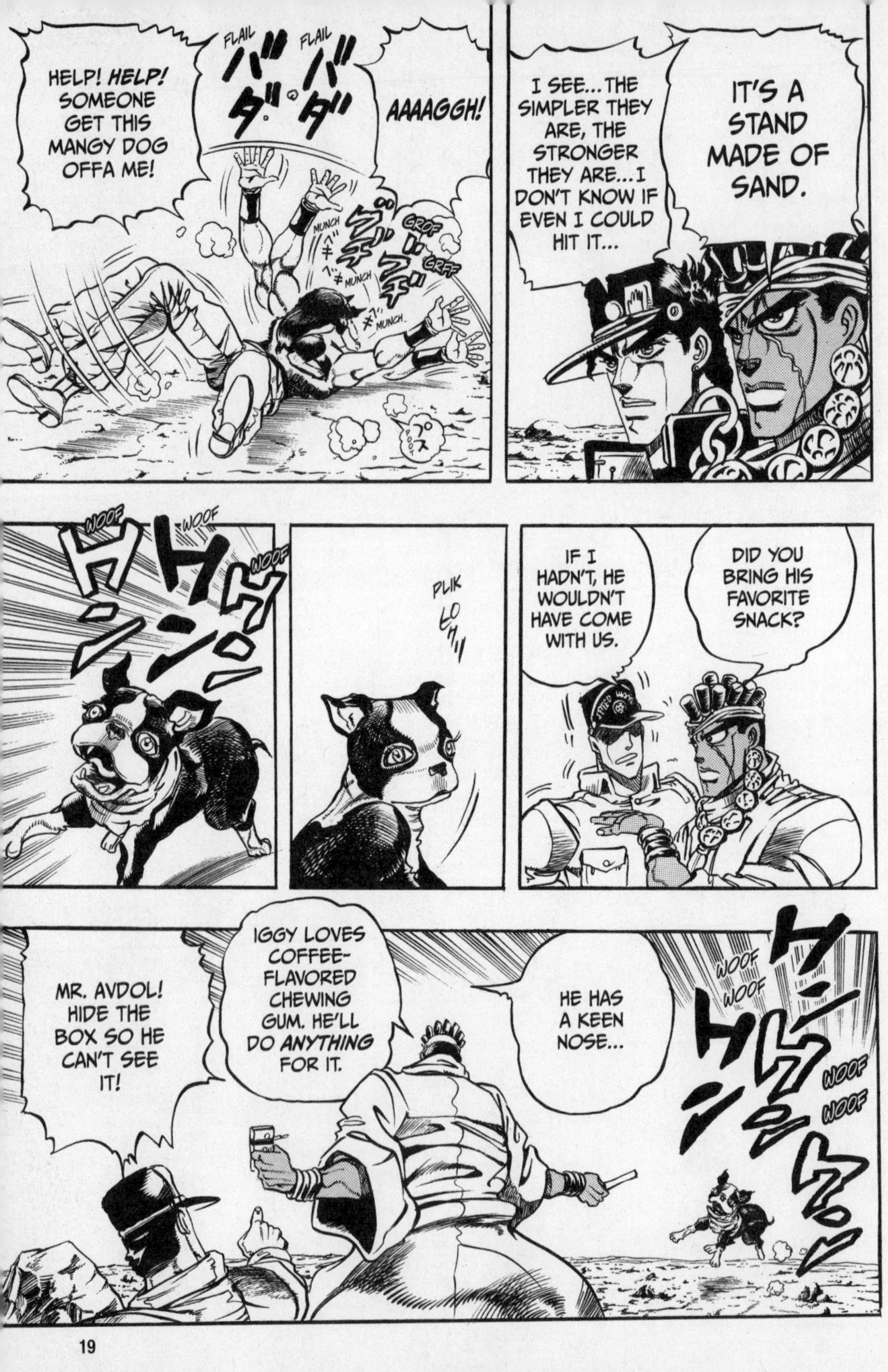
IT'S A STAND MADE OF SAND.
I SEE... THE SIMPLER THEY ARE, THE STRONGER THEY ARE... I DON'T KNOW IF EVEN I COULD HIT IT...
FLAIL
FLAIL
AAAAGH!
HELP! *HELP!* SOMEONE GET THIS MANGY DOG OFFA ME!
GROF
MUNCH
GRFF
MUNCH
MUNCH
DID YOU BRING HIS FAVORITE SNACK?
IF I HADN'T, HE WOULDN'T HAVE COME WITH US.
PLIK
WOOF
WOOF
WOOF
WOOF
WOOF
WOOF
WOOF
HE HAS A KEEN NOSE...
IGGY LOVES COFFEE-FLAVORED CHEWING GUM. HE'LL DO *ANYTHING* FOR IT.
MR. AVDOL! HIDE THE BOX SO HE CAN'T SEE IT!

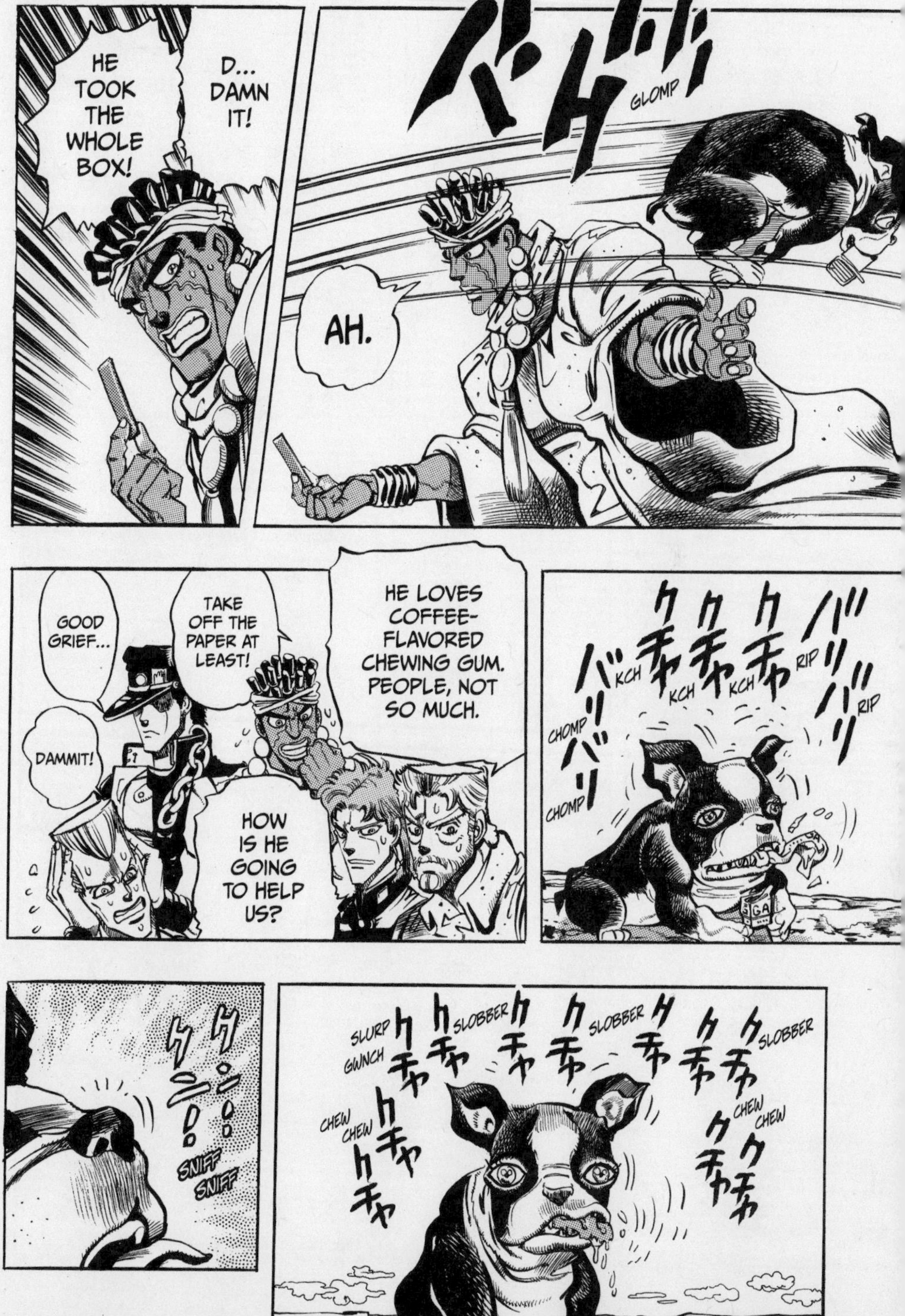
GLOMP
AH.
D... DAMN IT!
HE TOOK THE WHOLE BOX!
KCH KCH KCH
RIP RIP
CHOMP CHOMP
HE LOVES COFFEE-FLAVORED CHEWING GUM. PEOPLE, NOT SO MUCH.
TAKE OFF THE PAPER AT LEAST!
GOOD GRIEF...
DAMMIT!
HOW IS HE GOING TO HELP US?
SLOBBER
SLOBBER
SLOBBER
SLURP GWNCH
CHEW CHEW
CHEW CHEW
SNIFF SNIFF

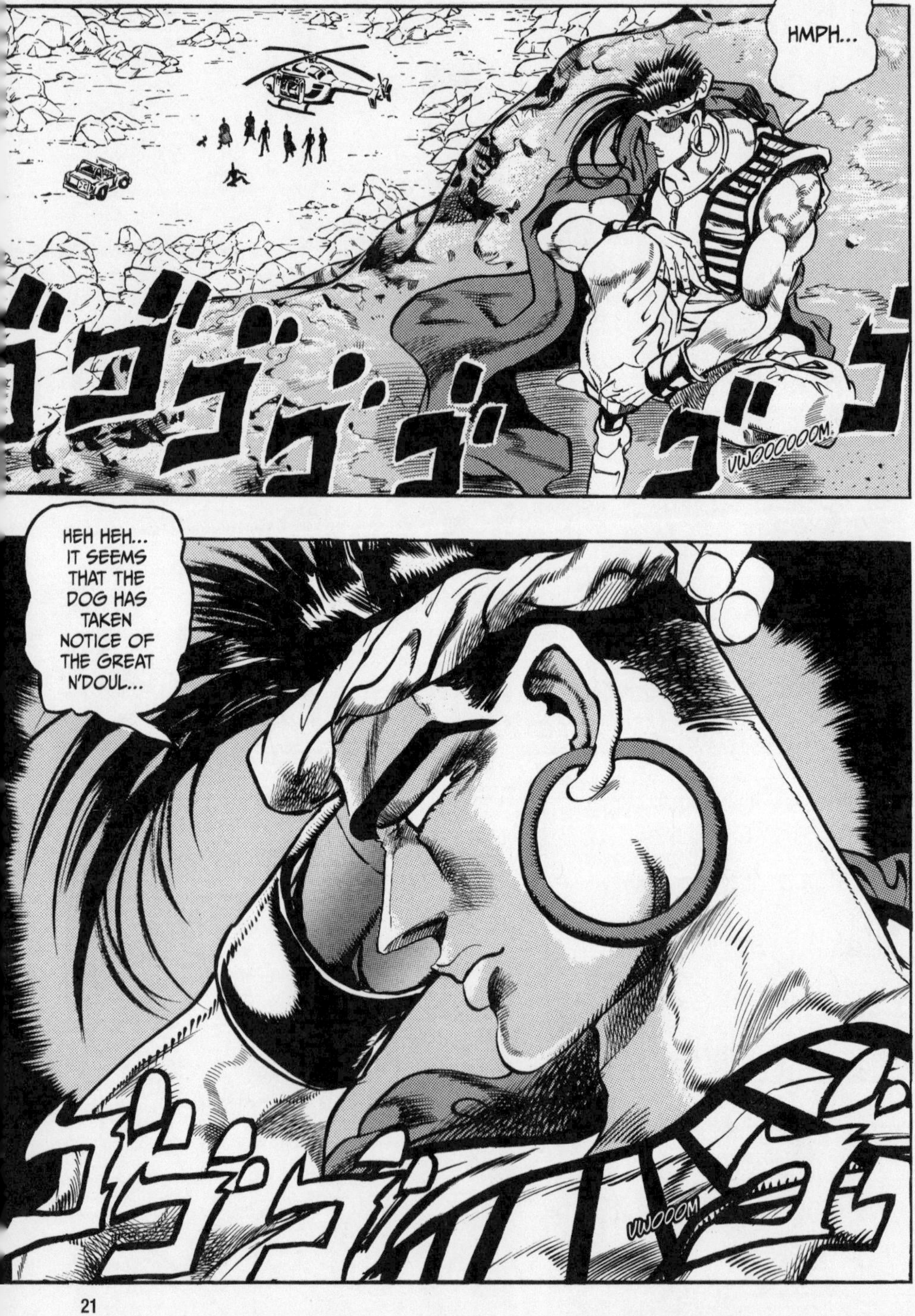
HMPH...
VWOOOOOOM
HEH HEH... IT SEEMS THAT THE DOG HAS TAKEN NOTICE OF THE GREAT N'DOUL...
VWOOOM

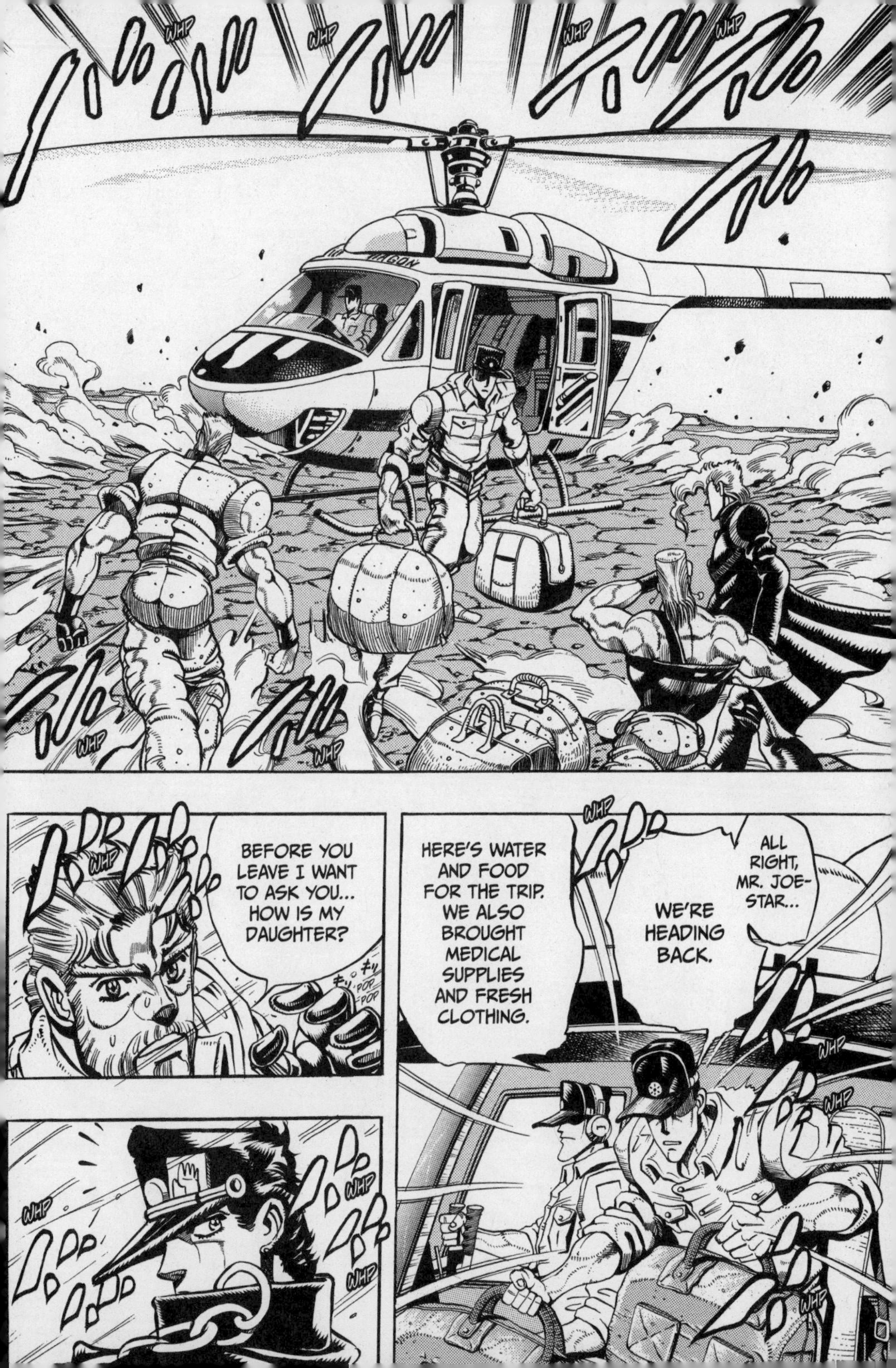

WHP
WHP
WHP
WHP
WHP
WHP
WHP
ALL RIGHT, MR. JOE-STAR...
WE'RE HEADING BACK.
HERE'S WATER AND FOOD FOR THE TRIP. WE ALSO BROUGHT MEDICAL SUPPLIES AND FRESH CLOTHING.
WHP
WHP
WHP
BEFORE YOU LEAVE I WANT TO ASK YOU... HOW IS MY DAUGHTER?
WHP
POP POP
WHP
WHP
WHP

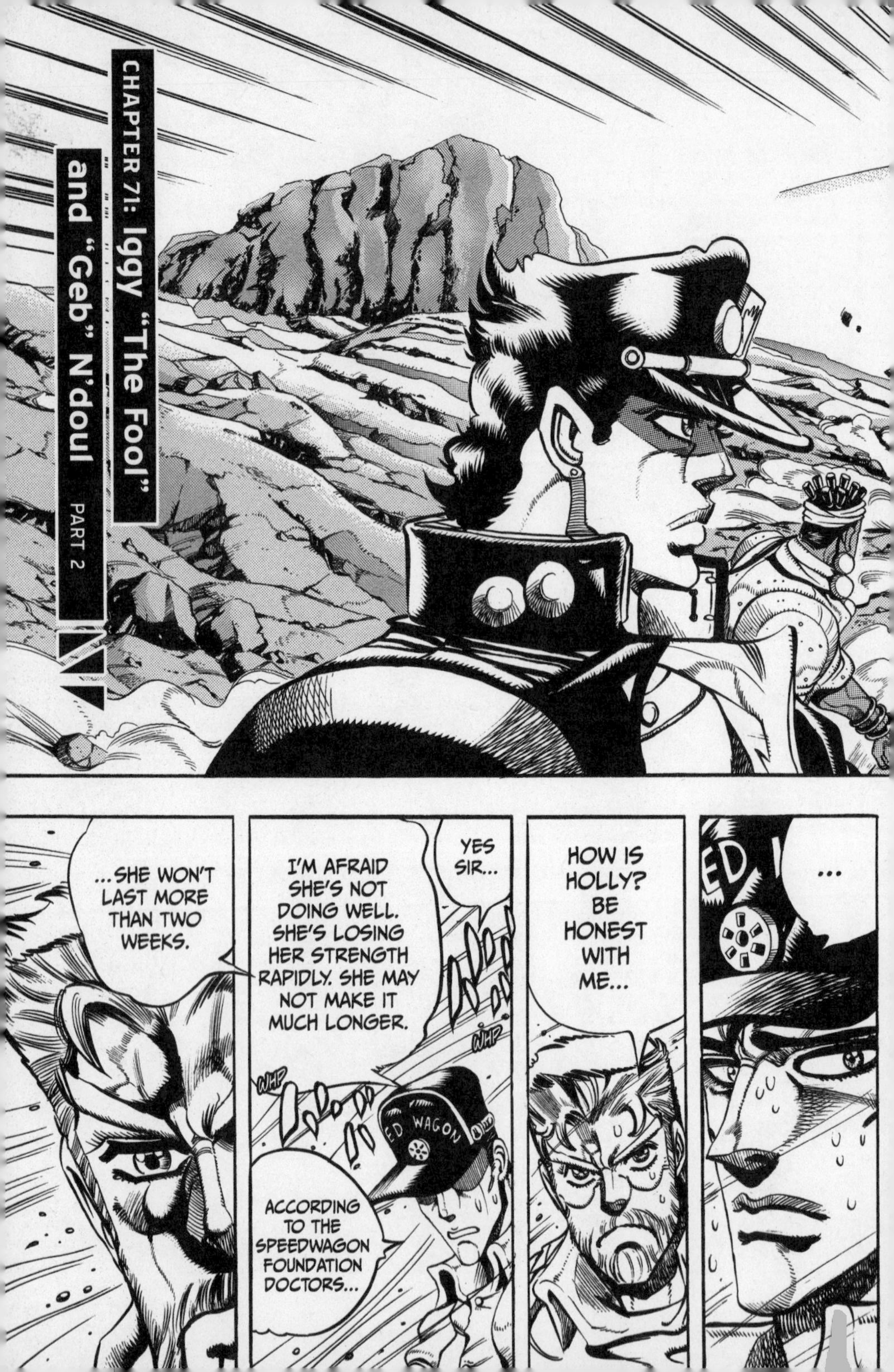
CHAPTER 71: Iggy "The Fool" and "Geb" N'doul PART 2
...
HOW IS HOLLY? BE HONEST WITH ME...
YES SIR...
I'M AFRAID SHE'S NOT DOING WELL. SHE'S LOSING HER STRENGTH RAPIDLY. SHE MAY NOT MAKE IT MUCH LONGER.
WHP
WHP
ED WAGON
ACCORDING TO THE SPEEDWAGON FOUNDATION DOCTORS...
...SHE WON'T LAST MORE THAN TWO WEEKS.

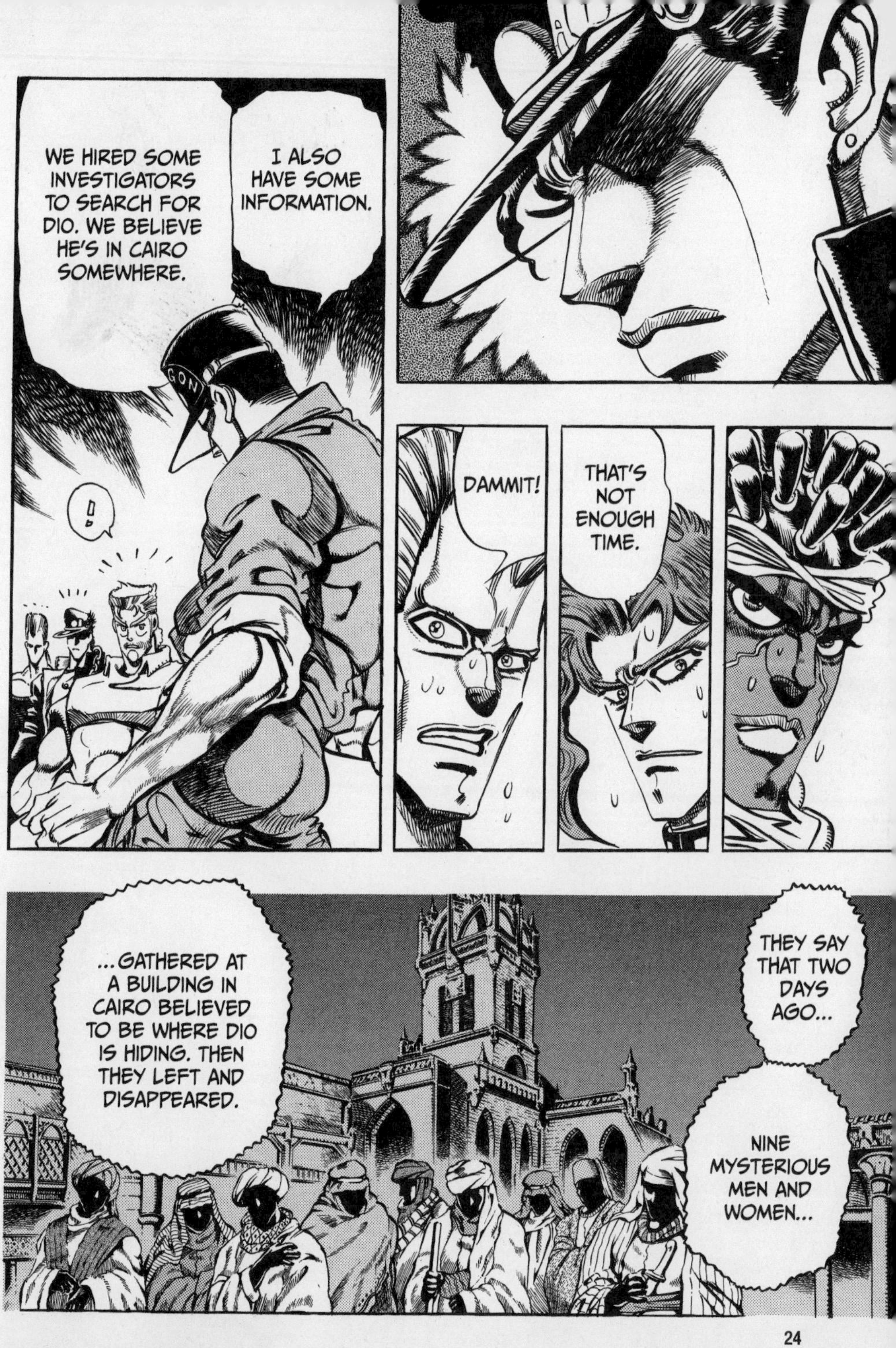
THAT'S NOT ENOUGH TIME.
DAMMIT!
I ALSO HAVE SOME INFORMATION.
WE HIRED SOME INVESTIGATORS TO SEARCH FOR DIO. WE BELIEVE HE'S IN CAIRO SOMEWHERE.
!
THEY SAY THAT TWO DAYS AGO...
NINE MYSTERIOUS MEN AND WOMEN...
...GATHERED AT A BUILDING IN CAIRO BELIEVED TO BE WHERE DIO IS HIDING. THEN THEY LEFT AND DISAPPEARED.

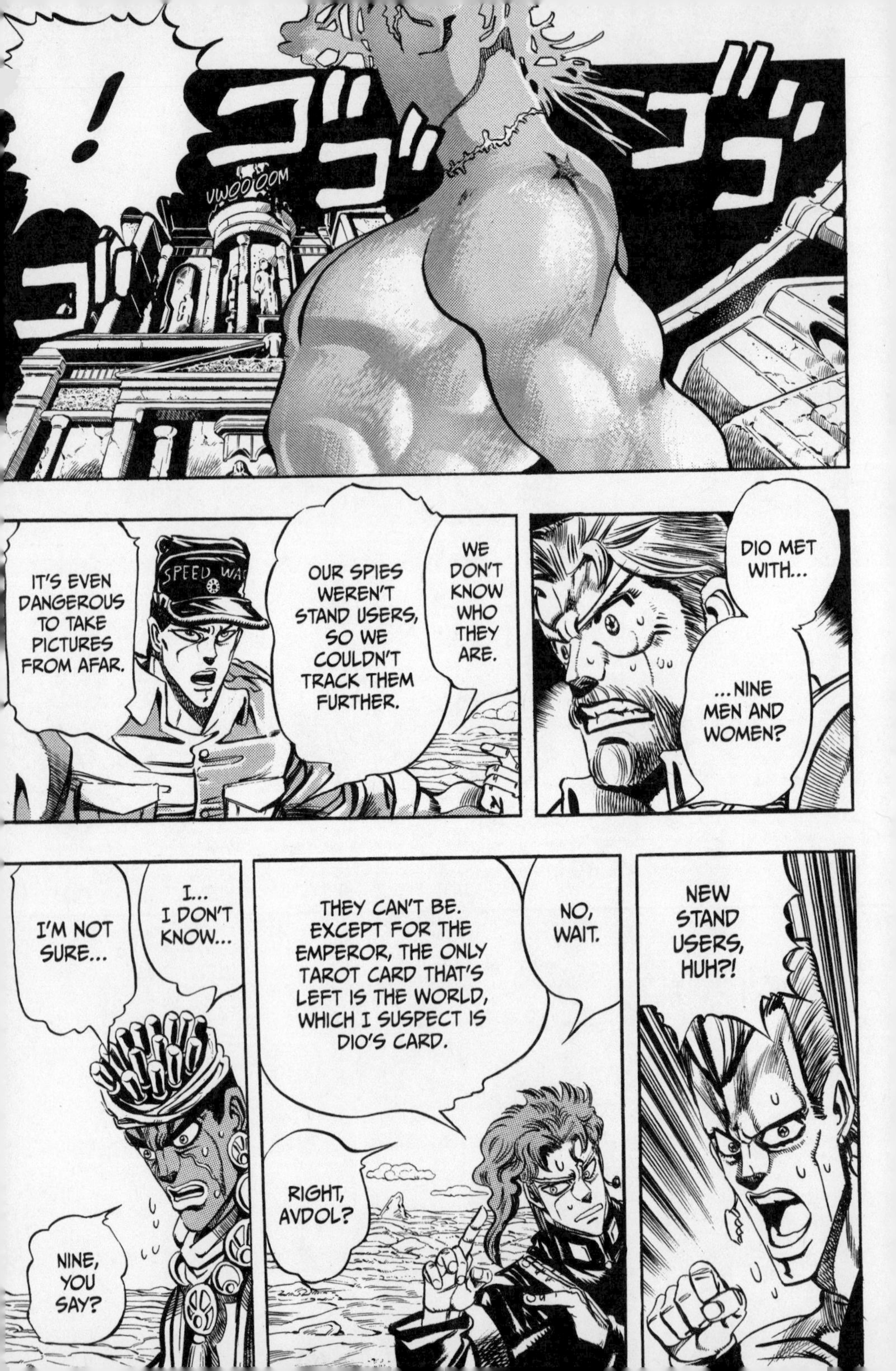

!
VWOOOOM
DIO MET WITH...
...NINE MEN AND WOMEN?
WE DON'T KNOW WHO THEY ARE.
OUR SPIES WEREN'T STAND USERS, SO WE COULDN'T TRACK THEM FURTHER.
IT'S EVEN DANGEROUS TO TAKE PICTURES FROM AFAR.
NEW STAND USERS, HUH?!
NO, WAIT.
THEY CAN'T BE. EXCEPT FOR THE EMPEROR, THE ONLY TAROT CARD THAT'S LEFT IS THE WORLD, WHICH I SUSPECT IS DIO'S CARD.
RIGHT, AVDOL?
I... I DON'T KNOW...
I'M NOT SURE...
NINE, YOU SAY?

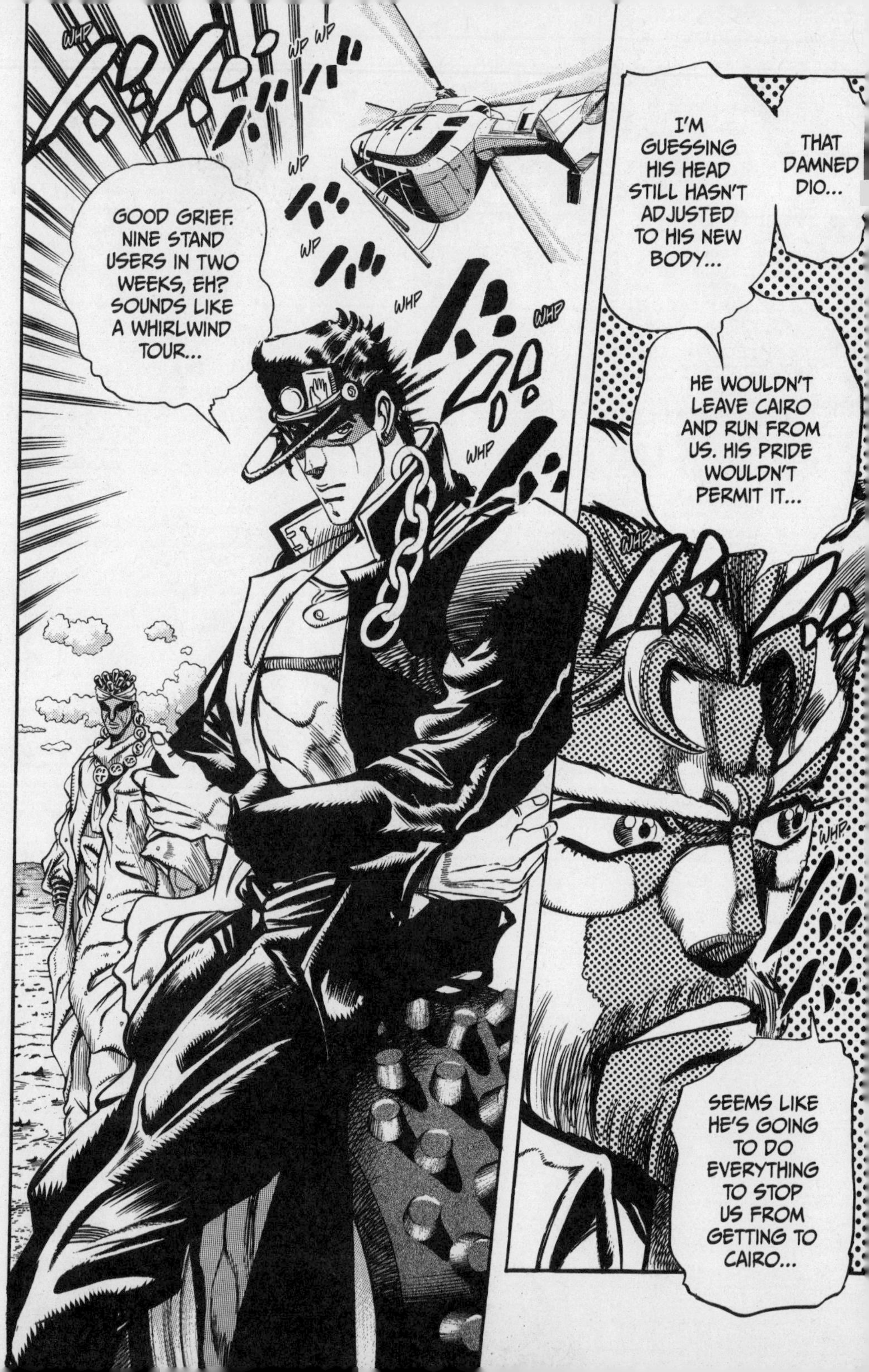
THAT DAMNED DIO...
I'M GUESSING HIS HEAD STILL HASN'T ADJUSTED TO HIS NEW BODY...
HE WOULDN'T LEAVE CAIRO AND RUN FROM US. HIS PRIDE WOULDN'T PERMIT IT...
WHP
WHP
SEEMS LIKE HE'S GOING TO DO EVERYTHING TO STOP US FROM GETTING TO CAIRO...
WP WP
WHP
WP
WP
WHP
WHP
GOOD GRIEF. NINE STAND USERS IN TWO WEEKS, EH? SOUNDS LIKE A WHIRLWIND TOUR...
WHP

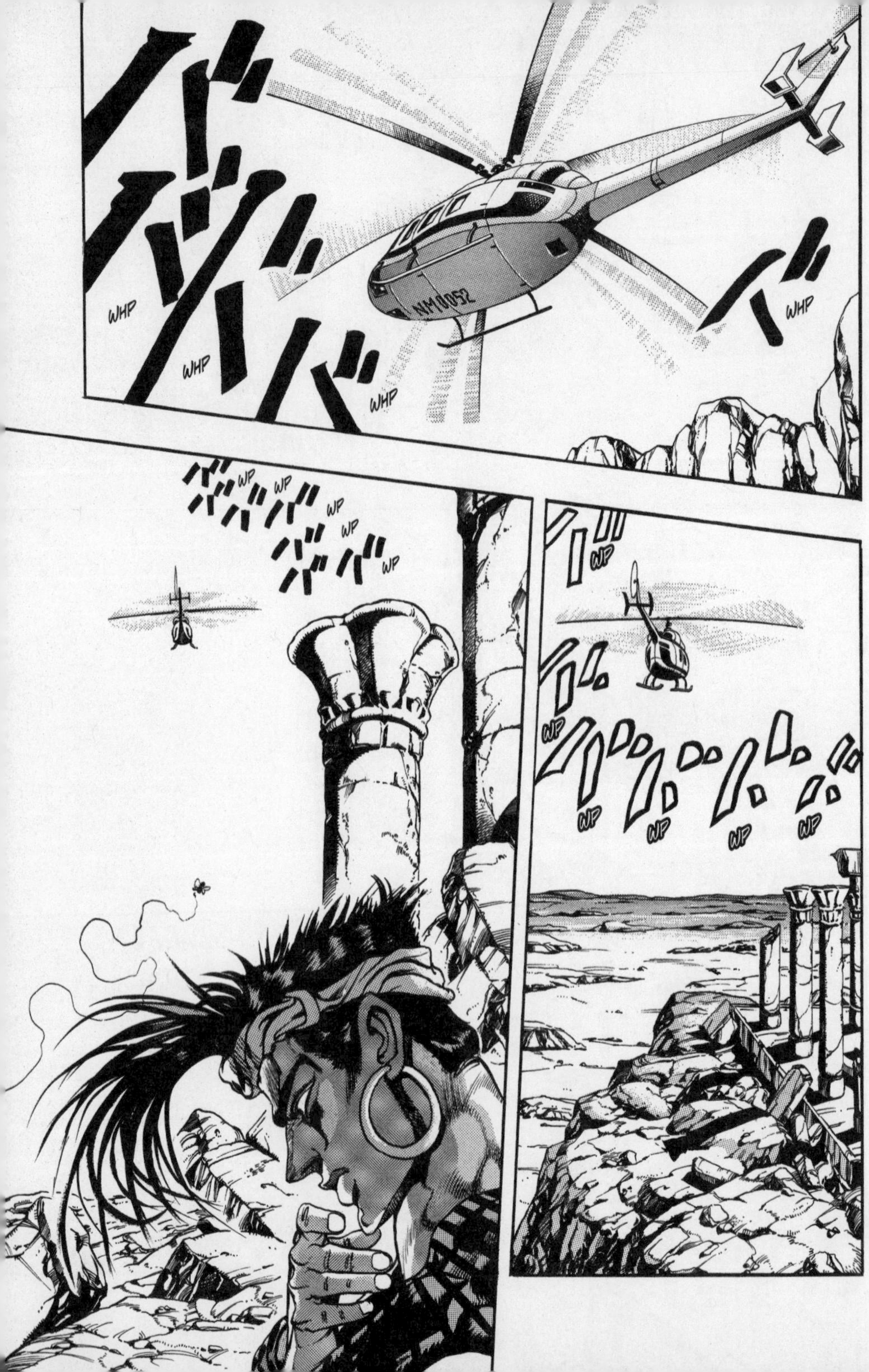
WHP
WHP
WHP
WHP
WP
WP
WP
WP
WP
WP
WP
WP
WP
WP
WP
WP

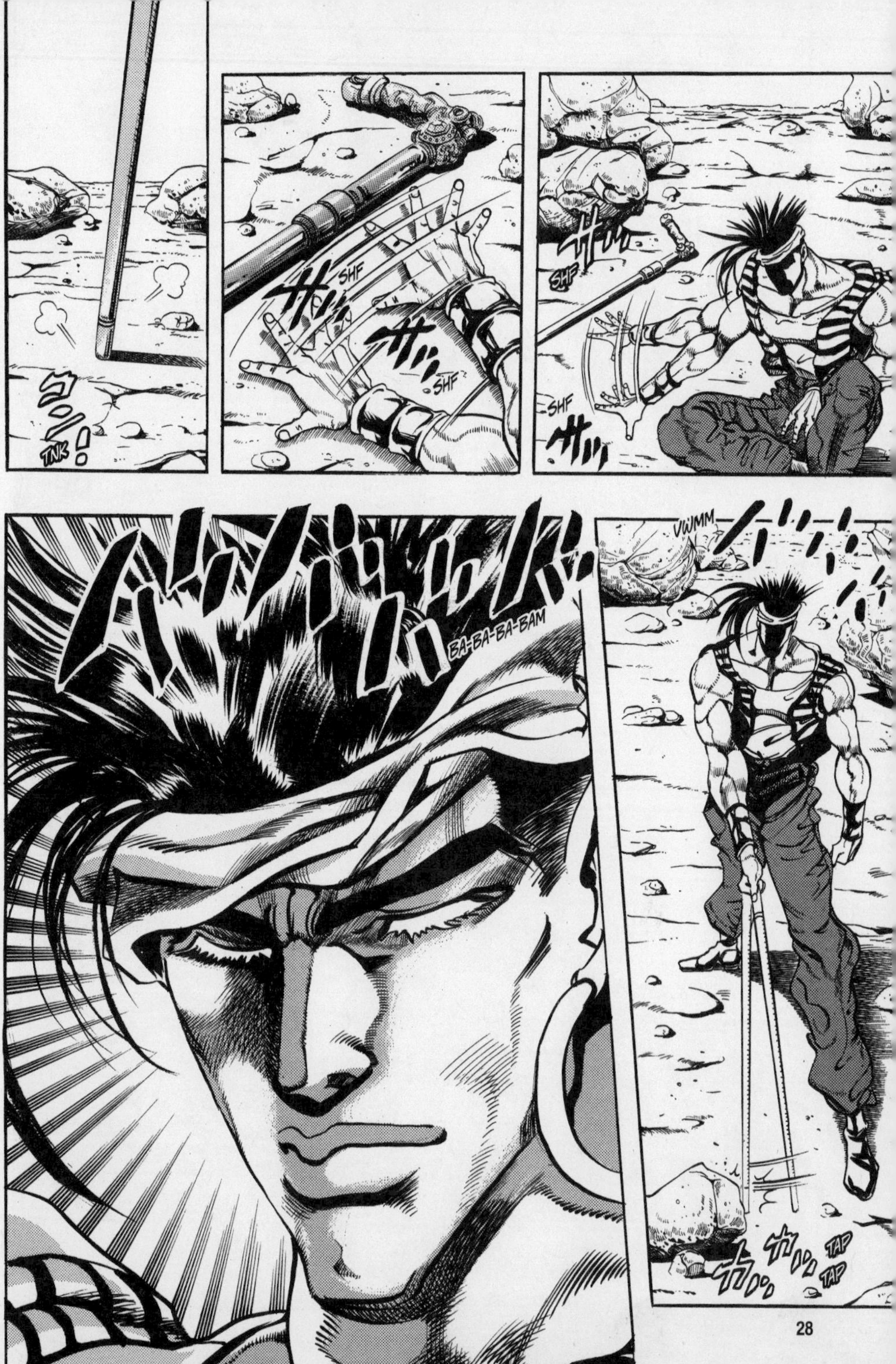
SHF
SHF
SHF
SHF
TNK
VWMM
TAP
TAP
BA-BA-BA-BAM

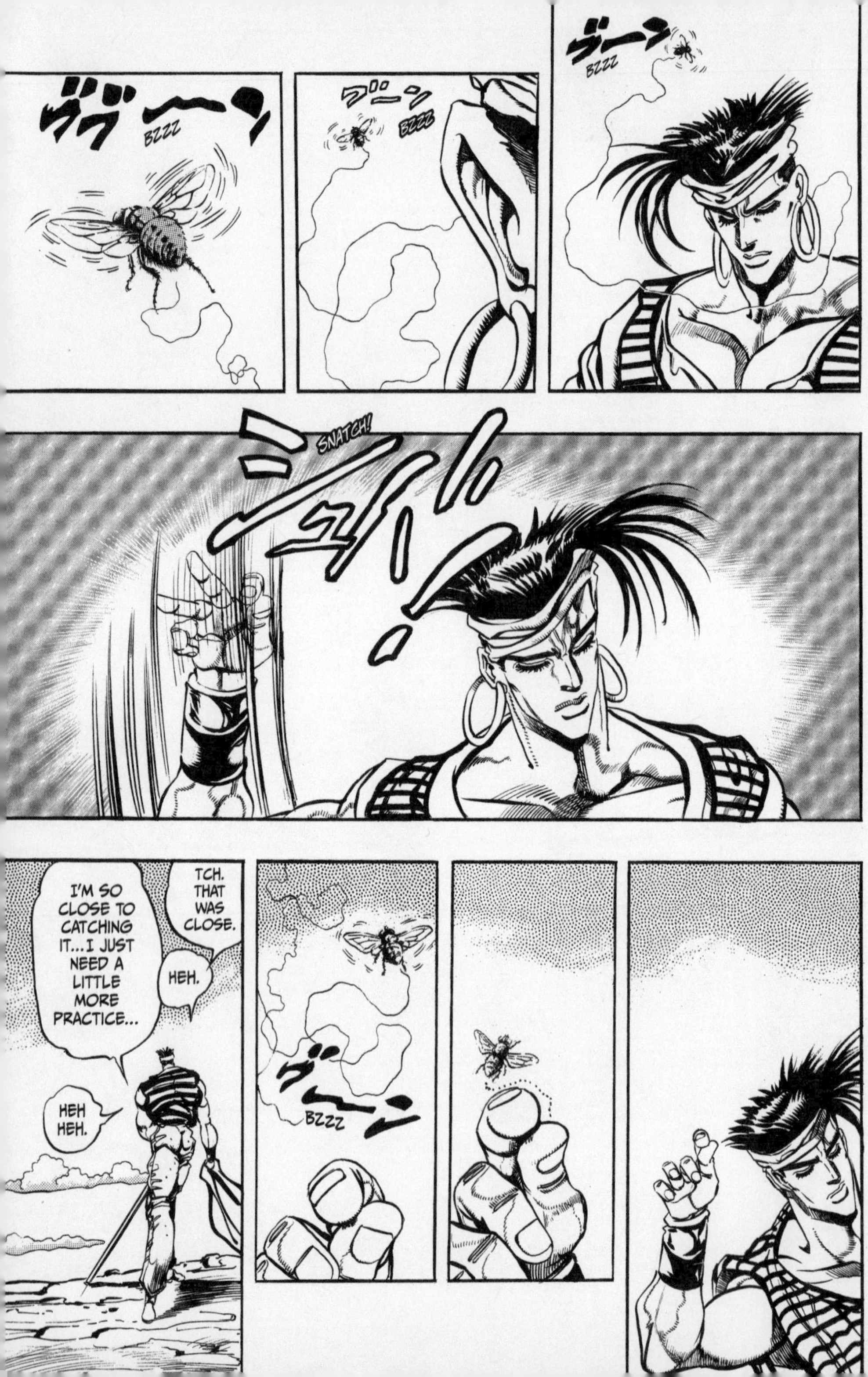
BZZZ
BZZZ
BZZZ
SNATCH!
BZZZ
TCH. THAT WAS CLOSE.
I'M SO CLOSE TO CATCHING IT... I JUST NEED A LITTLE MORE PRACTICE...
HEH.
HEH HEH.

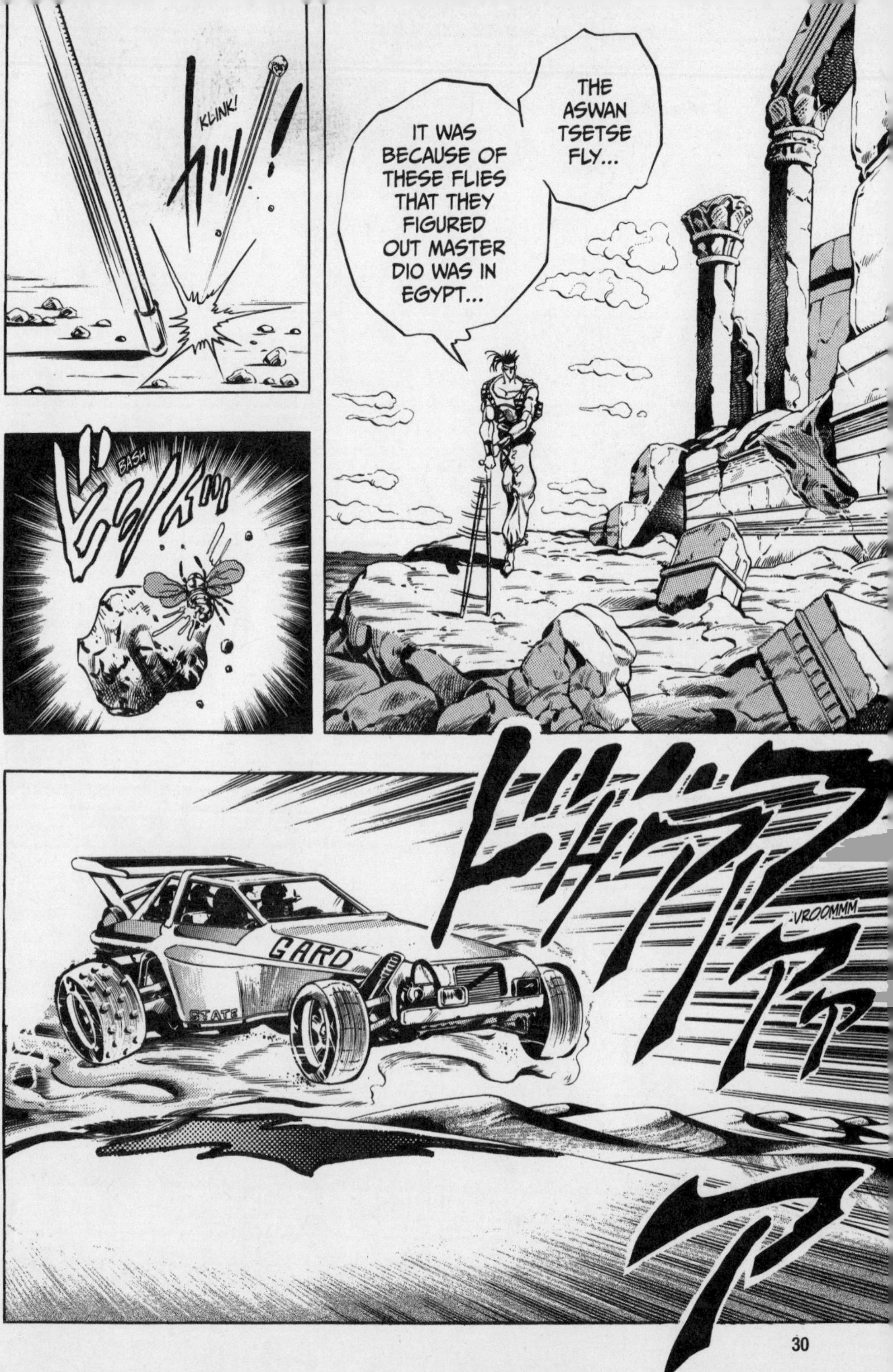
THE ASWAN TSETSE FLY...
IT WAS BECAUSE OF THESE FLIES THAT THEY FIGURED OUT MASTER DIO WAS IN EGYPT...
KLINK!
カッ！
BASH
ビシィッ
GARD
STATE
VROOMMM
ドゥワァァァ

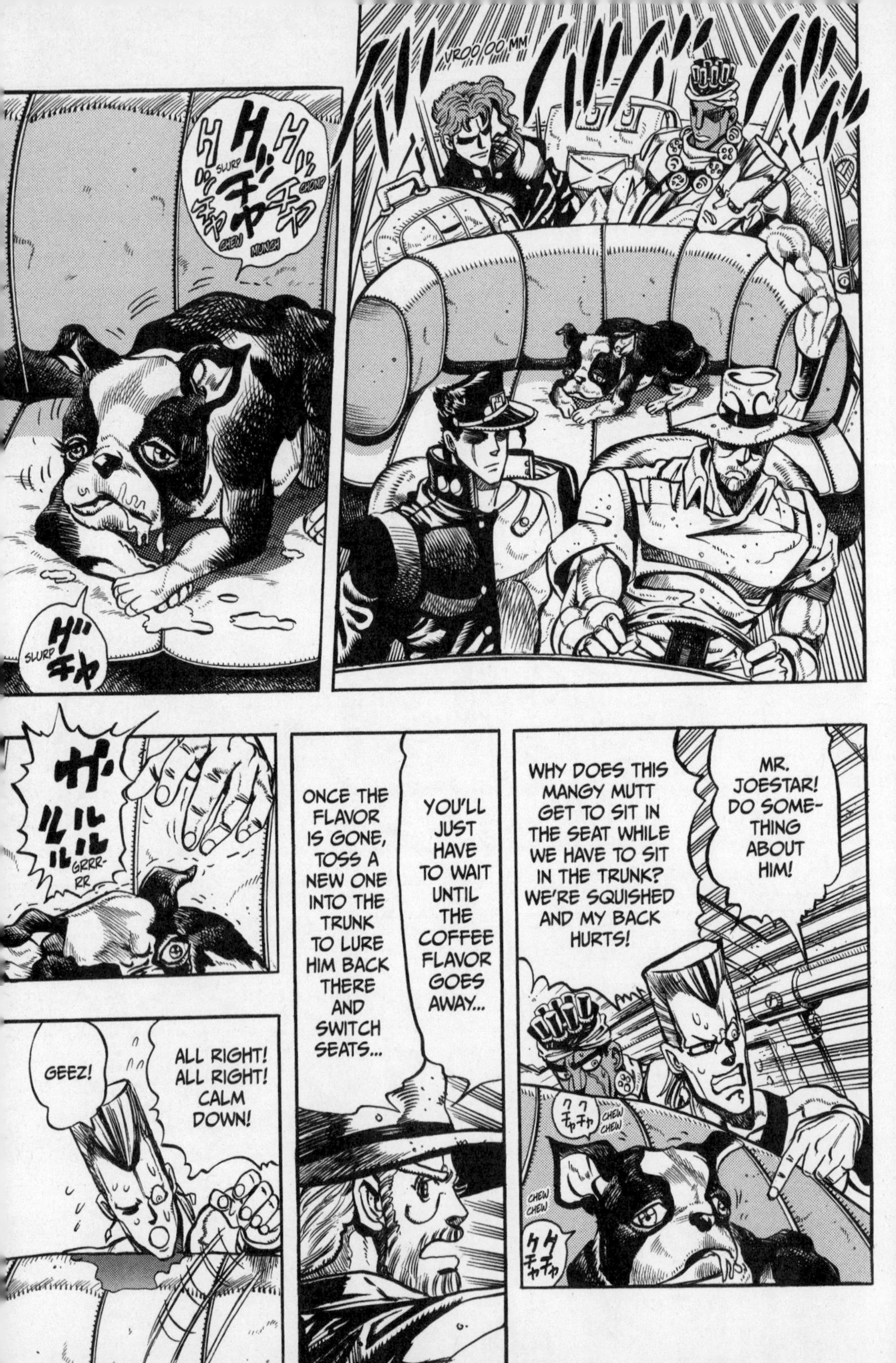
VROO OO MM
SLURP
CHEW
MUNCH
CHOMP
SLURP
MR. JOESTAR! DO SOME-THING ABOUT HIM!
WHY DOES THIS MANGY MUTT GET TO SIT IN THE SEAT WHILE WE HAVE TO SIT IN THE TRUNK? WE'RE SQUISHED AND MY BACK HURTS!
CHEW CHEW
CHEW CHEW
YOU'LL JUST HAVE TO WAIT UNTIL THE COFFEE FLAVOR GOES AWAY...
ONCE THE FLAVOR IS GONE, TOSS A NEW ONE INTO THE TRUNK TO LURE HIM BACK THERE AND SWITCH SEATS...
GRRR-RR
ALL RIGHT! ALL RIGHT! CALM DOWN!
GEEZ!

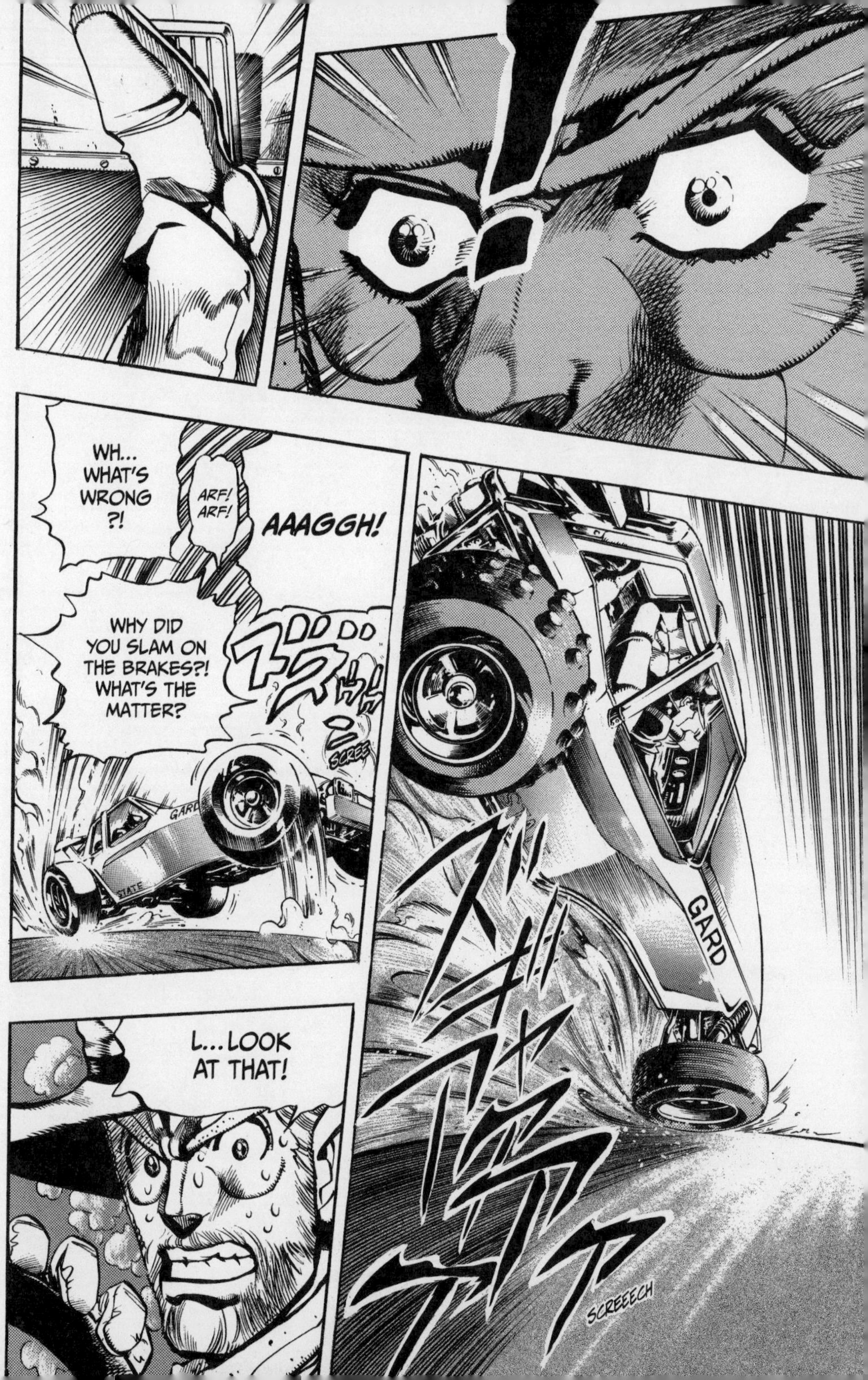
GARD
SCREEECH
AAAGGH!
ARF! ARF!
WH... WHAT'S WRONG ?!
WHY DID YOU SLAM ON THE BRAKES?! WHAT'S THE MATTER?
SCREE
GARD
STATE
L...LOOK AT THAT!

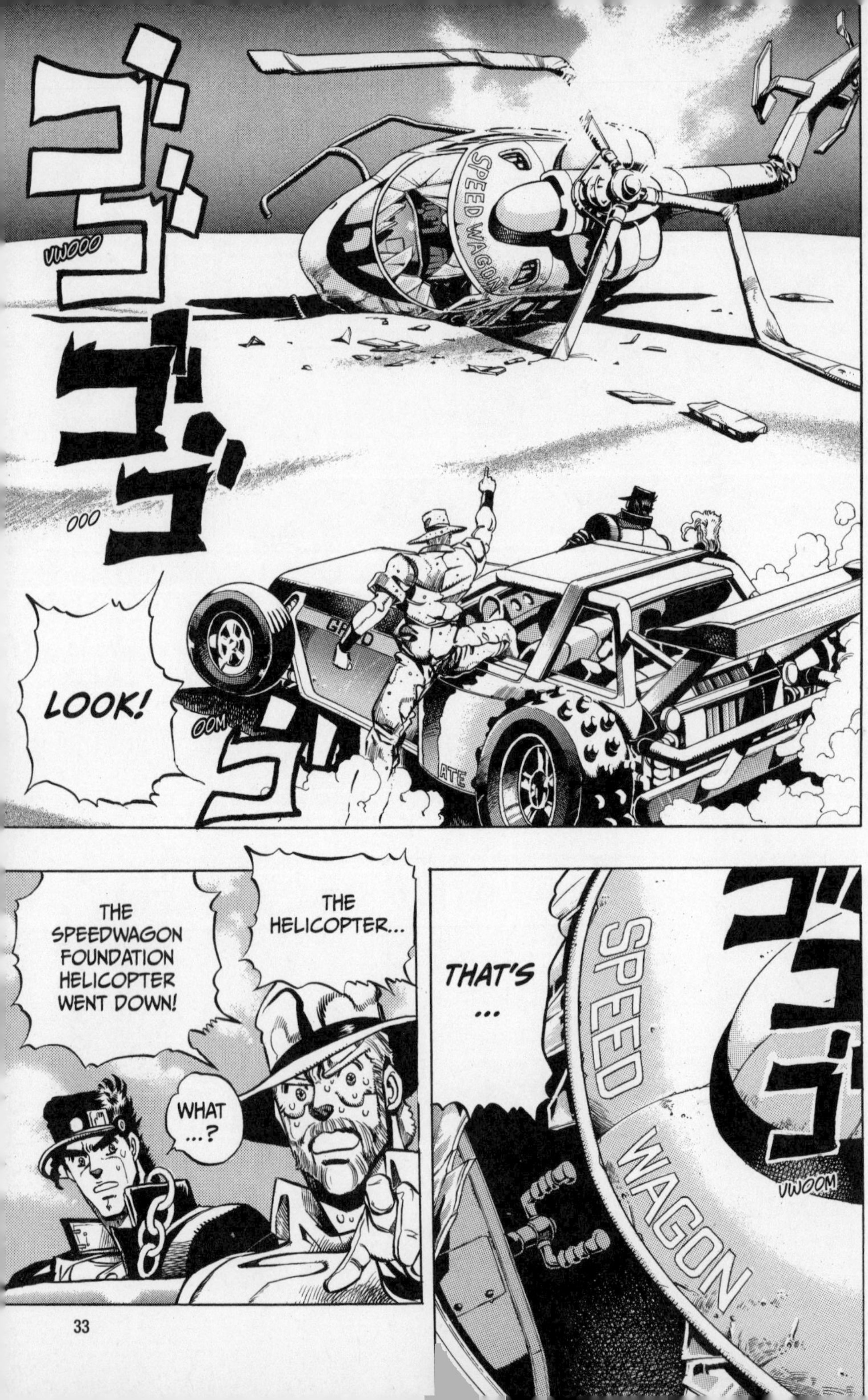
SPEED WAGON
VWOOO
OOO
LOOK!
OOM
THAT'S ...
SPEED WAGON
VWOOM
THE HELICOPTER...
THE SPEEDWAGON FOUNDATION HELICOPTER WENT DOWN!
WHAT ...?

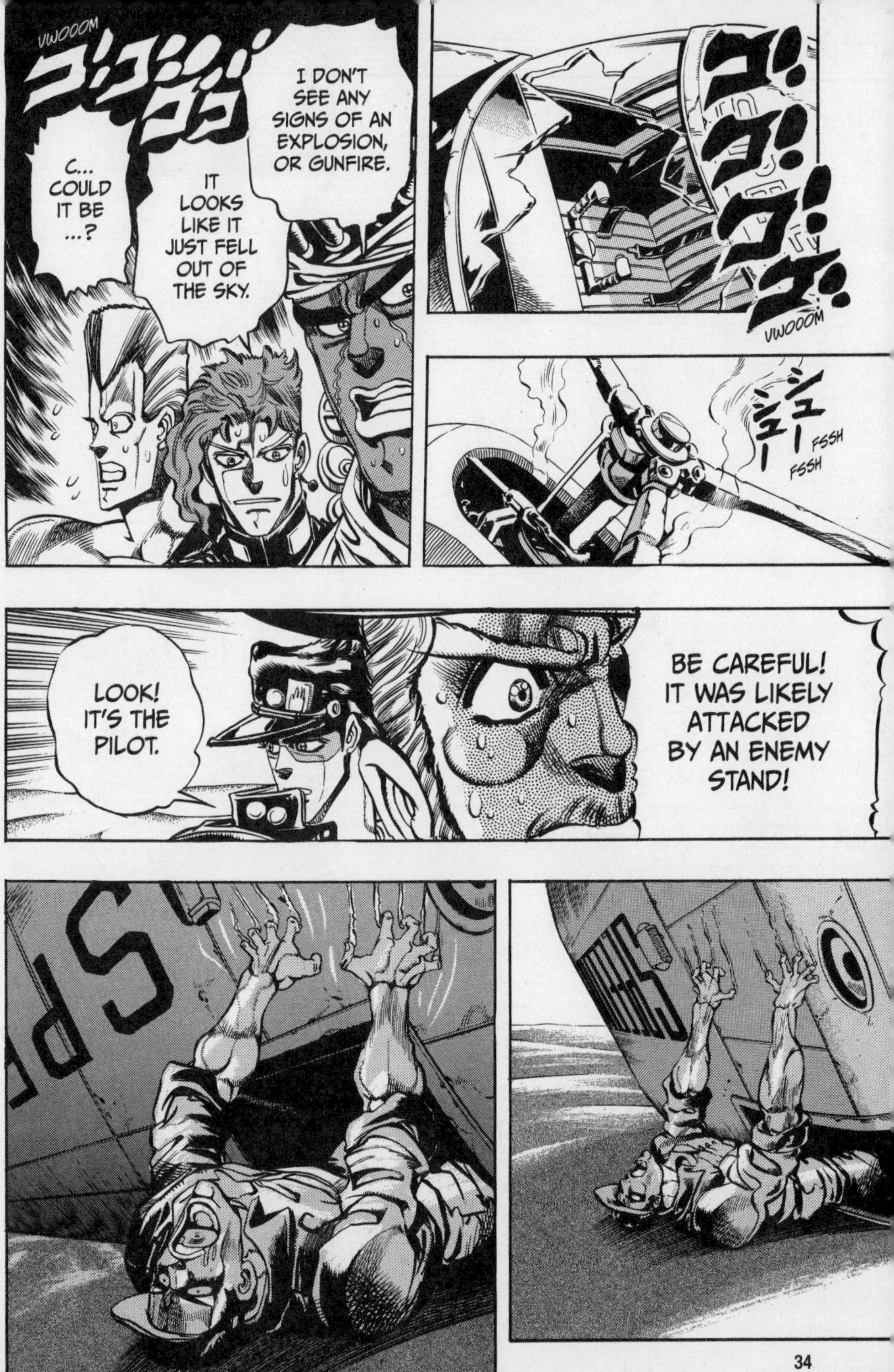

ゴゴゴゴ
VWOOOM
シューシュー
FSSH
FSSH
VWOOOM
ゴゴゴゴ
I DON'T SEE ANY SIGNS OF AN EXPLOSION, OR GUNFIRE.
IT LOOKS LIKE IT JUST FELL OUT OF THE SKY.
C... COULD IT BE ...?
BE CAREFUL! IT WAS LIKELY ATTACKED BY AN ENEMY STAND!
LOOK! IT'S THE PILOT.

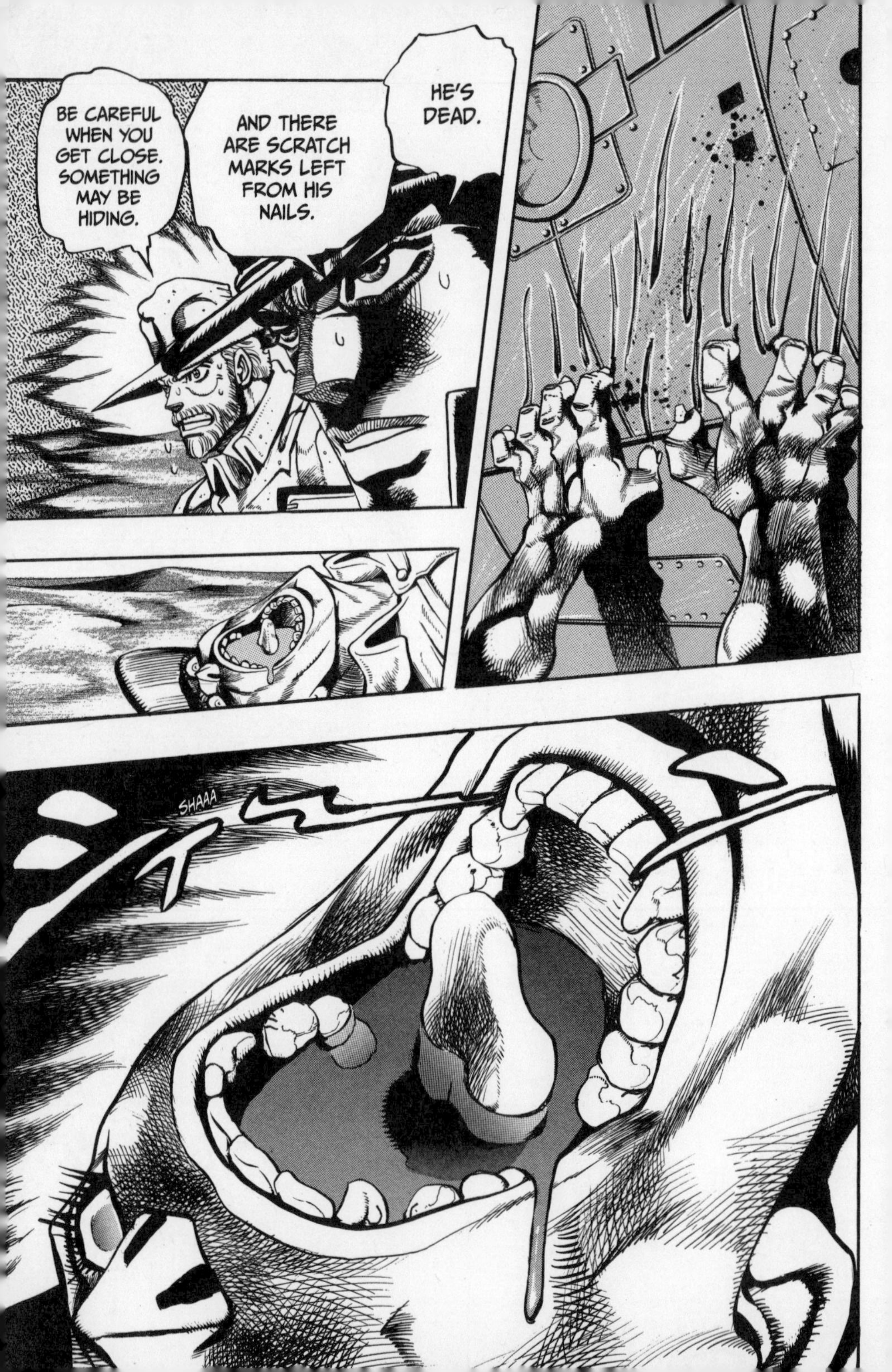
HE'S DEAD.
AND THERE ARE SCRATCH MARKS LEFT FROM HIS NAILS.
BE CAREFUL WHEN YOU GET CLOSE. SOMETHING MAY BE HIDING.
SHAAA

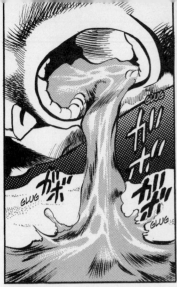

GLUG
GLUG

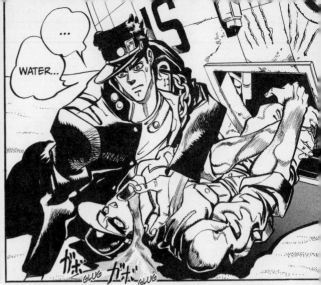

...

WATER...

GLUG GLUG GLUG

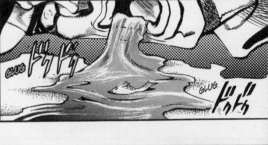

GLUG

GLUG

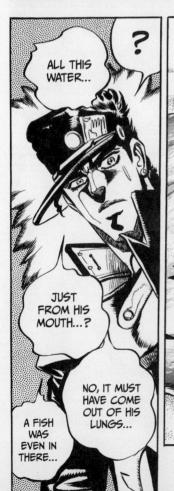

?

ALL THIS
WATER...

JUST
FROM HIS
MOUTH...?

NO, IT MUST
HAVE COME
OUT OF HIS
LUNGS...

A FISH
WAS
EVEN IN
THERE...

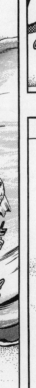

FLIP
FLIP

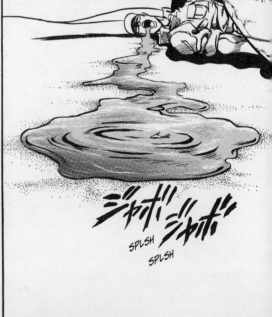

SPLSH

SPLSH

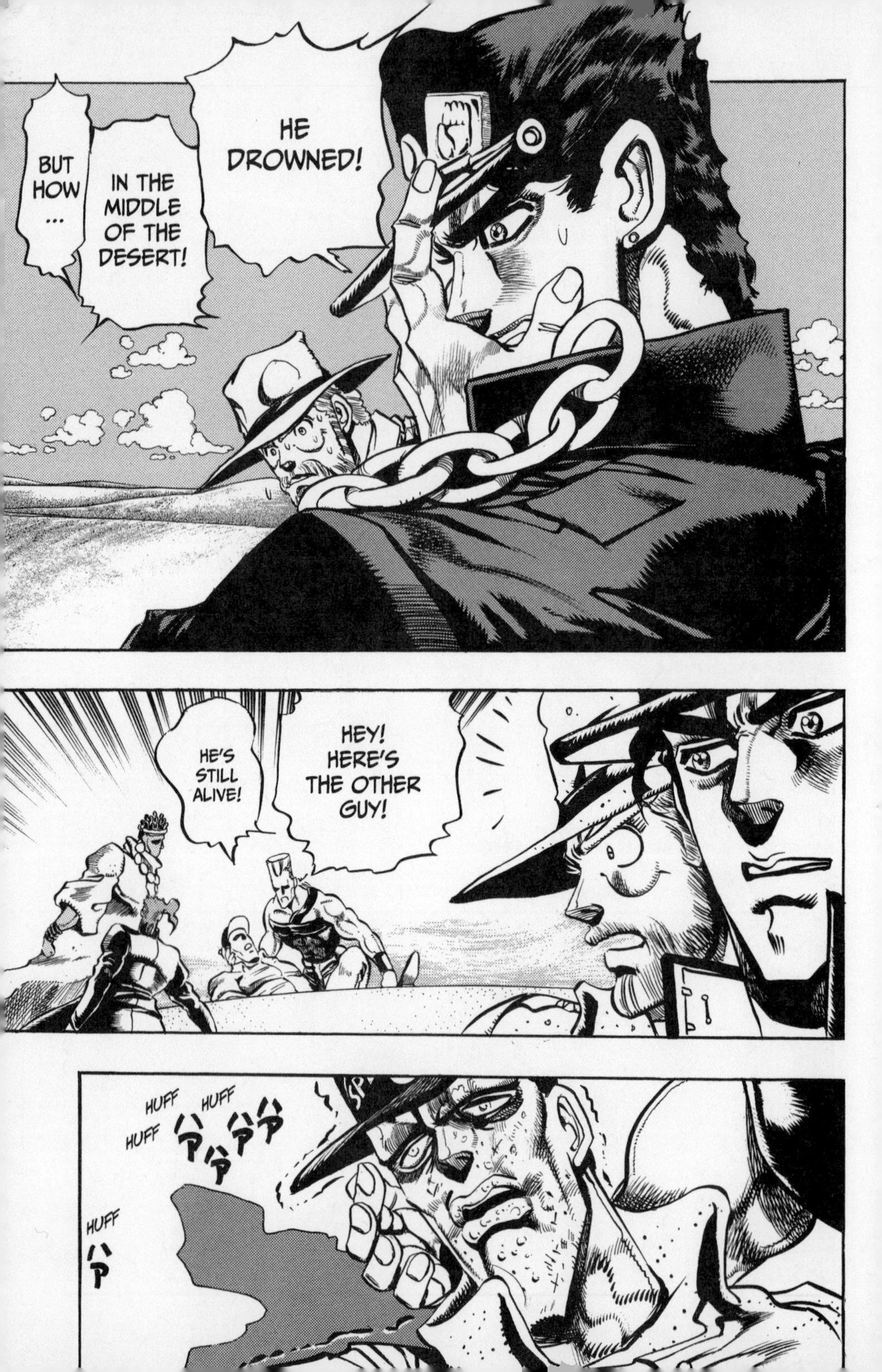
HE DROWNED!
IN THE MIDDLE OF THE DESERT!
BUT HOW ...
HEY! HERE'S THE OTHER GUY!
HE'S STILL ALIVE!
HUFF HUFF HUFF
ハァハァハァハァ
HUFF
ハァ

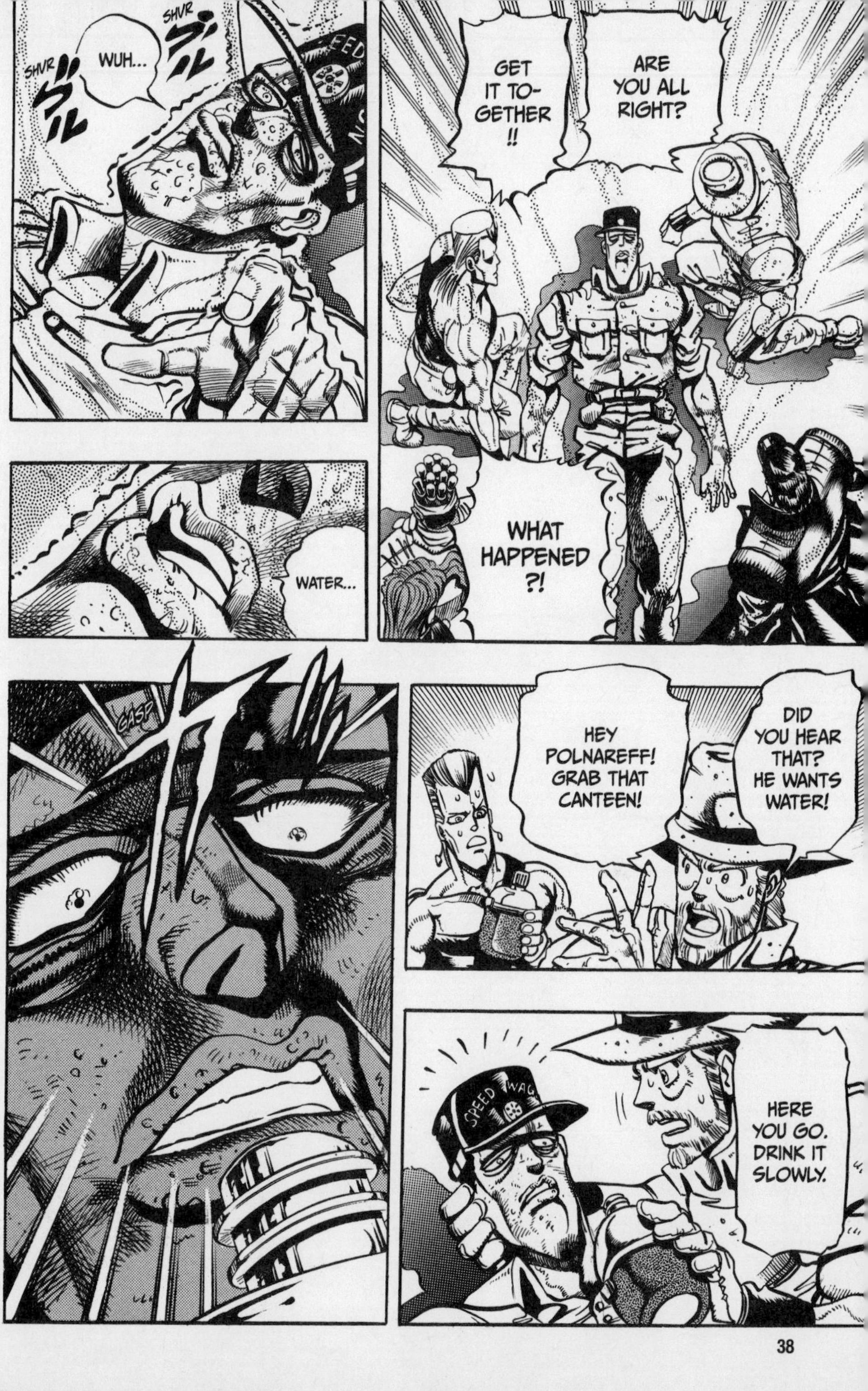
ARE YOU ALL RIGHT?
GET IT TO-GETHER !!
WHAT HAPPENED ?!
SHVR
WUH...
SHVR
WATER...
DID YOU HEAR THAT? HE WANTS WATER!
HEY POLNAREFF! GRAB THAT CANTEEN!
HERE YOU GO. DRINK IT SLOWLY.
GASP

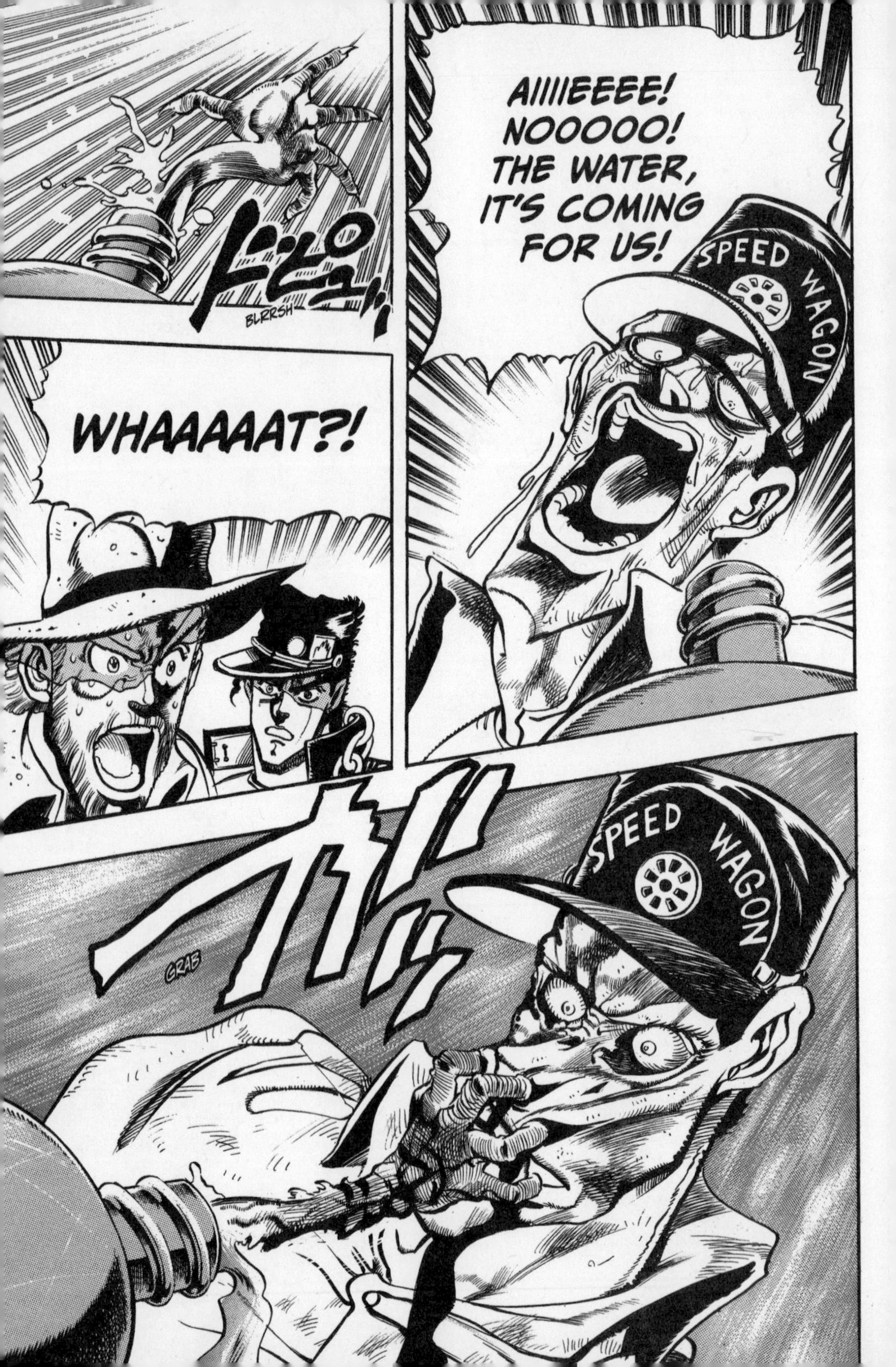
AIIIIEEEE! NOOOOO! THE WATER, IT'S COMING FOR US!
SPEED WAGON
BLRRSH
WHAAAAAT?!
SPEED WAGON
GRAB

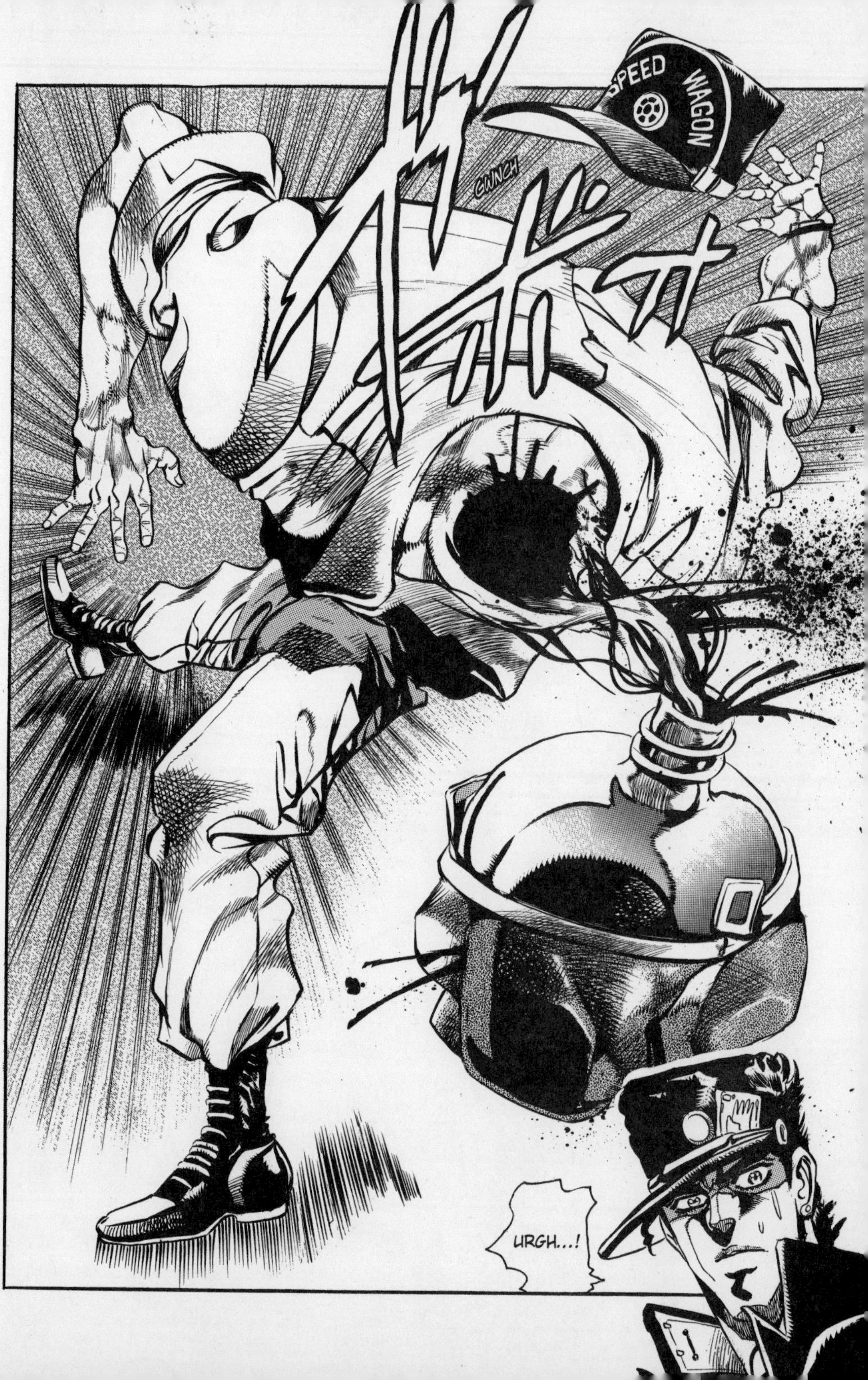
SPEED WAGON
GWNCH
URGH...!

CHAPTER 72: Iggy "The Fool" and "Geb" N'doul PART 3

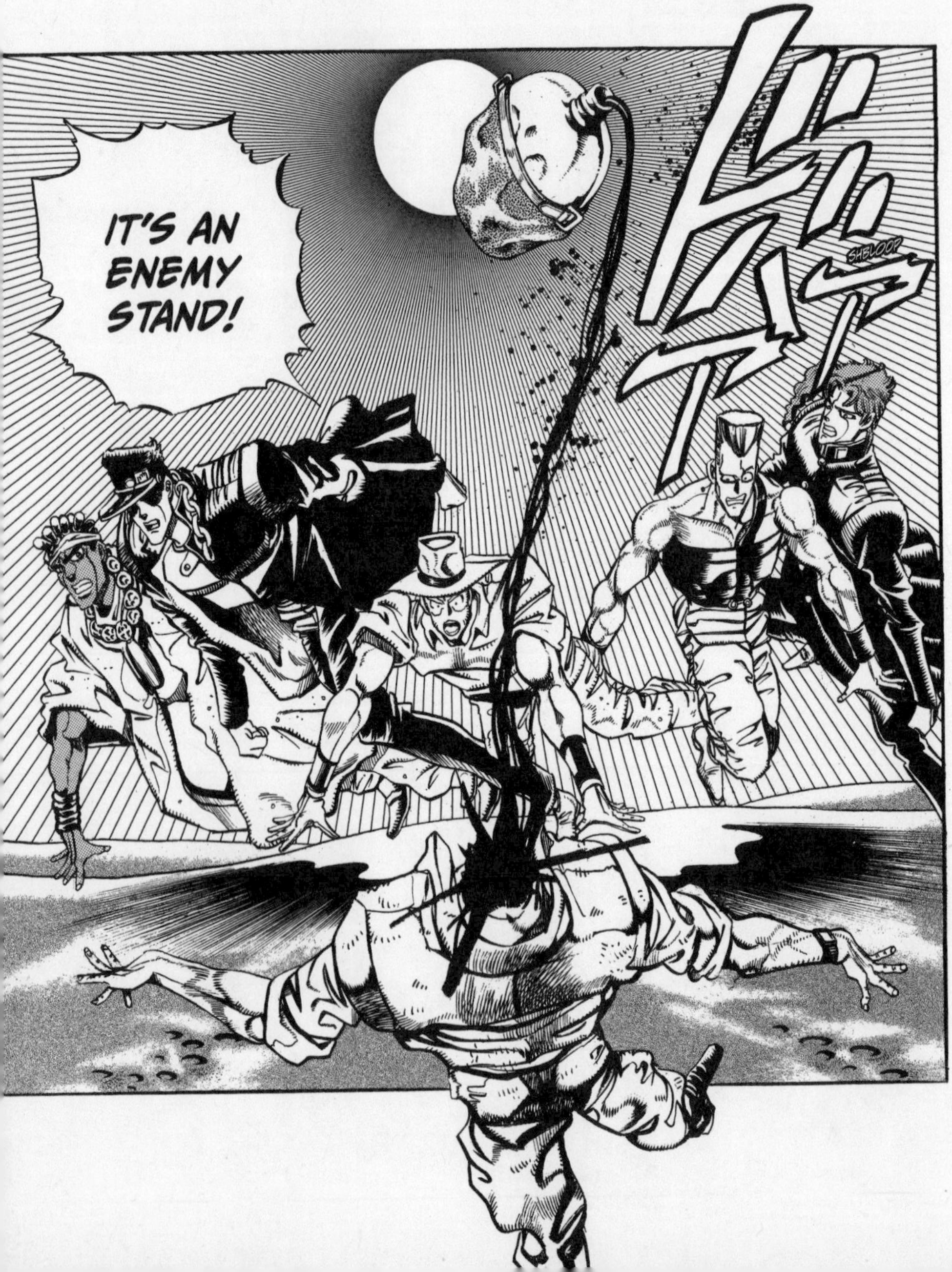
IT'S AN ENEMY STAND!
SHBLOOP

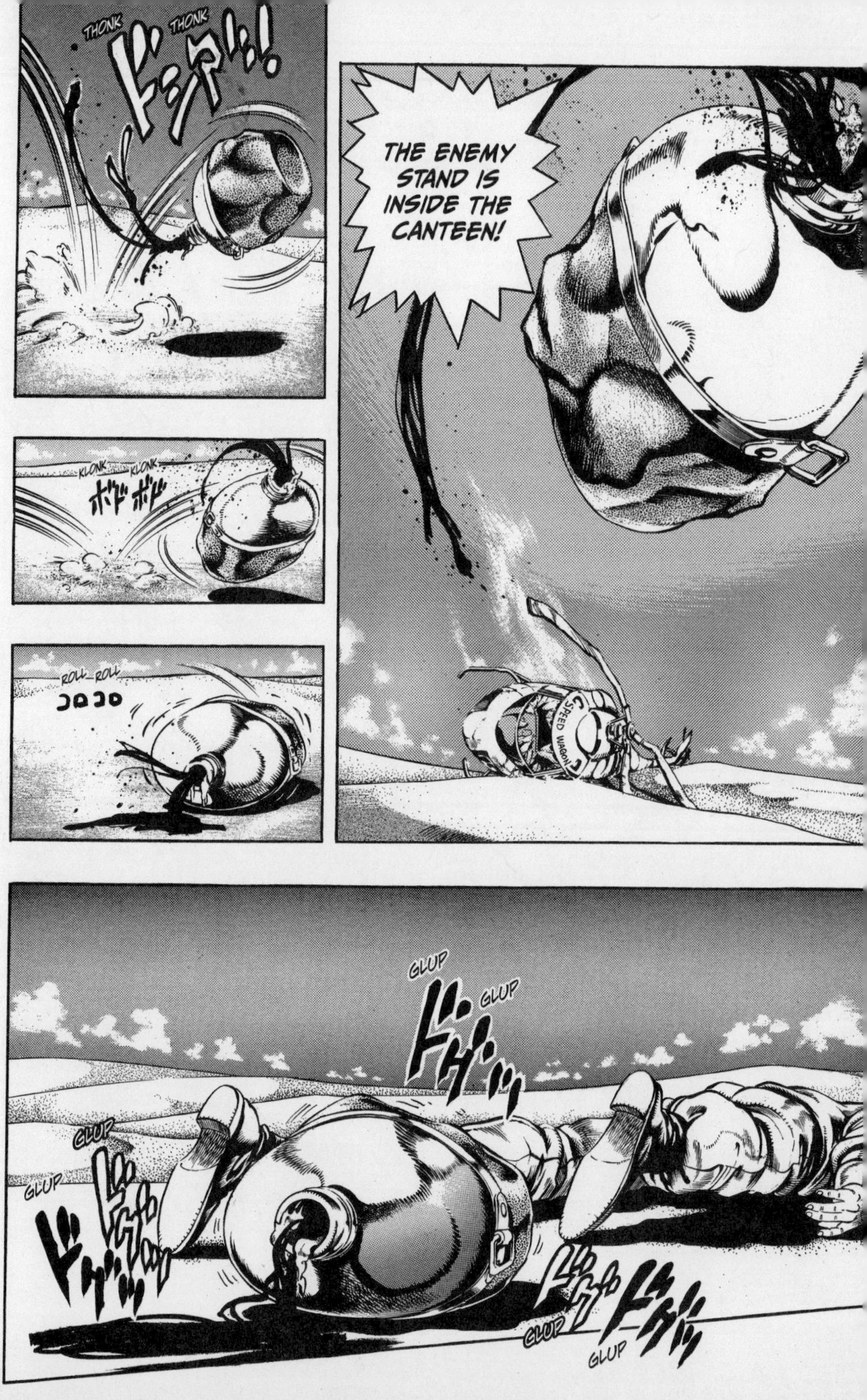
THE ENEMY STAND IS INSIDE THE CANTEEN!
SPEED WAGON
THONK THONK
KLONK KLONK
ボドボド
ROLL ROLL
コロコロ
GLUP GLUP
GLUP GLUP
GLUP GLUP

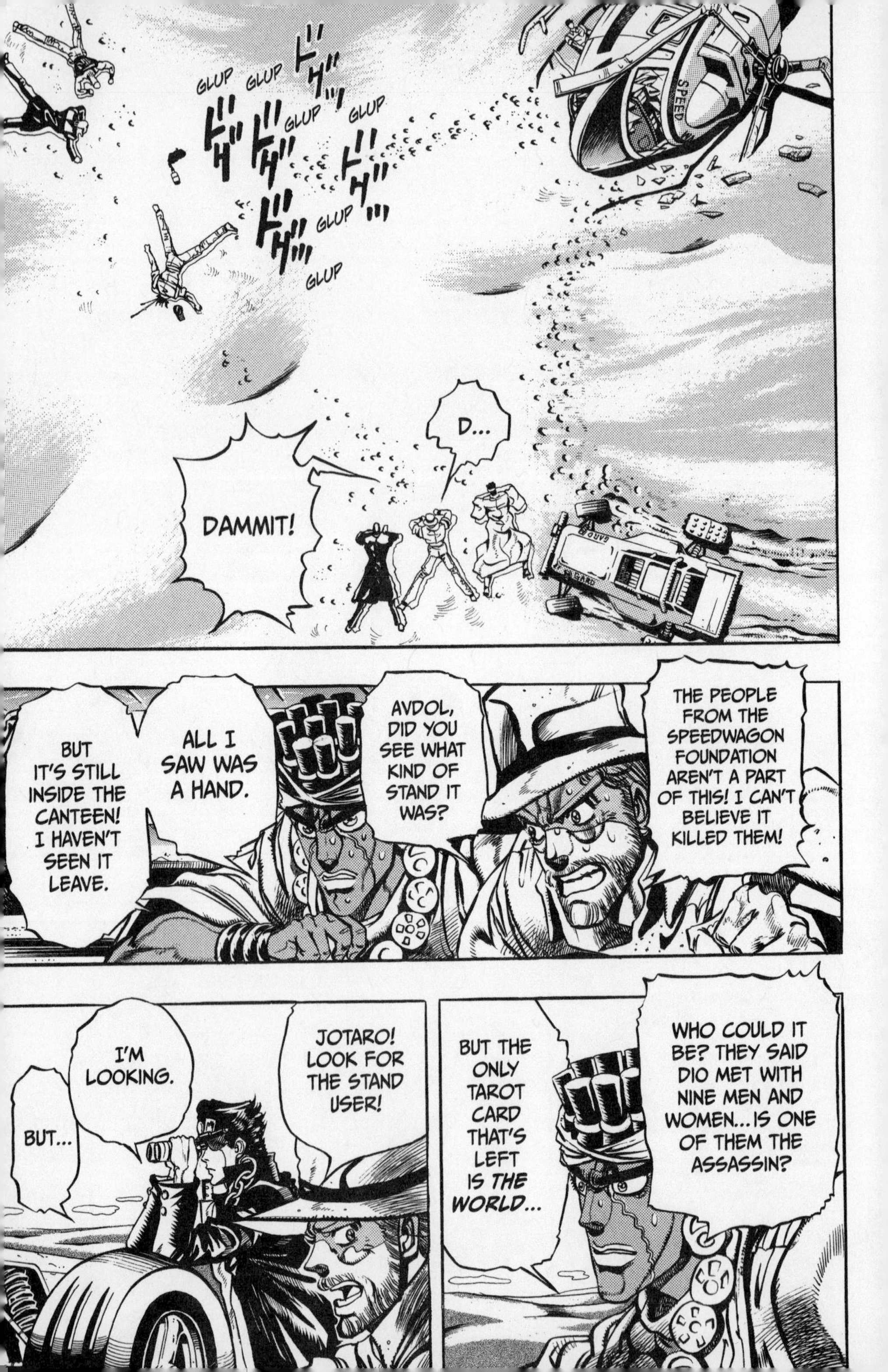
GLUP GLUP
GLUP GLUP
GLUP
GLUP
D...
DAMMIT!
THE PEOPLE FROM THE SPEEDWAGON FOUNDATION AREN'T A PART OF THIS! I CAN'T BELIEVE IT KILLED THEM!
AVDOL, DID YOU SEE WHAT KIND OF STAND IT WAS?
ALL I SAW WAS A HAND.
BUT IT'S STILL INSIDE THE CANTEEN! I HAVEN'T SEEN IT LEAVE.
WHO COULD IT BE? THEY SAID DIO MET WITH NINE MEN AND WOMEN...IS ONE OF THEM THE ASSASSIN?
BUT THE ONLY TAROT CARD THAT'S LEFT IS *THE WORLD*...
JOTARO! LOOK FOR THE STAND USER!
I'M LOOKING.
BUT...

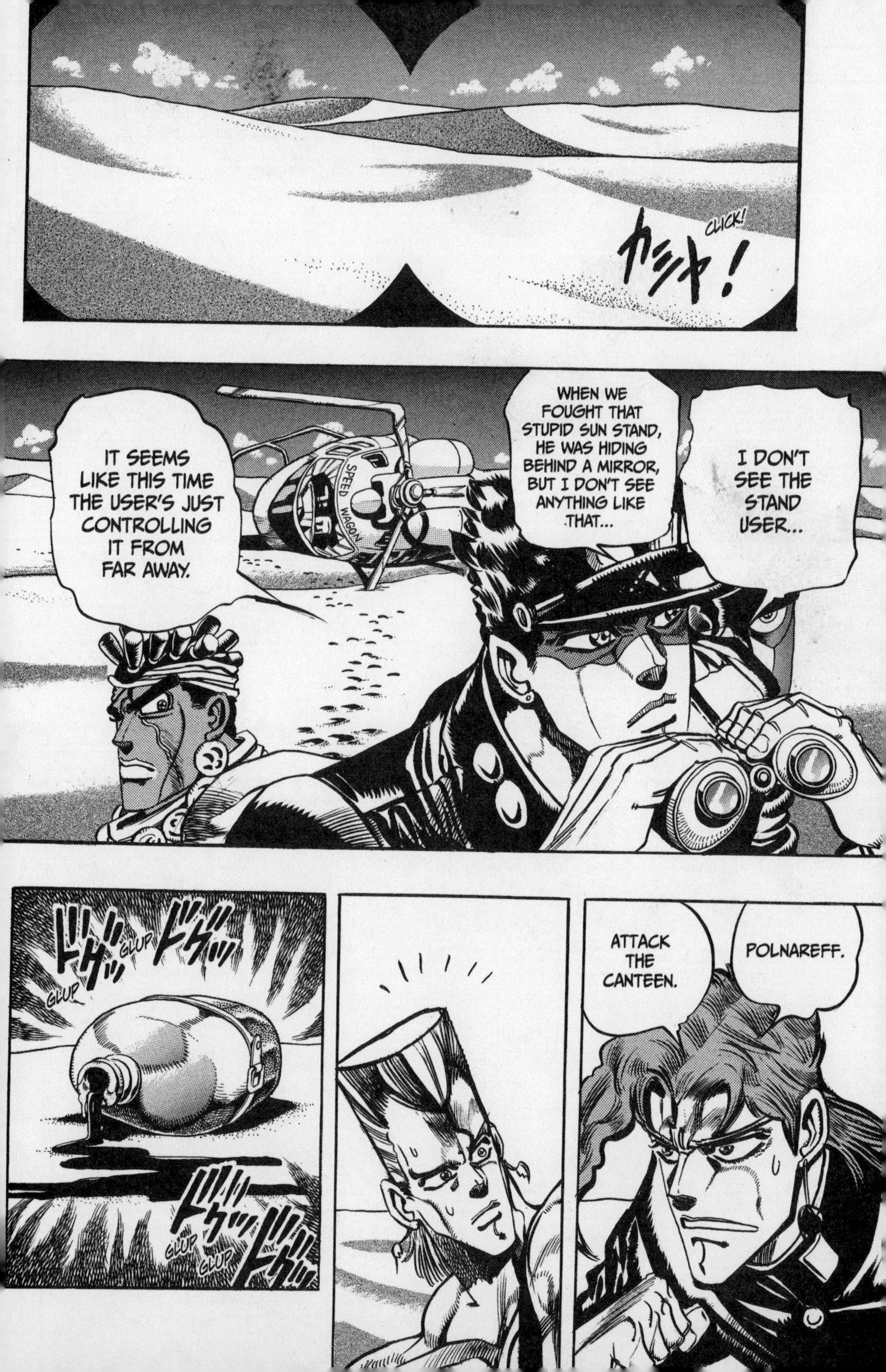
カシャ!
CLICK!
I DON'T SEE THE STAND USER...
WHEN WE FOUGHT THAT STUPID SUN STAND, HE WAS HIDING BEHIND A MIRROR, BUT I DON'T SEE ANYTHING LIKE THAT...
IT SEEMS LIKE THIS TIME THE USER'S JUST CONTROLLING IT FROM FAR AWAY.
SPEED WAGON
POLNAREFF.
ATTACK THE CANTEEN.
GLUP
GLUP
GLUP
GLUP

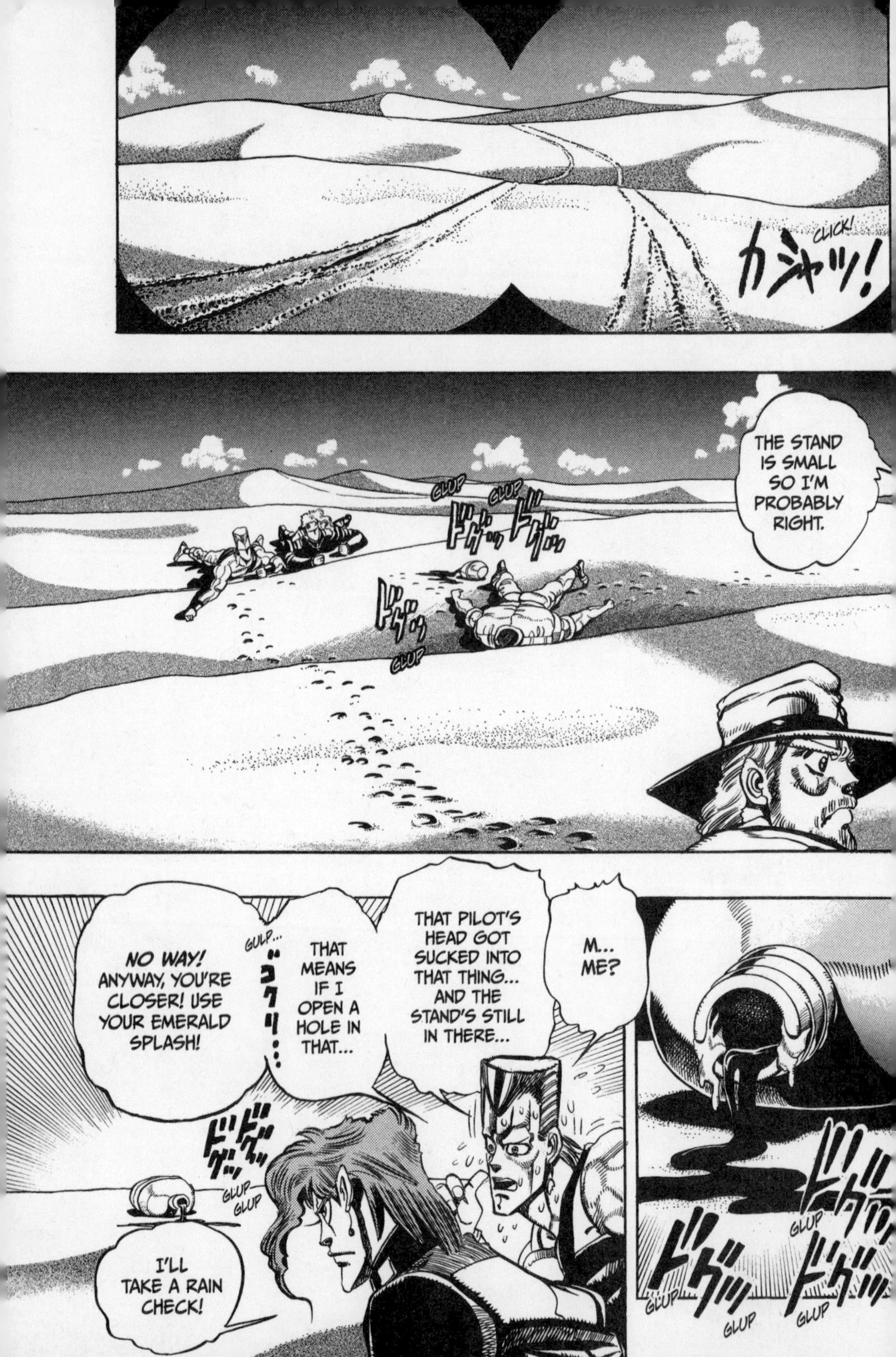

CLICK!
カシャッ!
THE STAND IS SMALL SO I'M PROBABLY RIGHT.
GLUP
GLUP
GLUP
GLUP
GLUP
GLUP
GLUP
M... ME?
THAT PILOT'S HEAD GOT SUCKED INTO THAT THING... AND THE STAND'S STILL IN THERE...
THAT MEANS IF I OPEN A HOLE IN THAT...
GULP...
ゴクリ...
NO WAY! ANYWAY, YOU'RE CLOSER! USE YOUR EMERALD SPLASH!
GLUP GLUP
I'LL TAKE A RAIN CHECK!

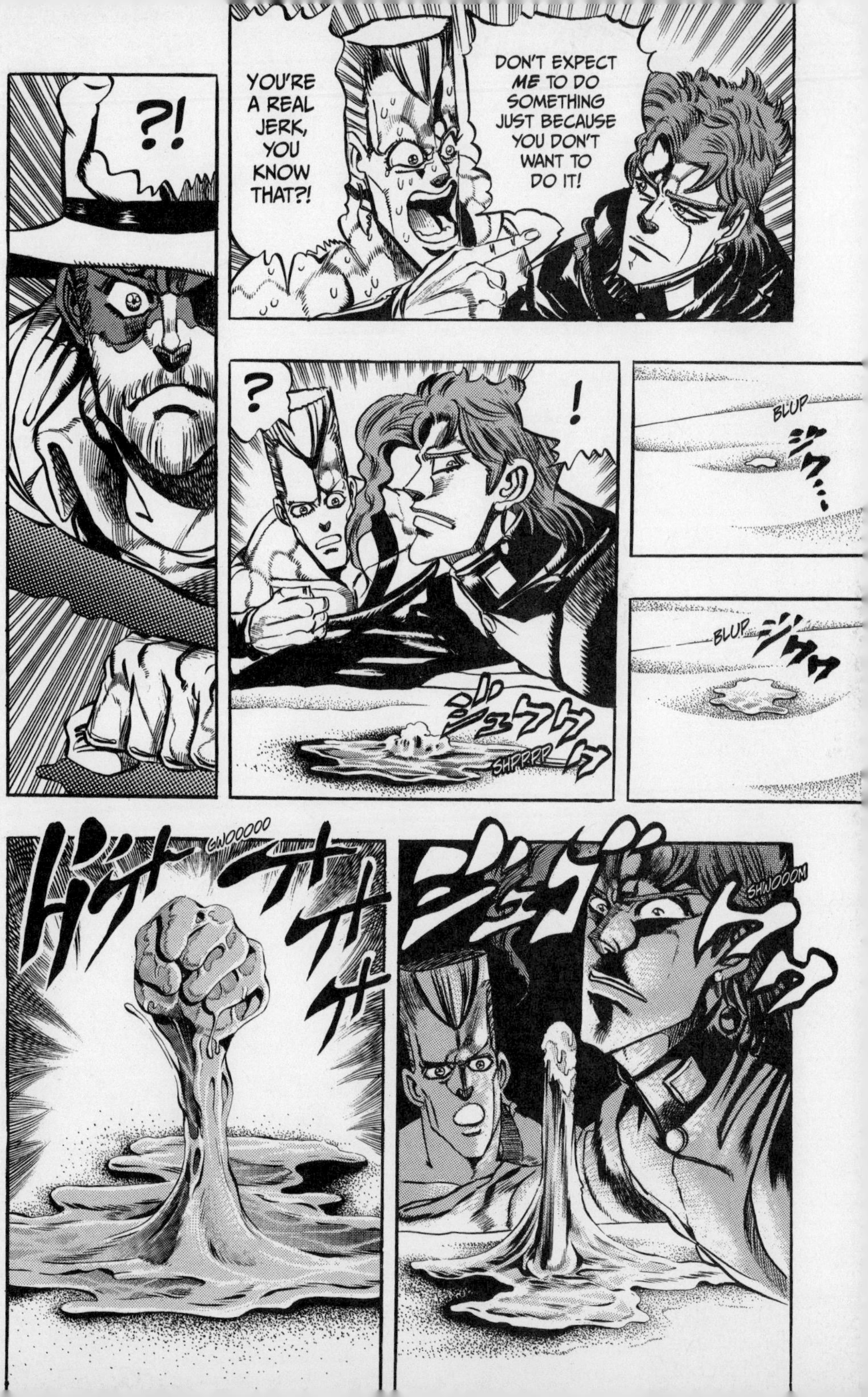
DON'T EXPECT *ME* TO DO SOMETHING JUST BECAUSE YOU DON'T WANT TO DO IT!
YOU'RE A REAL JERK, YOU KNOW THAT?!
BLUP
BLUP
!
?
SHRRRR
?!
SHWOOOM
GWOOOOO

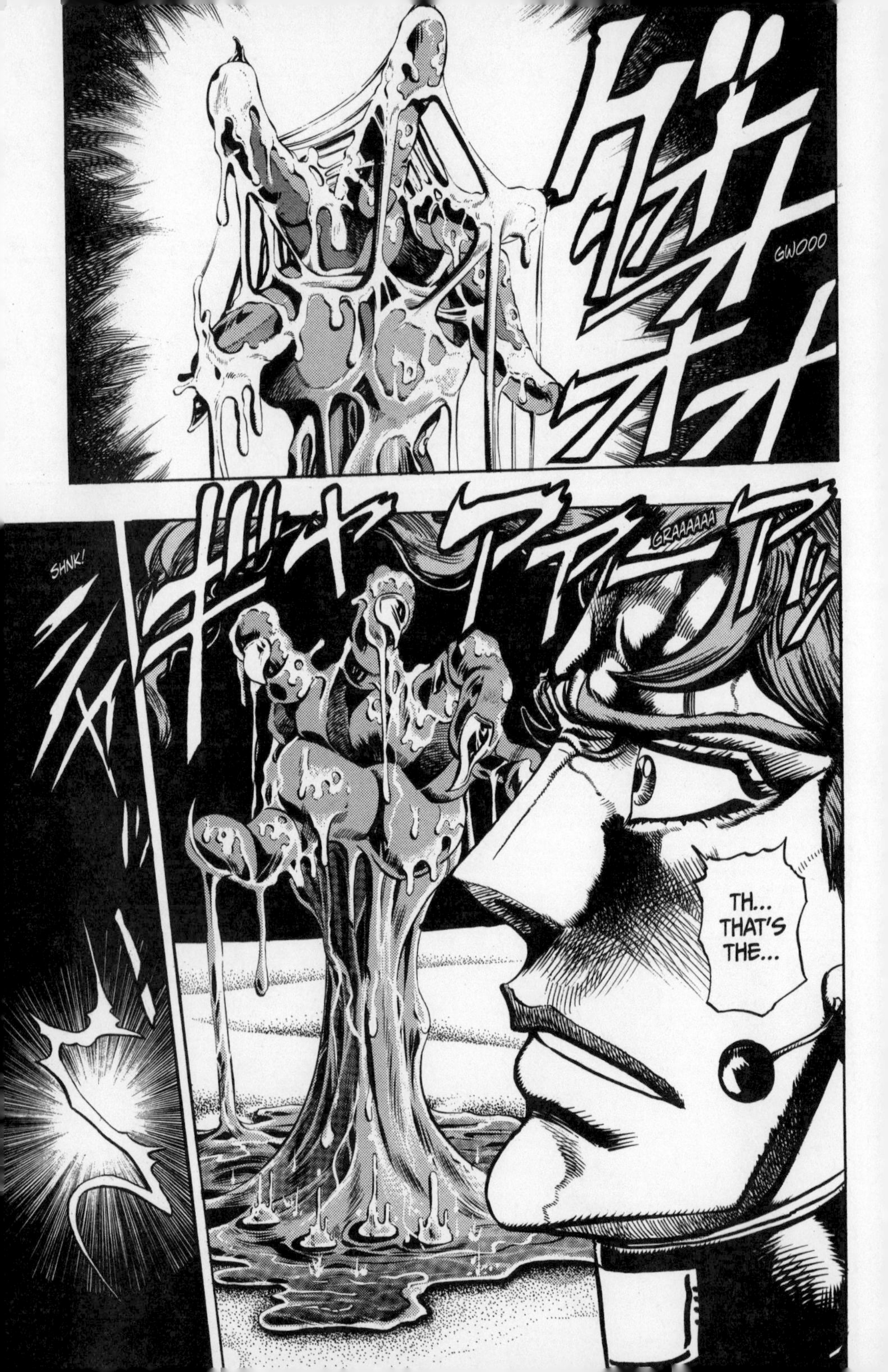
GWOOO
GRAAAAAA
TH... THAT'S THE...
SHNK!

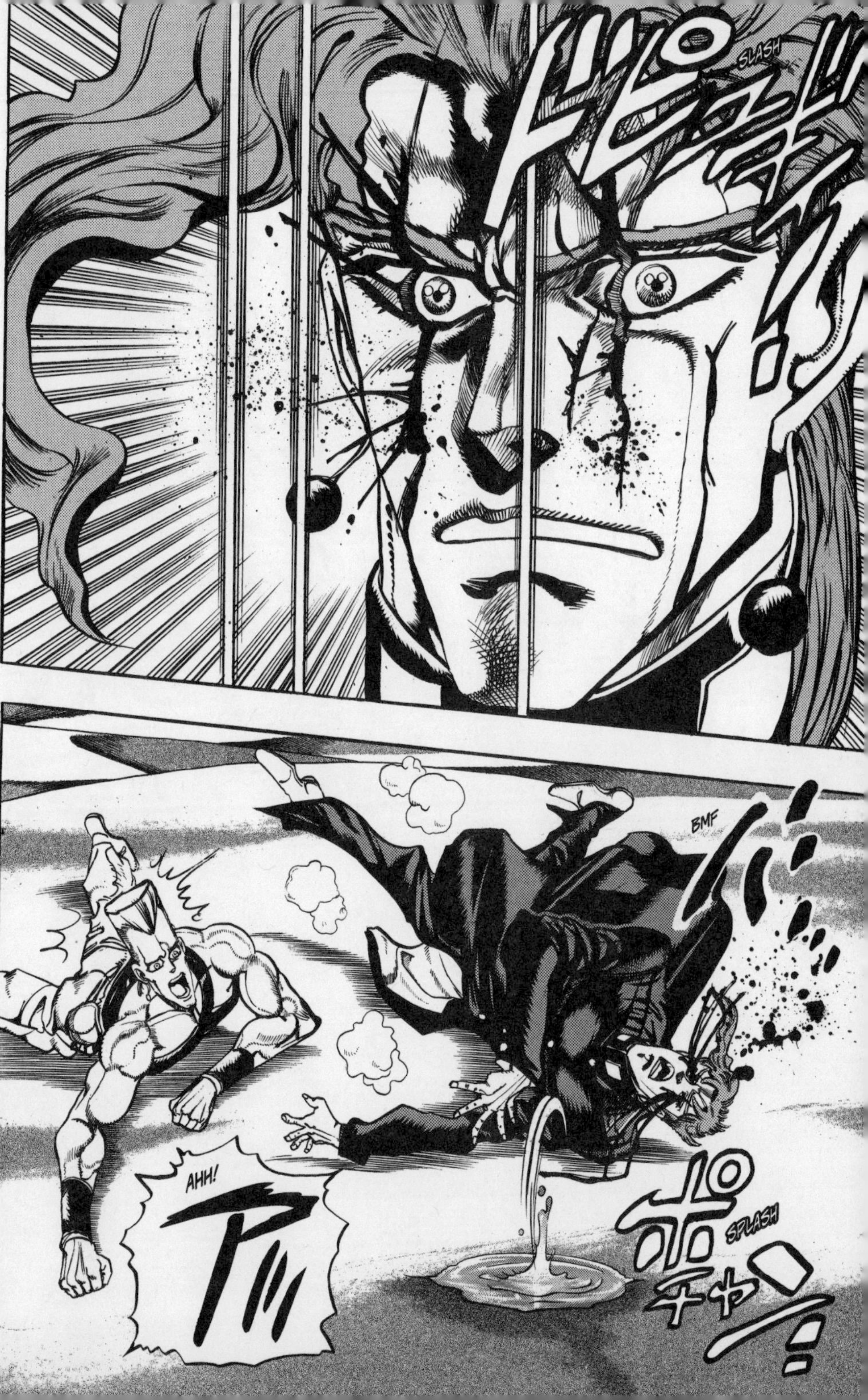
SLASH
BMF
SPLASH
AHH!

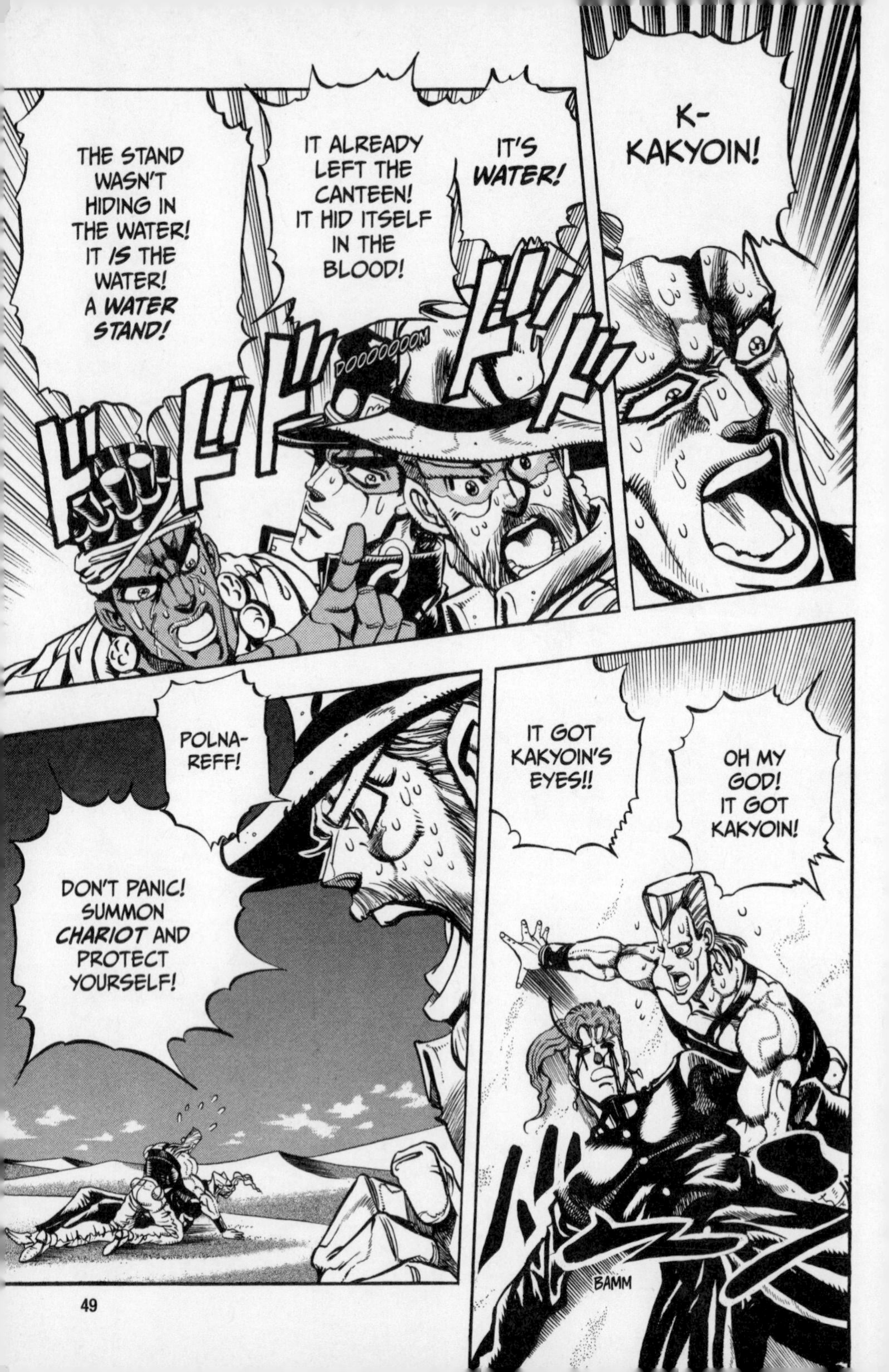
K-
KAKYOIN!
IT'S WATER!
IT ALREADY LEFT THE CANTEEN! IT HID ITSELF IN THE BLOOD!
THE STAND WASN'T HIDING IN THE WATER! IT *IS* THE WATER! A *WATER STAND!*
DOOOOOOOOM
OH MY GOD! IT GOT KAKYOIN!
IT GOT KAKYOIN'S EYES!!
BAMM
POLNA-
REFF!
DON'T PANIC! SUMMON *CHARIOT* AND PROTECT YOURSELF!

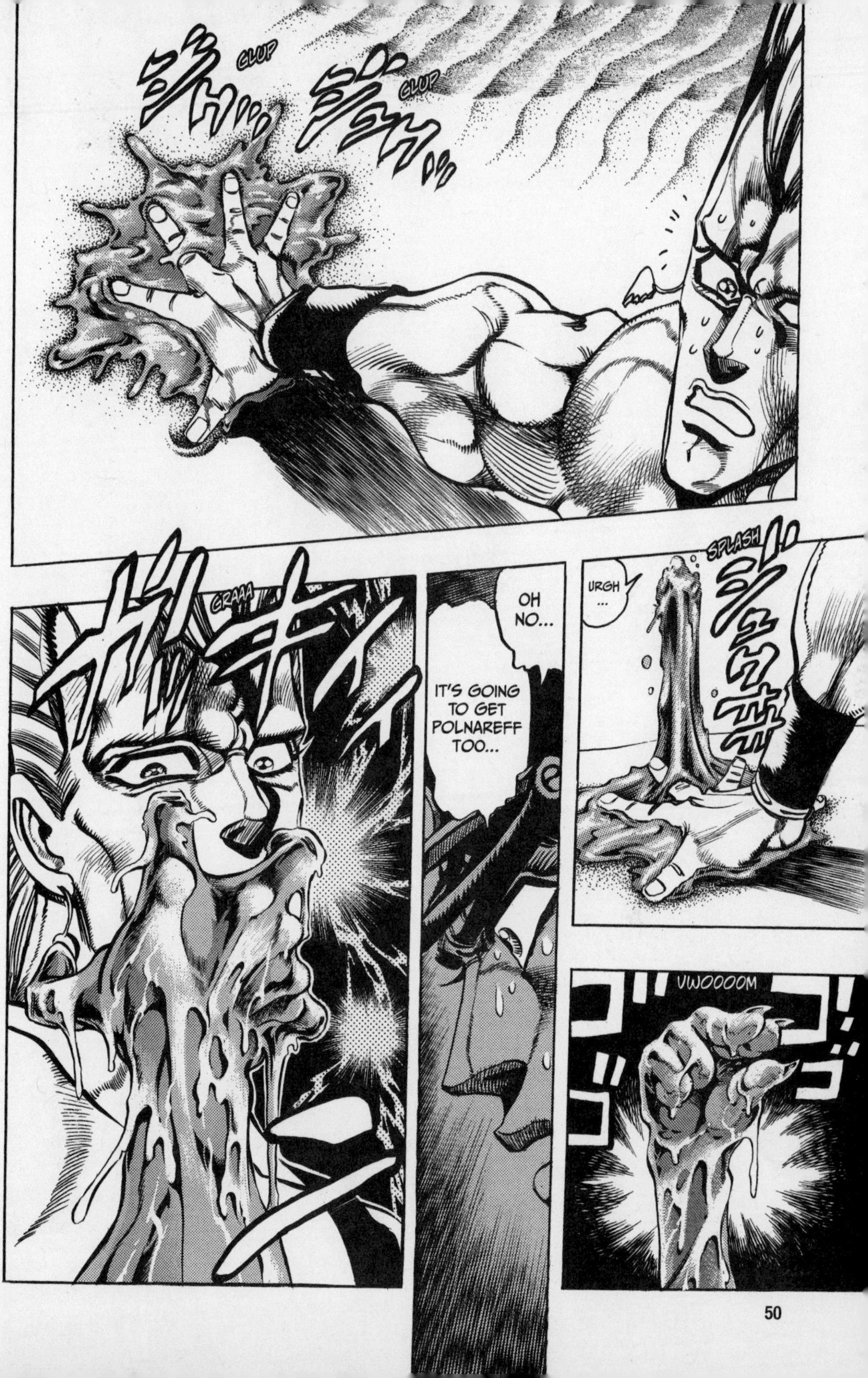
CLUP
CLUP
SPLASH
URGH ...
VWOOOOM
OH NO...
IT'S GOING TO GET POLNAREFF TOO...
GRAAA

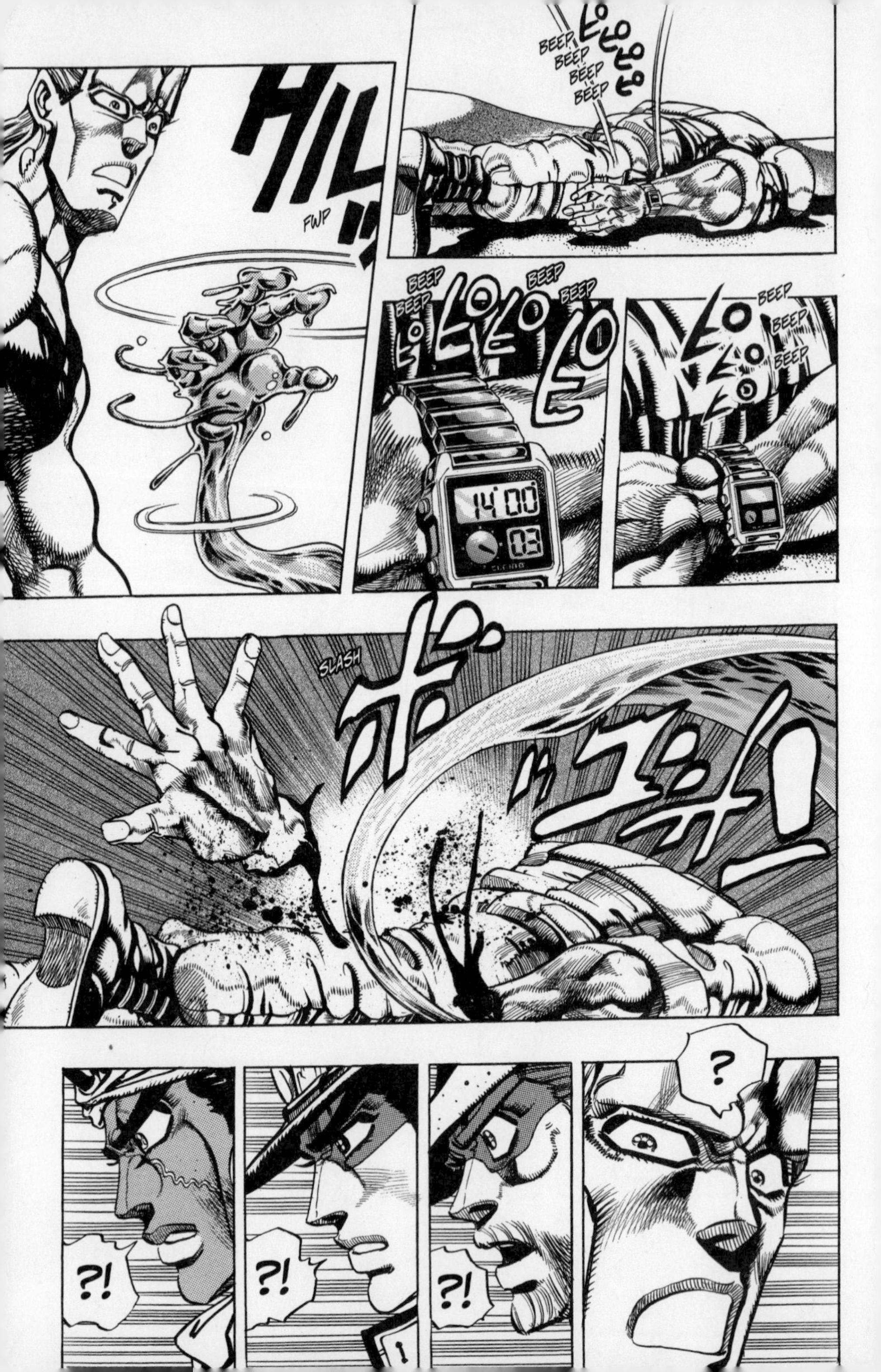
BEEP
BEEP
BEEP
BEEP
BEEP
BEEP
BEEP
BEEP
BEEP
BEEP
BEEP
FWP
SLASH
?
?!
?!
?!

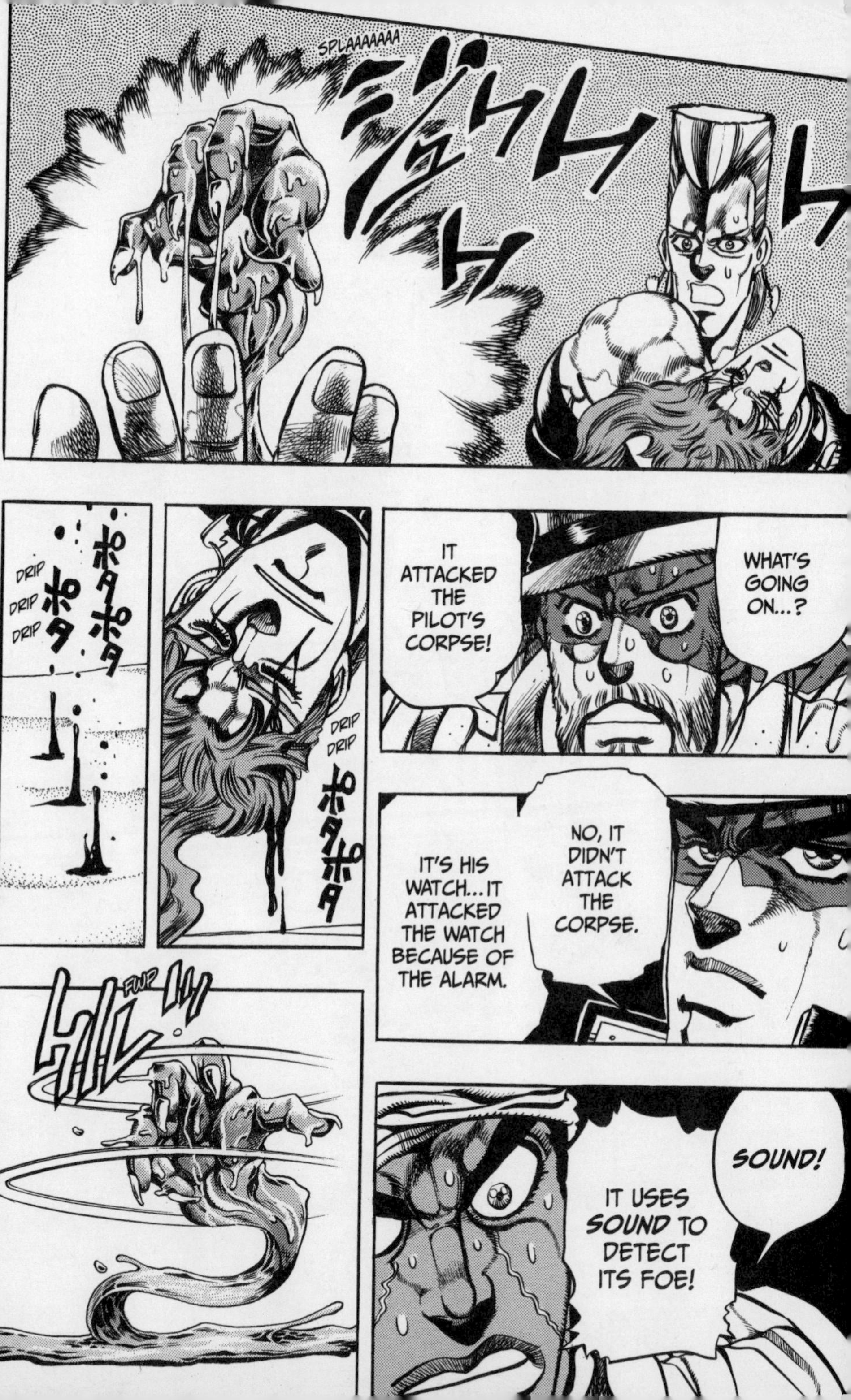
SPLAAAAAAA
WHAT'S GOING ON...?
IT ATTACKED THE PILOT'S CORPSE!
NO, IT DIDN'T ATTACK THE CORPSE.
IT'S HIS WATCH...IT ATTACKED THE WATCH BECAUSE OF THE ALARM.
DRIP DRIP
ポタポタ
DRIP DRIP DRIP
ポタポタポタ
SOUND!
IT USES *SOUND* TO DETECT ITS FOE!
FWIP

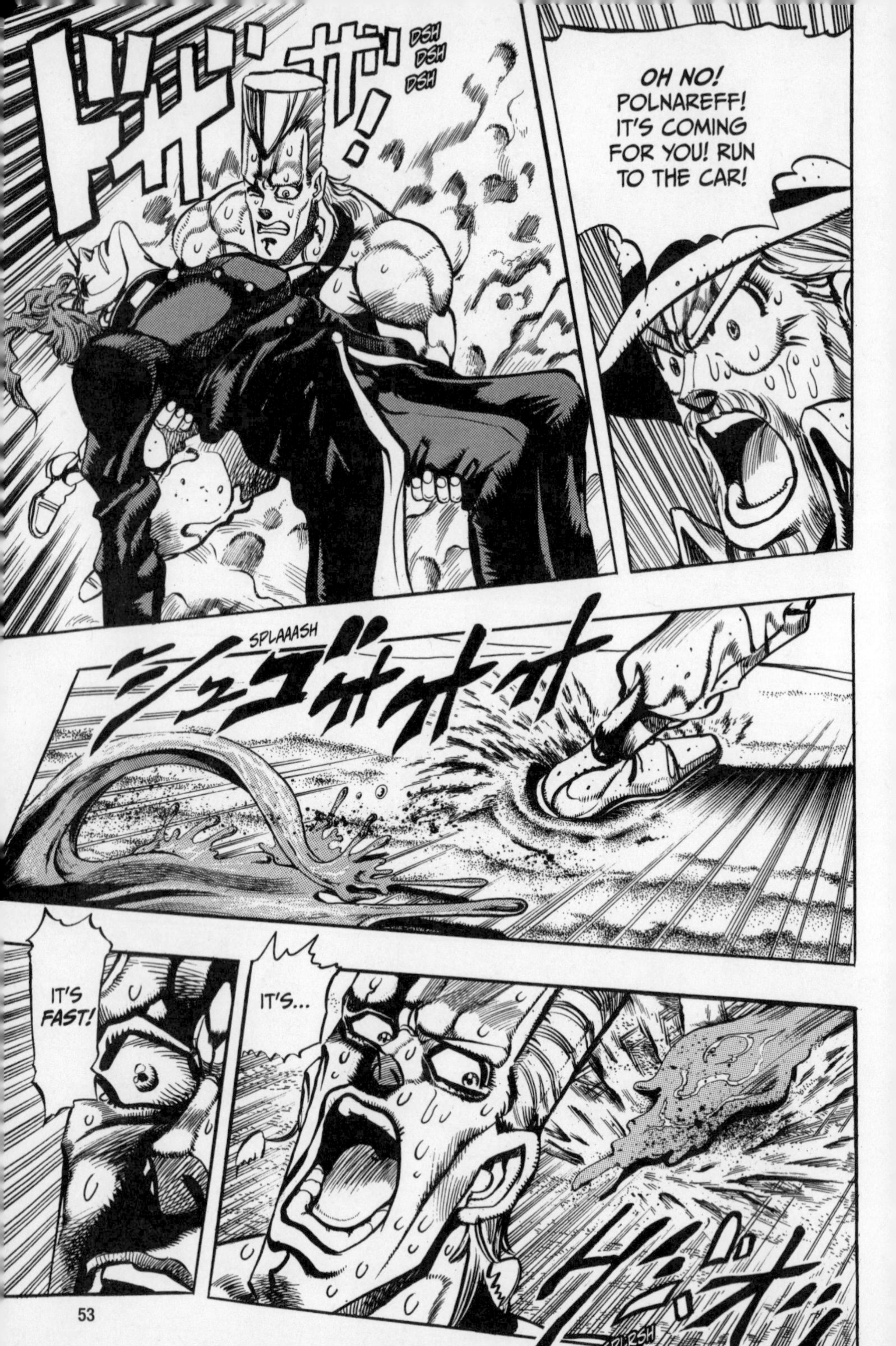
OH NO! POLNAREFF! IT'S COMING FOR YOU! RUN TO THE CAR!
DSH DSH DSH
SPLAAASH
SPLRSH
IT'S...
IT'S FAST!

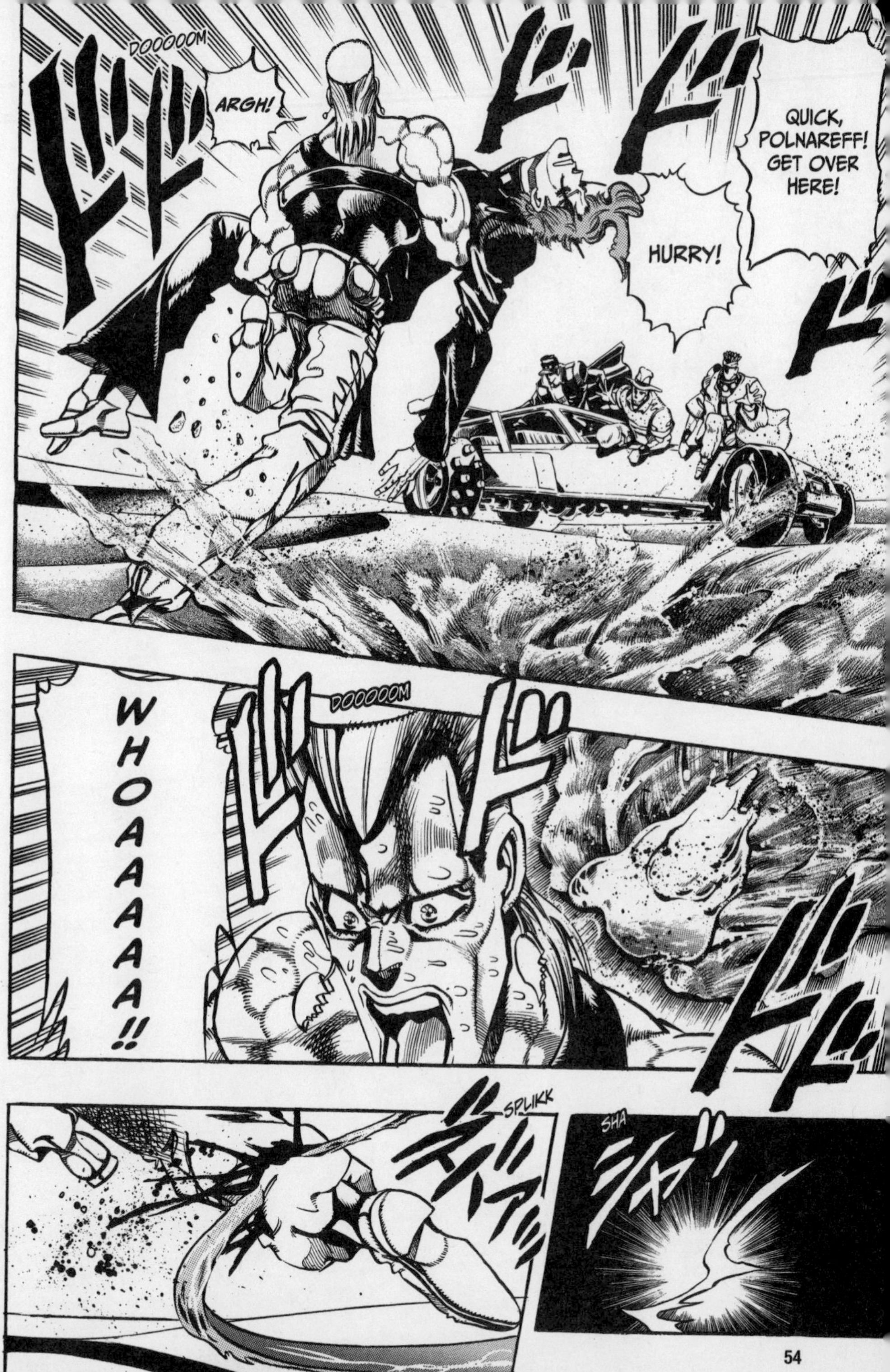
QUICK, POLNAREFF! GET OVER HERE!
HURRY!
ARGH!
DOOOOOM
DOOOOOM
WHOAAAAAAA!!
SHA
SPLIKK

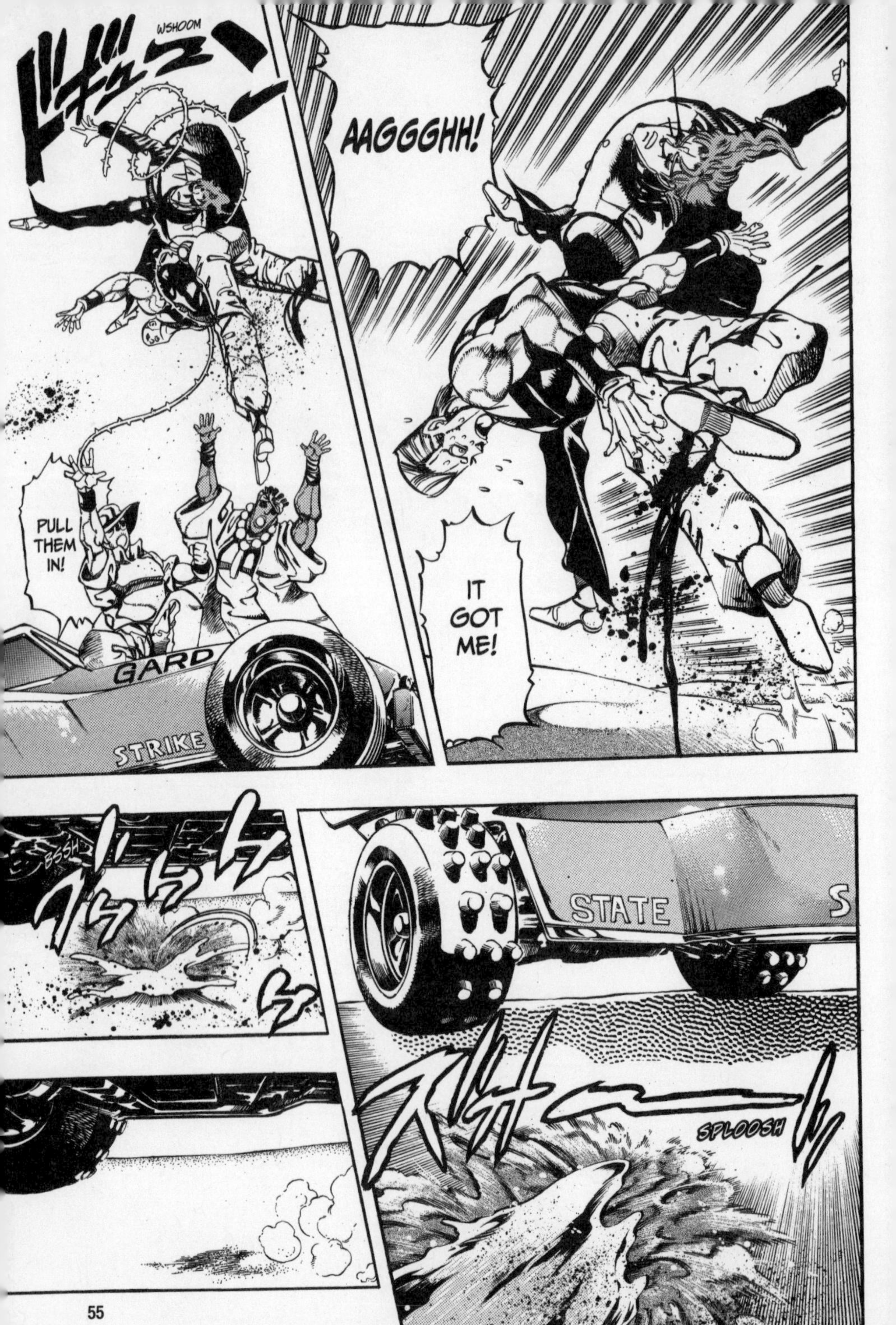
AAGGGHH!
IT GOT ME!
WSHOOM
PULL THEM IN!
GARD
STRIKE
STATE
S
SPLOOSH
BSSH

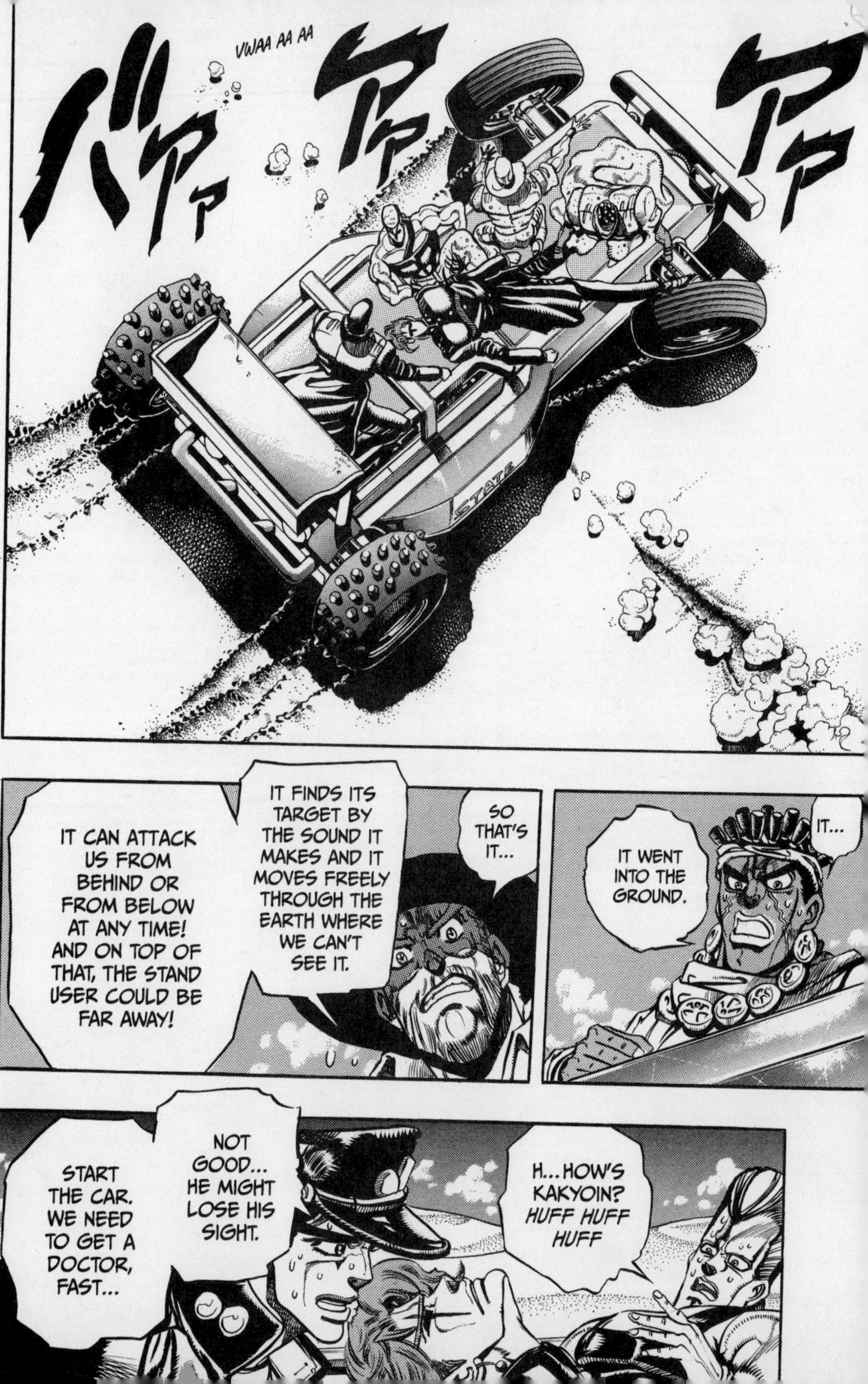
VWAA AA AA
IT...
IT WENT INTO THE GROUND.
SO THAT'S IT...
IT FINDS ITS TARGET BY THE SOUND IT MAKES AND IT MOVES FREELY THROUGH THE EARTH WHERE WE CAN'T SEE IT.
IT CAN ATTACK US FROM BEHIND OR FROM BELOW AT ANY TIME! AND ON TOP OF THAT, THE STAND USER COULD BE FAR AWAY!
H...HOW'S KAKYOIN? HUFF HUFF HUFF
NOT GOOD... HE MIGHT LOSE HIS SIGHT.
START THE CAR. WE NEED TO GET A DOCTOR, FAST...

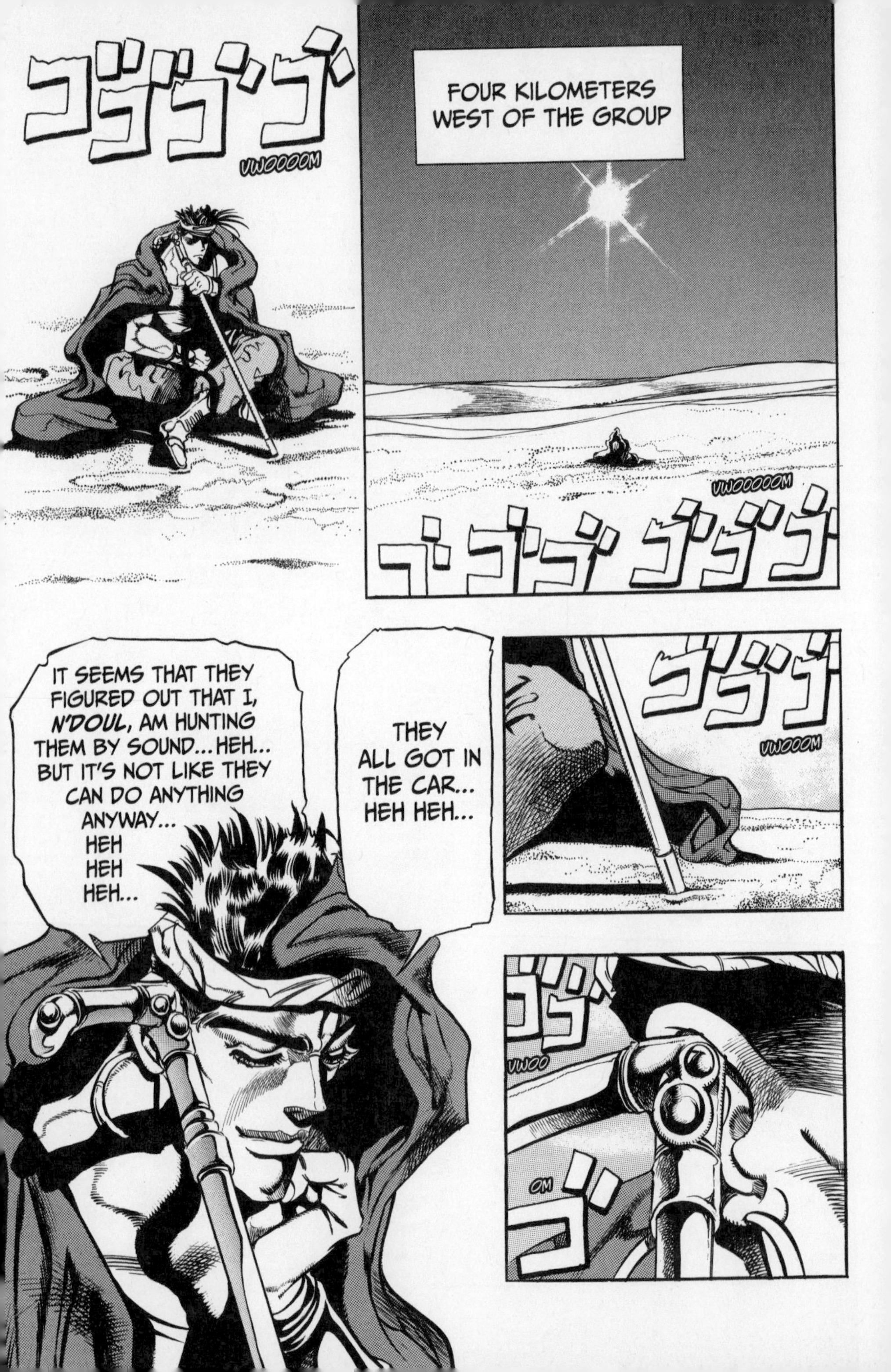
FOUR KILOMETERS WEST OF THE GROUP
VWOOOOOM
ゴゴゴゴ ゴゴゴゴ
ゴゴゴゴ
VWOOOOM
ゴゴゴ
VWOOOM
ゴゴ
VWOO
OM
ゴ
THEY ALL GOT IN THE CAR... HEH HEH...
IT SEEMS THAT THEY FIGURED OUT THAT I, *N'DOUL*, AM HUNTING THEM BY SOUND... HEH... BUT IT'S NOT LIKE THEY CAN DO ANYTHING ANYWAY... HEH HEH HEH...

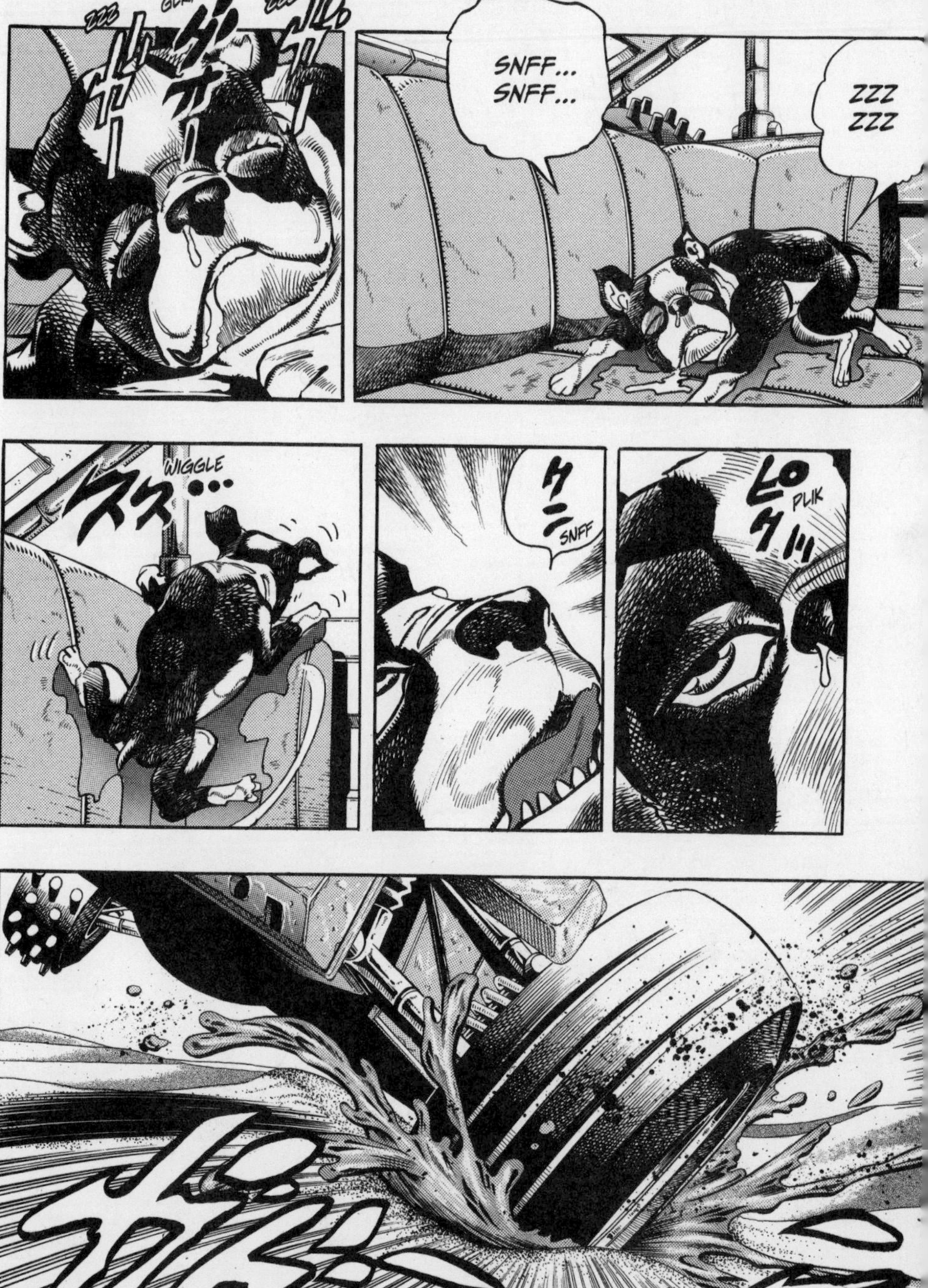
ZZZ
ZZZ
SNFF...
SNFF...
ZZZ
GLRF
ZZZ
PLIK
SNFF
WIGGLE
CLRSSH

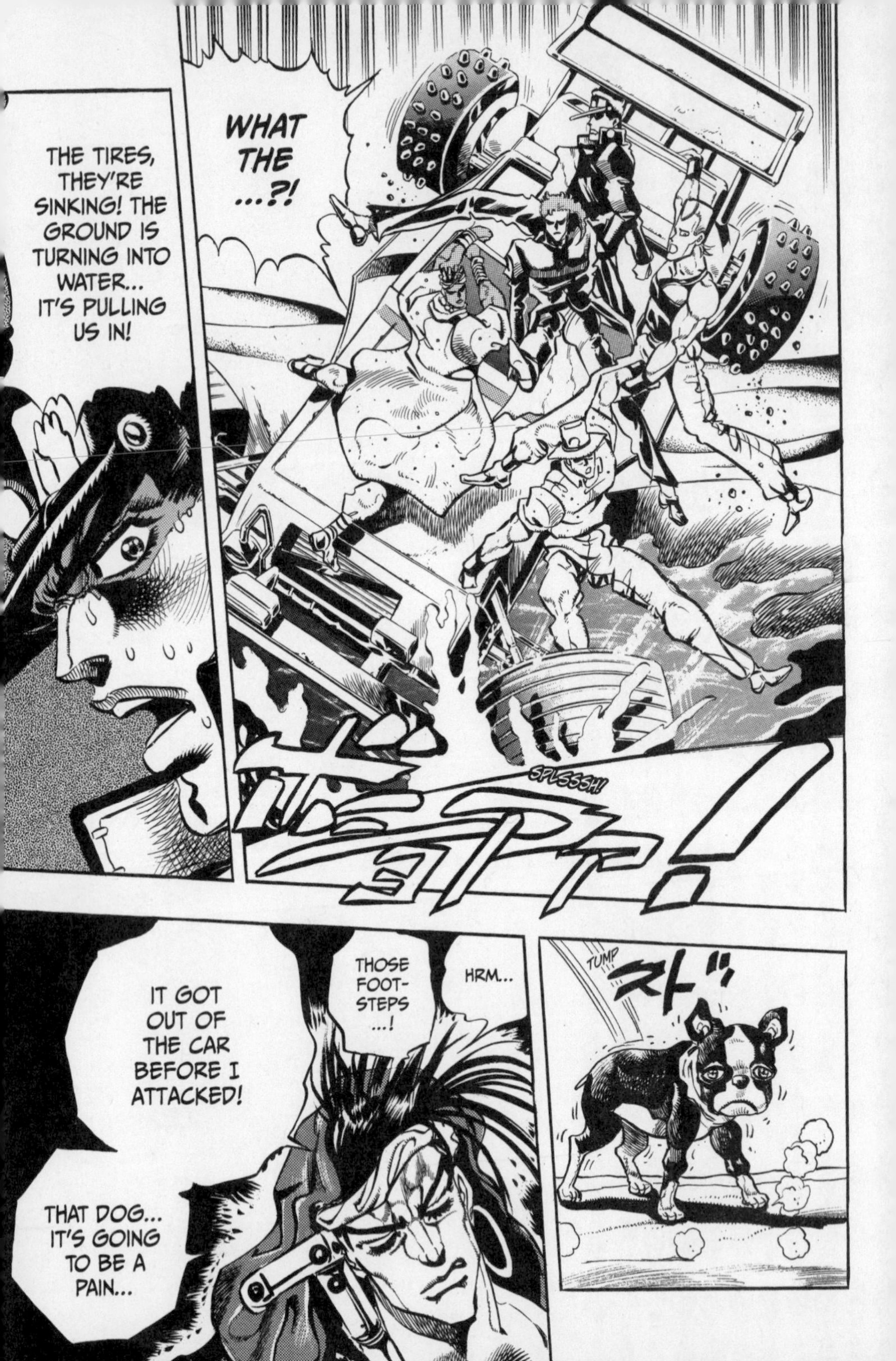

WHAT THE ...?!
SPLSSSH!
THE TIRES, THEY'RE SINKING! THE GROUND IS TURNING INTO WATER... IT'S PULLING US IN!
TUMP
HRM...
THOSE FOOT-STEPS ...!
IT GOT OUT OF THE CAR BEFORE I ATTACKED!
THAT DOG... IT'S GOING TO BE A PAIN...

LUCK LAND
THE FOOL 0

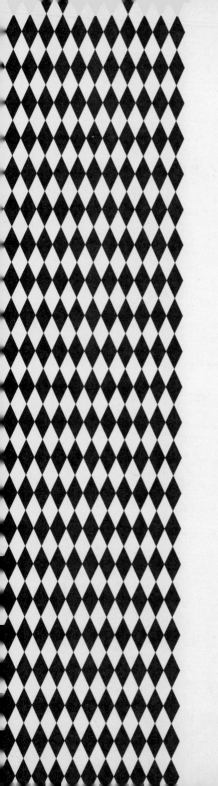

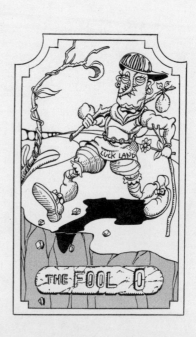

CHAPTER 73: Iggy "The Fool" and "Geb" N'doul PART 4

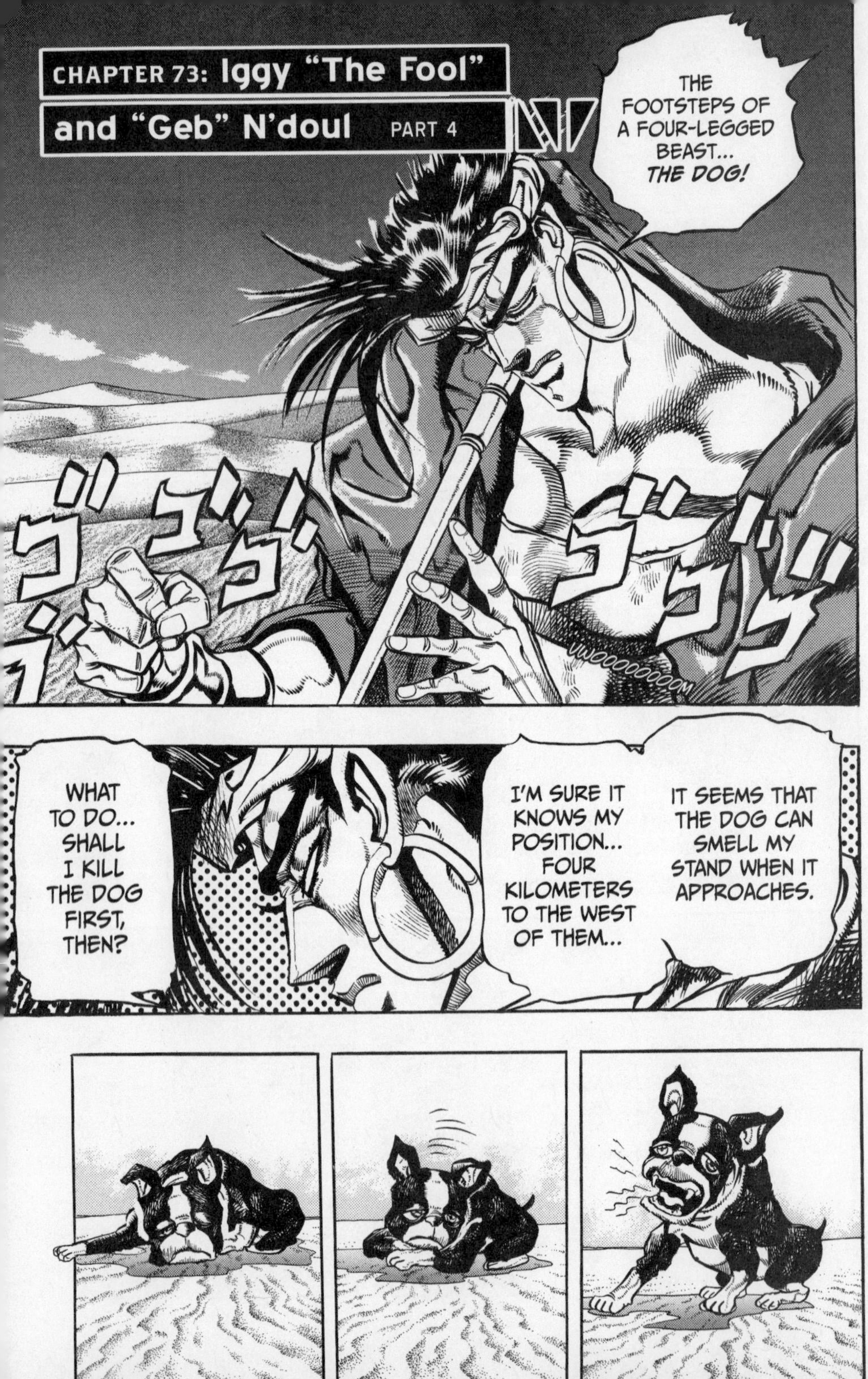
THE FOOTSTEPS OF A FOUR-LEGGED BEAST... *THE DOG!*
VWOOOOOOOOOM
IT SEEMS THAT THE DOG CAN SMELL MY STAND WHEN IT APPROACHES.
I'M SURE IT KNOWS MY POSITION... FOUR KILOMETERS TO THE WEST OF THEM...
WHAT TO DO... SHALL I KILL THE DOG FIRST, THEN?

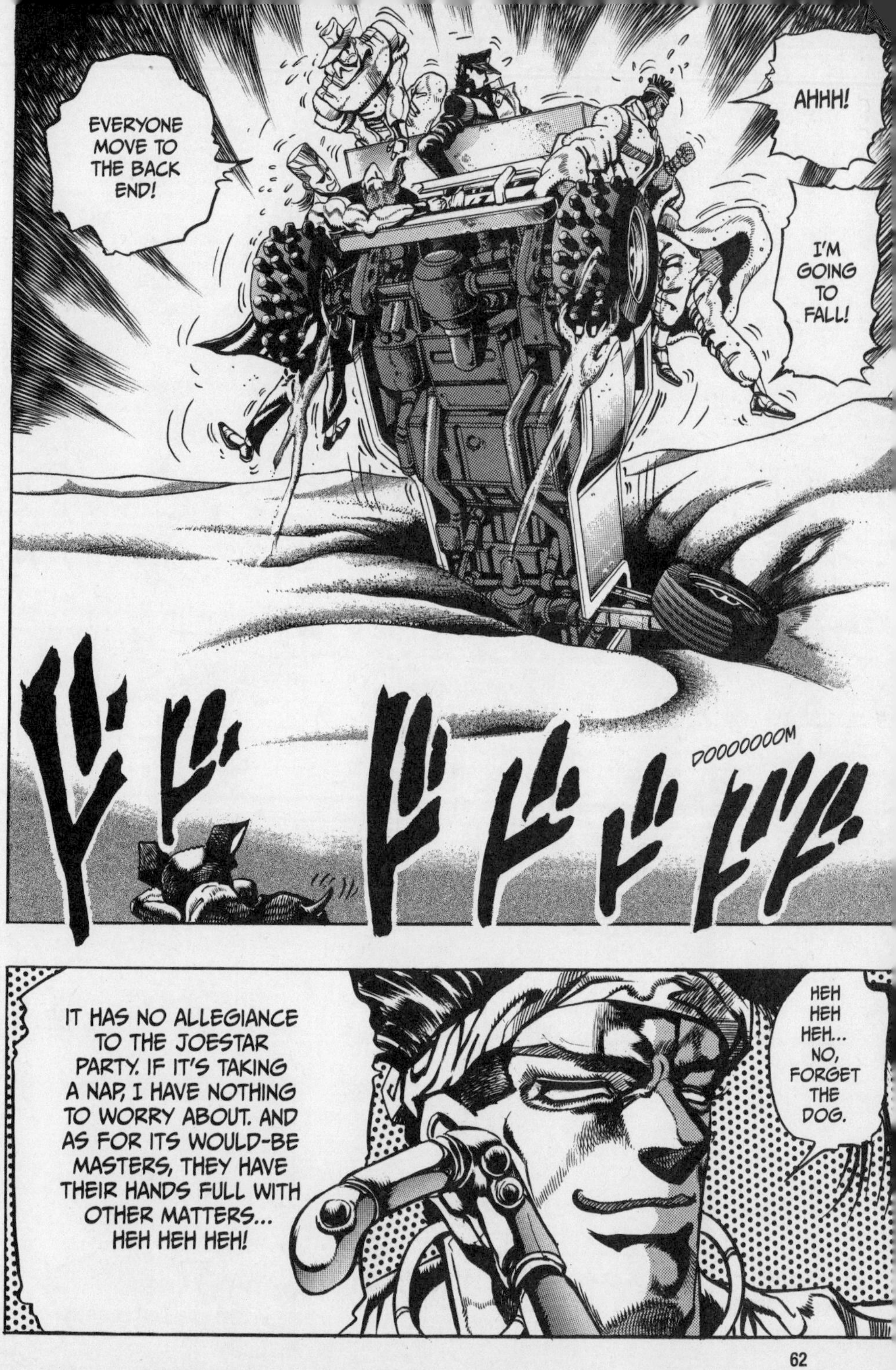
AHHH!
I'M GOING TO FALL!
EVERYONE MOVE TO THE BACK END!
DOOOOOOOM
HEH HEH HEH... NO, FORGET THE DOG.
IT HAS NO ALLEGIANCE TO THE JOESTAR PARTY. IF IT'S TAKING A NAP, I HAVE NOTHING TO WORRY ABOUT. AND AS FOR ITS WOULD-BE MASTERS, THEY HAVE THEIR HANDS FULL WITH OTHER MATTERS... HEH HEH HEH!

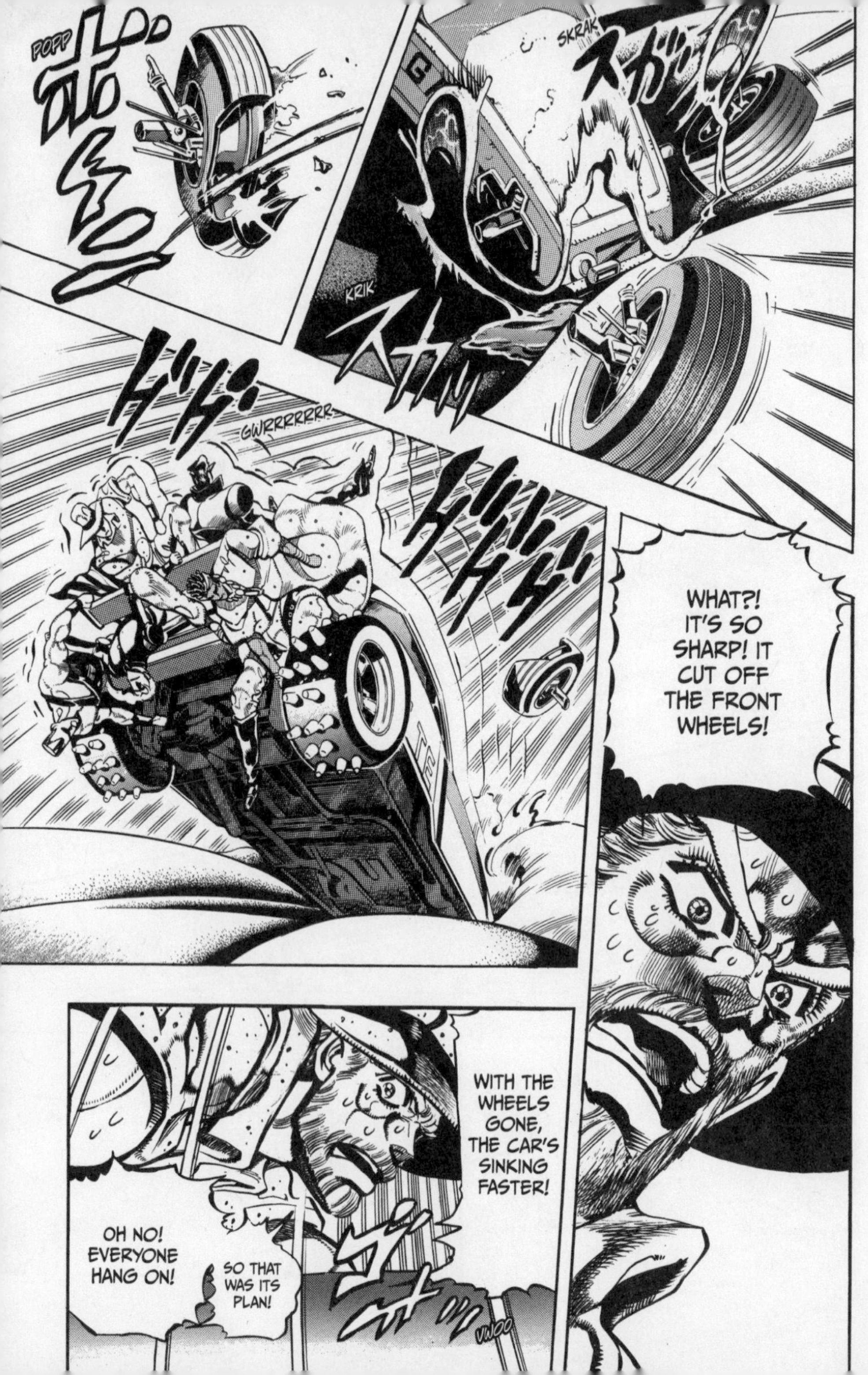
SKRAK
KRIK
POPP
WHAT?! IT'S SO SHARP! IT CUT OFF THE FRONT WHEELS!
GWRRRRRRR
WITH THE WHEELS GONE, THE CAR'S SINKING FASTER!
OH NO! EVERYONE HANG ON!
SO THAT WAS ITS PLAN!
VWOO

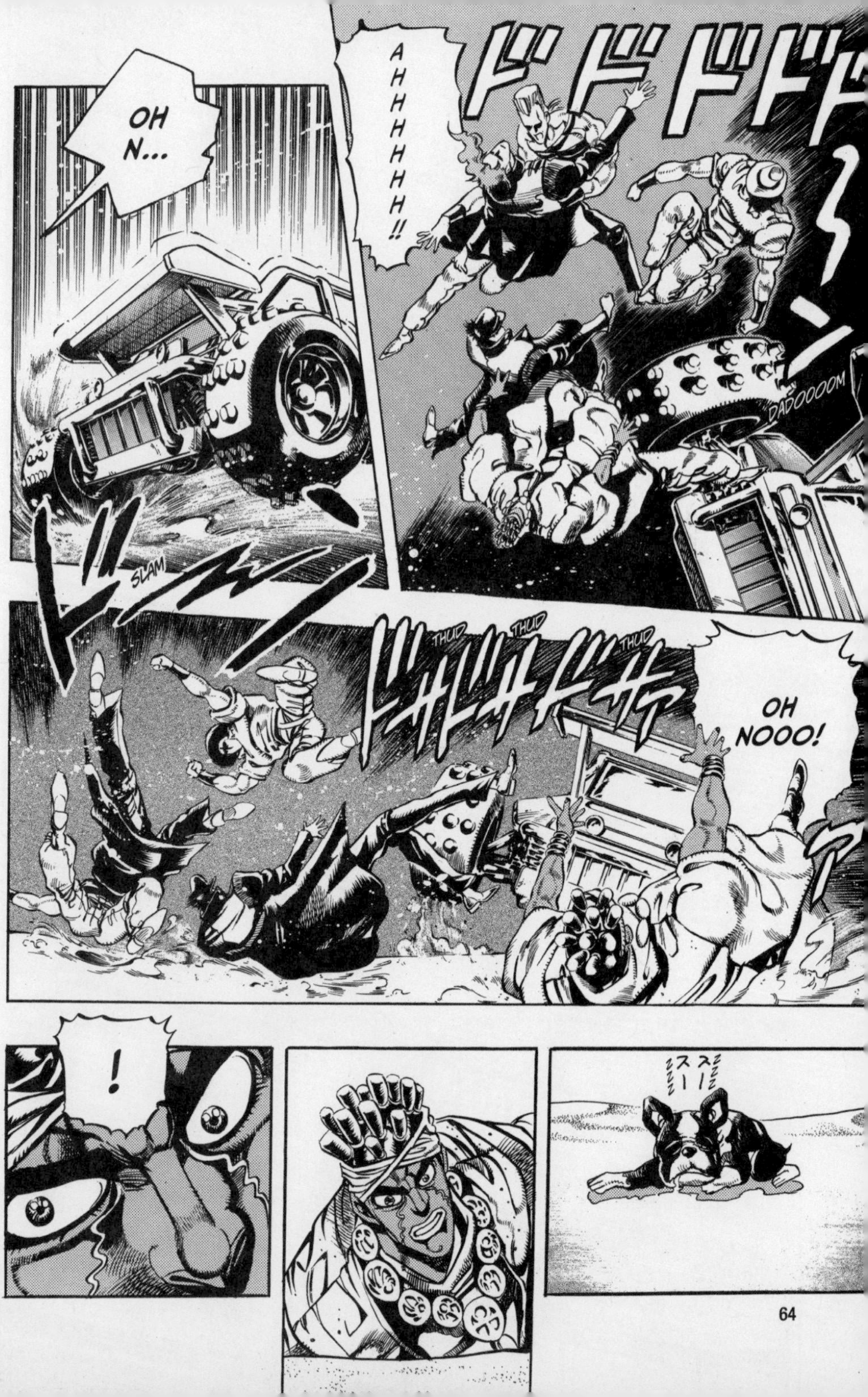
AHHHHHHHH!!
DADOOOOM
OH N...
SLAM
THUD THUD THUD
OH NOOO!
!

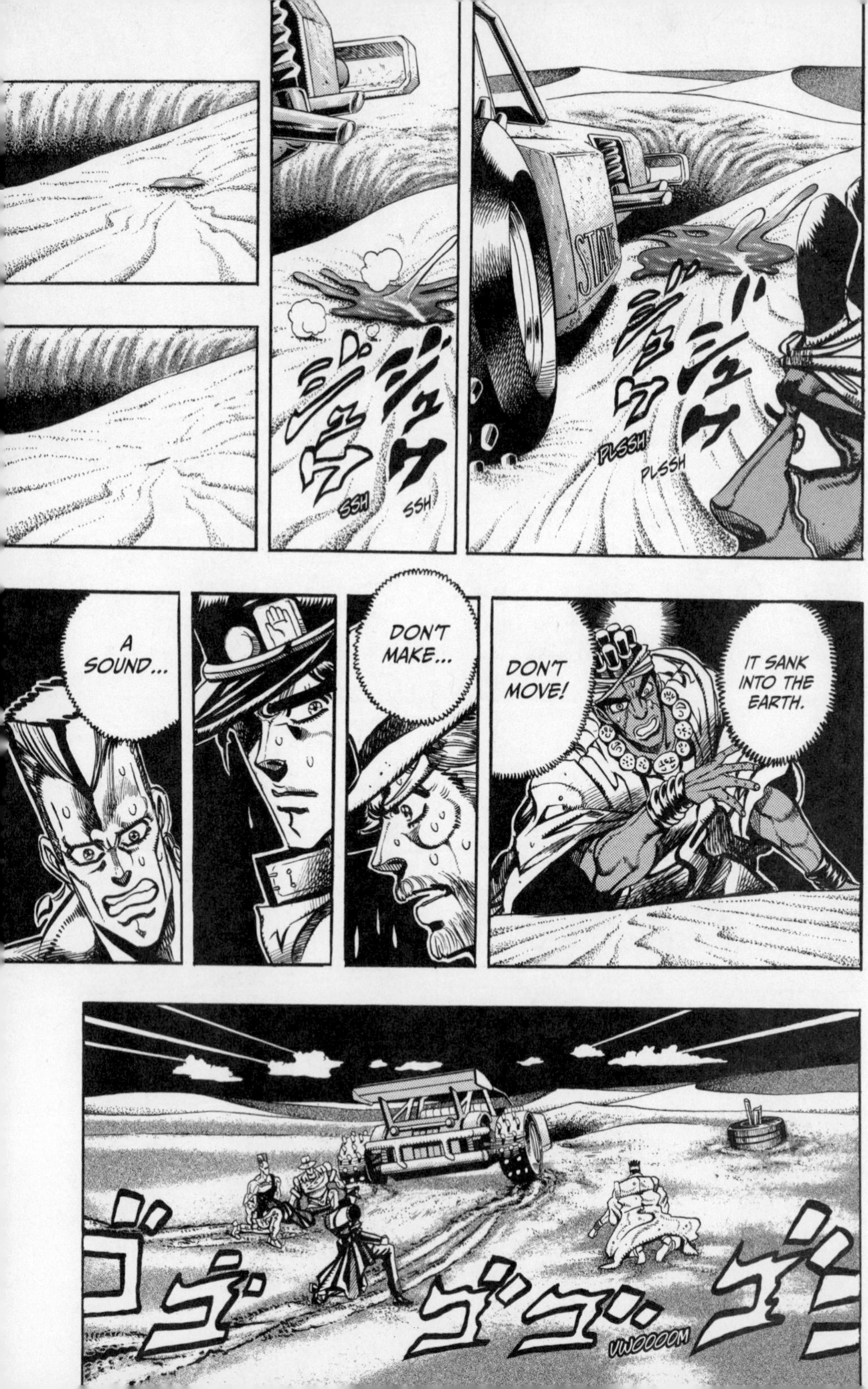
PLSSH
PLSSH
SSH
SSH
IT SANK INTO THE EARTH.
DON'T MOVE!
DON'T MAKE...
A SOUND...
UWOOOOM

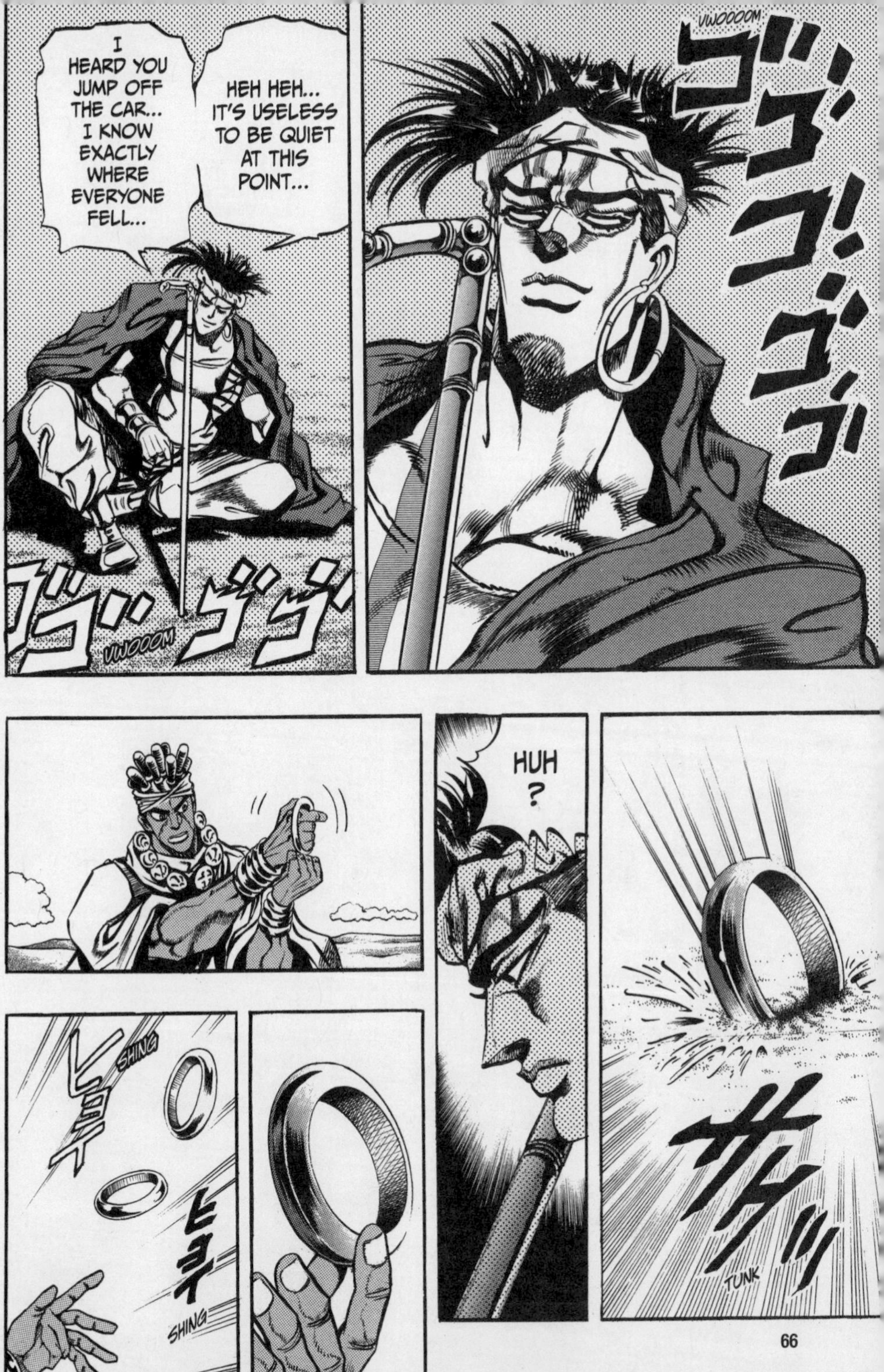
VWOOOOM
HEH HEH... IT'S USELESS TO BE QUIET AT THIS POINT...
I HEARD YOU JUMP OFF THE CAR... I KNOW EXACTLY WHERE EVERYONE FELL...
VWOOOM
TUNK
HUH ?
SHING
SHING

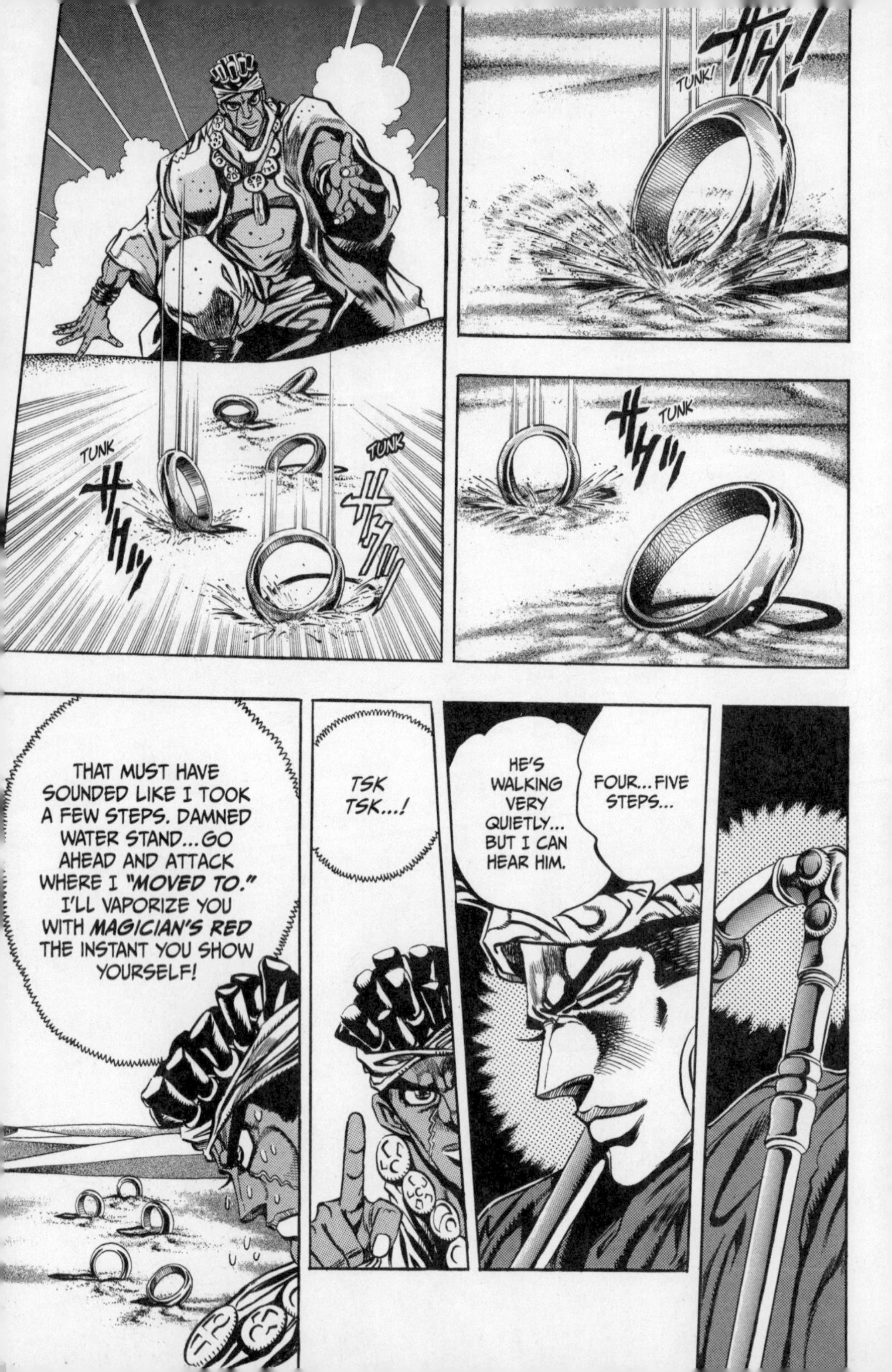
TUNK!
TUNK
TUNK
TUNK
FOUR...FIVE STEPS...
HE'S WALKING VERY QUIETLY... BUT I CAN HEAR HIM.
TSK TSK...!
THAT MUST HAVE SOUNDED LIKE I TOOK A FEW STEPS. DAMNED WATER STAND...GO AHEAD AND ATTACK WHERE I "MOVED TO." I'LL VAPORIZE YOU WITH MAGICIAN'S RED THE INSTANT YOU SHOW YOURSELF!

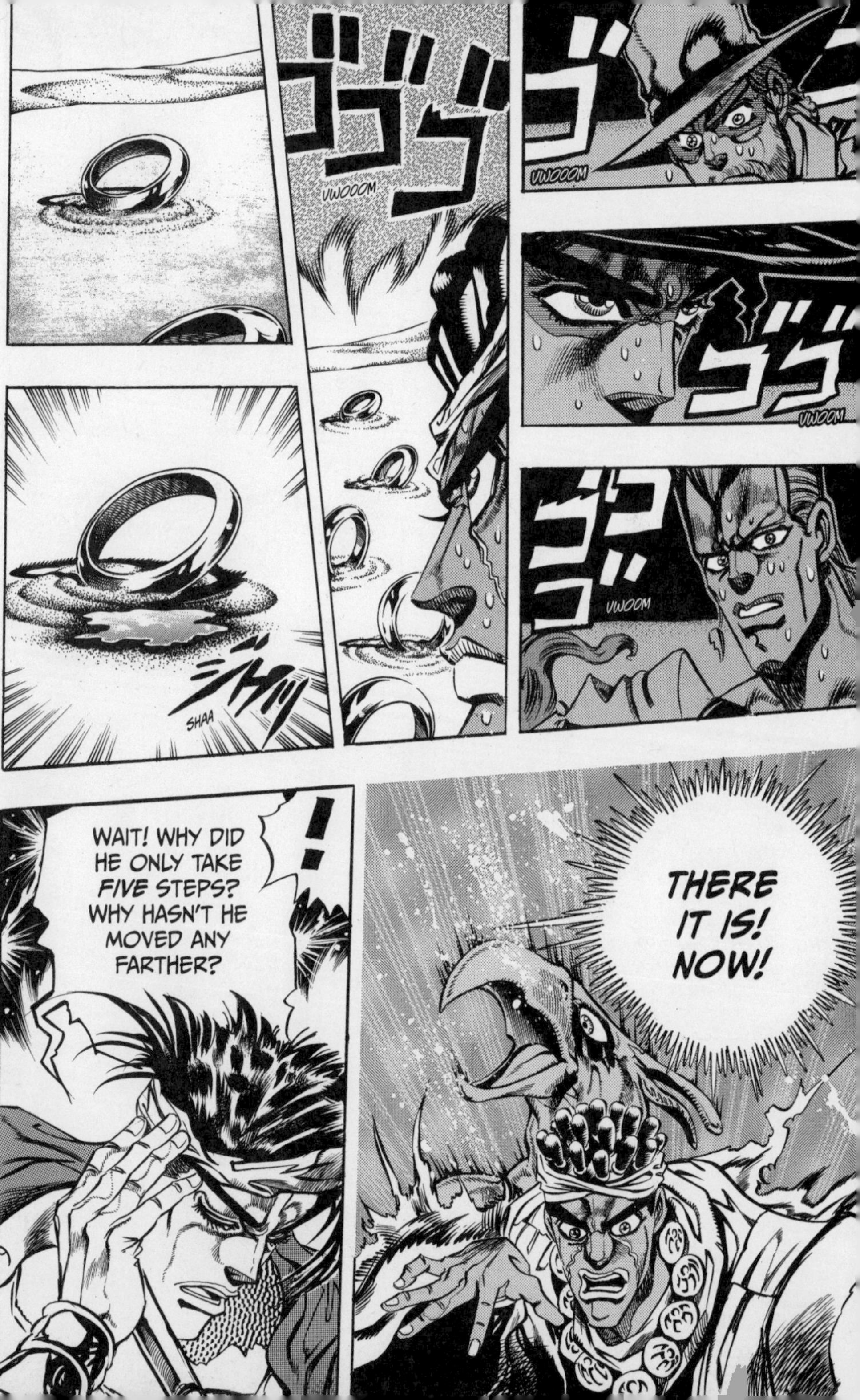
VWOOOM
VWOOM
VWOOM
VWOOOM
SHAA
THERE IT IS! NOW!
!
WAIT! WHY DID HE ONLY TAKE *FIVE* STEPS? WHY HASN'T HE MOVED ANY FARTHER?

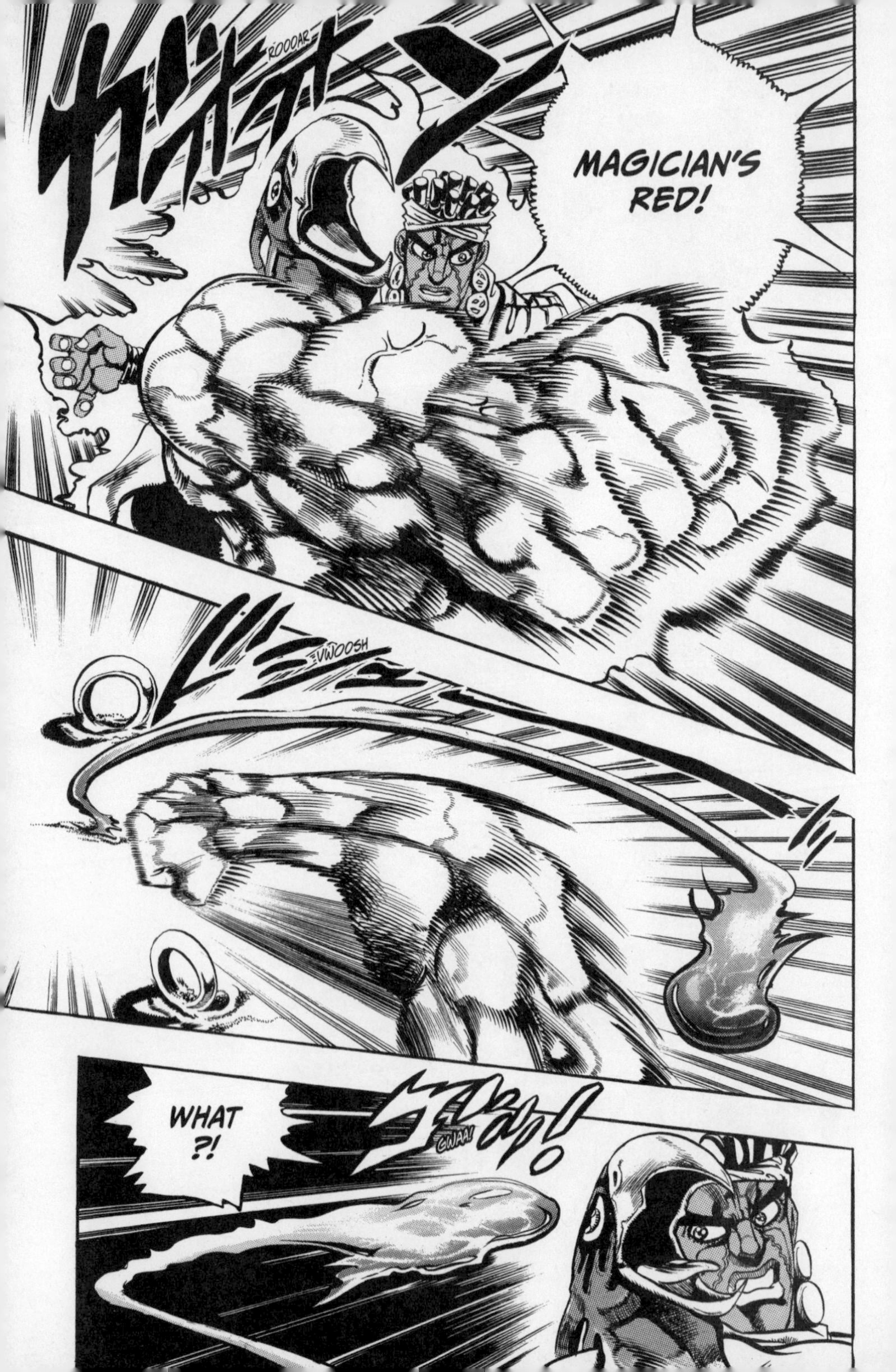
MAGICIAN'S RED!
ROOOAR
VWOOSH
CWAA!
WHAT ?!

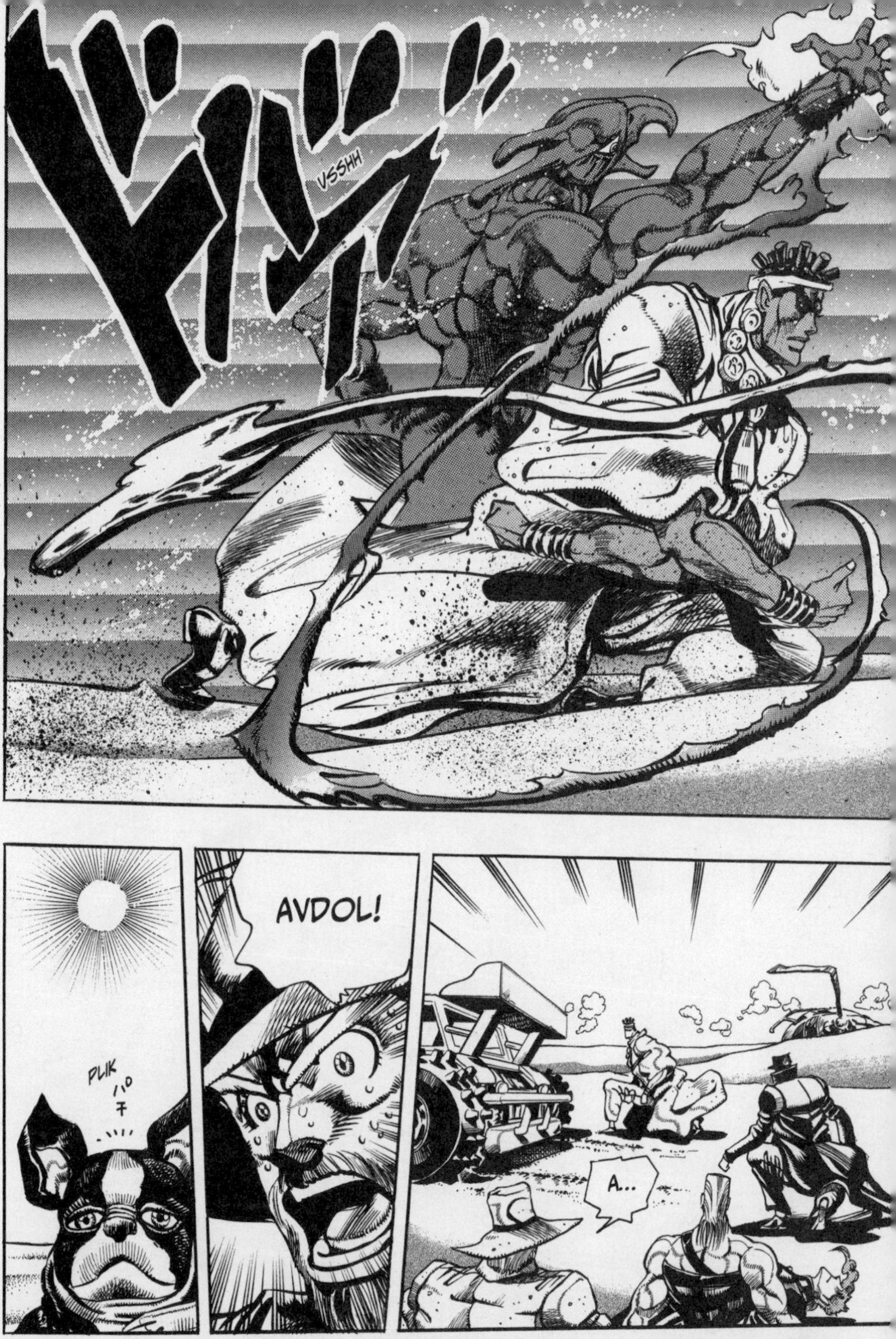
VSSHH
A...
AVDOL!
PLIK
パチ

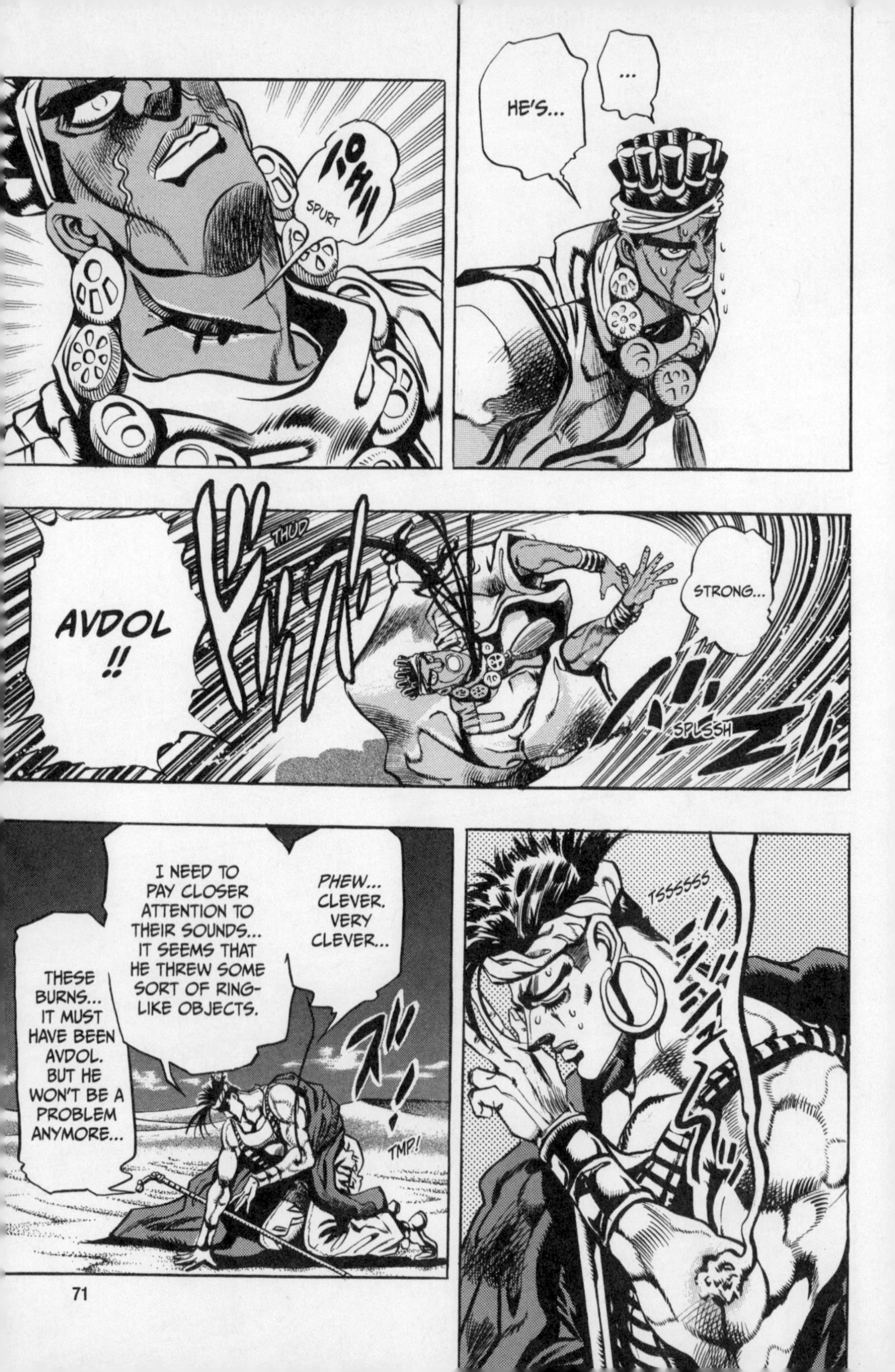
...
HE'S...
SPURT
STRONG...
SPLSSH
THUD
AVDOL !!
TSSSSSS
PHEW... CLEVER. VERY CLEVER...
I NEED TO PAY CLOSER ATTENTION TO THEIR SOUNDS... IT SEEMS THAT HE THREW SOME SORT OF RING-LIKE OBJECTS.
THESE BURNS... IT MUST HAVE BEEN AVDOL. BUT HE WON'T BE A PROBLEM ANYMORE...
TMP!

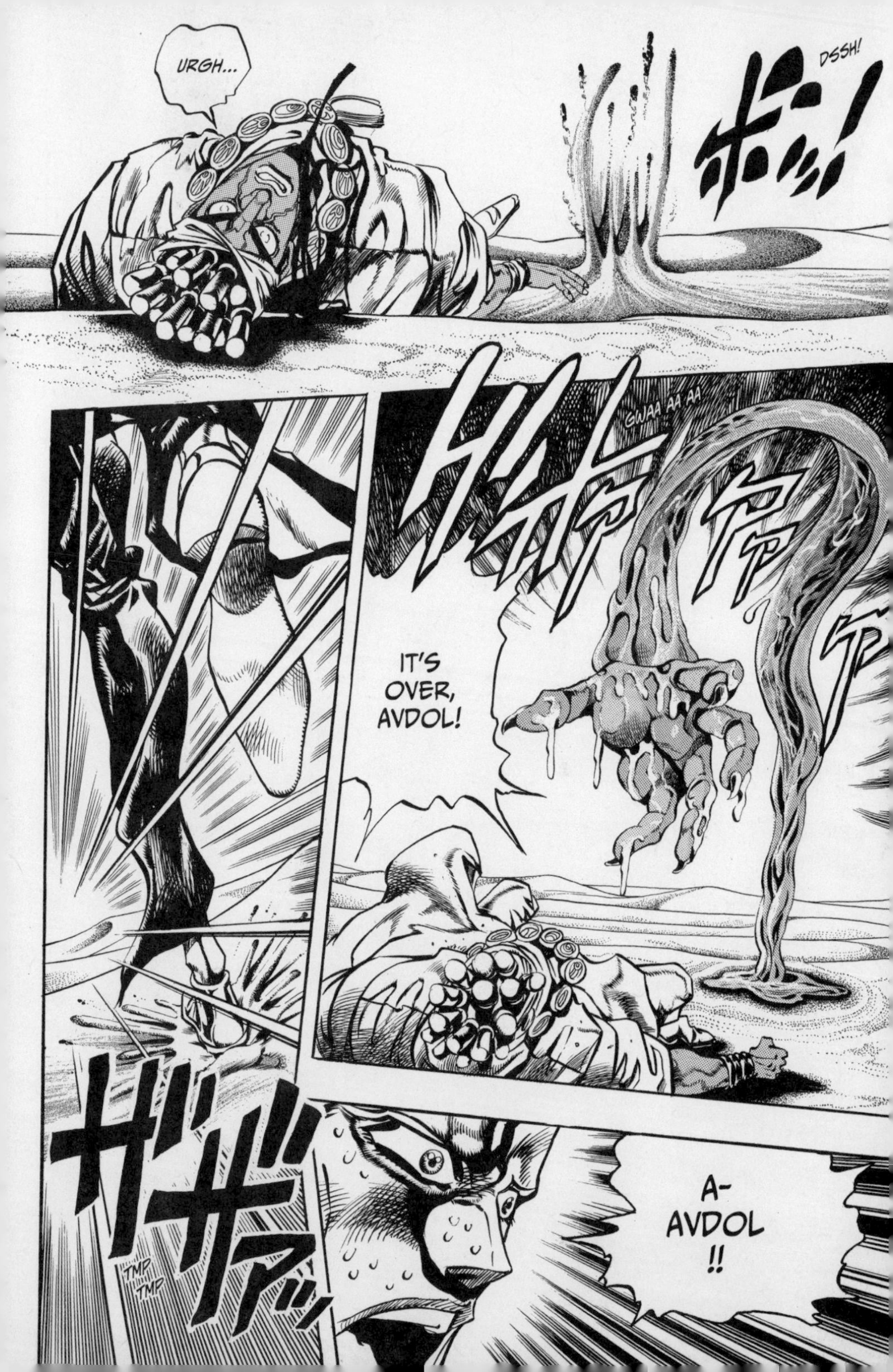
DSSH!
URGH...
GWAA AA AA
IT'S OVER, AVDOL!
A-AVDOL!!
TMP TMP

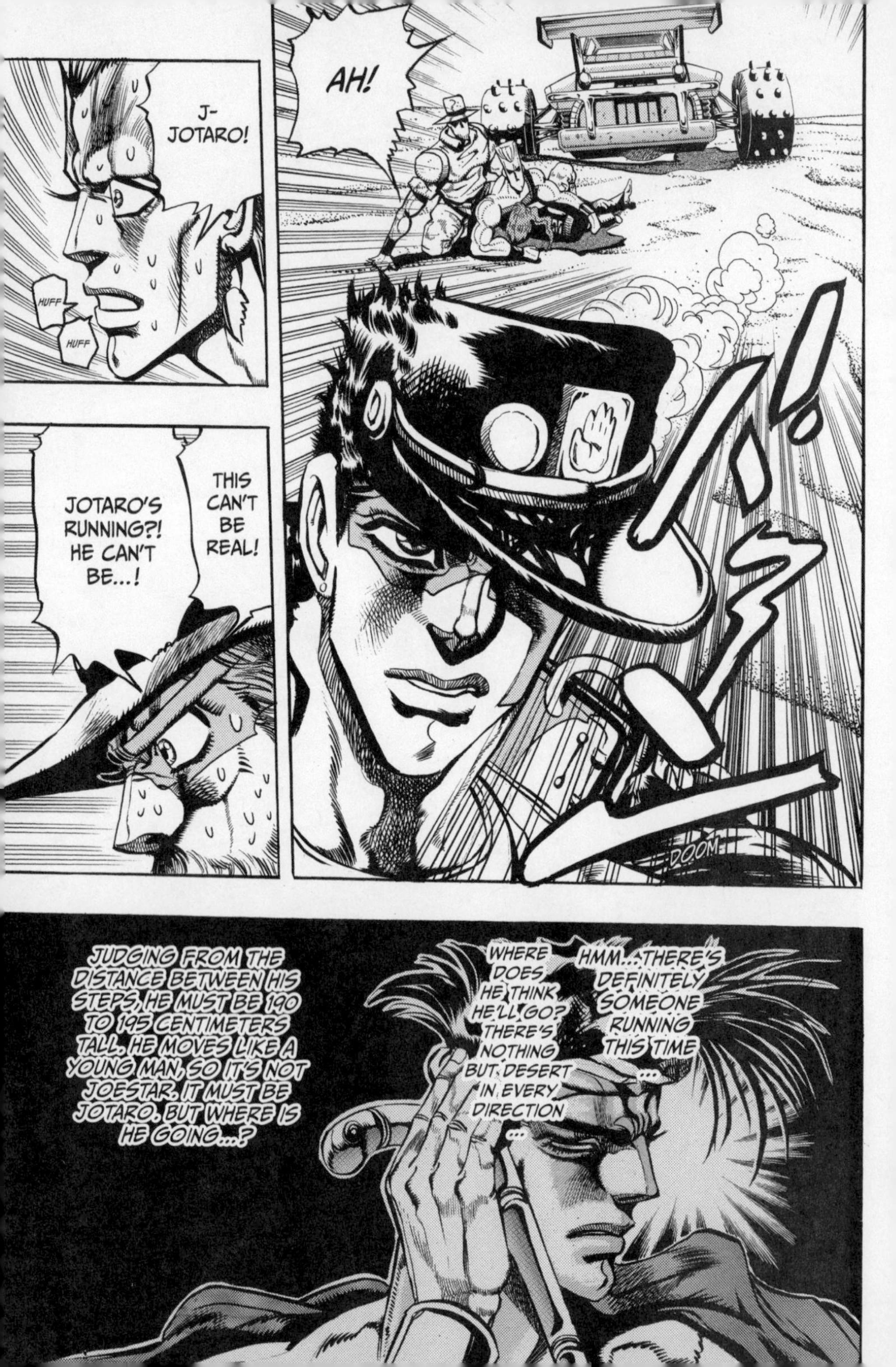
AH!
DOOM
J- JOTARO!
HUFF
HUFF
THIS CAN'T BE REAL!
JOTARO'S RUNNING?! HE CAN'T BE...!
HMM... THERE'S DEFINITELY SOMEONE RUNNING THIS TIME ...
WHERE DOES HE THINK HE'LL GO? THERE'S NOTHING BUT DESERT IN EVERY DIRECTION ...
JUDGING FROM THE DISTANCE BETWEEN HIS STEPS, HE MUST BE 190 TO 195 CENTIMETERS TALL. HE MOVES LIKE A YOUNG MAN, SO IT'S NOT JOESTAR. IT MUST BE JOTARO. BUT WHERE IS HE GOING...?

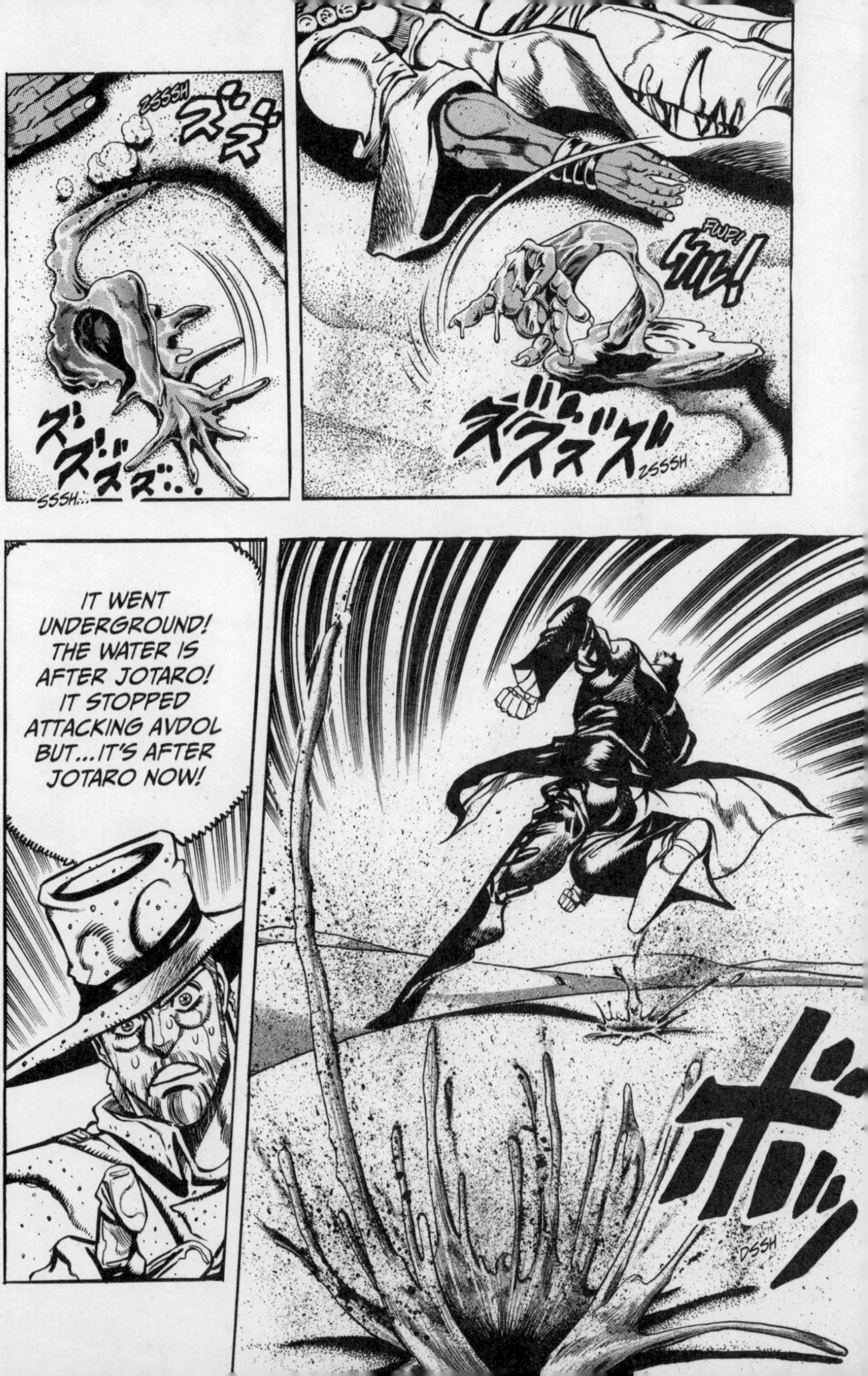

FWUP!
ZSSSH
ZSSSH
SSSH...
DSSH
IT WENT UNDERGROUND! THE WATER IS AFTER JOTARO! IT STOPPED ATTACKING AVDOL BUT...IT'S AFTER JOTARO NOW!

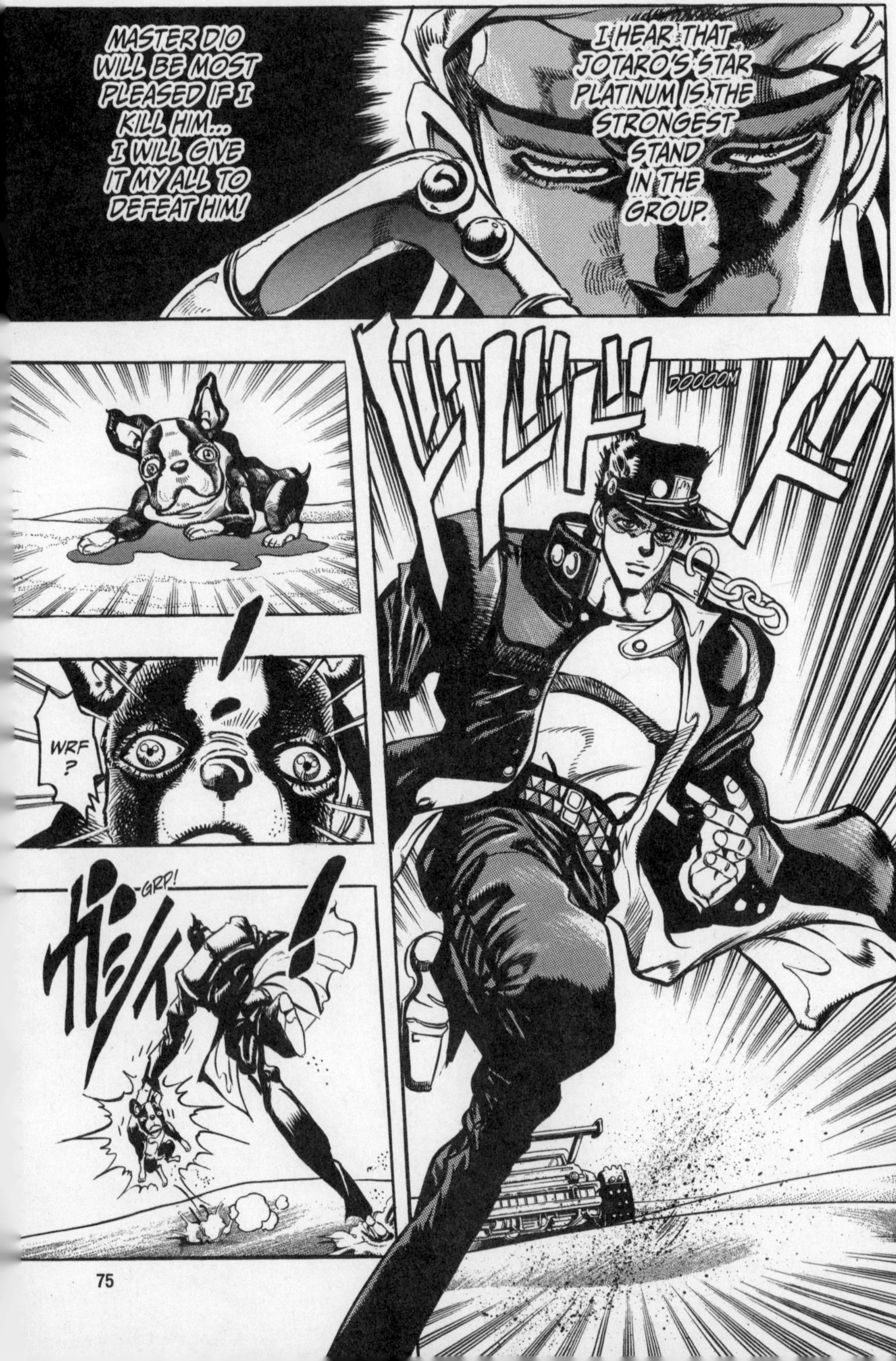
I HEAR THAT JOTARO'S STAR PLATINUM IS THE STRONGEST STAND IN THE GROUP.
MASTER DIO WILL BE MOST PLEASED IF I KILL HIM... I WILL GIVE IT MY ALL TO DEFEAT HIM!
DOOOOM
WRF ?
GRP!

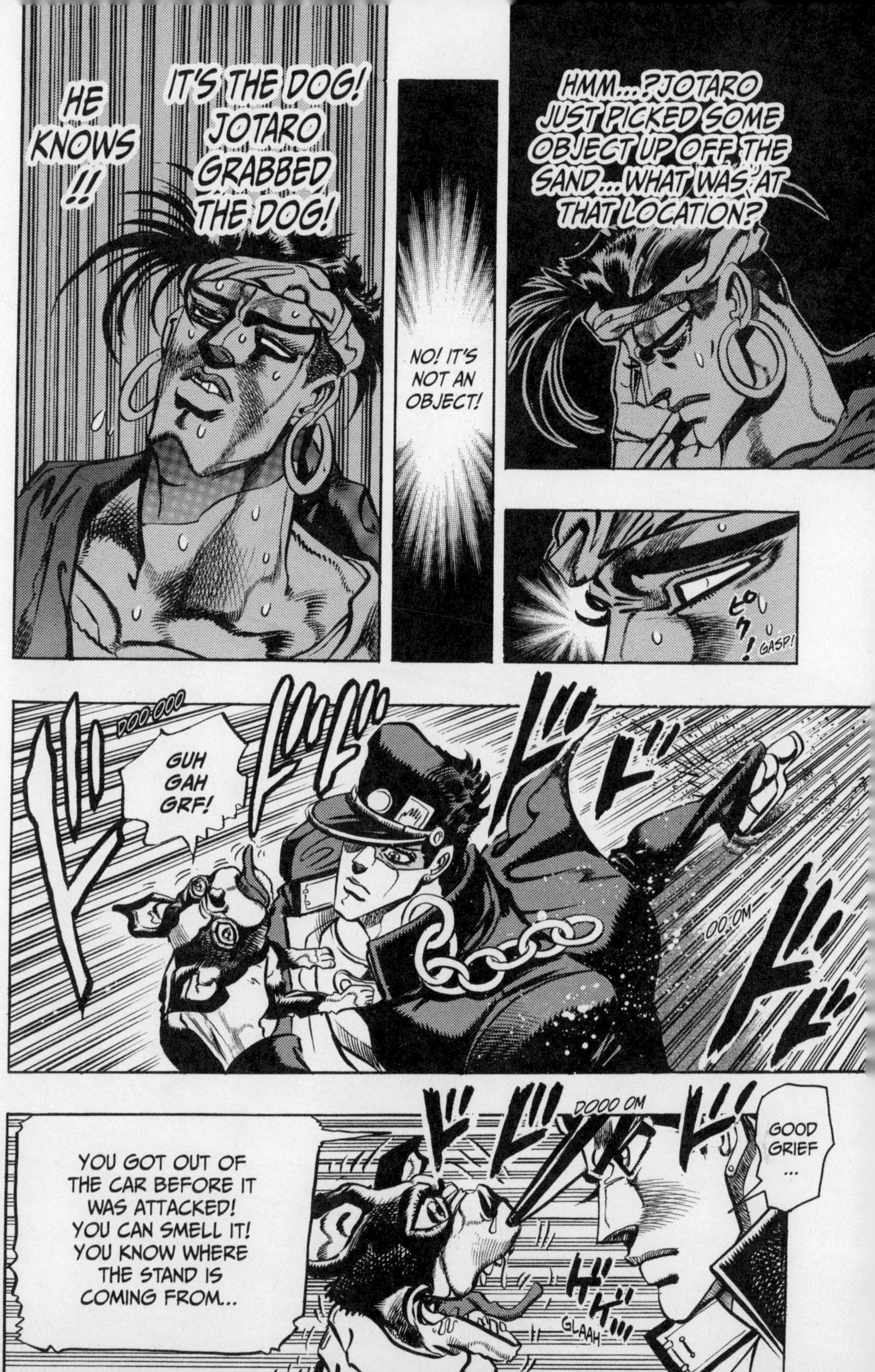

HMM...? JOTARO JUST PICKED SOME OBJECT UP OFF THE SAND... WHAT WAS AT THAT LOCATION?
ピクッ!
GASP!
NO! IT'S NOT AN OBJECT!
IT'S THE DOG! JOTARO GRABBED THE DOG!
HE KNOWS!!
OO OM
DOO OOO
GUH GAH GRF!
GOOD GRIEF...
DOOO OM
GLAAH
YOU GOT OUT OF THE CAR BEFORE IT WAS ATTACKED! YOU CAN SMELL IT! YOU KNOW WHERE THE STAND IS COMING FROM...

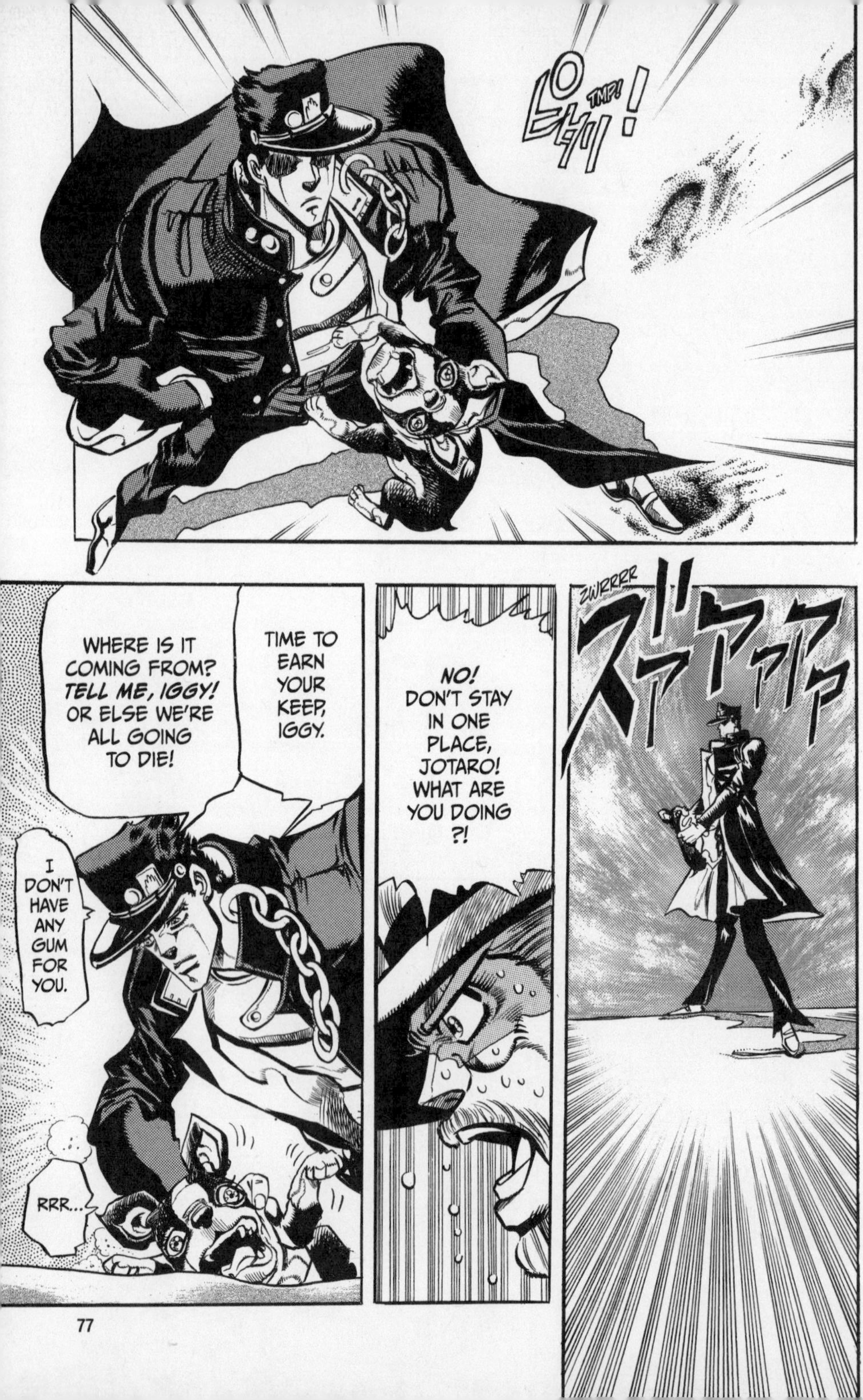
TMP!
ZWRRRR
NO! DON'T STAY IN ONE PLACE, JOTARO! WHAT ARE YOU DOING?!
TIME TO EARN YOUR KEEP, IGGY.
WHERE IS IT COMING FROM? *TELL ME, IGGY!* OR ELSE WE'RE ALL GOING TO DIE!
I DON'T HAVE ANY GUM FOR YOU.
RRR...

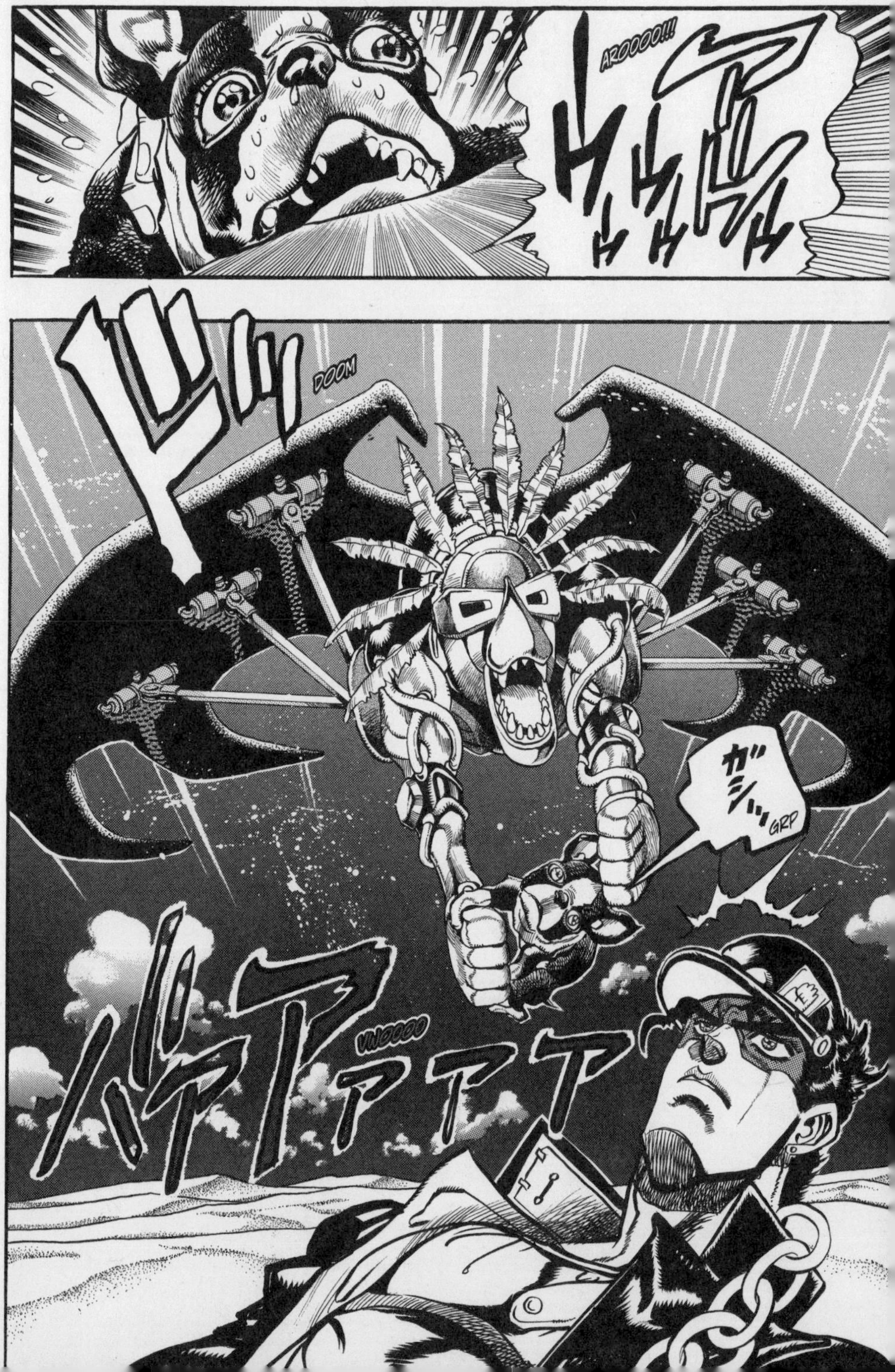
AROOOOO!!!
DOOM
ガシッ
GRP
VWOOOO

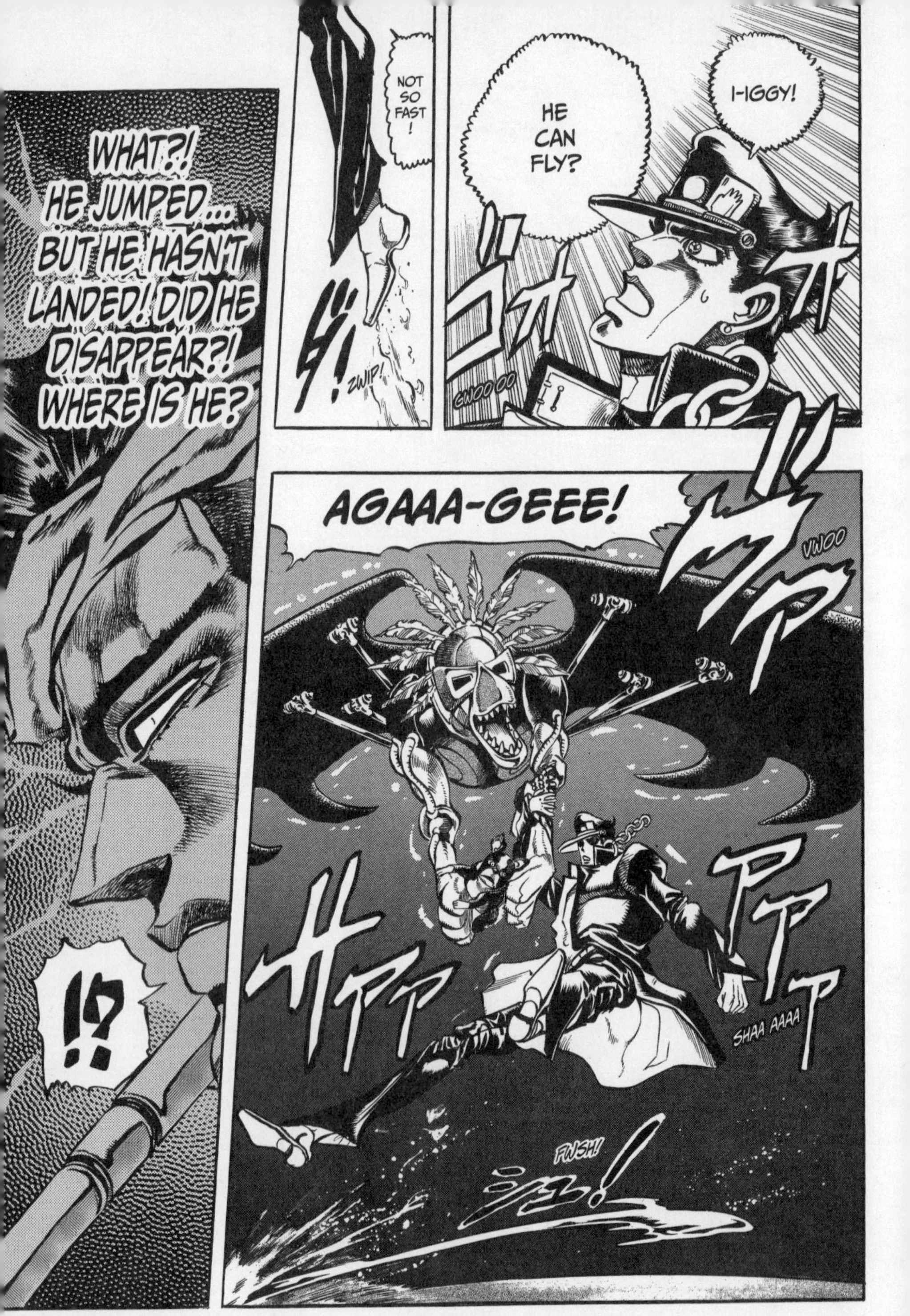
I-IGGY!
HE CAN FLY?
GWOO OO
NOT SO FAST!
ZWIP!
AGAAA-GEEE!
VWOO
SHAA AAAA
FWSH!
WHAT?! HE JUMPED... BUT HE HASN'T LANDED! DID HE DISAPPEAR?! WHERE IS HE?
!?

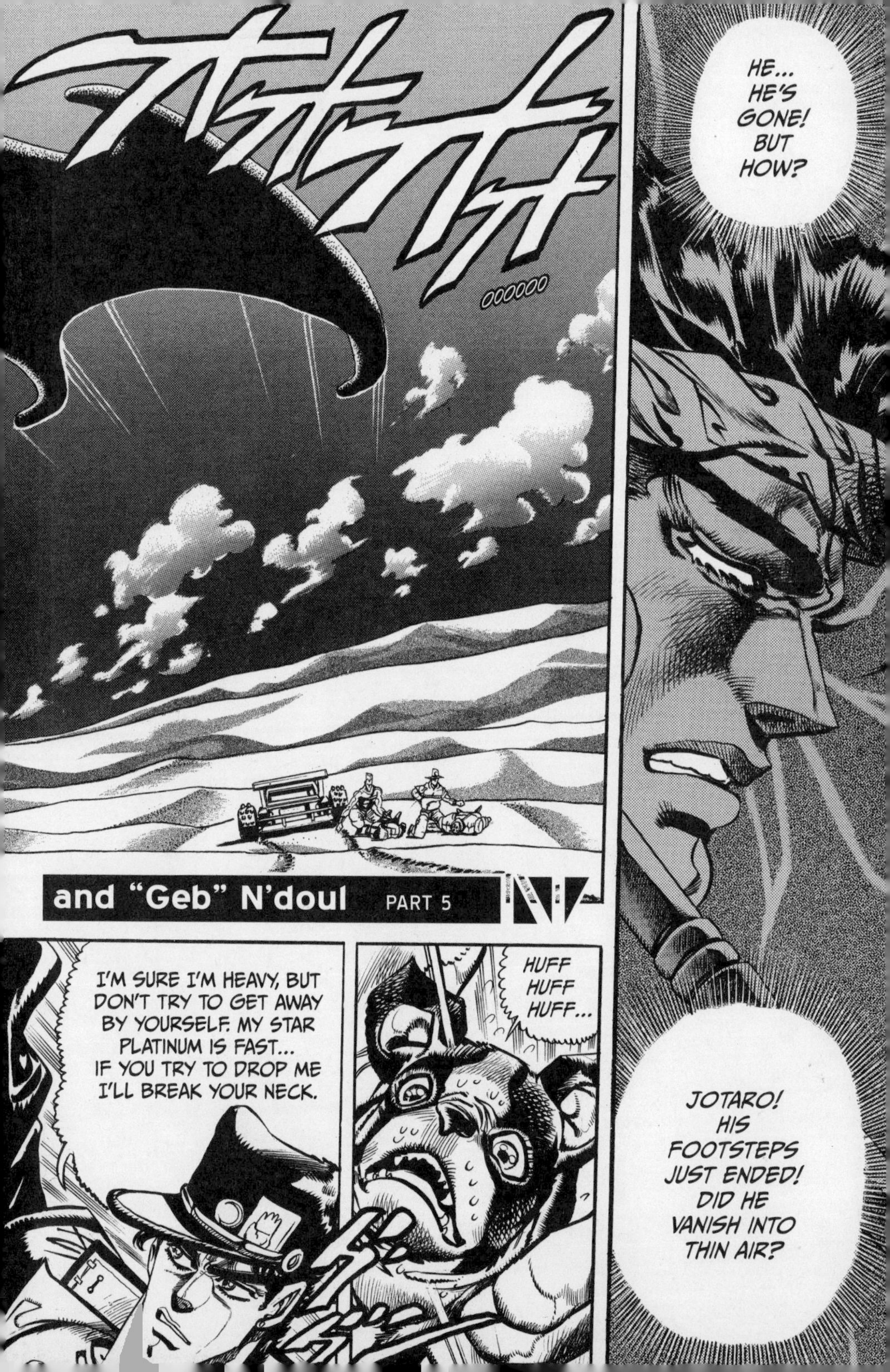
HE... HE'S GONE! BUT HOW?
JOTARO! HIS FOOTSTEPS JUST ENDED! DID HE VANISH INTO THIN AIR?
oooooo
and "Geb" N'doul PART 5
HUFF HUFF HUFF...
I'M SURE I'M HEAVY, BUT DON'T TRY TO GET AWAY BY YOURSELF. MY STAR PLATINUM IS FAST... IF YOU TRY TO DROP ME I'LL BREAK YOUR NECK.

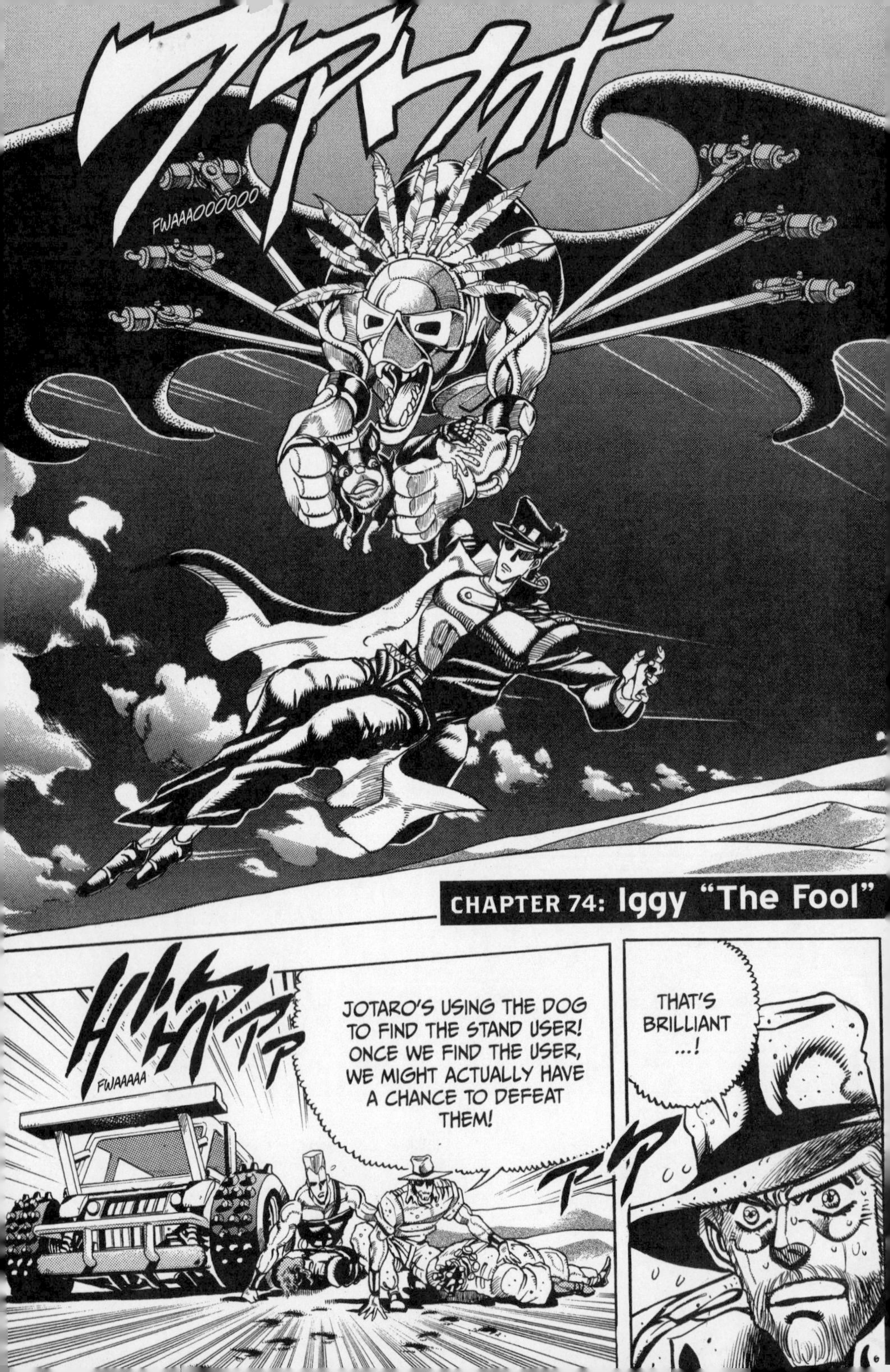
FWAAAOOOOOO
CHAPTER 74: Iggy "The Fool"
THAT'S BRILLIANT ...!
JOTARO'S USING THE DOG TO FIND THE STAND USER! ONCE WE FIND THE USER, WE MIGHT ACTUALLY HAVE A CHANCE TO DEFEAT THEM!
FWAAAAA

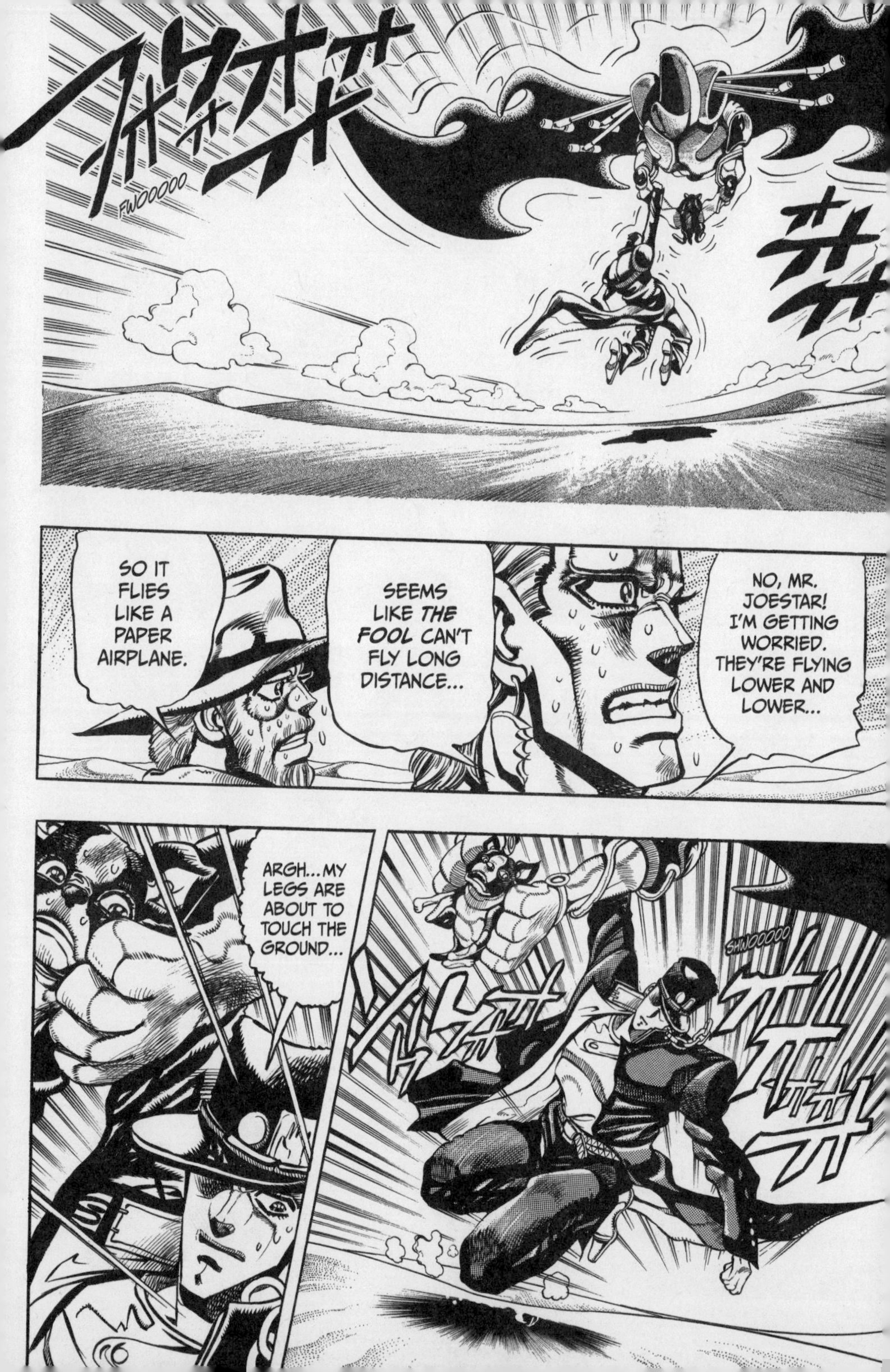
FWOOOOO
NO, MR. JOESTAR! I'M GETTING WORRIED. THEY'RE FLYING LOWER AND LOWER...
SEEMS LIKE *THE FOOL* CAN'T FLY LONG DISTANCE...
SO IT FLIES LIKE A PAPER AIRPLANE.
SHWOOOOO
ARGH...MY LEGS ARE ABOUT TO TOUCH THE GROUND...

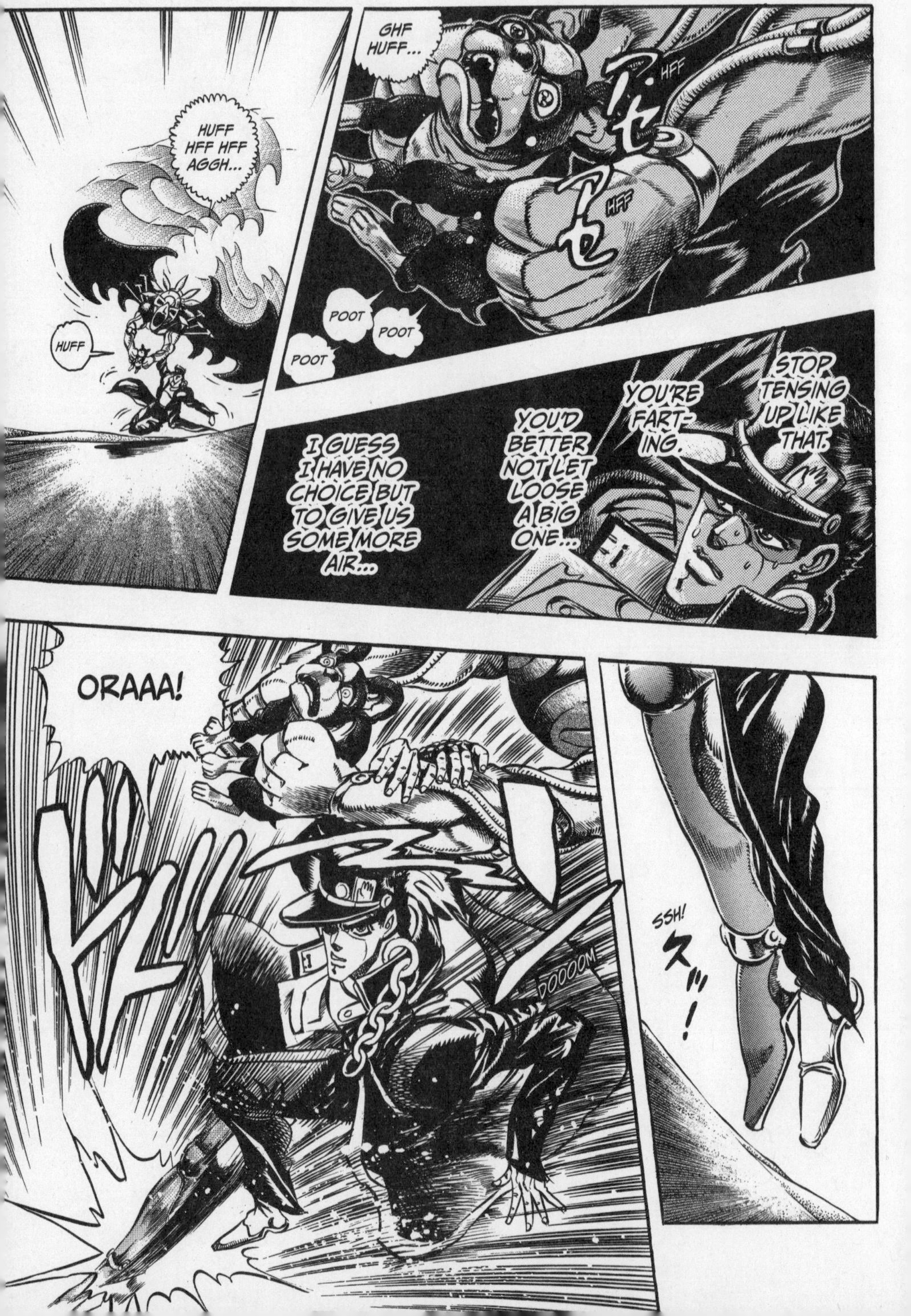
GHF HUFF...
HFF
HFF
POOT
POOT
POOT
STOP TENSING UP LIKE THAT.
YOU'RE FARTING.
YOU'D BETTER NOT LET LOOSE A BIG ONE...
I GUESS I HAVE NO CHOICE BUT TO GIVE US SOME MORE AIR...
HUFF HFF HFF AGGH...
HUFF
SSH!
ORAAA!
DOOOOM

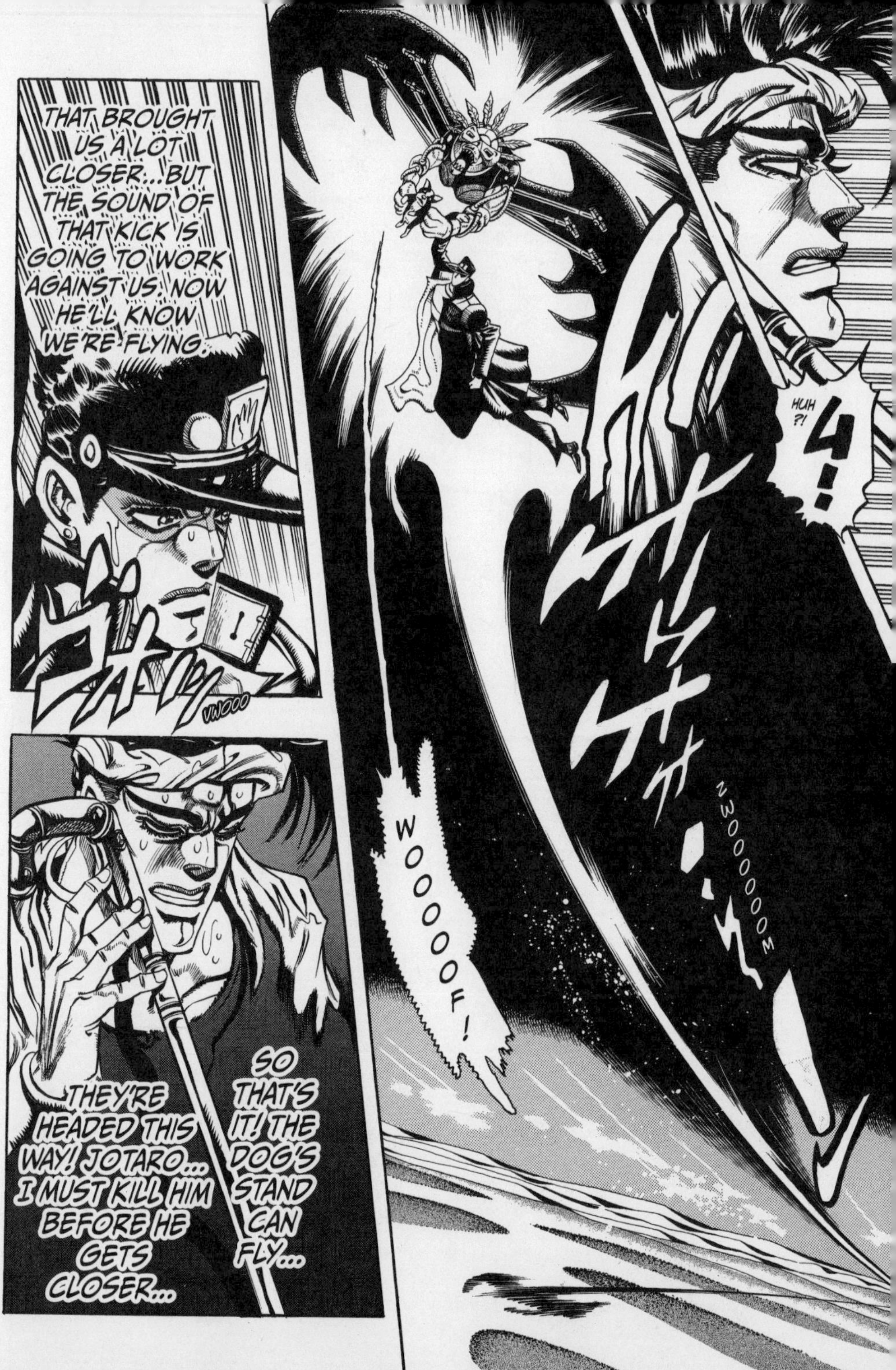
HUH ?!
WOOOOOF!
ZWOOOOOOOM
THAT BROUGHT US A LOT CLOSER... BUT THE SOUND OF THAT KICK IS GOING TO WORK AGAINST US. NOW HE'LL KNOW WE'RE FLYING.
VWOOO
SO THAT'S IT! THE DOG'S STAND CAN FLY...
THEY'RE HEADED THIS WAY! JOTARO... I MUST KILL HIM BEFORE HE GETS CLOSER...

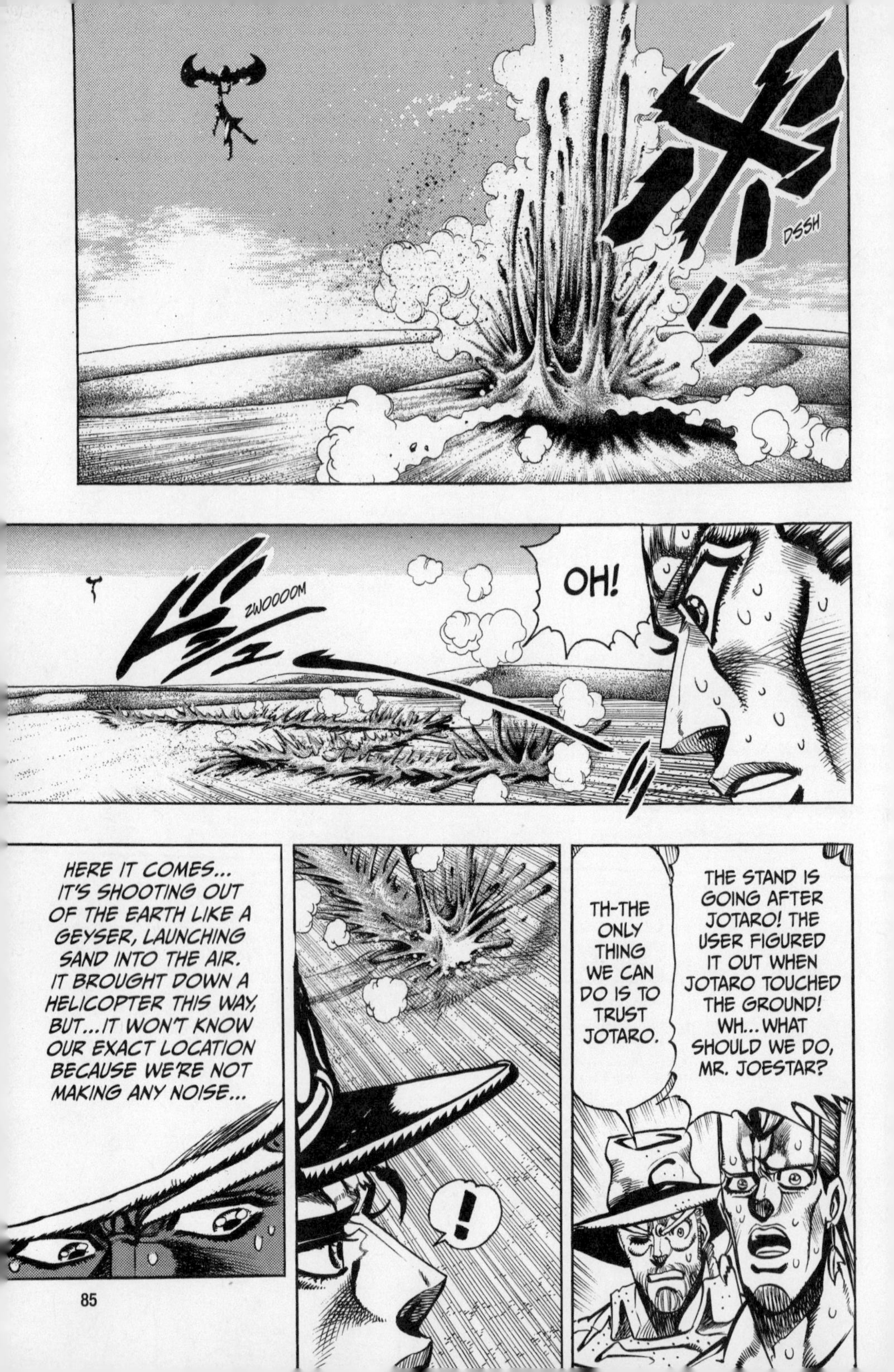
DSSH
ZWOOOOM
OH!
THE STAND IS GOING AFTER JOTARO! THE USER FIGURED IT OUT WHEN JOTARO TOUCHED THE GROUND! WH...WHAT SHOULD WE DO, MR. JOESTAR?
TH-THE ONLY THING WE CAN DO IS TO TRUST JOTARO.
!
HERE IT COMES... IT'S SHOOTING OUT OF THE EARTH LIKE A GEYSER, LAUNCHING SAND INTO THE AIR. IT BROUGHT DOWN A HELICOPTER THIS WAY, BUT...IT WON'T KNOW OUR EXACT LOCATION BECAUSE WE'RE NOT MAKING ANY NOISE...

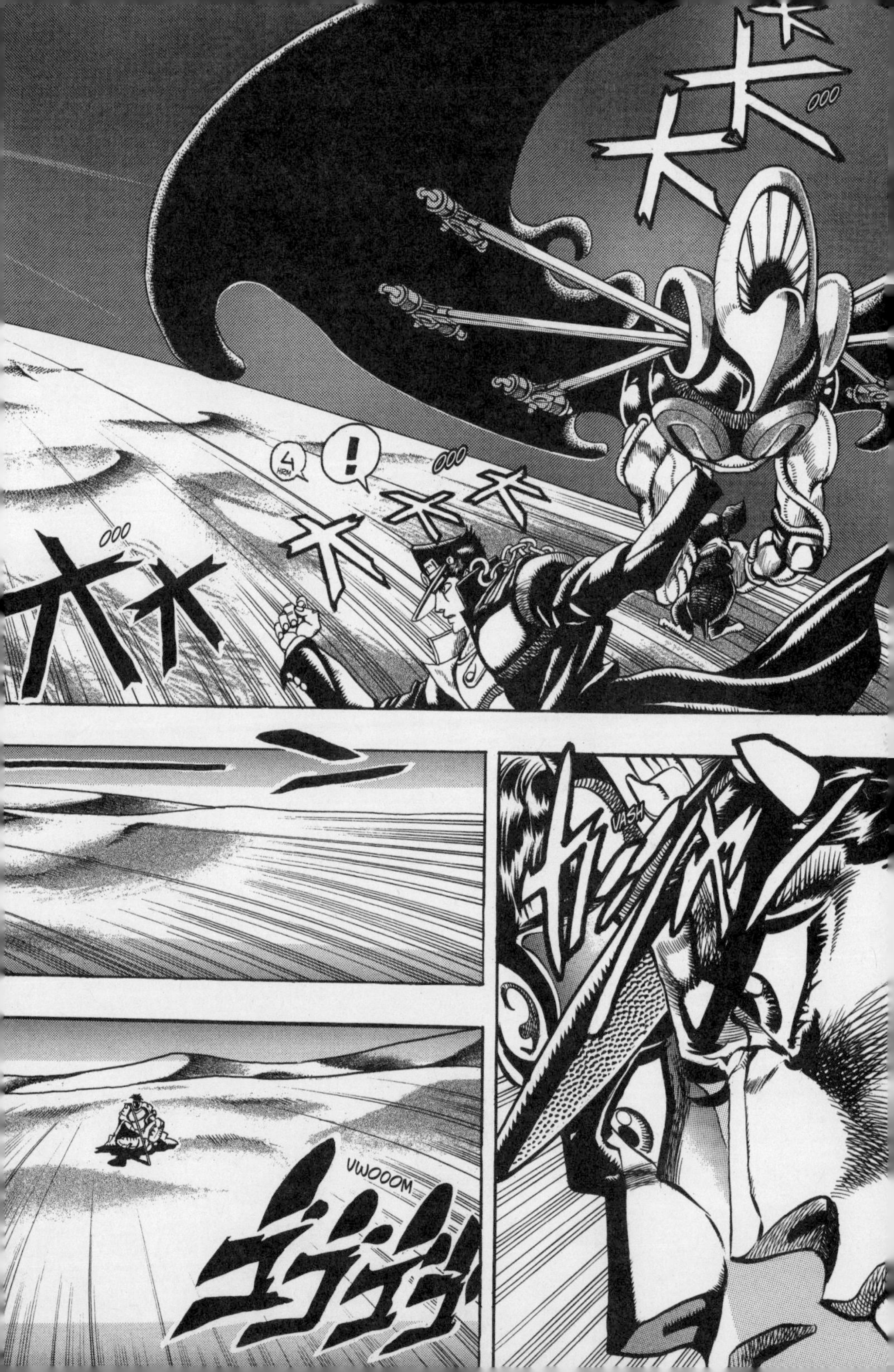
OOO
!
HRM
OOO
OOO
VASH
VWOOOM

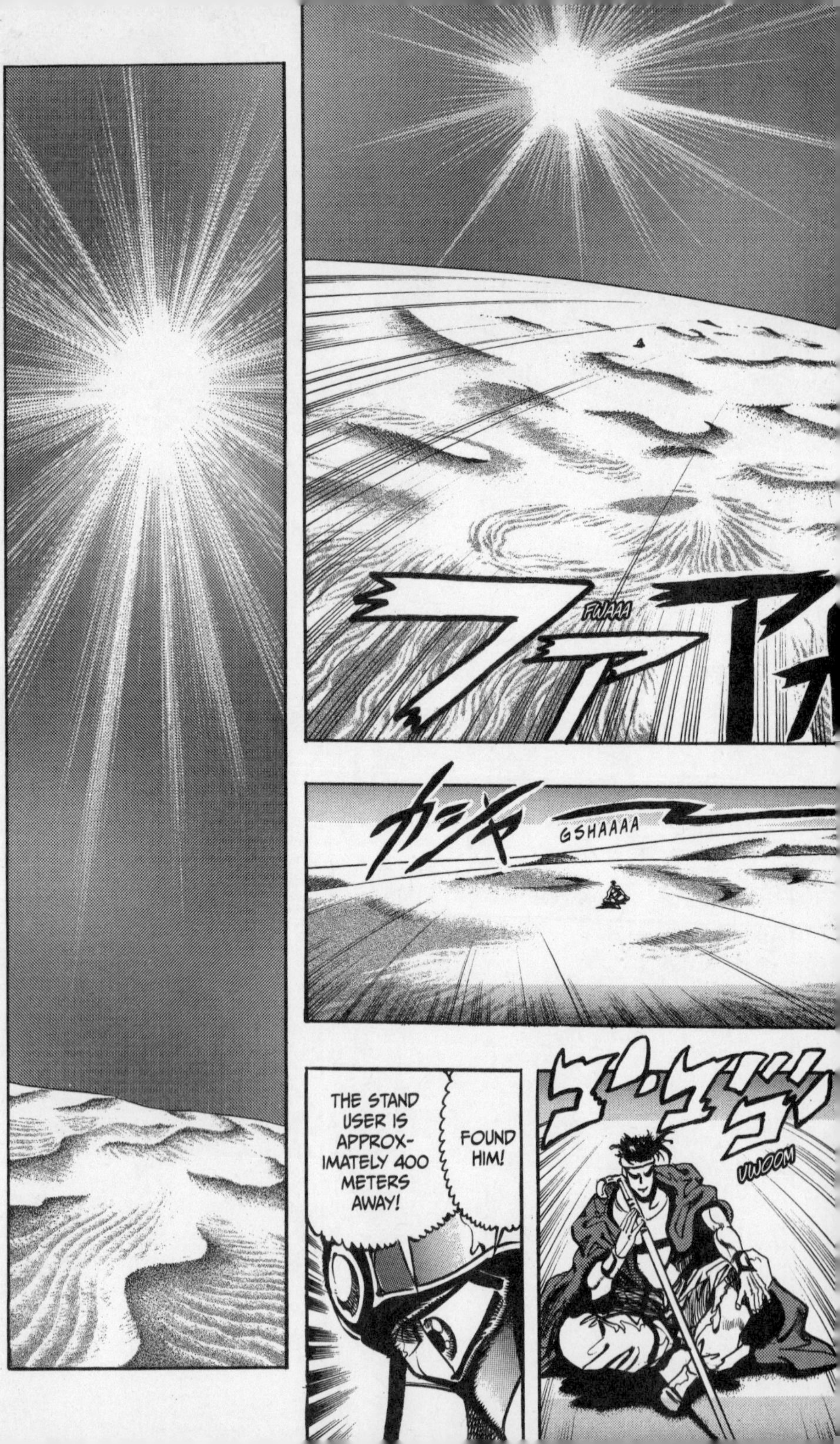
FWAAA
GSHAAAA
UWOOM
FOUND HIM!
THE STAND USER IS APPROXIMATELY 400 METERS AWAY!

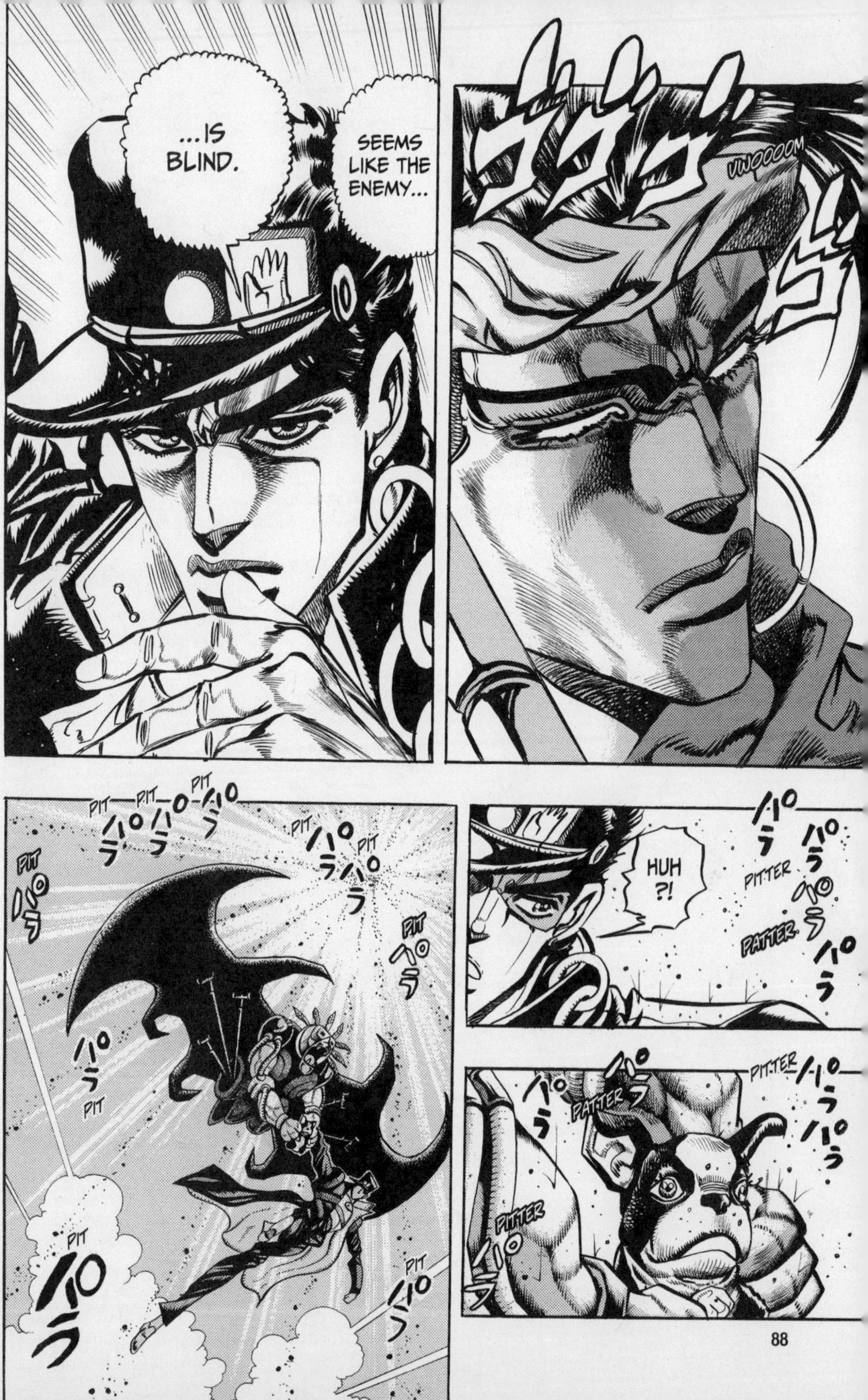
UWOOOOM
SEEMS LIKE THE ENEMY...
...IS BLIND.
PITTER
HUH ?!
PATTER
PITTER
PATTER
PITTER
PIT
PIT
PIT
PIT
PIT
PIT
PIT
PIT
PIT
PIT
PIT

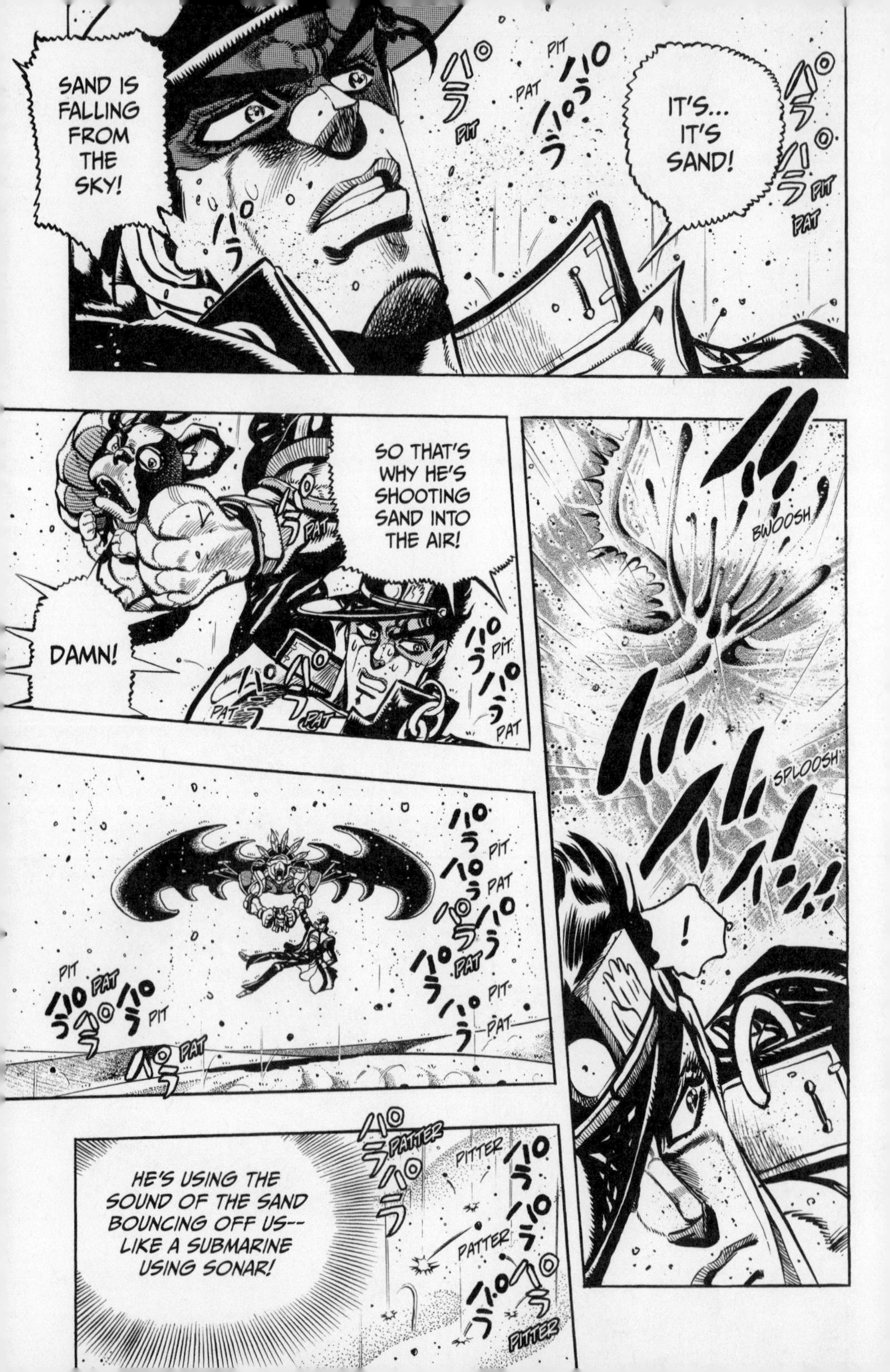
PIT
PAT
IT'S... IT'S SAND!
PIT
PAT
SAND IS FALLING FROM THE SKY!
BWOOSH
SPLOOSH
!
SO THAT'S WHY HE'S SHOOTING SAND INTO THE AIR!
PAT
DAMN!
PIT
PAT
PAT
PAT
PIT
PAT
PAT
PIT
PAT
PIT
PAT
PIT
PAT
PATTER
PITTER
HE'S USING THE SOUND OF THE SAND BOUNCING OFF US-- LIKE A SUBMARINE USING SONAR!
PATTER
PITTER

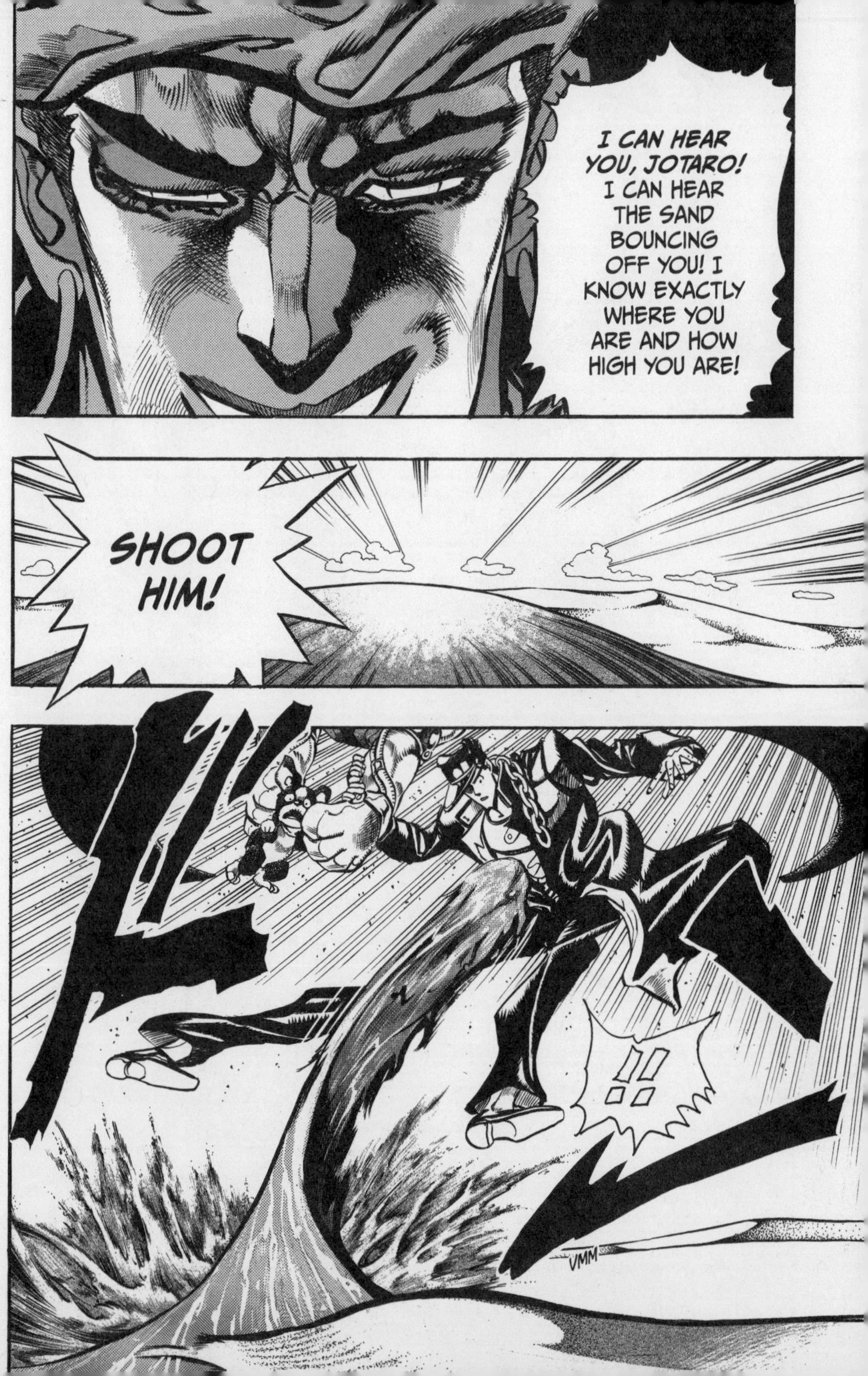
I CAN HEAR YOU, JOTARO! I CAN HEAR THE SAND BOUNCING OFF YOU! I KNOW EXACTLY WHERE YOU ARE AND HOW HIGH YOU ARE!
SHOOT HIM!
!!
VMM

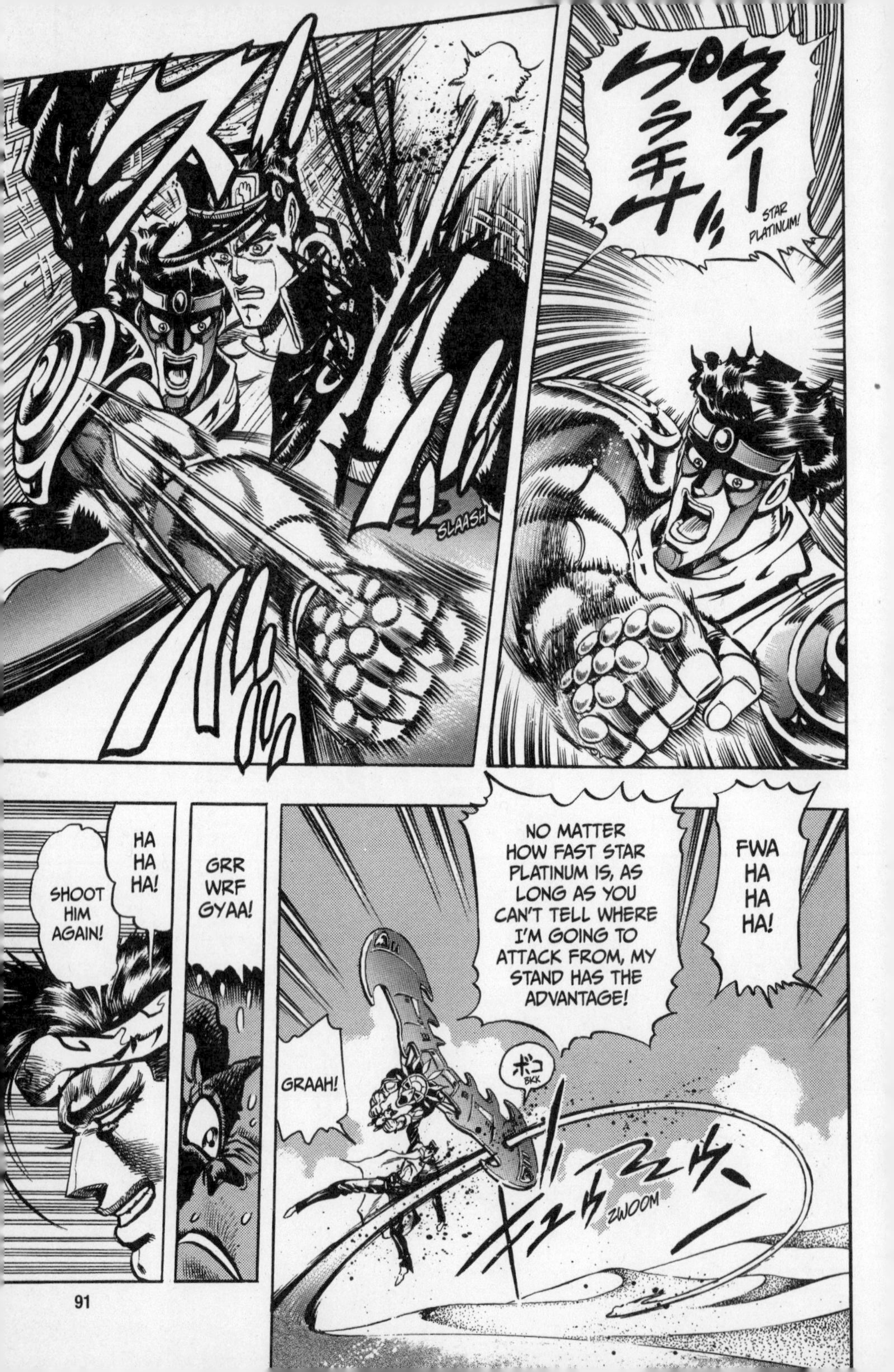
スタープラチナ!!
STAR PLATINUM!
SLAASH
FWA HA HA HA HA!
NO MATTER HOW FAST STAR PLATINUM IS, AS LONG AS YOU CAN'T TELL WHERE I'M GOING TO ATTACK FROM, MY STAND HAS THE ADVANTAGE!
ボコ
BKK
GRAAH!
ZWOOM
GRR WRF GYAA!
HA HA HA!
SHOOT HIM AGAIN!

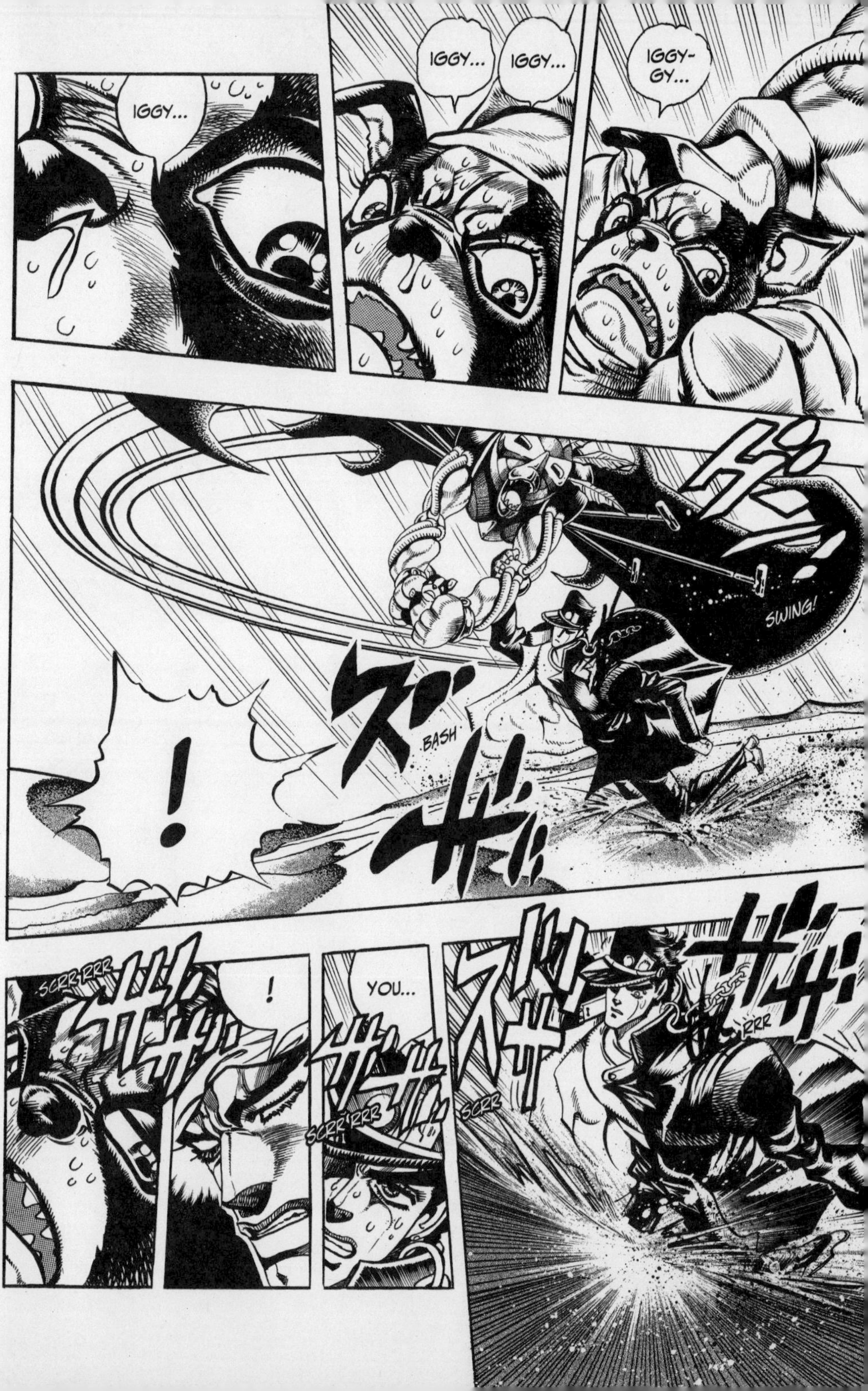
IGGY-
GY...
IGGY...
IGGY...
IGGY...
SWING!
BASH
!
RRR
SCRR
YOU...
SCRR'RRR
!
SCRR'RRR

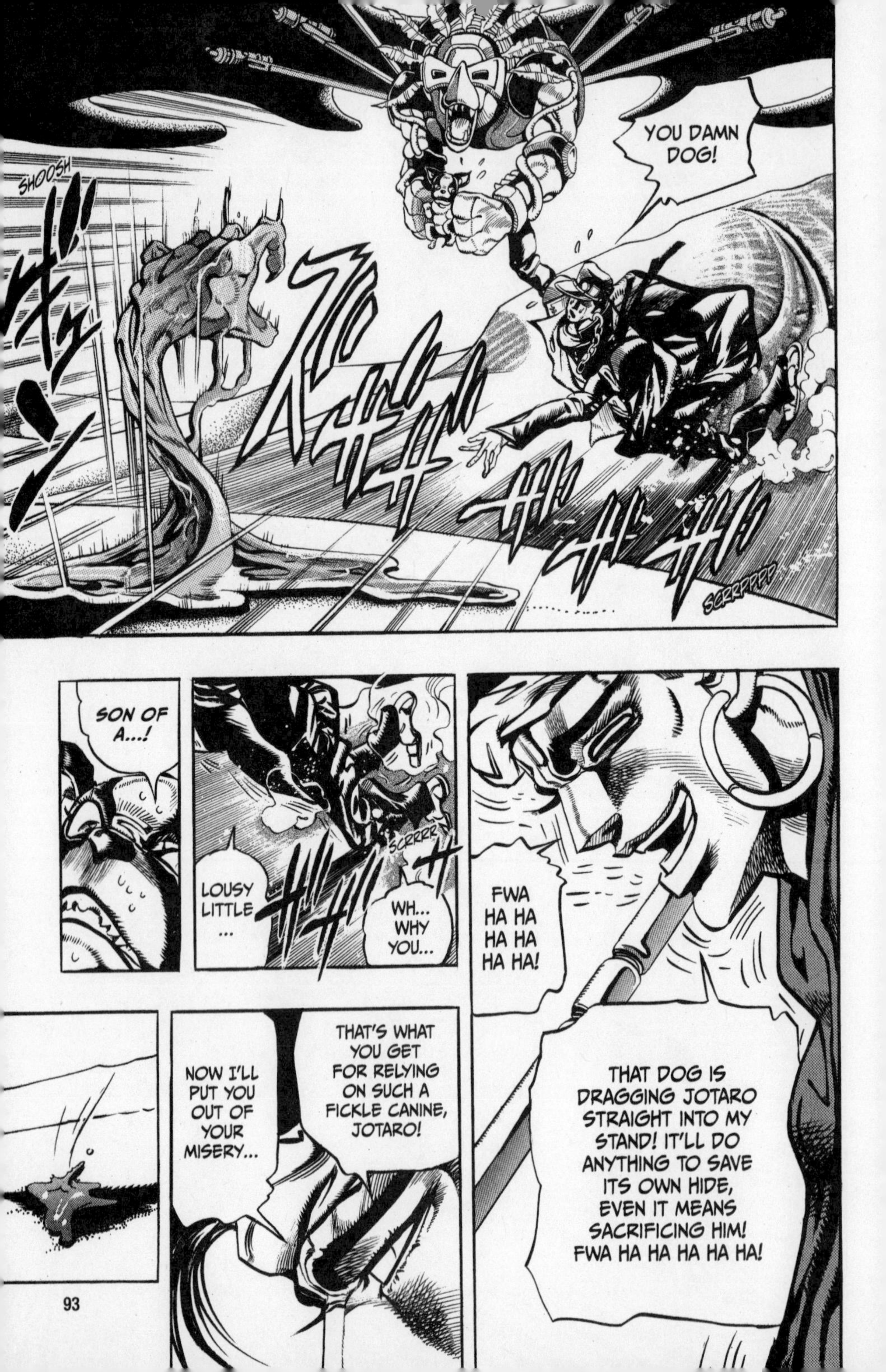
YOU DAMN DOG!
SCRRPPPP
SHOOSH
FWA HA HA HA HA HA HA!
WH... WHY YOU...
SCRRRR
LOUSY LITTLE ...
SON OF A...!
THAT DOG IS DRAGGING JOTARO STRAIGHT INTO MY STAND! IT'LL DO ANYTHING TO SAVE ITS OWN HIDE, EVEN IT MEANS SACRIFICING HIM! FWA HA HA HA HA HA!
THAT'S WHAT YOU GET FOR RELYING ON SUCH A FICKLE CANINE, JOTARO!
NOW I'LL PUT YOU OUT OF YOUR MISERY...

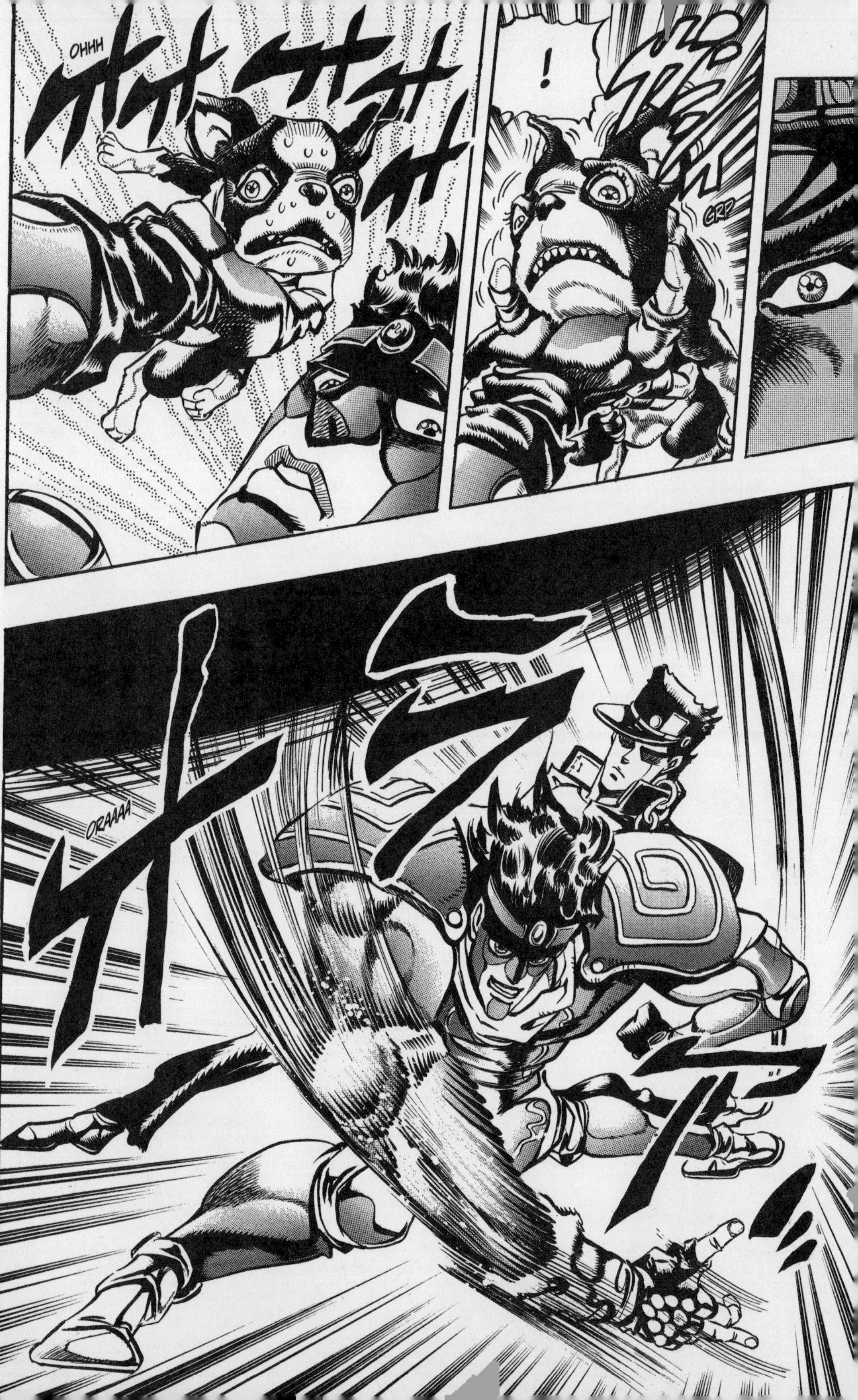
!
GRP
OHHH
ORAAAA

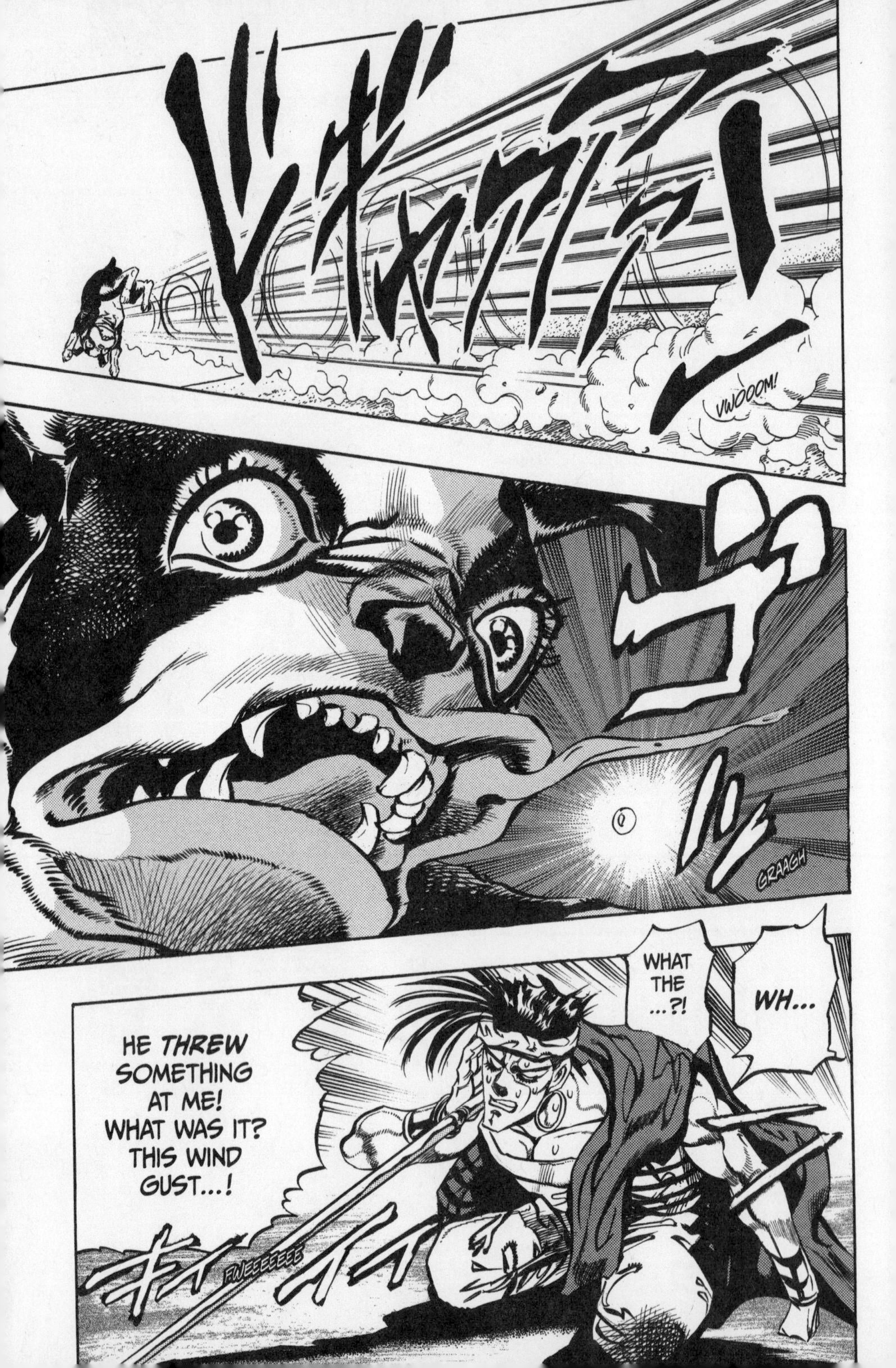

VWOOOM!
GRAAGH
WH...
WHAT THE ...?!
HE *THREW* SOMETHING AT ME! WHAT WAS IT? THIS WIND GUST...!
FWEEEEEEEE

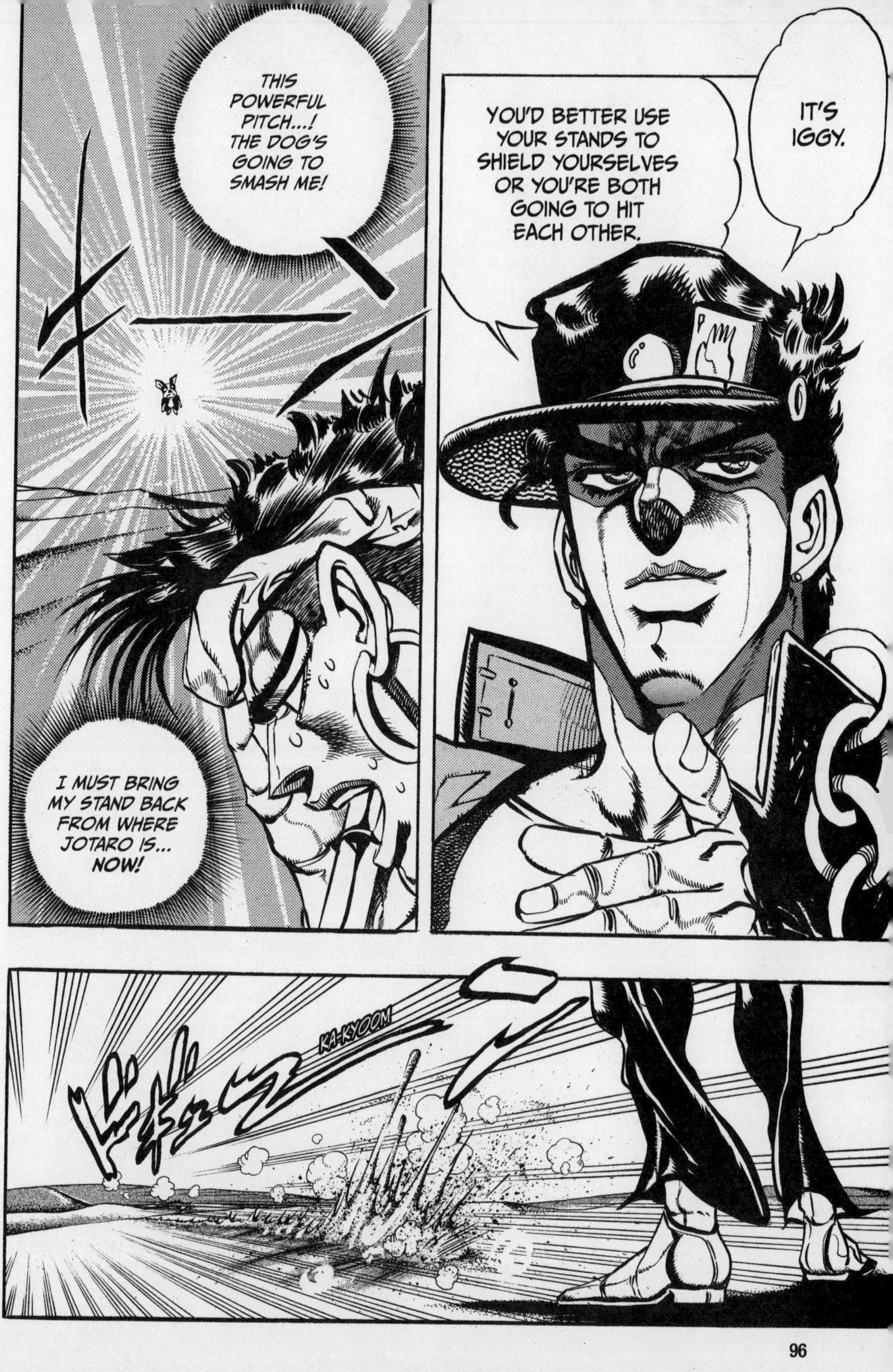
IT'S IGGY.
YOU'D BETTER USE YOUR STANDS TO SHIELD YOURSELVES OR YOU'RE BOTH GOING TO HIT EACH OTHER.
THIS POWERFUL PITCH...! THE DOG'S GOING TO SMASH ME!
I MUST BRING MY STAND BACK FROM WHERE JOTARO IS... NOW!
KA-KYOOM

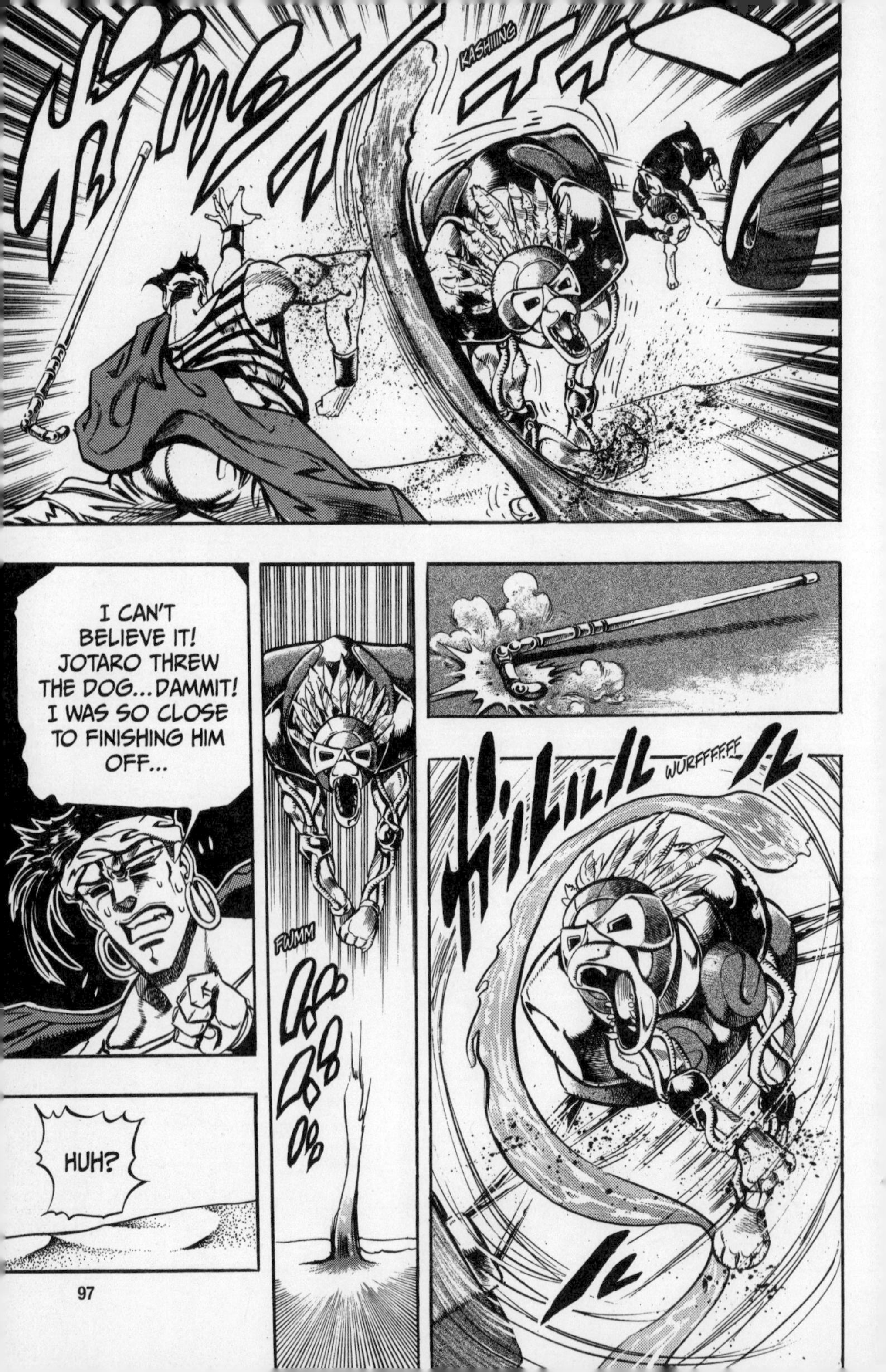
KASHIIING
WURFFFFF
FWMM
I CAN'T BELIEVE IT! JOTARO THREW THE DOG...DAMMIT! I WAS SO CLOSE TO FINISHING HIM OFF...
HUH?

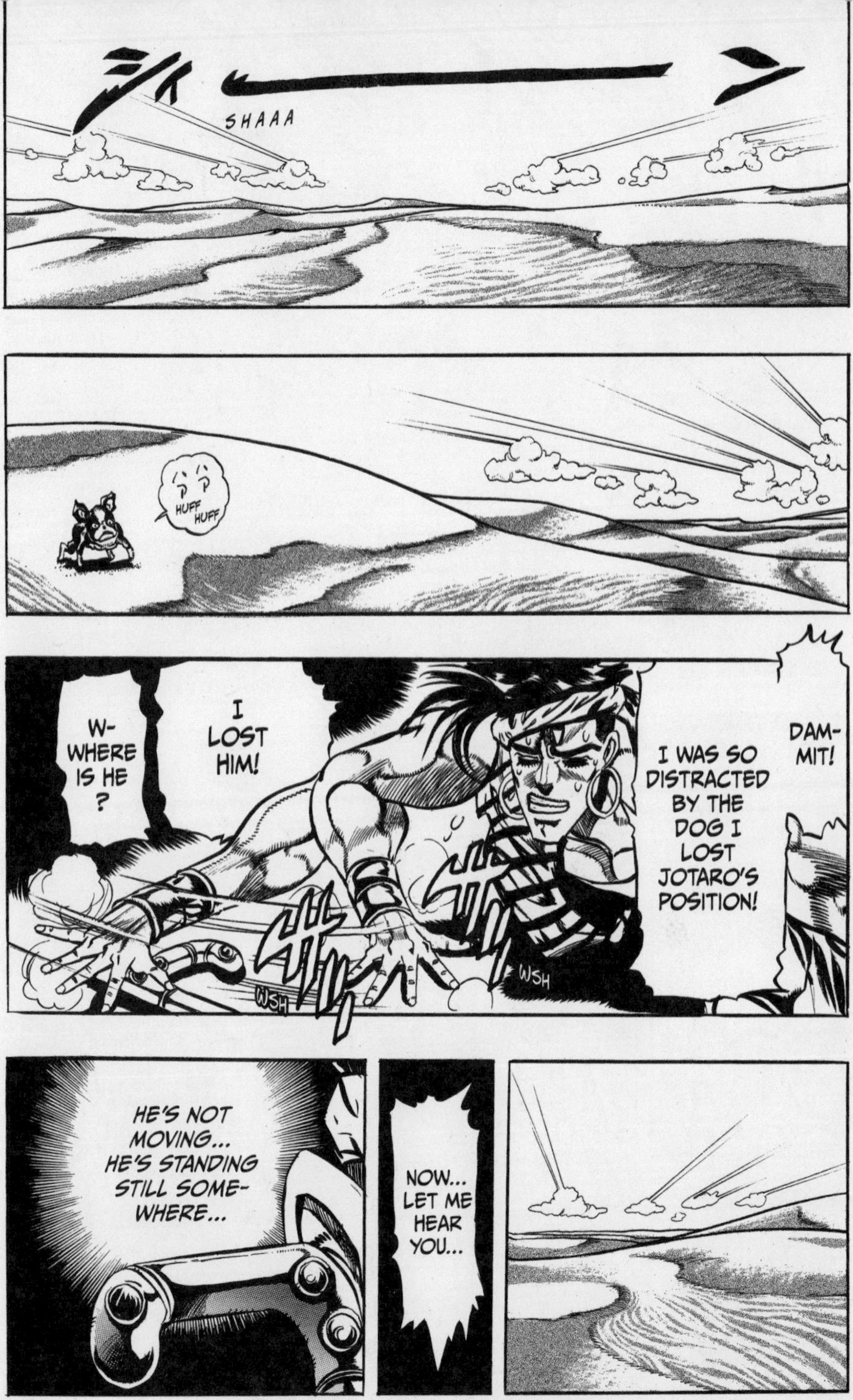
SHAAA
HUFF HUFF
DAM-MIT!
I WAS SO DISTRACTED BY THE DOG I LOST JOTARO'S POSITION!
I LOST HIM!
W-WHERE IS HE?
WSH
WSH
NOW... LET ME HEAR YOU...
HE'S NOT MOVING... HE'S STANDING STILL SOME-WHERE...

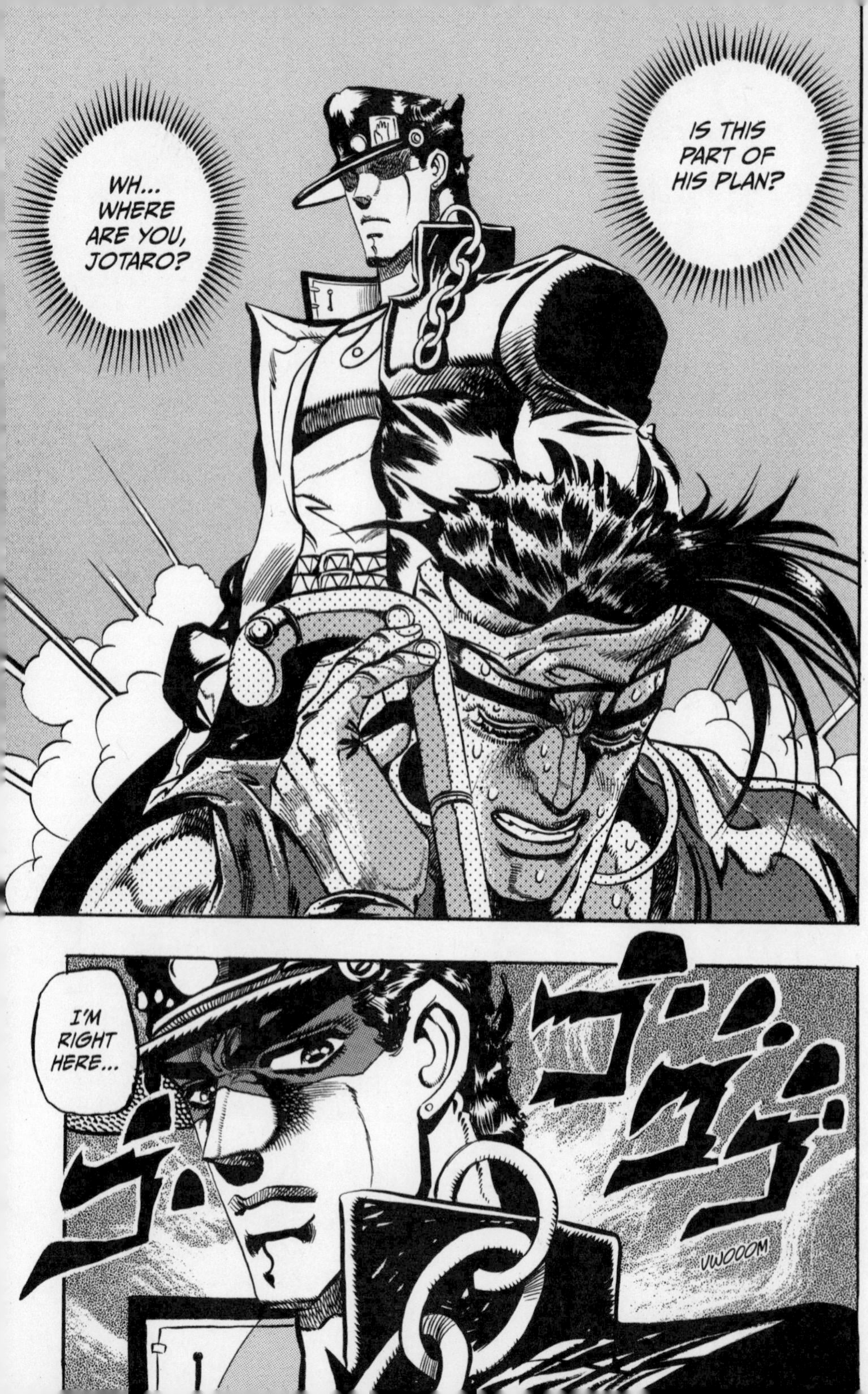
IS THIS PART OF HIS PLAN?
WH... WHERE ARE YOU, JOTARO?
I'M RIGHT HERE...
VWOOOM

3
GEB

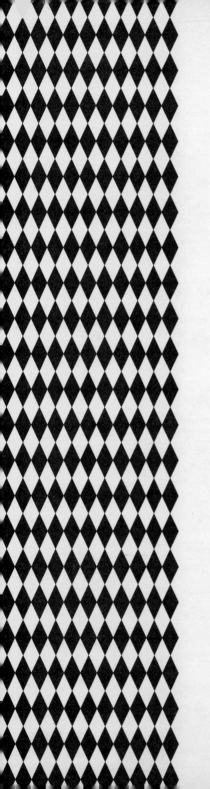

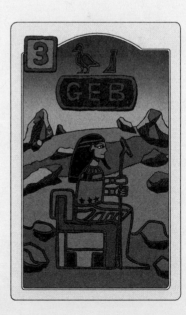

CHAPTER 75: Iggy "The Fool" and "Geb" N'doul PART 6

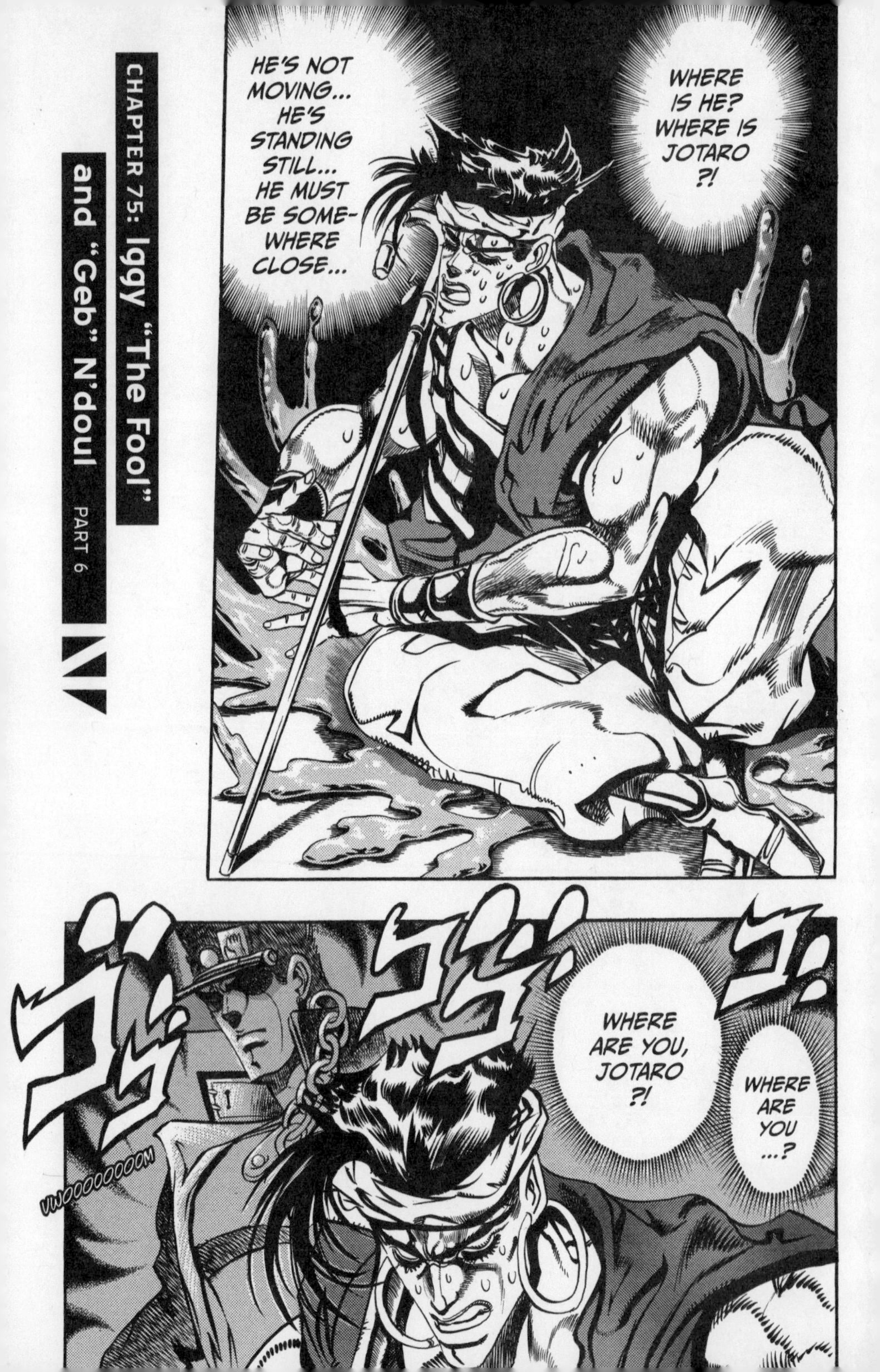
WHERE IS HE? WHERE IS JOTARO ?!
HE'S NOT MOVING... HE'S STANDING STILL... HE MUST BE SOME-WHERE CLOSE...
ゴゴゴゴ
WHERE ARE YOU ...?
WHERE ARE YOU, JOTARO ?!
VWOOOOOOOOM

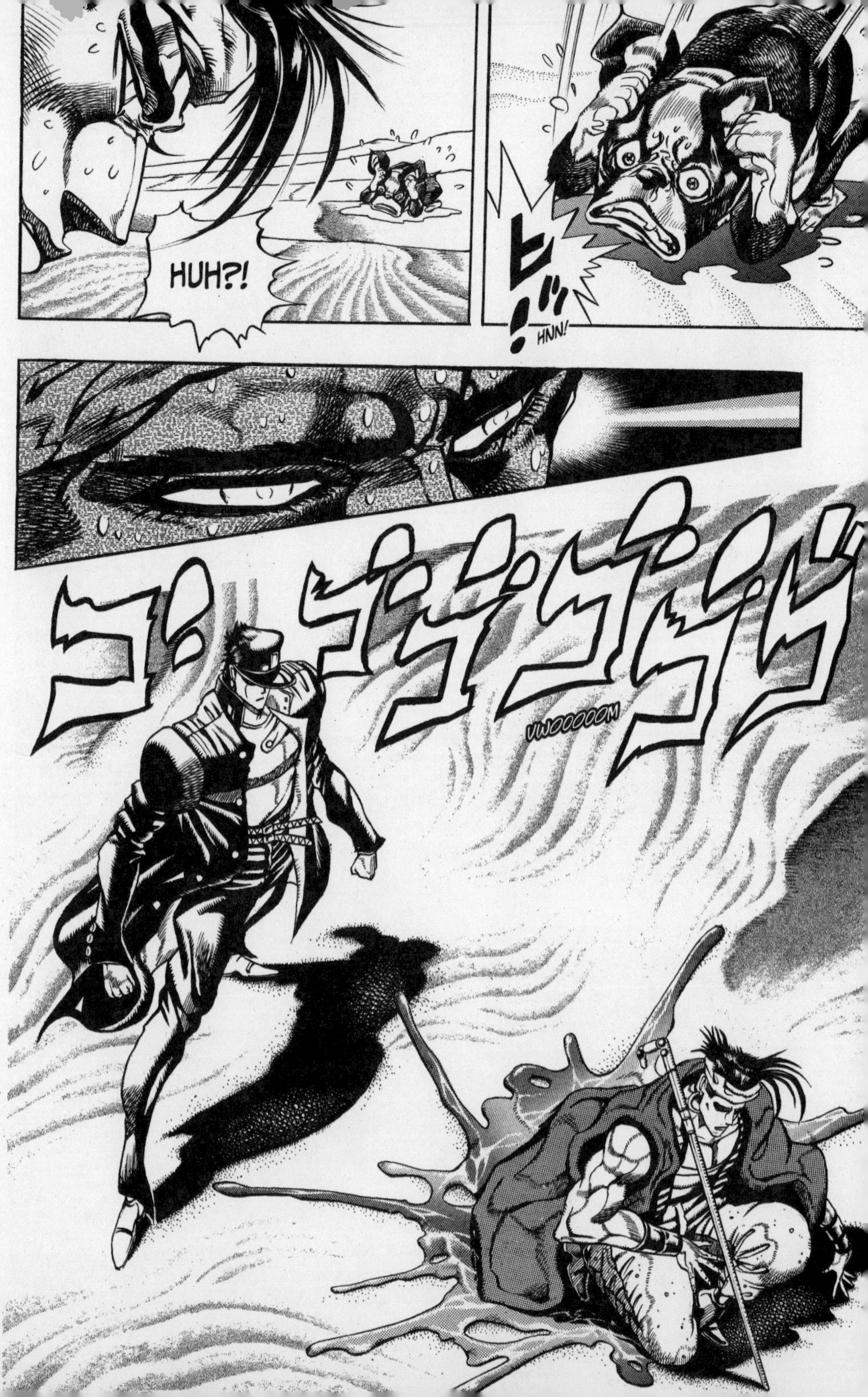
ヒッ!
HNN!
HUH?!
ゴゴゴゴゴゴ
VWOOOOOM

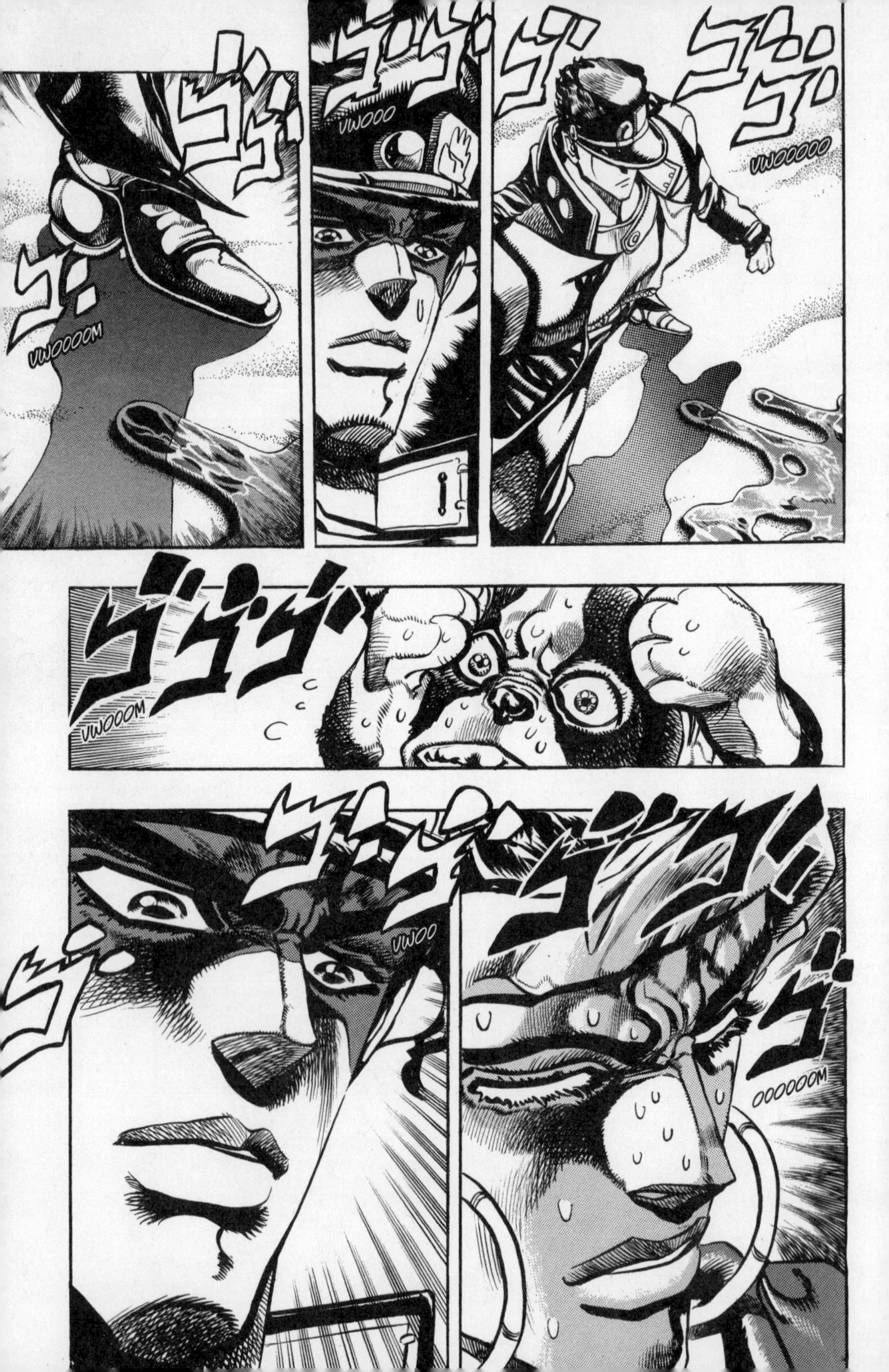
VWOOOOO
VWOOO
VWOOOOM
VWOOOM
OOOOOOM
VWOO

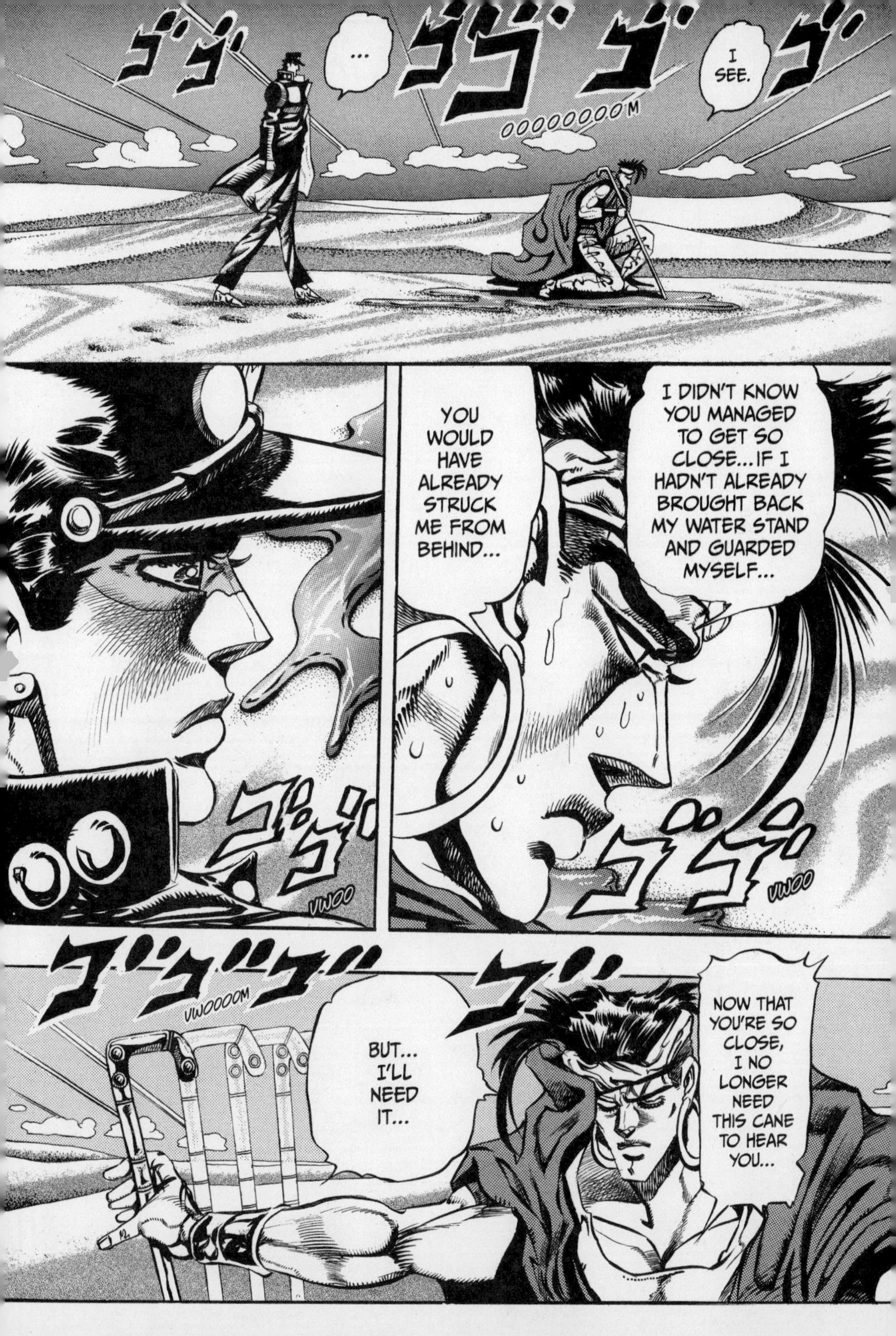
I SEE.
OOOOOOOOOM
...
I DIDN'T KNOW YOU MANAGED TO GET SO CLOSE... IF I HADN'T ALREADY BROUGHT BACK MY WATER STAND AND GUARDED MYSELF...
YOU WOULD HAVE ALREADY STRUCK ME FROM BEHIND...
VWOO
VWOO
NOW THAT YOU'RE SO CLOSE, I NO LONGER NEED THIS CANE TO HEAR YOU...
BUT... I'LL NEED IT...
VWOOOOM

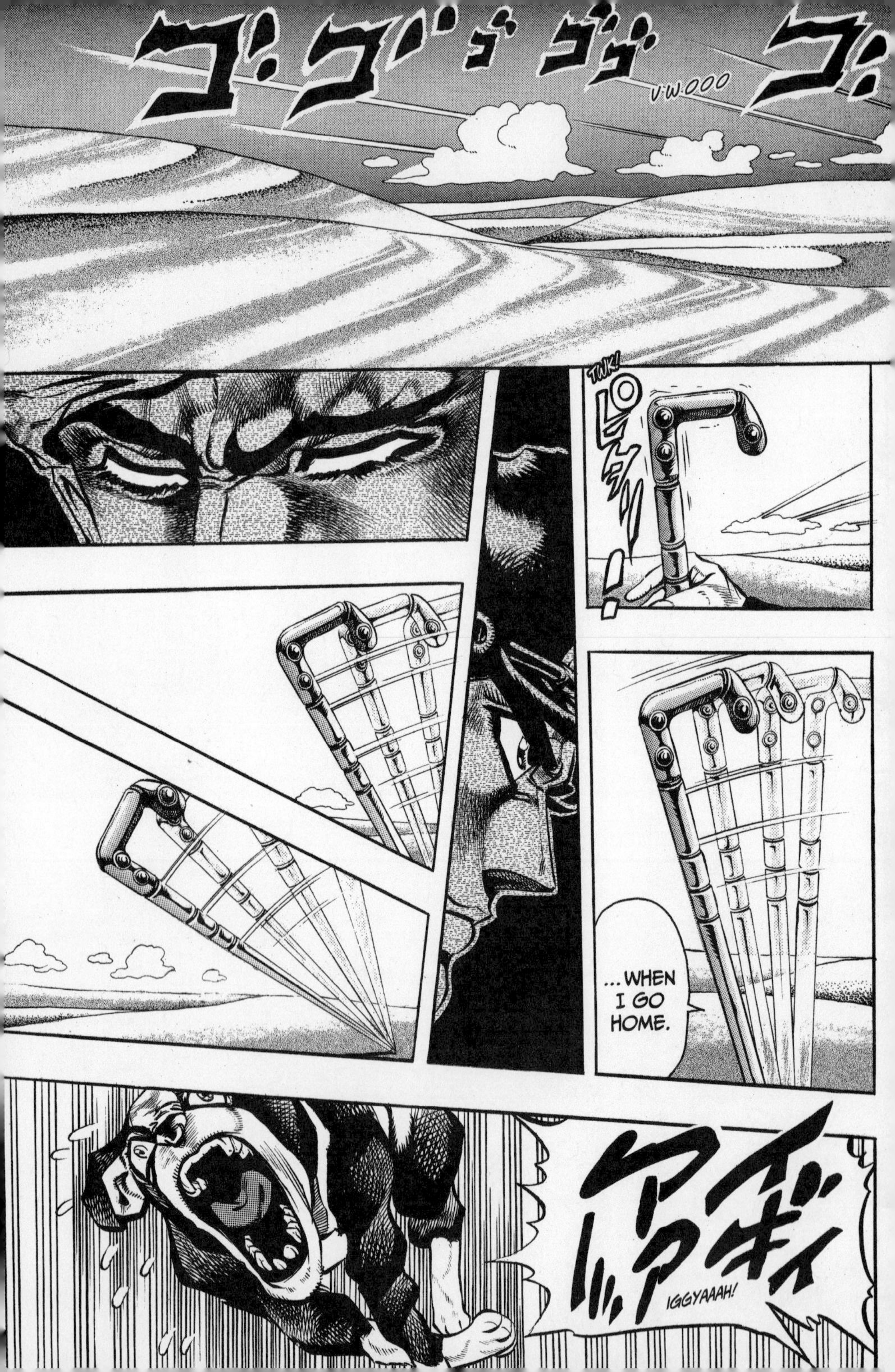
V-W-OOO
TWK!
...WHEN I GO HOME.
IGGYAAAH!

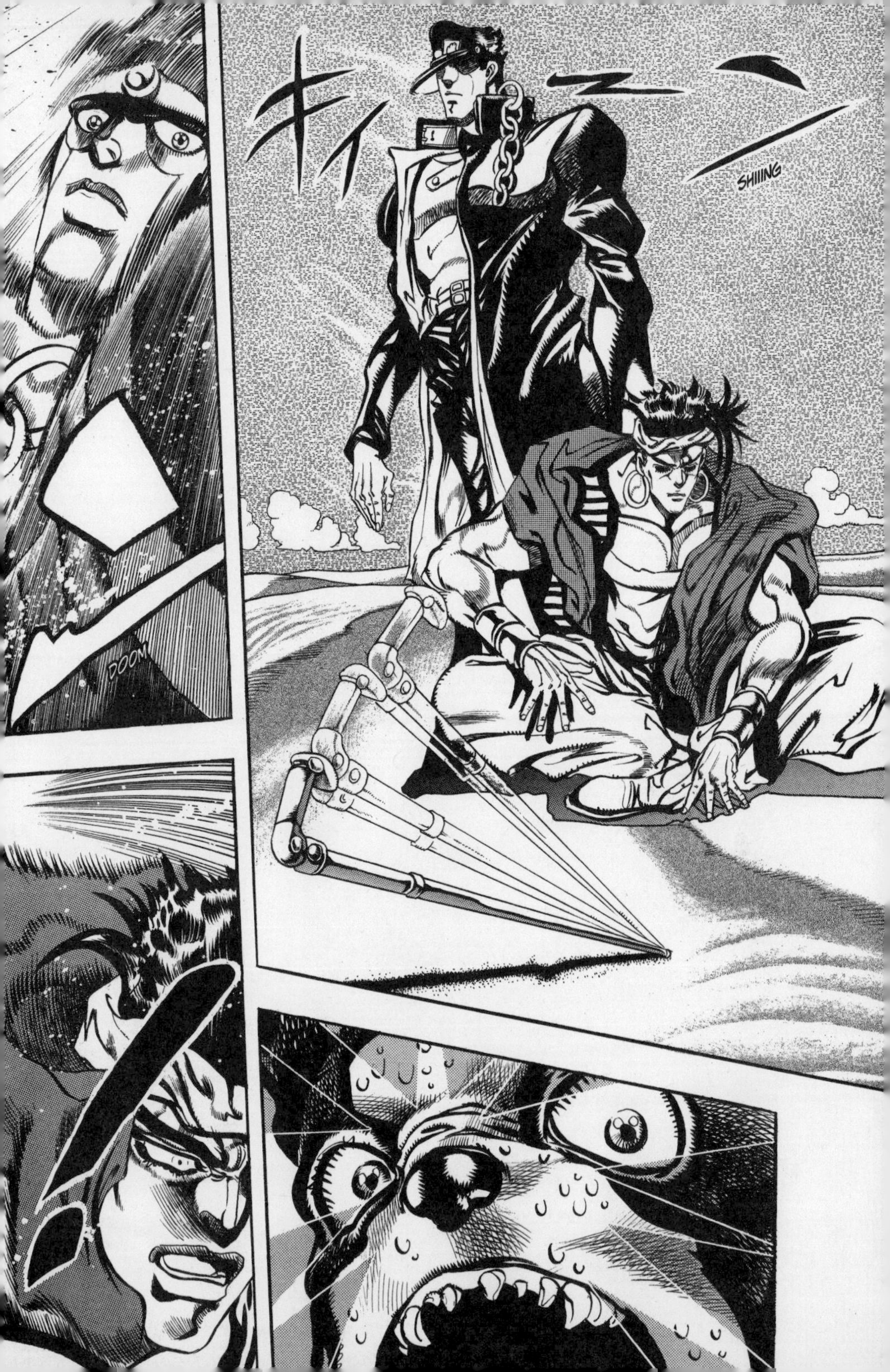

SHIIING
DOOM

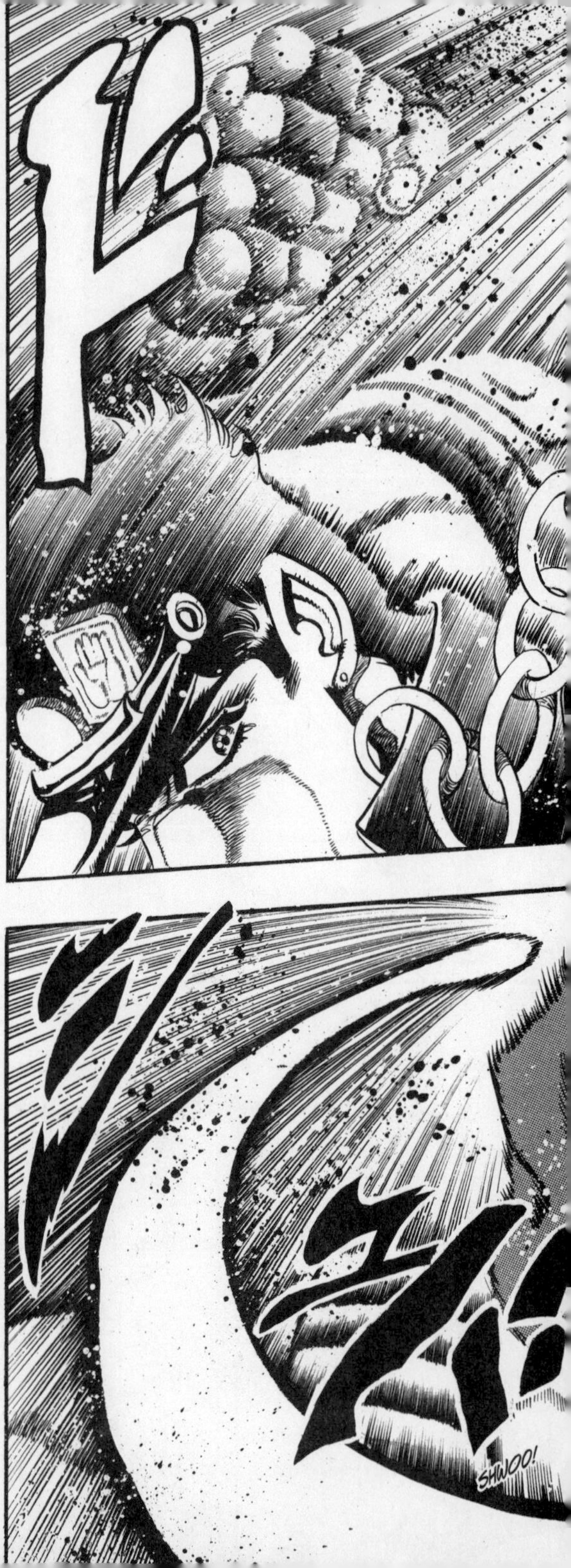
SHWOO!

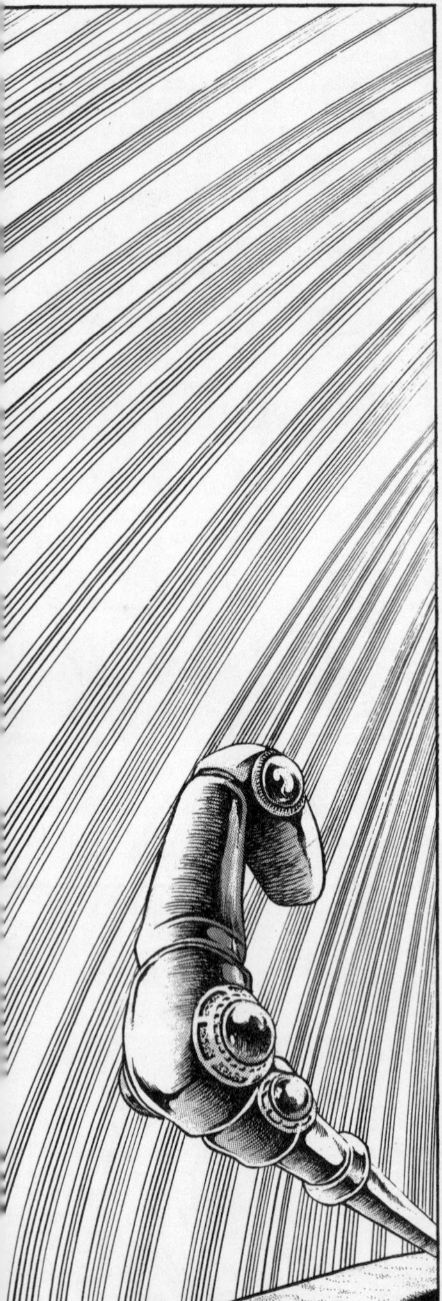

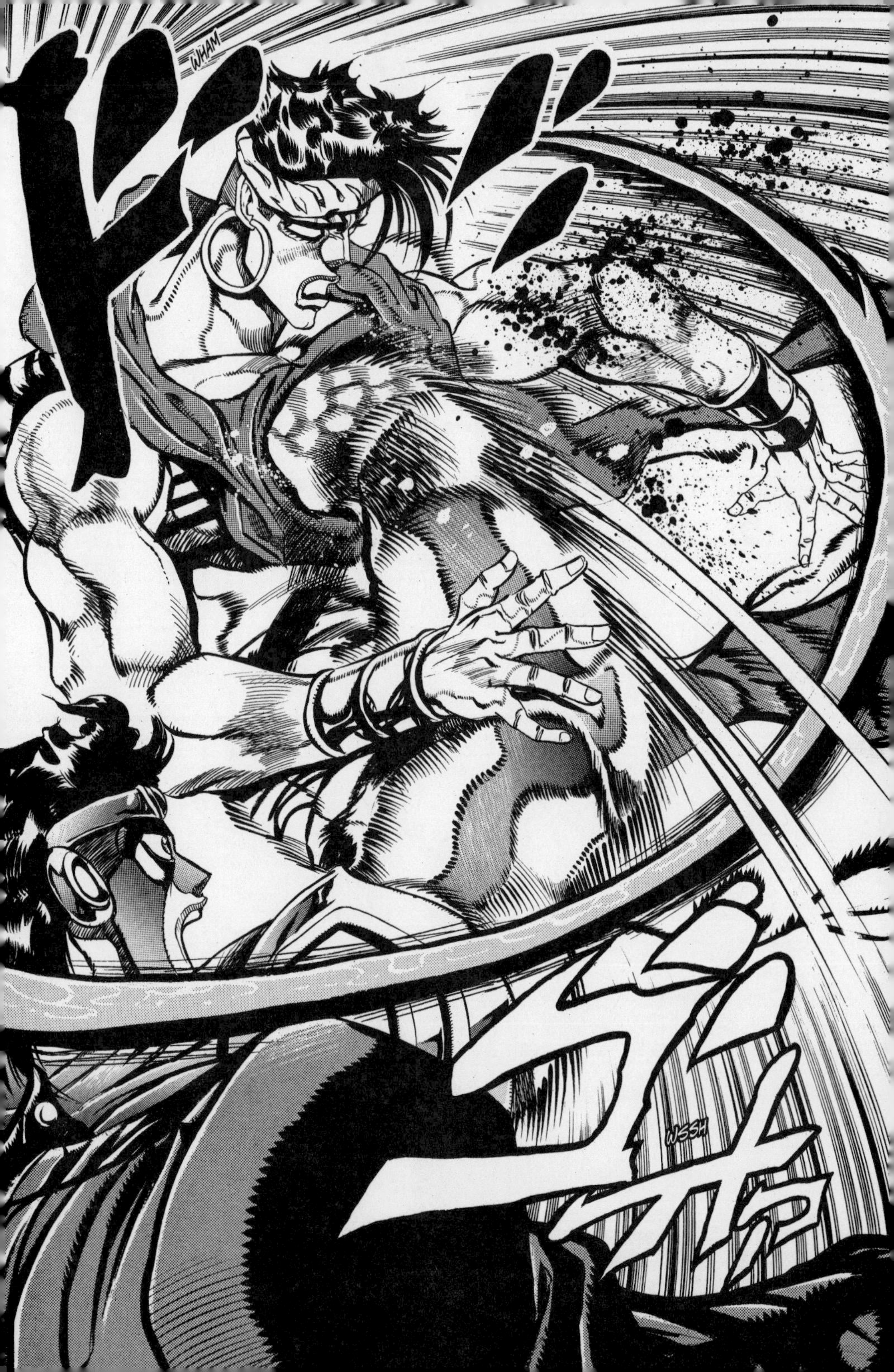
WHAM
WSSH

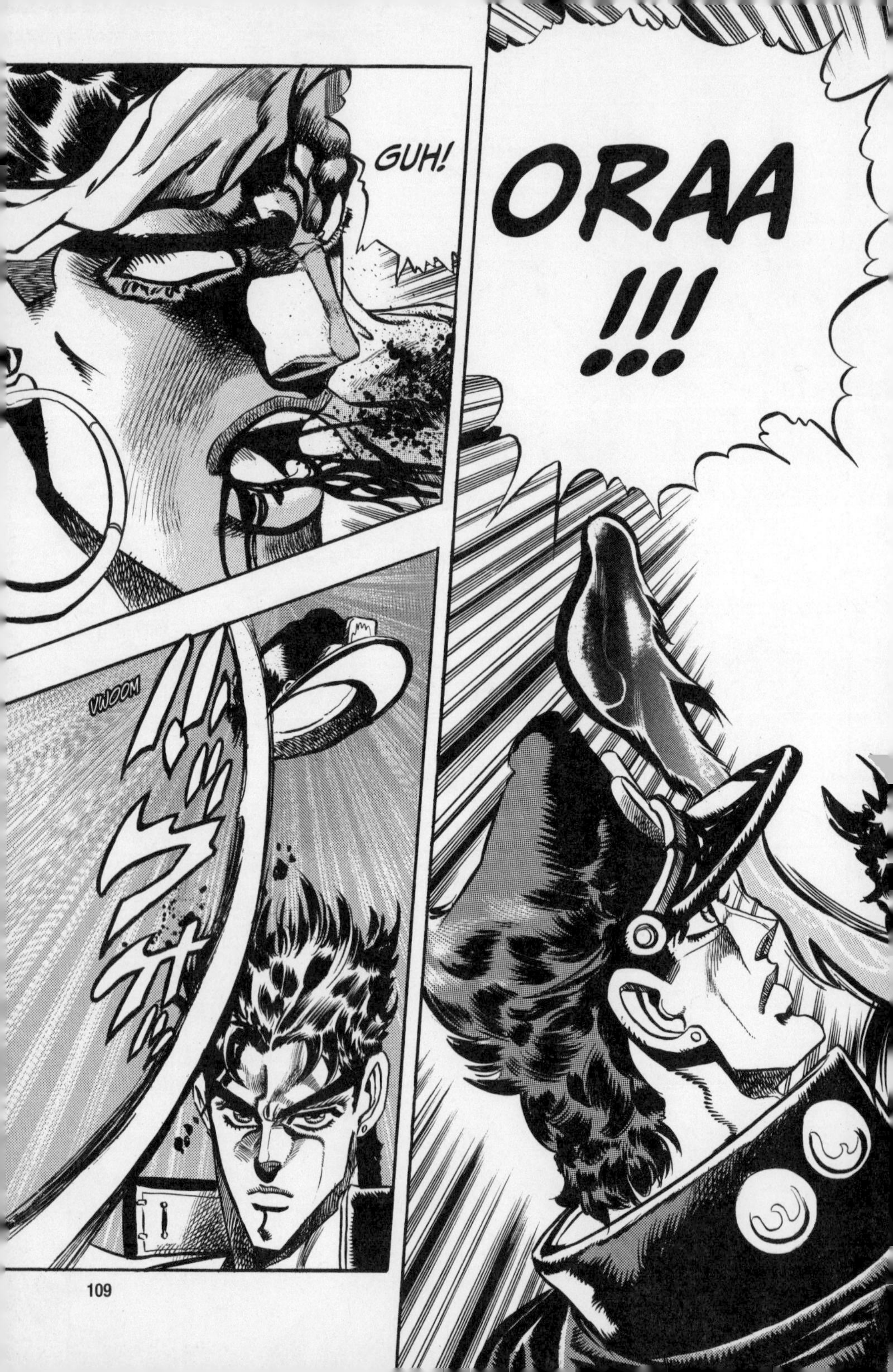
ORAA!!!
GUH!
VWOOM

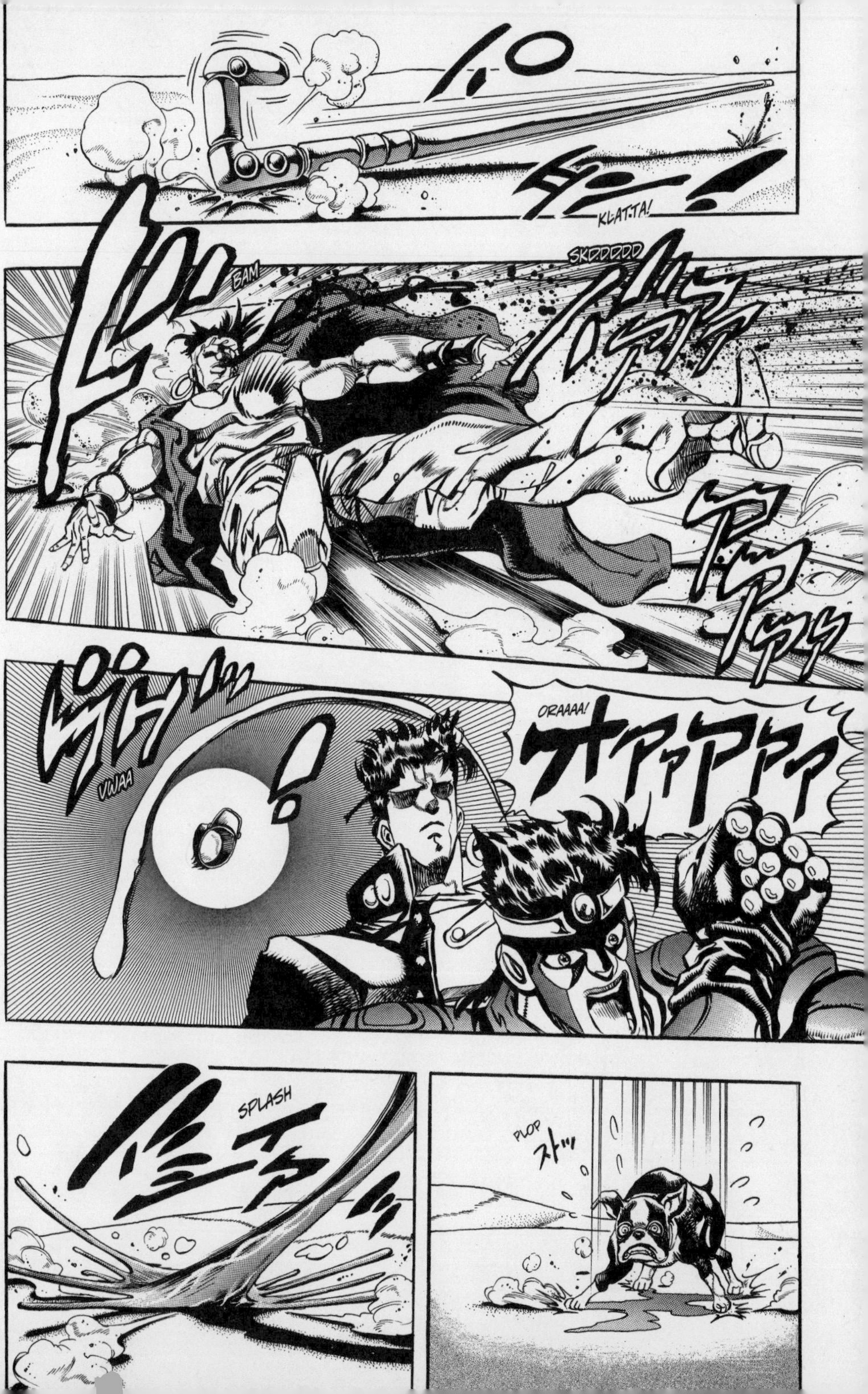
KLATTA!
SKDDDDD
BAM
ORAAAA!
VWAA
PLOP
SPLASH

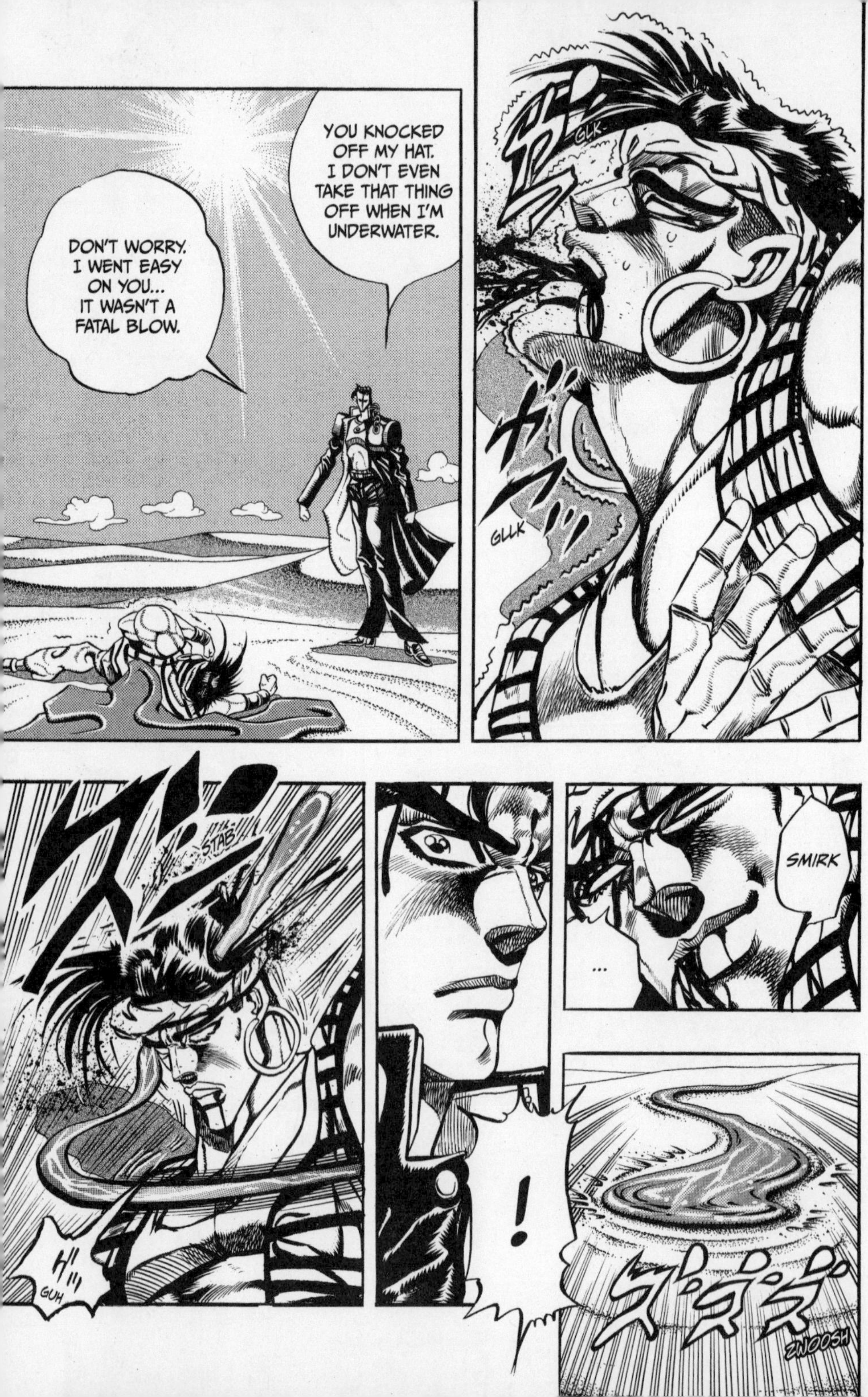
GLK
GLLK
YOU KNOCKED OFF MY HAT. I DON'T EVEN TAKE THAT THING OFF WHEN I'M UNDERWATER.
DON'T WORRY. I WENT EASY ON YOU... IT WASN'T A FATAL BLOW.
SMIRK
...
ZWOOSH
!
STAB
GUH

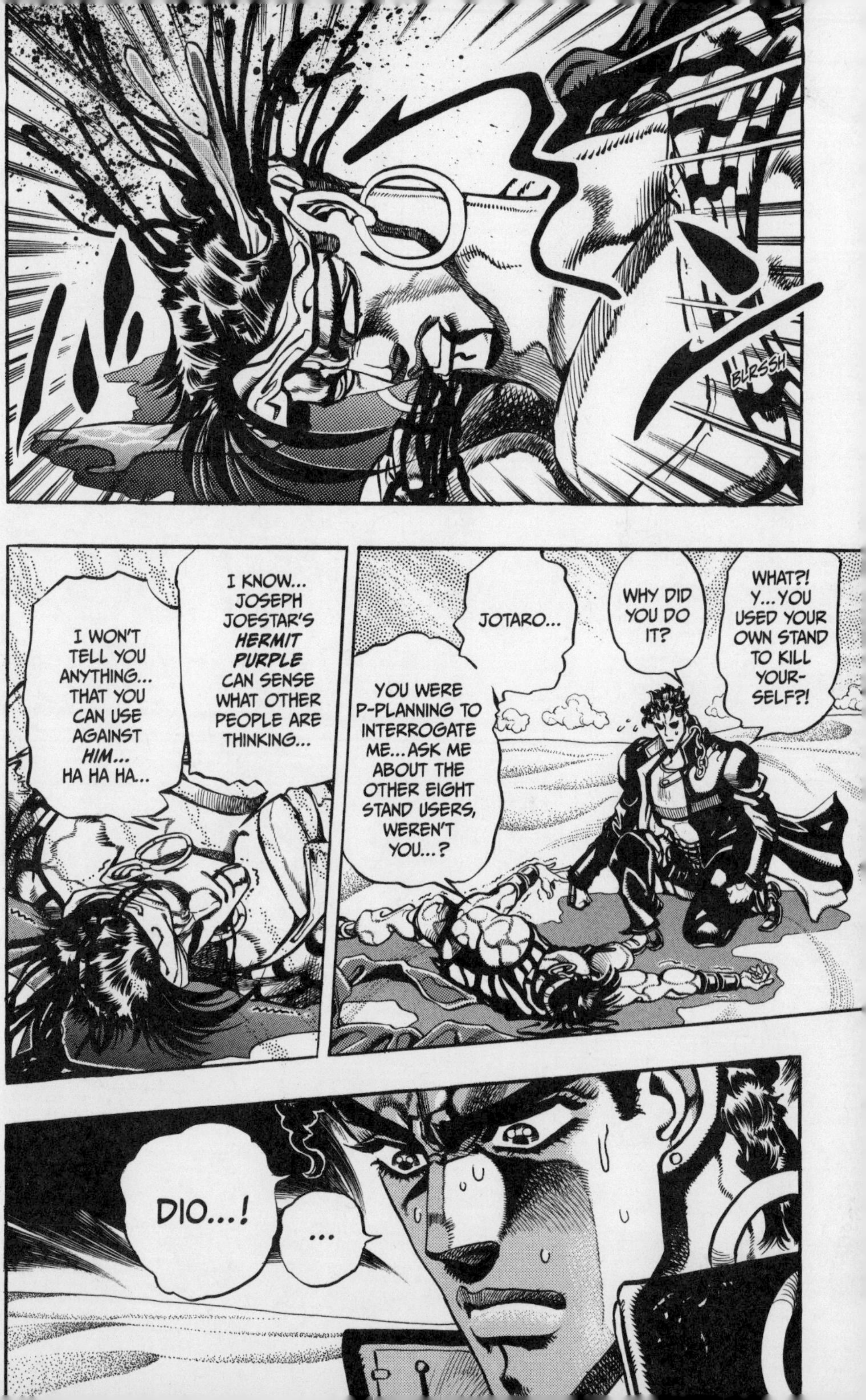
BLRSSH
WHAT?! Y...YOU USED YOUR OWN STAND TO KILL YOURSELF?!
WHY DID YOU DO IT?
JOTARO...
YOU WERE P-PLANNING TO INTERROGATE ME...ASK ME ABOUT THE OTHER EIGHT STAND USERS, WEREN'T YOU...?
I KNOW... JOSEPH JOESTAR'S *HERMIT PURPLE* CAN SENSE WHAT OTHER PEOPLE ARE THINKING...
I WON'T TELL YOU ANYTHING... THAT YOU CAN USE AGAINST *HIM*... HA HA HA...
...
DIO...!

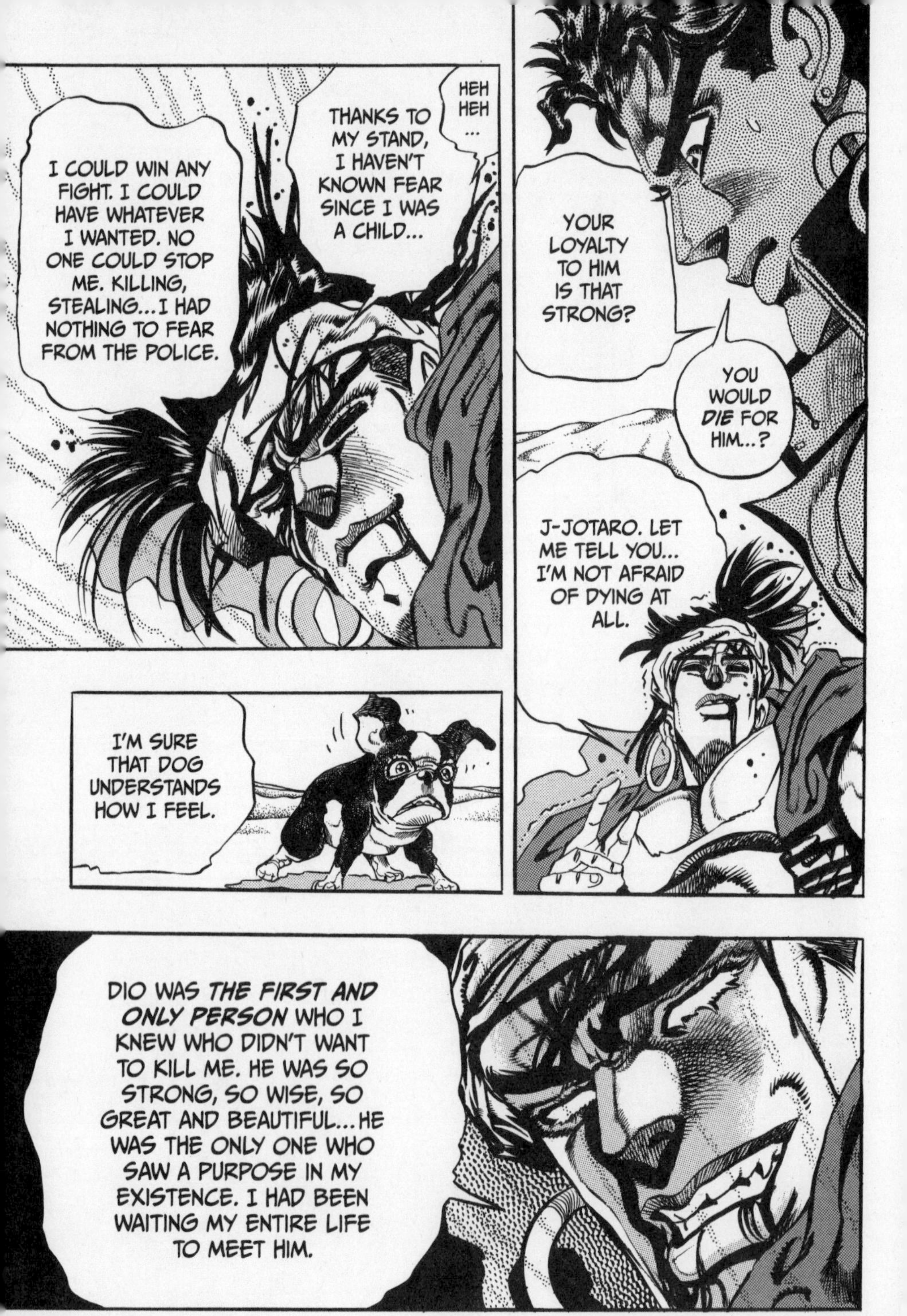
YOUR LOYALTY TO HIM IS THAT STRONG?
YOU WOULD *DIE* FOR HIM...?
J-JOTARO. LET ME TELL YOU... I'M NOT AFRAID OF DYING AT ALL.
HEH HEH ...
THANKS TO MY STAND, I HAVEN'T KNOWN FEAR SINCE I WAS A CHILD...
I COULD WIN ANY FIGHT. I COULD HAVE WHATEVER I WANTED. NO ONE COULD STOP ME. KILLING, STEALING...I HAD NOTHING TO FEAR FROM THE POLICE.
I'M SURE THAT DOG UNDERSTANDS HOW I FEEL.
DIO WAS *THE FIRST AND ONLY PERSON* WHO I KNEW WHO DIDN'T WANT TO KILL ME. HE WAS SO STRONG, SO WISE, SO GREAT AND BEAUTIFUL...HE WAS THE ONLY ONE WHO SAW A PURPOSE IN MY EXISTENCE. I HAD BEEN WAITING MY ENTIRE LIFE TO MEET HIM.

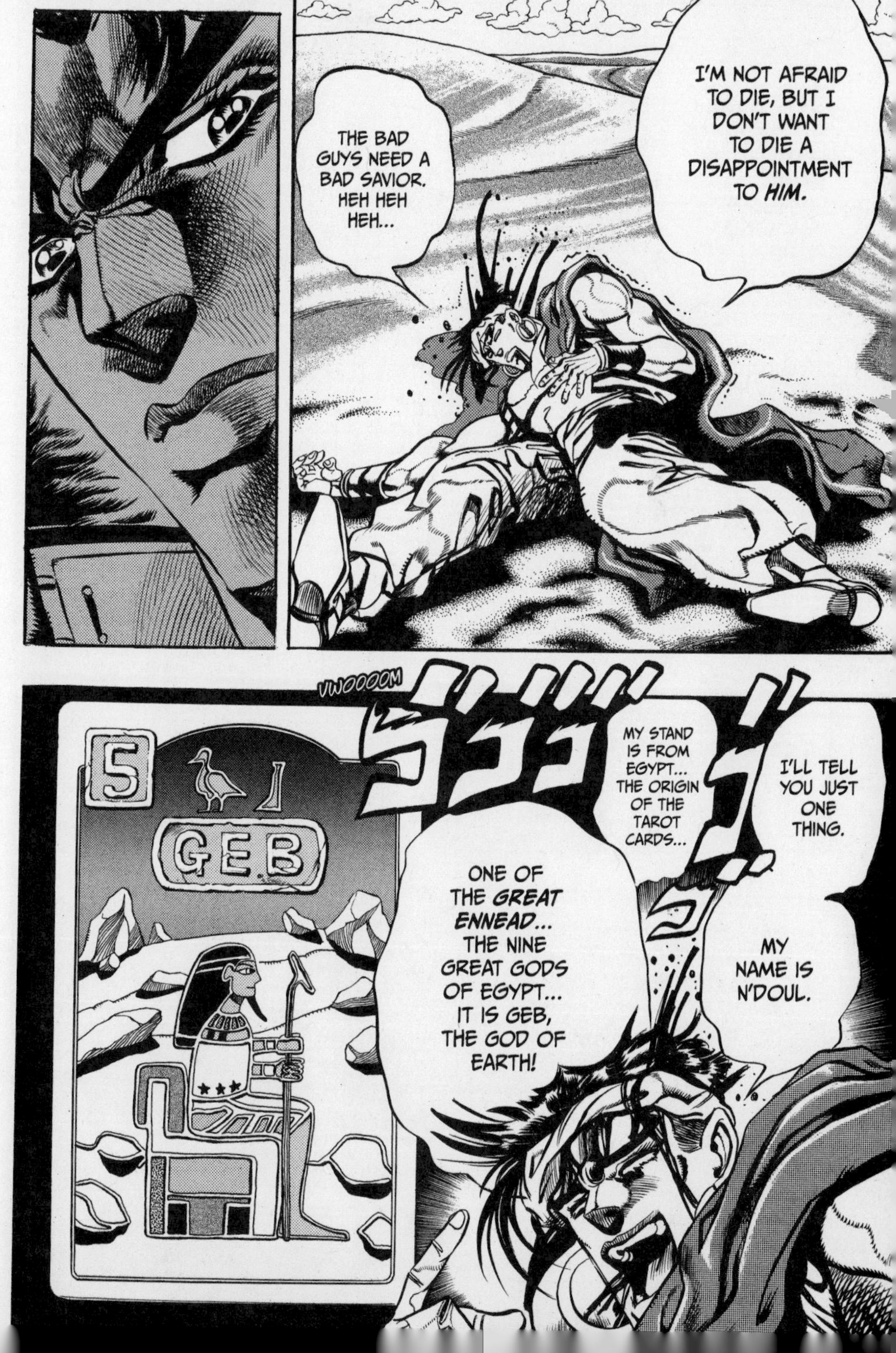
I'M NOT AFRAID TO DIE, BUT I DON'T WANT TO DIE A DISAPPOINTMENT TO *HIM*.
THE BAD GUYS NEED A BAD SAVIOR. HEH HEH HEH...
VWOOOOM
I'LL TELL YOU JUST ONE THING.
MY NAME IS N'DOUL.
MY STAND IS FROM EGYPT... THE ORIGIN OF THE TAROT CARDS...
ONE OF THE *GREAT ENNEAD*... THE NINE GREAT GODS OF EGYPT... IT IS GEB, THE GOD OF EARTH!
5
GEB

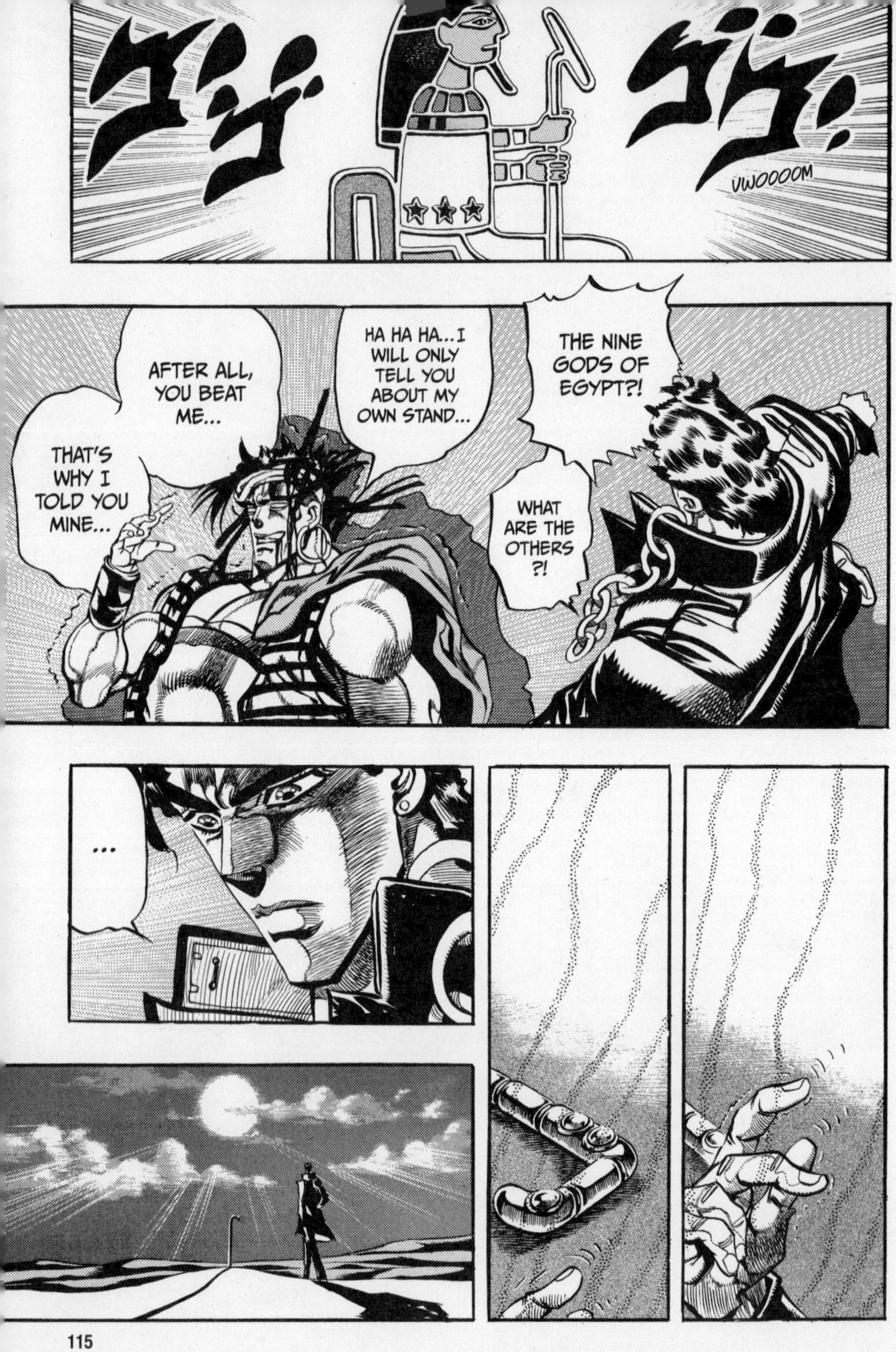
UWOOOOM
THE NINE GODS OF EGYPT?!
WHAT ARE THE OTHERS?!
HA HA HA...I WILL ONLY TELL YOU ABOUT MY OWN STAND...
AFTER ALL, YOU BEAT ME...
THAT'S WHY I TOLD YOU MINE...
...

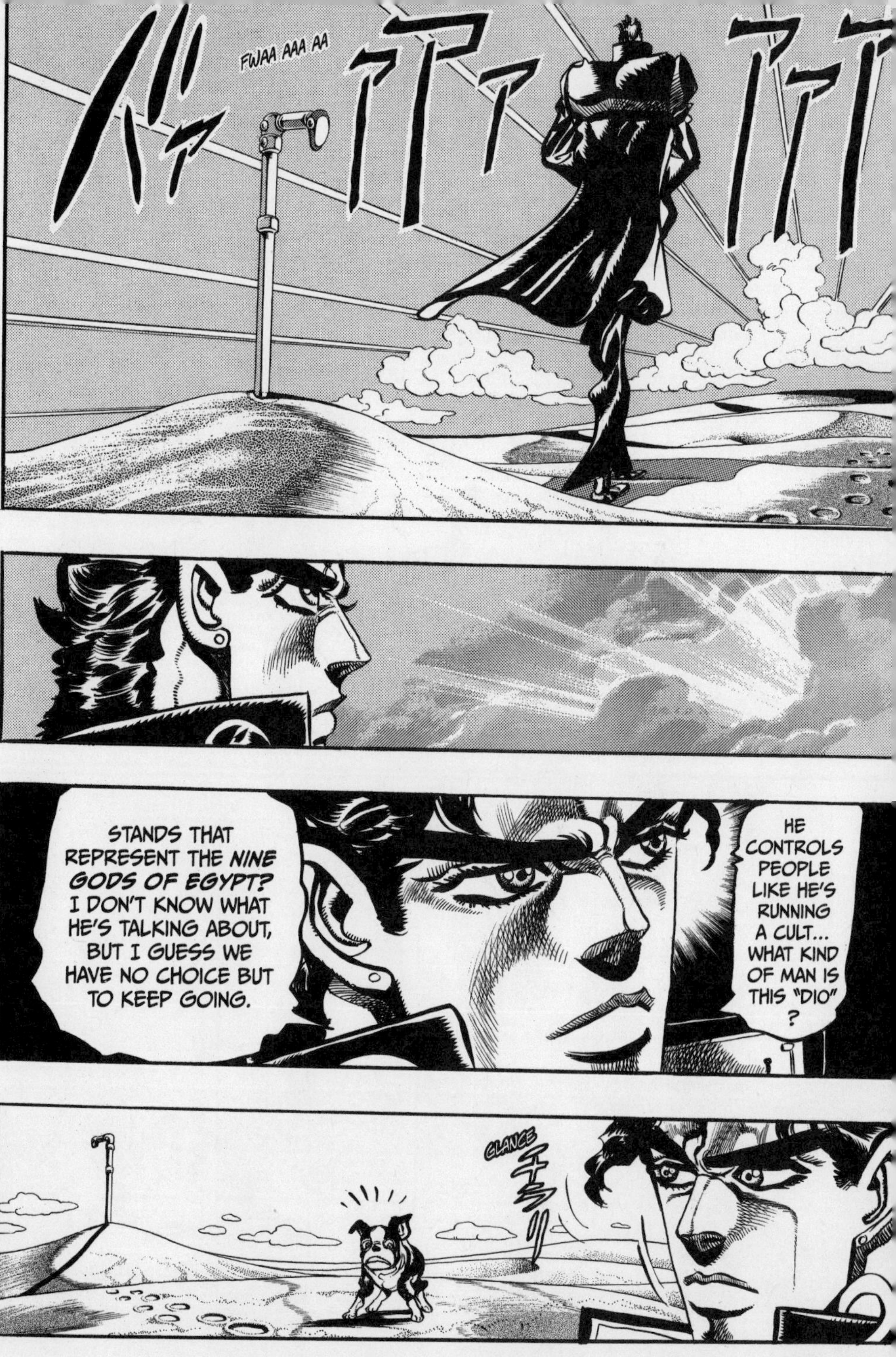
FWAA AAA AA
HE CONTROLS PEOPLE LIKE HE'S RUNNING A CULT... WHAT KIND OF MAN IS THIS "DIO" ?
STANDS THAT REPRESENT THE *NINE GODS OF EGYPT?* I DON'T KNOW WHAT HE'S TALKING ABOUT, BUT I GUESS WE HAVE NO CHOICE BUT TO KEEP GOING.
GLANCE

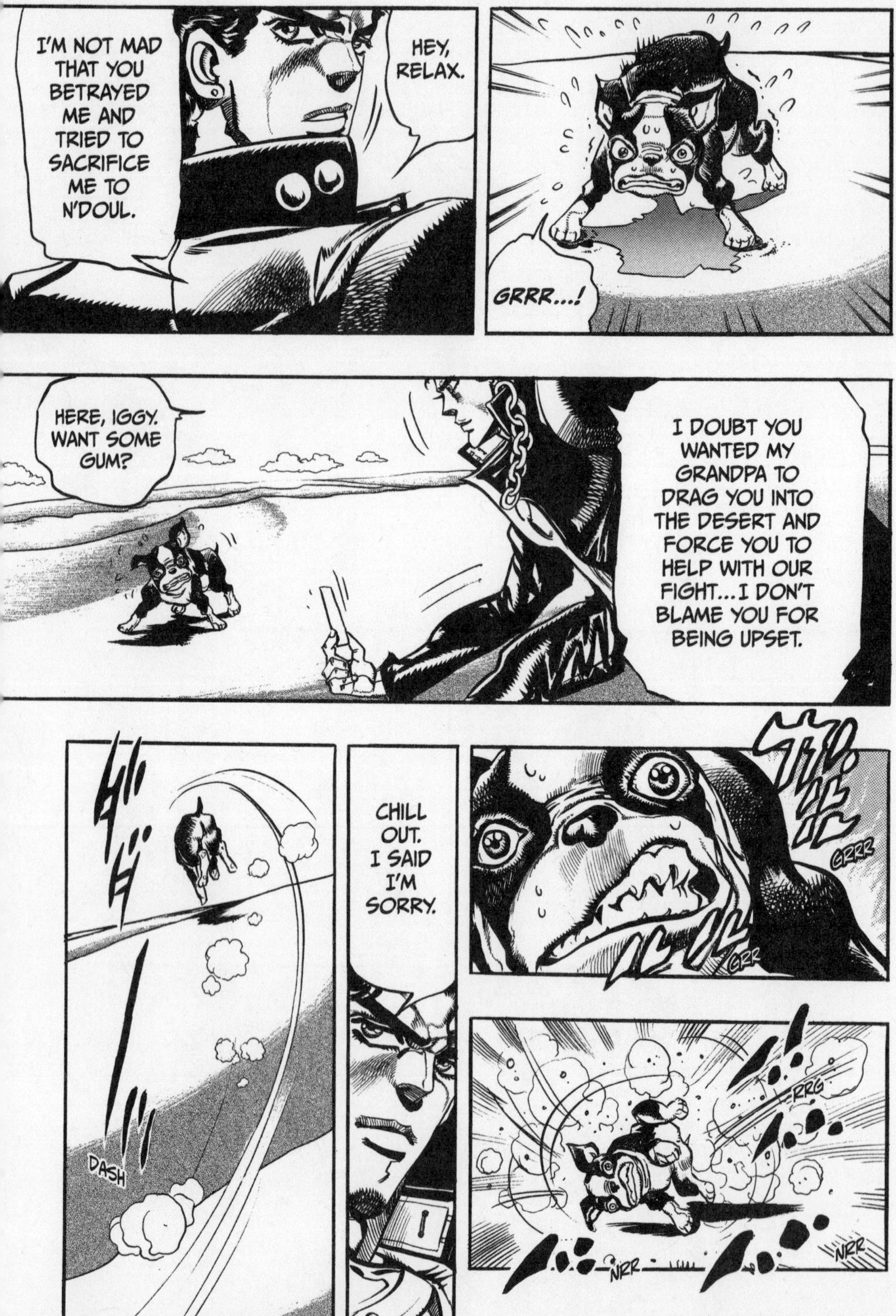
GRRR...!
HEY, RELAX.
I'M NOT MAD THAT YOU BETRAYED ME AND TRIED TO SACRIFICE ME TO N'DOUL.
I DOUBT YOU WANTED MY GRANDPA TO DRAG YOU INTO THE DESERT AND FORCE YOU TO HELP WITH OUR FIGHT...I DON'T BLAME YOU FOR BEING UPSET.
HERE, IGGY. WANT SOME GUM?
GRRR
GRR
RRG
NRR
NRR
CHILL OUT. I SAID I'M SORRY.
DASH

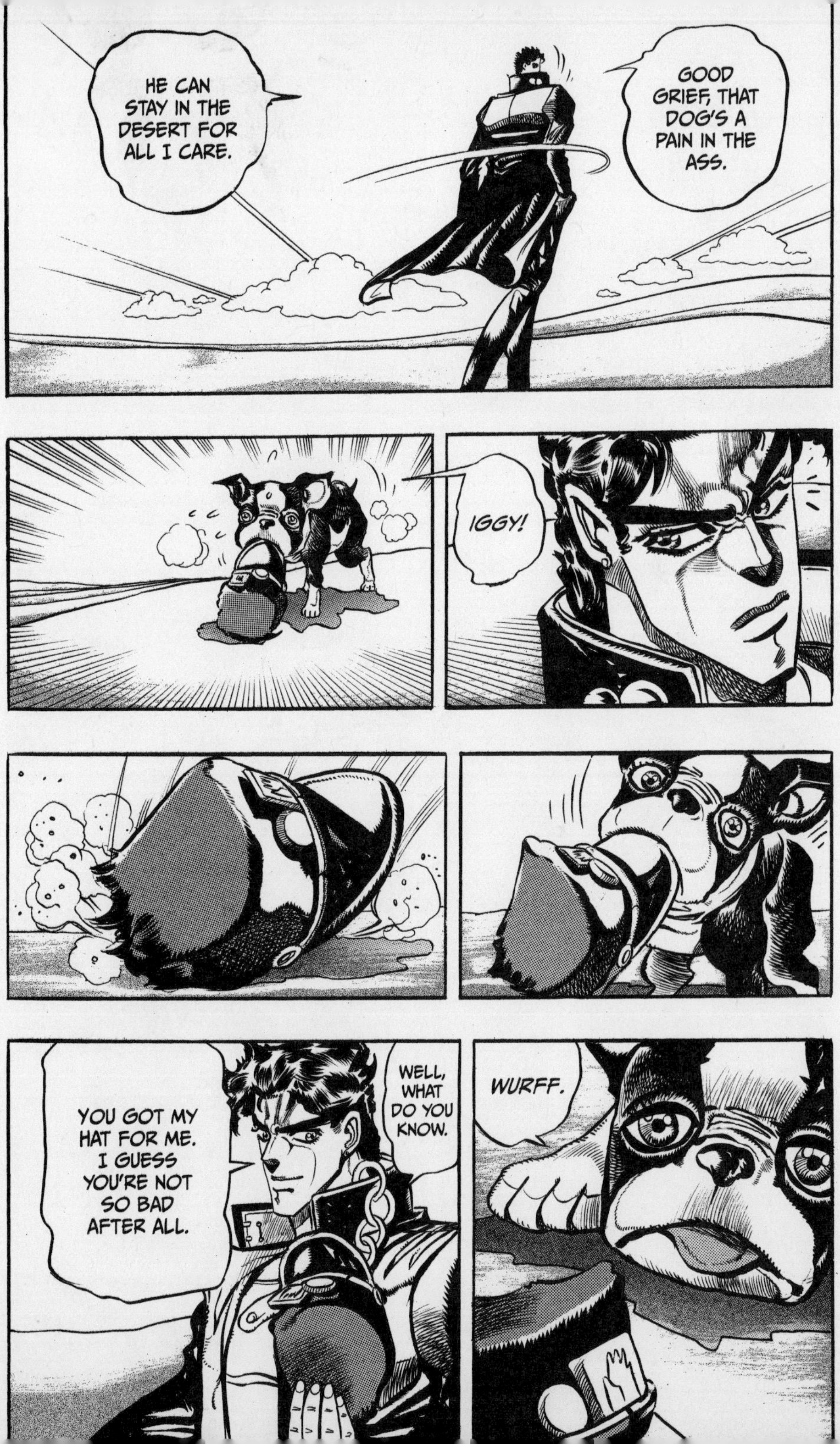
GOOD GRIEF, THAT DOG'S A PAIN IN THE ASS.
HE CAN STAY IN THE DESERT FOR ALL I CARE.
IGGY!
WURFF.
WELL, WHAT DO YOU KNOW.
YOU GOT MY HAT FOR ME. I GUESS YOU'RE NOT SO BAD AFTER ALL.

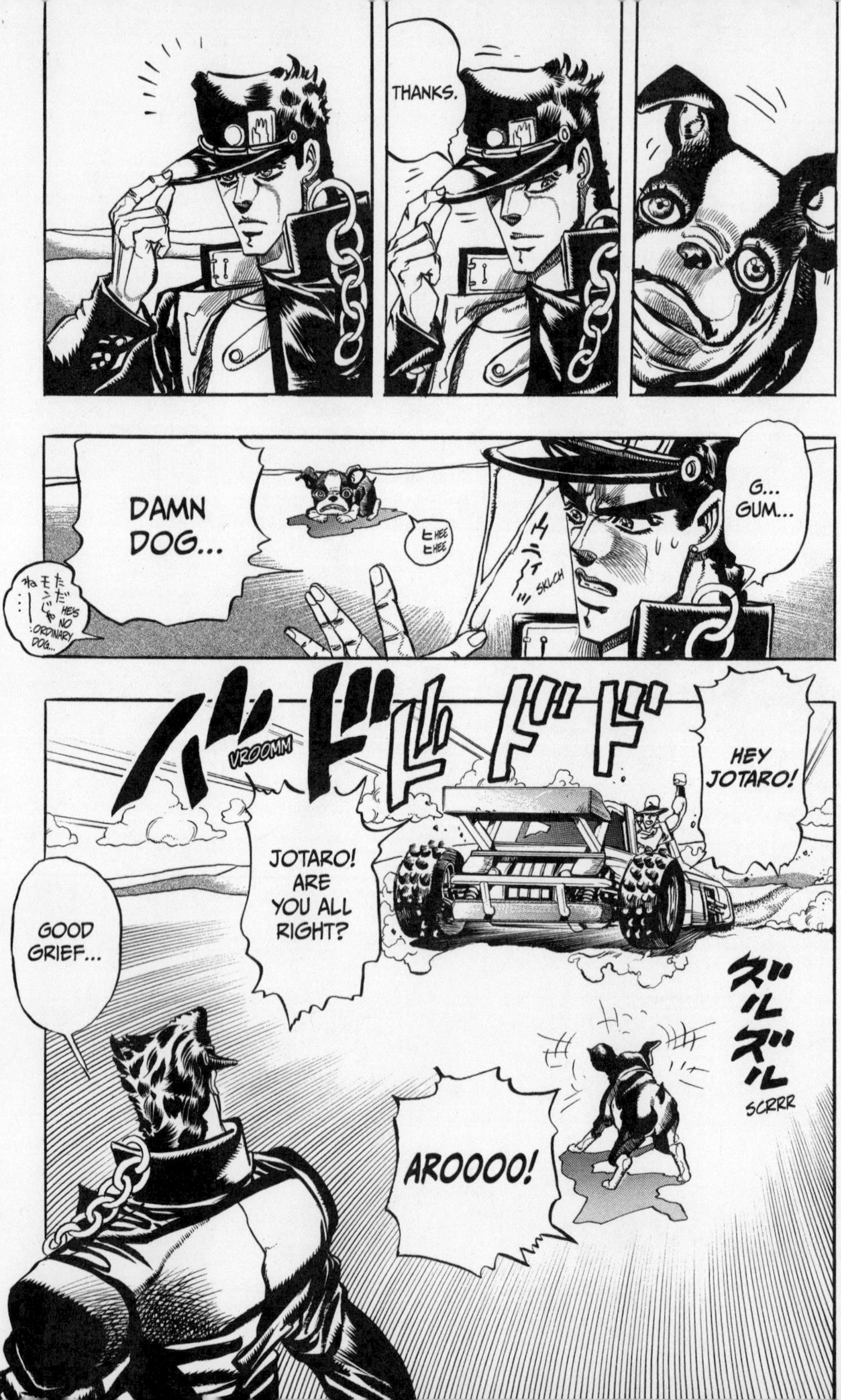
THANKS.
G... GUM...
SKLCH
ヒHEE ヒHEE
DAMN DOG...
ただモンじゃねー… HE'S NO ORDINARY DOG...
HEY JOTARO!
バドドドド VROOMM
JOTARO! ARE YOU ALL RIGHT?
GOOD GRIEF...
ズルズル SCRRR
AROOOO!

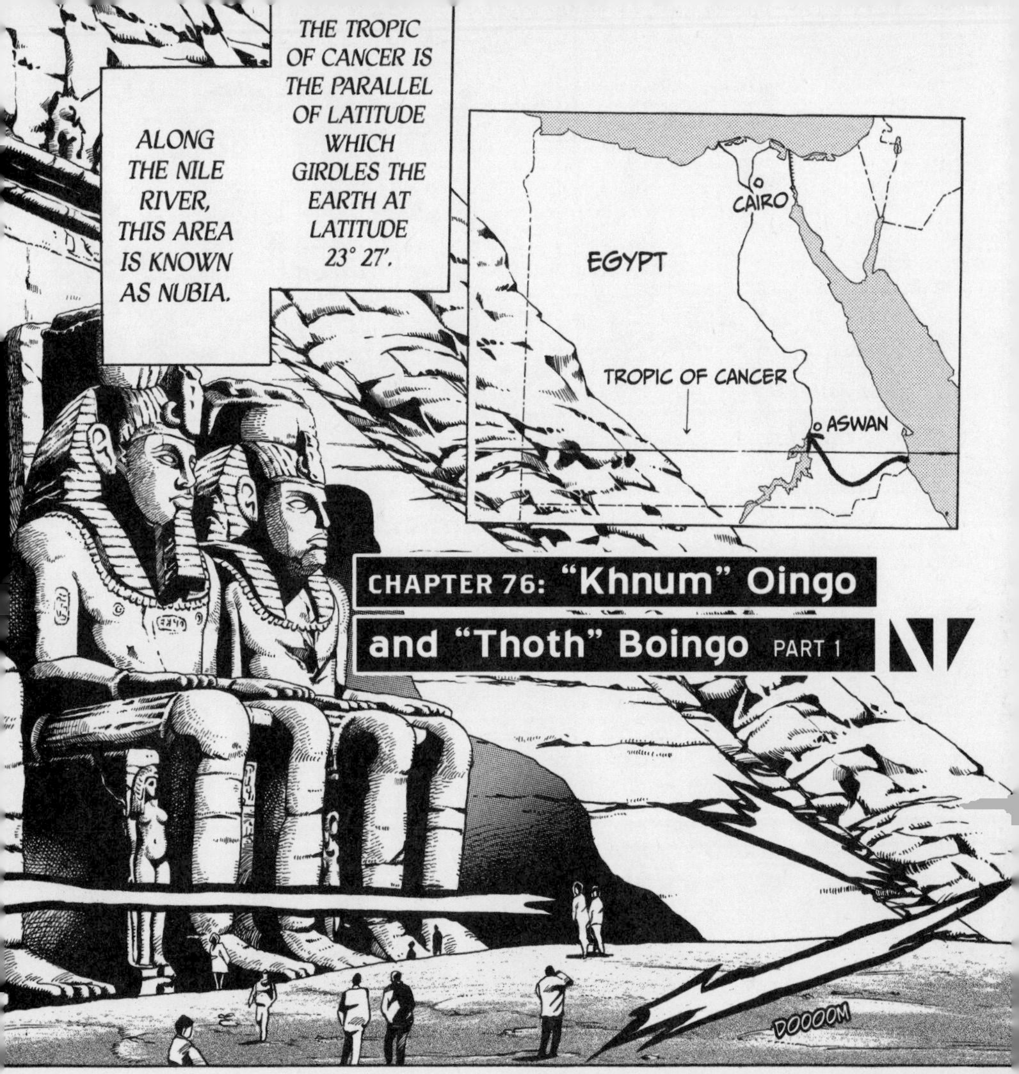
THE TROPIC OF CANCER IS THE PARALLEL OF LATITUDE WHICH GIRDLES THE EARTH AT LATITUDE 23° 27′.
ALONG THE NILE RIVER, THIS AREA IS KNOWN AS NUBIA.
CAIRO
EGYPT
TROPIC OF CANCER
ASWAN
CHAPTER 76: "Khnum" Oingo and "Thoth" Boingo PART 1
DOOOOM

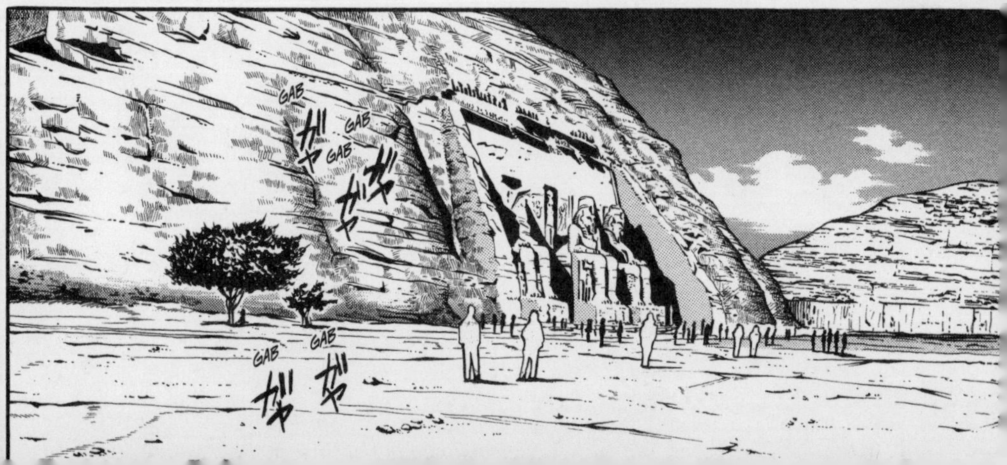
GAB ガヤ
GAB ガヤ
GAB ガヤ
GAB ガヤ
GAB ガヤ

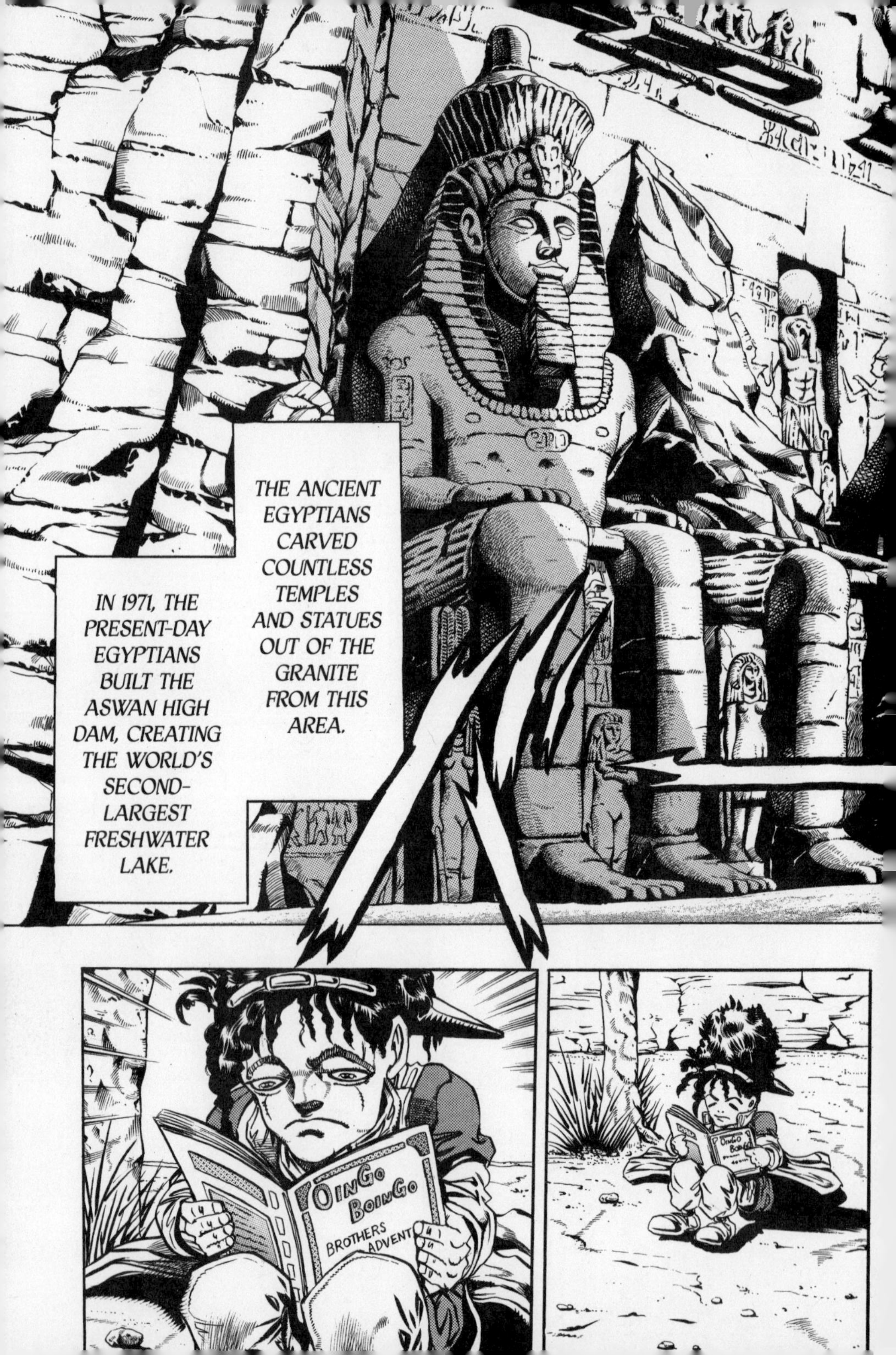
THE ANCIENT EGYPTIANS CARVED COUNTLESS TEMPLES AND STATUES OUT OF THE GRANITE FROM THIS AREA.
IN 1971, THE PRESENT-DAY EGYPTIANS BUILT THE ASWAN HIGH DAM, CREATING THE WORLD'S SECOND-LARGEST FRESHWATER LAKE.
OINGO BOINGO BROTHERS ADVENT

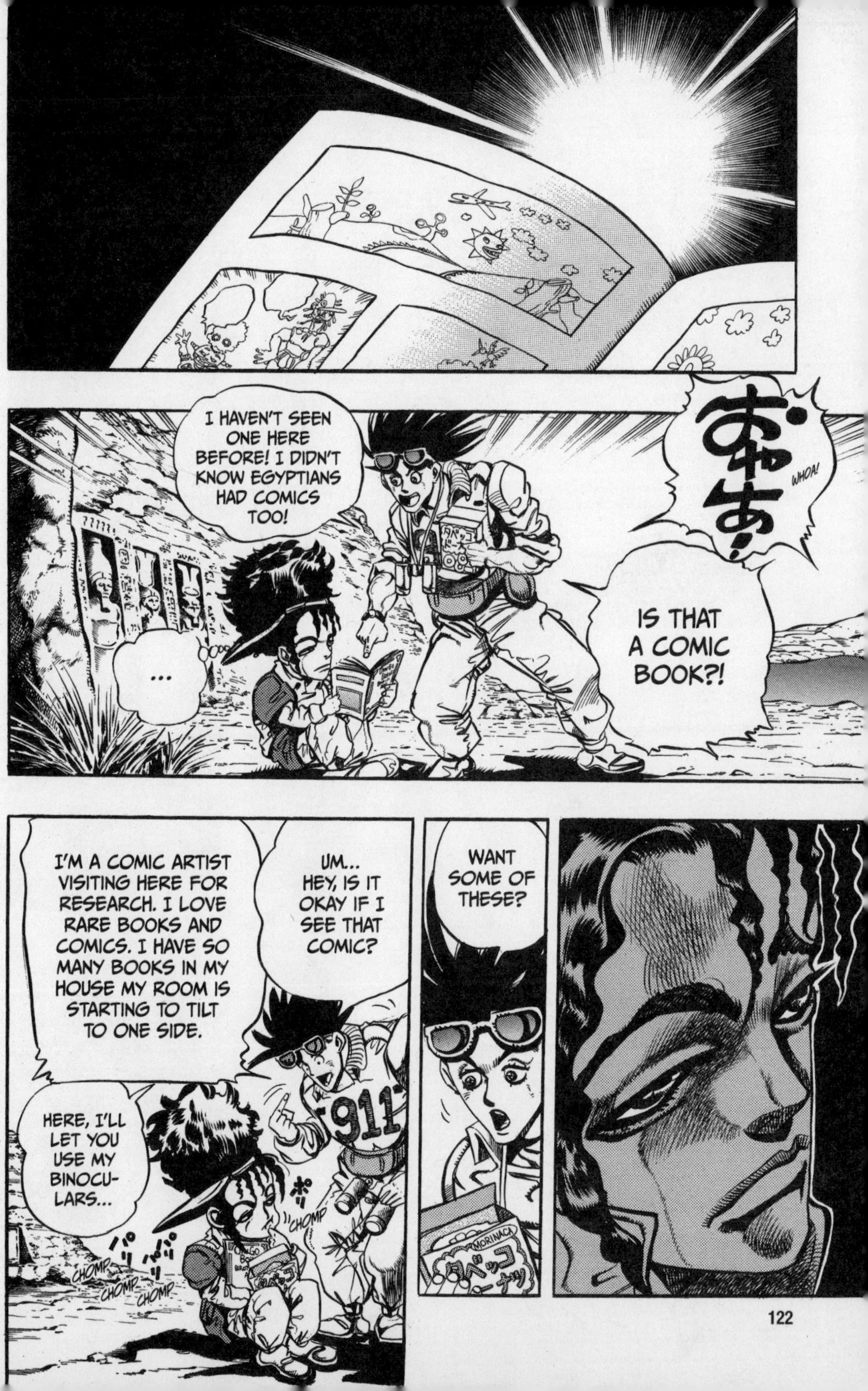
WHOA!
IS THAT A COMIC BOOK?!
I HAVEN'T SEEN ONE HERE BEFORE! I DIDN'T KNOW EGYPTIANS HAD COMICS TOO!
...
WANT SOME OF THESE?
MORINAGA
UM... HEY, IS IT OKAY IF I SEE THAT COMIC?
I'M A COMIC ARTIST VISITING HERE FOR RESEARCH. I LOVE RARE BOOKS AND COMICS. I HAVE SO MANY BOOKS IN MY HOUSE MY ROOM IS STARTING TO TILT TO ONE SIDE.
HERE, I'LL LET YOU USE MY BINOCULARS...
CHOMP
CHOMP CHOMP CHOMP

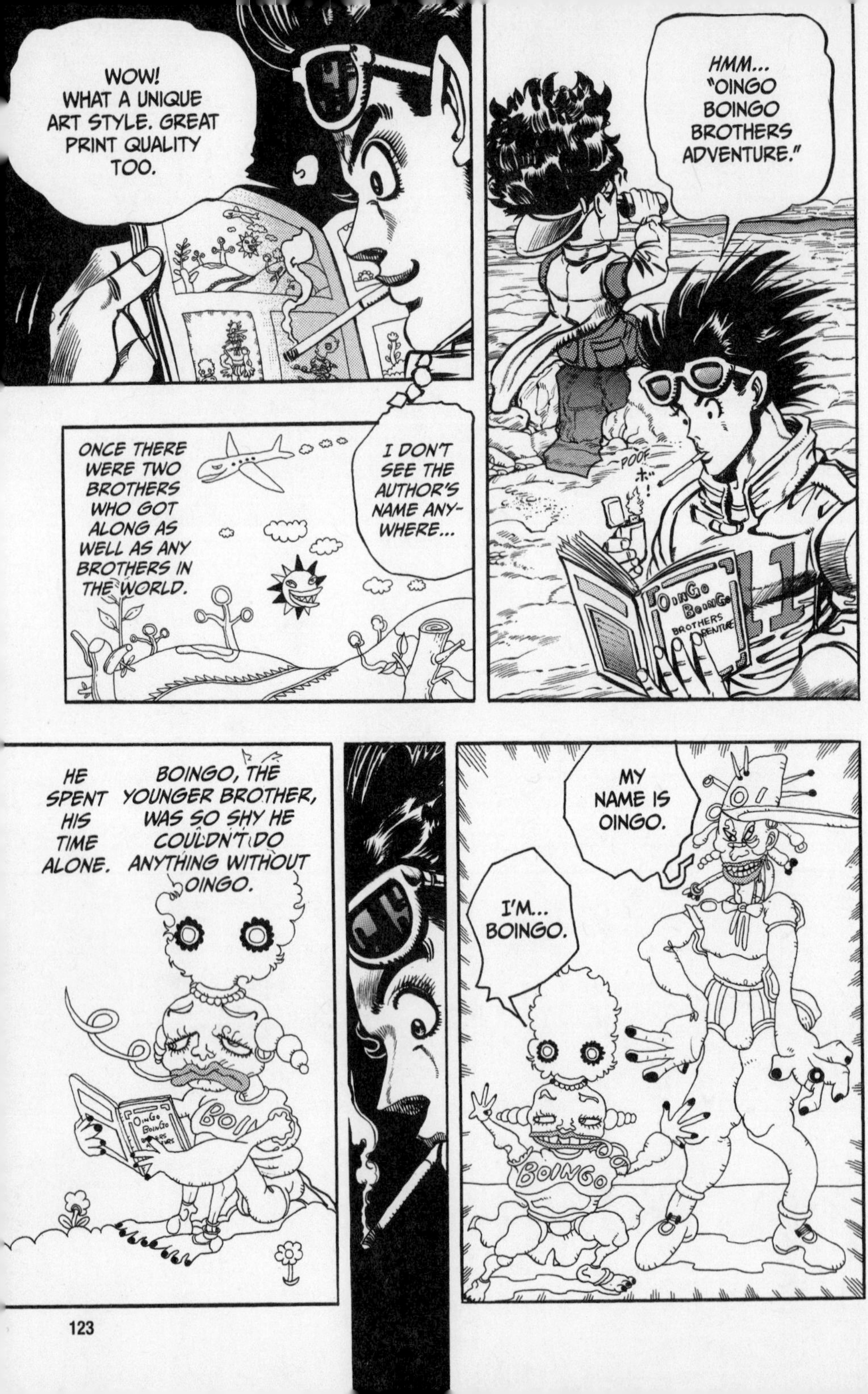
HMM... "OINGO BOINGO BROTHERS ADVENTURE."
POOF
ボ
OINGO BOINGO BROTHERS ADVENTURE
WOW! WHAT A UNIQUE ART STYLE. GREAT PRINT QUALITY TOO.
I DON'T SEE THE AUTHOR'S NAME ANY-WHERE...
ONCE THERE WERE TWO BROTHERS WHO GOT ALONG AS WELL AS ANY BROTHERS IN THE WORLD.
MY NAME IS OINGO.
I'M... BOINGO.
BOINGO
BOINGO, THE YOUNGER BROTHER, WAS SO SHY HE COULDN'T DO ANYTHING WITHOUT OINGO.
HE SPENT HIS TIME ALONE.

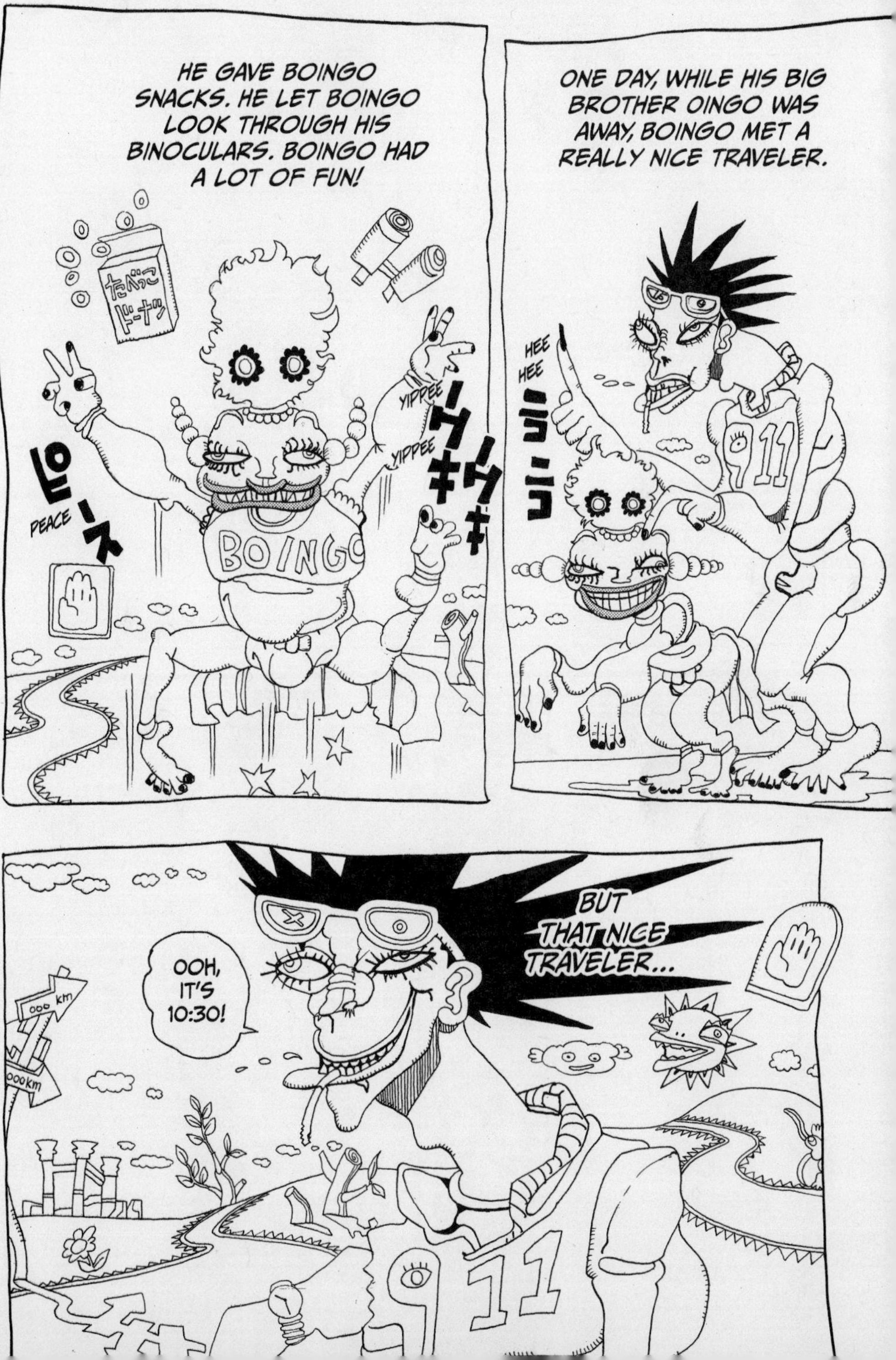
ONE DAY, WHILE HIS BIG BROTHER OINGO WAS AWAY, BOINGO MET A REALLY NICE TRAVELER.
HEE HEE
HE GAVE BOINGO SNACKS. HE LET BOINGO LOOK THROUGH HIS BINOCULARS. BOINGO HAD A LOT OF FUN!
ウキウキ
YIPPEE YIPPEE
ピース
PEACE
BOINGO
BUT THAT NICE TRAVELER...
OOH, IT'S 10:30!
ooo km
ooo km

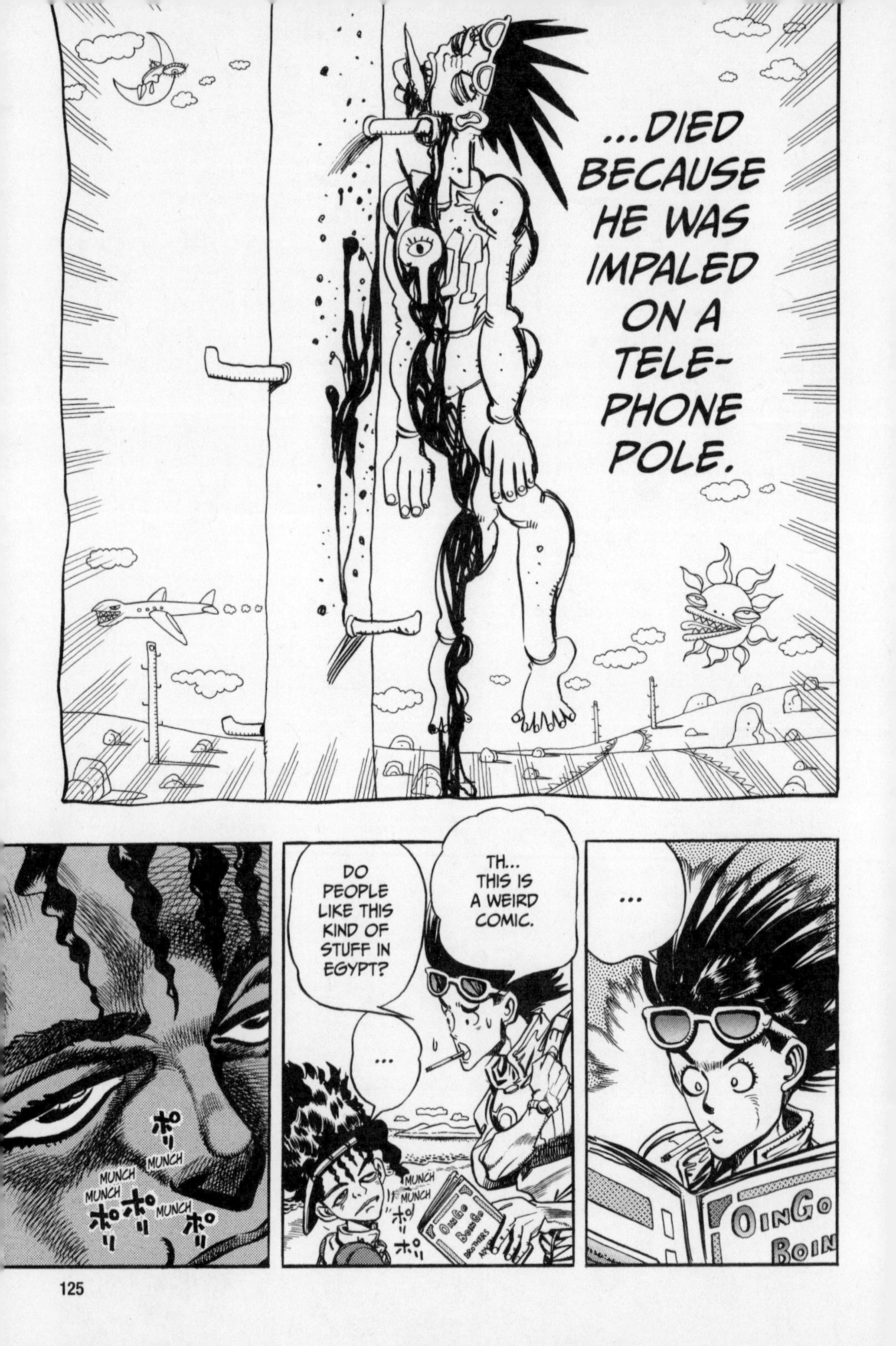
...DIED BECAUSE HE WAS IMPALED ON A TELE-PHONE POLE.
...
TH... THIS IS A WEIRD COMIC.
DO PEOPLE LIKE THIS KIND OF STUFF IN EGYPT?
...
MUNCH MUNCH ポリ ポリ
MUNCH MUNCH MUNCH ポリ ポリ ポリ
MUNCH

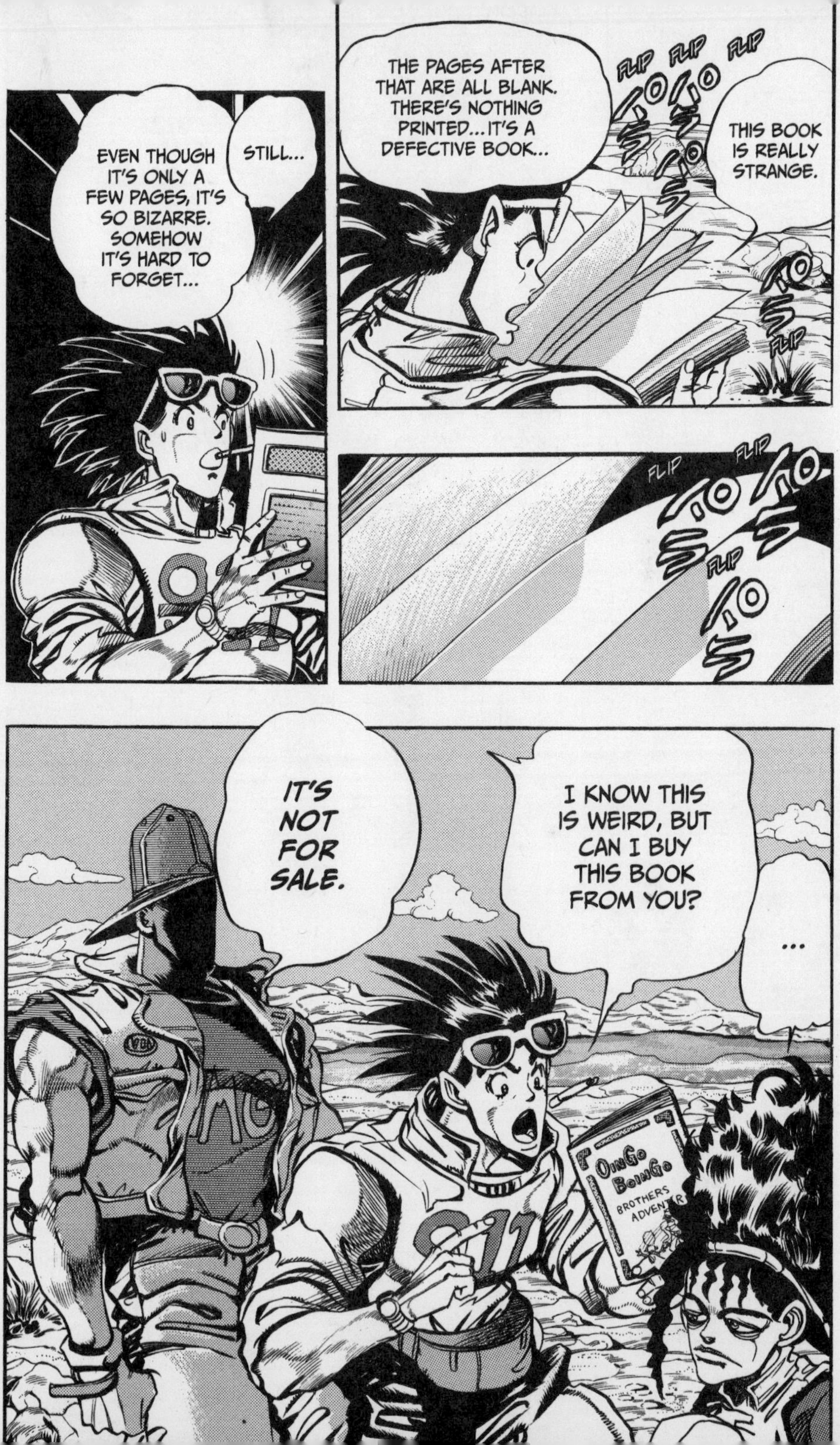
FLIP FLIP FLIP
THIS BOOK IS REALLY STRANGE.
THE PAGES AFTER THAT ARE ALL BLANK. THERE'S NOTHING PRINTED...IT'S A DEFECTIVE BOOK...
FLIP
FLIP
FLIP
FLIP
STILL...
EVEN THOUGH IT'S ONLY A FEW PAGES, IT'S SO BIZARRE. SOMEHOW IT'S HARD TO FORGET...
...
I KNOW THIS IS WEIRD, BUT CAN I BUY THIS BOOK FROM YOU?
IT'S NOT FOR SALE.
OINGO BOINGO
BROTHERS ADVENT

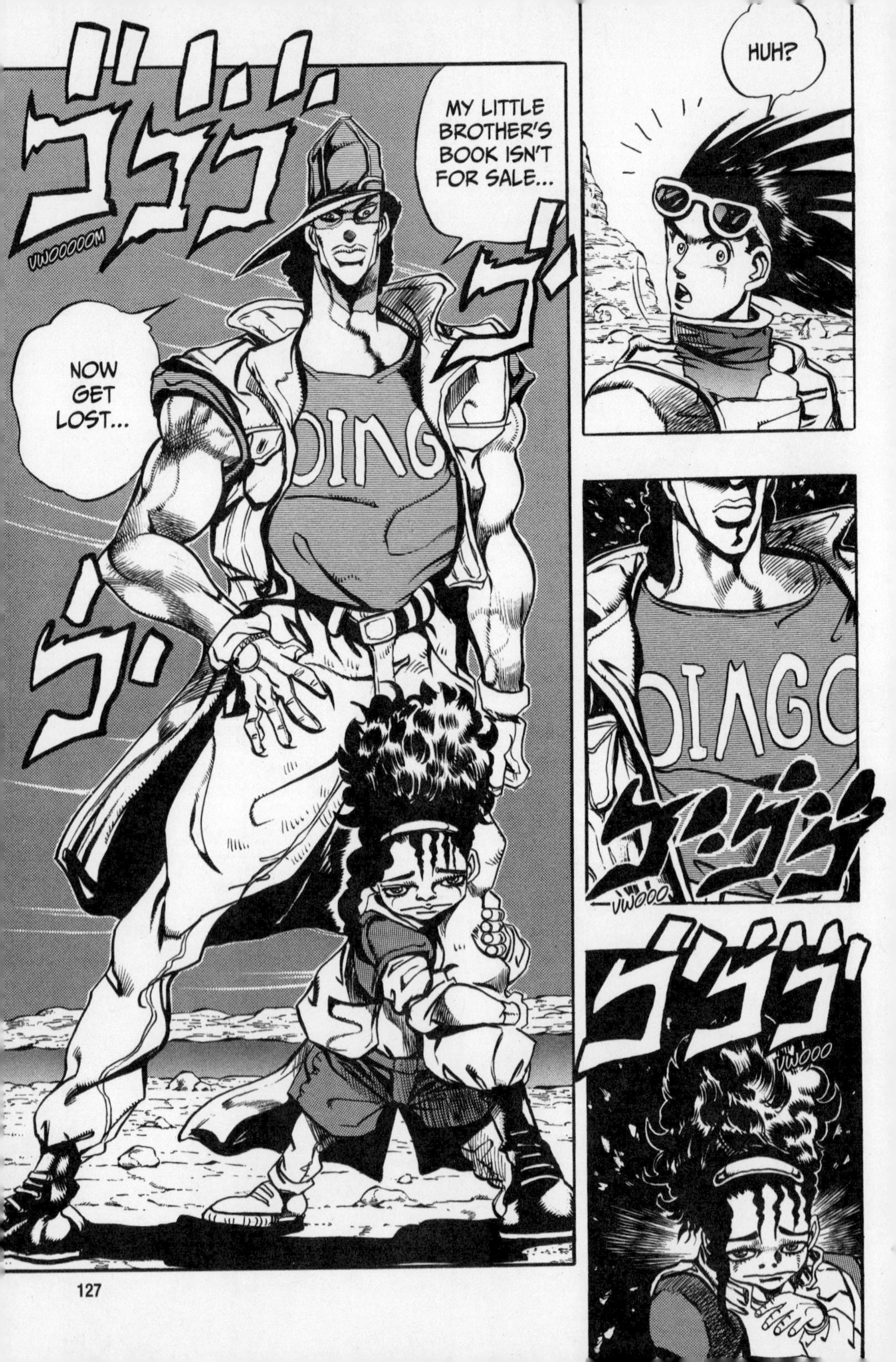
HUH?
VWOOO
VWOOO
MY LITTLE BROTHER'S BOOK ISN'T FOR SALE...
VWOOOOOM
NOW GET LOST...

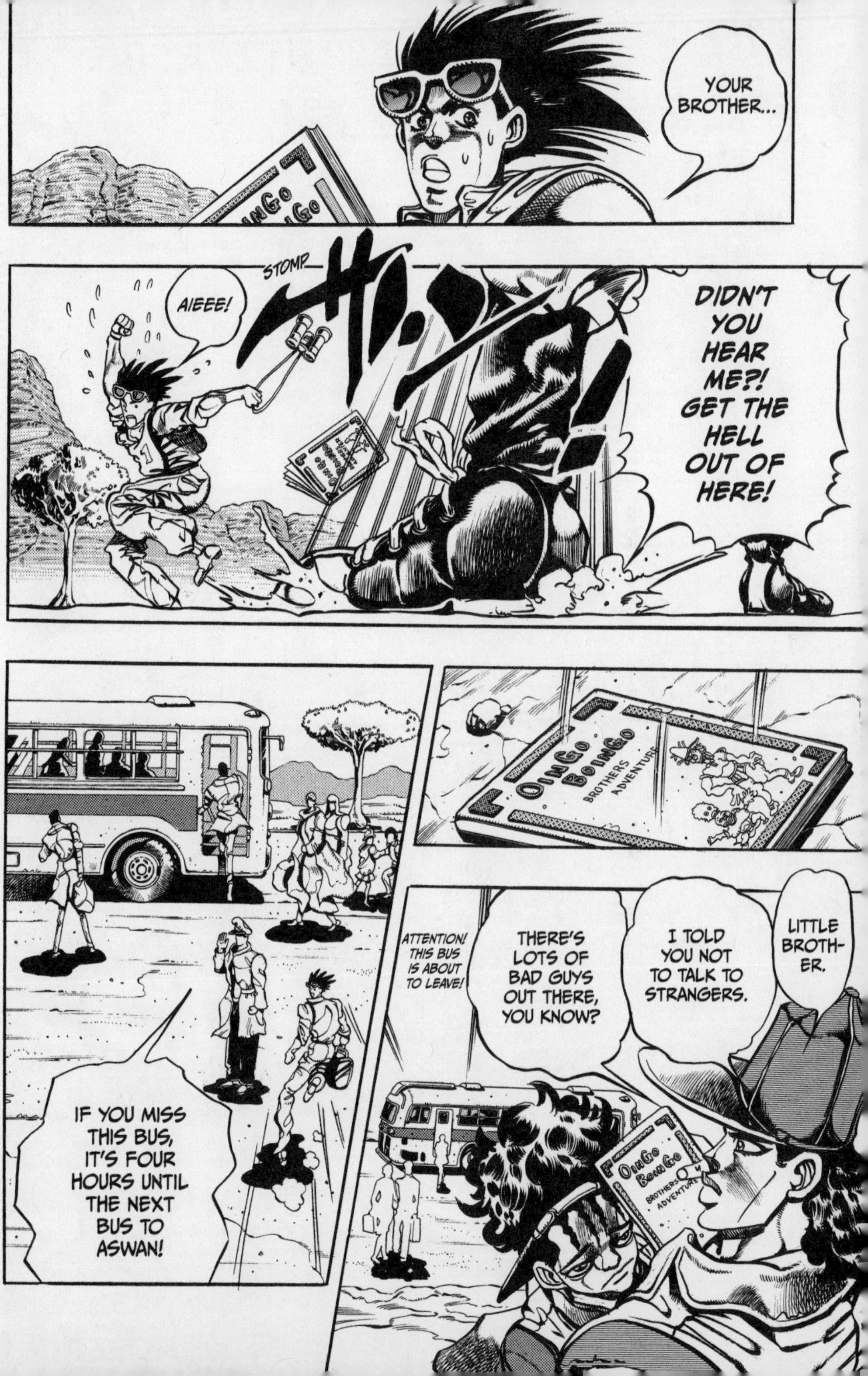
YOUR BROTHER...
DIDN'T YOU HEAR ME?! GET THE HELL OUT OF HERE!
STOMP
AIEEE!
OINGO BOINGO BROTHERS ADVENTURE
LITTLE BROTH-ER.
I TOLD YOU NOT TO TALK TO STRANGERS.
THERE'S LOTS OF BAD GUYS OUT THERE, YOU KNOW?
ATTENTION! THIS BUS IS ABOUT TO LEAVE!
IF YOU MISS THIS BUS, IT'S FOUR HOURS UNTIL THE NEXT BUS TO ASWAN!

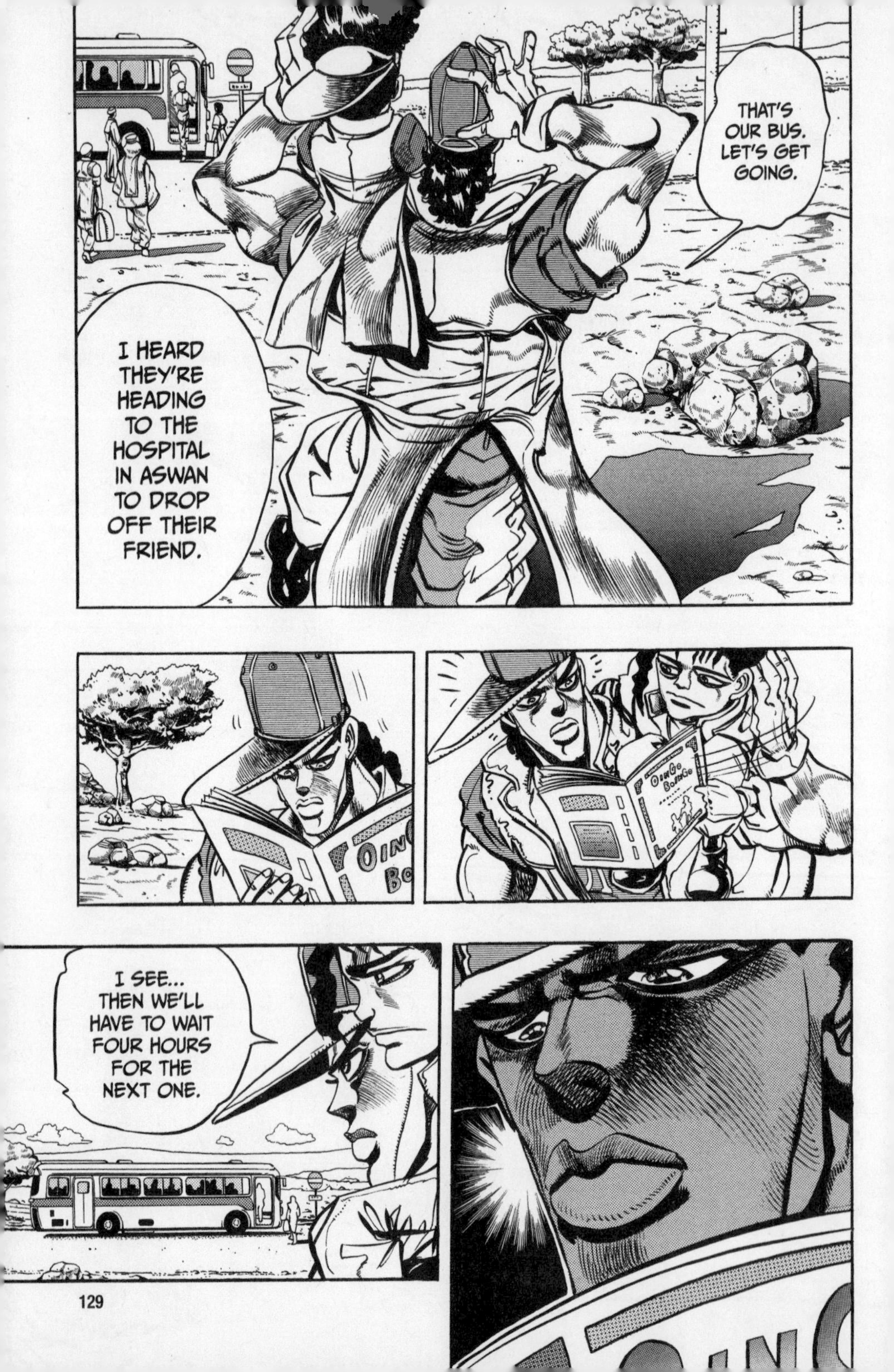
THAT'S OUR BUS. LET'S GET GOING.
I HEARD THEY'RE HEADING TO THE HOSPITAL IN ASWAN TO DROP OFF THEIR FRIEND.
I SEE... THEN WE'LL HAVE TO WAIT FOUR HOURS FOR THE NEXT ONE.

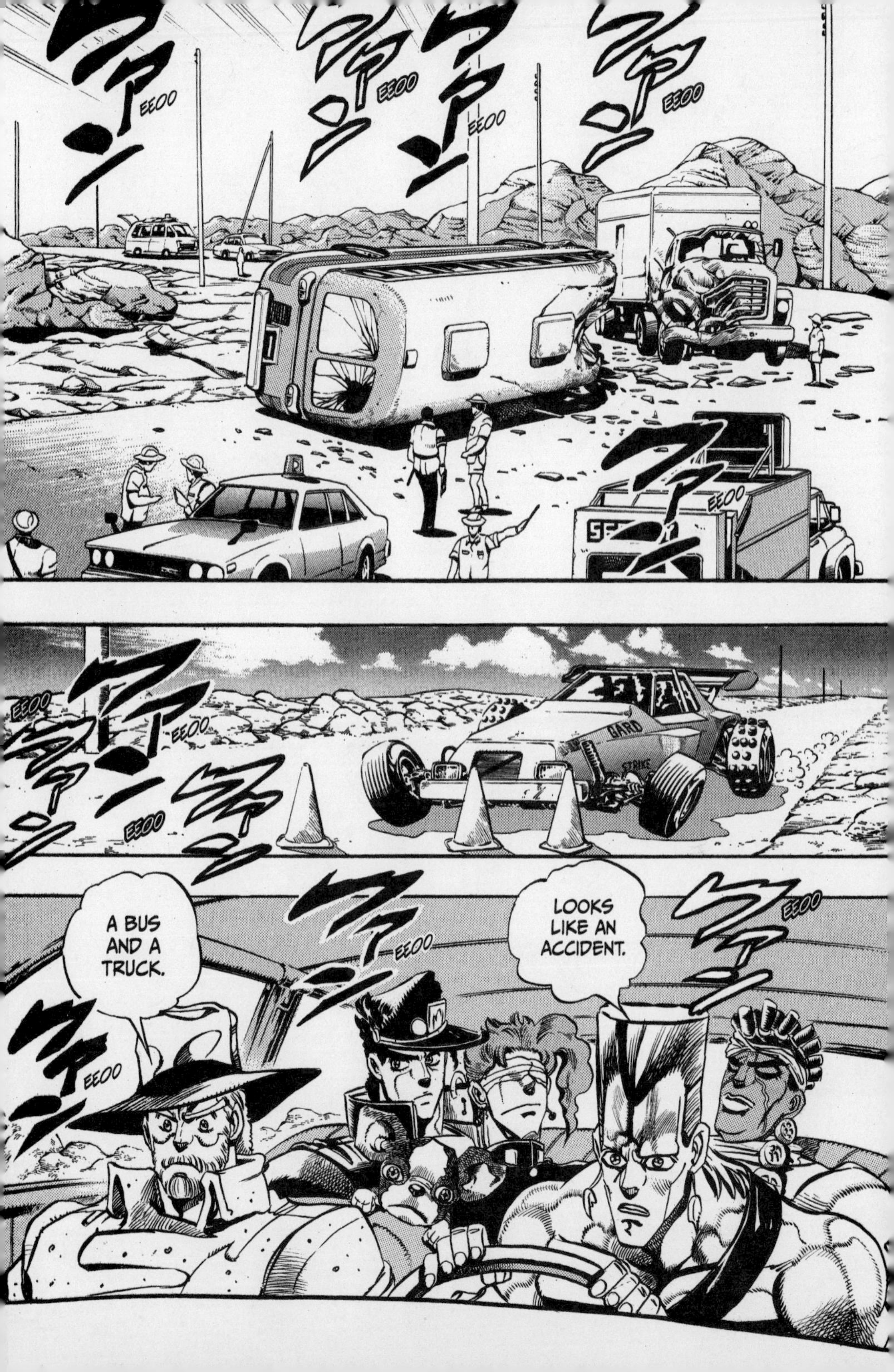
EEOO
EEOO
EEOO
EEOO
EEOO
EEOO
EEOO
EEOO
LOOKS LIKE AN ACCIDENT.
EEOO
EEOO
A BUS AND A TRUCK.
EEOO

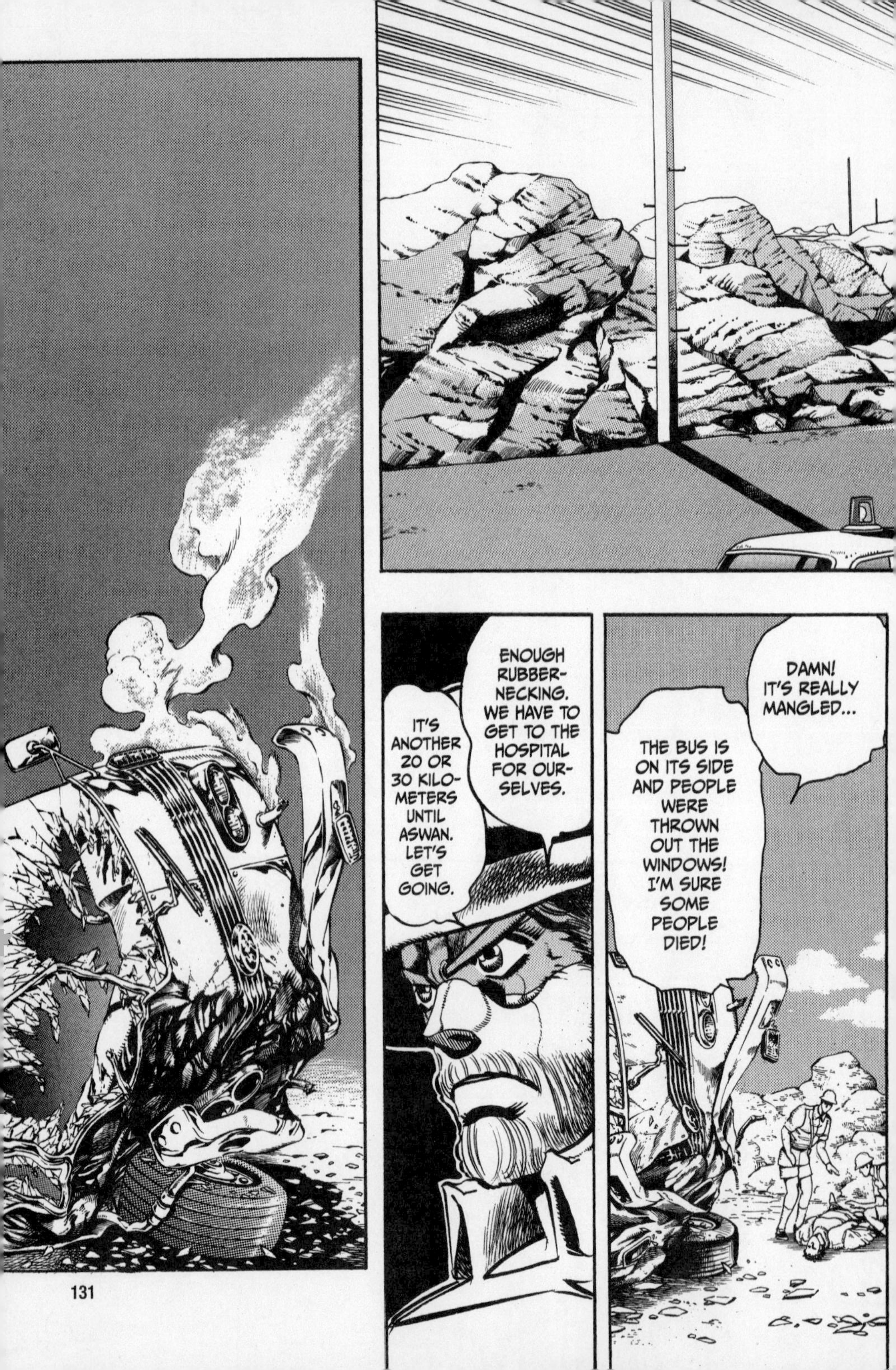
DAMN! IT'S REALLY MANGLED...
THE BUS IS ON ITS SIDE AND PEOPLE WERE THROWN OUT THE WINDOWS! I'M SURE SOME PEOPLE DIED!
ENOUGH RUBBER-NECKING. WE HAVE TO GET TO THE HOSPITAL FOR OUR-SELVES.
IT'S ANOTHER 20 OR 30 KILO-METERS UNTIL ASWAN. LET'S GET GOING.

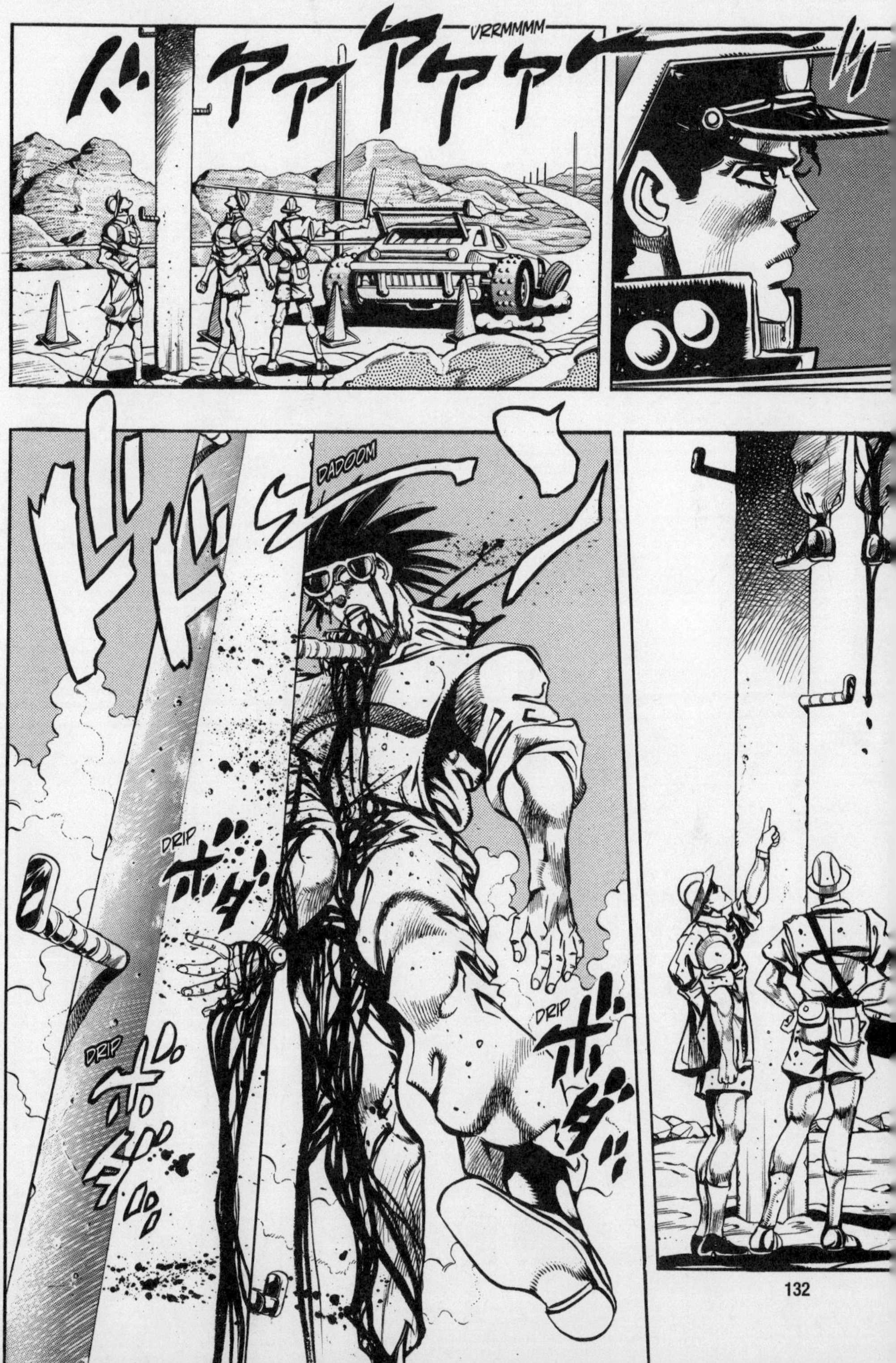
VRRMMMM
DADOOM
DRIP
DRIP
DRIP

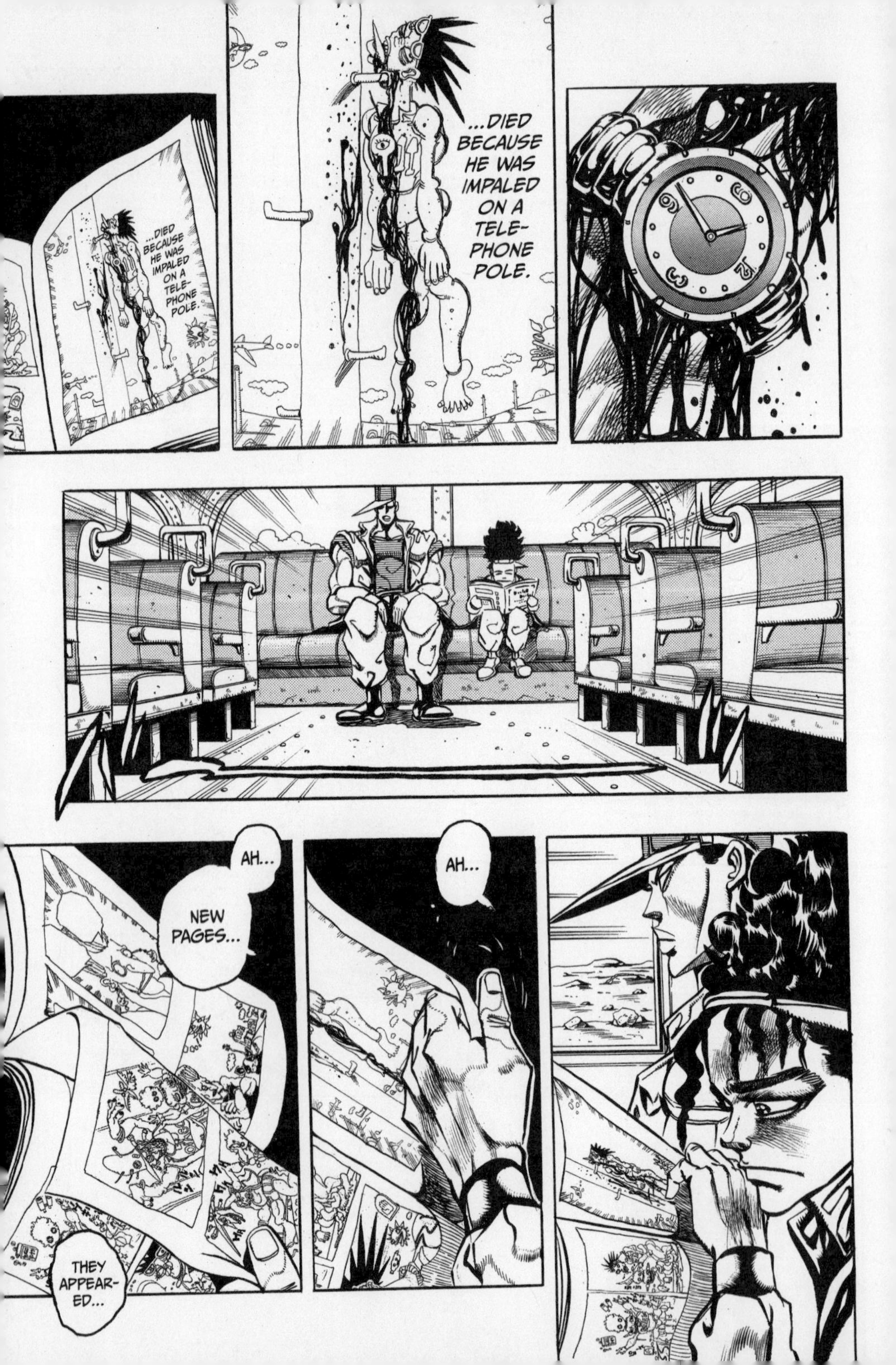
...DIED BECAUSE HE WAS IMPALED ON A TELE-PHONE POLE.
...DIED BECAUSE HE WAS IMPALED ON A TELE-PHONE POLE.
AH...
AH...
NEW PAGES...
THEY APPEAR-ED...

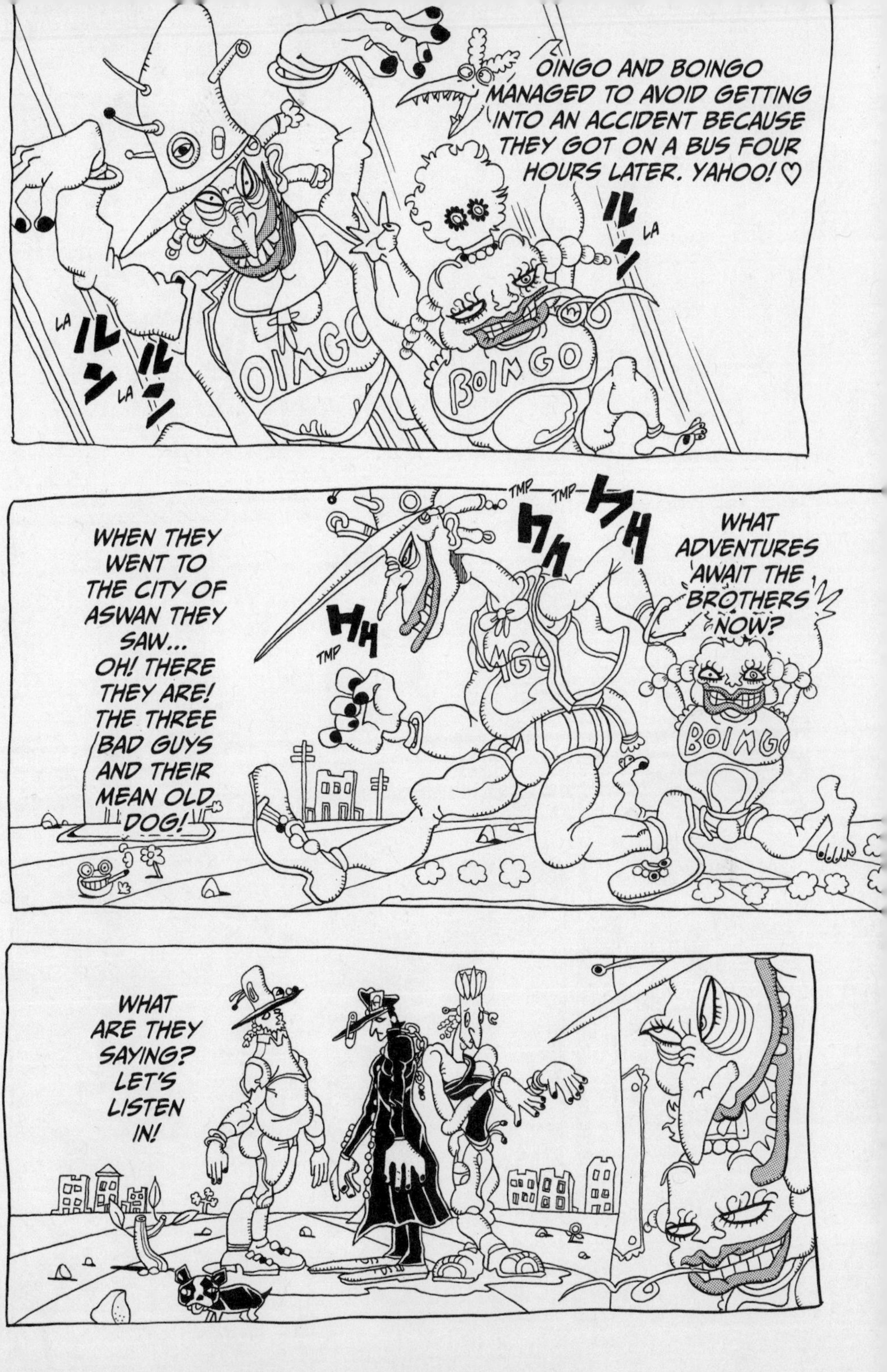
OINGO AND BOINGO MANAGED TO AVOID GETTING INTO AN ACCIDENT BECAUSE THEY GOT ON A BUS FOUR HOURS LATER. YAHOO! ♡
LA
LA
LA
WHAT ADVENTURES AWAIT THE BROTHERS NOW?
TMP
TMP
TMP
WHEN THEY WENT TO THE CITY OF ASWAN THEY SAW... OH! THERE THEY ARE! THE THREE BAD GUYS AND THEIR MEAN OLD DOG!
WHAT ARE THEY SAYING? LET'S LISTEN IN!

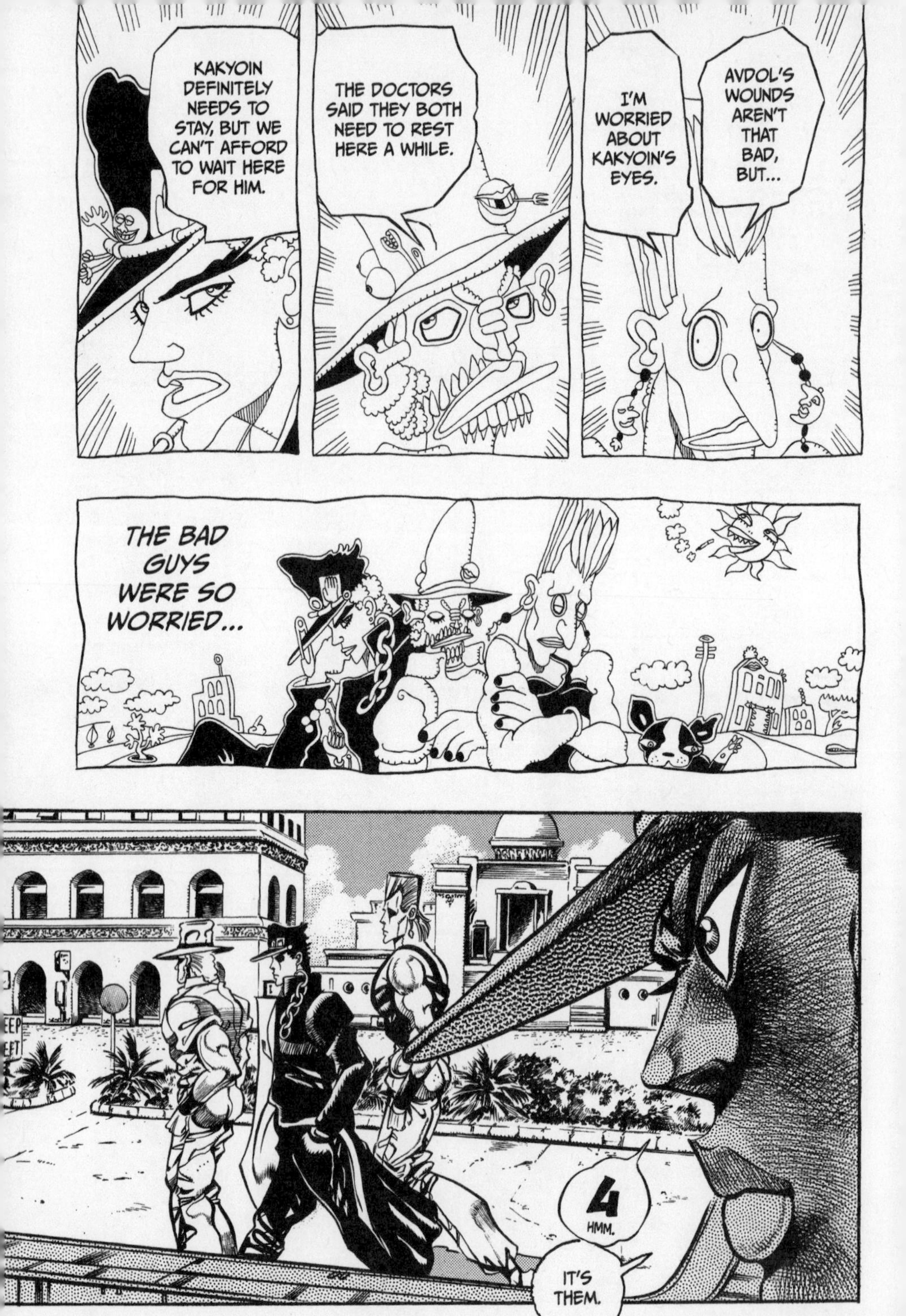
AVDOL'S WOUNDS AREN'T THAT BAD, BUT...
I'M WORRIED ABOUT KAKYOIN'S EYES.
THE DOCTORS SAID THEY BOTH NEED TO REST HERE A WHILE.
KAKYOIN DEFINITELY NEEDS TO STAY, BUT WE CAN'T AFFORD TO WAIT HERE FOR HIM.
THE BAD GUYS WERE SO WORRIED...
4
HMM.
IT'S THEM.

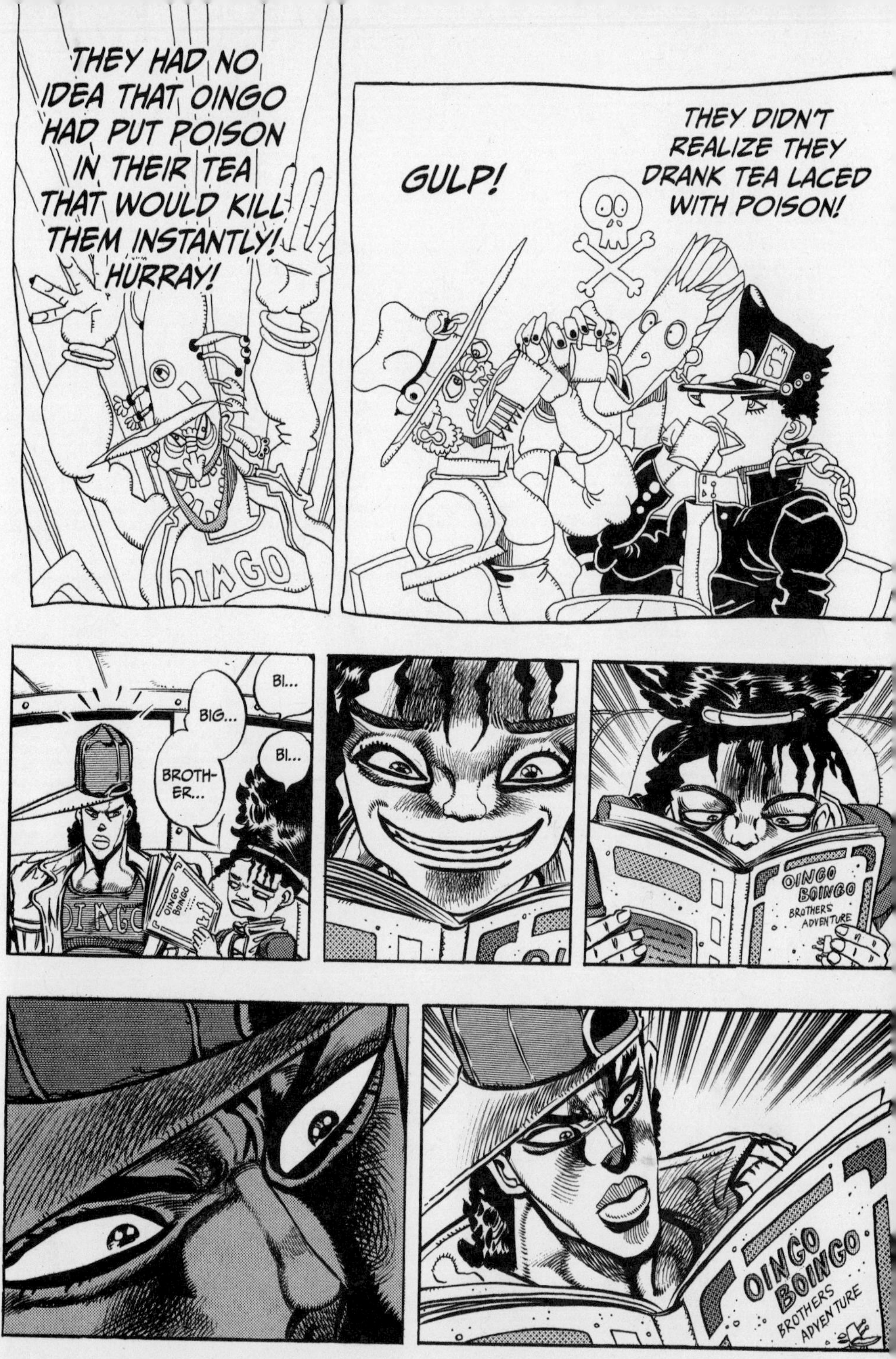
THEY DIDN'T REALIZE THEY DRANK TEA LACED WITH POISON!
GULP!
THEY HAD NO IDEA THAT OINGO HAD PUT POISON IN THEIR TEA THAT WOULD KILL THEM INSTANTLY! HURRAY!
OINGO
OINGO BOINGO BROTHERS' ADVENTURE
BI...
BIG...
BI...
BROTHER-ER...
OINGO BOINGO
OINGO
OINGO BOINGO BROTHERS ADVENTURE

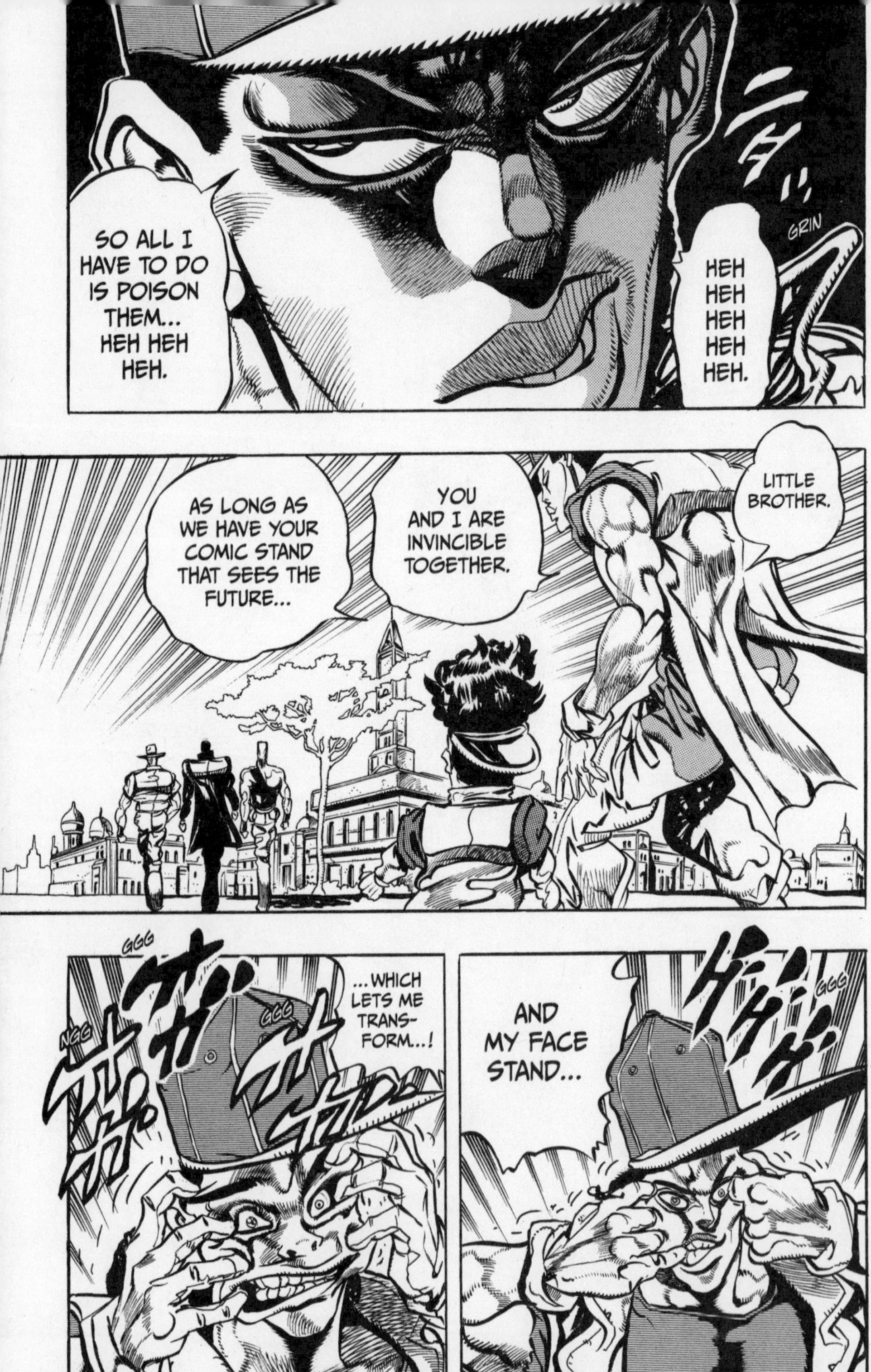
GRIN
HEH HEH HEH HEH HEH.
SO ALL I HAVE TO DO IS POISON THEM... HEH HEH HEH.
LITTLE BROTHER.
YOU AND I ARE INVINCIBLE TOGETHER.
AS LONG AS WE HAVE YOUR COMIC STAND THAT SEES THE FUTURE...
GGG
AND MY FACE STAND...
...WHICH LETS ME TRANS-FORM...!
GGG
GGG
NGG

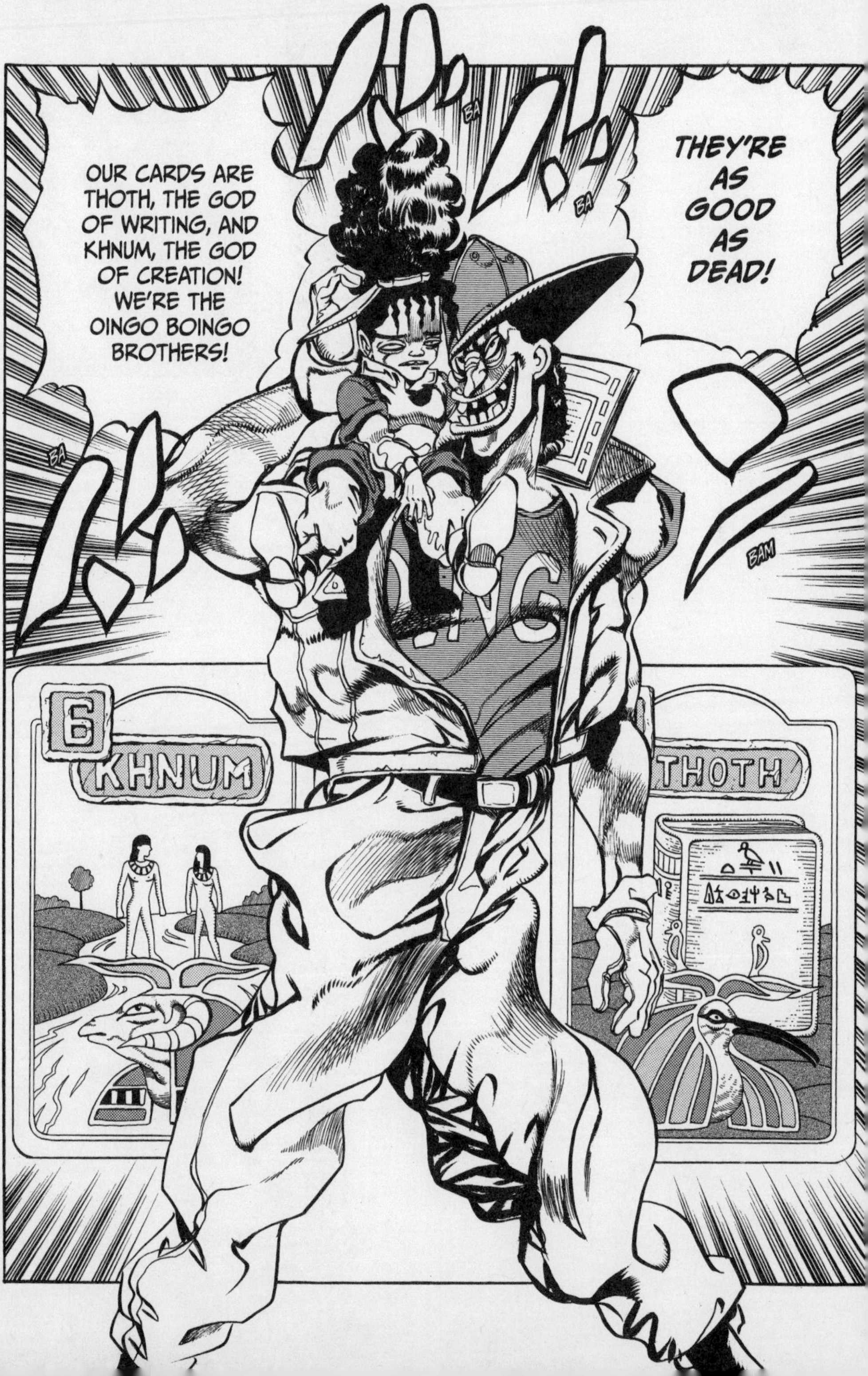
BA
BA
THEY'RE AS GOOD AS DEAD!
OUR CARDS ARE THOTH, THE GOD OF WRITING, AND KHNUM, THE GOD OF CREATION! WE'RE THE OINGO BOINGO BROTHERS!
BAM
BA
THOTH
6
KHNUM

KHNUM

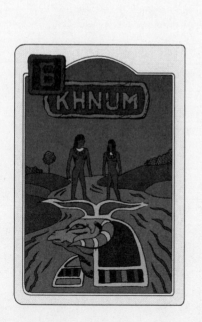

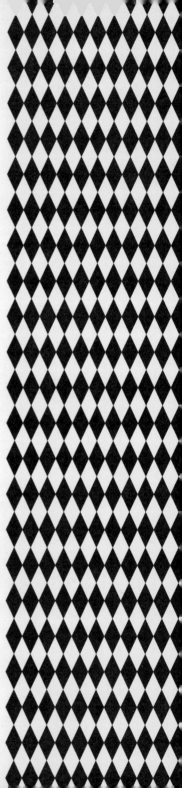

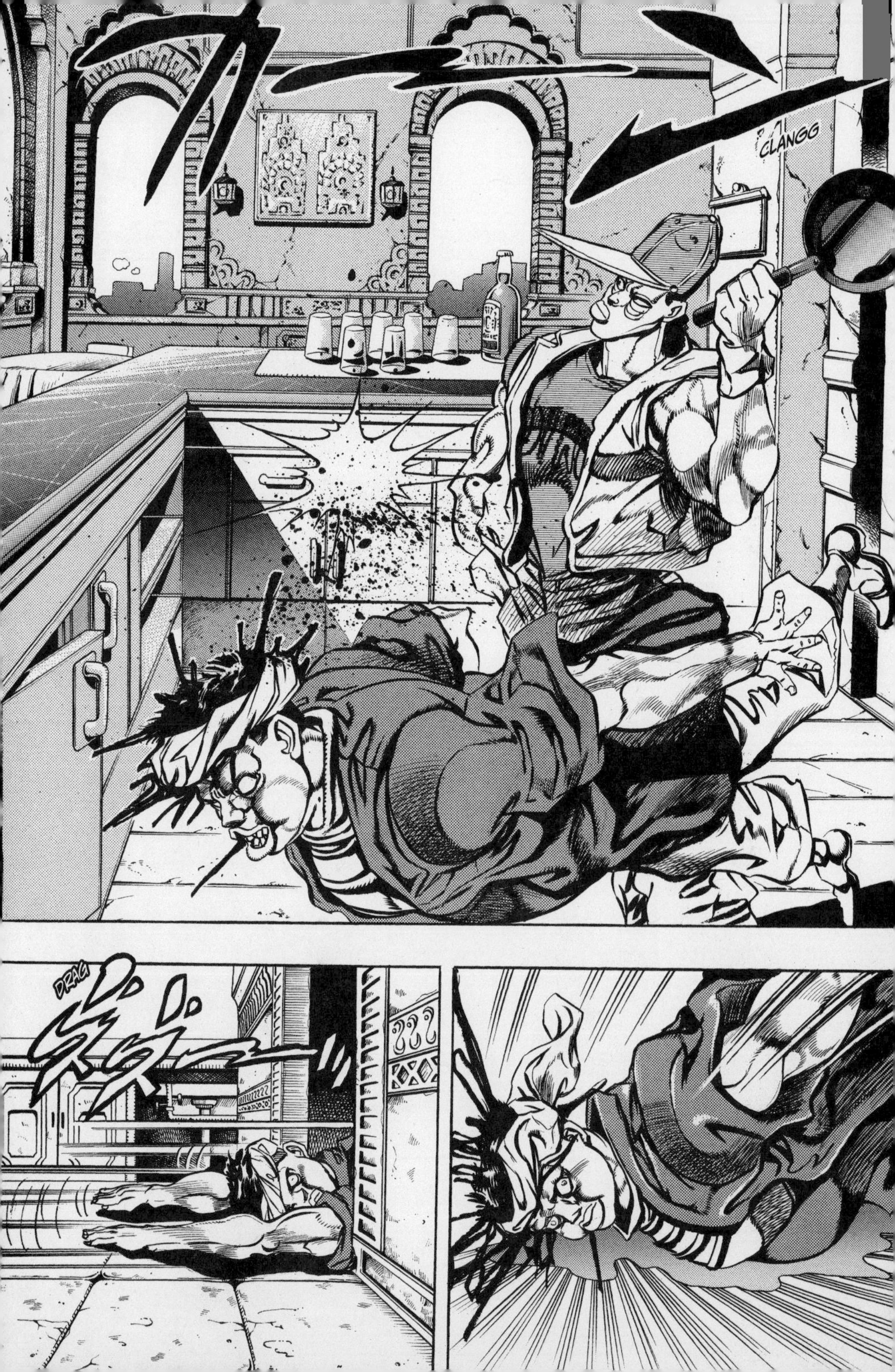
CLANGG
DRAG

CHAPTER 77: "Khnum" Oingo and "Thoth" Boingo PART 2

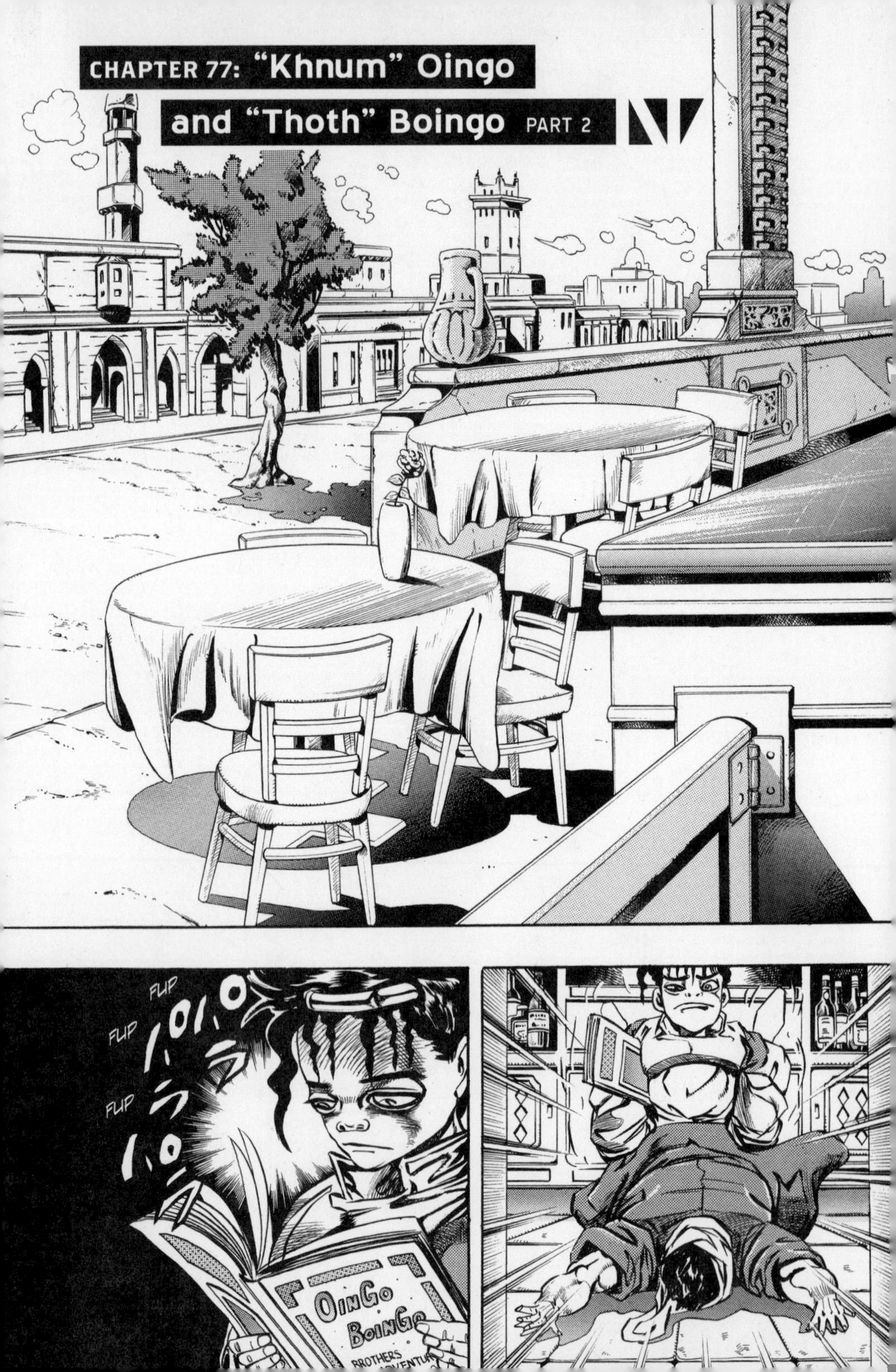
FLIP
FLIP
FLIP
OINGO BOINGO
BROTHERS

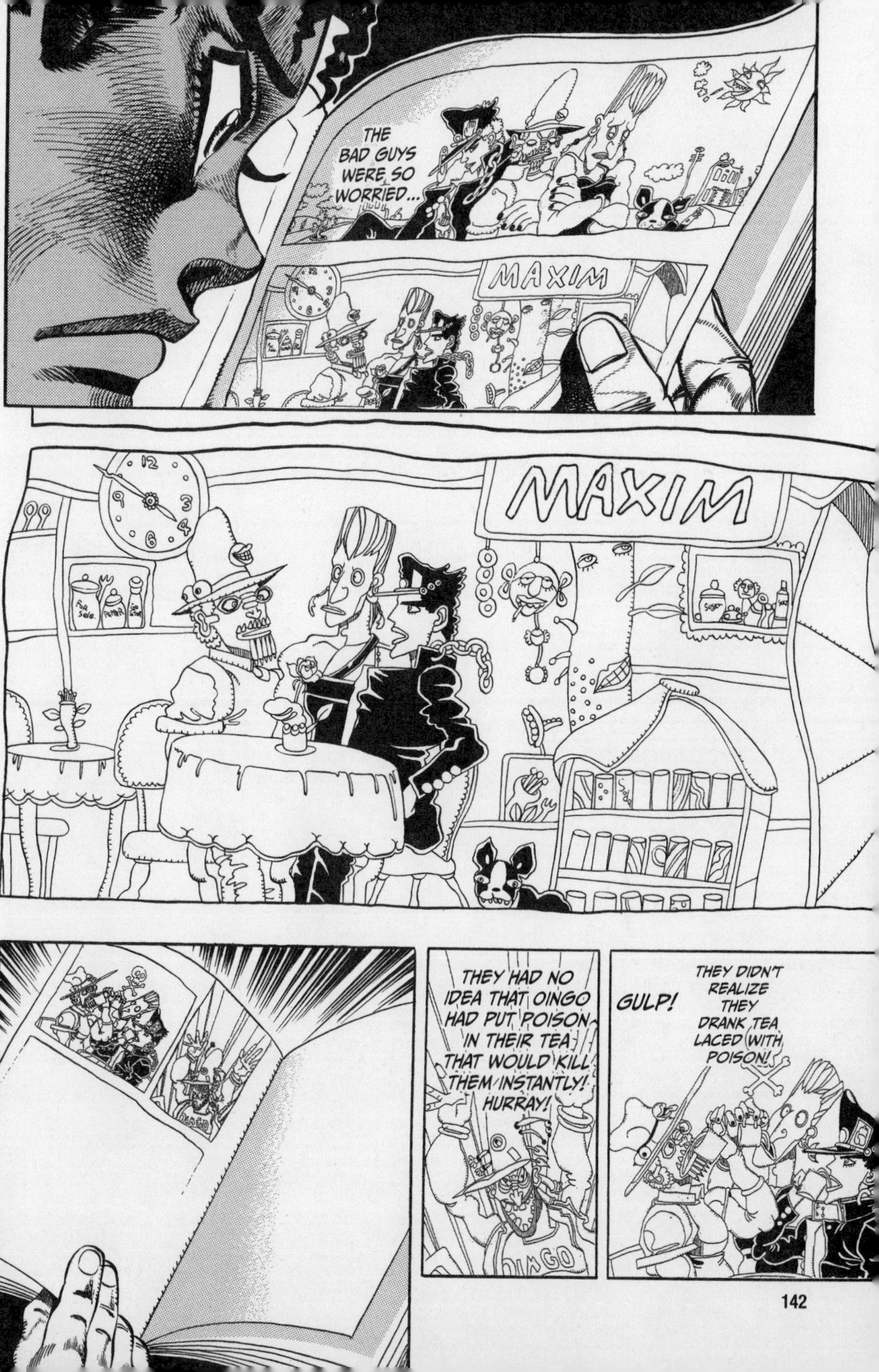
THE BAD GUYS WERE SO WORRIED...
MAXIM
MAXIM
THEY DIDN'T REALIZE THEY DRANK TEA LACED WITH POISON!
GULP!
THEY HAD NO IDEA THAT OINGO HAD PUT POISON IN THEIR TEA THAT WOULD KILL THEM INSTANTLY! HURRAY!

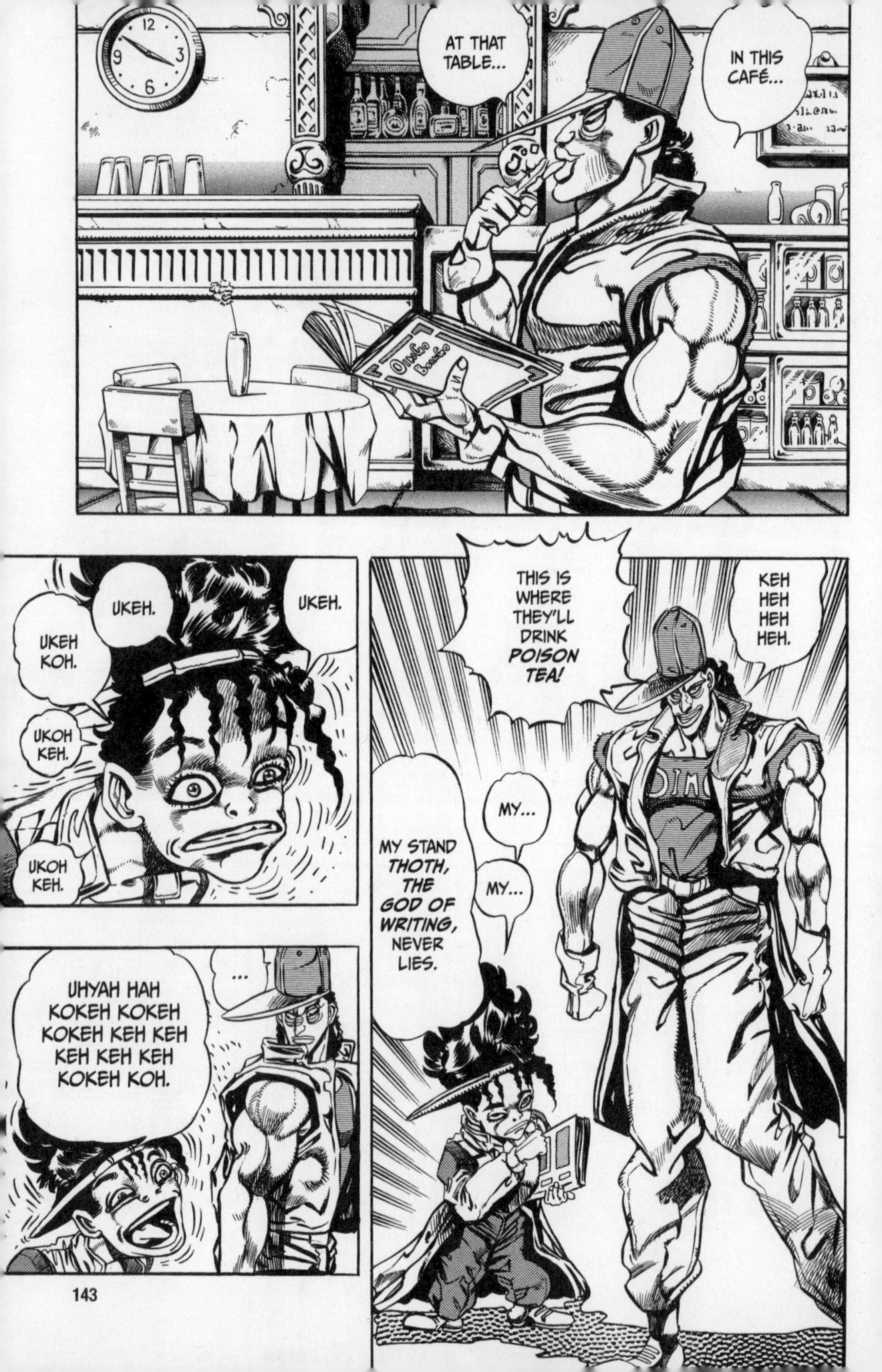

IN THIS CAFÉ...
AT THAT TABLE...
KEH HEH HEH HEH.
THIS IS WHERE THEY'LL DRINK *POISON TEA!*
MY...
MY...
MY STAND *THOTH, THE GOD OF WRITING,* NEVER LIES.
UKEH.
UKEH.
UKEH KOH.
UKOH KEH.
UKOH KEH.
...
UHYAH HAH KOKEH KOKEH KOKEH KEH KEH KEH KEH KEH KOKEH KOH.

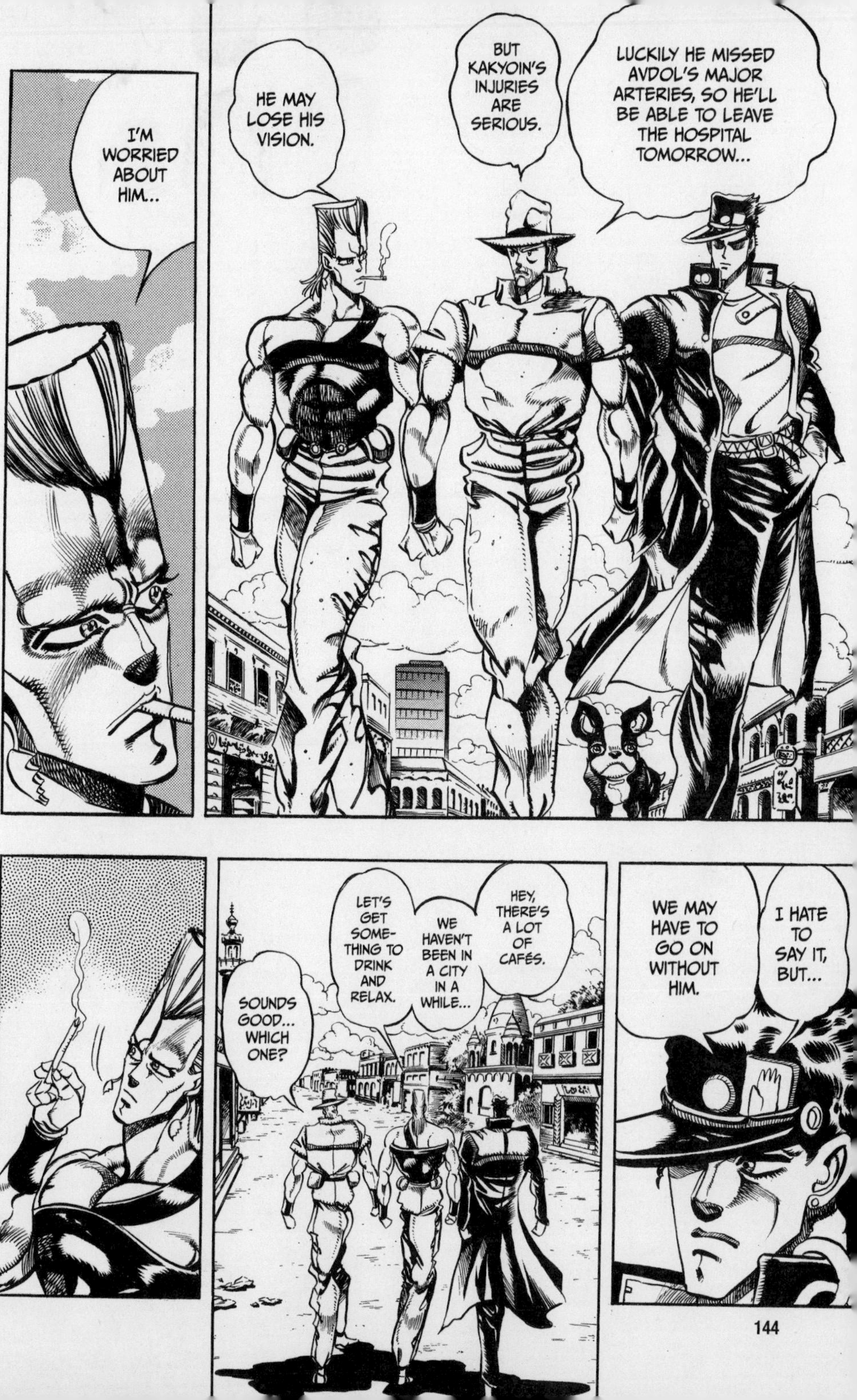
LUCKILY HE MISSED AVDOL'S MAJOR ARTERIES, SO HE'LL BE ABLE TO LEAVE THE HOSPITAL TOMORROW...
BUT KAKYOIN'S INJURIES ARE SERIOUS.
HE MAY LOSE HIS VISION.
I'M WORRIED ABOUT HIM...
I HATE TO SAY IT, BUT...
WE MAY HAVE TO GO ON WITHOUT HIM.
HEY, THERE'S A LOT OF CAFÉS.
WE HAVEN'T BEEN IN A CITY IN A WHILE...
LET'S GET SOME-THING TO DRINK AND RELAX.
SOUNDS GOOD... WHICH ONE?

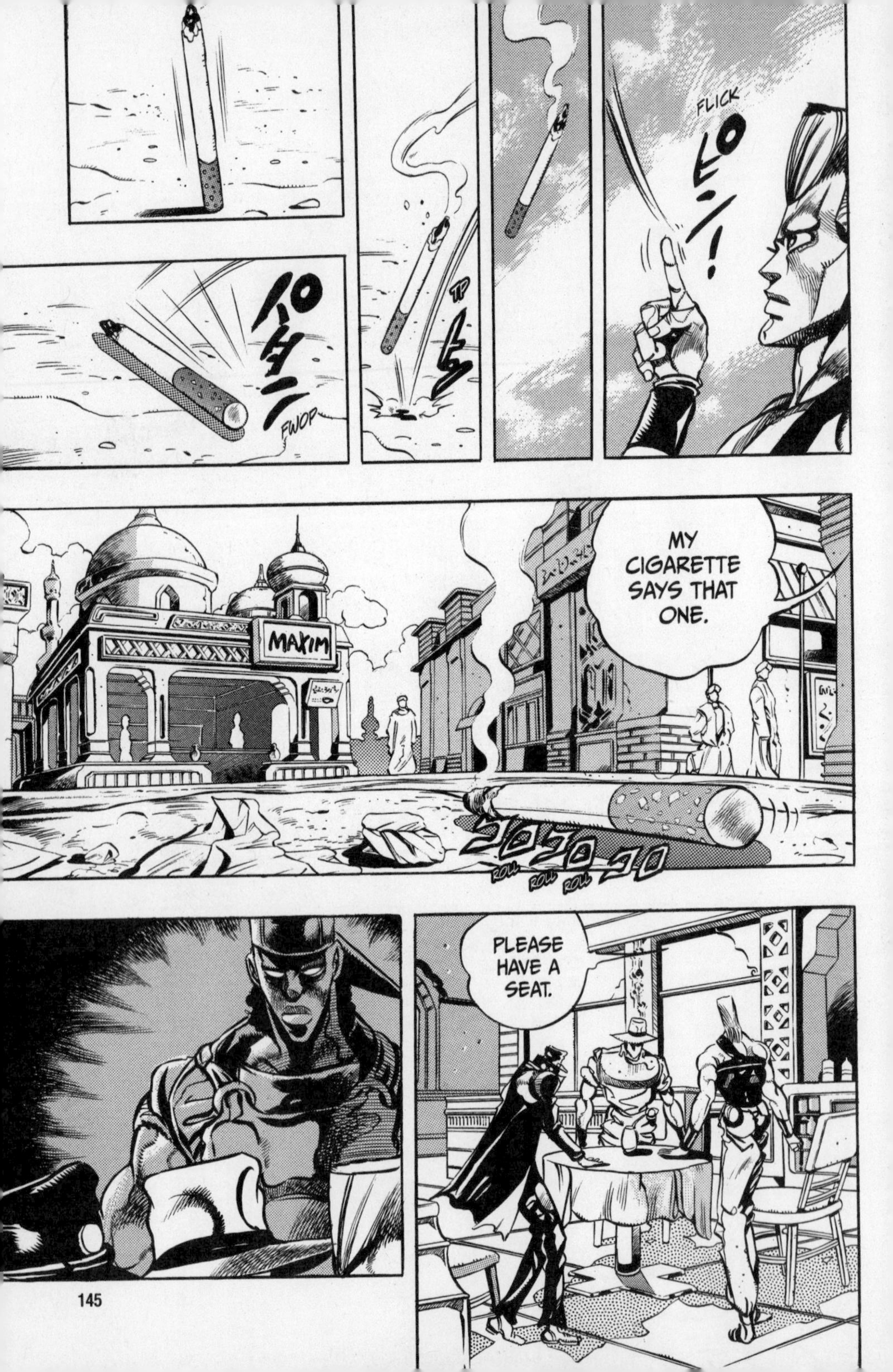
FLICK
TP
FWOP
MY CIGARETTE SAYS THAT ONE.
MAXIM
ROLL
ROLL
ROLL
PLEASE HAVE A SEAT.

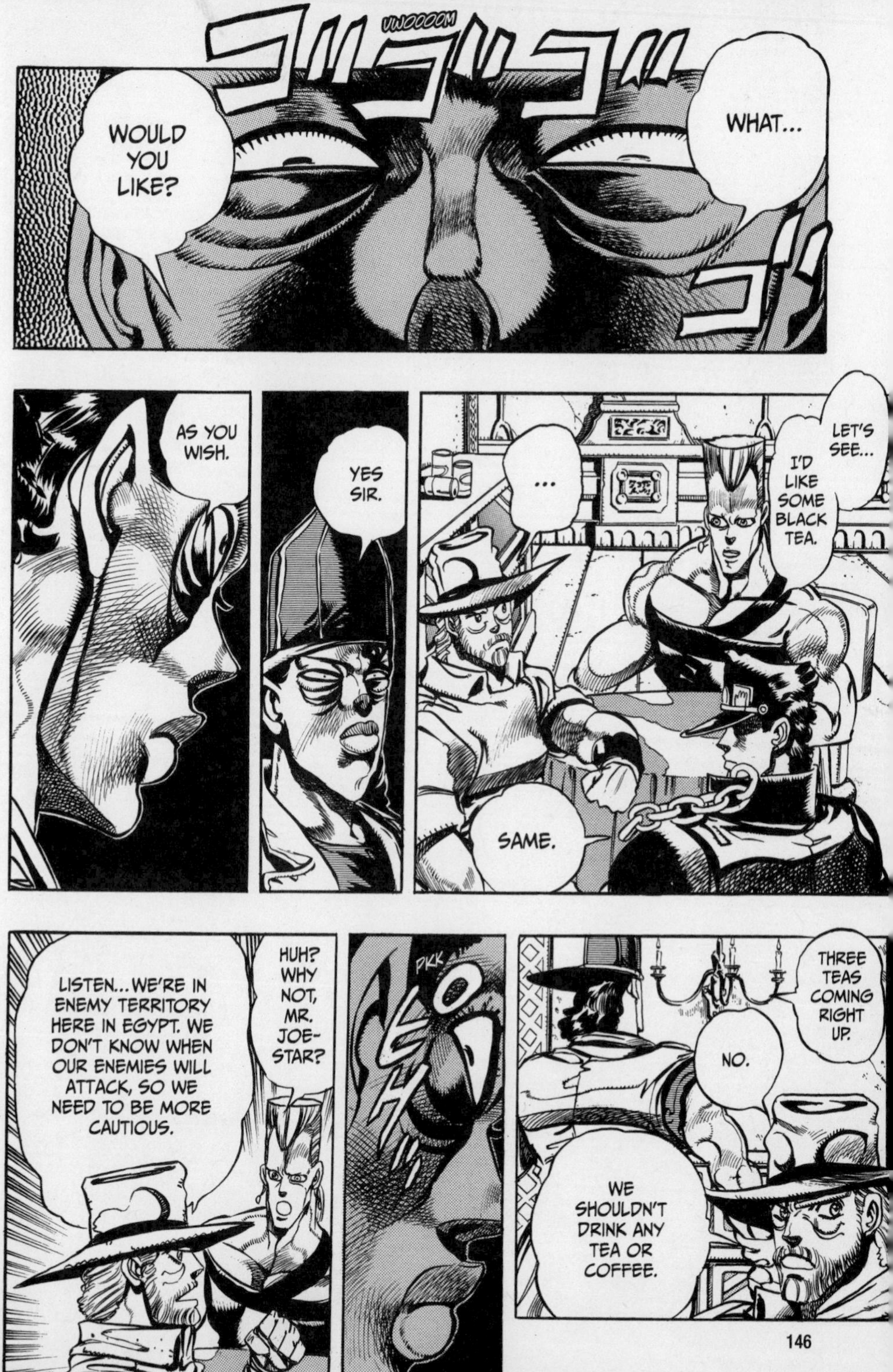
VWOOOOM
WHAT...
WOULD YOU LIKE?
LET'S SEE...
I'D LIKE SOME BLACK TEA.
...
SAME.
YES SIR.
AS YOU WISH.
THREE TEAS COMING RIGHT UP.
NO.
WE SHOULDN'T DRINK ANY TEA OR COFFEE.
PKK
HUH? WHY NOT, MR. JOE-STAR?
LISTEN...WE'RE IN ENEMY TERRITORY HERE IN EGYPT. WE DON'T KNOW WHEN OUR ENEMIES WILL ATTACK, SO WE NEED TO BE MORE CAUTIOUS.

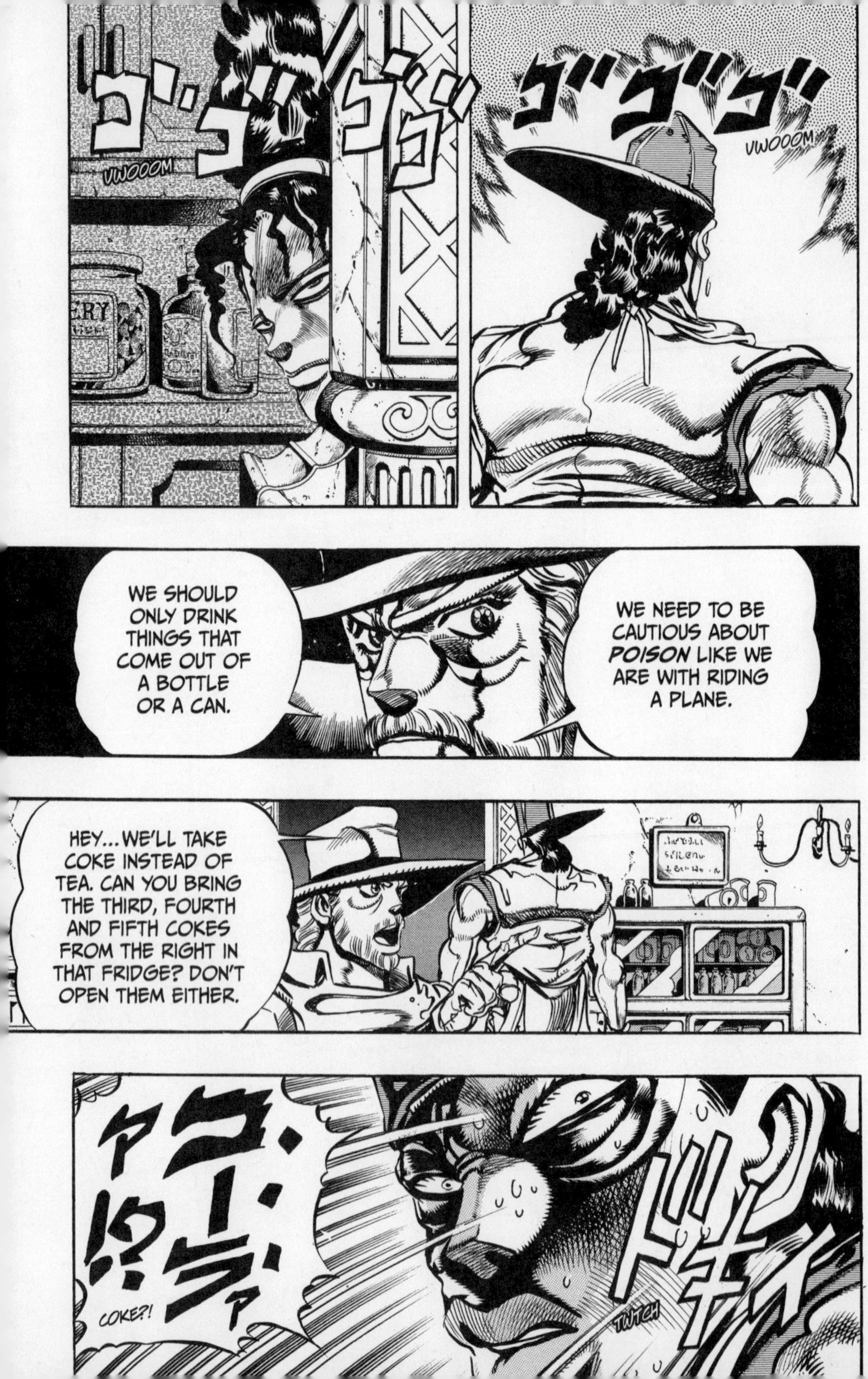
VWOOOM
VWOOOM
WE NEED TO BE CAUTIOUS ABOUT *POISON* LIKE WE ARE WITH RIDING A PLANE.
WE SHOULD ONLY DRINK THINGS THAT COME OUT OF A BOTTLE OR A CAN.
HEY...WE'LL TAKE COKE INSTEAD OF TEA. CAN YOU BRING THE THIRD, FOURTH AND FIFTH COKES FROM THE RIGHT IN THAT FRIDGE? DON'T OPEN THEM EITHER.
TWITCH
COKE?!

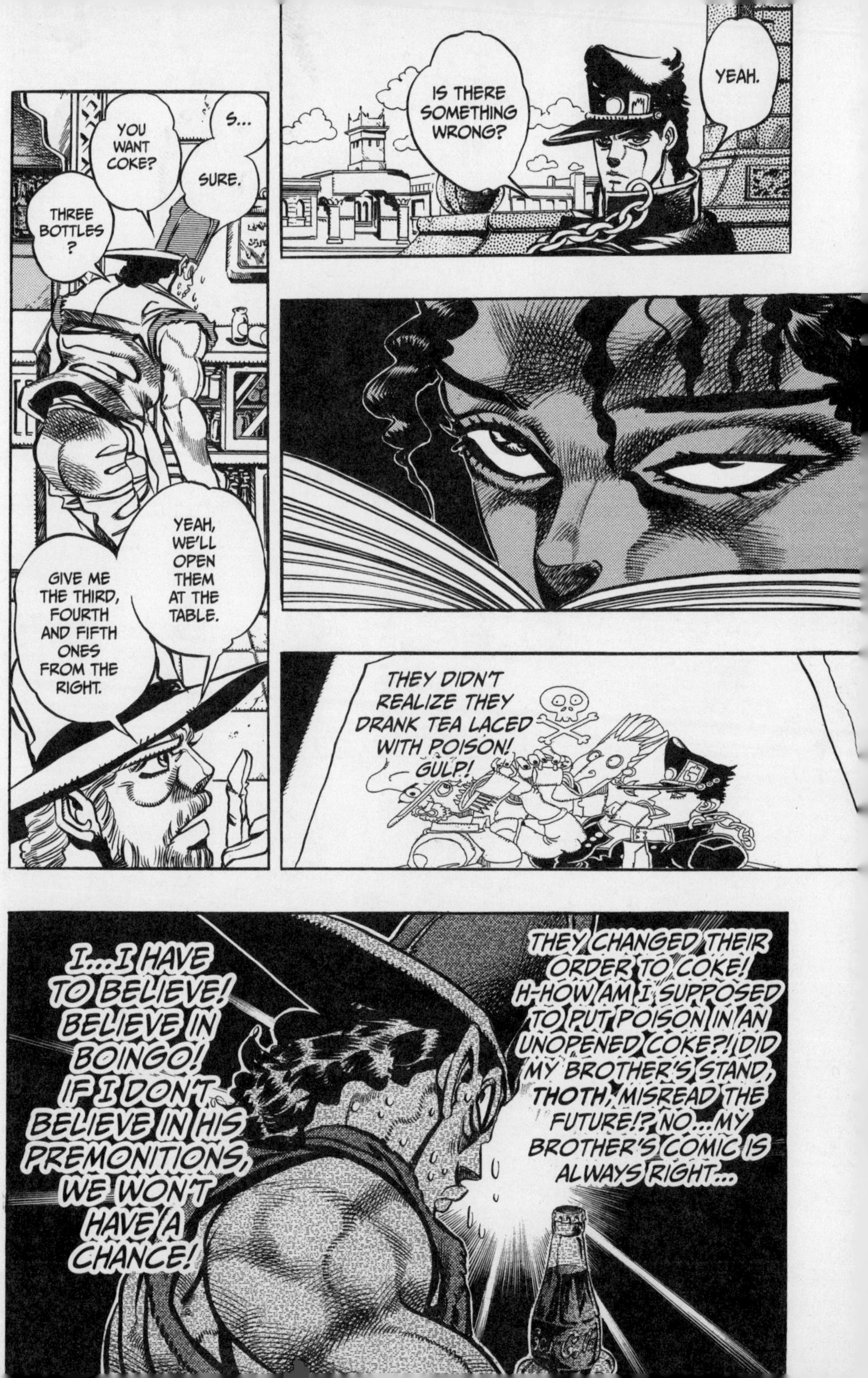
YEAH.
IS THERE SOMETHING WRONG?
THEY DIDN'T REALIZE THEY DRANK TEA LACED WITH POISON!
GULP!
S...
YOU WANT COKE?
SURE.
THREE BOTTLES?
YEAH, WE'LL OPEN THEM AT THE TABLE.
GIVE ME THE THIRD, FOURTH AND FIFTH ONES FROM THE RIGHT.
THEY CHANGED THEIR ORDER TO COKE! H-HOW AM I SUPPOSED TO PUT POISON IN AN UNOPENED COKE?! DID MY BROTHER'S STAND, THOTH, MISREAD THE FUTURE!? NO...MY BROTHER'S COMIC IS ALWAYS RIGHT...
I...I HAVE TO BELIEVE! BELIEVE IN BOINGO! IF I DON'T BELIEVE IN HIS PREMONITIONS, WE WON'T HAVE A CHANCE!

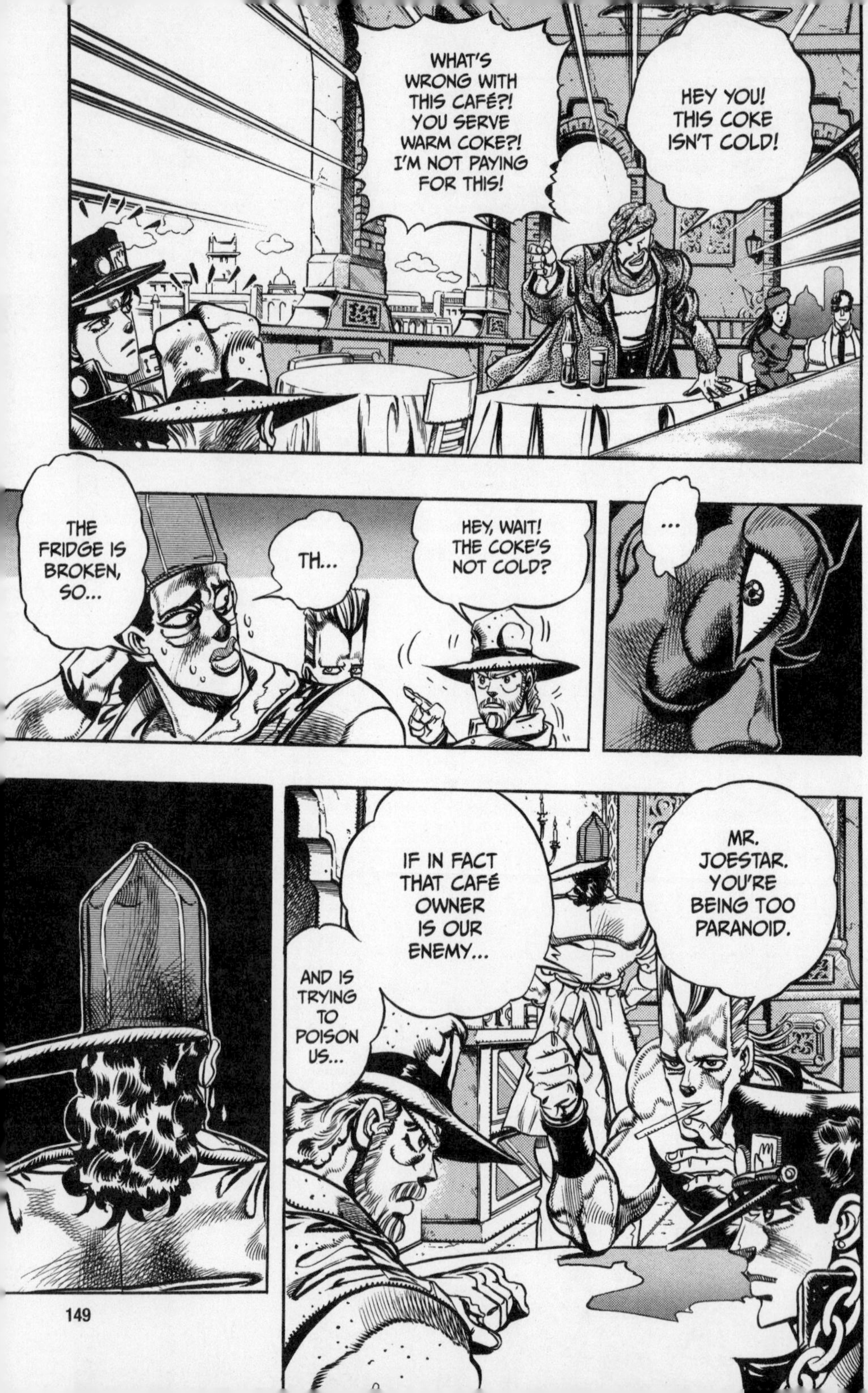
HEY YOU! THIS COKE ISN'T COLD!
WHAT'S WRONG WITH THIS CAFÉ?! YOU SERVE WARM COKE?! I'M NOT PAYING FOR THIS!
...
HEY, WAIT! THE COKE'S NOT COLD?
TH...
THE FRIDGE IS BROKEN, SO...
MR. JOESTAR. YOU'RE BEING TOO PARANOID.
IF IN FACT THAT CAFÉ OWNER IS OUR ENEMY...
AND IS TRYING TO POISON US...

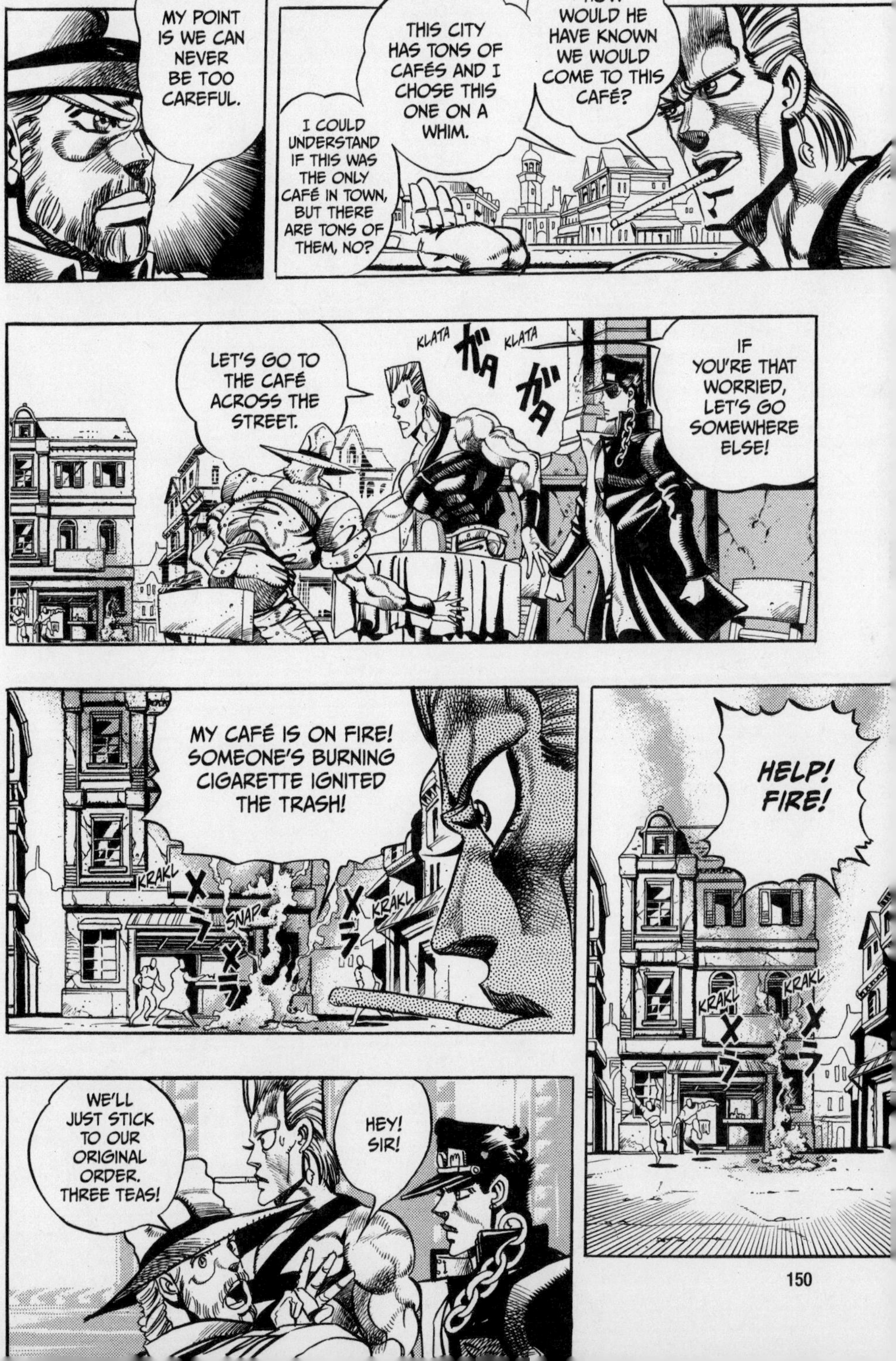
HOW WOULD HE HAVE KNOWN WE WOULD COME TO THIS CAFÉ?
THIS CITY HAS TONS OF CAFÉS AND I CHOSE THIS ONE ON A WHIM.
I COULD UNDERSTAND IF THIS WAS THE ONLY CAFÉ IN TOWN, BUT THERE ARE TONS OF THEM, NO?
MY POINT IS WE CAN NEVER BE TOO CAREFUL.
IF YOU'RE THAT WORRIED, LET'S GO SOMEWHERE ELSE!
KLATA
ガタ
KLATA
ガタ
LET'S GO TO THE CAFÉ ACROSS THE STREET.
HELP! FIRE!
KRAKL
メラ
KRAKL
メラ
MY CAFÉ IS ON FIRE! SOMEONE'S BURNING CIGARETTE IGNITED THE TRASH!
KRAKL
メラ
KRAKL
メラ
SNAP
メラ
HEY! SIR!
WE'LL JUST STICK TO OUR ORIGINAL ORDER. THREE TEAS!

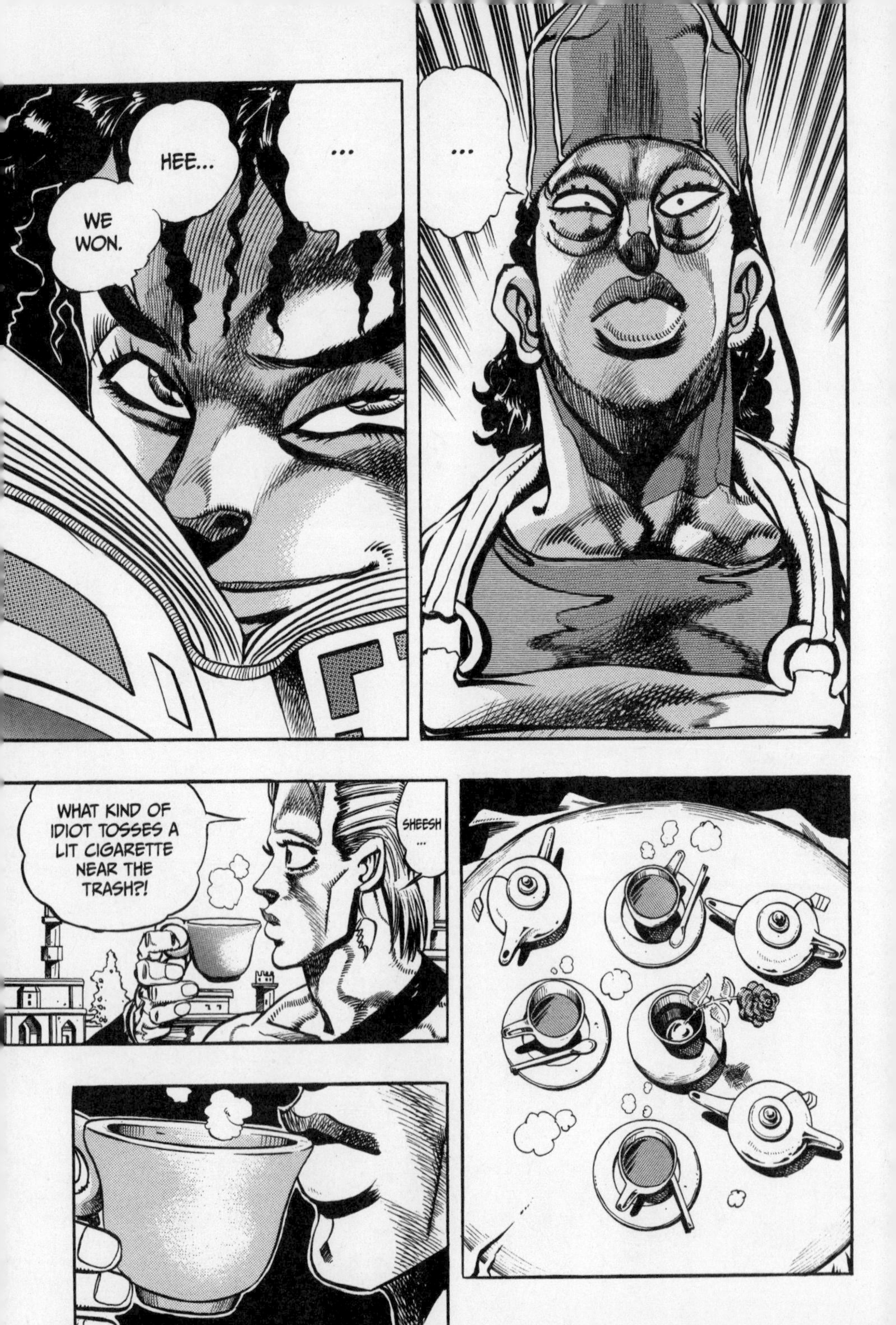
...
...
HEE...
WE WON.
SHEESH ...
WHAT KIND OF IDIOT TOSSES A LIT CIGARETTE NEAR THE TRASH?!

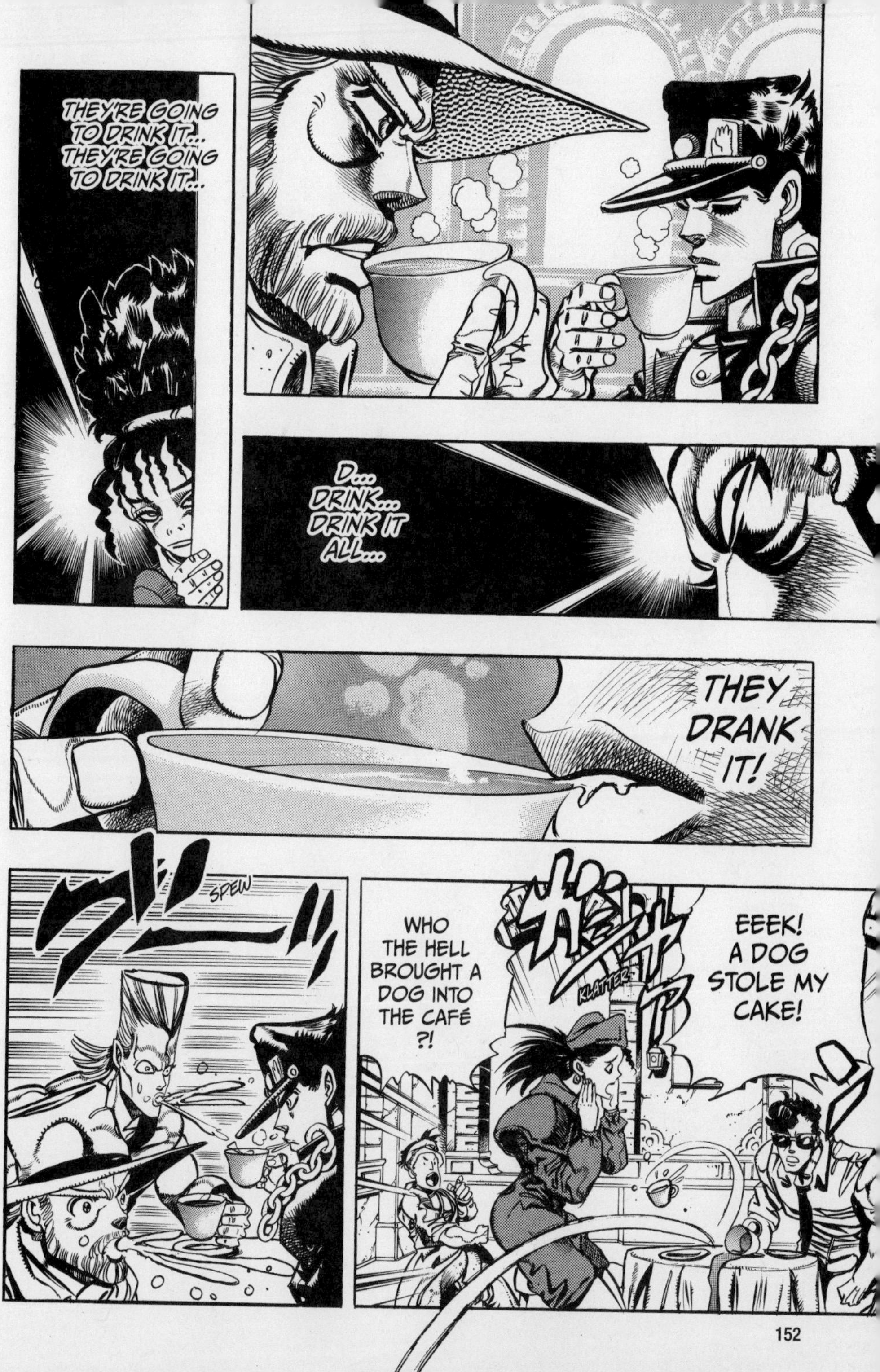
D... DRINK... DRINK IT ALL...
THEY'RE GOING TO DRINK IT... THEY'RE GOING TO DRINK IT...
THEY DRANK IT!
EEEK! A DOG STOLE MY CAKE!
KLATTER
WHO THE HELL BROUGHT A DOG INTO THE CAFÉ ?!
SPEW

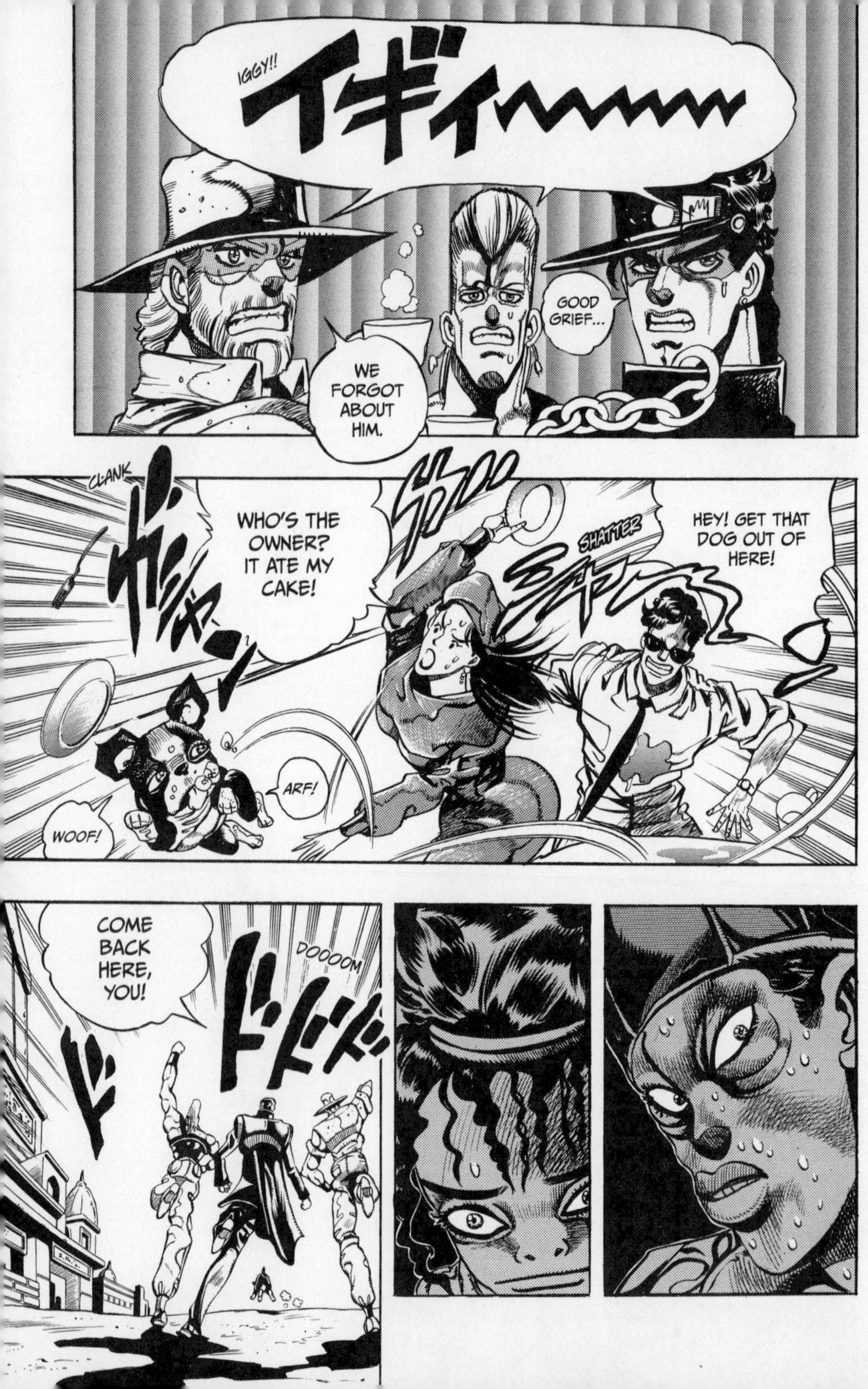
IGGY!!
イギィ
GOOD GRIEF...
WE FORGOT ABOUT HIM.
HEY! GET THAT DOG OUT OF HERE!
SHATTER
WHO'S THE OWNER? IT ATE MY CAKE!
CLANK
ARF!
WOOF!
COME BACK HERE, YOU!
DOOOOM

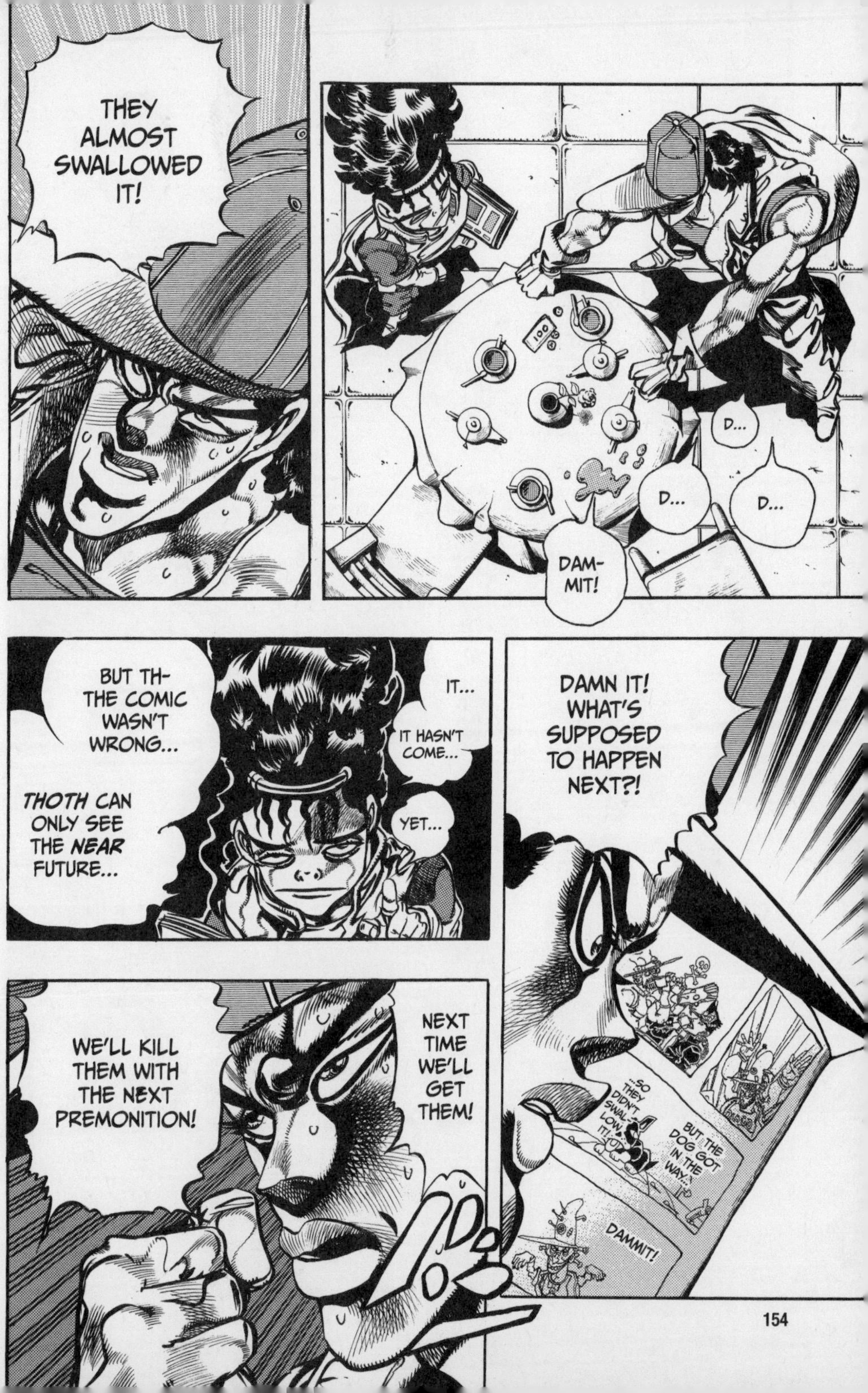
D...
D...
D...
DAM-MIT!
THEY ALMOST SWALLOWED IT!
DAMN IT! WHAT'S SUPPOSED TO HAPPEN NEXT?!
BUT THE DOG GOT IN THE WAY...
...SO THEY DIDN'T SWAL-LOW IT!
DAMMIT!
IT...
IT HASN'T COME...
YET...
BUT TH- THE COMIC WASN'T WRONG...
THOTH CAN ONLY SEE THE *NEAR* FUTURE...
NEXT TIME WE'LL GET THEM!
WE'LL KILL THEM WITH THE NEXT PREMONITION!

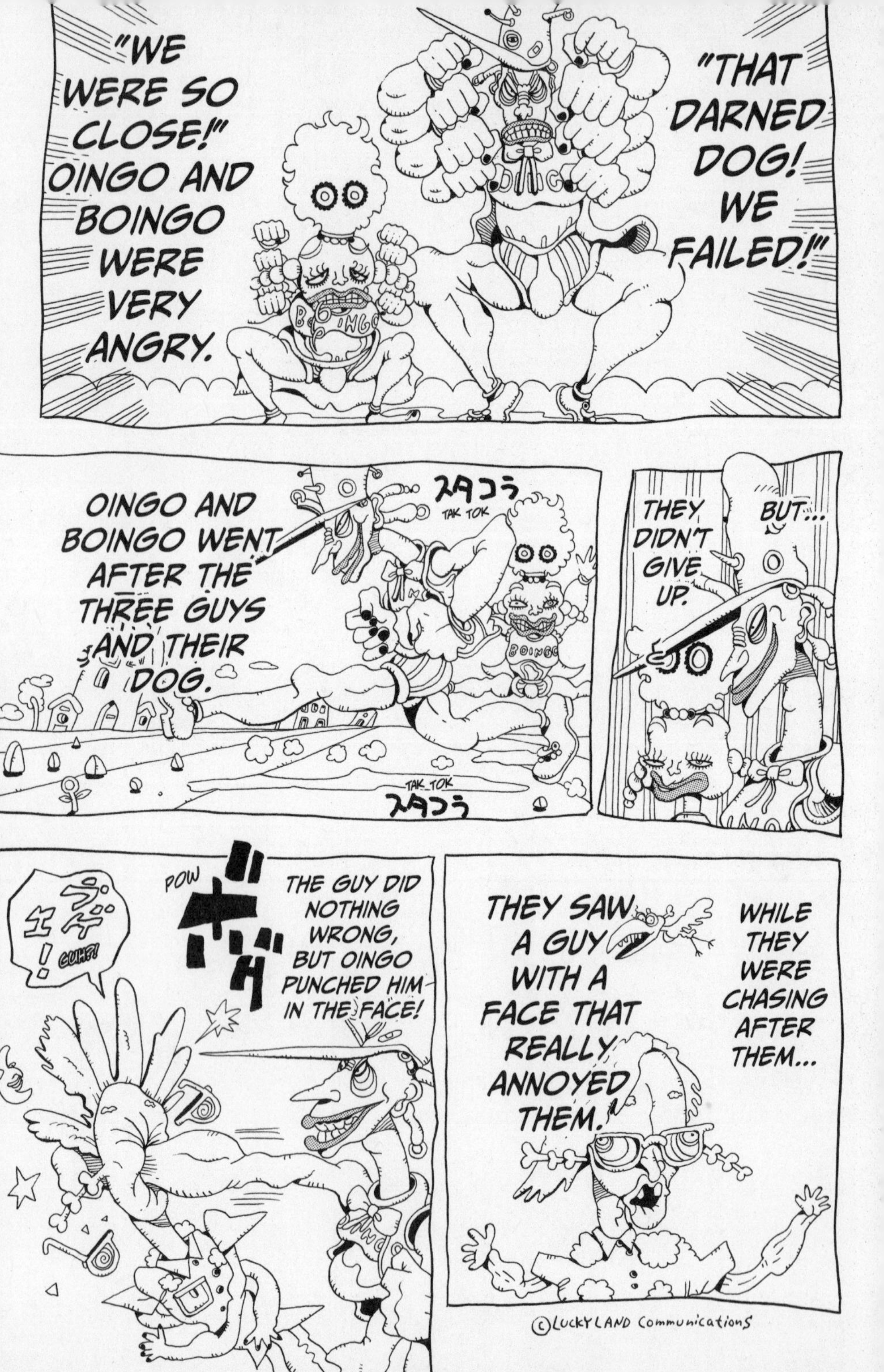
"WE WERE SO CLOSE!" OINGO AND BOINGO WERE VERY ANGRY.
"THAT DARNED DOG! WE FAILED!"
BUT...
THEY DIDN'T GIVE UP.
スタコラ
TAK TOK
OINGO AND BOINGO WENT AFTER THE THREE GUYS AND THEIR DOG.
TAK TOK
スタコラ
WHILE THEY WERE CHASING AFTER THEM...
THEY SAW A GUY WITH A FACE THAT REALLY ANNOYED THEM.
THE GUY DID NOTHING WRONG, BUT OINGO PUNCHED HIM IN THE FACE!
POW
ブゲエ!
GUH?!

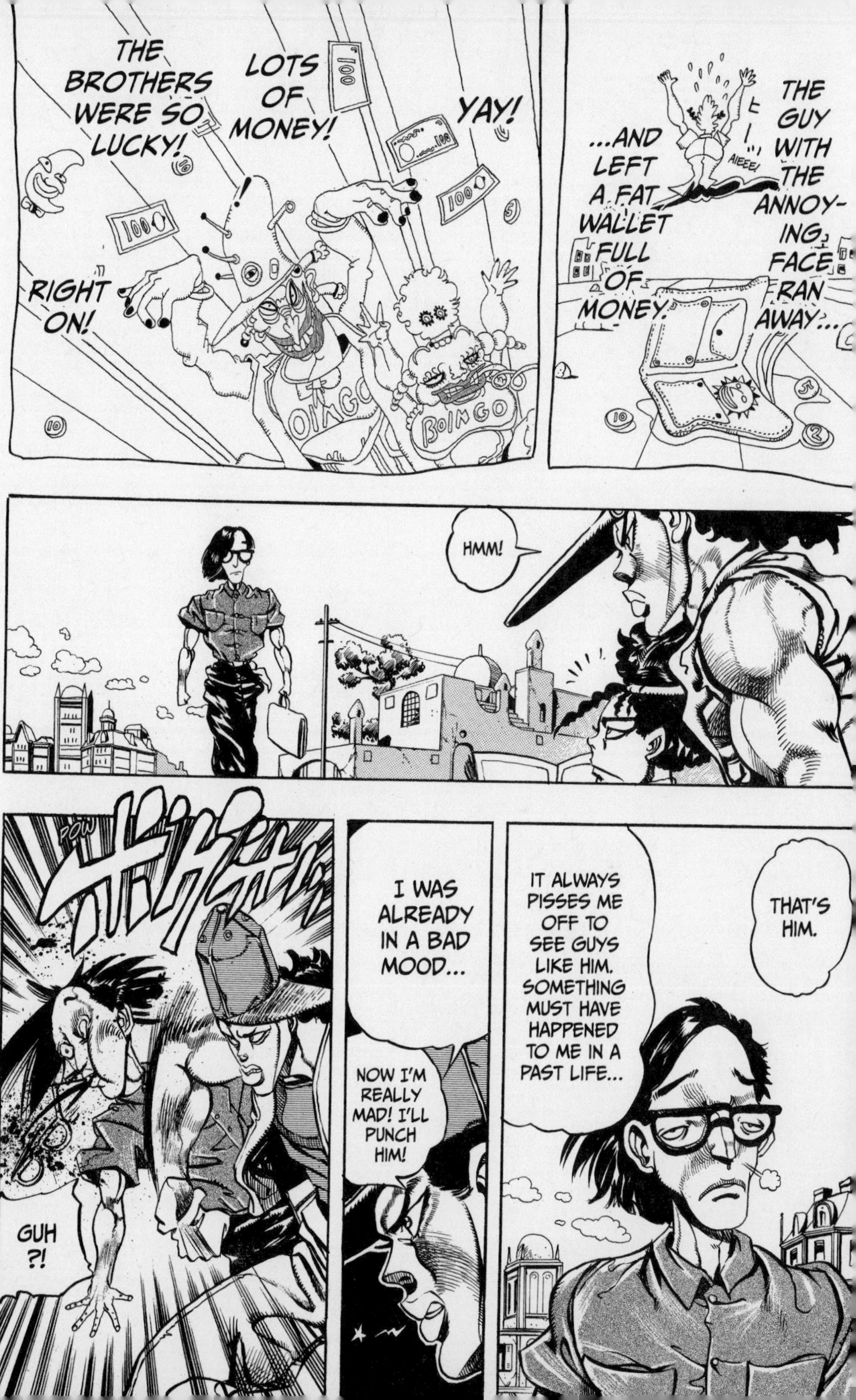
THE GUY WITH THE ANNOYING FACE RAN AWAY...
AIEEE!
...AND LEFT A FAT WALLET FULL OF MONEY.
YAY!
LOTS OF MONEY!
THE BROTHERS WERE SO LUCKY!
RIGHT ON!
HMM!
THAT'S HIM.
IT ALWAYS PISSES ME OFF TO SEE GUYS LIKE HIM. SOMETHING MUST HAVE HAPPENED TO ME IN A PAST LIFE...
I WAS ALREADY IN A BAD MOOD...
NOW I'M REALLY MAD! I'LL PUNCH HIM!
POW
GUH?!

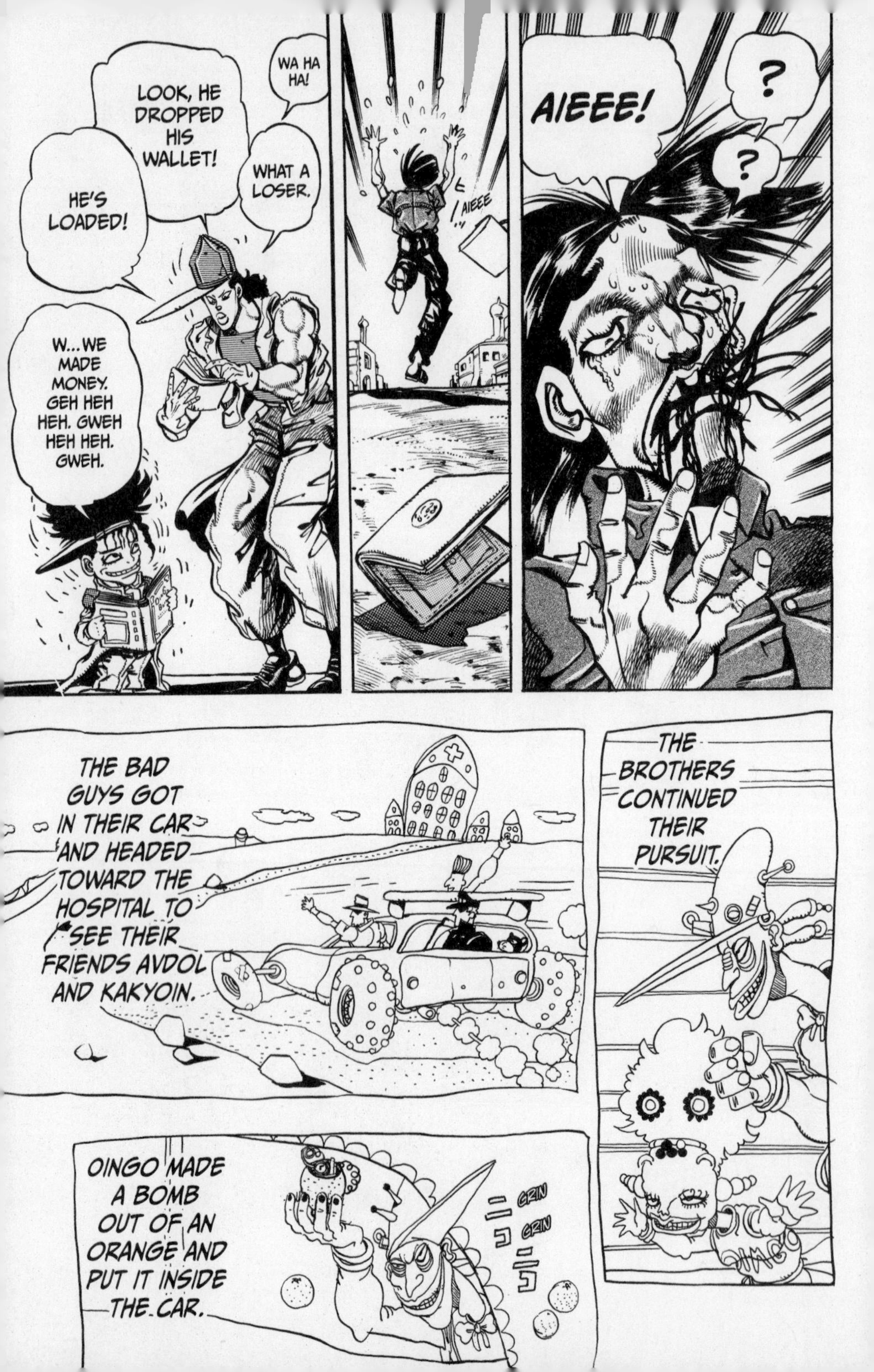
?
?
AIEEE!
AIEEE
WA HA HA!
LOOK, HE DROPPED HIS WALLET!
WHAT A LOSER.
HE'S LOADED!
W...WE MADE MONEY. GEH HEH HEH. GWEH HEH HEH. GWEH.
THE BROTHERS CONTINUED THEIR PURSUIT.
THE BAD GUYS GOT IN THEIR CAR AND HEADED TOWARD THE HOSPITAL TO SEE THEIR FRIENDS AVDOL AND KAKYOIN.
OINGO MADE A BOMB OUT OF AN ORANGE AND PUT IT INSIDE THE CAR.
GRIN
GRIN

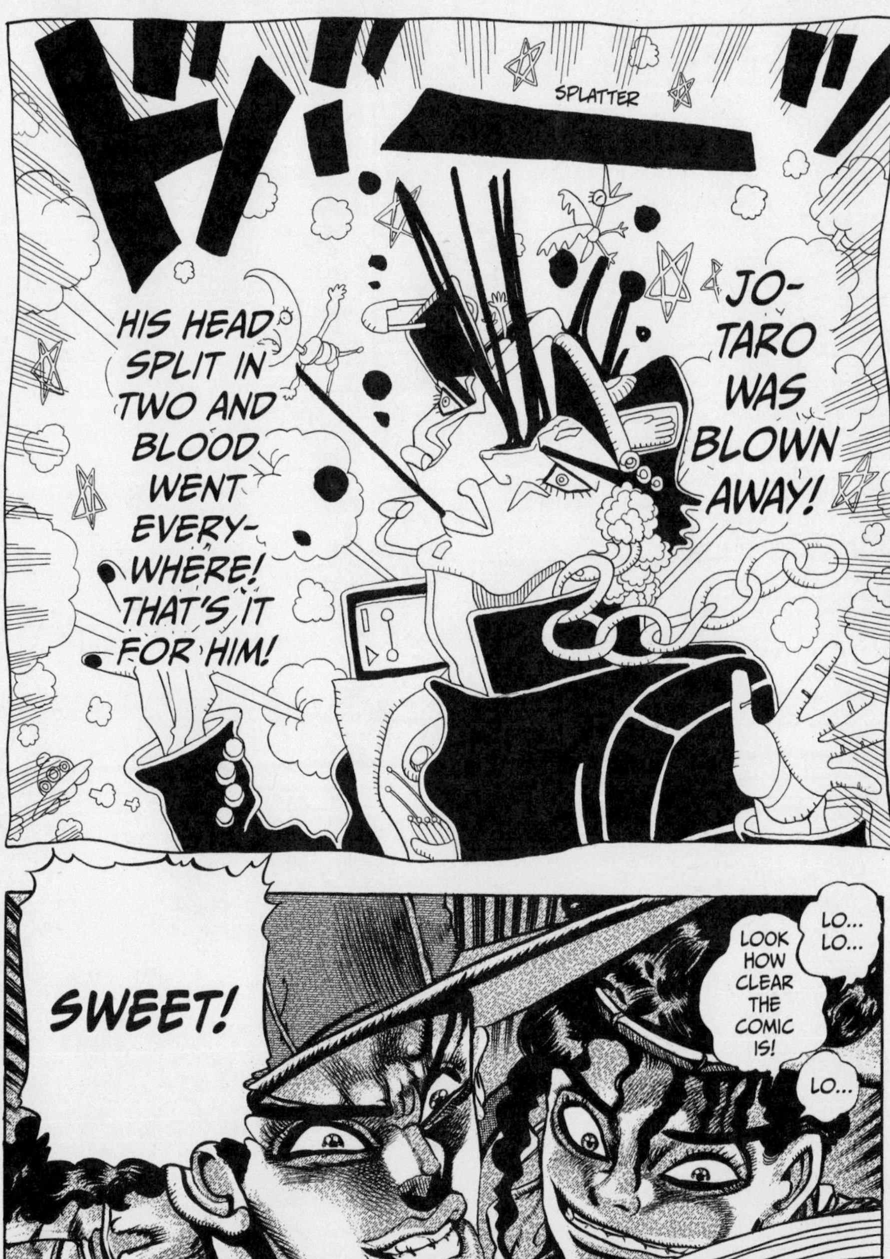
SPLATTER
JO-TARO WAS BLOWN AWAY!
HIS HEAD SPLIT IN TWO AND BLOOD WENT EVERY-WHERE! THAT'S IT FOR HIM!
LO... LO...
LOOK HOW CLEAR THE COMIC IS!
LO...
SWEET!

7
THOTH

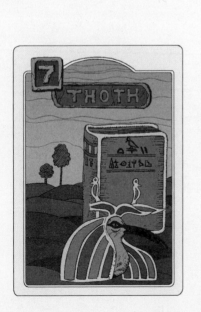

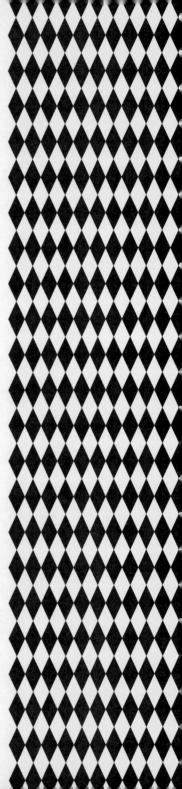

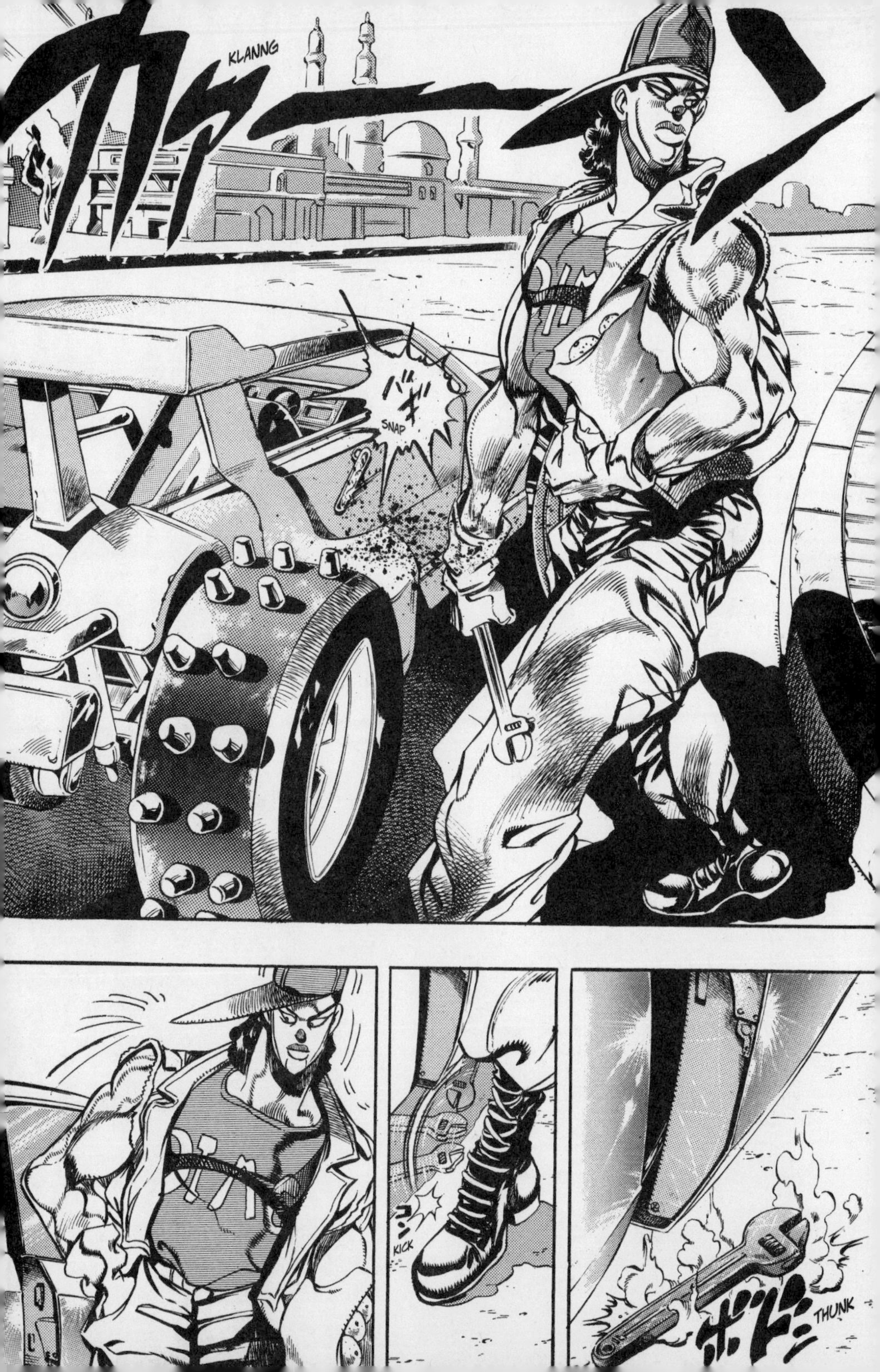
KLANNG
SNAP
THUNK
KICK

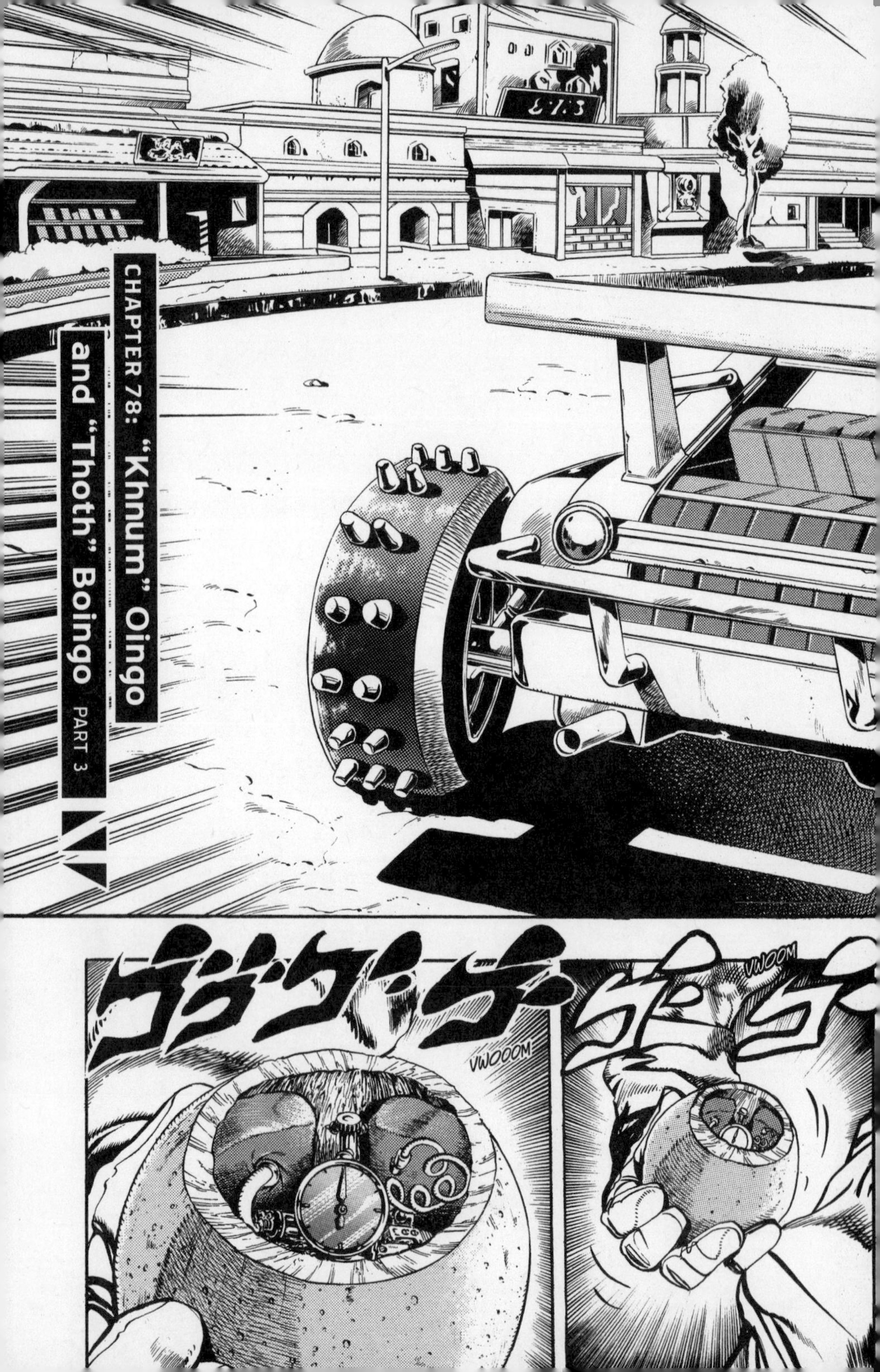
CHAPTER 78: "Khnum" Oingo and "Thoth" Boingo PART 3
VWOOM
VWOOOM

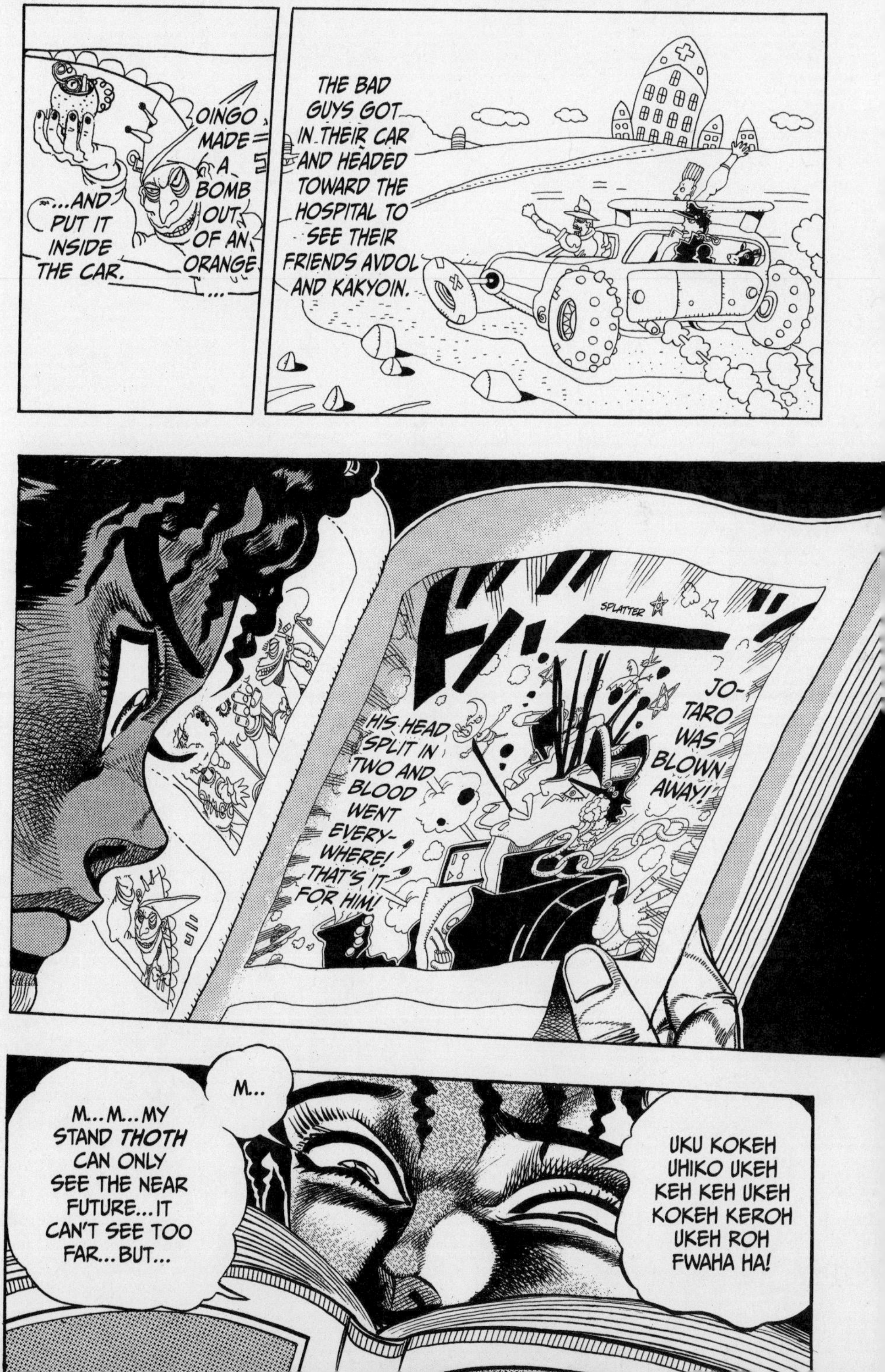
THE BAD GUYS GOT IN THEIR CAR AND HEADED TOWARD THE HOSPITAL TO SEE THEIR FRIENDS AVDOL AND KAKYOIN.
OINGO MADE A BOMB OUT OF AN ORANGE...
...AND PUT IT INSIDE THE CAR.
SPLATTER
JO-TARO WAS BLOWN AWAY!
HIS HEAD SPLIT IN TWO AND BLOOD WENT EVERY-WHERE! THAT'S IT FOR HIM!
UKU KOKEH UHIKO UKEH KEH KEH UKEH KOKEH KEROH UKEH ROH FWAHA HA!
M...
M...M...MY STAND THOTH CAN ONLY SEE THE NEAR FUTURE...IT CAN'T SEE TOO FAR...BUT...

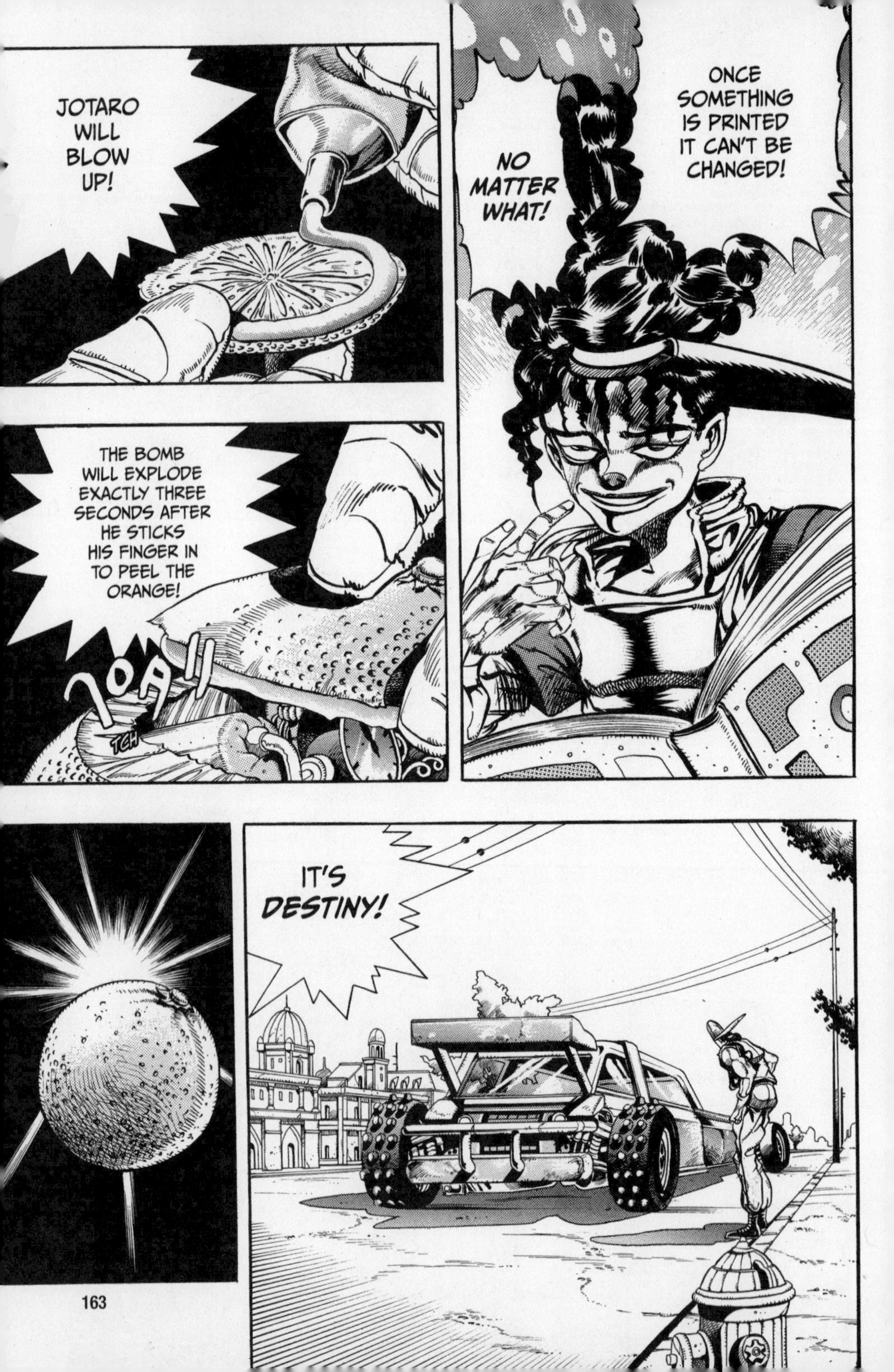
ONCE SOMETHING IS PRINTED IT CAN'T BE CHANGED!
NO MATTER WHAT!
JOTARO WILL BLOW UP!
THE BOMB WILL EXPLODE EXACTLY THREE SECONDS AFTER HE STICKS HIS FINGER IN TO PEEL THE ORANGE!
TCH
IT'S DESTINY!

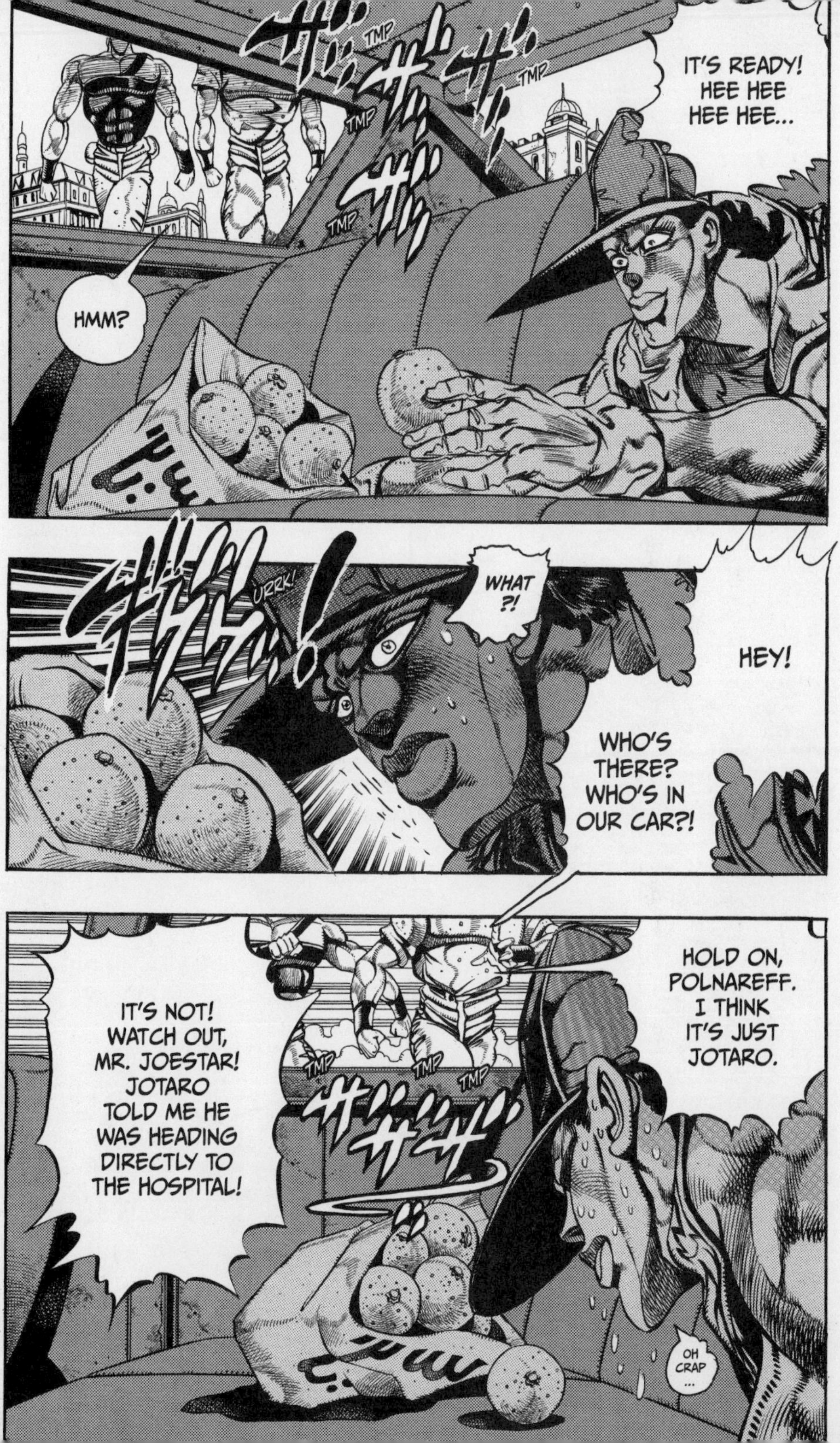

IT'S READY! HEE HEE HEE HEE...
TMP
TMP
TMP
TMP
HMM?
HEY!
WHO'S THERE? WHO'S IN OUR CAR?!
WHAT ?!
URRK!
HOLD ON, POLNAREFF. I THINK IT'S JUST JOTARO.
TMP
TMP
TMP
IT'S NOT! WATCH OUT, MR. JOESTAR! JOTARO TOLD ME HE WAS HEADING DIRECTLY TO THE HOSPITAL!
OH CRAP ...

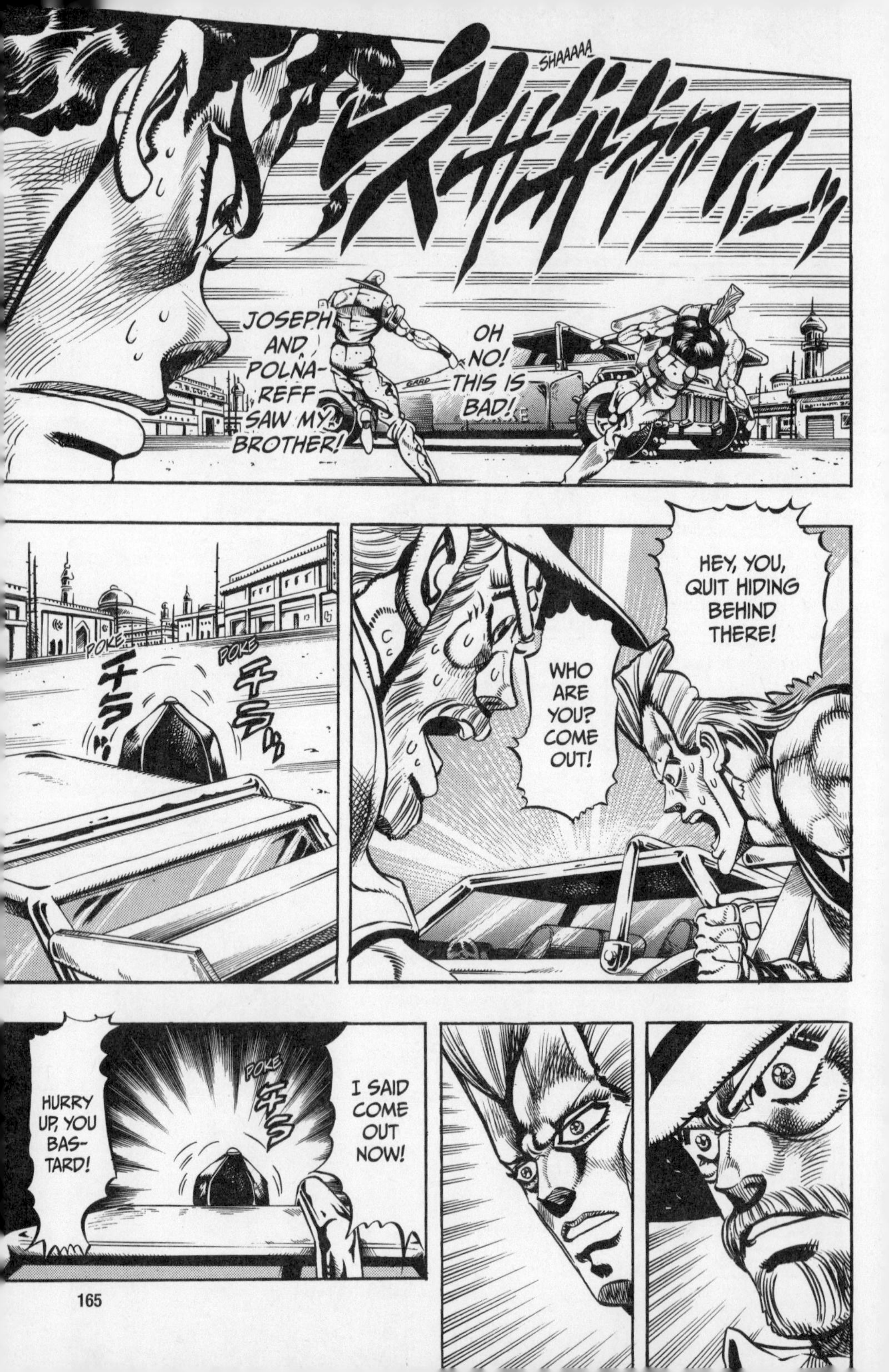
SHAAAAA
OH NO! THIS IS BAD!
JOSEPH AND POLNAREFF SAW MY BROTHER!
HEY, YOU, QUIT HIDING BEHIND THERE!
WHO ARE YOU? COME OUT!
POKE
POKE
POKE
I SAID COME OUT NOW!
HURRY UP, YOU BASTARD!

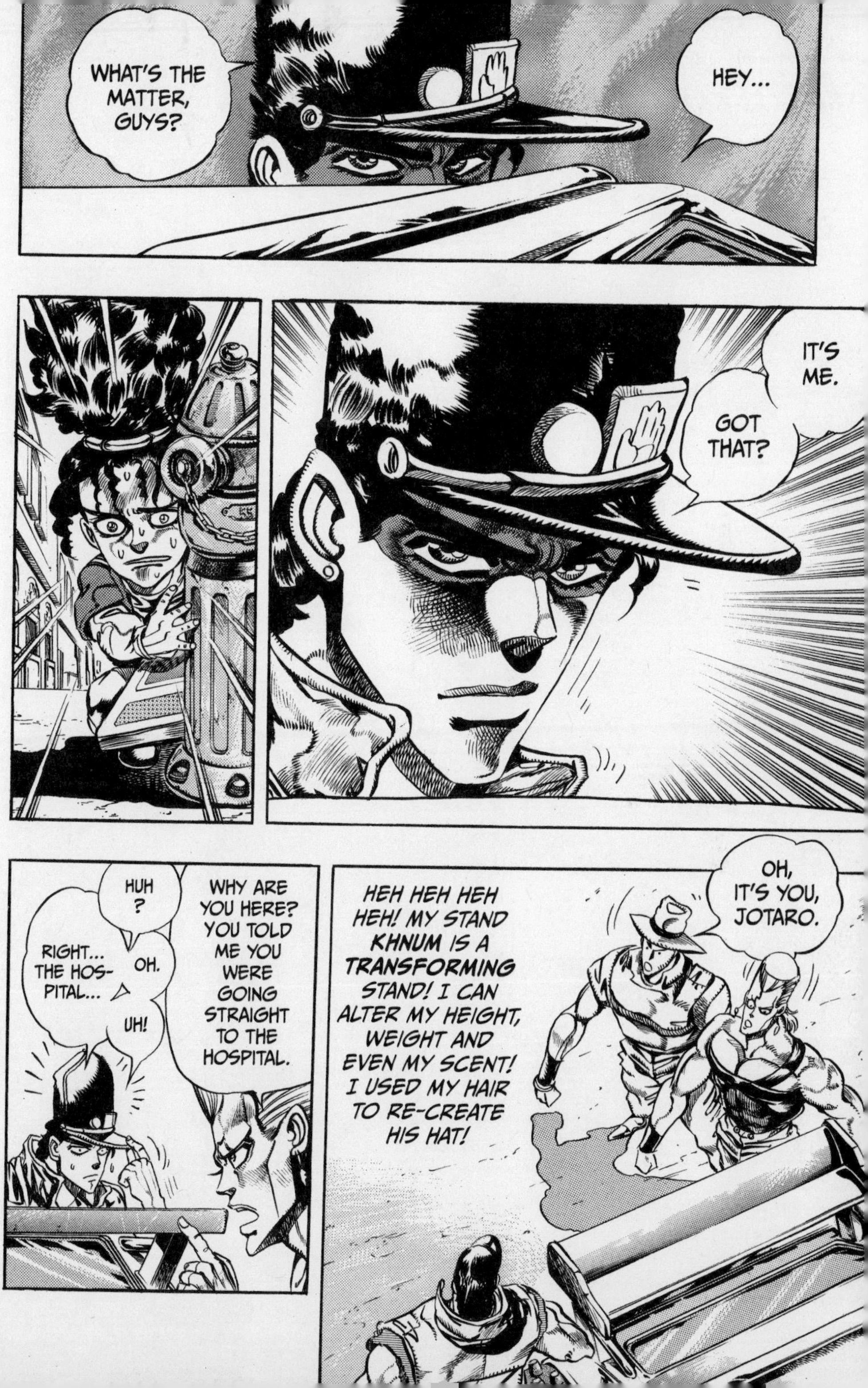
HEY...
WHAT'S THE MATTER, GUYS?
IT'S ME.
GOT THAT?
OH, IT'S YOU, JOTARO.
HEH HEH HEH HEH! MY STAND KHNUM IS A TRANSFORMING STAND! I CAN ALTER MY HEIGHT, WEIGHT AND EVEN MY SCENT! I USED MY HAIR TO RE-CREATE HIS HAT!
WHY ARE YOU HERE? YOU TOLD ME YOU WERE GOING STRAIGHT TO THE HOSPITAL.
HUH?
OH.
UH!
RIGHT... THE HOSPITAL...

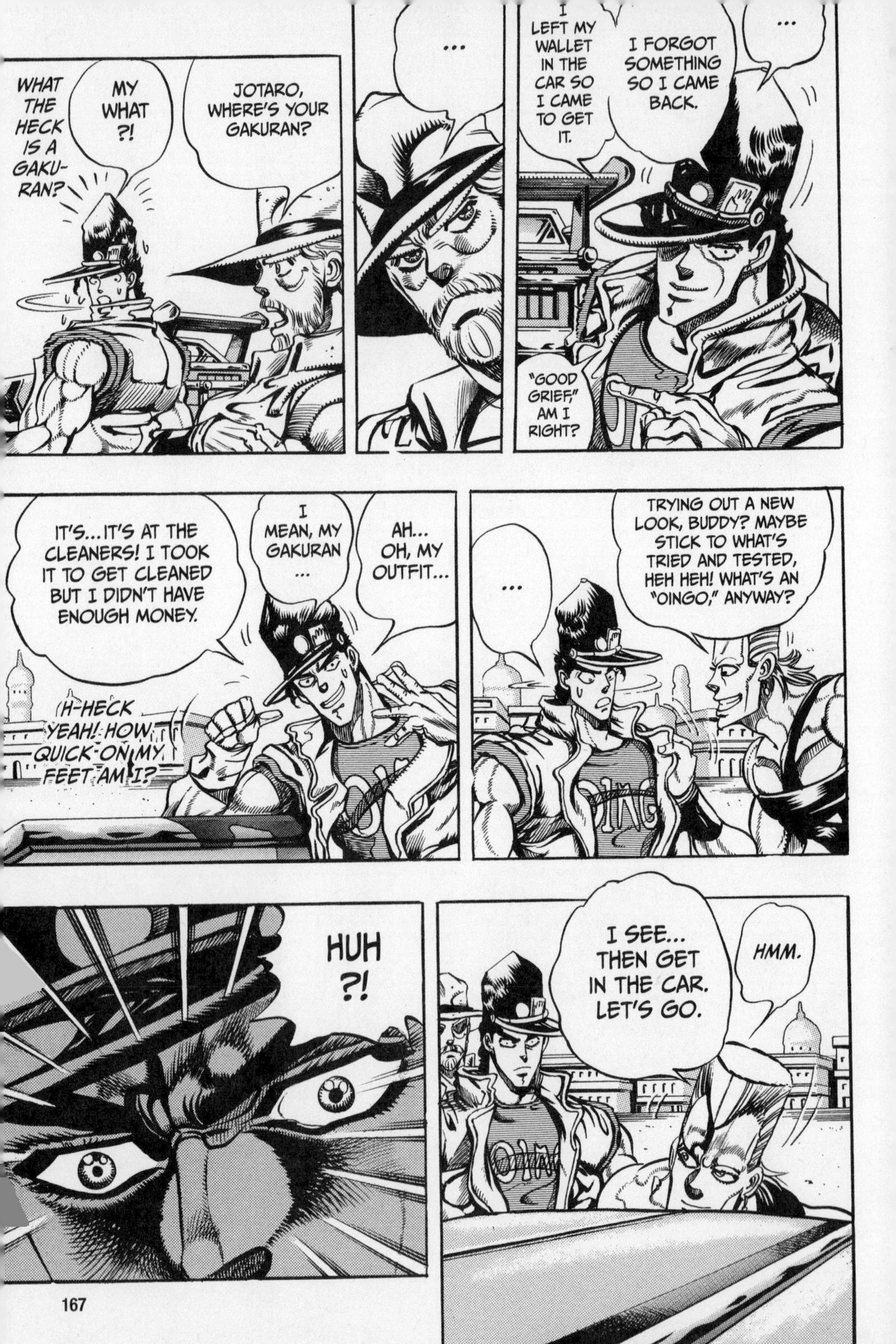
...
I FORGOT SOMETHING SO I CAME BACK.
I LEFT MY WALLET IN THE CAR SO I CAME TO GET IT.
"GOOD GRIEF," AM I RIGHT?
...
JOTARO, WHERE'S YOUR GAKURAN?
MY WHAT ?!
WHAT THE HECK IS A GAKU-RAN?
TRYING OUT A NEW LOOK, BUDDY? MAYBE STICK TO WHAT'S TRIED AND TESTED, HEH HEH! WHAT'S AN "OINGO," ANYWAY?
...
AH... OH, MY OUTFIT...
I MEAN, MY GAKURAN ...
IT'S...IT'S AT THE CLEANERS! I TOOK IT TO GET CLEANED BUT I DIDN'T HAVE ENOUGH MONEY.
H-HECK YEAH! HOW QUICK ON MY FEET AM I?
HMM.
I SEE... THEN GET IN THE CAR. LET'S GO.
HUH ?!

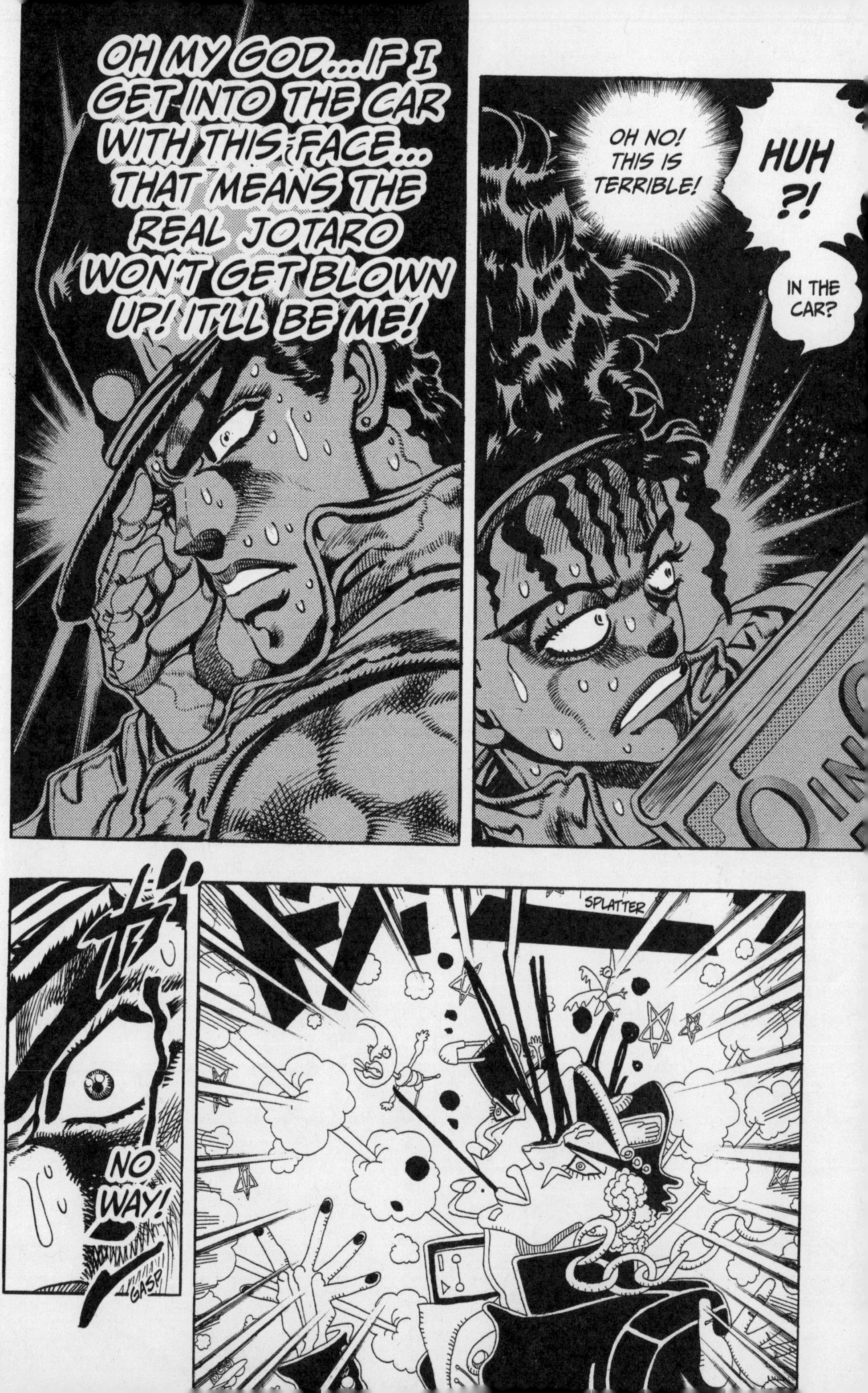
HUH ?!
IN THE CAR?
OH NO! THIS IS TERRIBLE!
OH MY GOD...IF I GET INTO THE CAR WITH THIS FACE... THAT MEANS THE REAL JOTARO WON'T GET BLOWN UP! IT'LL BE ME!
SPLATTER
NO WAY!
GASP

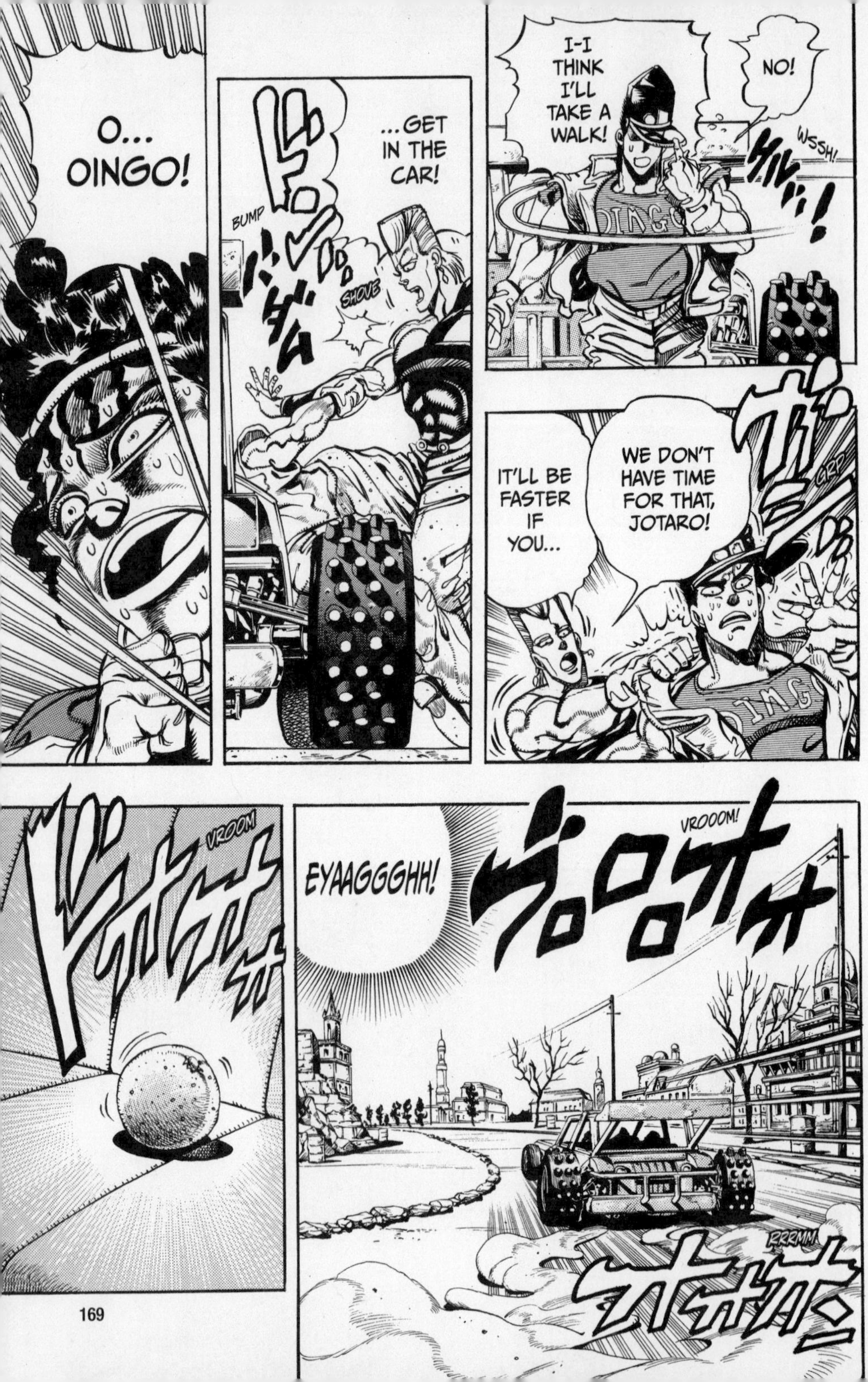
NO!
I-I THINK I'LL TAKE A WALK!
WSSH!
WE DON'T HAVE TIME FOR THAT, JOTARO!
IT'LL BE FASTER IF YOU...
GRP
...GET IN THE CAR!
BUMP
SHOVE
O... OINGO!
VROOOM!
EYAAGGGHH!
RRRMM
VROOM

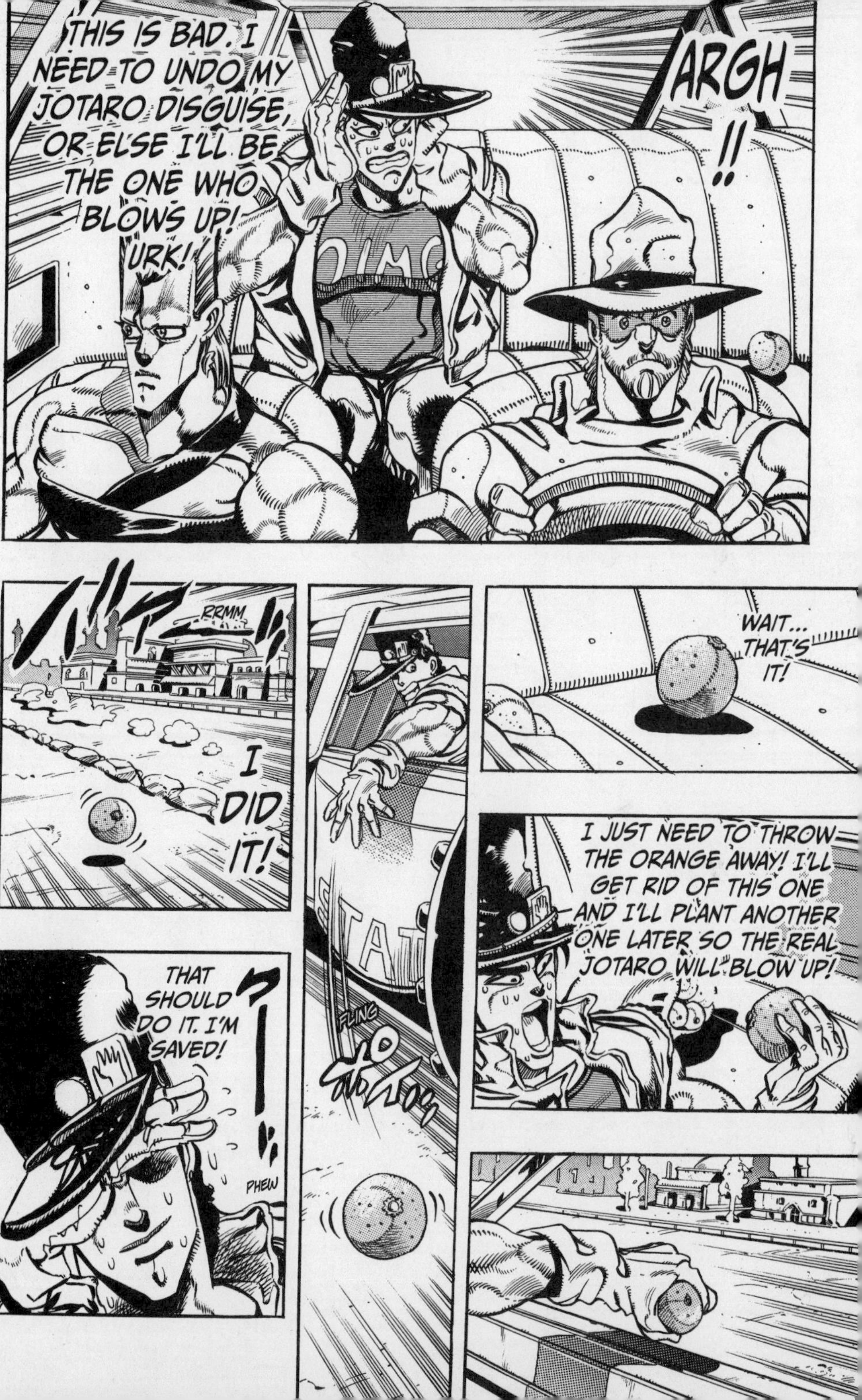
ARGH !!
THIS IS BAD. I NEED TO UNDO MY JOTARO DISGUISE, OR ELSE I'LL BE THE ONE WHO BLOWS UP! URK!
WAIT... THAT'S IT!
I JUST NEED TO THROW THE ORANGE AWAY! I'LL GET RID OF THIS ONE AND I'LL PLANT ANOTHER ONE LATER SO THE REAL JOTARO WILL BLOW UP!
FLING
RRMM
I DID IT!
THAT SHOULD DO IT. I'M SAVED!
PHEW

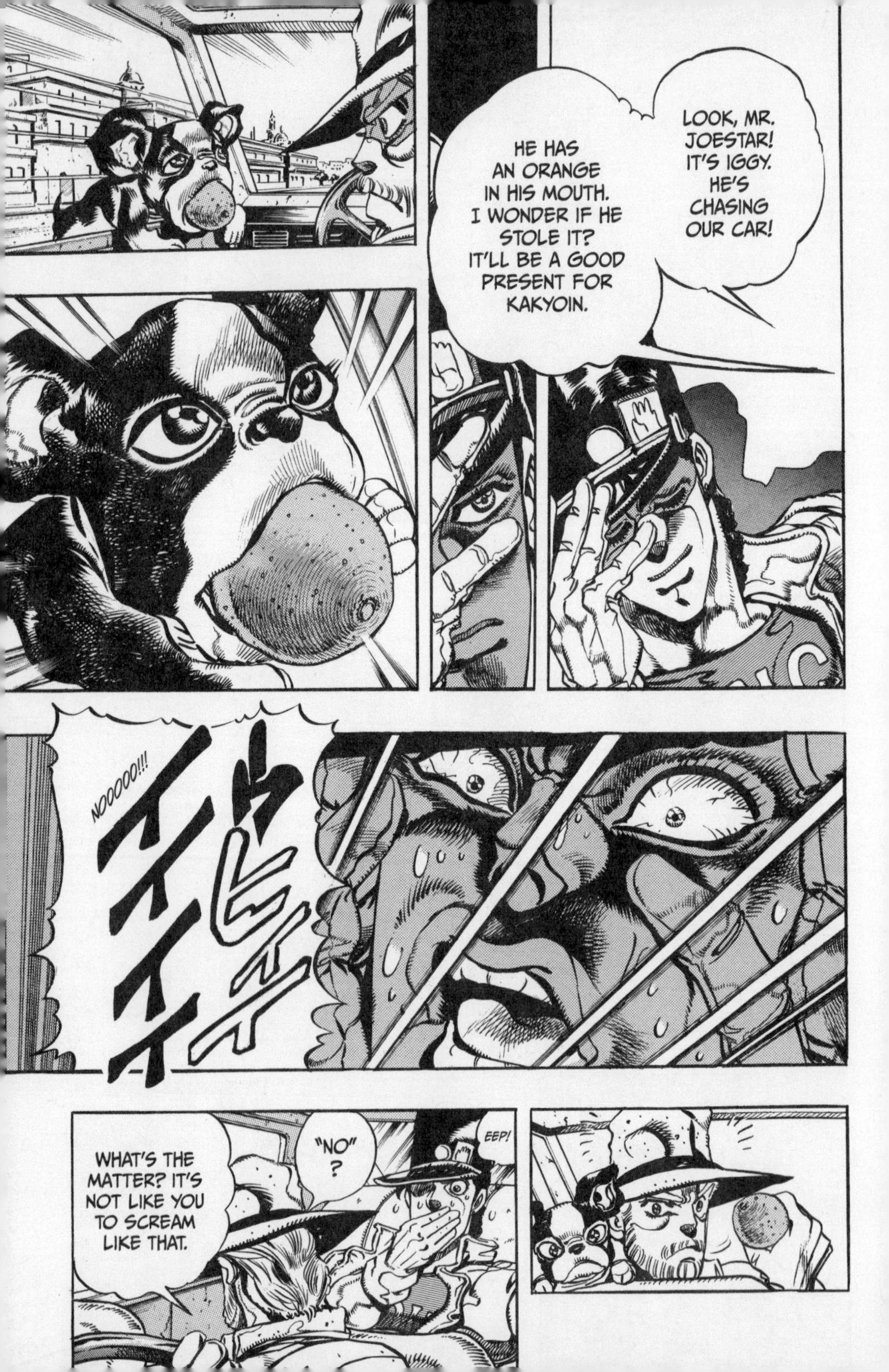

LOOK, MR. JOESTAR! IT'S IGGY. HE'S CHASING OUR CAR!
HE HAS AN ORANGE IN HIS MOUTH. I WONDER IF HE STOLE IT? IT'LL BE A GOOD PRESENT FOR KAKYOIN.
NOOOOO!!!
EEP!
"NO"?
WHAT'S THE MATTER? IT'S NOT LIKE YOU TO SCREAM LIKE THAT.

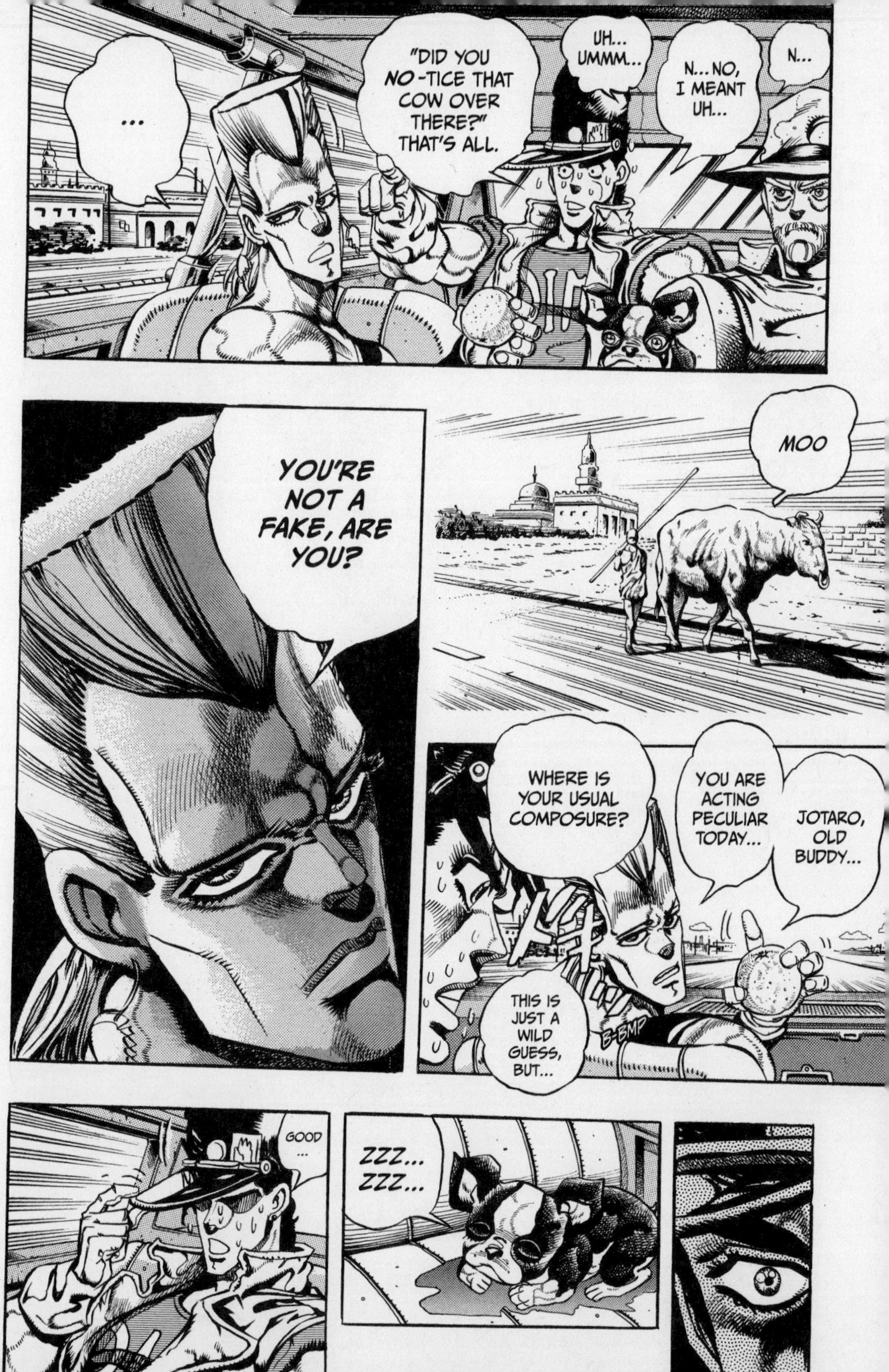
N...
N... NO, I MEANT UH...
UH... UMMM...
"DID YOU NO-TICE THAT COW OVER THERE?" THAT'S ALL.
...
MOO
JOTARO, OLD BUDDY...
YOU ARE ACTING PECULIAR TODAY...
WHERE IS YOUR USUAL COMPOSURE?
THIS IS JUST A WILD GUESS, BUT...
B-BMP
YOU'RE NOT A FAKE, ARE YOU?
ZZZ... ZZZ...
GOOD ...

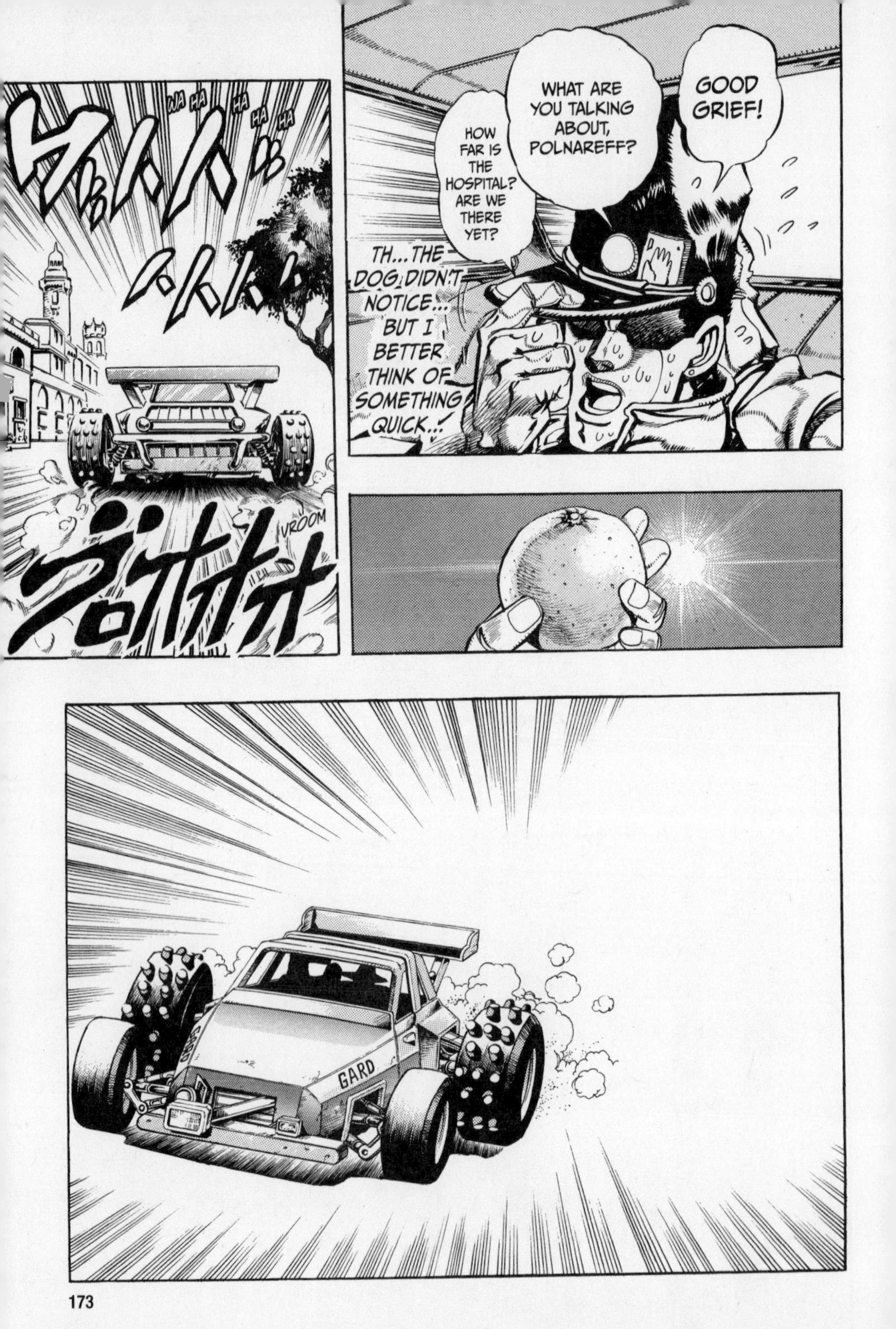
GOOD GRIEF!
WHAT ARE YOU TALKING ABOUT, POLNAREFF?
HOW FAR IS THE HOSPITAL? ARE WE THERE YET?
TH...THE DOG DIDN'T NOTICE... BUT I BETTER THINK OF SOMETHING QUICK...!
WA HA HA HA HA
VROOM

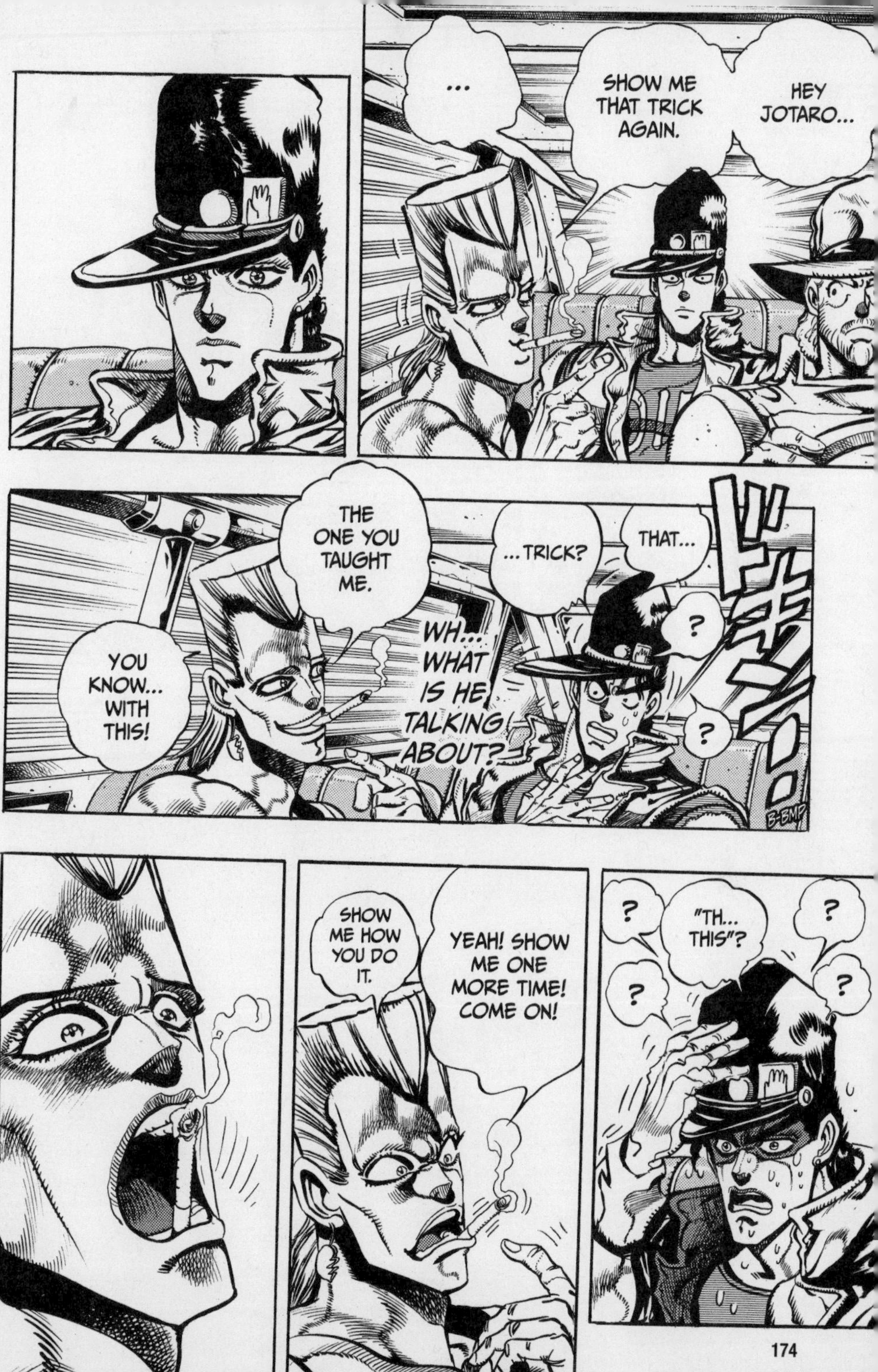
HEY JOTARO...
SHOW ME THAT TRICK AGAIN.
...
B-BMP
?
?
THAT...
...TRICK?
THE ONE YOU TAUGHT ME.
WH... WHAT IS HE TALKING ABOUT?
YOU KNOW... WITH THIS!
?
"TH... THIS"?
?
?
?
YEAH! SHOW ME ONE MORE TIME! COME ON!
SHOW ME HOW YOU DO IT.

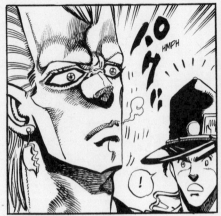

HMPH
OH, YOU'VE GOTTEN BETTER, POLNA-REFF.
HEH.
HEH HEH HEH HEH.
OH.
TH... THAT!
YOU MEAN THAT TRICK!
WHEW! I KNOW HOW TO DO THAT! IT'S DANGEROUS BUT I CAN PULL IT OFF! FOR A MINUTE I HAD NO IDEA WHAT HE WAS TALKING ABOUT.
SURE. IT'S EASY.
OKAY! DO THE ONE WITH FIVE CIGARETTES!
POP
...
GULP

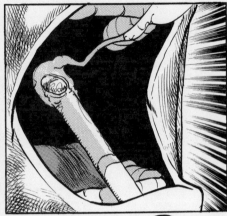

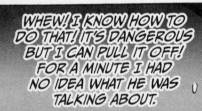

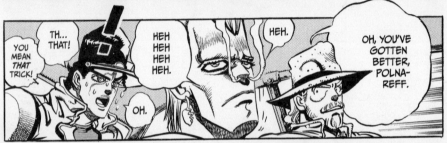

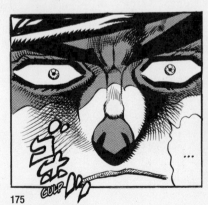

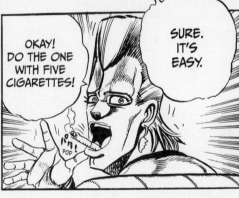

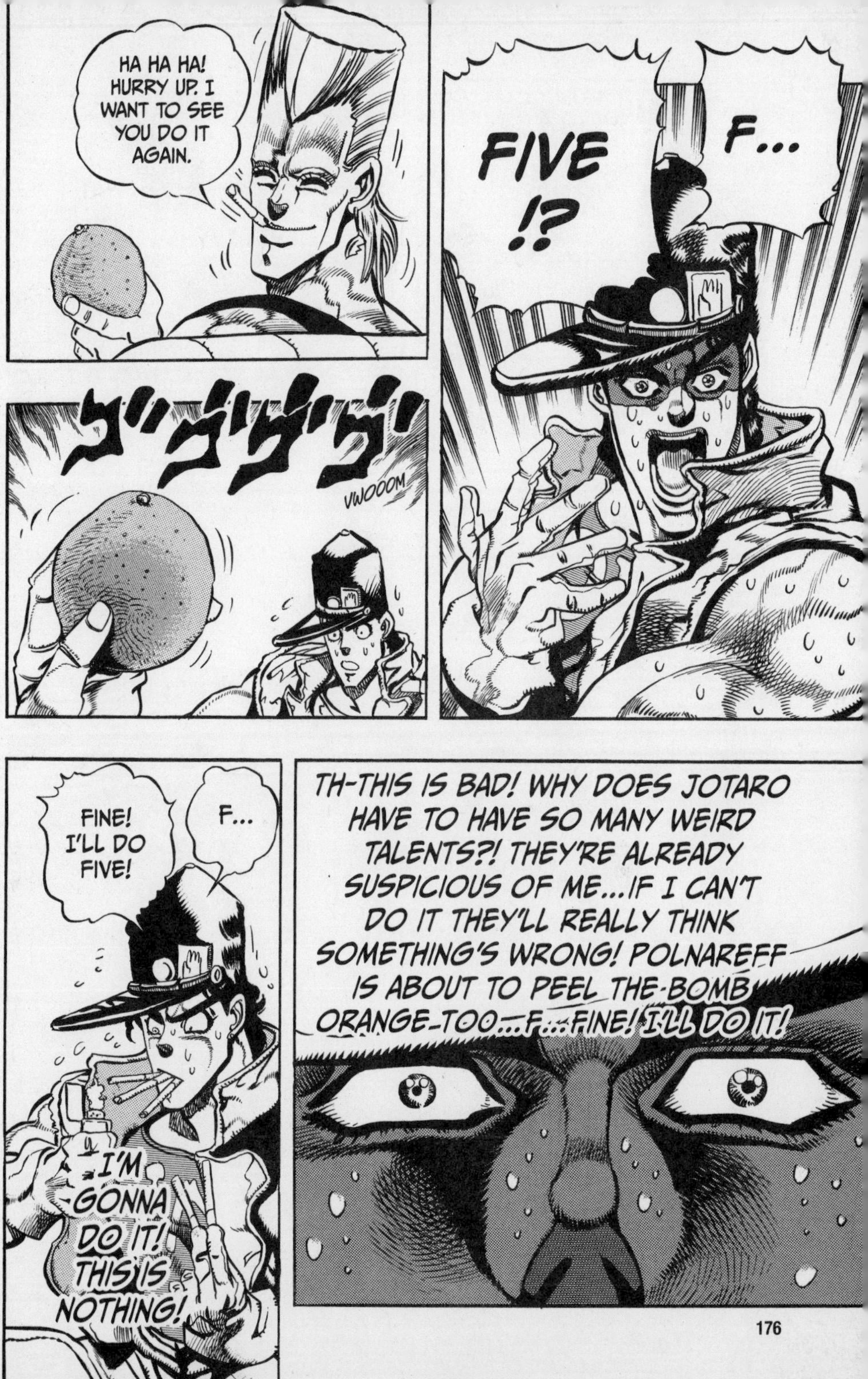

F...
FIVE !?
HA HA HA! HURRY UP. I WANT TO SEE YOU DO IT AGAIN.
ゴゴゴゴ
VWOOOM
TH-THIS IS BAD! WHY DOES JOTARO HAVE TO HAVE SO MANY WEIRD TALENTS?! THEY'RE ALREADY SUSPICIOUS OF ME...IF I CAN'T DO IT THEY'LL REALLY THINK SOMETHING'S WRONG! POLNAREFF IS ABOUT TO PEEL THE BOMB ORANGE TOO...F...FINE! I'LL DO IT!
F...
FINE! I'LL DO FIVE!
I'M GONNA DO IT! THIS IS NOTHING!

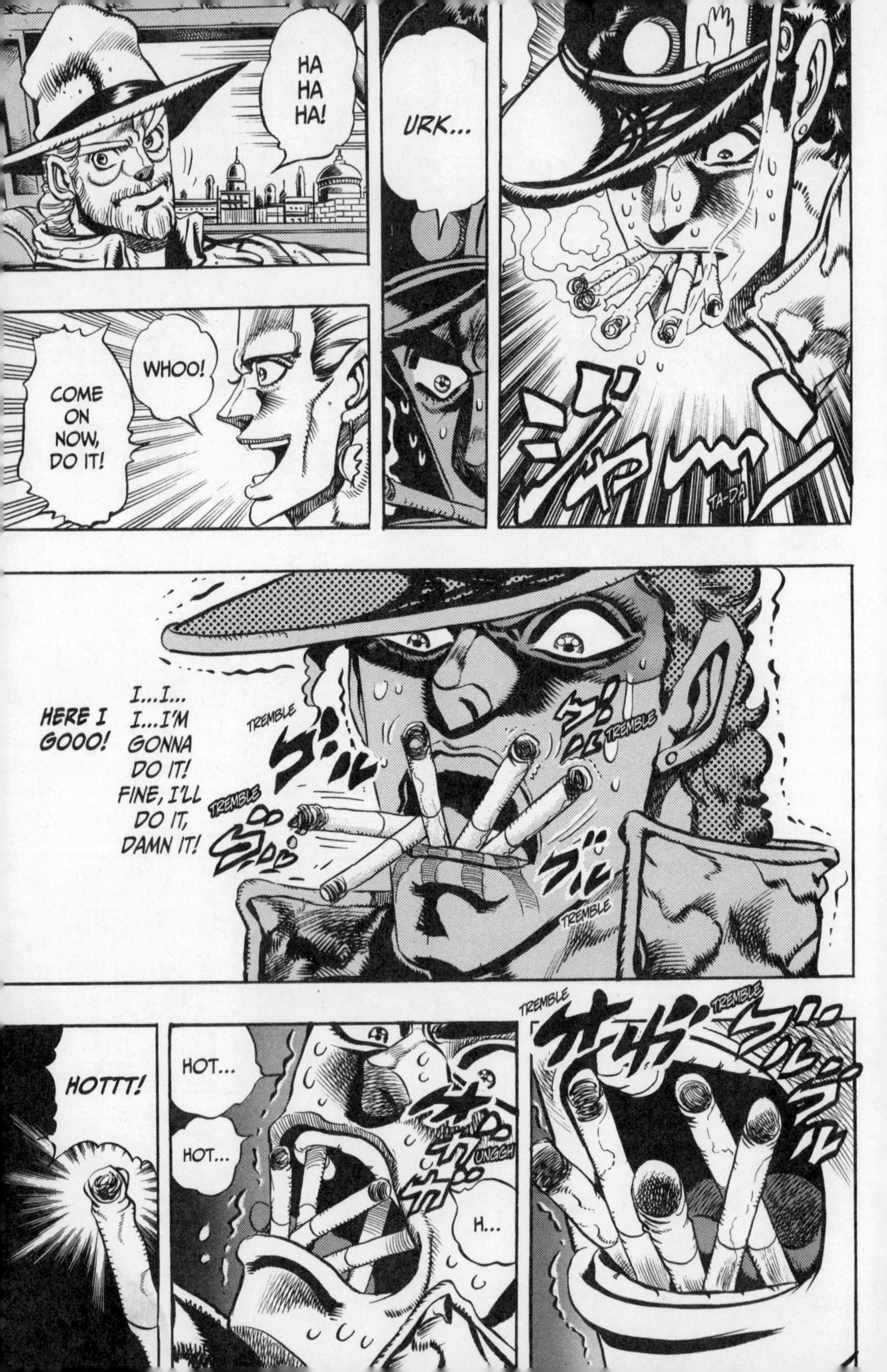
TA-DA
URK...
HA HA HA!
WHOO!
COME ON NOW, DO IT!
TREMBLE
TREMBLE
TREMBLE
TREMBLE
I...I... I...I'M GONNA DO IT! FINE, I'LL DO IT, DAMN IT!
HERE I GOOO!
TREMBLE
TREMBLE
UNGGH
HOT...
HOT...
H...
HOTTT!

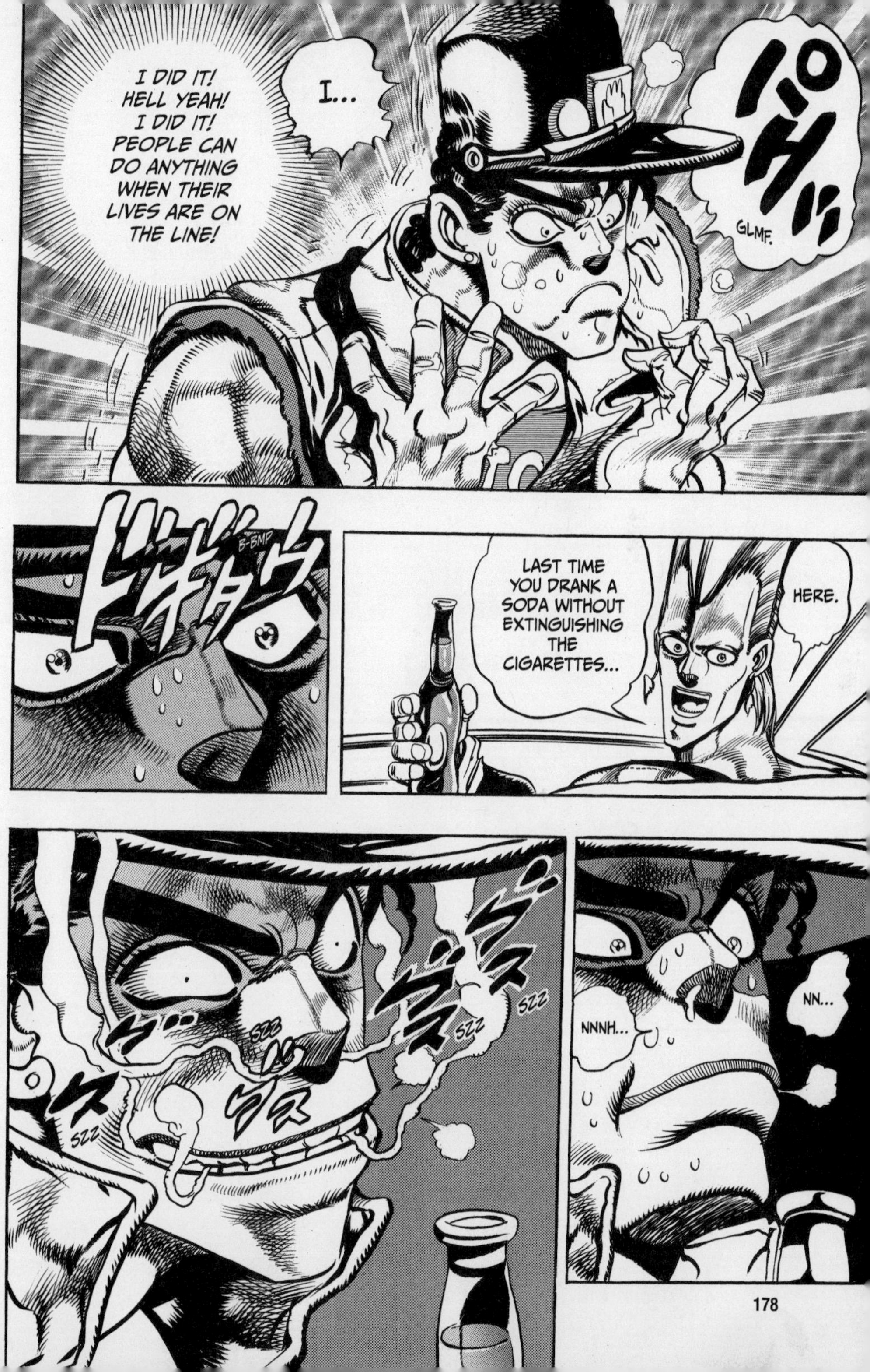
GLMF.
I...
I DID IT! HELL YEAH! I DID IT! PEOPLE CAN DO ANYTHING WHEN THEIR LIVES ARE ON THE LINE!
HERE.
LAST TIME YOU DRANK A SODA WITHOUT EXTINGUISHING THE CIGARETTES...
B-BMP
NN...
NNNH...
SZZ
SZZ
SZZ
SZZ

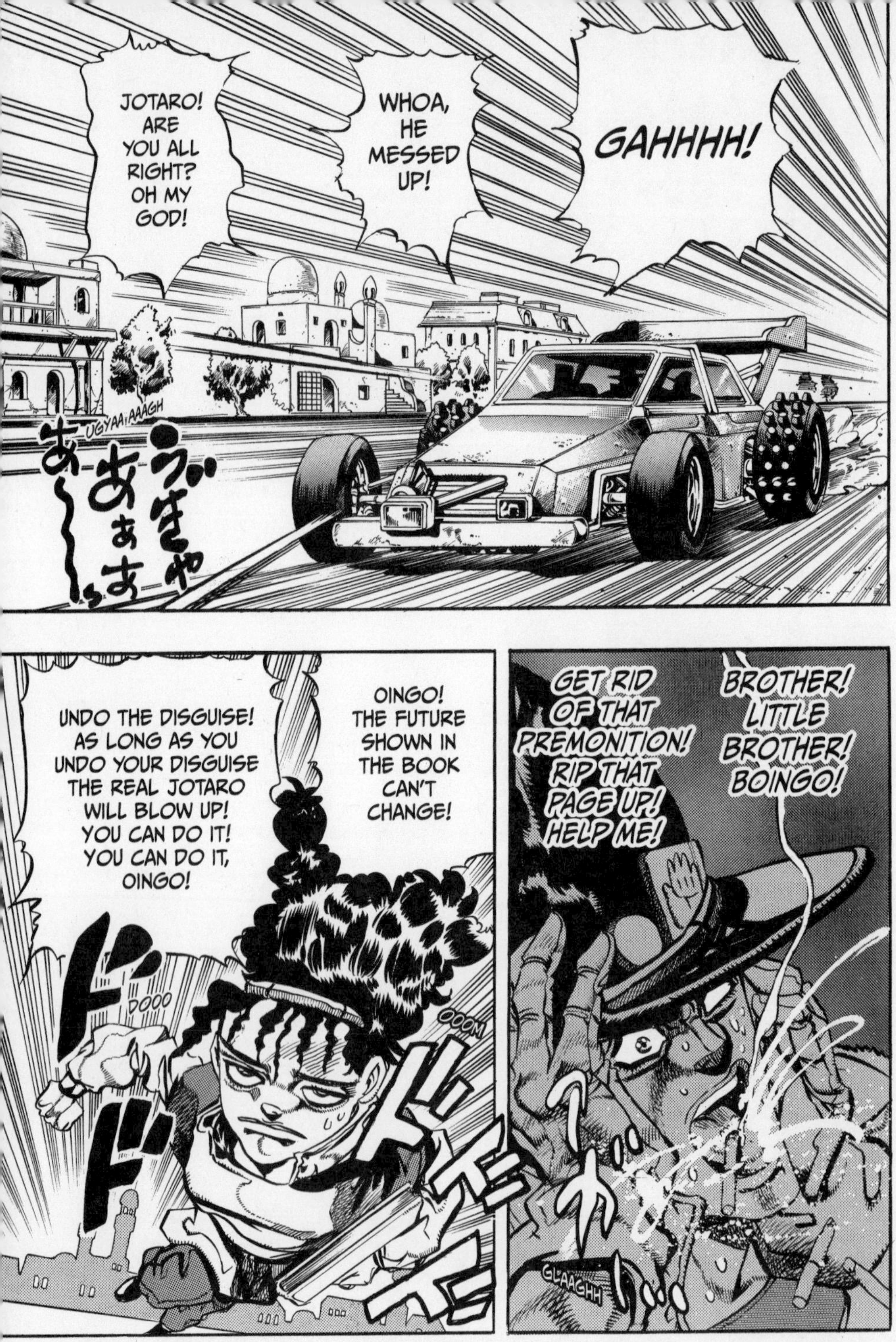
GAHHHH!
WHOA, HE MESSED UP!
JOTARO! ARE YOU ALL RIGHT? OH MY GOD!
UGYAAAAAGH
うぎゃあぁぁあ〜〜〜
BROTHER! LITTLE BROTHER! BOINGO!
GET RID OF THAT PREMONITION! RIP THAT PAGE UP! HELP ME!
GLAAGHH
OINGO! THE FUTURE SHOWN IN THE BOOK CAN'T CHANGE!
UNDO THE DISGUISE! AS LONG AS YOU UNDO YOUR DISGUISE THE REAL JOTARO WILL BLOW UP! YOU CAN DO IT! YOU CAN DO IT, OINGO!
DOOOOOOM
ドドド

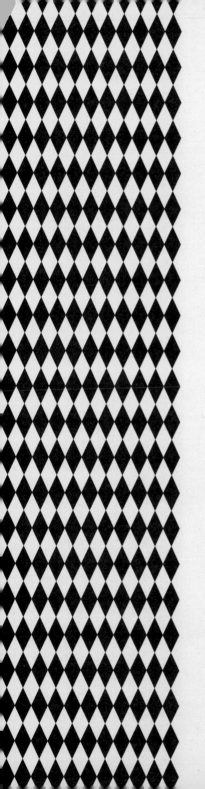

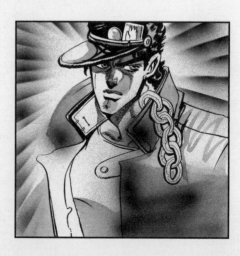

CHAPTER 79: "Khnum" Oingo and "Thoth" Boingo PART 4

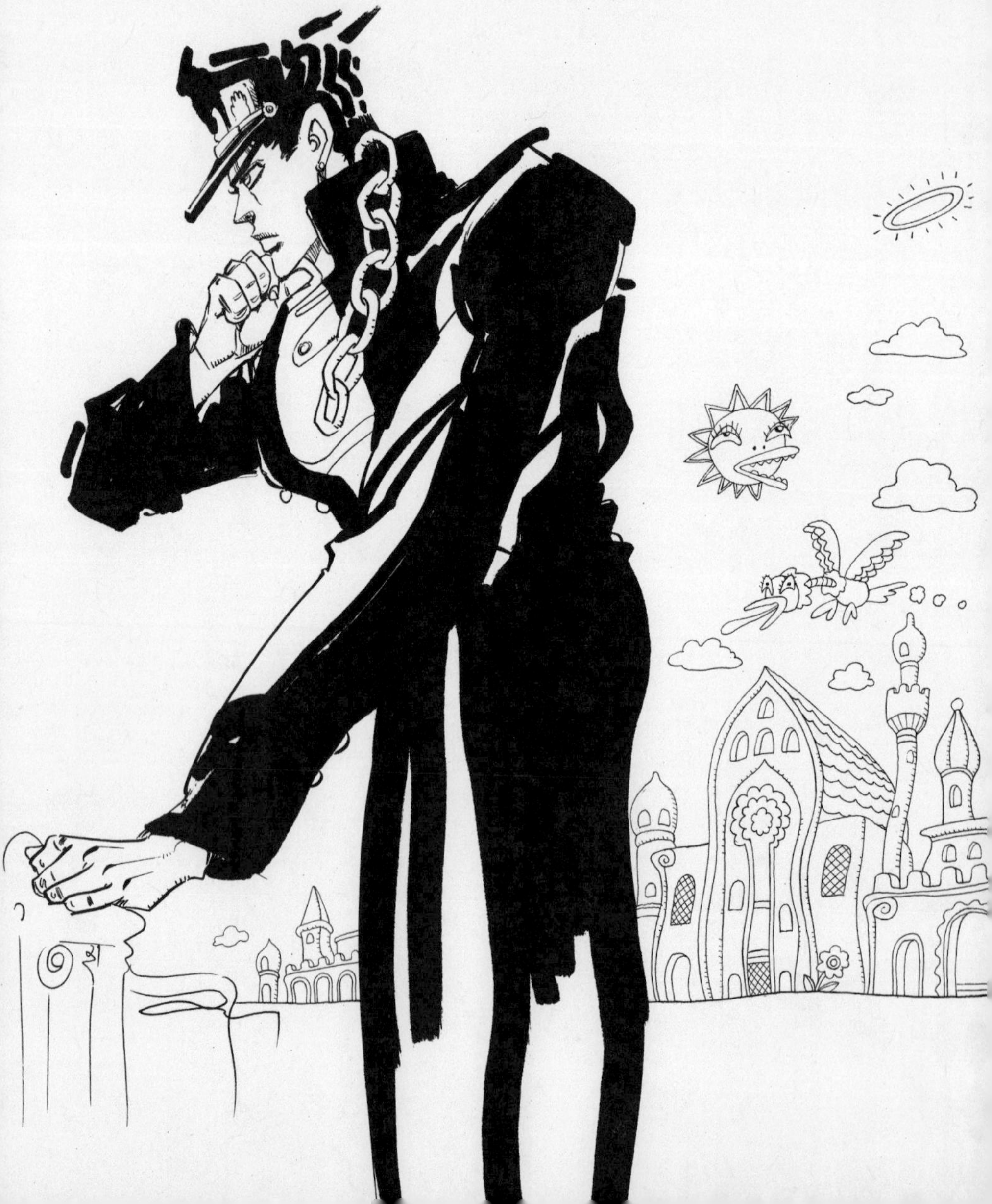

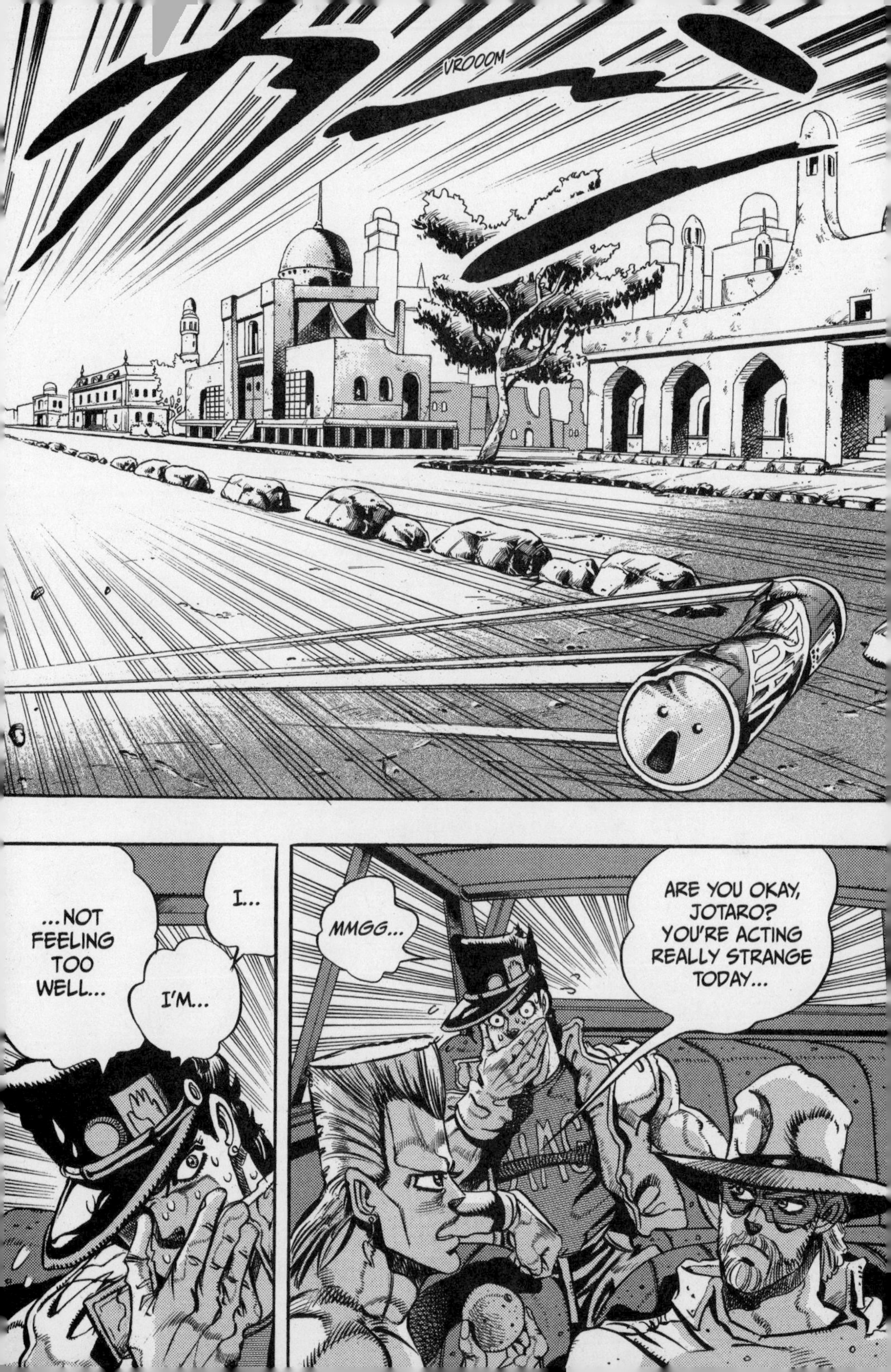
VROOOM
ARE YOU OKAY, JOTARO? YOU'RE ACTING REALLY STRANGE TODAY...
MMGG...
I...
I'M...
...NOT FEELING TOO WELL...

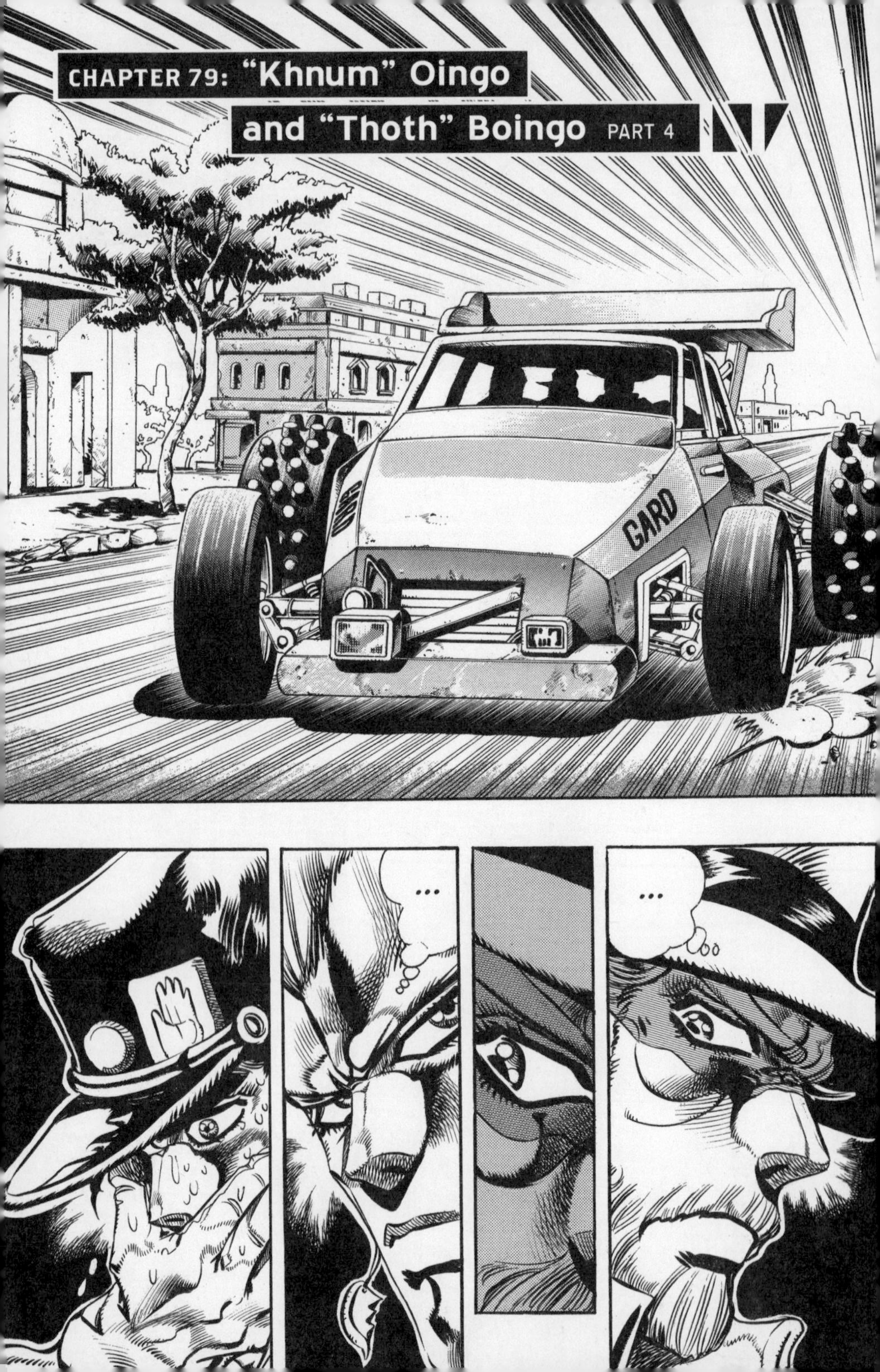
CHAPTER 79: "Khnum" Oingo and "Thoth" Boingo PART 4
GARD
...
...

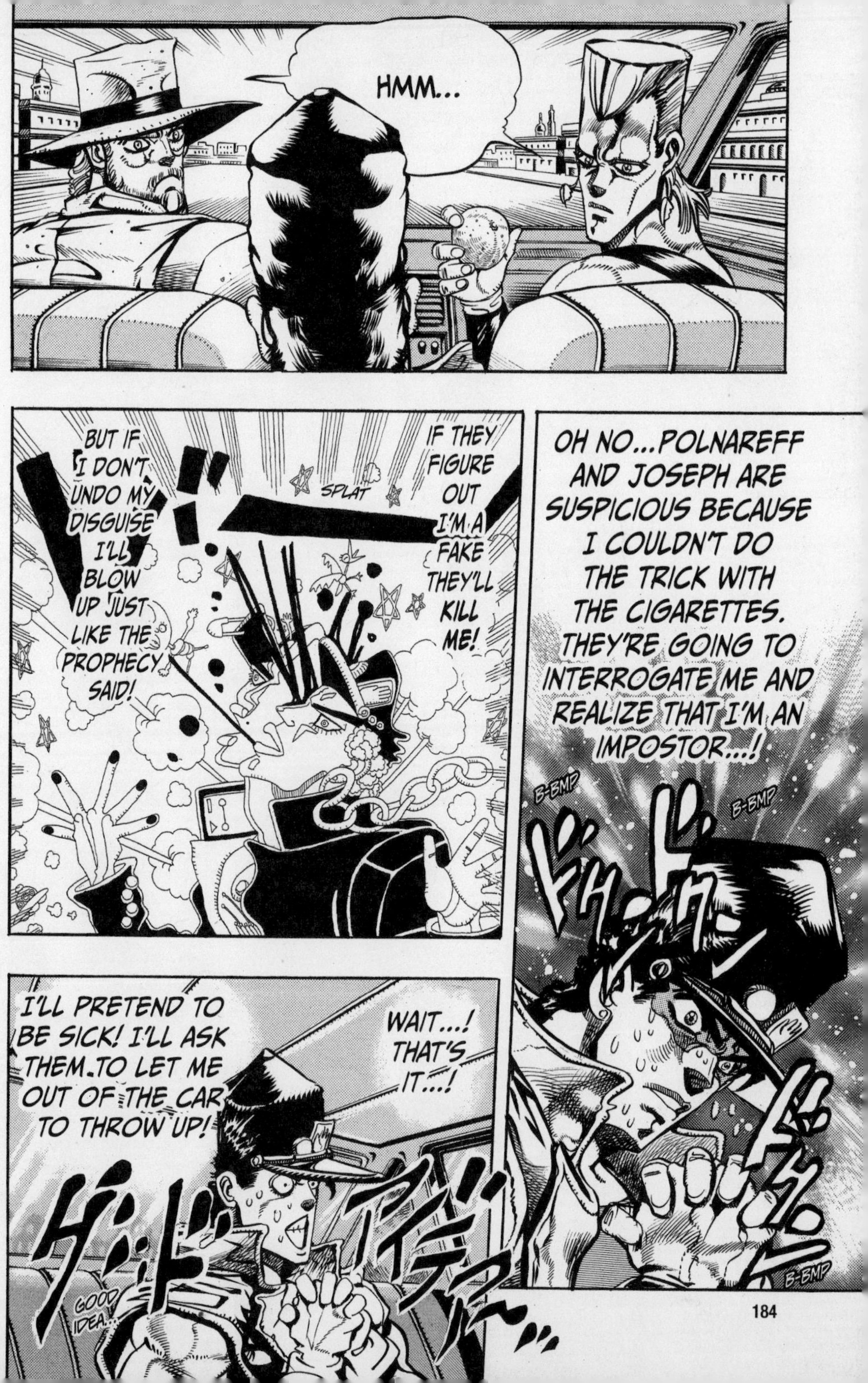
HMM...
OH NO...POLNAREFF AND JOSEPH ARE SUSPICIOUS BECAUSE I COULDN'T DO THE TRICK WITH THE CIGARETTES. THEY'RE GOING TO INTERROGATE ME AND REALIZE THAT I'M AN IMPOSTOR...!
B-BMP
B-BMP
B-BMP
IF THEY FIGURE OUT I'M A FAKE THEY'LL KILL ME!
SPLAT
BUT IF I DON'T UNDO MY DISGUISE I'LL BLOW UP JUST LIKE THE PROPHECY SAID!
WAIT...! THAT'S IT...!
I'LL PRETEND TO BE SICK! I'LL ASK THEM TO LET ME OUT OF THE CAR TO THROW UP!
GOOD IDEA...

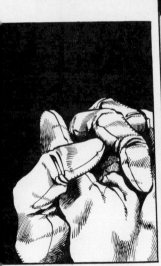

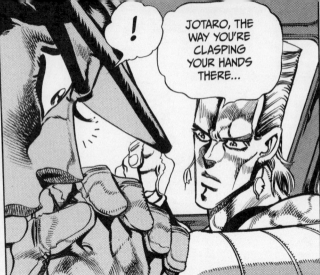

!

JOTARO, THE WAY YOU'RE CLASPING YOUR HANDS THERE...

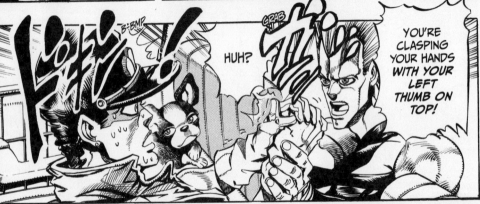

HUH?

GRAB

B-BMP

YOU'RE CLASPING YOUR HANDS WITH YOUR LEFT THUMB ON TOP!

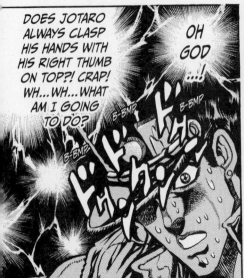

DOES JOTARO ALWAYS CLASP HIS HANDS WITH HIS RIGHT THUMB ON TOP?! CRAP! WH...WH...WHAT AM I GOING TO DO?

B-BMP

B-BMP

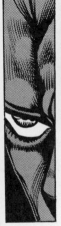

OH GOD ...!

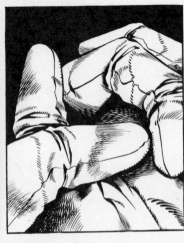

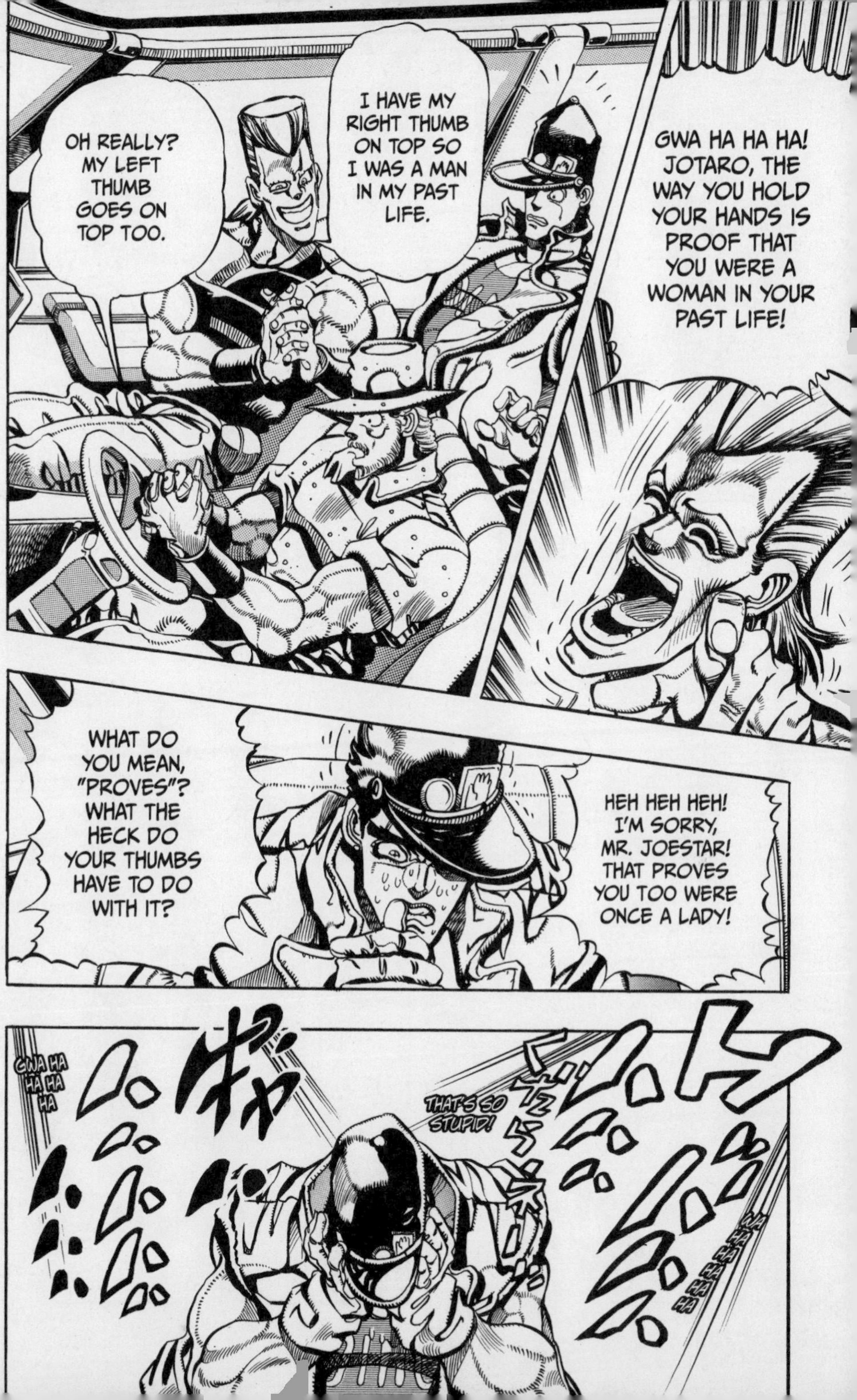
GWA HA HA HA! JOTARO, THE WAY YOU HOLD YOUR HANDS IS PROOF THAT YOU WERE A WOMAN IN YOUR PAST LIFE!
I HAVE MY RIGHT THUMB ON TOP SO I WAS A MAN IN MY PAST LIFE.
OH REALLY? MY LEFT THUMB GOES ON TOP TOO.
HEH HEH HEH! I'M SORRY, MR. JOESTAR! THAT PROVES YOU TOO WERE ONCE A LADY!
WHAT DO YOU MEAN, "PROVES"? WHAT THE HECK DO YOUR THUMBS HAVE TO DO WITH IT?
THAT'S SO STUPID!
GWA HA HA HA HA

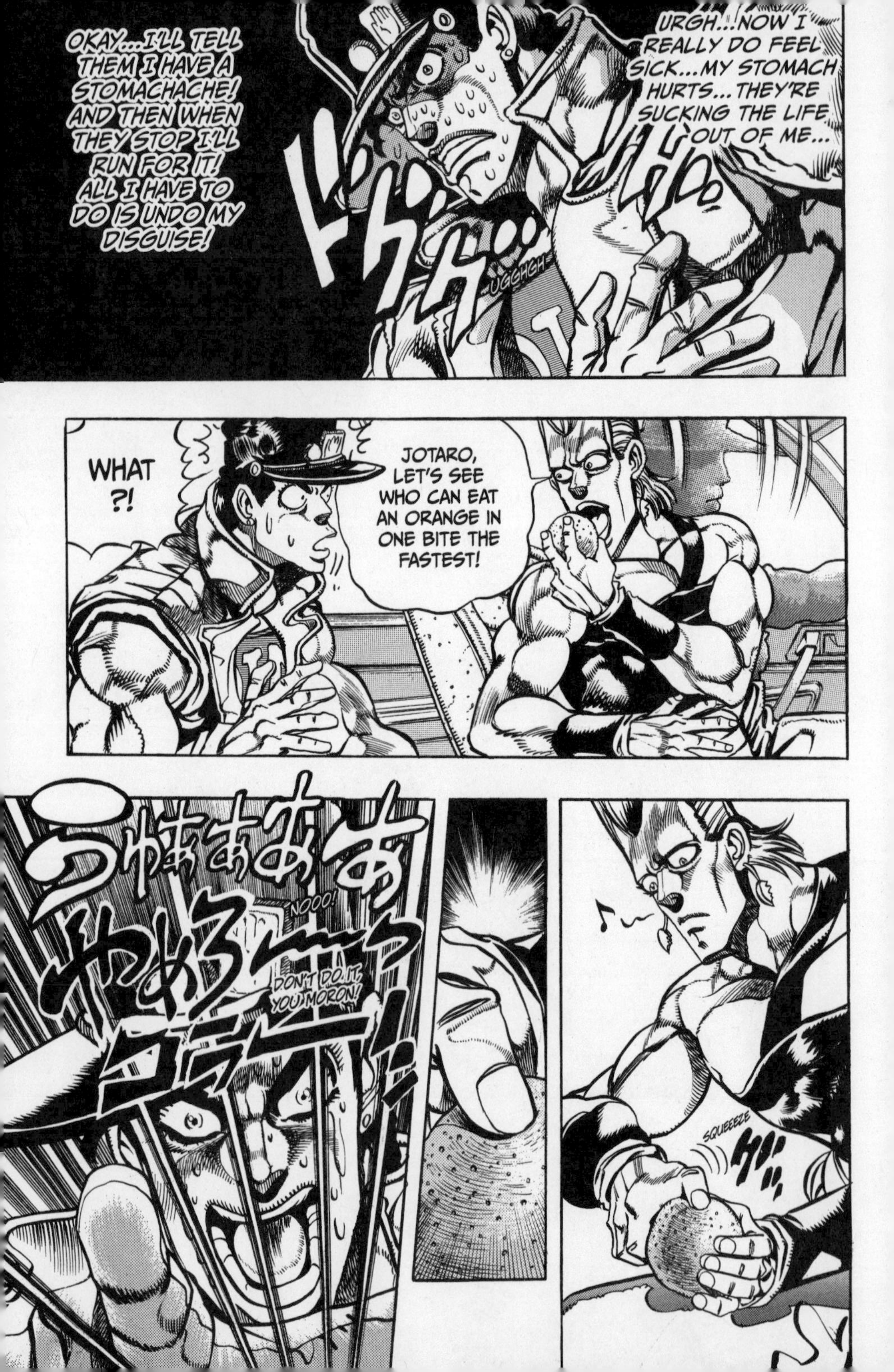
URGH...NOW I REALLY DO FEEL SICK...MY STOMACH HURTS...THEY'RE SUCKING THE LIFE OUT OF ME...
OKAY...I'LL TELL THEM I HAVE A STOMACHACHE! AND THEN WHEN THEY STOP I'LL RUN FOR IT! ALL I HAVE TO DO IS UNDO MY DISGUISE!
UGGHGH
JOTARO, LET'S SEE WHO CAN EAT AN ORANGE IN ONE BITE THE FASTEST!
WHAT ?!
SQUEEEZE
NOOO!
DON'T DO IT, YOU MORON!

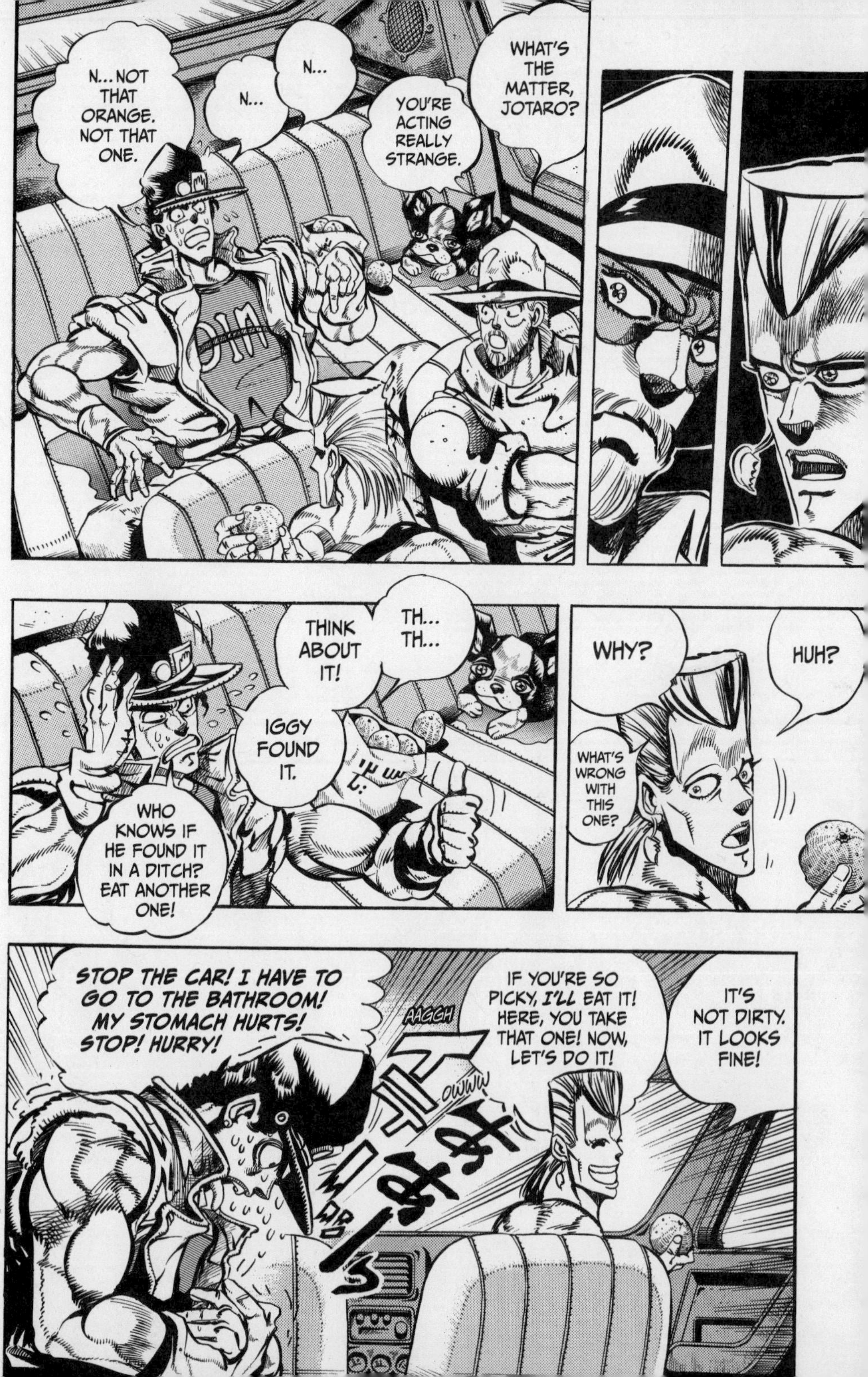
WHAT'S THE MATTER, JOTARO?
YOU'RE ACTING REALLY STRANGE.
N...
N...
N... NOT THAT ORANGE. NOT THAT ONE.
HUH?
WHY?
WHAT'S WRONG WITH THIS ONE?
TH... TH...
THINK ABOUT IT!
IGGY FOUND IT.
WHO KNOWS IF HE FOUND IT IN A DITCH? EAT ANOTHER ONE!
IT'S NOT DIRTY. IT LOOKS FINE!
IF YOU'RE SO PICKY, I'LL EAT IT! HERE, YOU TAKE THAT ONE! NOW, LET'S DO IT!
OWWW
AAGGH
STOP THE CAR! I HAVE TO GO TO THE BATHROOM! MY STOMACH HURTS! STOP! HURRY!

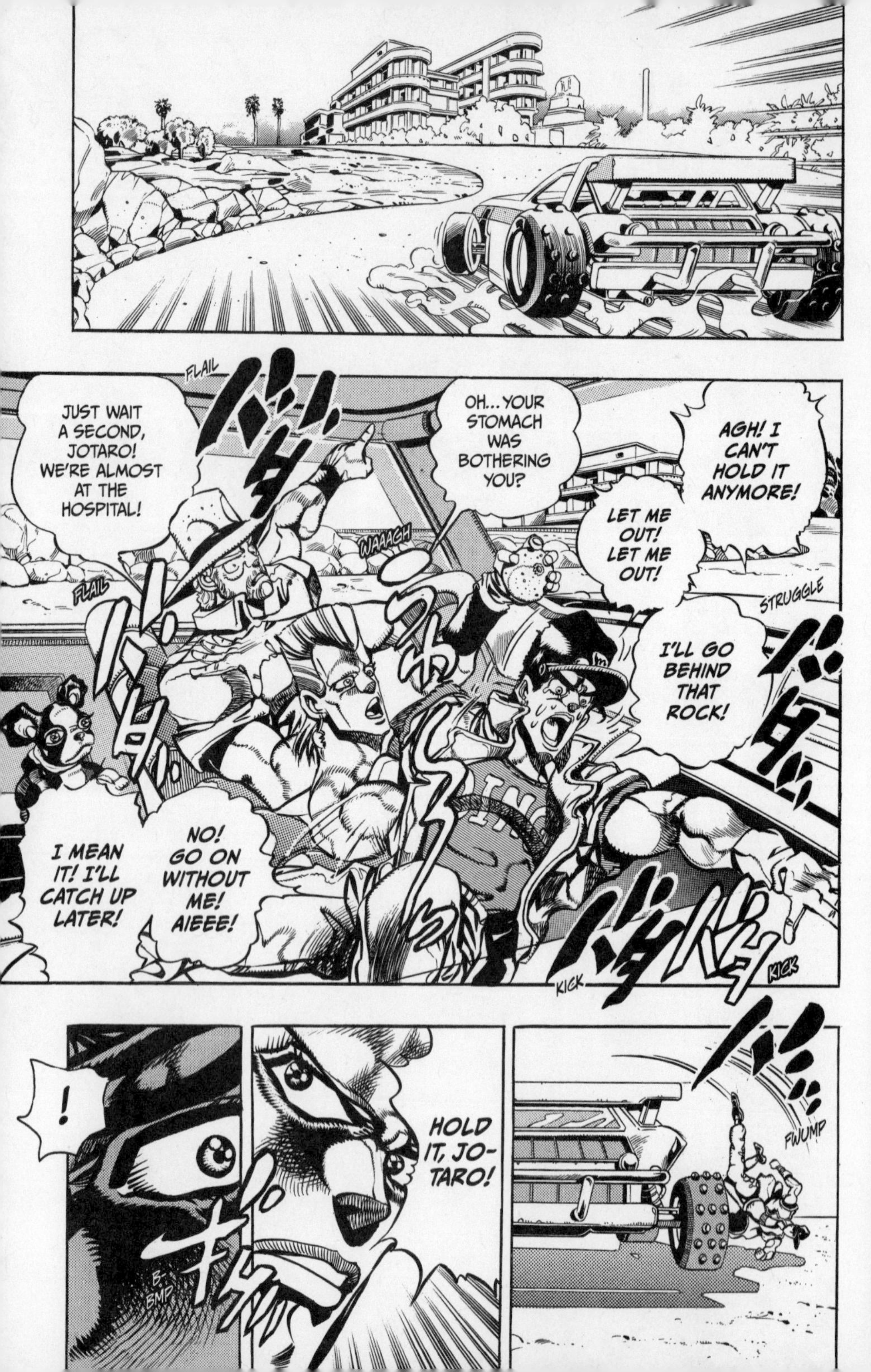
STRUGGLE
AGH! I CAN'T HOLD IT ANYMORE!
LET ME OUT! LET ME OUT!
OH... YOUR STOMACH WAS BOTHERING YOU?
WAAAGH
FLAIL
JUST WAIT A SECOND, JOTARO! WE'RE ALMOST AT THE HOSPITAL!
FLAIL
I'LL GO BEHIND THAT ROCK!
KICK
KICK
NO! GO ON WITHOUT ME! AIEEE!
I MEAN IT! I'LL CATCH UP LATER!
FWUMP
HOLD IT, JO-TARO!
!
B-BMP

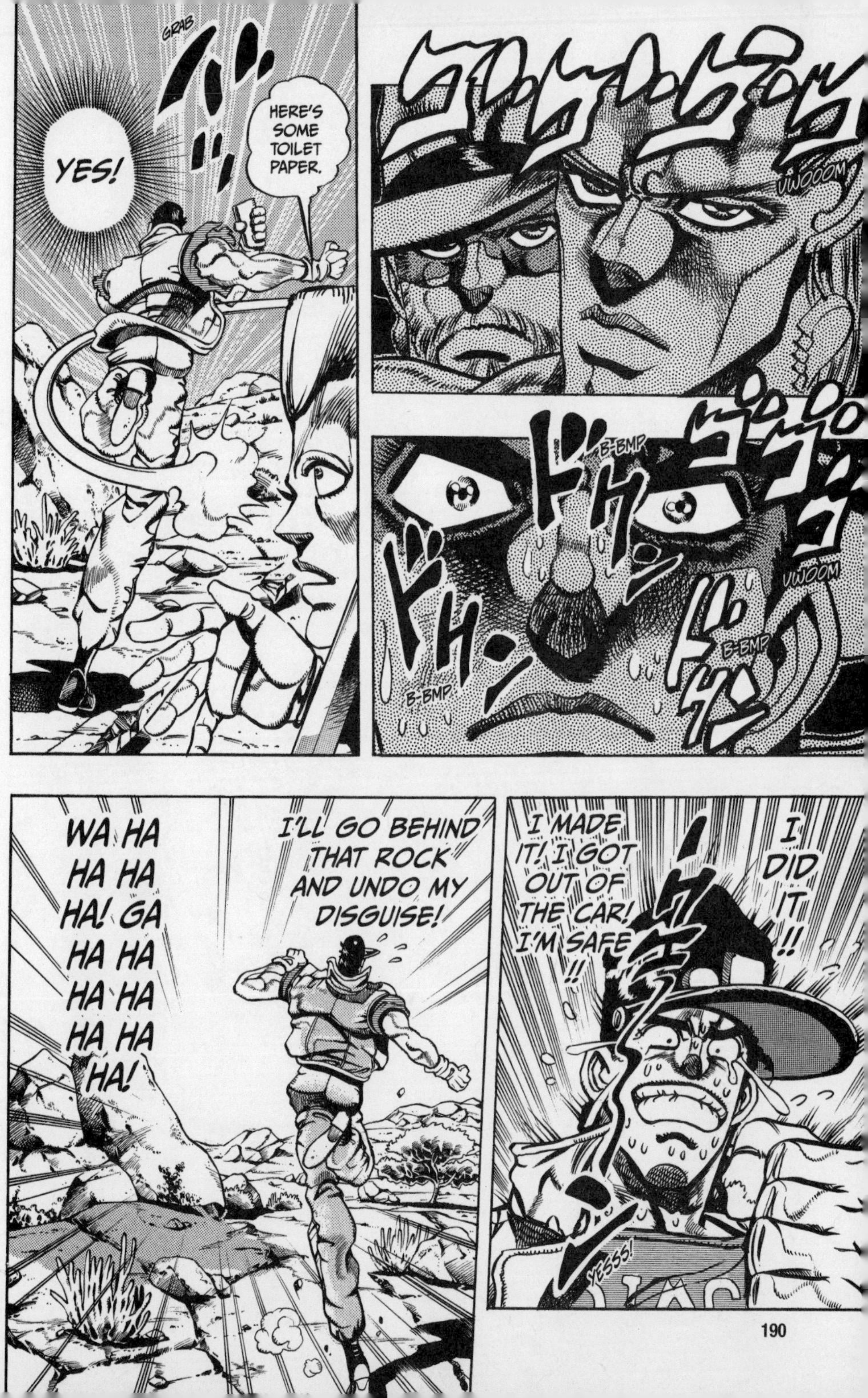
VWOOOM
B-BMP
VWOOM
B-BMP
B-BMP
GRAB
HERE'S SOME TOILET PAPER.
YES!
I DID IT!!
I MADE IT! I GOT OUT OF THE CAR! I'M SAFE!!
YESSS!
I'LL GO BEHIND THAT ROCK AND UNDO MY DISGUISE!
WA HA HA HA HA! GA HA HA HA HA HA HA HA!

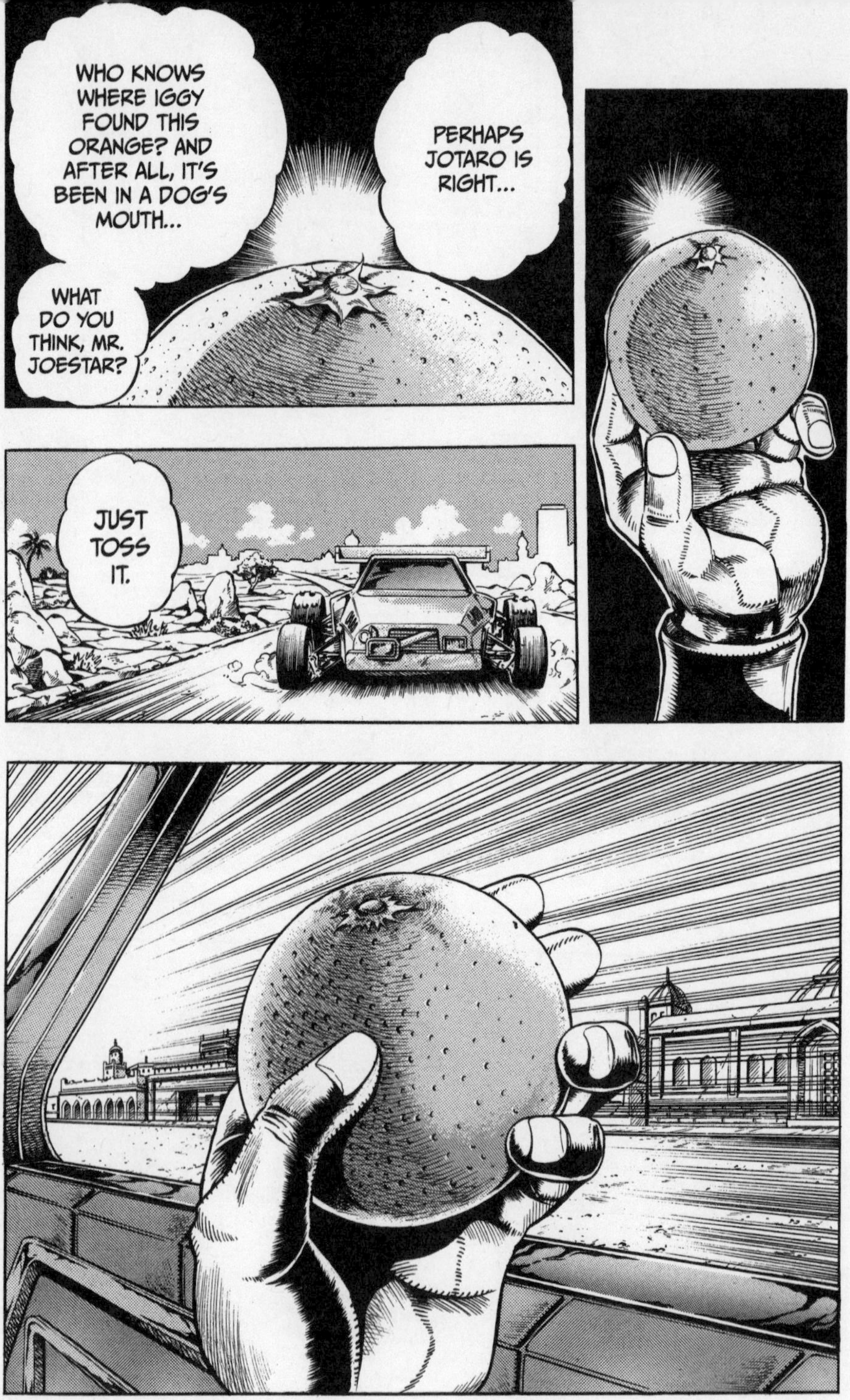
PERHAPS JOTARO IS RIGHT...
WHO KNOWS WHERE IGGY FOUND THIS ORANGE? AND AFTER ALL, IT'S BEEN IN A DOG'S MOUTH...
WHAT DO YOU THINK, MR. JOESTAR?
JUST TOSS IT.

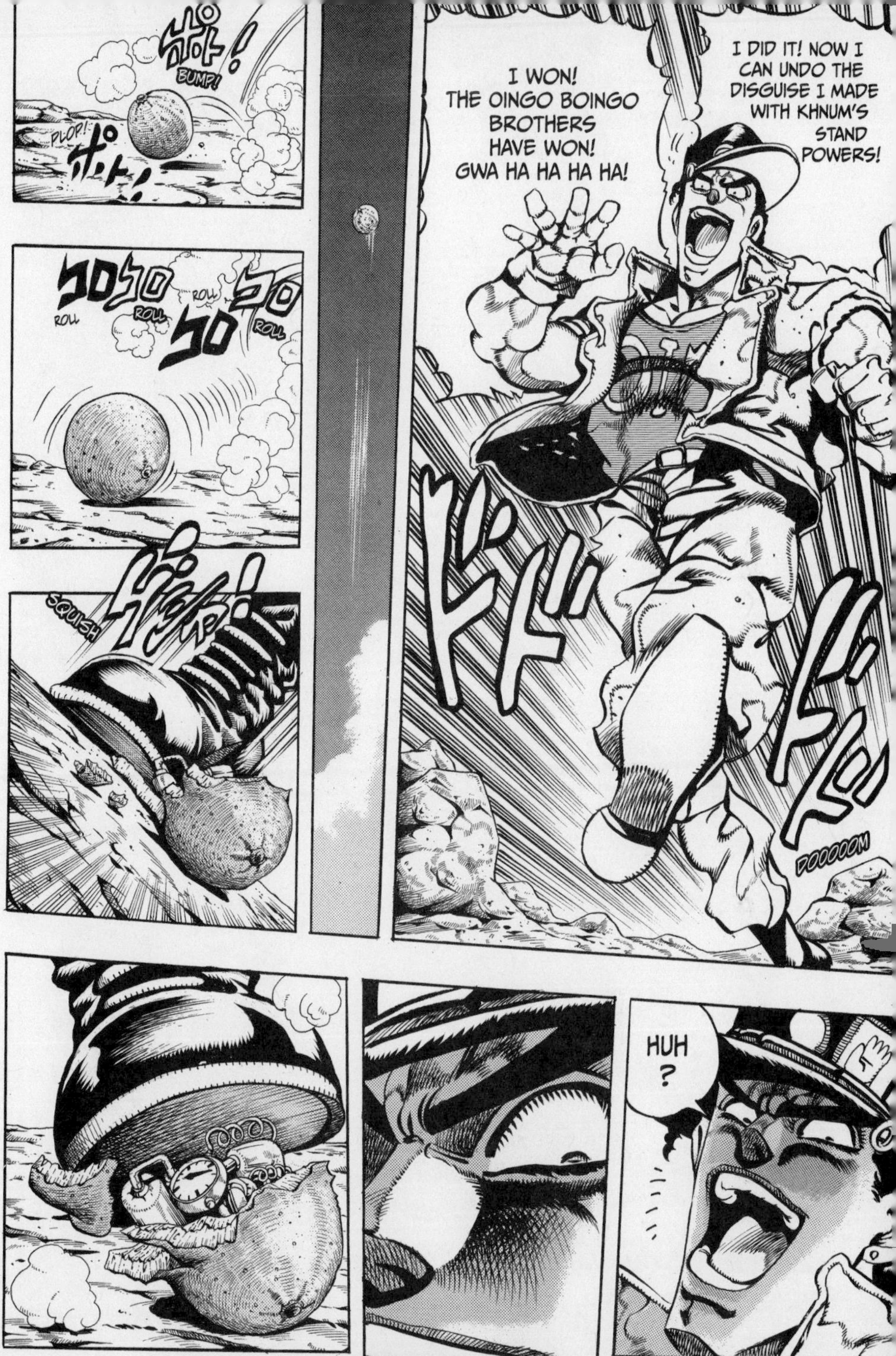
I DID IT! NOW I CAN UNDO THE DISGUISE I MADE WITH KHNUM'S STAND POWERS!
I WON! THE OINGO BOINGO BROTHERS HAVE WON! GWA HA HA HA HA!
DOOOOOM
BUMP!
PLOP!
ROLL
ROLL
ROLL
ROLL
SQUISH
HUH ?

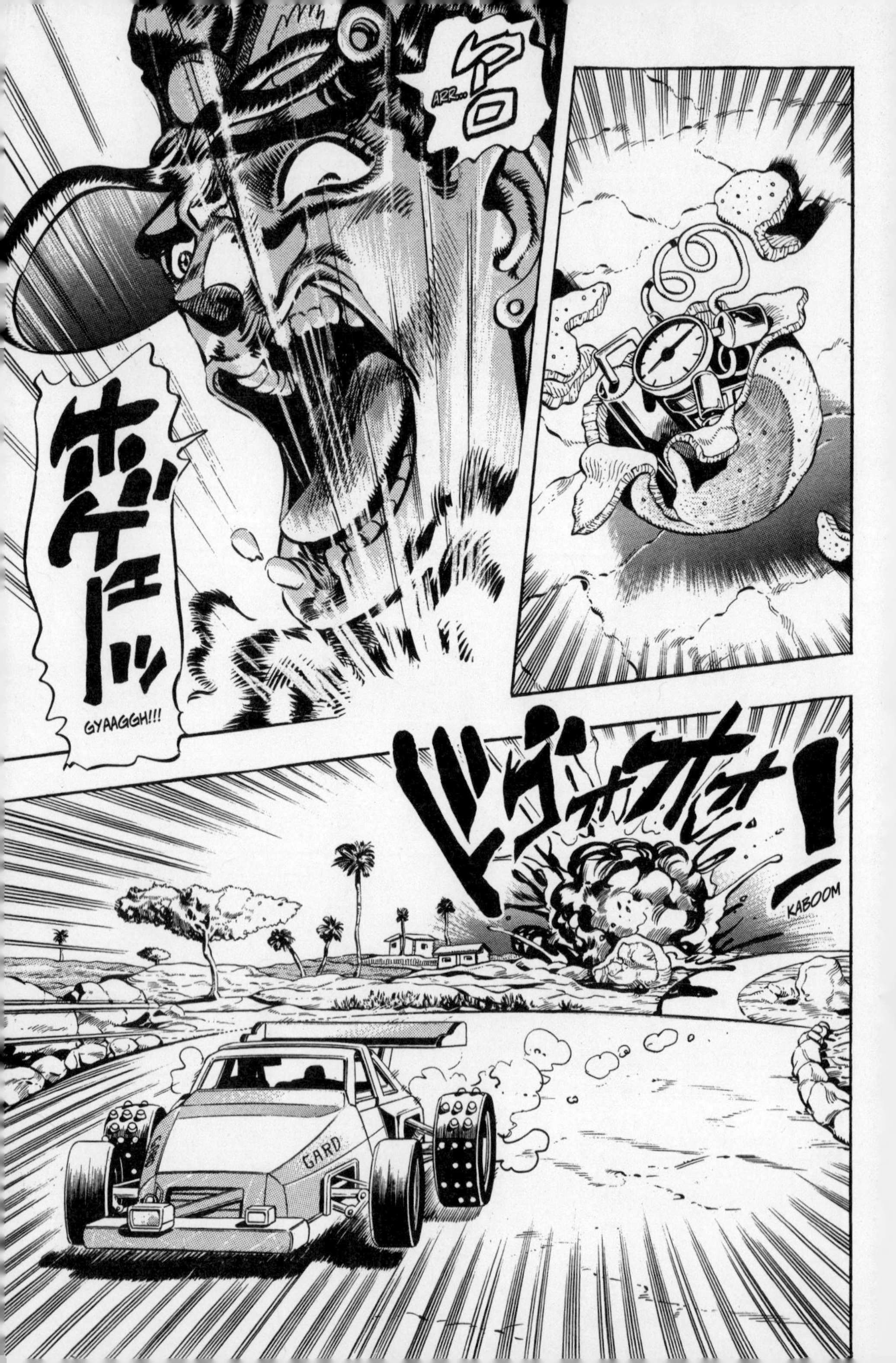

ARR...
GYAAGGH!!!
KABOOM
GARD

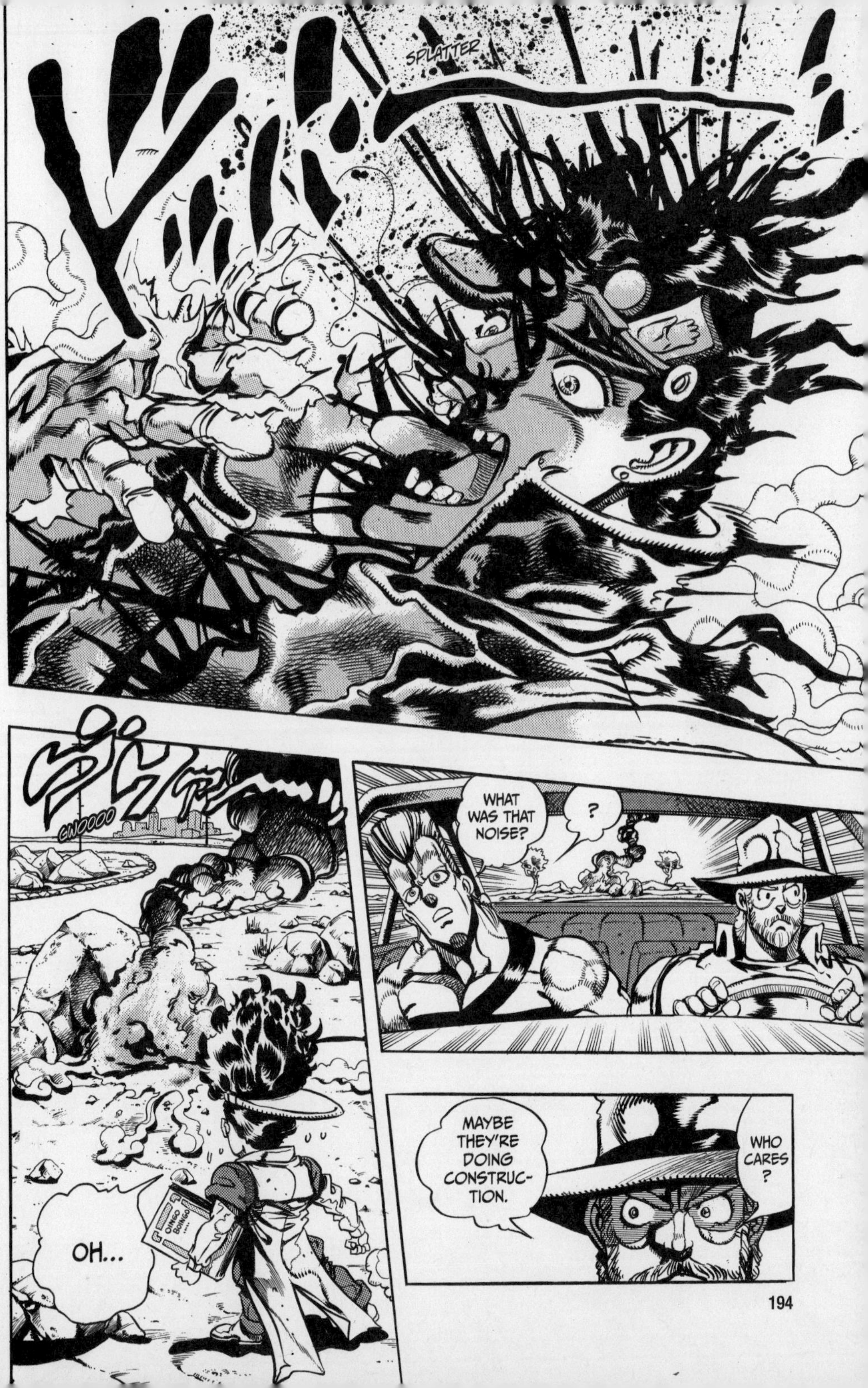
SPLATTER
?
WHAT WAS THAT NOISE?
WHO CARES?
MAYBE THEY'RE DOING CONSTRUC-TION.
GWOOOO
OH...
QINGO BOINGO

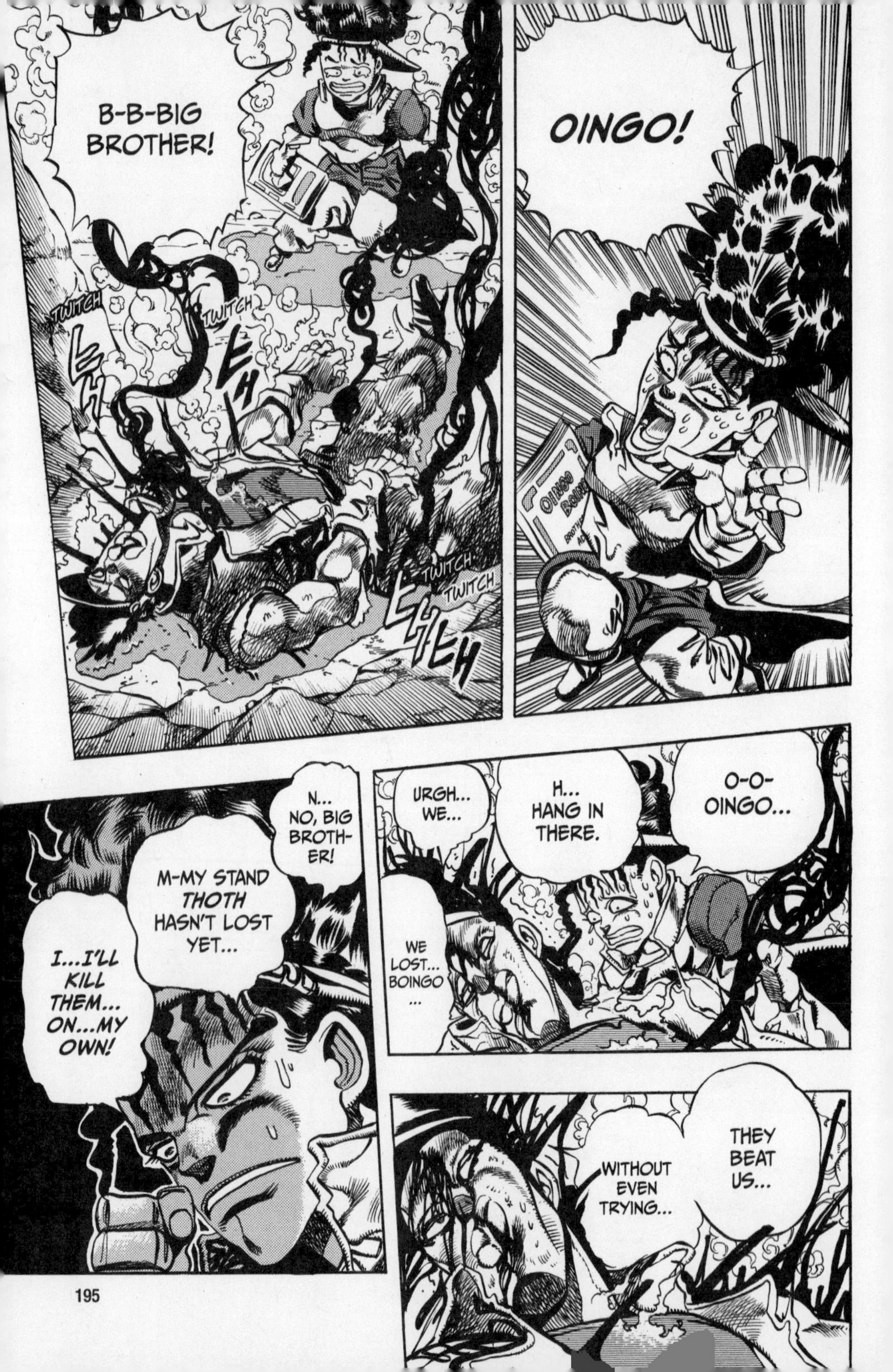
OINGO!
B-B-BIG BROTHER!
TWITCH
TWITCH
TWITCH
TWITCH
O-O-OINGO...
H... HANG IN THERE.
URGH... WE...
WE LOST... BOINGO...
THEY BEAT US...
WITHOUT EVEN TRYING...
N... NO, BIG BROTHER!
M-MY STAND *THOTH* HASN'T LOST YET...
I...I'LL KILL THEM... ON...MY OWN!

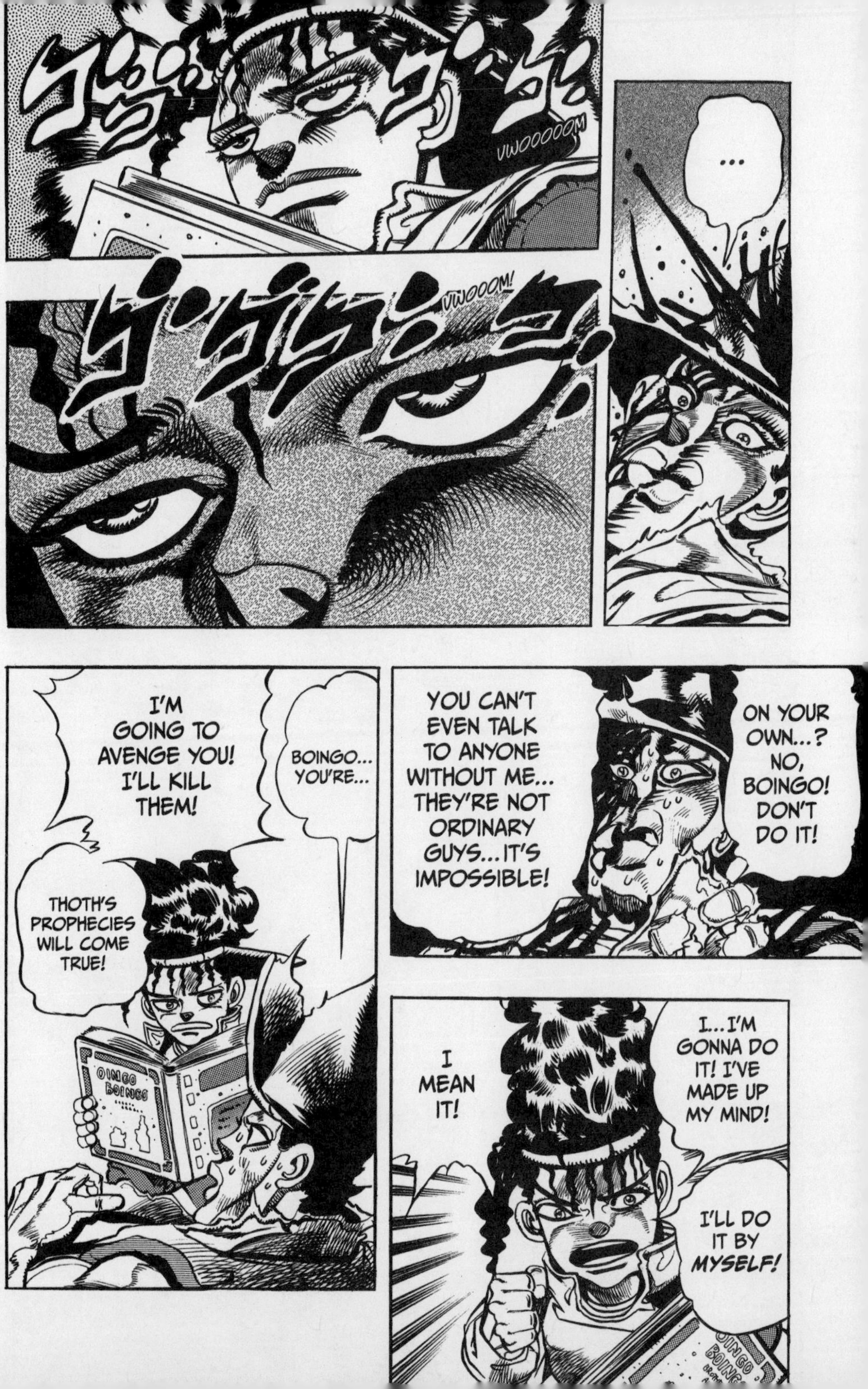
...
VWOOOOOM
VWOOOM!
ON YOUR OWN...? NO, BOINGO! DON'T DO IT!
YOU CAN'T EVEN TALK TO ANYONE WITHOUT ME... THEY'RE NOT ORDINARY GUYS... IT'S IMPOSSIBLE!
I... I'M GONNA DO IT! I'VE MADE UP MY MIND!
I MEAN IT!
I'LL DO IT BY *MYSELF!*
BOINGO... YOU'RE...
I'M GOING TO AVENGE YOU! I'LL KILL THEM!
THOTH'S PROPHECIES WILL COME TRUE!
OINGO BOINGO

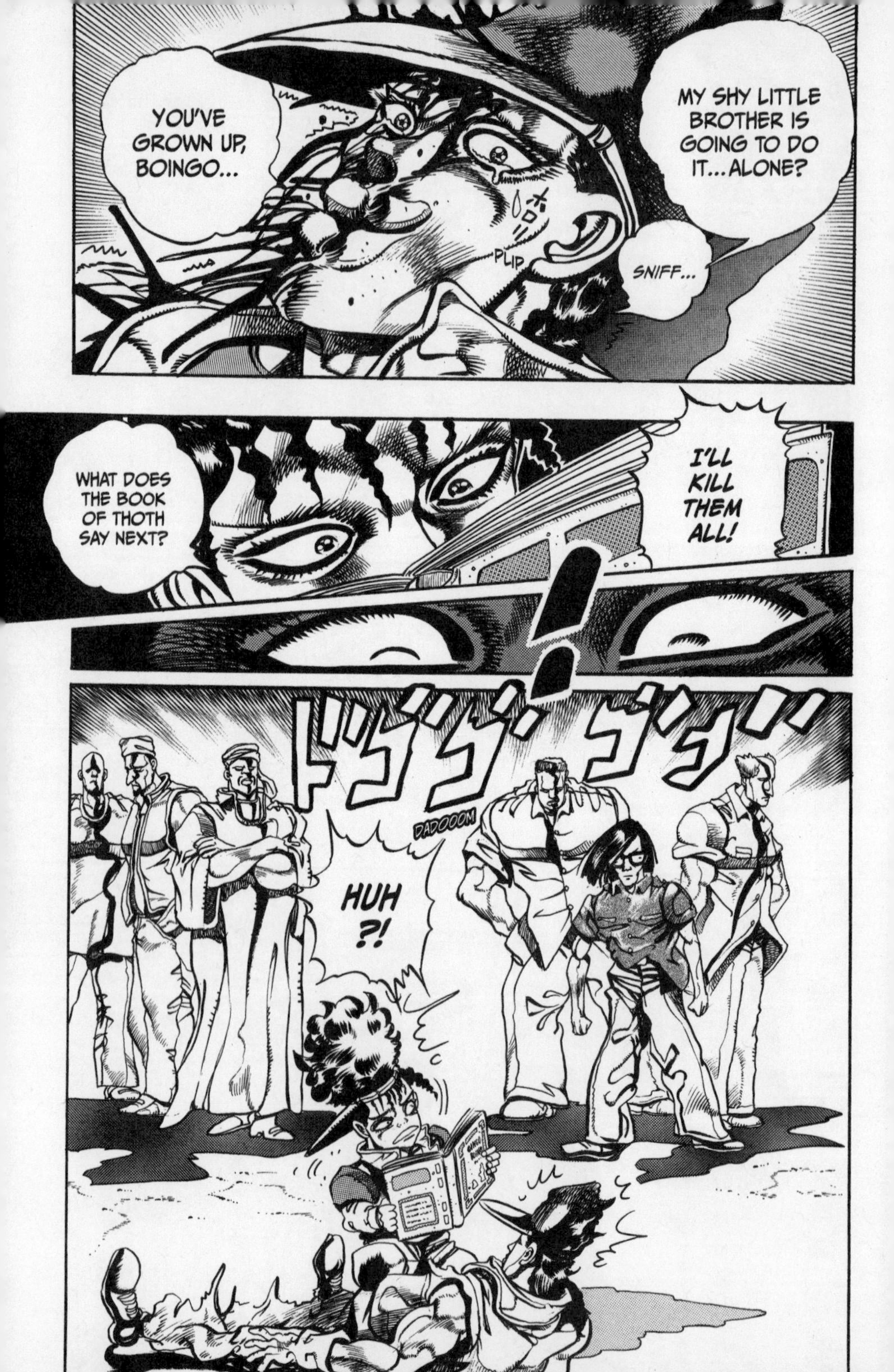
MY SHY LITTLE BROTHER IS GOING TO DO IT... ALONE?
SNIFF...
PLIP
YOU'VE GROWN UP, BOINGO...
I'LL KILL THEM ALL!
WHAT DOES THE BOOK OF THOTH SAY NEXT?
DADOOOM
HUH ?!

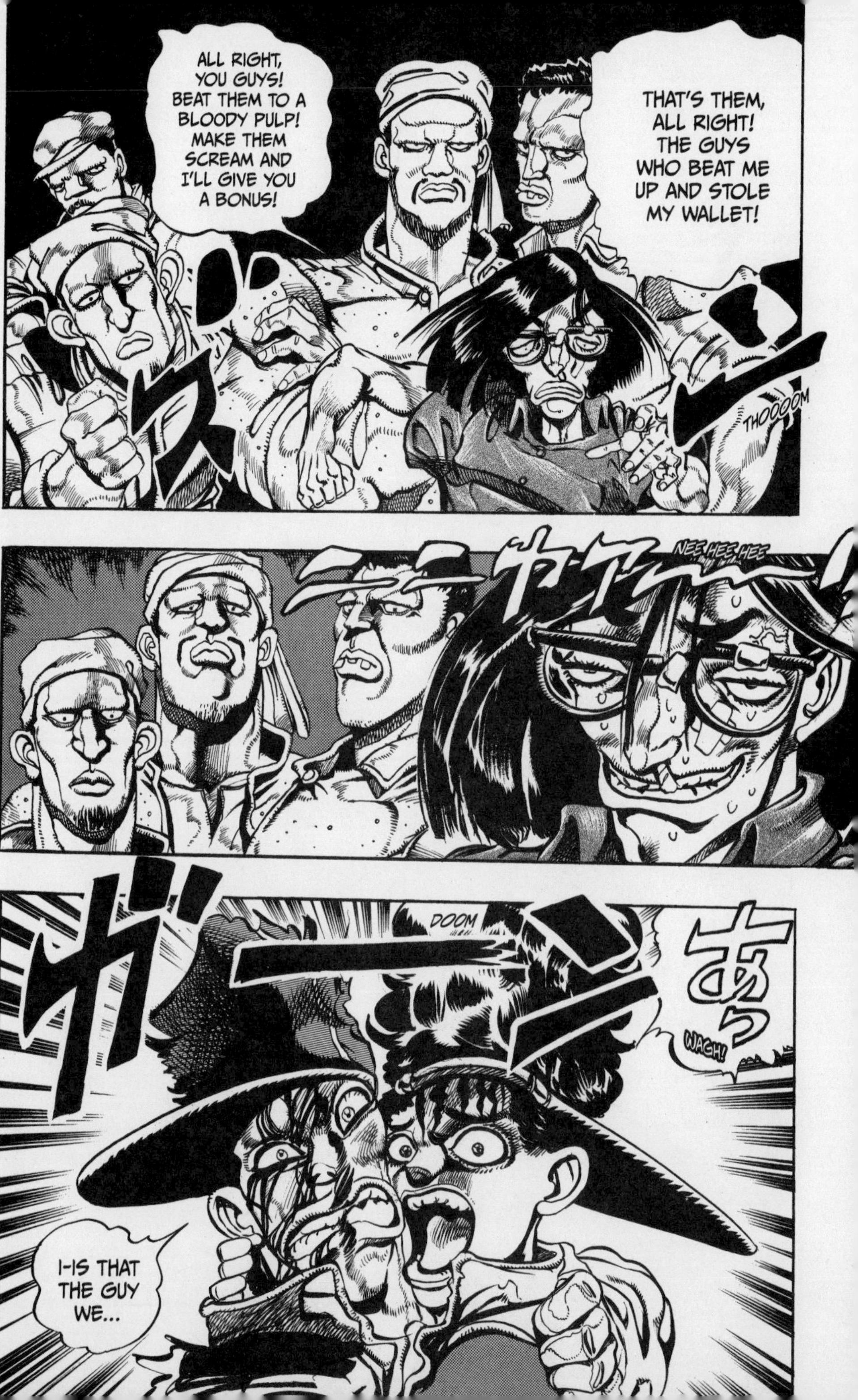
THAT'S THEM, ALL RIGHT! THE GUYS WHO BEAT ME UP AND STOLE MY WALLET!
ALL RIGHT, YOU GUYS! BEAT THEM TO A BLOODY PULP! MAKE THEM SCREAM AND I'LL GIVE YOU A BONUS!
THOOOOM
NEE HEE HEE
WACH!
DOOM
I-IS THAT THE GUY WE...

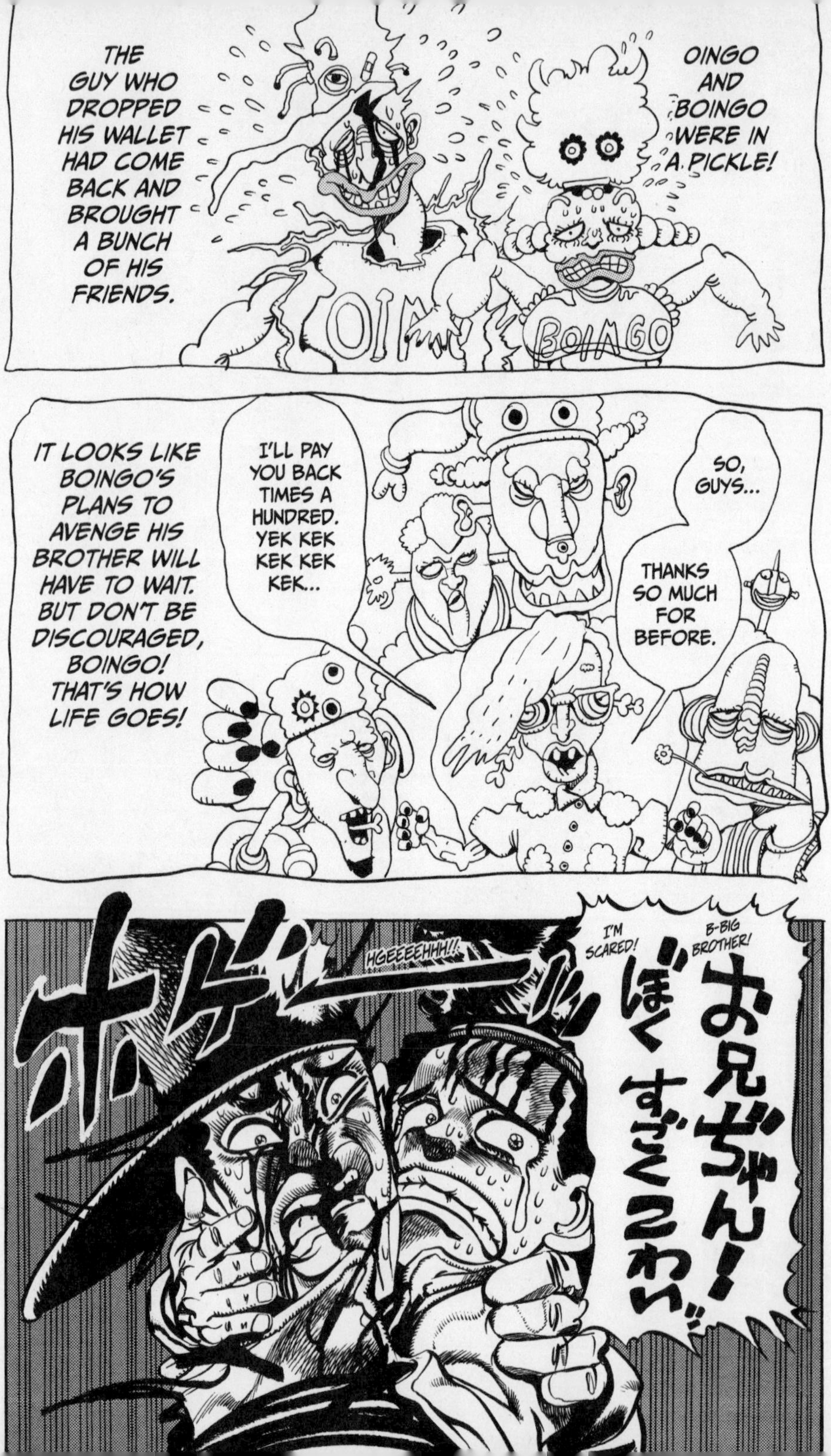
OINGO AND BOINGO WERE IN A PICKLE!
THE GUY WHO DROPPED HIS WALLET HAD COME BACK AND BROUGHT A BUNCH OF HIS FRIENDS.
BOINGO
SO, GUYS...
THANKS SO MUCH FOR BEFORE.
I'LL PAY YOU BACK TIMES A HUNDRED. YEK KEK KEK KEK KEK...
IT LOOKS LIKE BOINGO'S PLANS TO AVENGE HIS BROTHER WILL HAVE TO WAIT. BUT DON'T BE DISCOURAGED, BOINGO! THAT'S HOW LIFE GOES!
お兄ぢゃん！
B-BIG BROTHER!
ぼく すごくこわい
I'M SCARED!
ホゲー
HGEEEEEHHH!!

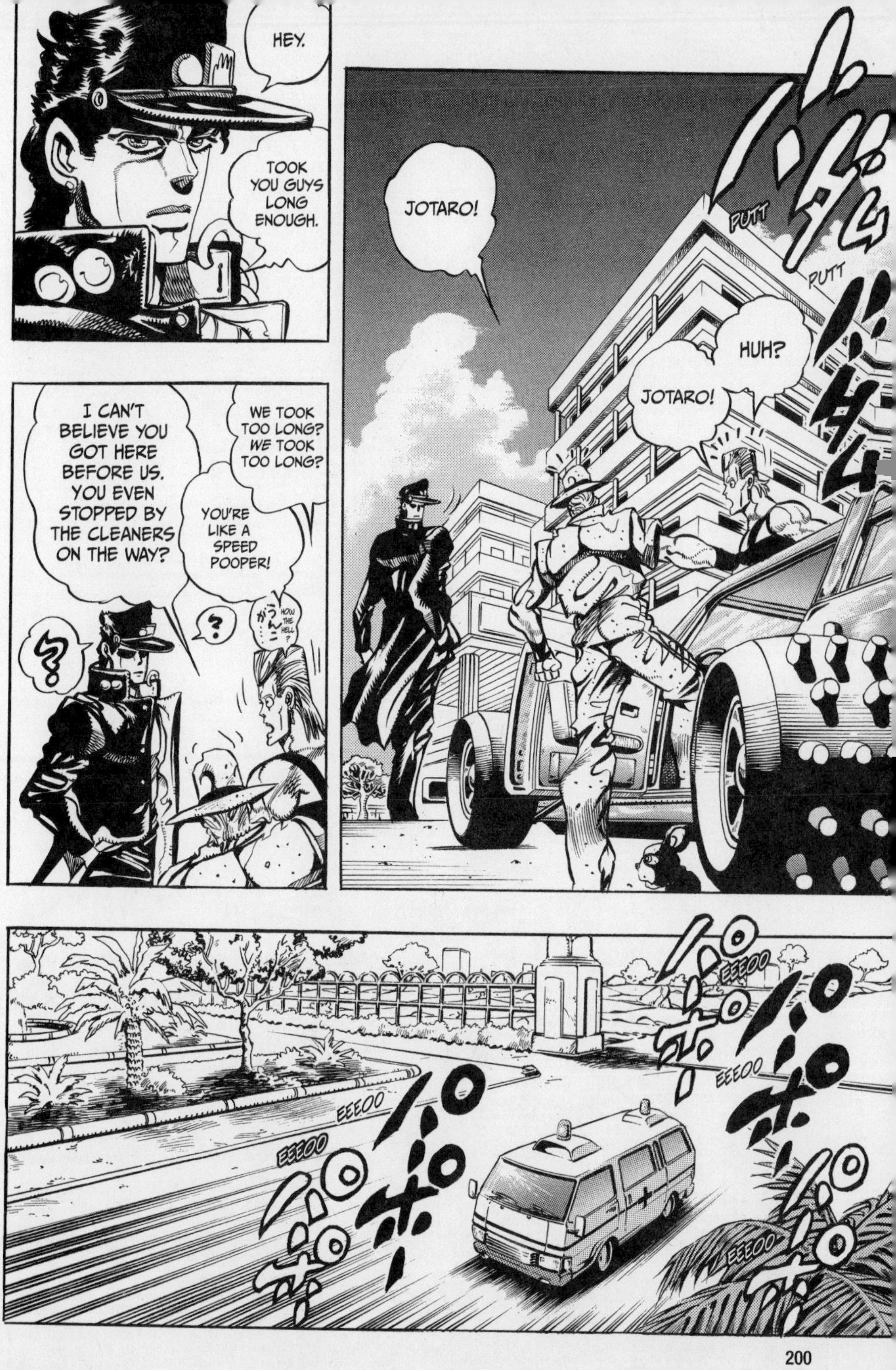
PUTT
PUTT
JOTARO!
HUH?
JOTARO!
HEY.
TOOK YOU GUYS LONG ENOUGH.
WE TOOK TOO LONG? WE TOOK TOO LONG?
YOU'RE LIKE A SPEED POOPER!
I CAN'T BELIEVE YOU GOT HERE BEFORE US. YOU EVEN STOPPED BY THE CLEANERS ON THE WAY?
HOW THE HELL?
?
?
EEEOO
EEEOO
EEEOO
EEEOO
EEEOO

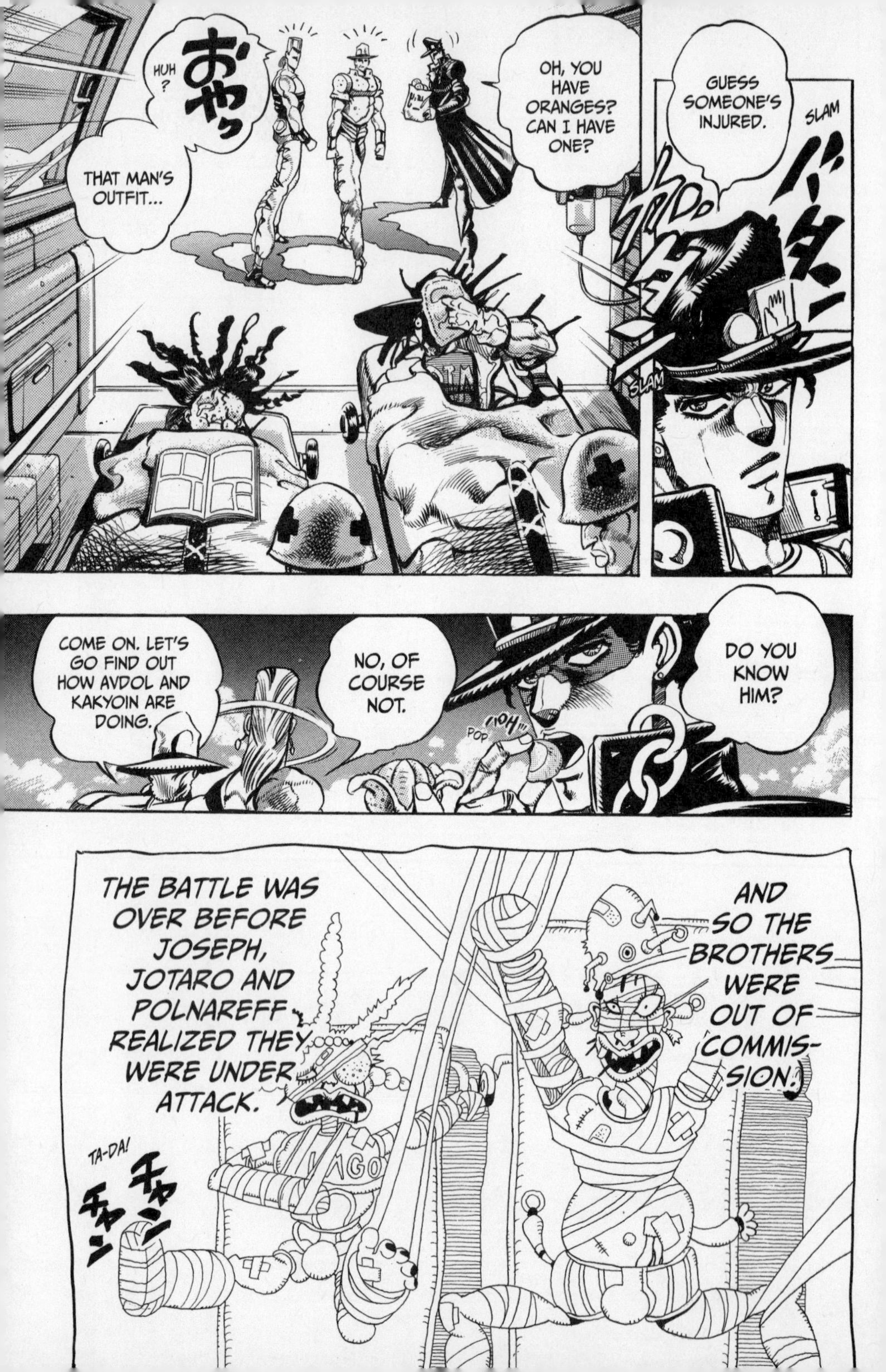
GUESS SOMEONE'S INJURED.
SLAM
バタン
SLAM
OH, YOU HAVE ORANGES? CAN I HAVE ONE?
おやっ
HUH?
THAT MAN'S OUTFIT...
DO YOU KNOW HIM?
POP
NO, OF COURSE NOT.
COME ON. LET'S GO FIND OUT HOW AVDOL AND KAKYOIN ARE DOING.
AND SO THE BROTHERS WERE OUT OF COMMISSION.
THE BATTLE WAS OVER BEFORE JOSEPH, JOTARO AND POLNAREFF REALIZED THEY WERE UNDER ATTACK.
TA-DA!
チャン チャン

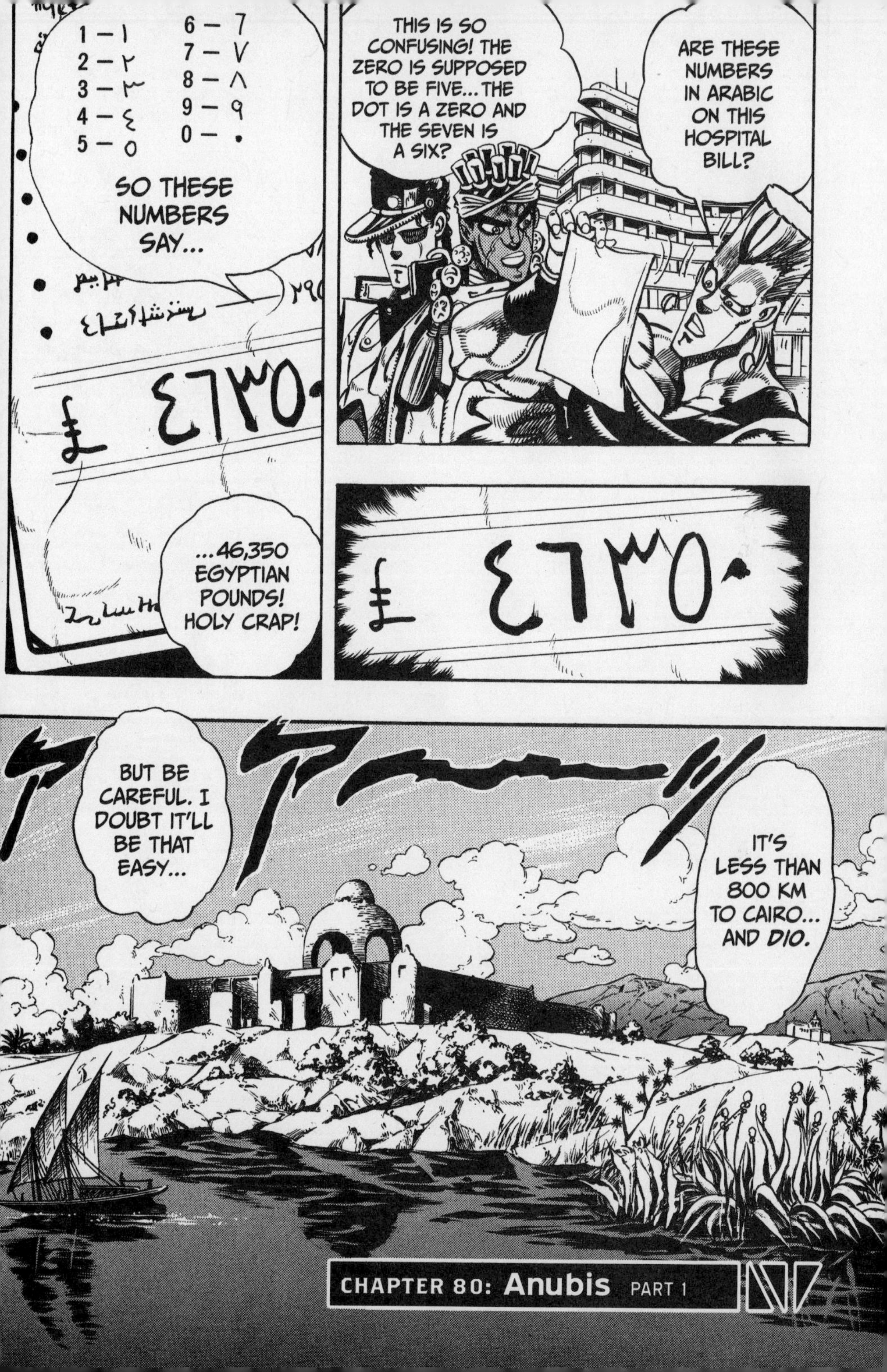

ARE THESE NUMBERS IN ARABIC ON THIS HOSPITAL BILL?
THIS IS SO CONFUSING! THE ZERO IS SUPPOSED TO BE FIVE... THE DOT IS A ZERO AND THE SEVEN IS A SIX?
£ ٤٦٣٥٠
1 — ١
2 — ٢
3 — ٣
4 — ٤
5 — ٥
6 — ٦
7 — ٧
8 — ٨
9 — ٩
0 — ٠
SO THESE NUMBERS SAY...
£ ٤٦٣٥٠
...46,350 EGYPTIAN POUNDS! HOLY CRAP!
アアーッ
IT'S LESS THAN 800 KM TO CAIRO... AND *DIO*.
BUT BE CAREFUL. I DOUBT IT'LL BE THAT EASY...
CHAPTER 80: Anubis PART 1

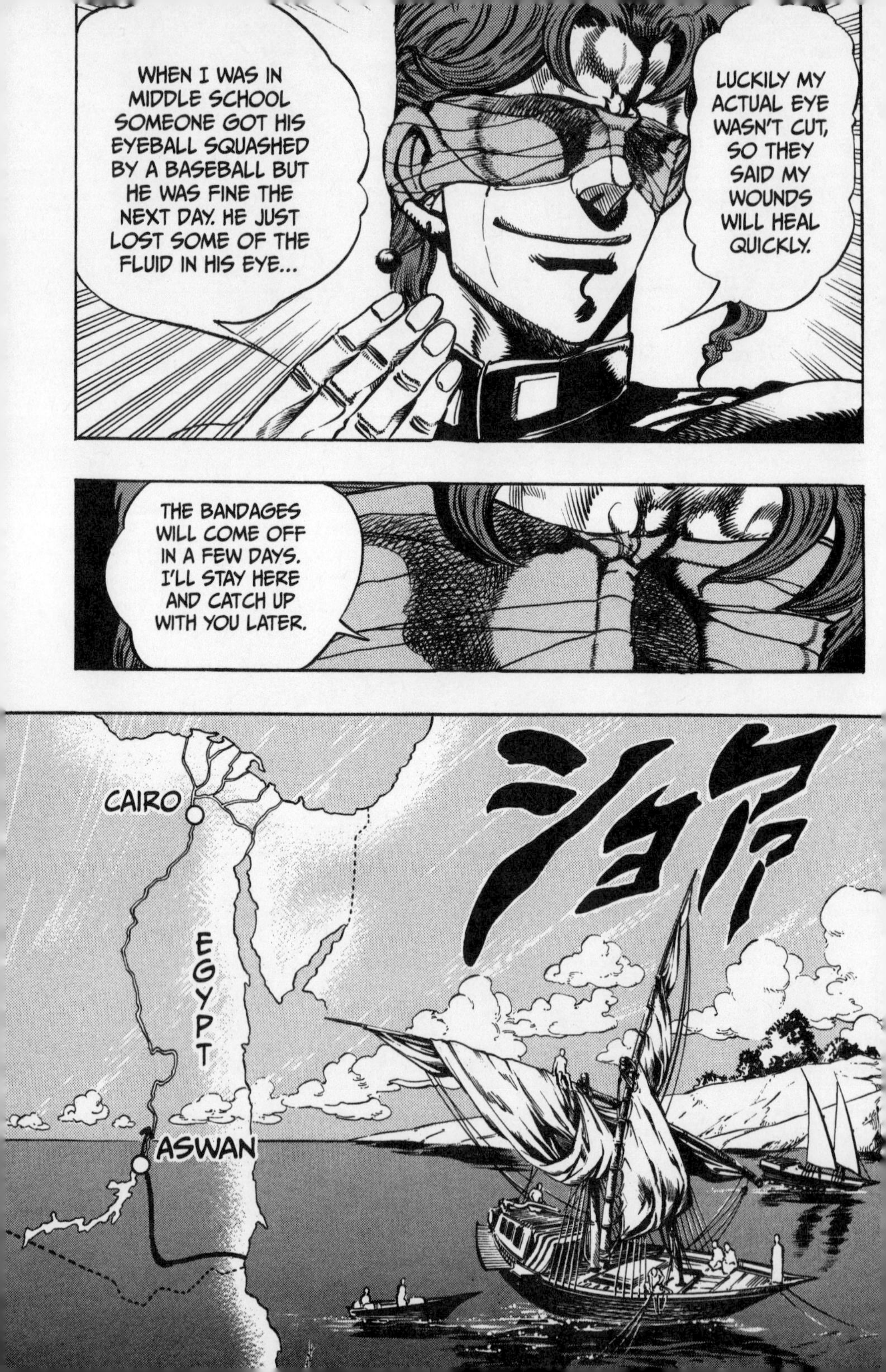

LUCKILY MY ACTUAL EYE WASN'T CUT, SO THEY SAID MY WOUNDS WILL HEAL QUICKLY.
WHEN I WAS IN MIDDLE SCHOOL SOMEONE GOT HIS EYEBALL SQUASHED BY A BASEBALL BUT HE WAS FINE THE NEXT DAY. HE JUST LOST SOME OF THE FLUID IN HIS EYE...
THE BANDAGES WILL COME OFF IN A FEW DAYS. I'LL STAY HERE AND CATCH UP WITH YOU LATER.
ショァ
CAIRO
EGYPT
ASWAN

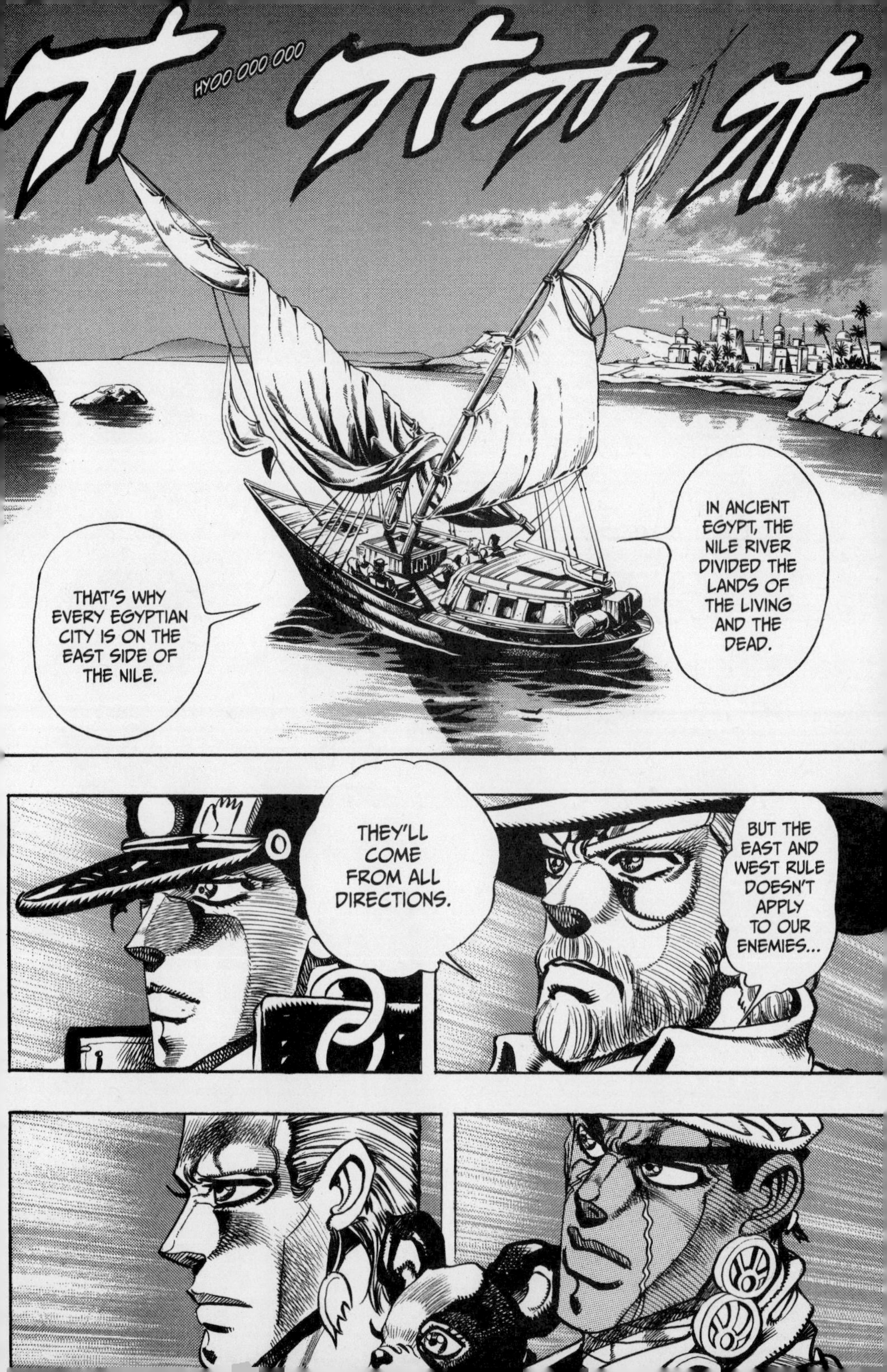
HYOO OOO OOO
IN ANCIENT EGYPT, THE NILE RIVER DIVIDED THE LANDS OF THE LIVING AND THE DEAD.
THAT'S WHY EVERY EGYPTIAN CITY IS ON THE EAST SIDE OF THE NILE.
BUT THE EAST AND WEST RULE DOESN'T APPLY TO OUR ENEMIES...
THEY'LL COME FROM ALL DIRECTIONS.

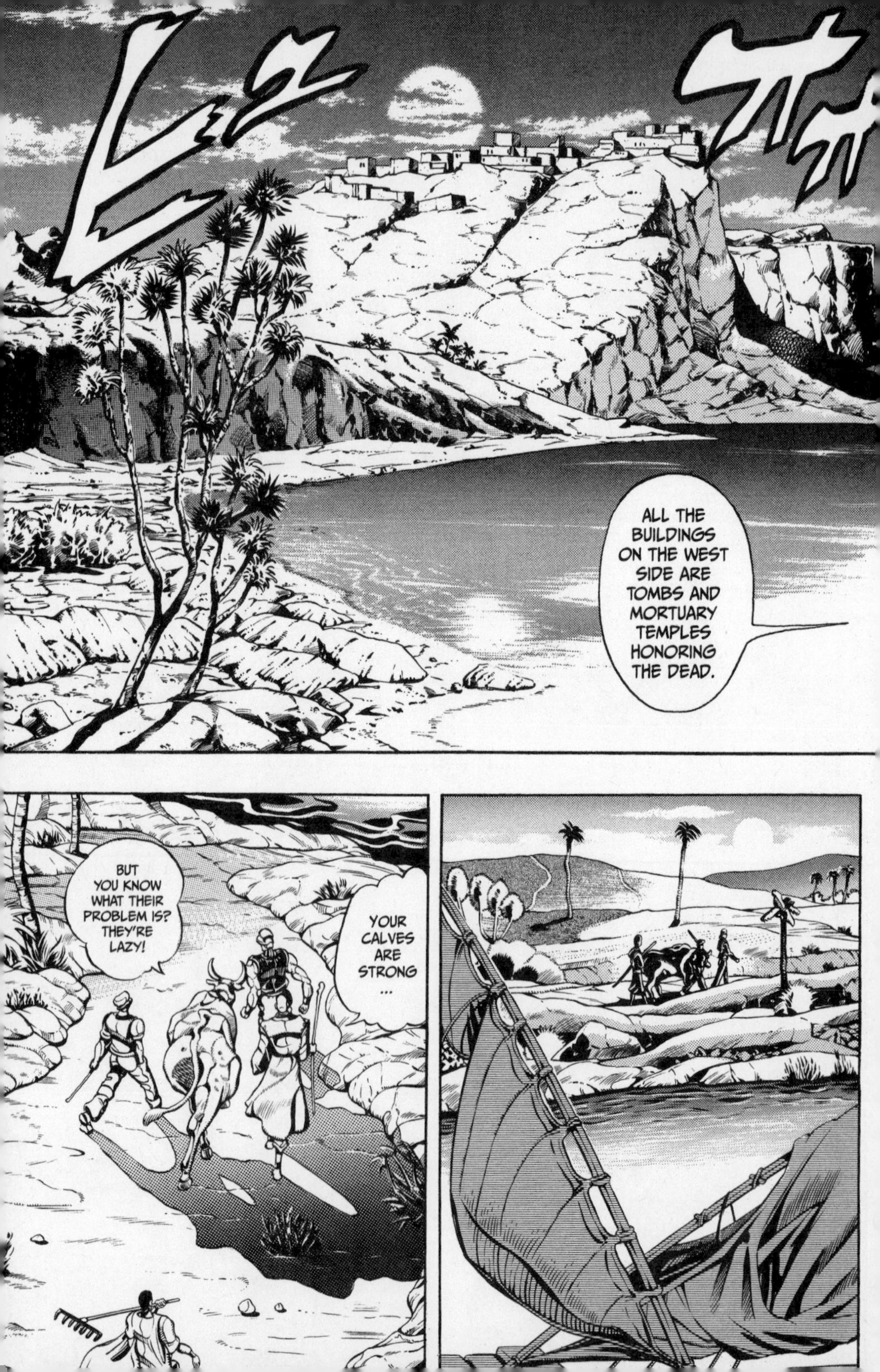
ALL THE BUILDINGS ON THE WEST SIDE ARE TOMBS AND MORTUARY TEMPLES HONORING THE DEAD.
YOUR CALVES ARE STRONG ...
BUT YOU KNOW WHAT THEIR PROBLEM IS? THEY'RE LAZY!

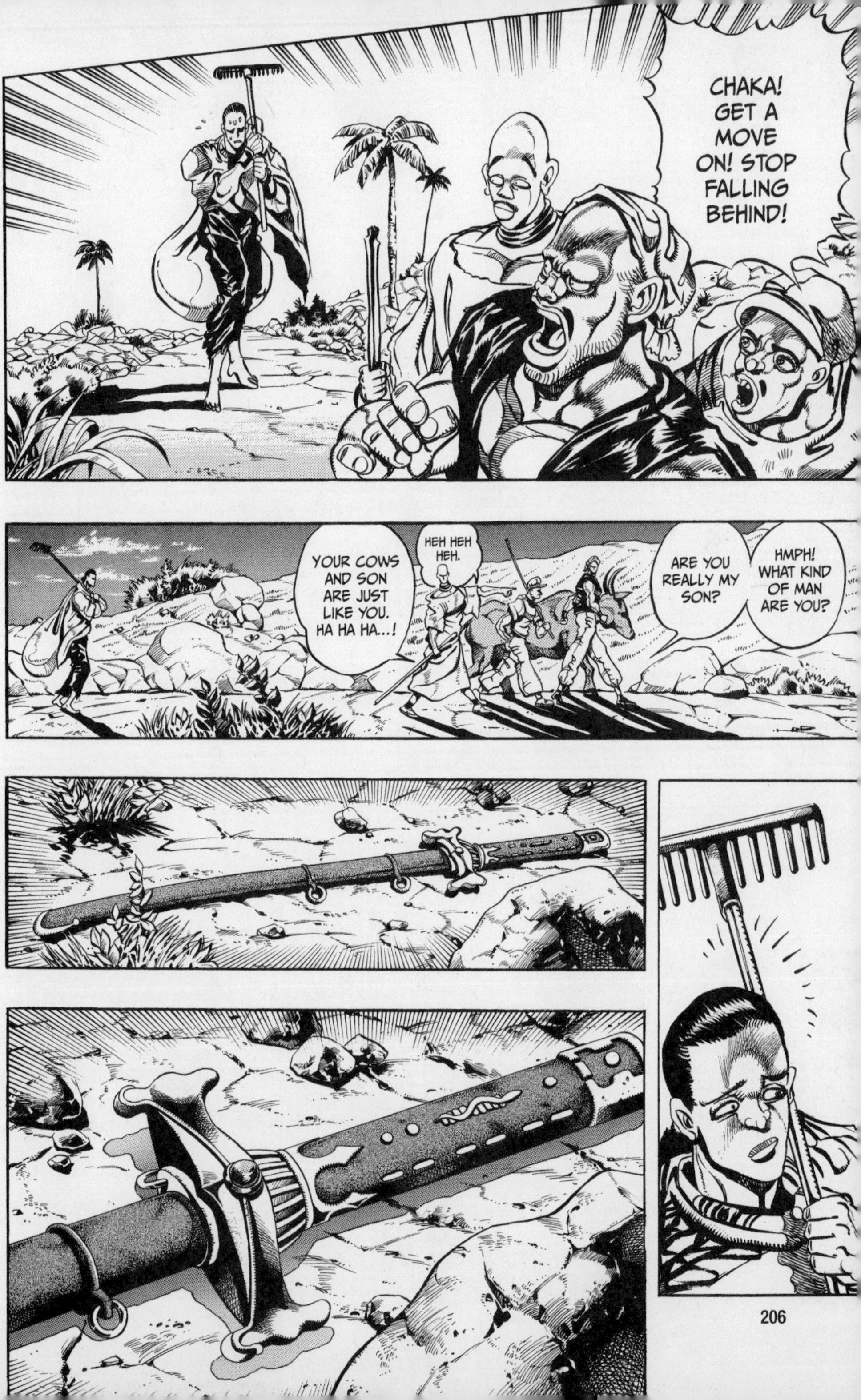
CHAKA! GET A MOVE ON! STOP FALLING BEHIND!
HMPH! WHAT KIND OF MAN ARE YOU?
ARE YOU REALLY MY SON?
HEH HEH HEH.
YOUR COWS AND SON ARE JUST LIKE YOU. HA HA HA...!

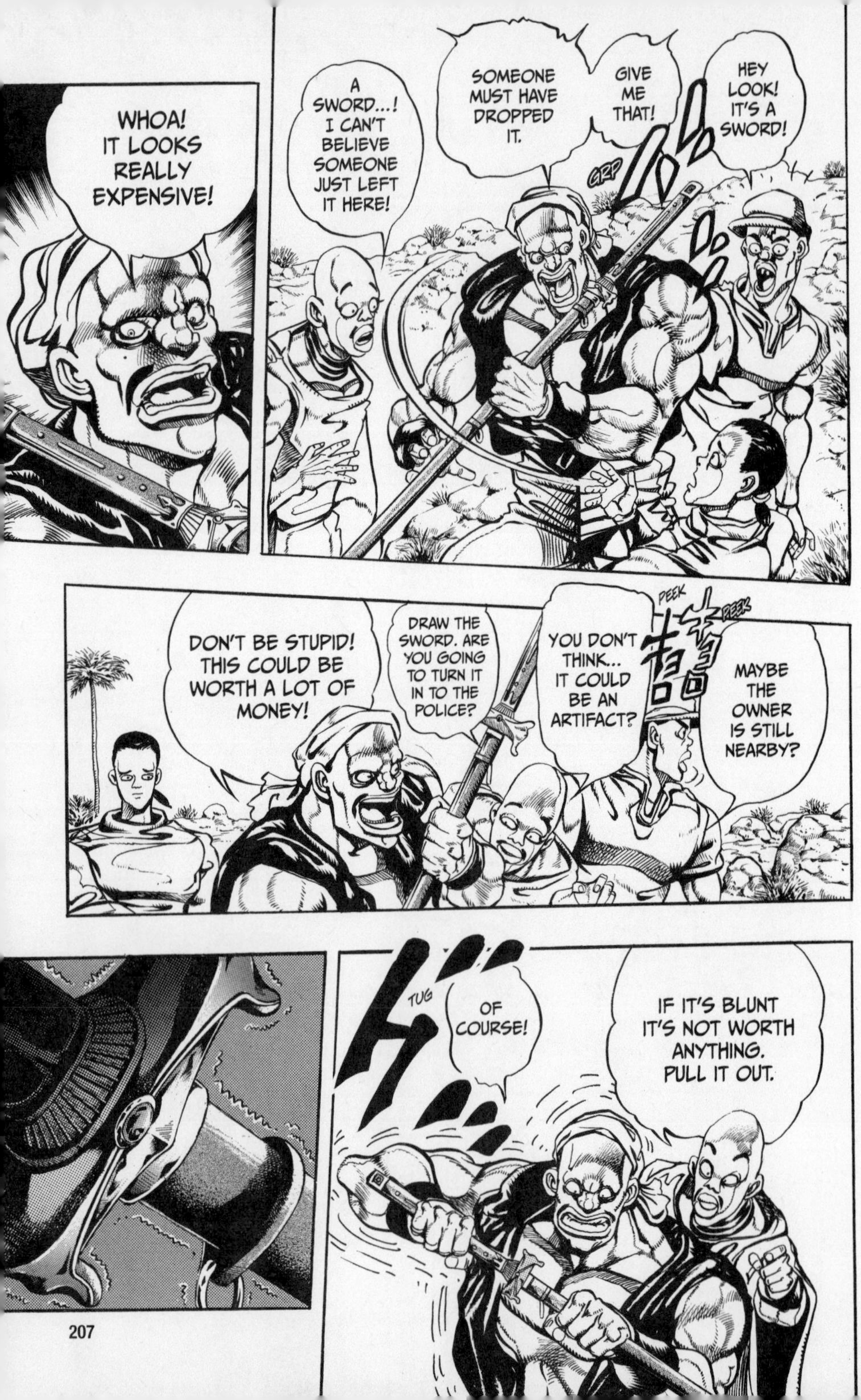
HEY LOOK! IT'S A SWORD!
GIVE ME THAT!
GRP
SOMEONE MUST HAVE DROPPED IT.
A SWORD...! I CAN'T BELIEVE SOMEONE JUST LEFT IT HERE!
WHOA! IT LOOKS REALLY EXPENSIVE!
MAYBE THE OWNER IS STILL NEARBY?
PEEK
PEEK
YOU DON'T THINK... IT COULD BE AN ARTIFACT?
DRAW THE SWORD. ARE YOU GOING TO TURN IT IN TO THE POLICE?
DON'T BE STUPID! THIS COULD BE WORTH A LOT OF MONEY!
IF IT'S BLUNT IT'S NOT WORTH ANYTHING. PULL IT OUT.
OF COURSE!
TUG

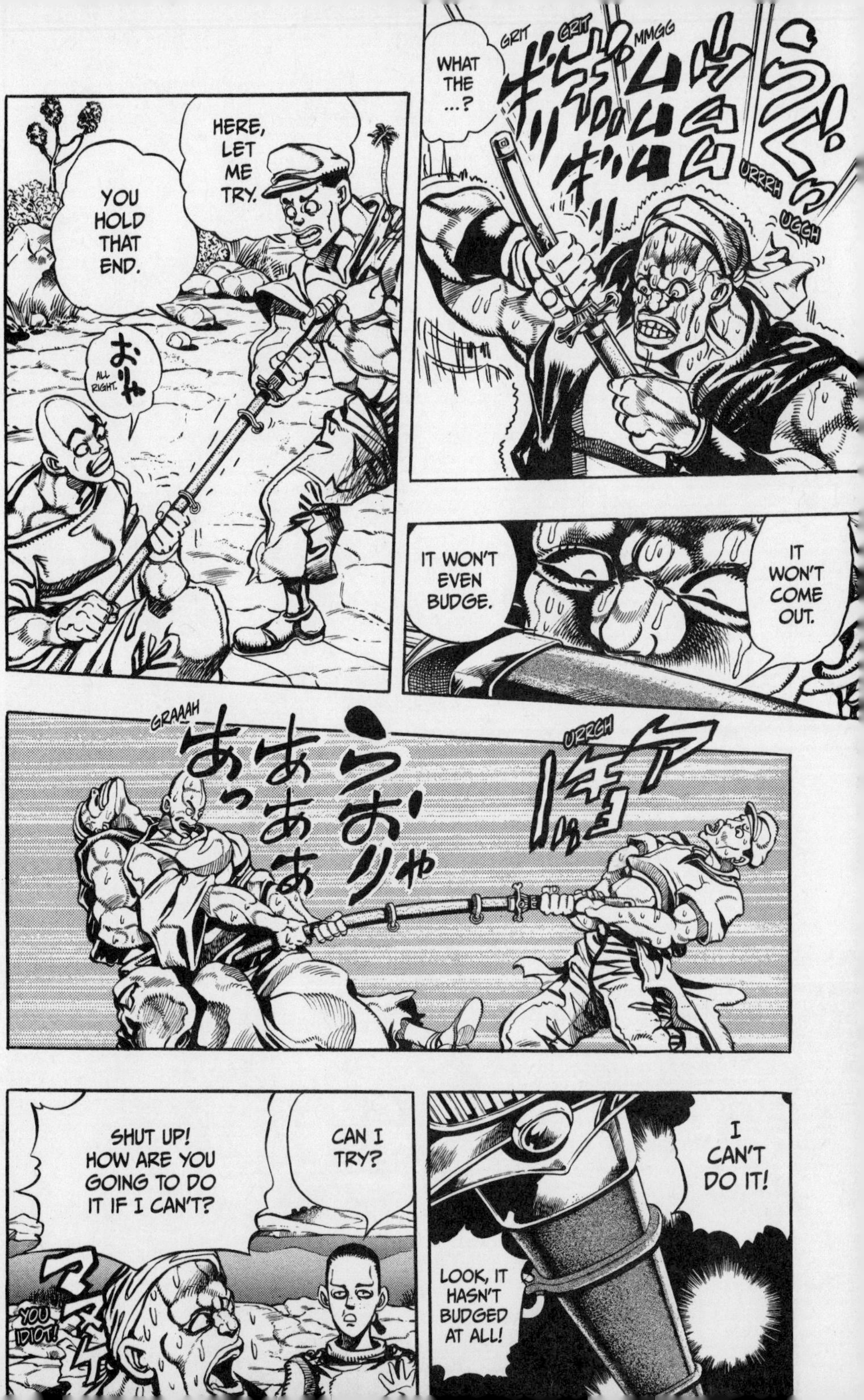
WHAT THE ...?
GRIT
GRIT
MMGG
URRRH
UGGH
IT WON'T COME OUT.
IT WON'T EVEN BUDGE.
HERE, LET ME TRY.
YOU HOLD THAT END.
ALL RIGHT.
URRGH
GRAAAH
I CAN'T DO IT!
LOOK, IT HASN'T BUDGED AT ALL!
CAN I TRY?
SHUT UP! HOW ARE YOU GOING TO DO IT IF I CAN'T?
YOU IDIOT!

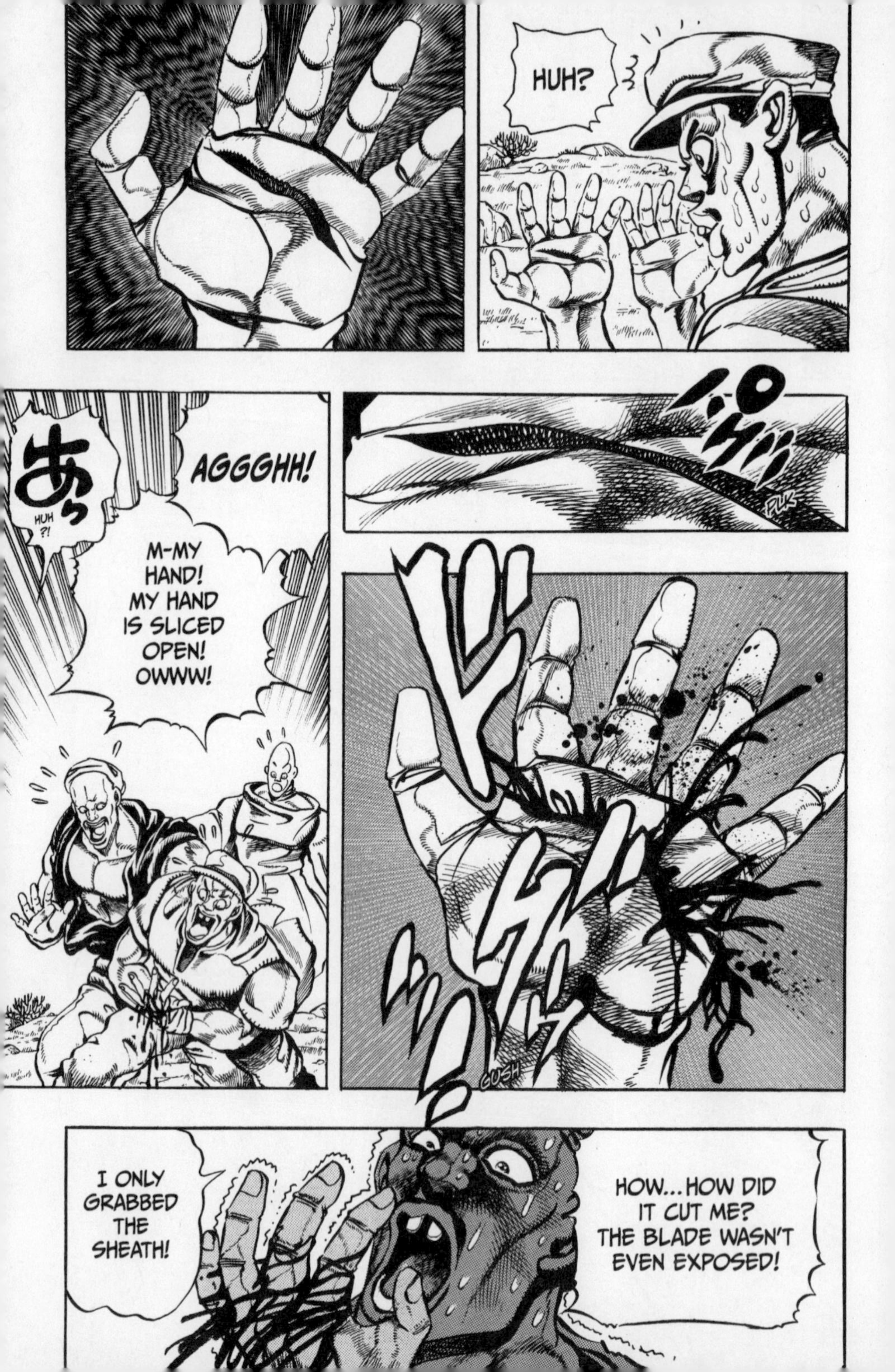
HUH?
PUK
GUSH
あっ
HUH?!
AGGGHH!
M-MY HAND! MY HAND IS SLICED OPEN! OWWW!
HOW...HOW DID IT CUT ME? THE BLADE WASN'T EVEN EXPOSED!
I ONLY GRABBED THE SHEATH!

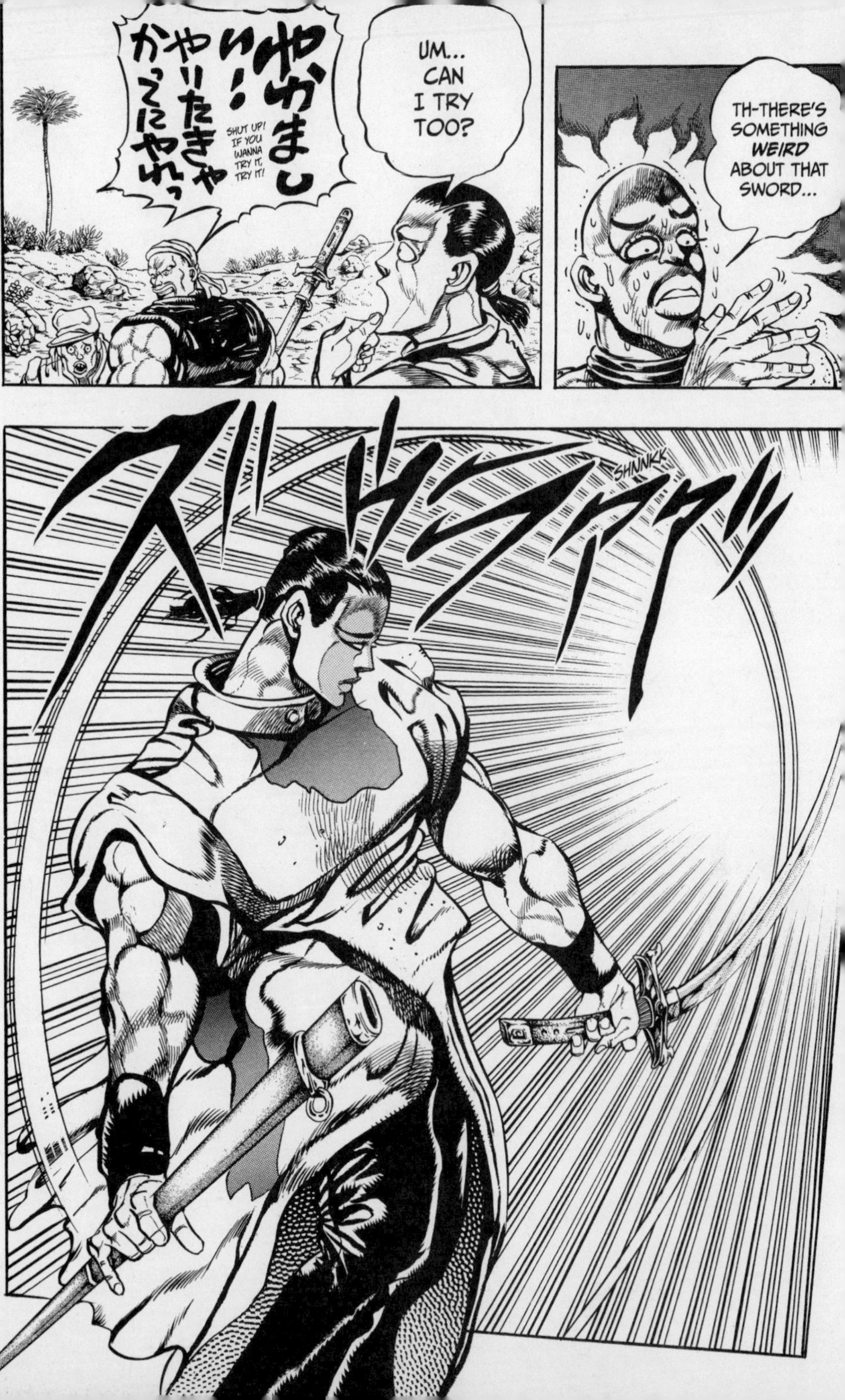
TH-THERE'S SOMETHING WEIRD ABOUT THAT SWORD...
UM... CAN I TRY TOO?
やかましい！やりたきゃかってにやれっ
SHUT UP! IF YOU WANNA TRY IT, TRY IT!
SHNNKK

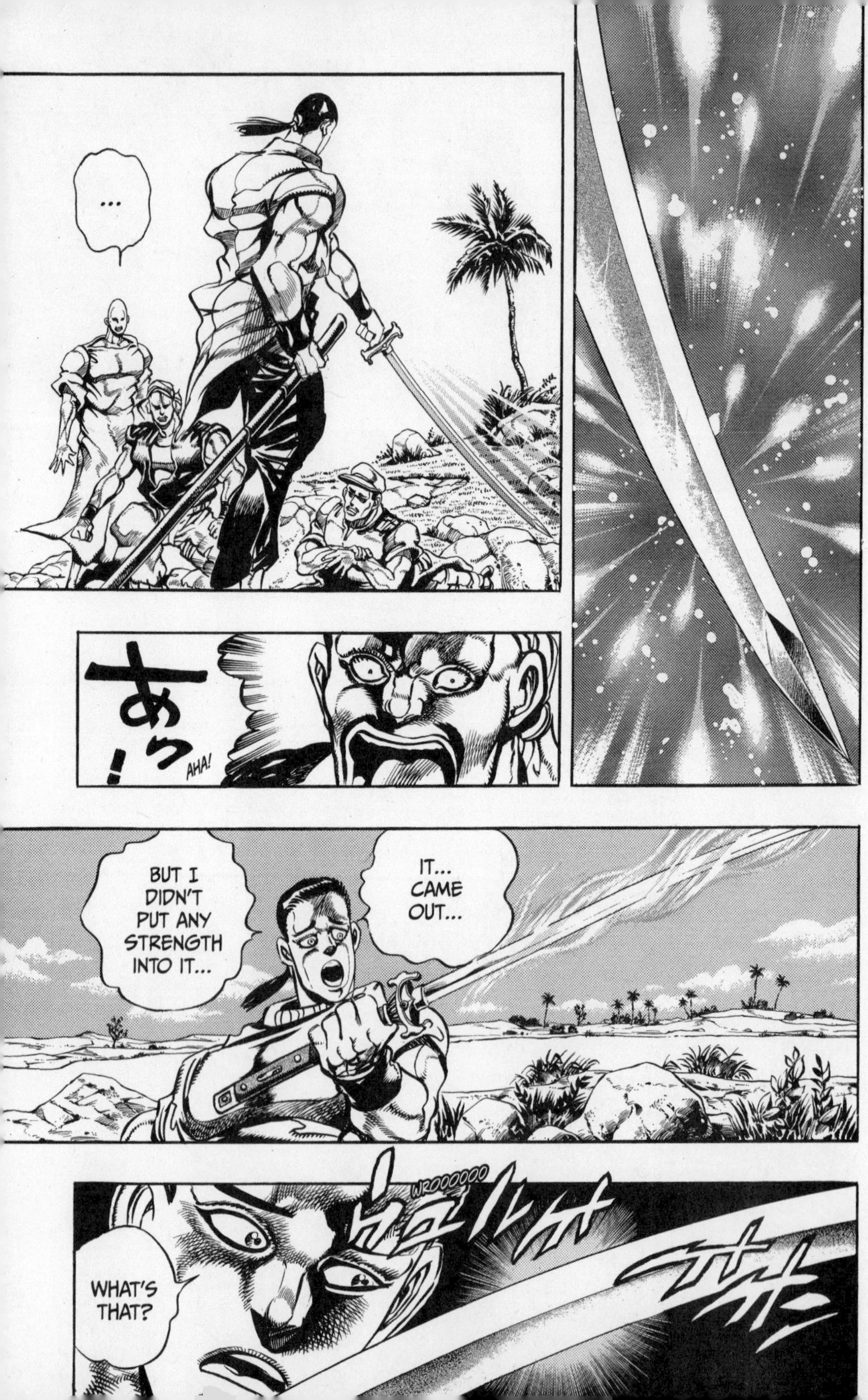
...
あっ!
AHA!
IT... CAME OUT...
BUT I DIDN'T PUT ANY STRENGTH INTO IT...
WROOOOOO
WHAT'S THAT?

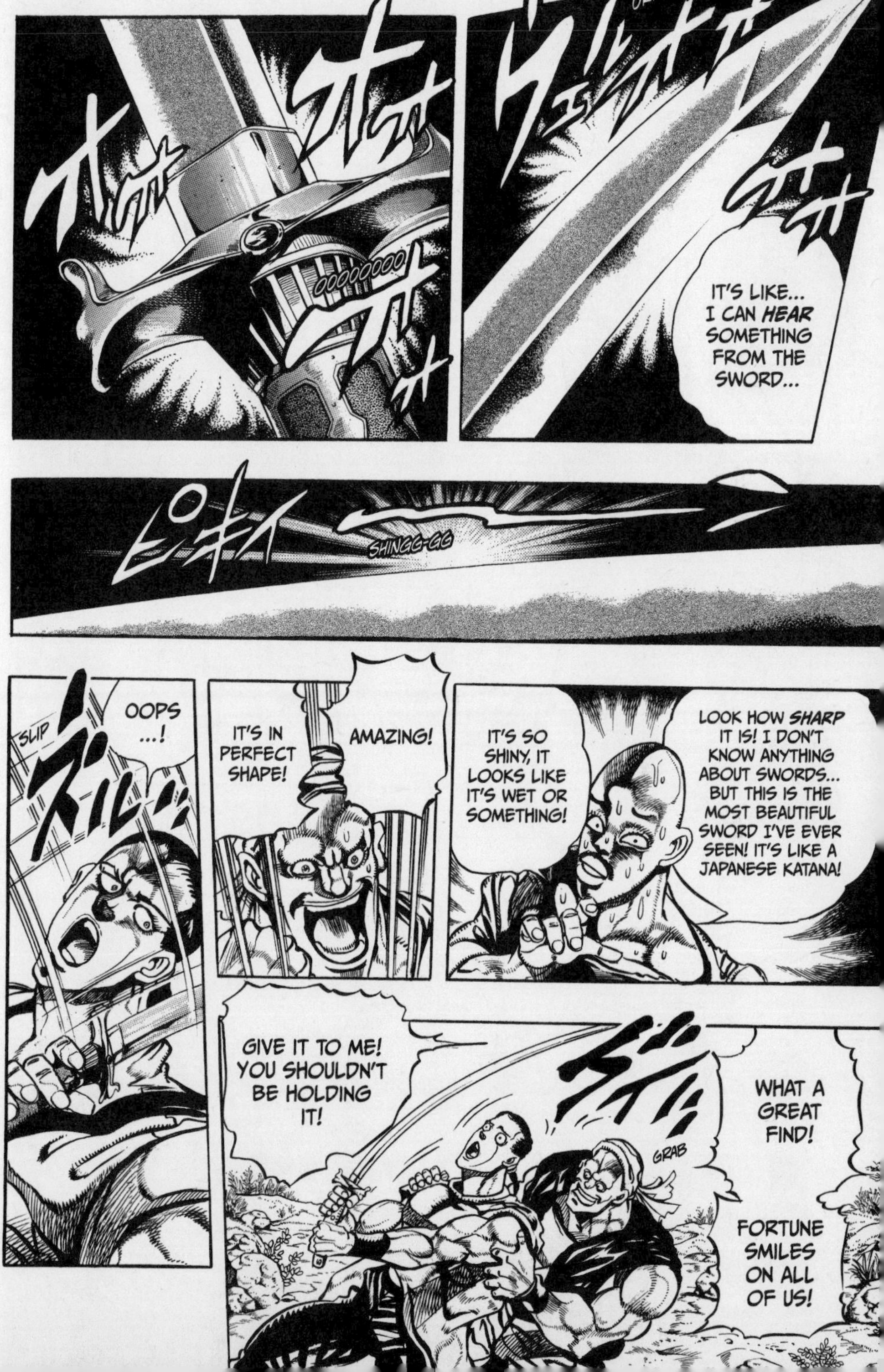
URROOO
IT'S LIKE... I CAN HEAR SOMETHING FROM THE SWORD...
OOOOOOOOO
SHINGG-GG
LOOK HOW SHARP IT IS! I DON'T KNOW ANYTHING ABOUT SWORDS... BUT THIS IS THE MOST BEAUTIFUL SWORD I'VE EVER SEEN! IT'S LIKE A JAPANESE KATANA!
IT'S SO SHINY, IT LOOKS LIKE IT'S WET OR SOMETHING!
AMAZING!
IT'S IN PERFECT SHAPE!
WHAT A GREAT FIND!
FORTUNE SMILES ON ALL OF US!
GRAB
GIVE IT TO ME! YOU SHOULDN'T BE HOLDING IT!
SLIP
OOPS ...!

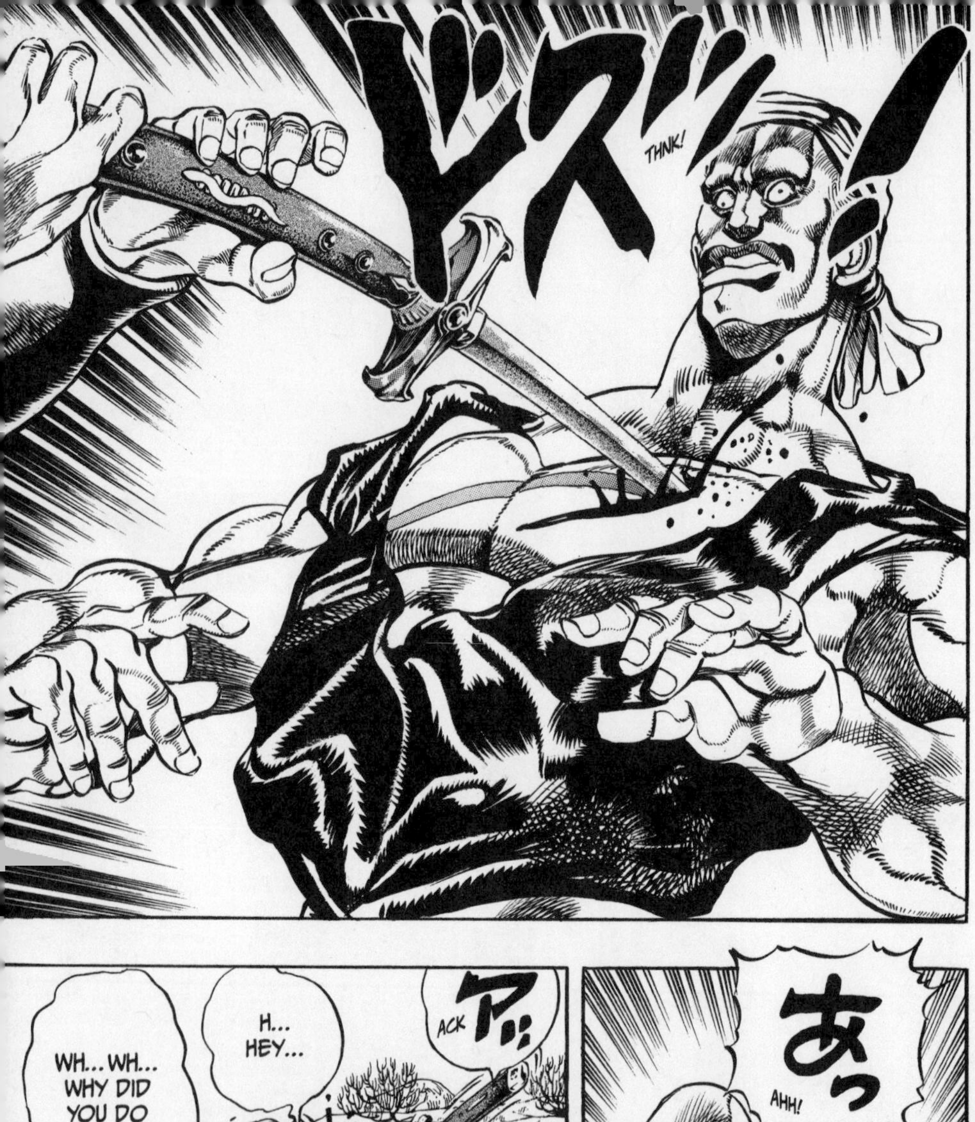
ドスッ
THNK!

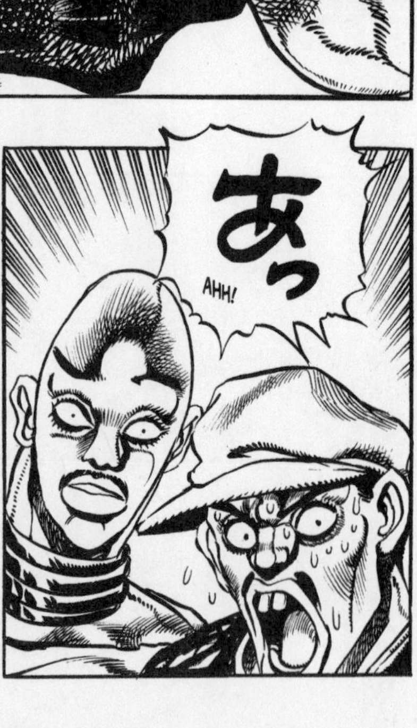
あっ
AHH!

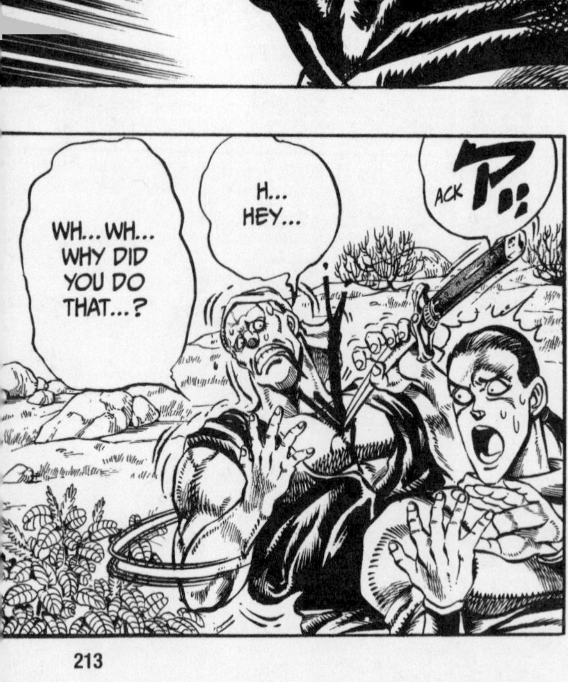
アッ
ACK
H... HEY...
WH... WH... WHY DID YOU DO THAT...?

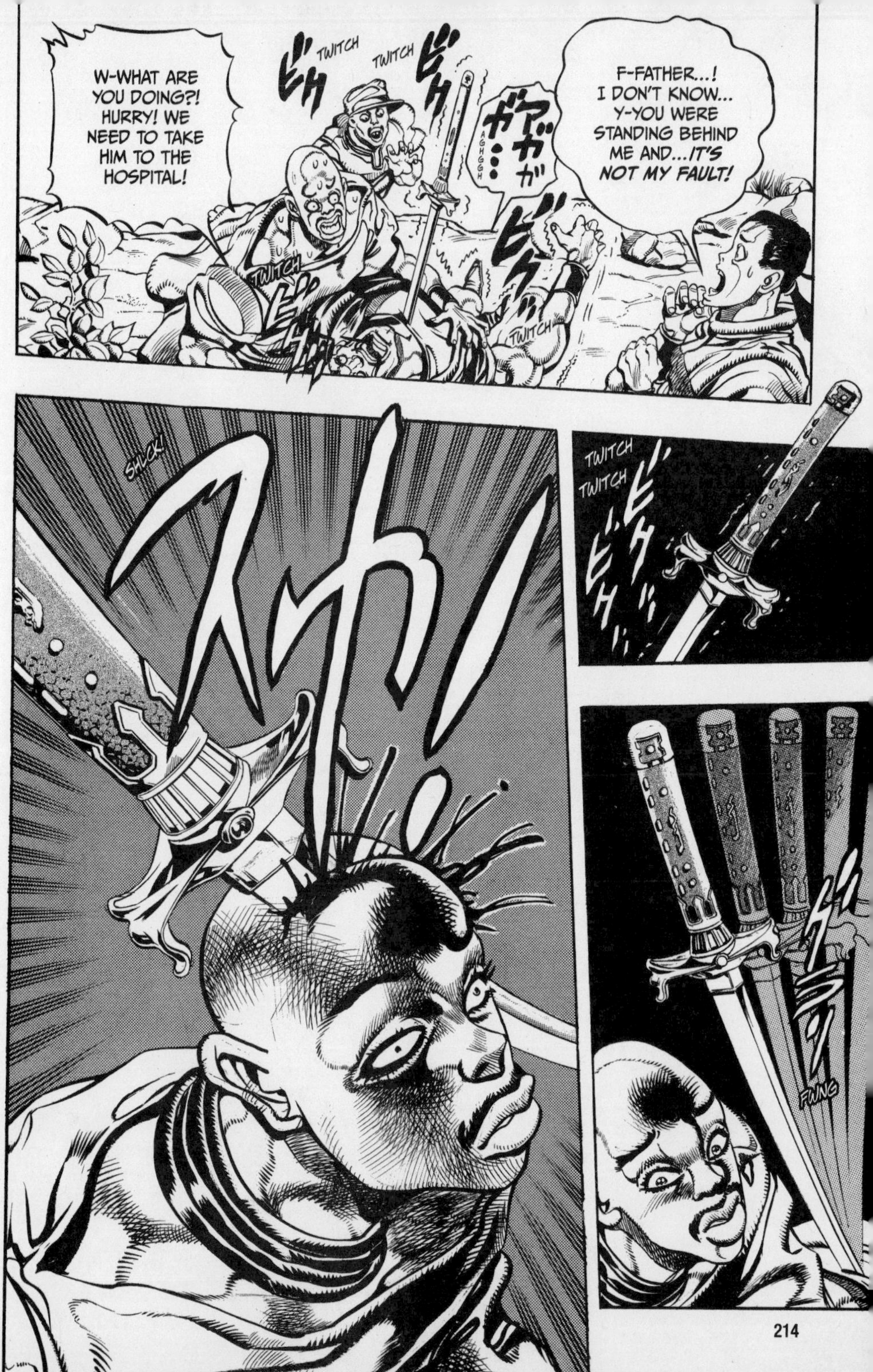
F-FATHER...! I DON'T KNOW... Y-YOU WERE STANDING BEHIND ME AND...*IT'S NOT MY FAULT!*
TWITCH
TWITCH
AGHGH
TWITCH
TWITCH
W-WHAT ARE YOU DOING?! HURRY! WE NEED TO TAKE HIM TO THE HOSPITAL!
TWITCH
TWITCH
FWING
SHLCK!

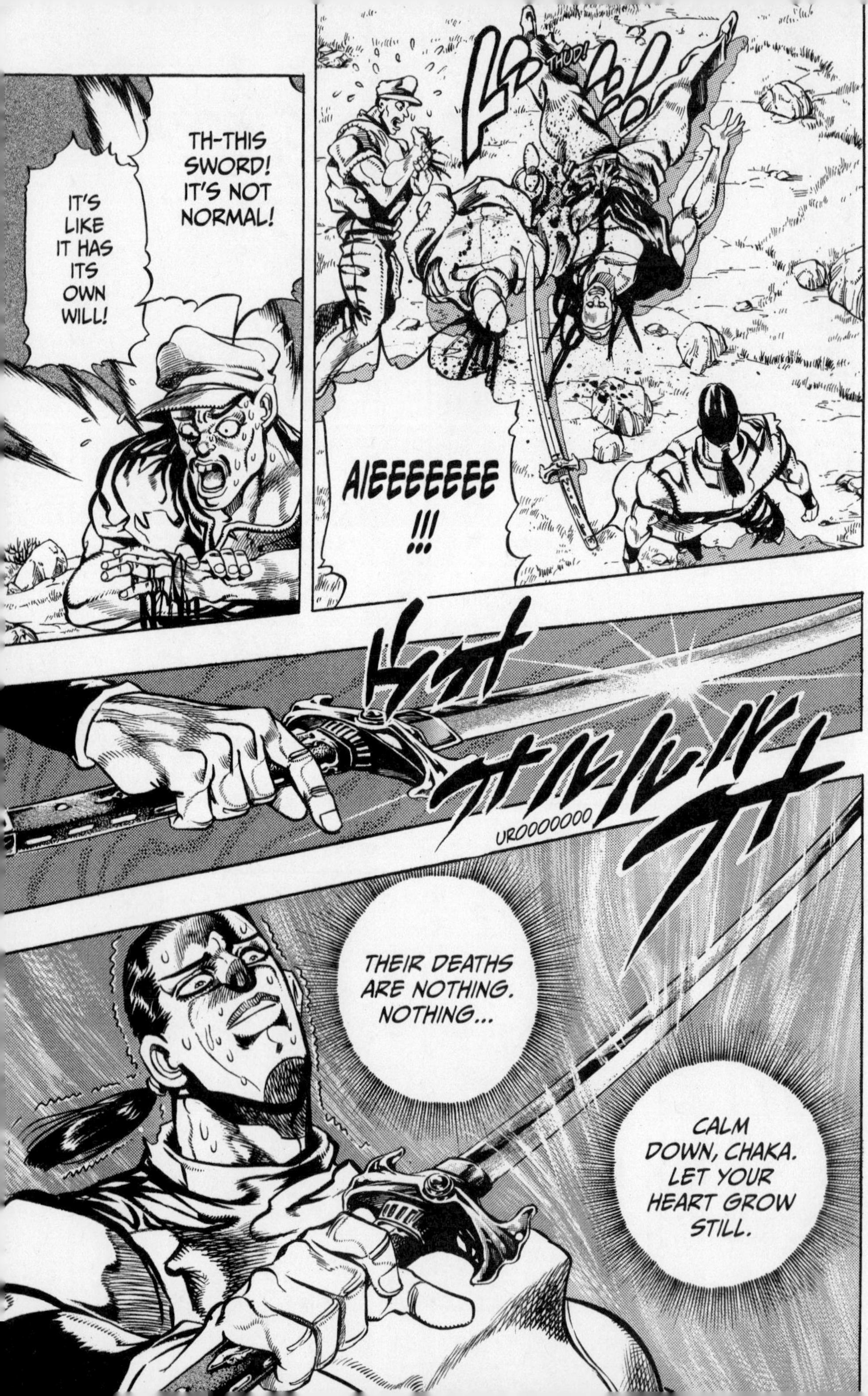
THUD!
AIEEEEEEE!!!
TH-THIS SWORD! IT'S NOT NORMAL!
IT'S LIKE IT HAS ITS OWN WILL!
UROOOOOOO
THEIR DEATHS ARE NOTHING. NOTHING...
CALM DOWN, CHAKA. LET YOUR HEART GROW STILL.

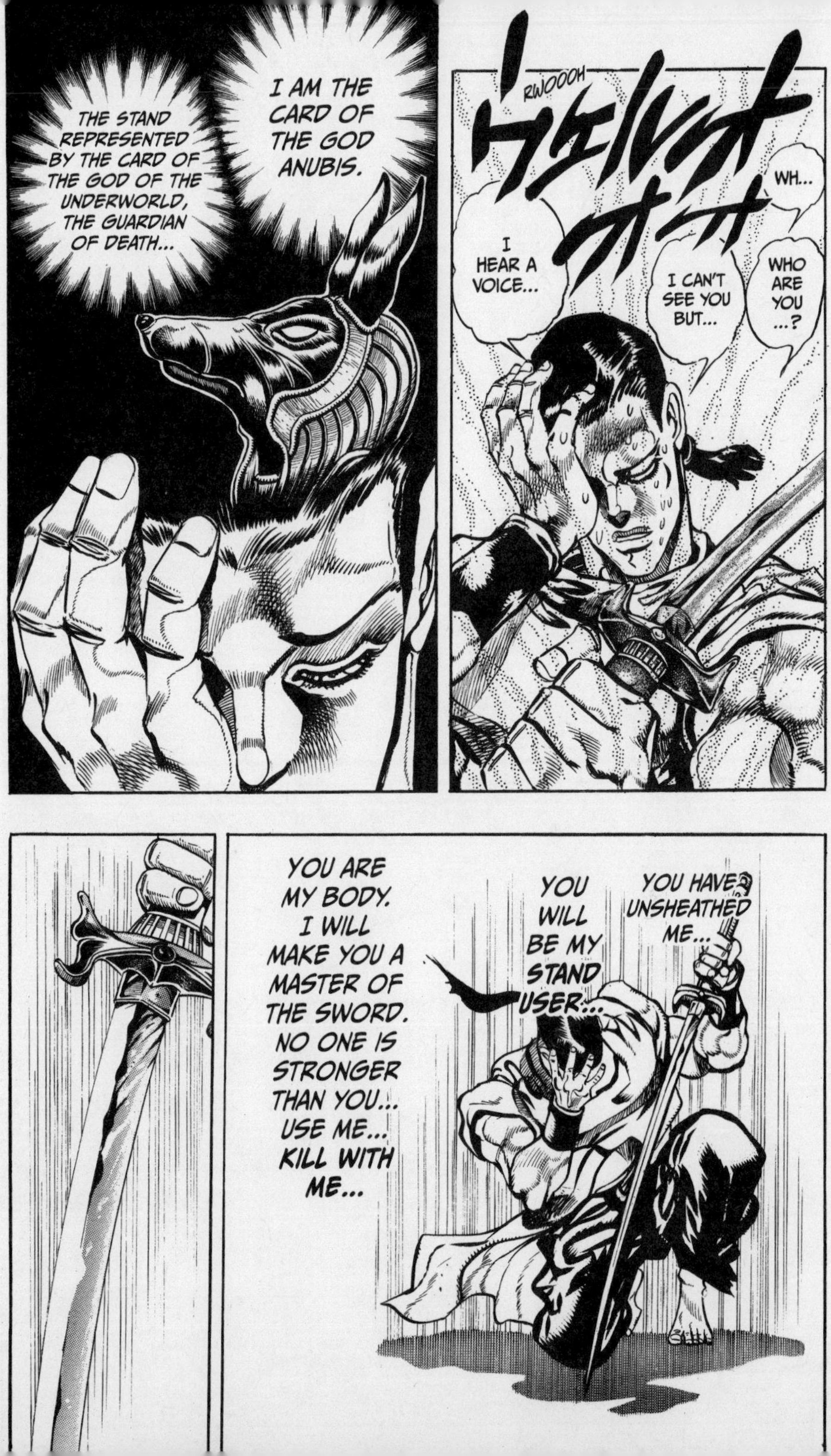
RWOOOH
WH...
I HEAR A VOICE...
I CAN'T SEE YOU BUT...
WHO ARE YOU ...?
I AM THE CARD OF THE GOD ANUBIS.
THE STAND REPRESENTED BY THE CARD OF THE GOD OF THE UNDERWORLD, THE GUARDIAN OF DEATH...
YOU HAVE UNSHEATHED ME...
YOU WILL BE MY STAND USER...
YOU ARE MY BODY. I WILL MAKE YOU A MASTER OF THE SWORD. NO ONE IS STRONGER THAN YOU... USE ME... KILL WITH ME...

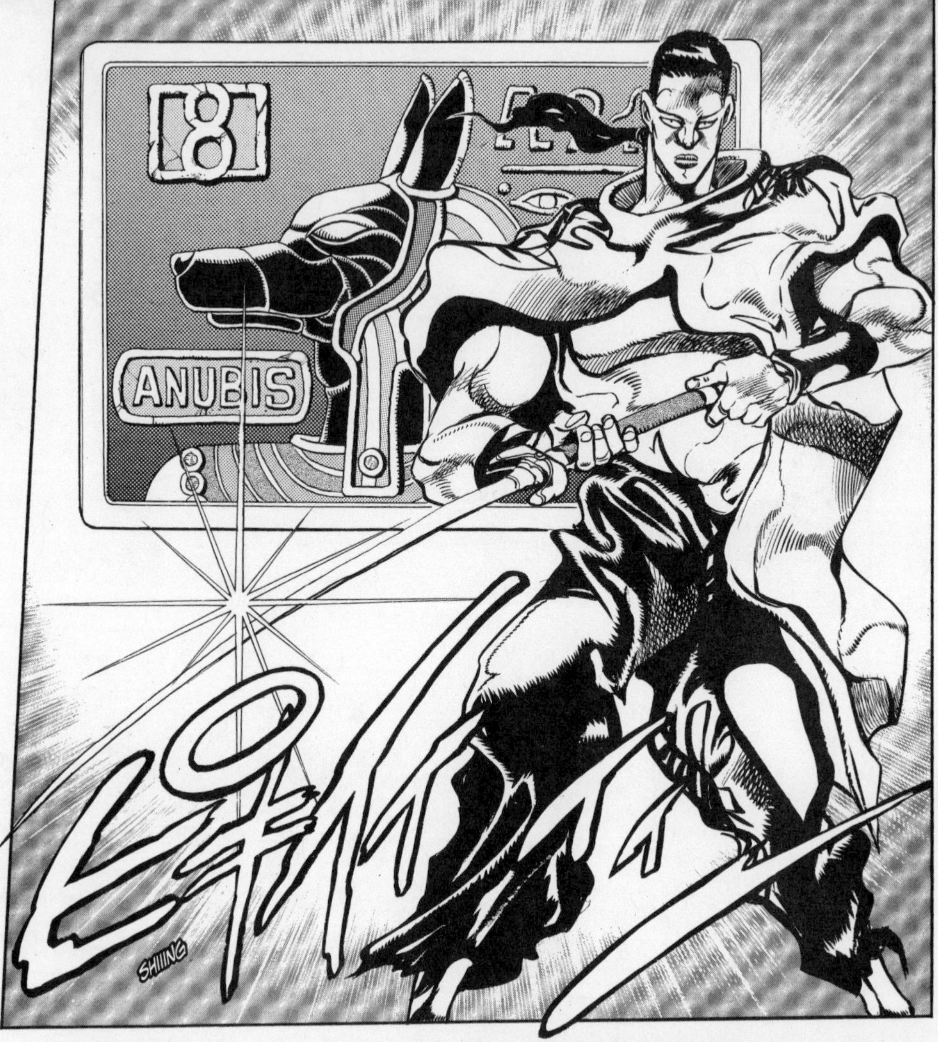
ANUBIS
SHIIING

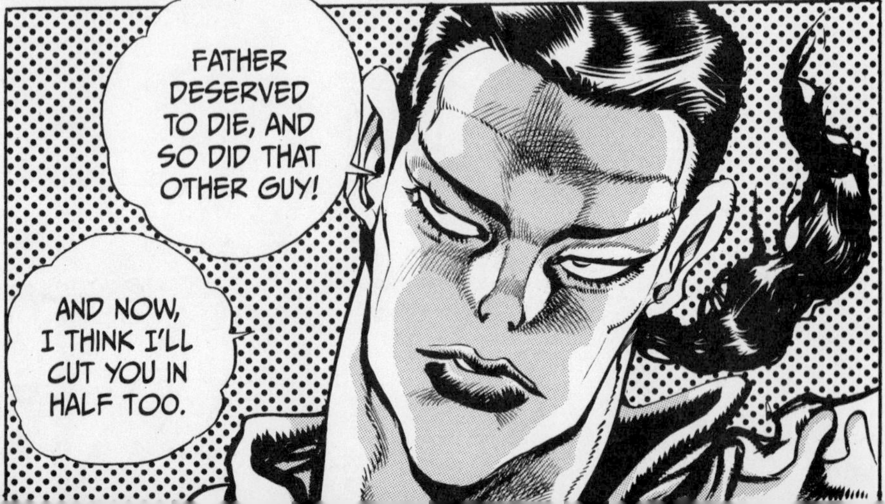
FATHER DESERVED TO DIE, AND SO DID THAT OTHER GUY!
AND NOW, I THINK I'LL CUT YOU IN HALF TOO.

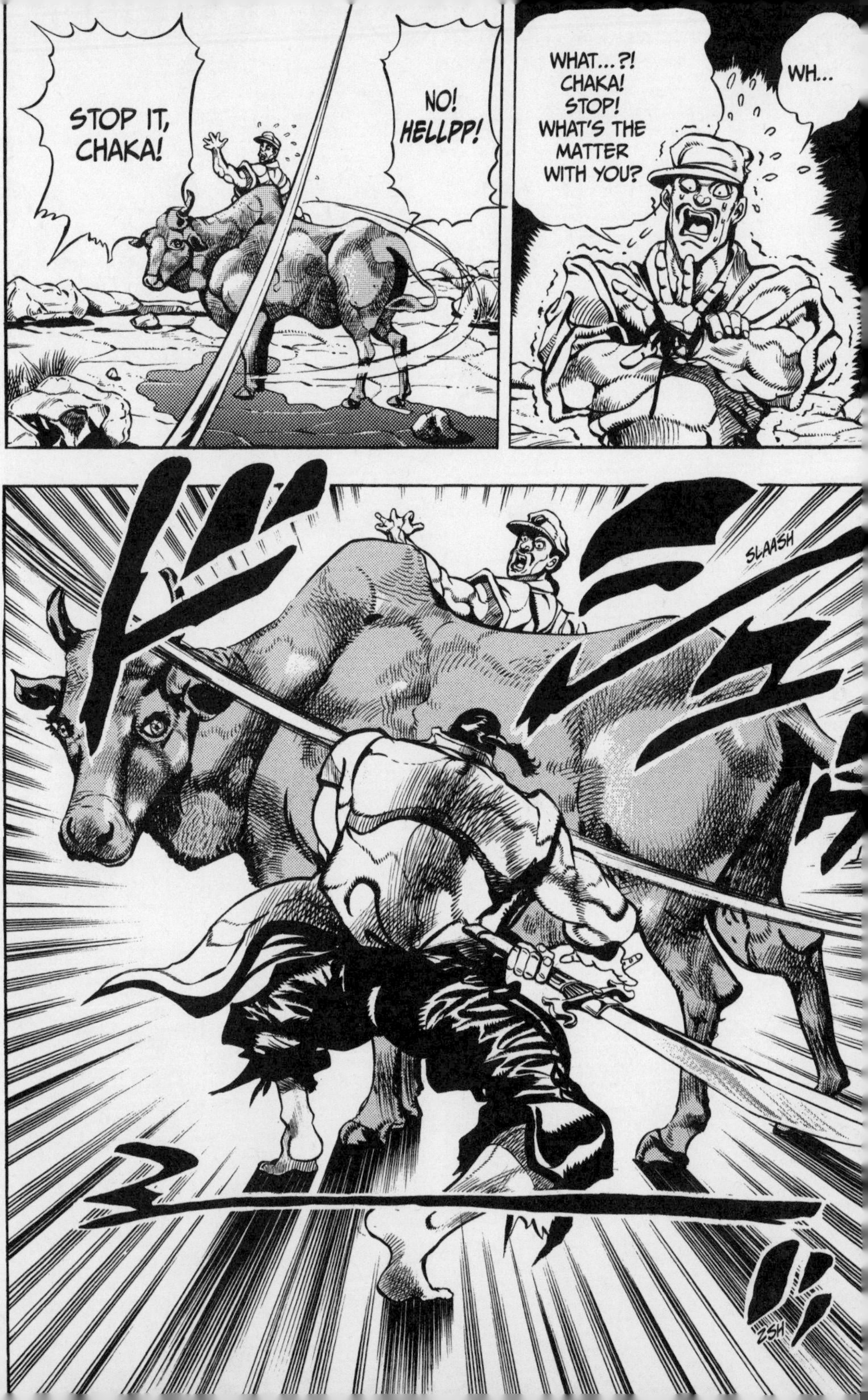
WH...
WHAT...?! CHAKA! STOP! WHAT'S THE MATTER WITH YOU?
NO! HELLPP!
STOP IT, CHAKA!
SLAASH
ZSH

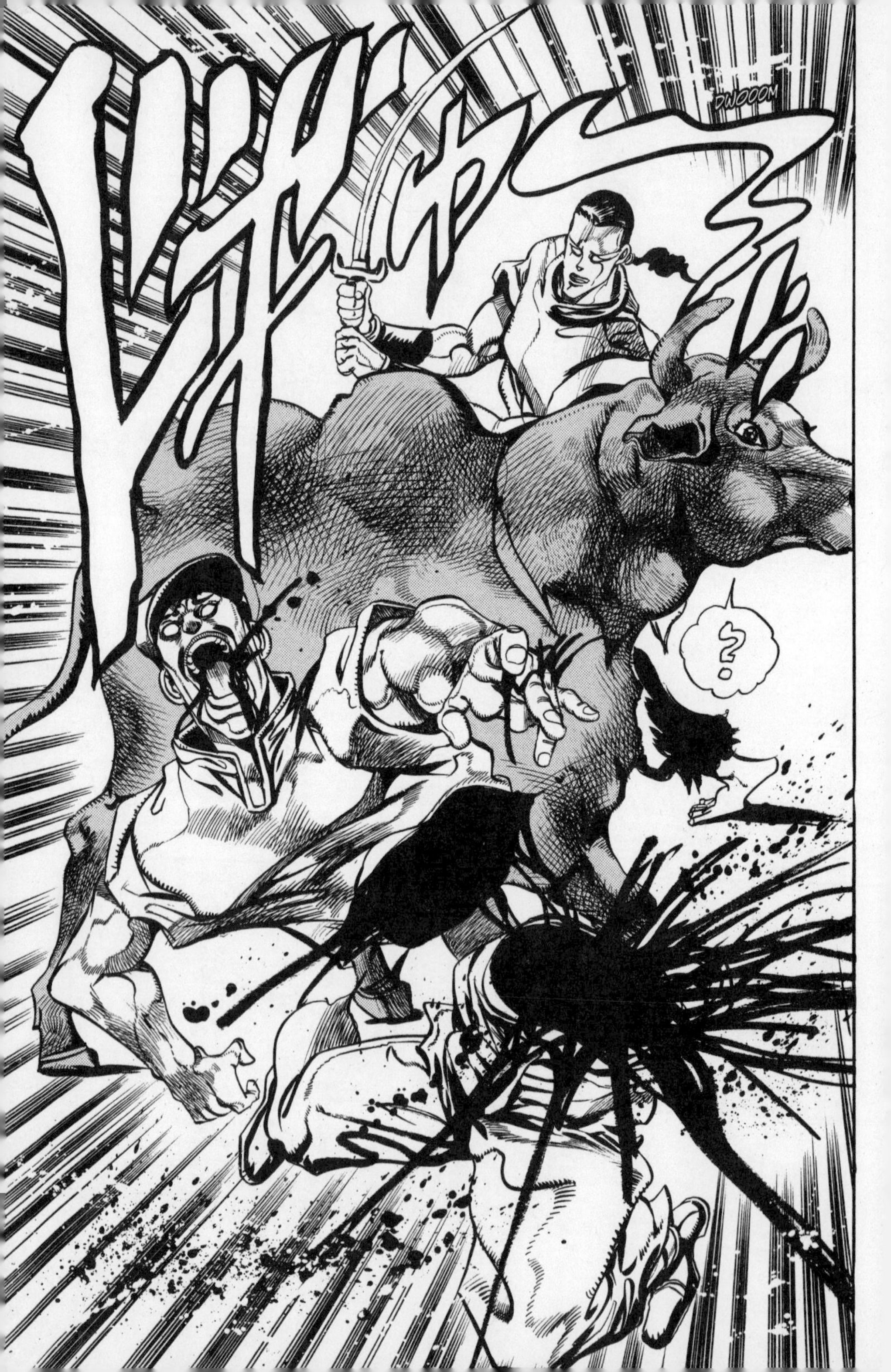
DWOOOM
?

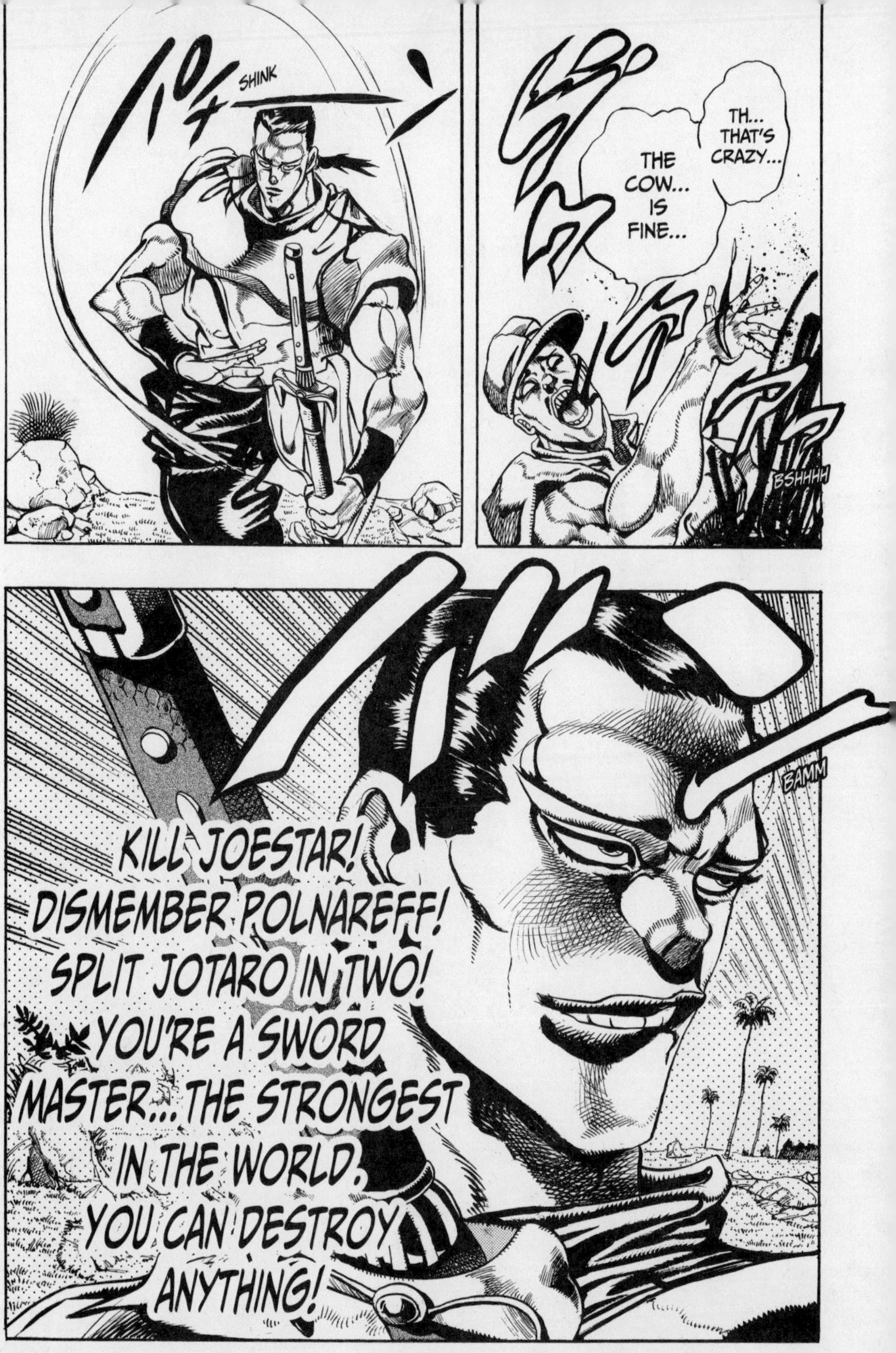
TH... THAT'S CRAZY...
THE COW... IS FINE...
BSHHHH
SHINK
BAMM
KILL JOESTAR! DISMEMBER POLNAREFF! SPLIT JOTARO IN TWO! YOU'RE A SWORD MASTER... THE STRONGEST IN THE WORLD. YOU CAN DESTROY ANYTHING!

CHAPTER 81: Anubis PART 2

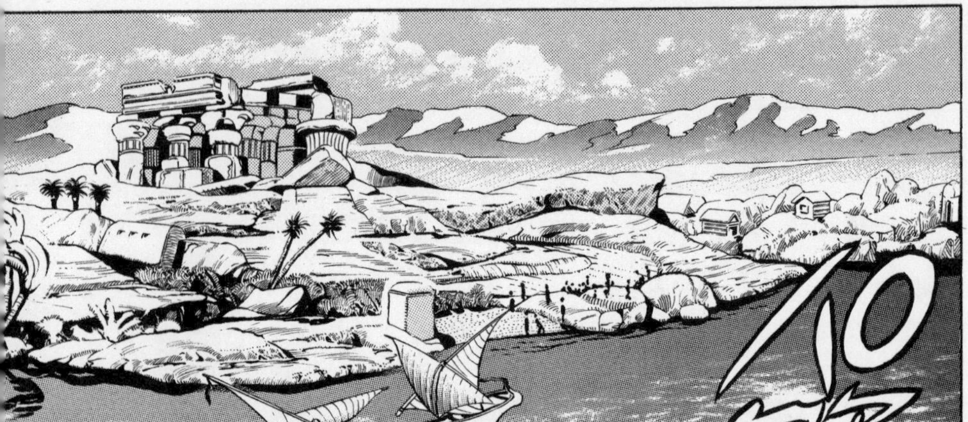
SHIIING
KOM OMBO

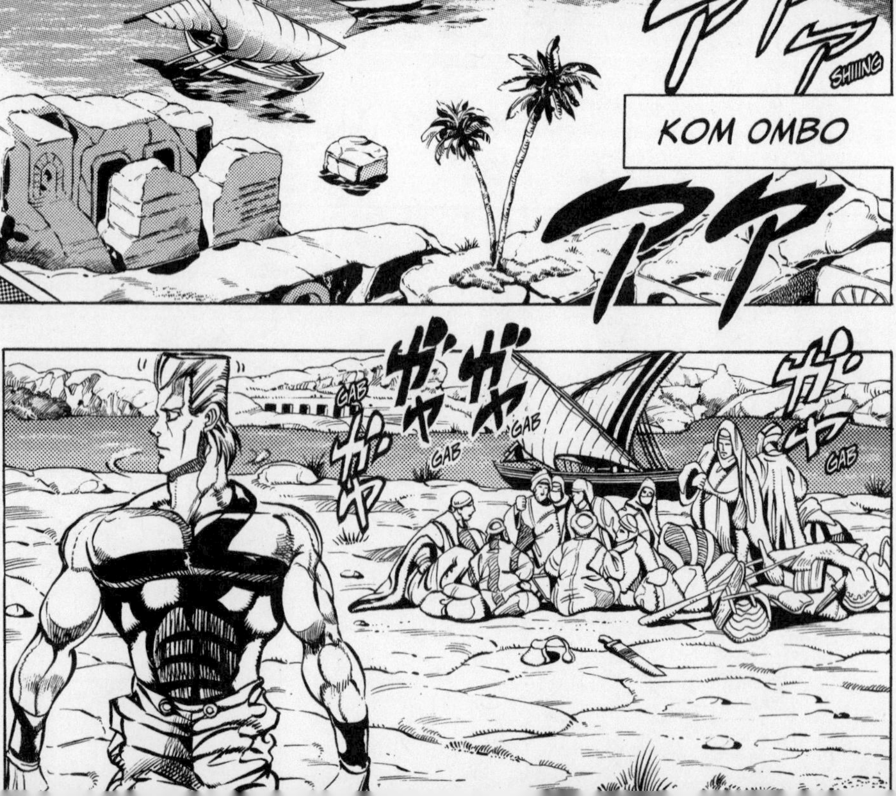
GAB
GAB
GAB
GAB
GAB

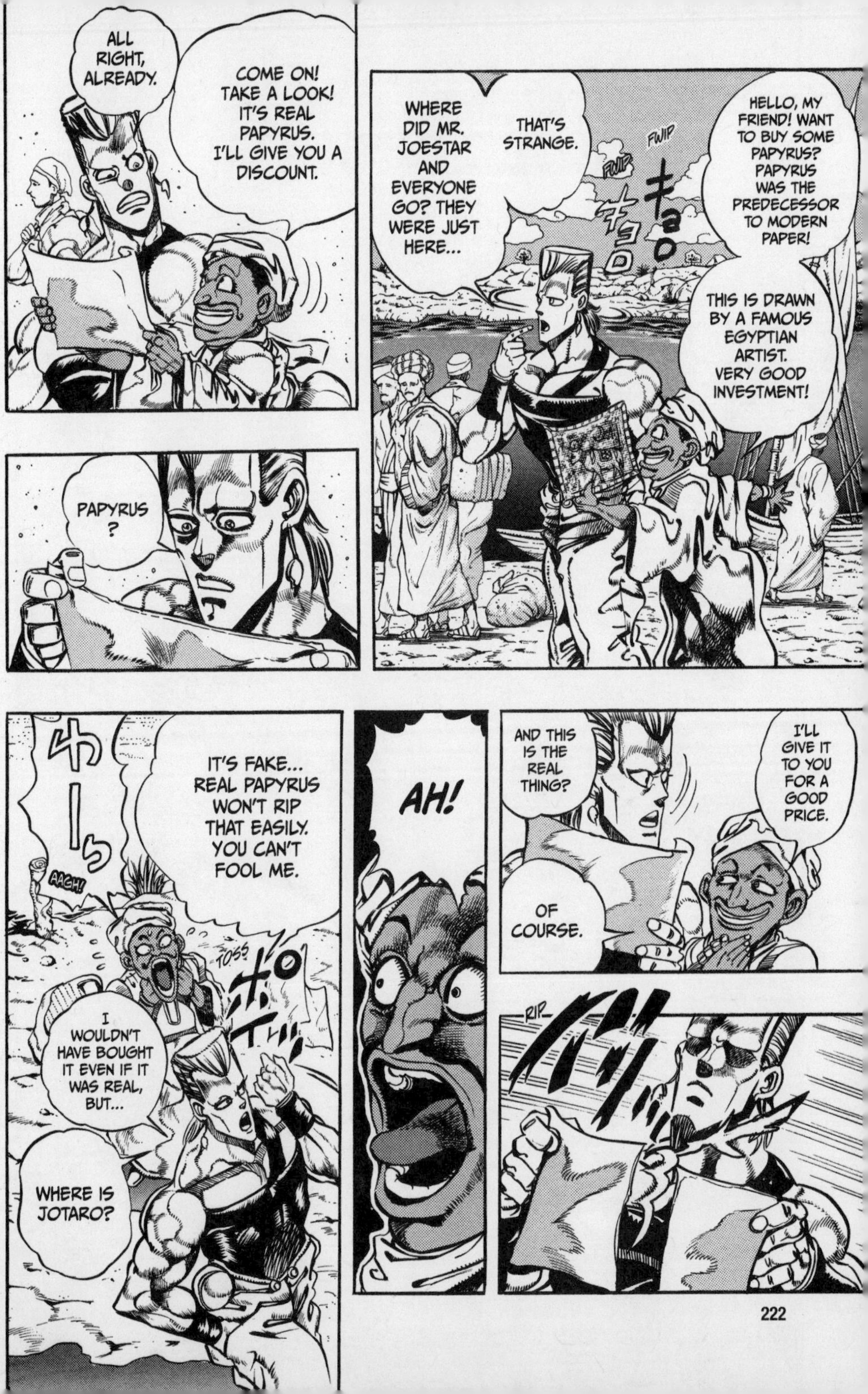
HELLO, MY FRIEND! WANT TO BUY SOME PAPYRUS? PAPYRUS WAS THE PREDECESSOR TO MODERN PAPER!
THAT'S STRANGE.
WHERE DID MR. JOESTAR AND EVERYONE GO? THEY WERE JUST HERE...
FWIP
FWIP
THIS IS DRAWN BY A FAMOUS EGYPTIAN ARTIST. VERY GOOD INVESTMENT!
COME ON! TAKE A LOOK! IT'S REAL PAPYRUS. I'LL GIVE YOU A DISCOUNT.
ALL RIGHT, ALREADY.
PAPYRUS ?
I'LL GIVE IT TO YOU FOR A GOOD PRICE.
AND THIS IS THE REAL THING?
OF COURSE.
RIP
AH!
IT'S FAKE... REAL PAPYRUS WON'T RIP THAT EASILY. YOU CAN'T FOOL ME.
AAGH!
TOSS
I WOULDN'T HAVE BOUGHT IT EVEN IF IT WAS REAL, BUT...
WHERE IS JOTARO?

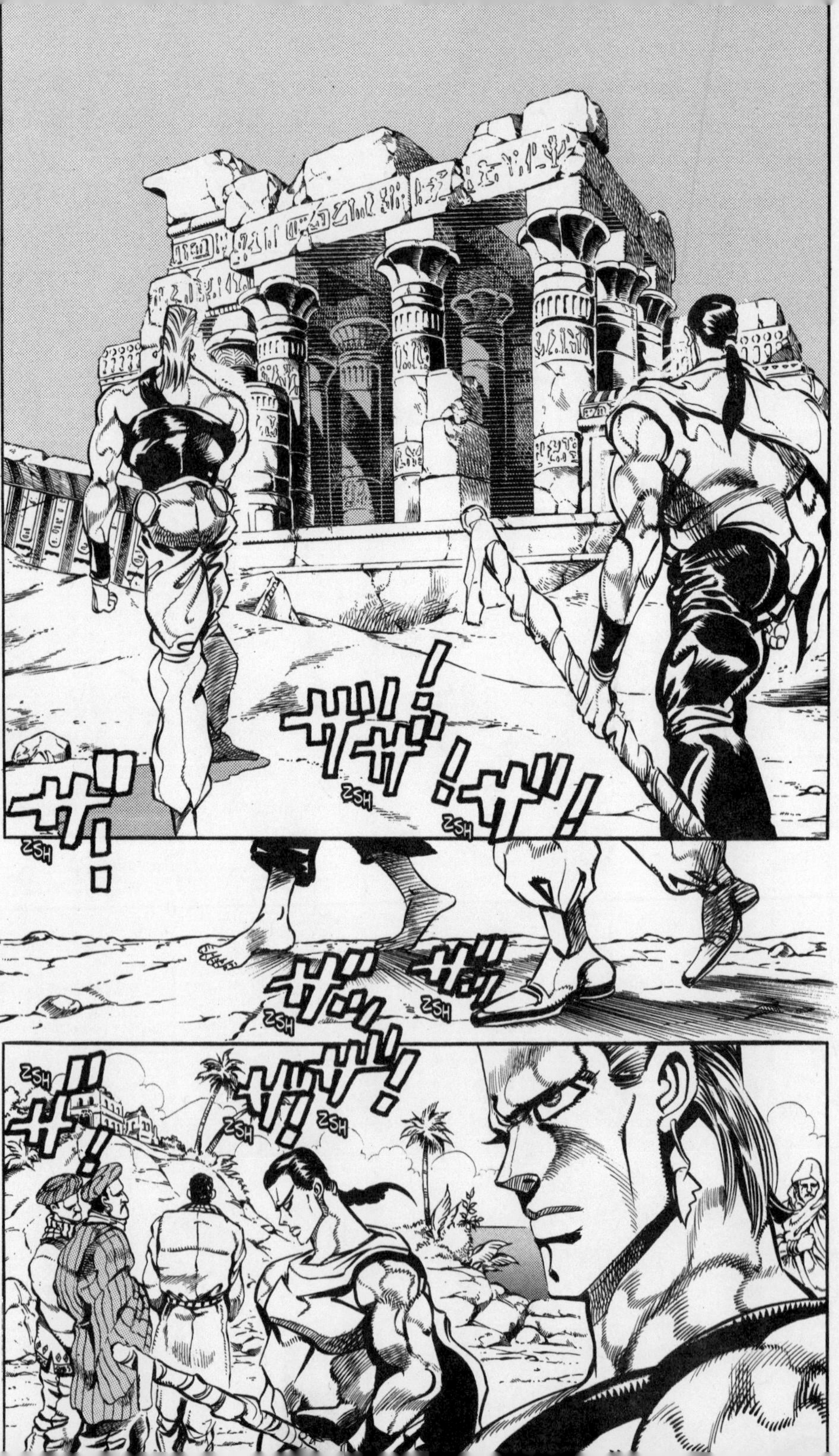
ZSH
ZSH
ZSH
ZSH
ZSH
ZSH
ZSH
ZSH

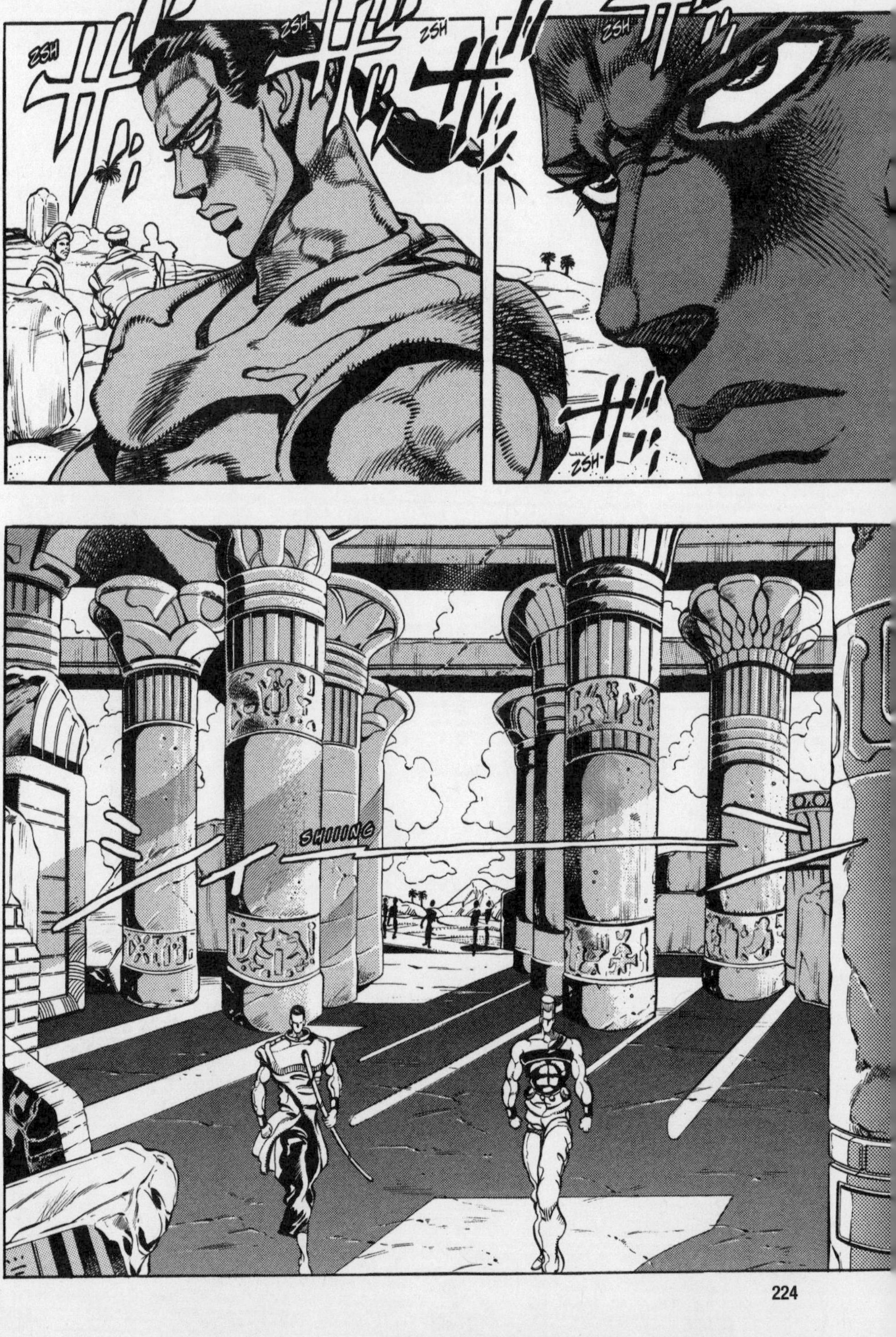
ZSH
ザッ
ZSH
ZSH
ZSH
SHIIING

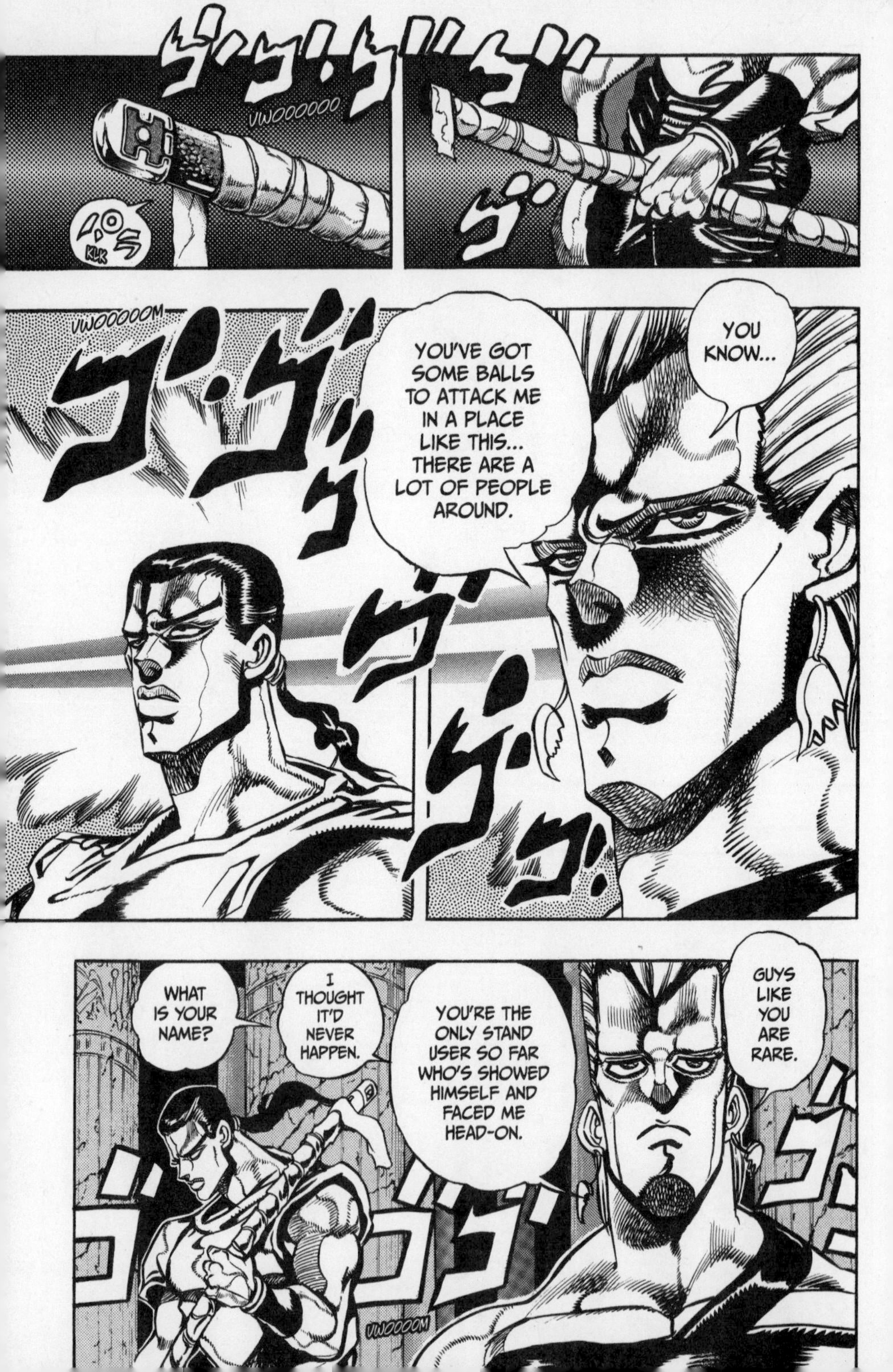
VWOOOOOO
KLIK
YOU KNOW...
YOU'VE GOT SOME BALLS TO ATTACK ME IN A PLACE LIKE THIS... THERE ARE A LOT OF PEOPLE AROUND.
VWOOOOOM
GUYS LIKE YOU ARE RARE.
YOU'RE THE ONLY STAND USER SO FAR WHO'S SHOWED HIMSELF AND FACED ME HEAD-ON.
I THOUGHT IT'D NEVER HAPPEN.
WHAT IS YOUR NAME?
VWOOOOM

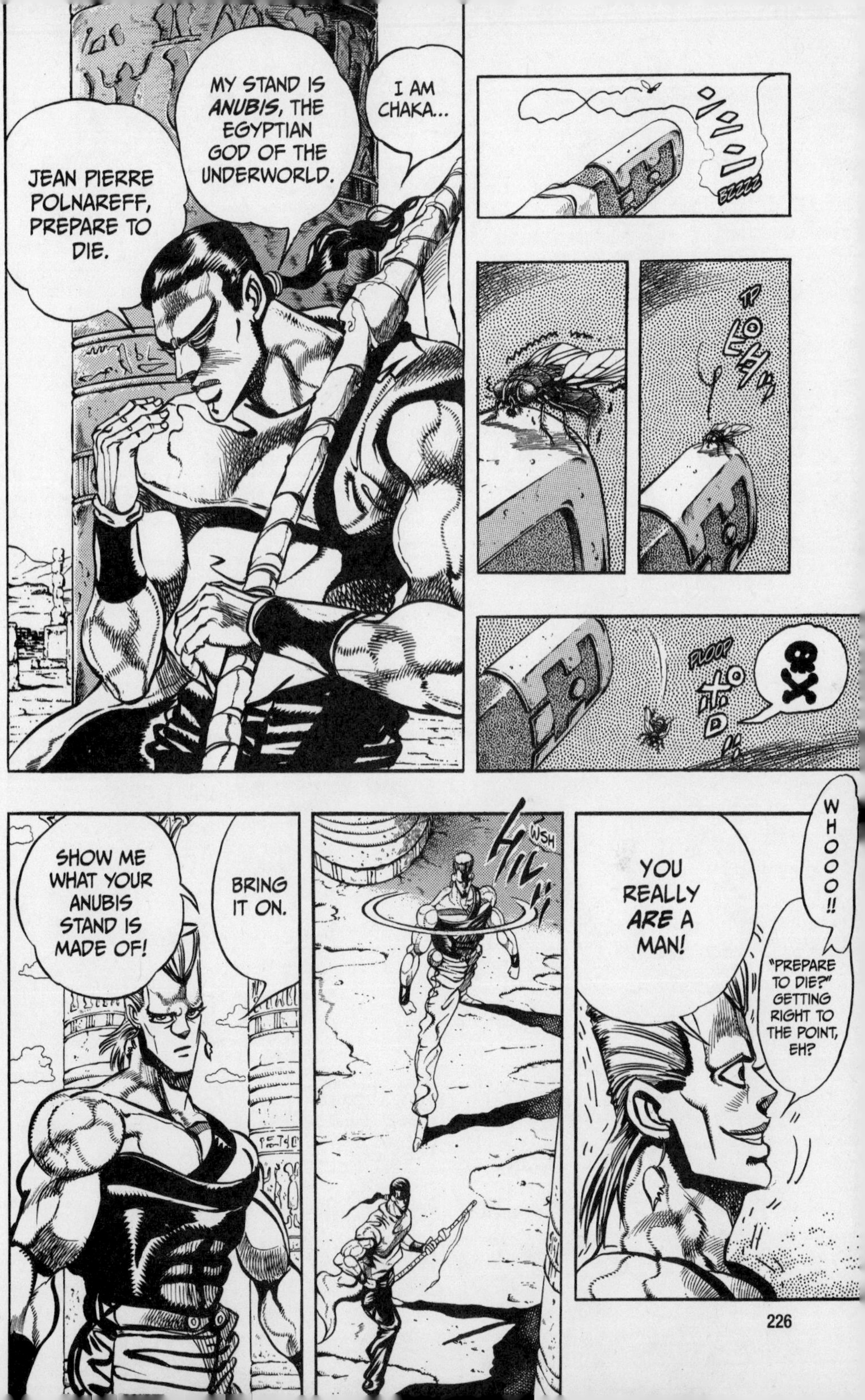
BZZZZ
TP
PLOOP
I AM CHAKA...
MY STAND IS *ANUBIS*, THE EGYPTIAN GOD OF THE UNDERWORLD.
JEAN PIERRE POLNAREFF, PREPARE TO DIE.
WHOOOO!!
YOU REALLY *ARE* A MAN!
"PREPARE TO DIE?" GETTING RIGHT TO THE POINT, EH?
WSH
BRING IT ON.
SHOW ME WHAT YOUR ANUBIS STAND IS MADE OF!

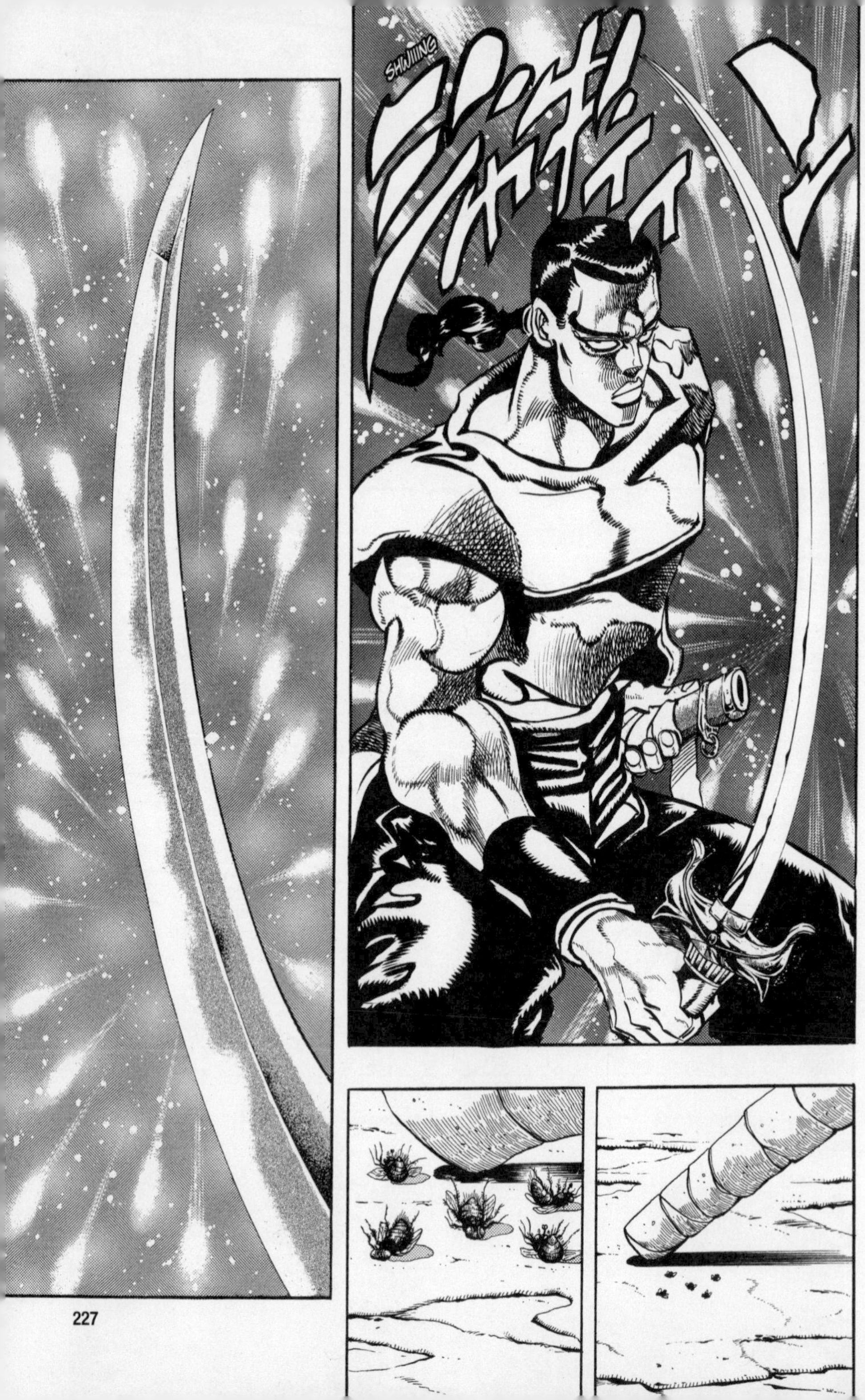
SHWIIING

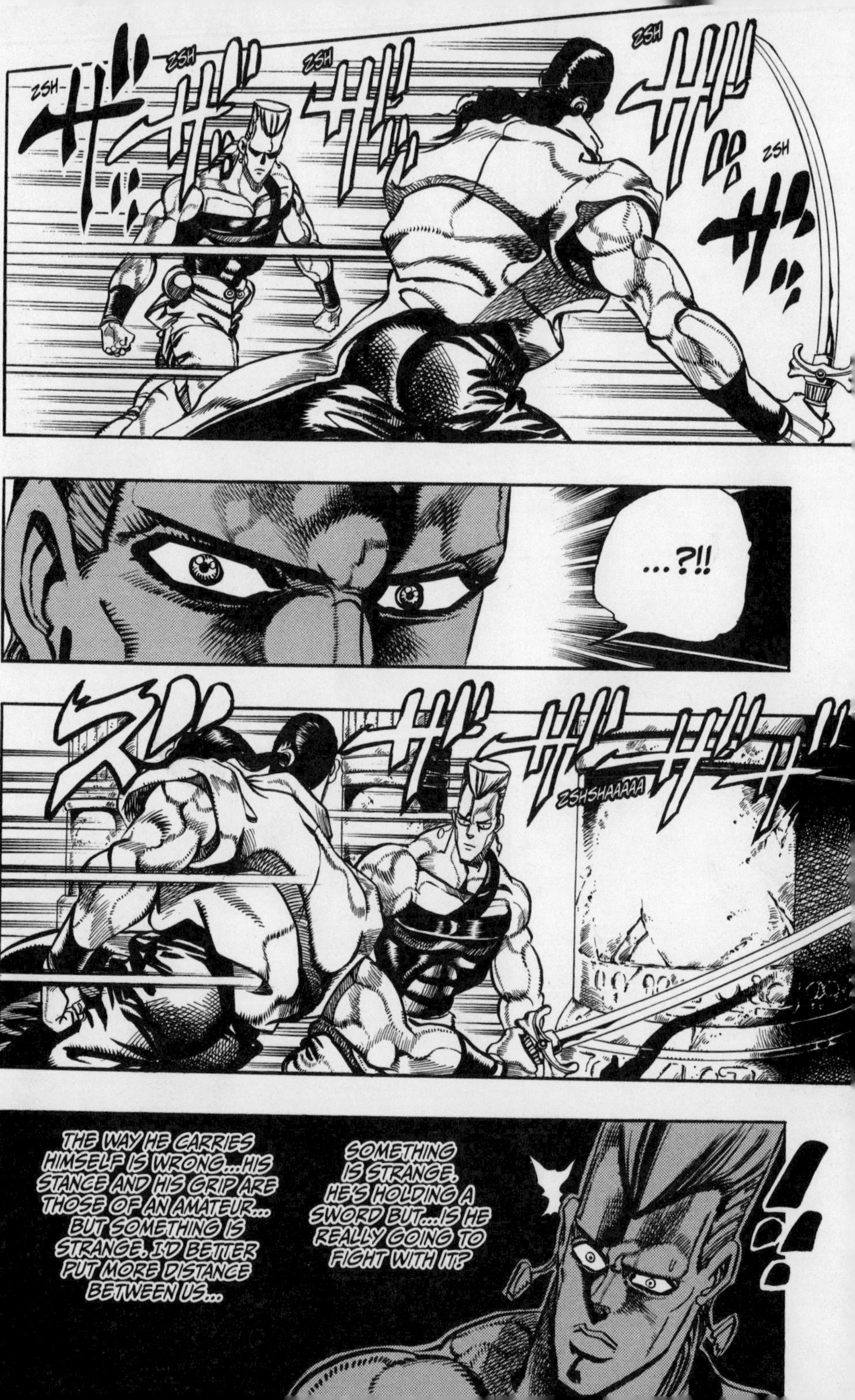
ZSH
ZSH
ZSH
ZSH
ZSH-
...?!!
ZSHSHAAAAA
SOMETHING IS STRANGE. HE'S HOLDING A SWORD BUT...IS HE REALLY GOING TO FIGHT WITH IT?
THE WAY HE CARRIES HIMSELF IS WRONG...HIS STANCE AND HIS GRIP ARE THOSE OF AN AMATEUR... BUT SOMETHING IS STRANGE. I'D BETTER PUT MORE DISTANCE BETWEEN US...

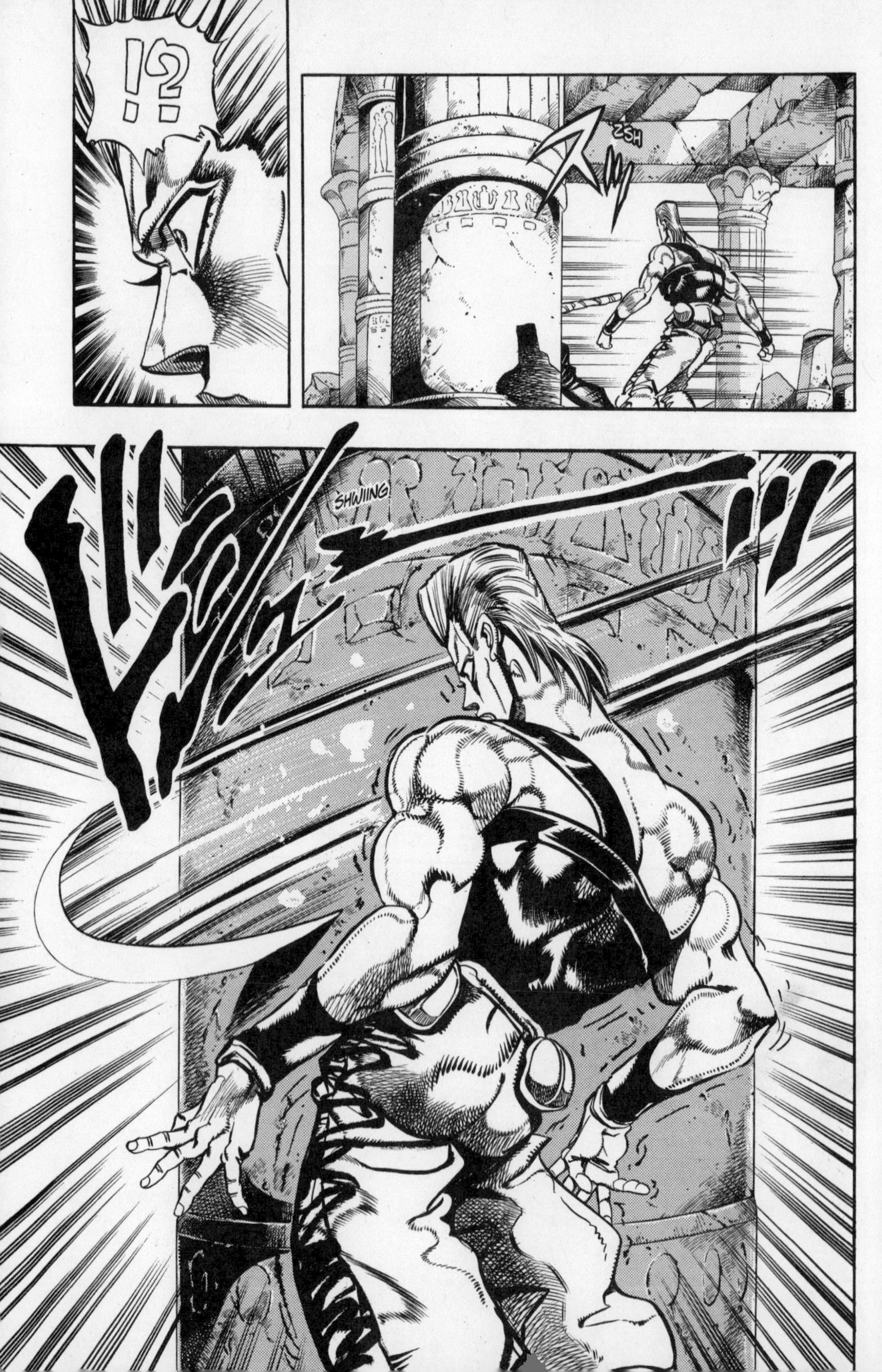
ZSH
!?
SHWIING

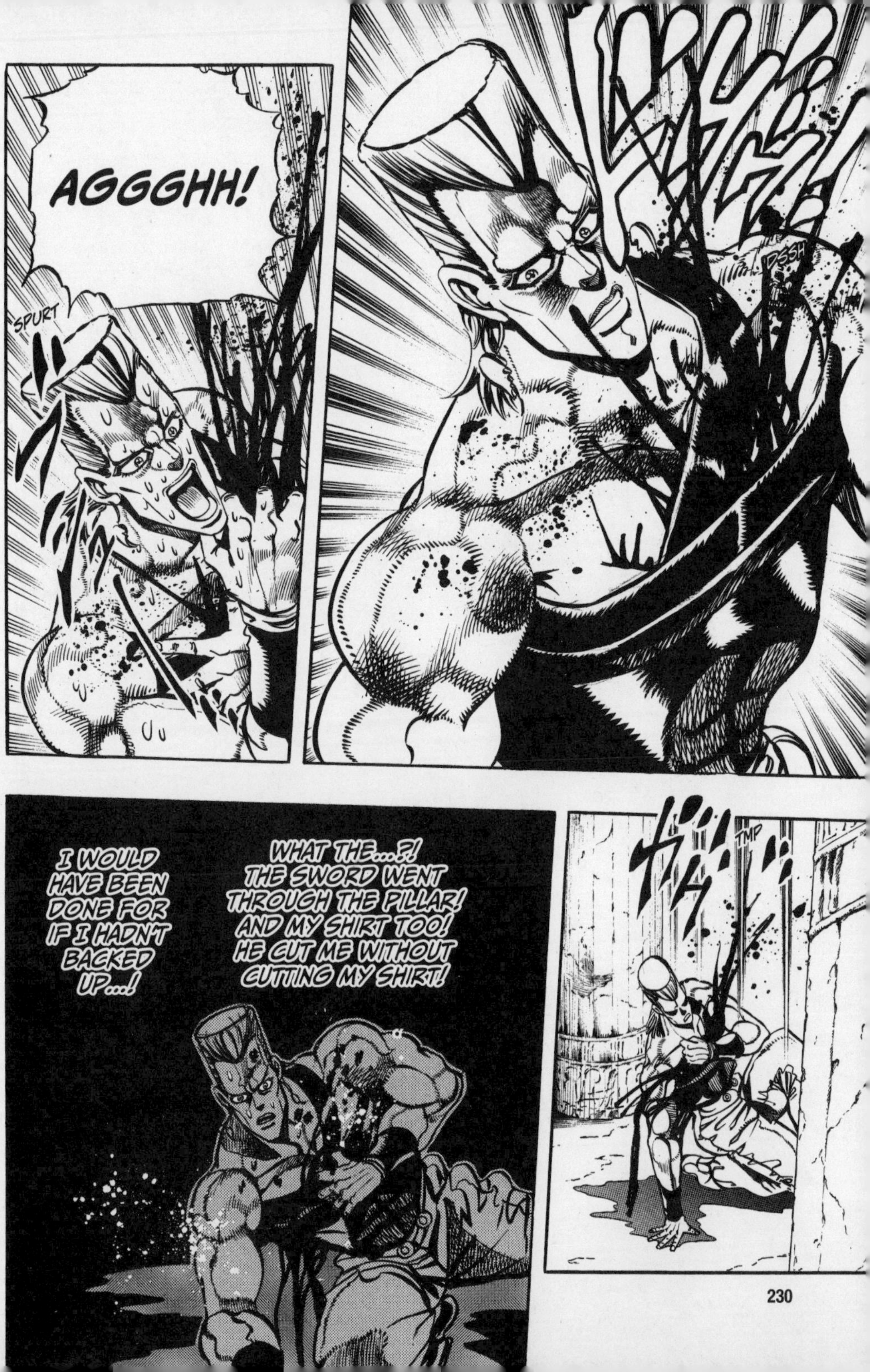
DSSH
AGGGHH!
SPURT
TMP
WHAT THE...?! THE SWORD WENT THROUGH THE PILLAR! AND MY SHIRT TOO! HE CUT ME WITHOUT CUTTING MY SHIRT!
I WOULD HAVE BEEN DONE FOR IF I HADN'T BACKED UP...!

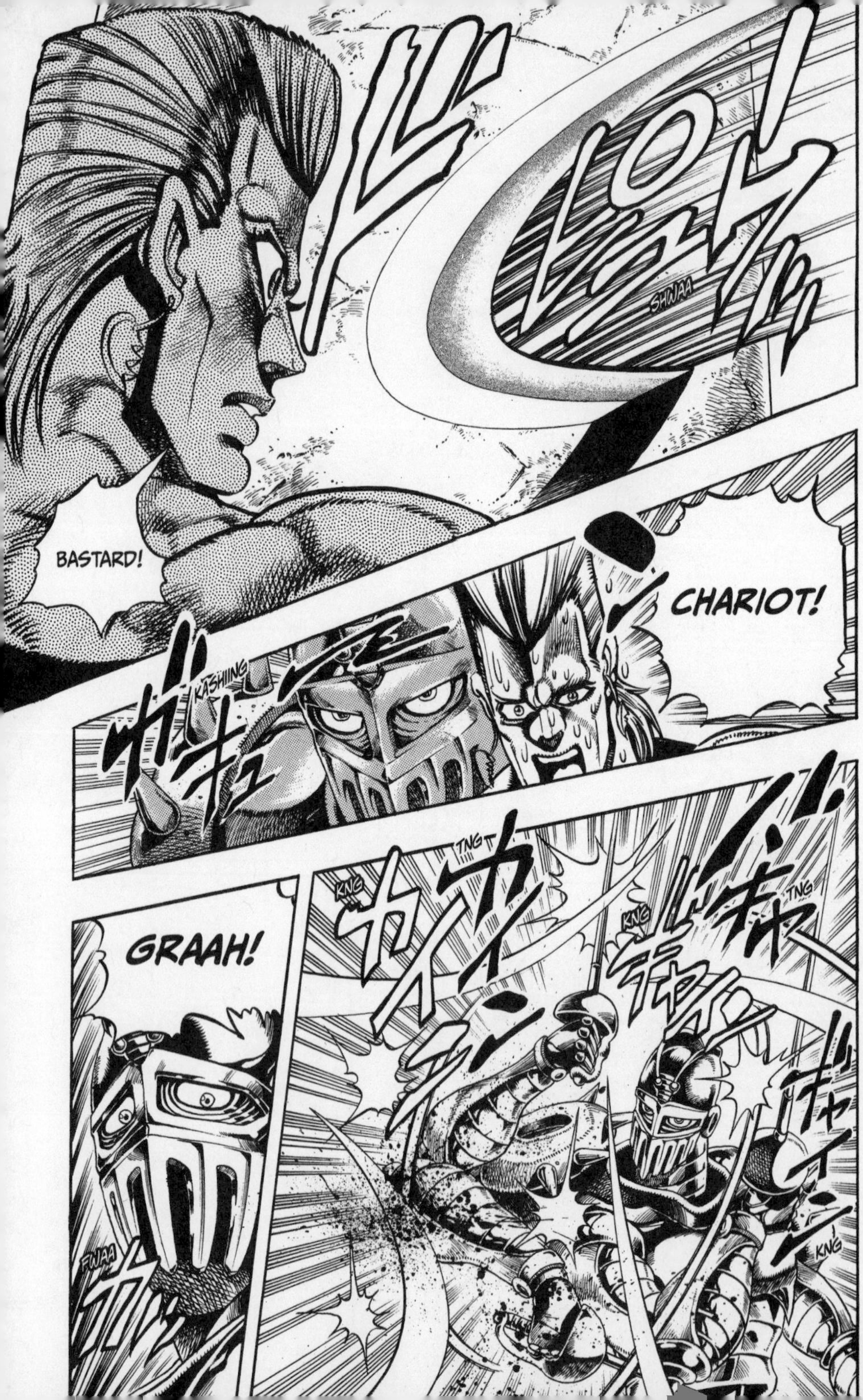
SHWAA
BASTARD!
CHARIOT!
KASHIING
TNG
KNG
TNG
KNG
KNG
GRAAH!
FWAA

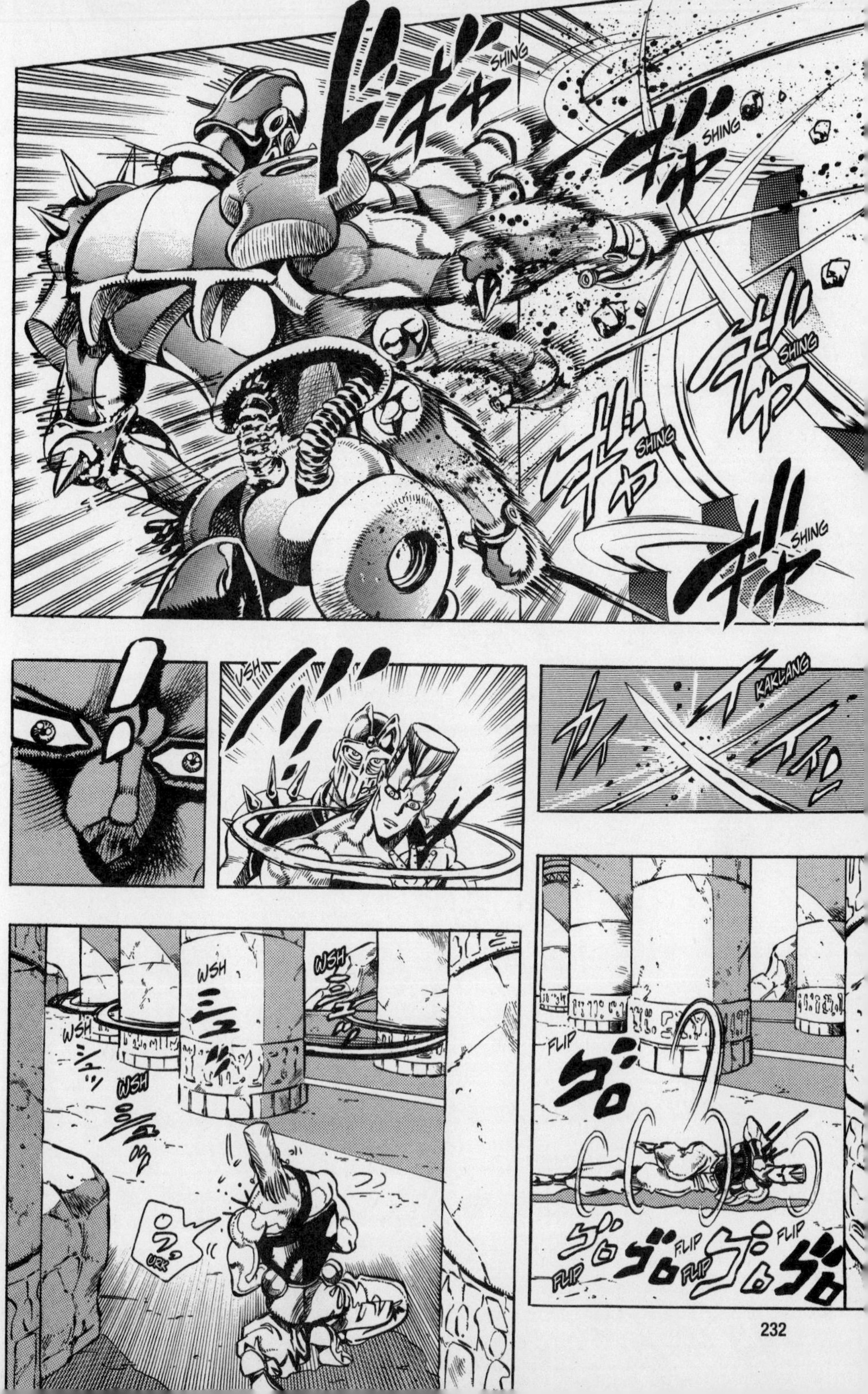
SHING
SHING
SHING
SHING
SHING
KAKLANG
WSH
FLIP
FLIP
FLIP
FLIP
FLIP
WSH
WSH
WSH
WSH
URK

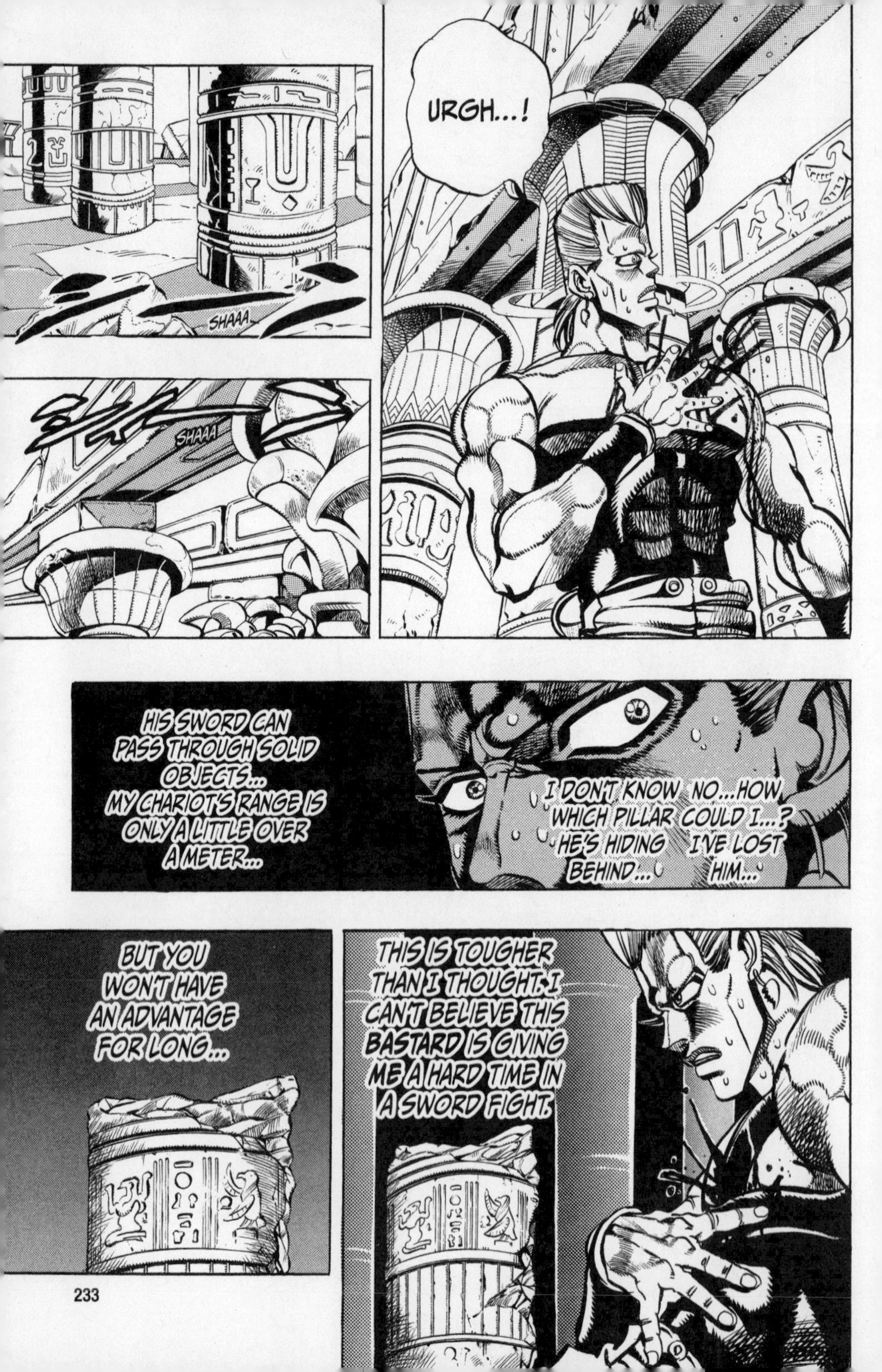
URGH...!
SHAAA
SHAAA
NO...HOW COULD I...? I'VE LOST HIM...
I DON'T KNOW WHICH PILLAR HE'S HIDING BEHIND...
HIS SWORD CAN PASS THROUGH SOLID OBJECTS... MY CHARIOT'S RANGE IS ONLY A LITTLE OVER A METER...
THIS IS TOUGHER THAN I THOUGHT. I CAN'T BELIEVE THIS BASTARD IS GIVING ME A HARD TIME IN A SWORD FIGHT.
BUT YOU WON'T HAVE AN ADVANTAGE FOR LONG...

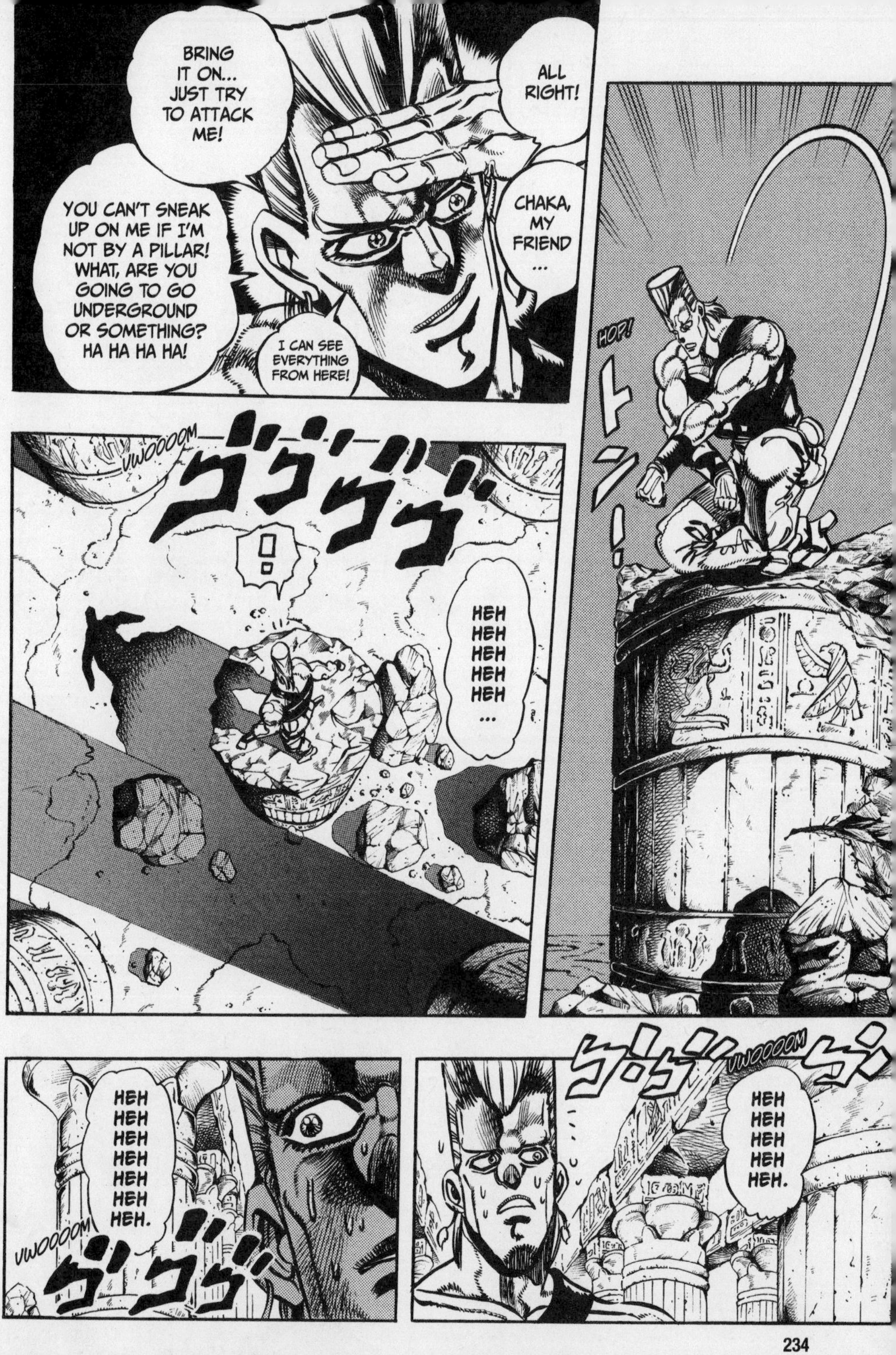

HOP!
ALL RIGHT!
CHAKA, MY FRIEND ...
BRING IT ON... JUST TRY TO ATTACK ME!
I CAN SEE EVERYTHING FROM HERE!
YOU CAN'T SNEAK UP ON ME IF I'M NOT BY A PILLAR! WHAT, ARE YOU GOING TO GO UNDERGROUND OR SOMETHING? HA HA HA HA!
VWOOOOM
!?
HEH HEH HEH HEH HEH ...
VWOOOOM
HEH HEH HEH HEH HEH.
HEH HEH HEH HEH HEH HEH HEH.
VWOOOOM

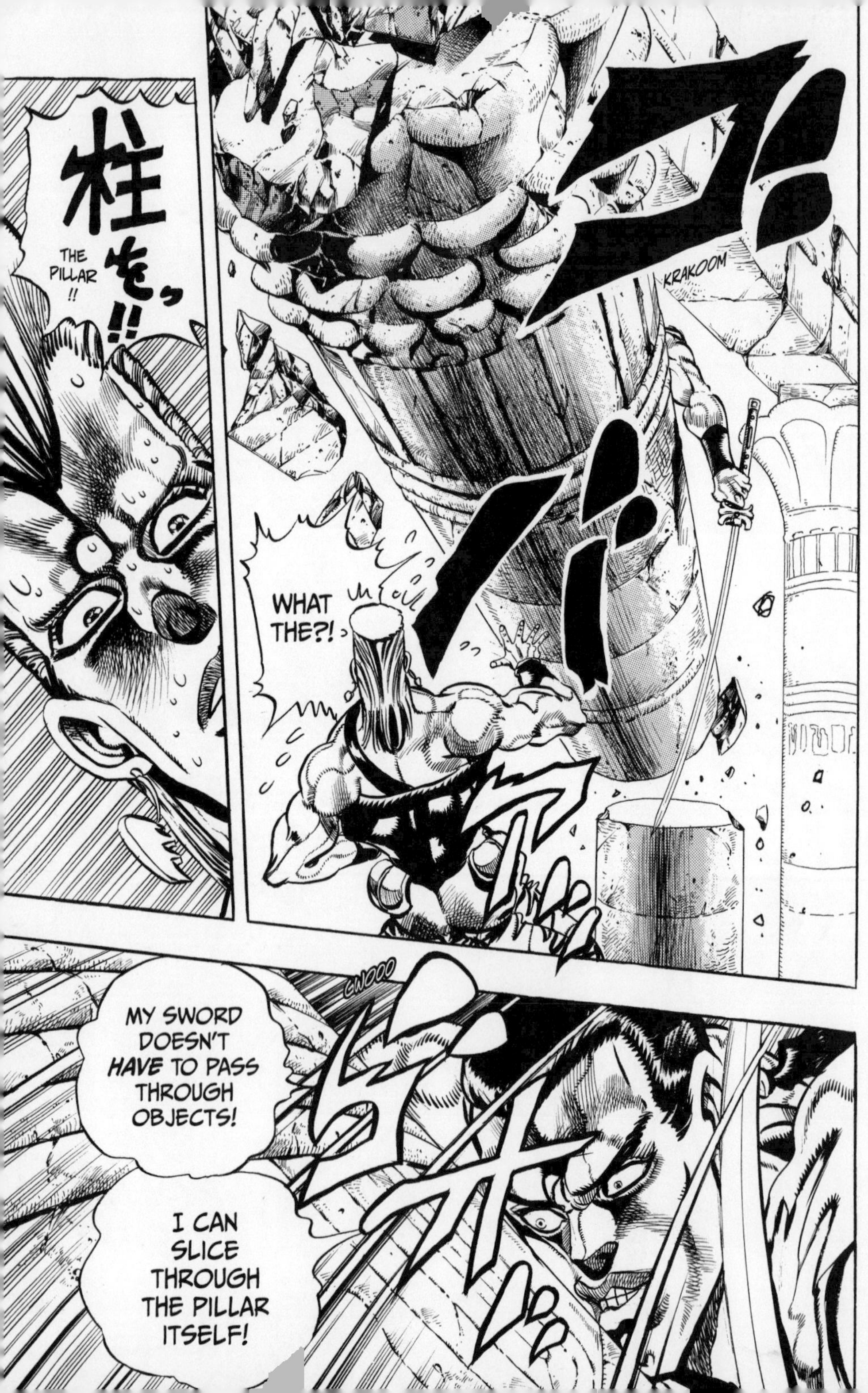
KRAKOOM
WHAT THE?!
柱をッ!!
THE PILLAR !!
GWOOO
MY SWORD DOESN'T *HAVE* TO PASS THROUGH OBJECTS!
I CAN SLICE THROUGH THE PILLAR ITSELF!

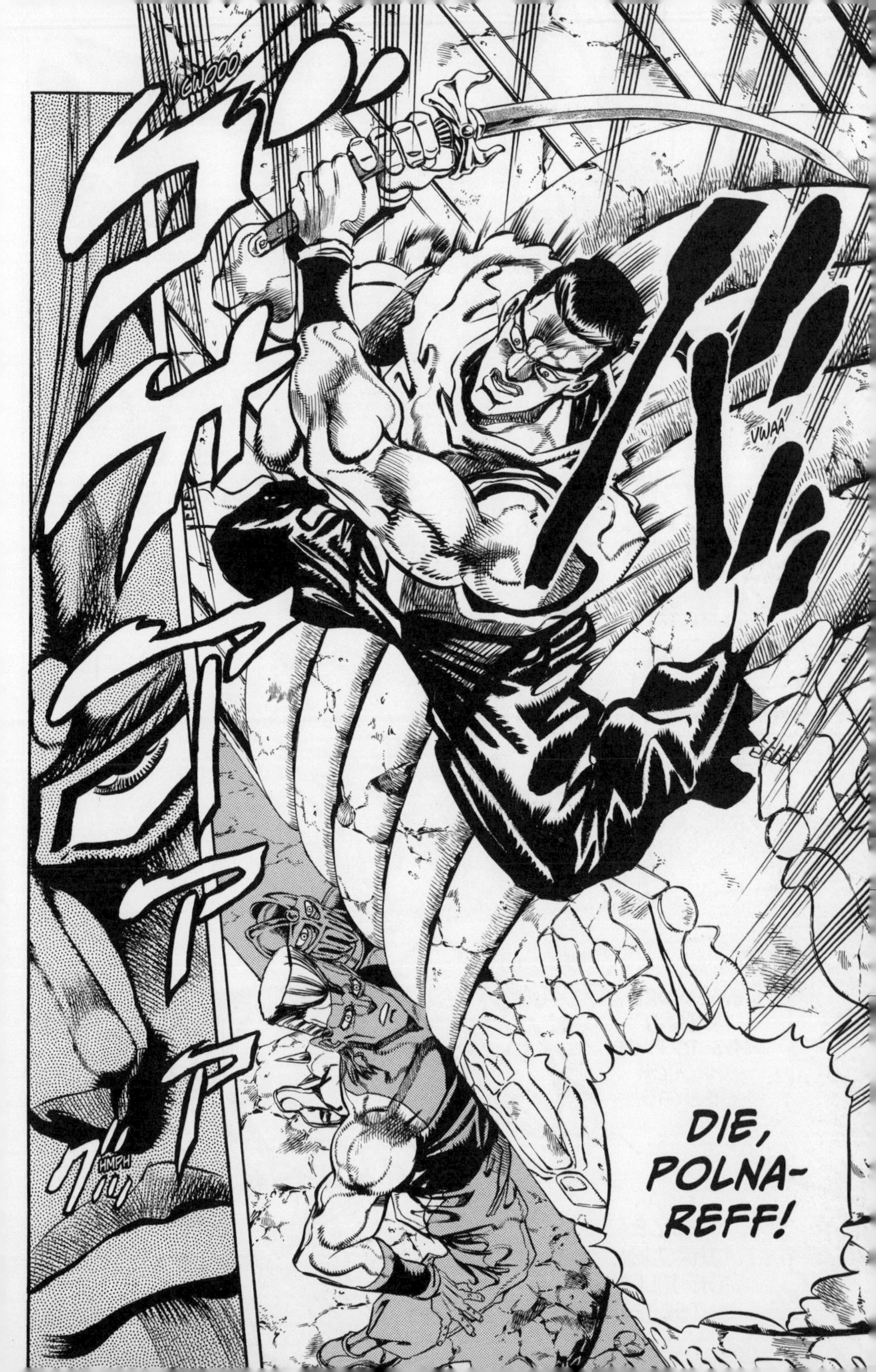
GWOOO
VWAA
DIE, POLNA-REFF!
HMPH

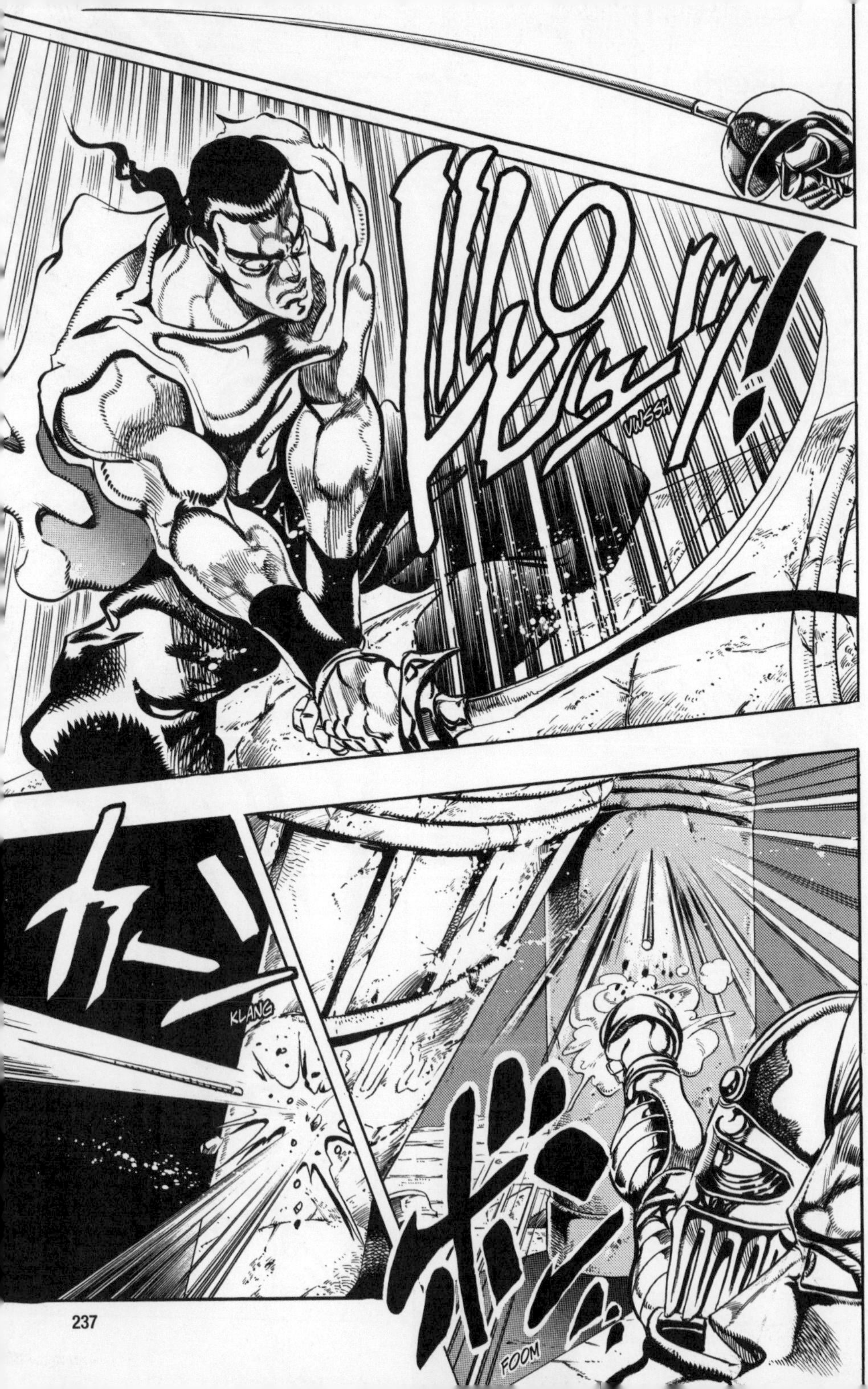
VWSSH
FOOM
カーン
KLANG

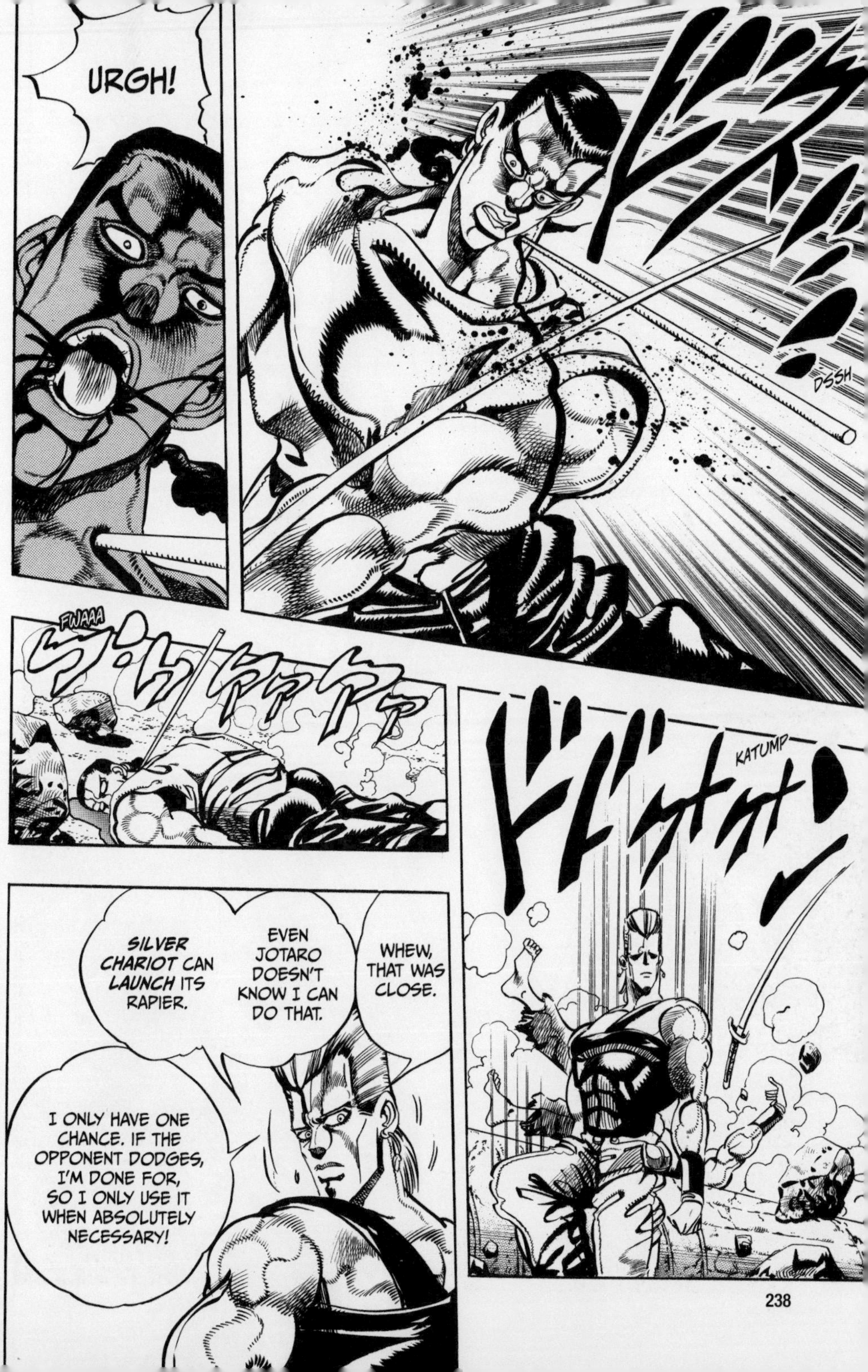
DSSH
URGH!
KATUMP
FWAAA
WHEW, THAT WAS CLOSE.
EVEN JOTARO DOESN'T KNOW I CAN DO THAT.
SILVER CHARIOT CAN LAUNCH ITS RAPIER.
I ONLY HAVE ONE CHANCE. IF THE OPPONENT DODGES, I'M DONE FOR, SO I ONLY USE IT WHEN ABSOLUTELY NECESSARY!

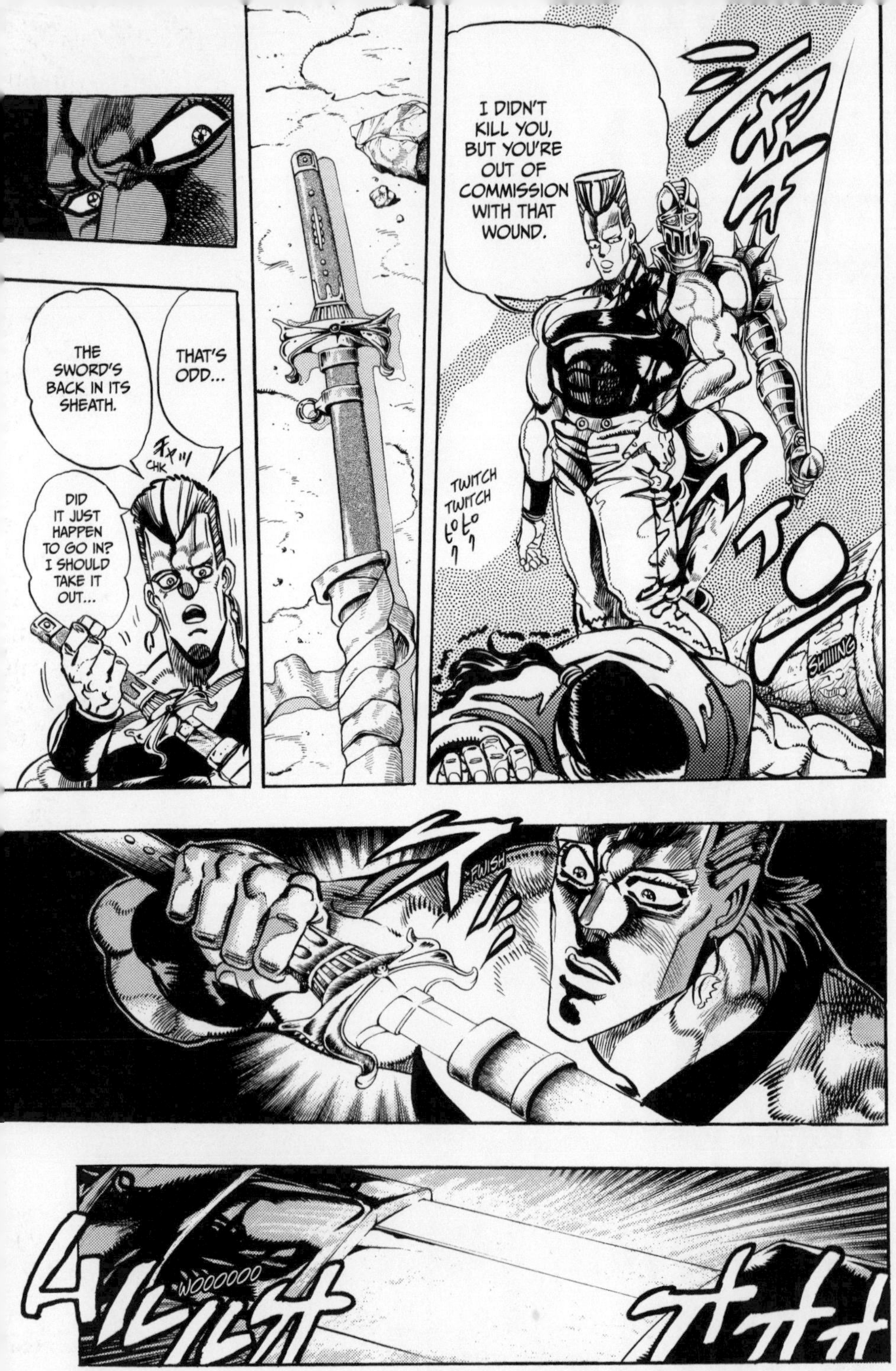
I DIDN'T KILL YOU, BUT YOU'RE OUT OF COMMISSION WITH THAT WOUND.
SHIIING
TWITCH TWITCH
THAT'S ODD...
THE SWORD'S BACK IN ITS SHEATH.
CHK
DID IT JUST HAPPEN TO GO IN? I SHOULD TAKE IT OUT...
FWISH
WOOOOOO

8
ANUBIS

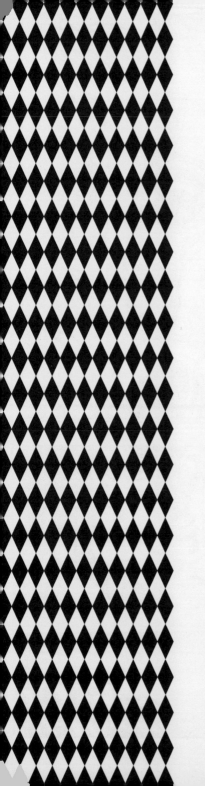

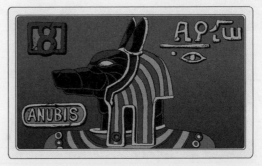

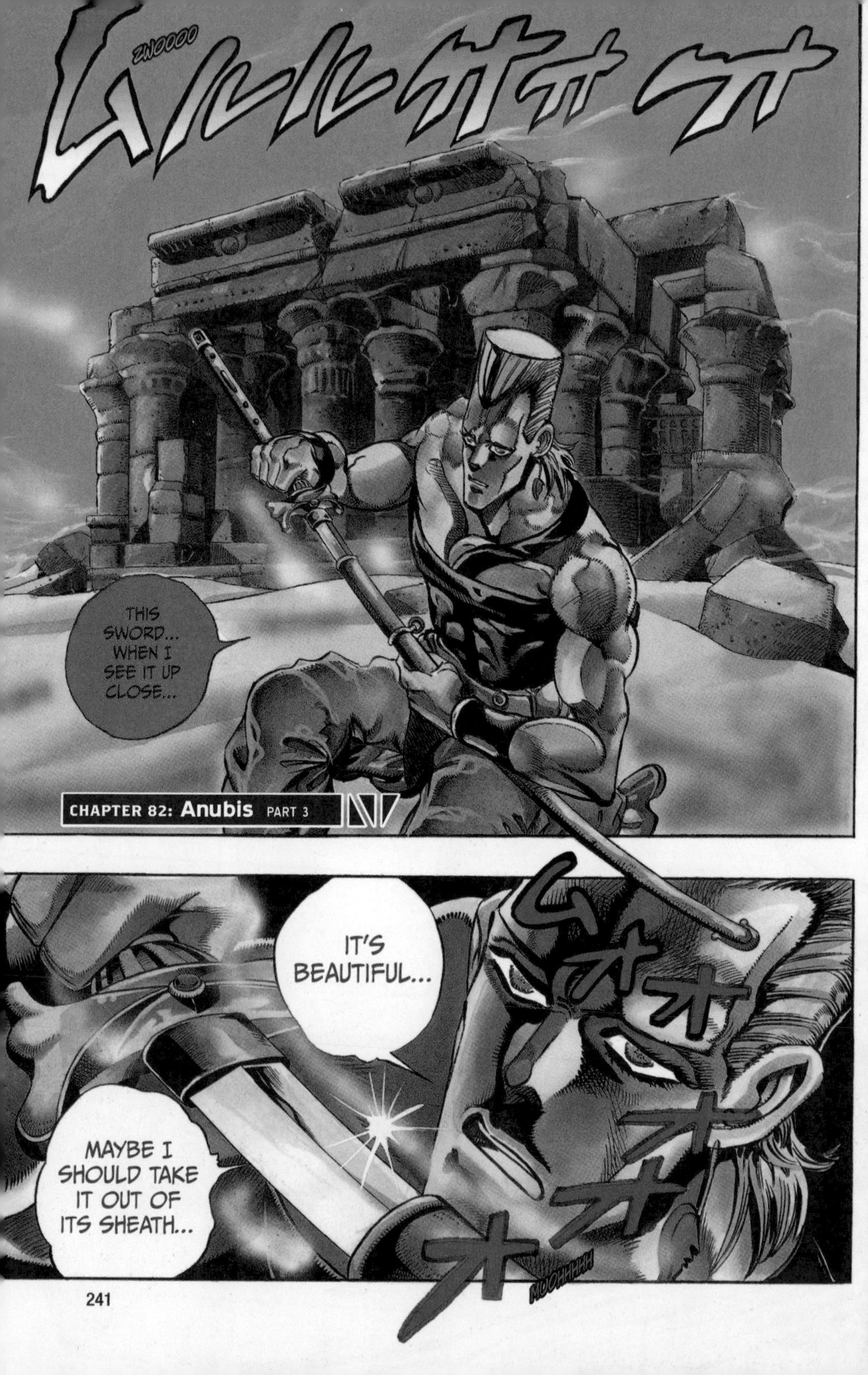
ZWOOOO
THIS SWORD... WHEN I SEE IT UP CLOSE...
CHAPTER 82: Anubis PART 3
IT'S BEAUTIFUL...
MAYBE I SHOULD TAKE IT OUT OF ITS SHEATH...
MUOHHHHH

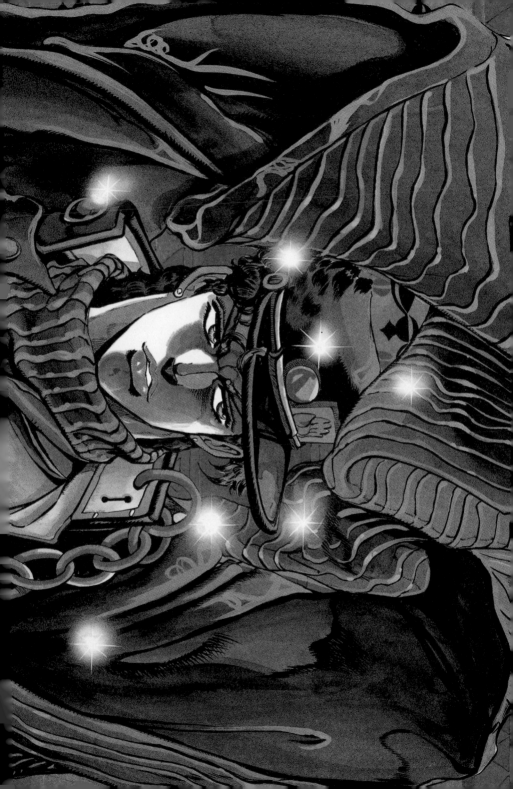

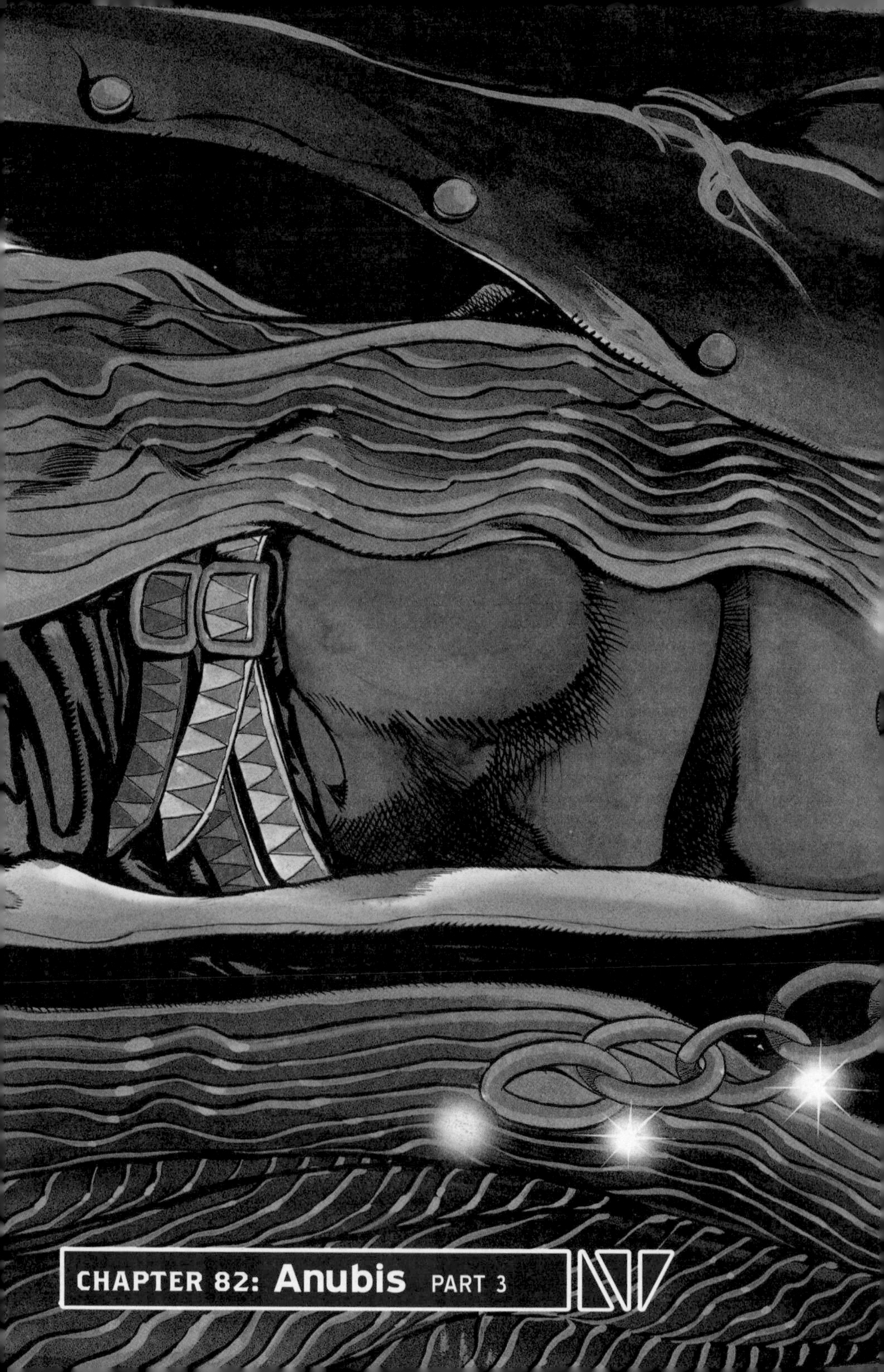

CHAPTER 82: Anubis PART 3

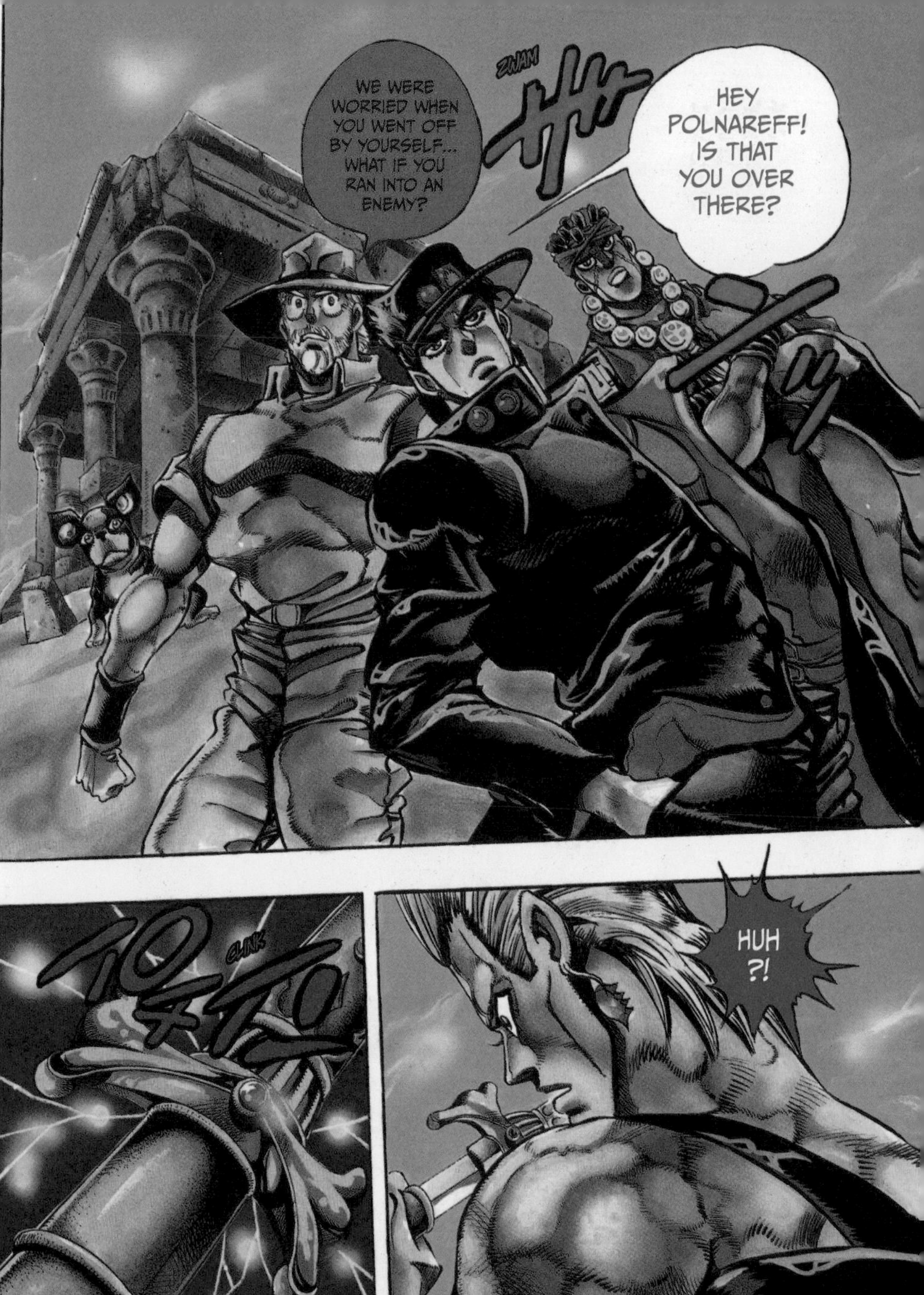
HEY POLNAREFF! IS THAT YOU OVER THERE?
ZWAM
WE WERE WORRIED WHEN YOU WENT OFF BY YOURSELF... WHAT IF YOU RAN INTO AN ENEMY?
HUH ?!
CLINK

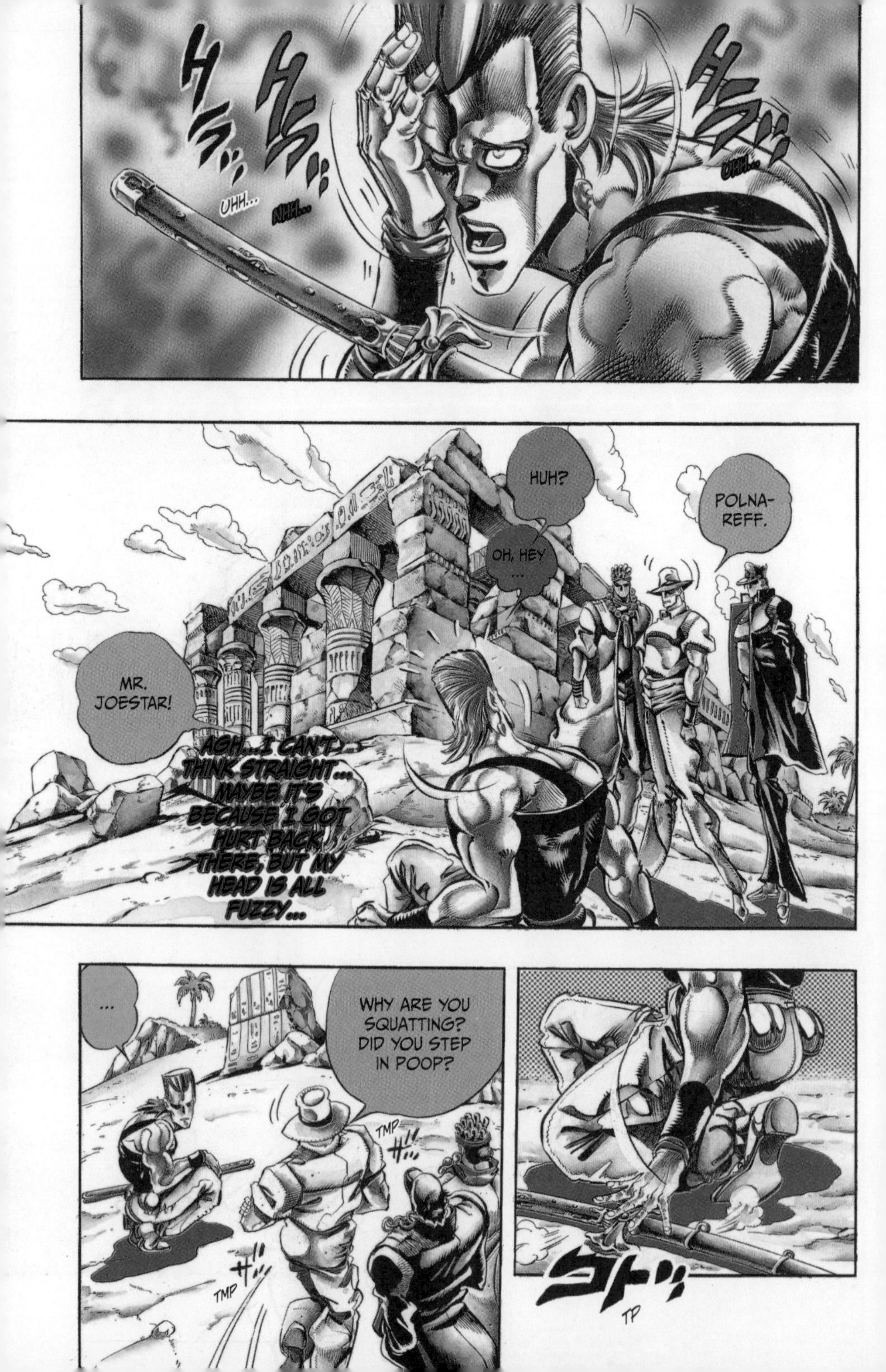
UHH...
NHH...
UHH...
POLNA-REFF.
HUH?
OH, HEY ...
MR. JOESTAR!
AGH...I CAN'T THINK STRAIGHT... MAYBE IT'S BECAUSE I GOT HURT BACK THERE, BUT MY HEAD IS ALL FUZZY...
TP
WHY ARE YOU SQUATTING? DID YOU STEP IN POOP?
TMP
...
TMP

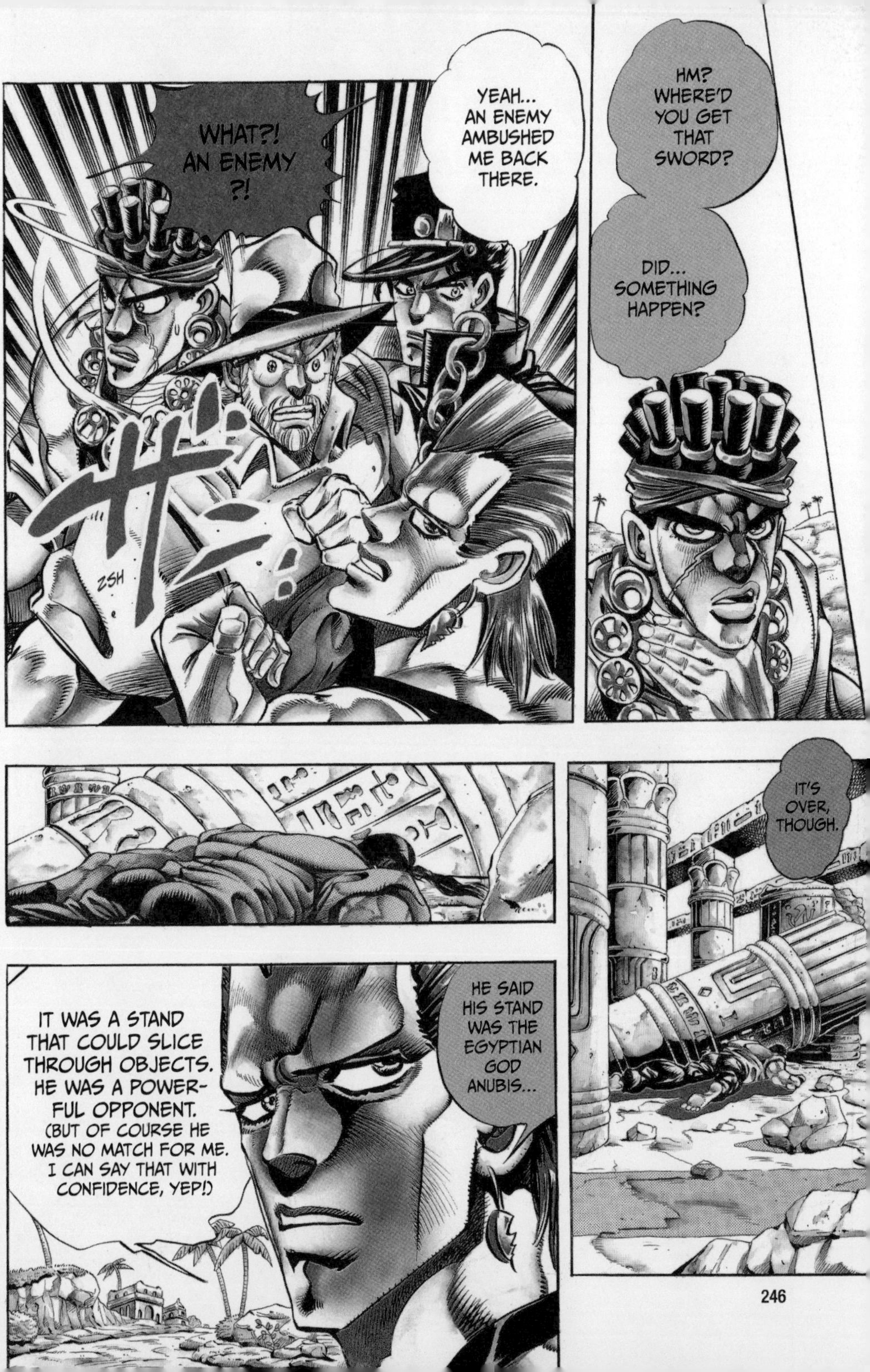
HM? WHERE'D YOU GET THAT SWORD?
DID... SOMETHING HAPPEN?
YEAH... AN ENEMY AMBUSHED ME BACK THERE.
WHAT?! AN ENEMY ?!
ZSH
IT'S OVER, THOUGH.
HE SAID HIS STAND WAS THE EGYPTIAN GOD ANUBIS...
IT WAS A STAND THAT COULD SLICE THROUGH OBJECTS. HE WAS A POWER-FUL OPPONENT.
(BUT OF COURSE HE WAS NO MATCH FOR ME. I CAN SAY THAT WITH CONFIDENCE, YEP!)

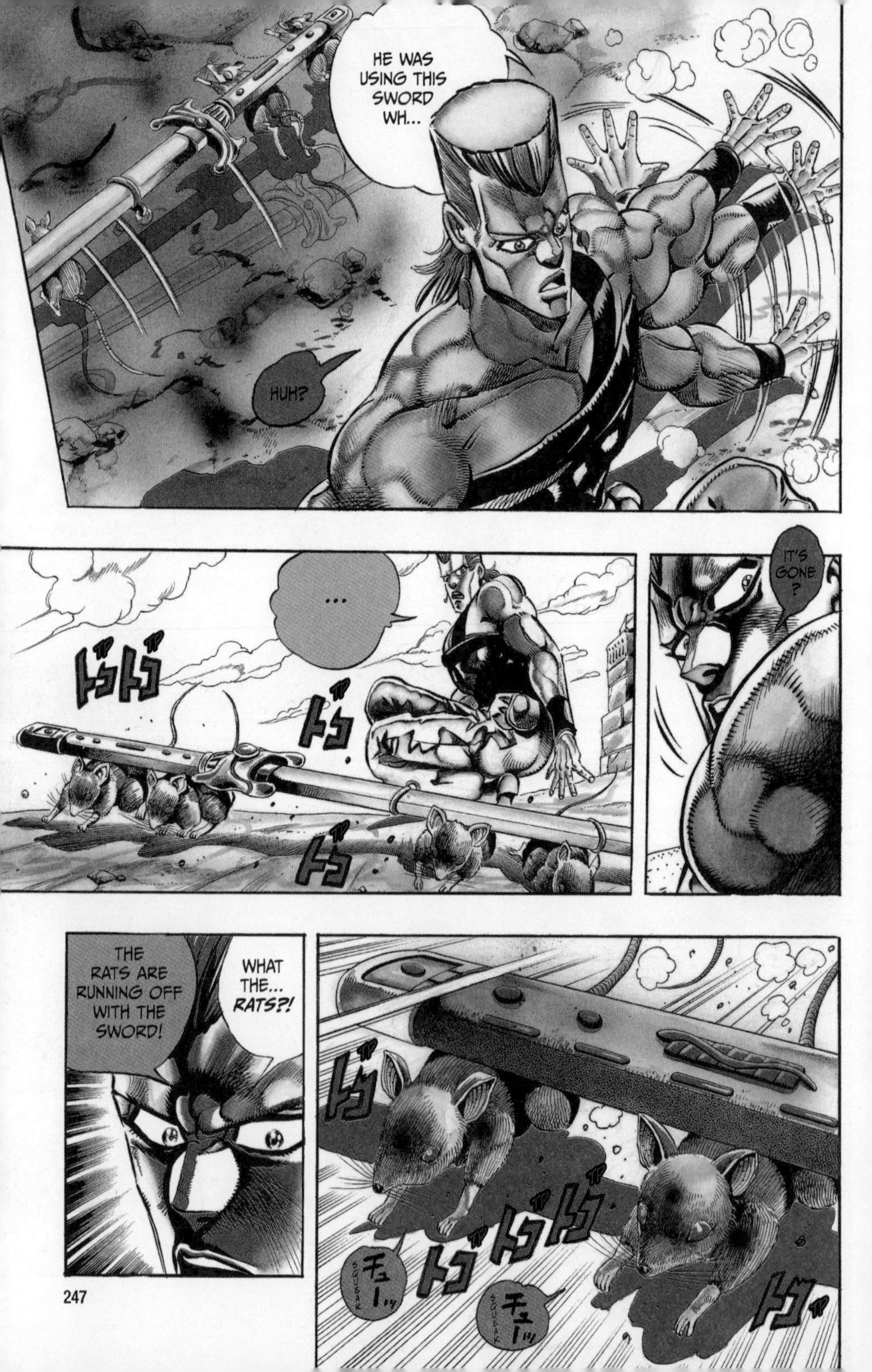
HE WAS USING THIS SWORD WH...
HUH?
IT'S GONE?
...
トットッ TP TP
トッ TP
トッ TP
WHAT THE... RATS?!
THE RATS ARE RUNNING OFF WITH THE SWORD!
トッ TP
トットットッ TP TP TP
トッ TP
チューッ SQUEAK
チューッ SQUEAK
トッ TP

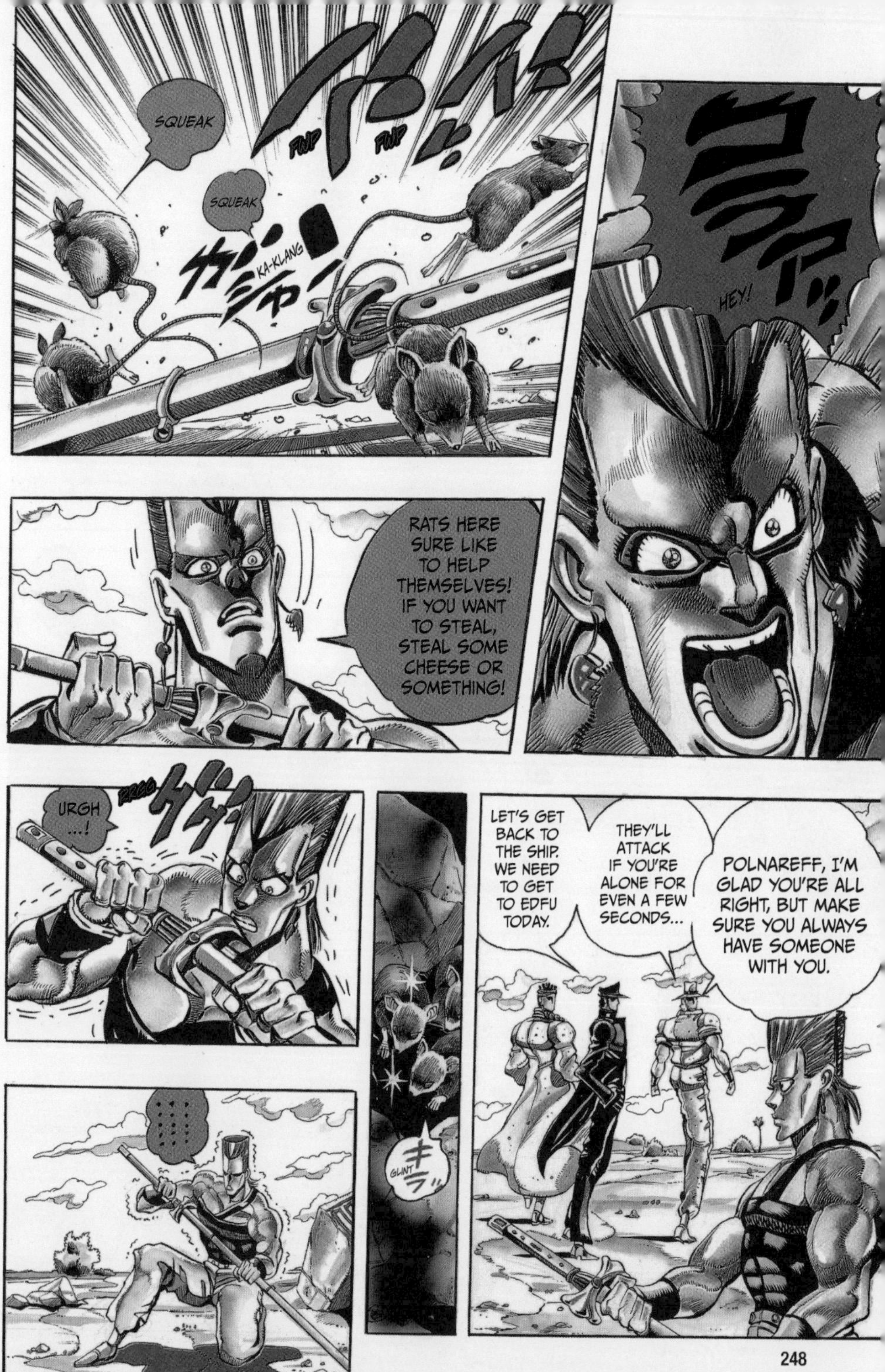
HEY!
SQUEAK
FWP
FWP
SQUEAK
KA-KLANG
RATS HERE SURE LIKE TO HELP THEMSELVES! IF YOU WANT TO STEAL, STEAL SOME CHEESE OR SOMETHING!
POLNAREFF, I'M GLAD YOU'RE ALL RIGHT, BUT MAKE SURE YOU ALWAYS HAVE SOMEONE WITH YOU.
THEY'LL ATTACK IF YOU'RE ALONE FOR EVEN A FEW SECONDS...
LET'S GET BACK TO THE SHIP. WE NEED TO GET TO EDFU TODAY.
GLINT
RRGG
URGH ...!

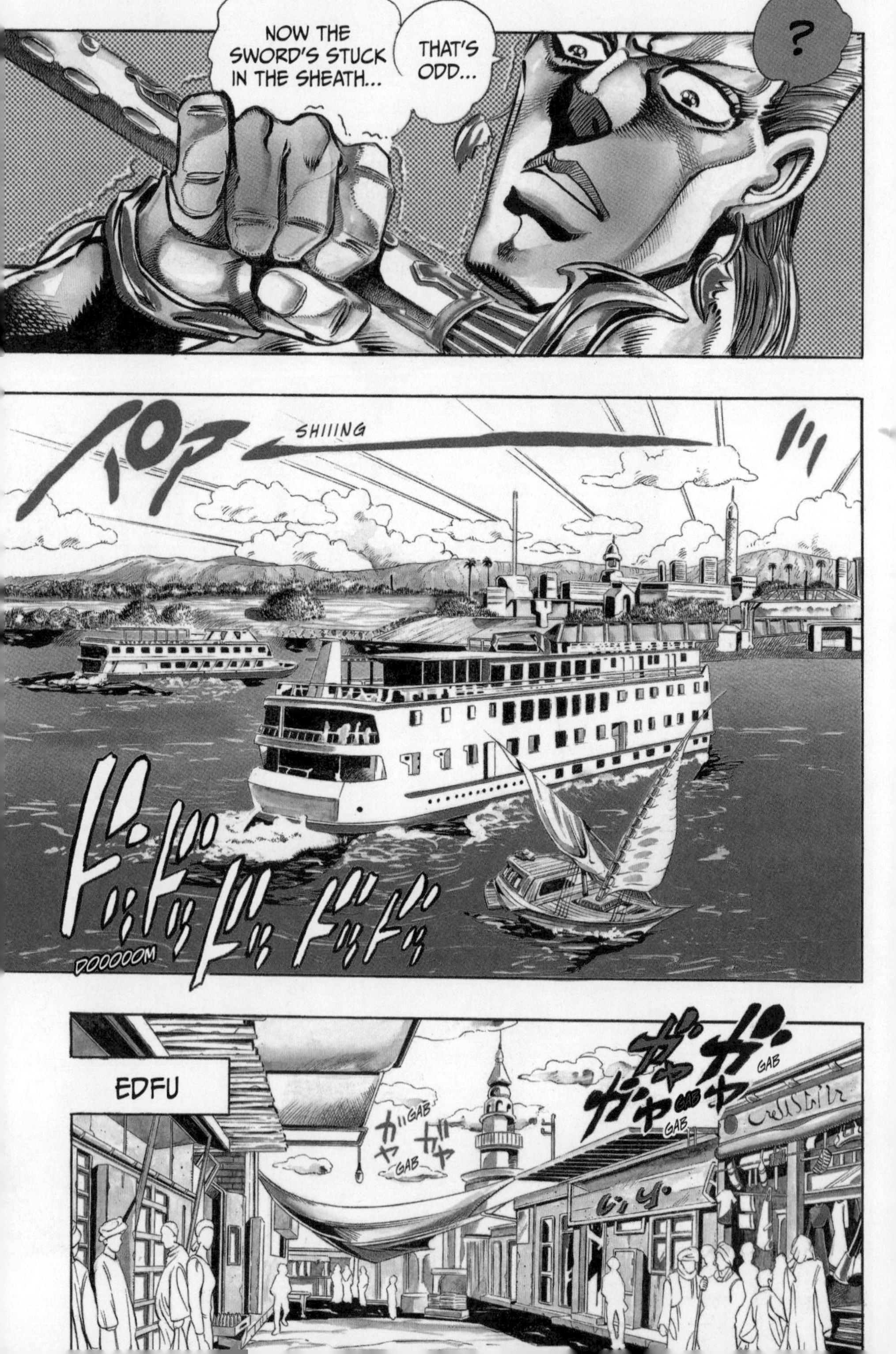
?
THAT'S ODD...
NOW THE SWORD'S STUCK IN THE SHEATH...
SHIIING
DOOOOOM
GAB GAB GAB
GAB GAB
EDFU

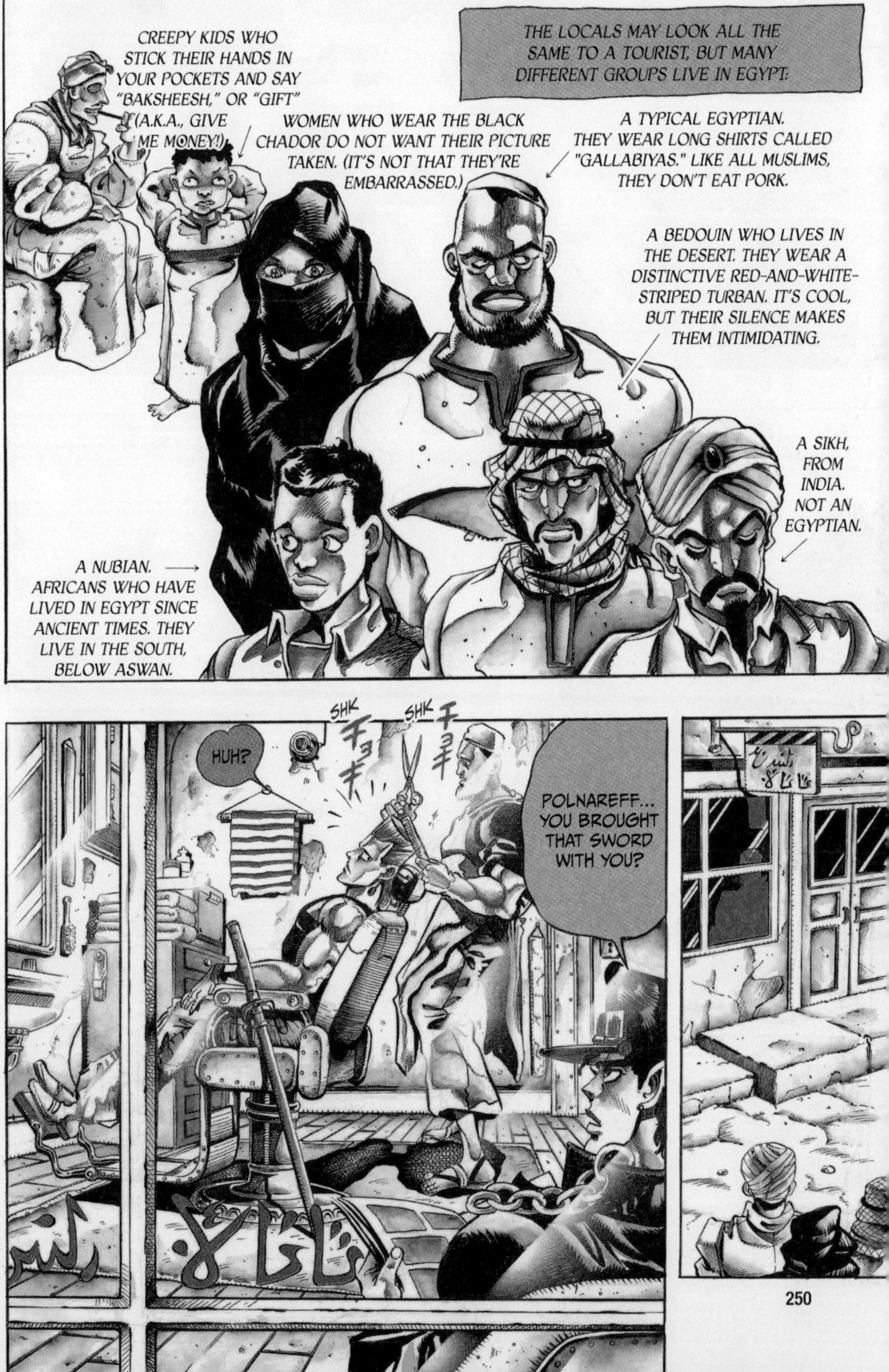
THE LOCALS MAY LOOK ALL THE SAME TO A TOURIST, BUT MANY DIFFERENT GROUPS LIVE IN EGYPT:
A TYPICAL EGYPTIAN. THEY WEAR LONG SHIRTS CALLED "GALLABIYAS." LIKE ALL MUSLIMS, THEY DON'T EAT PORK.
WOMEN WHO WEAR THE BLACK CHADOR DO NOT WANT THEIR PICTURE TAKEN. (IT'S NOT THAT THEY'RE EMBARRASSED.)
CREEPY KIDS WHO STICK THEIR HANDS IN YOUR POCKETS AND SAY "BAKSHEESH," OR "GIFT" (A.K.A., GIVE ME MONEY!)
A BEDOUIN WHO LIVES IN THE DESERT. THEY WEAR A DISTINCTIVE RED-AND-WHITE-STRIPED TURBAN. IT'S COOL, BUT THEIR SILENCE MAKES THEM INTIMIDATING.
A SIKH, FROM INDIA. NOT AN EGYPTIAN.
A NUBIAN. AFRICANS WHO HAVE LIVED IN EGYPT SINCE ANCIENT TIMES. THEY LIVE IN THE SOUTH, BELOW ASWAN.
POLNAREFF... YOU BROUGHT THAT SWORD WITH YOU?
SHK
SHK
HUH?

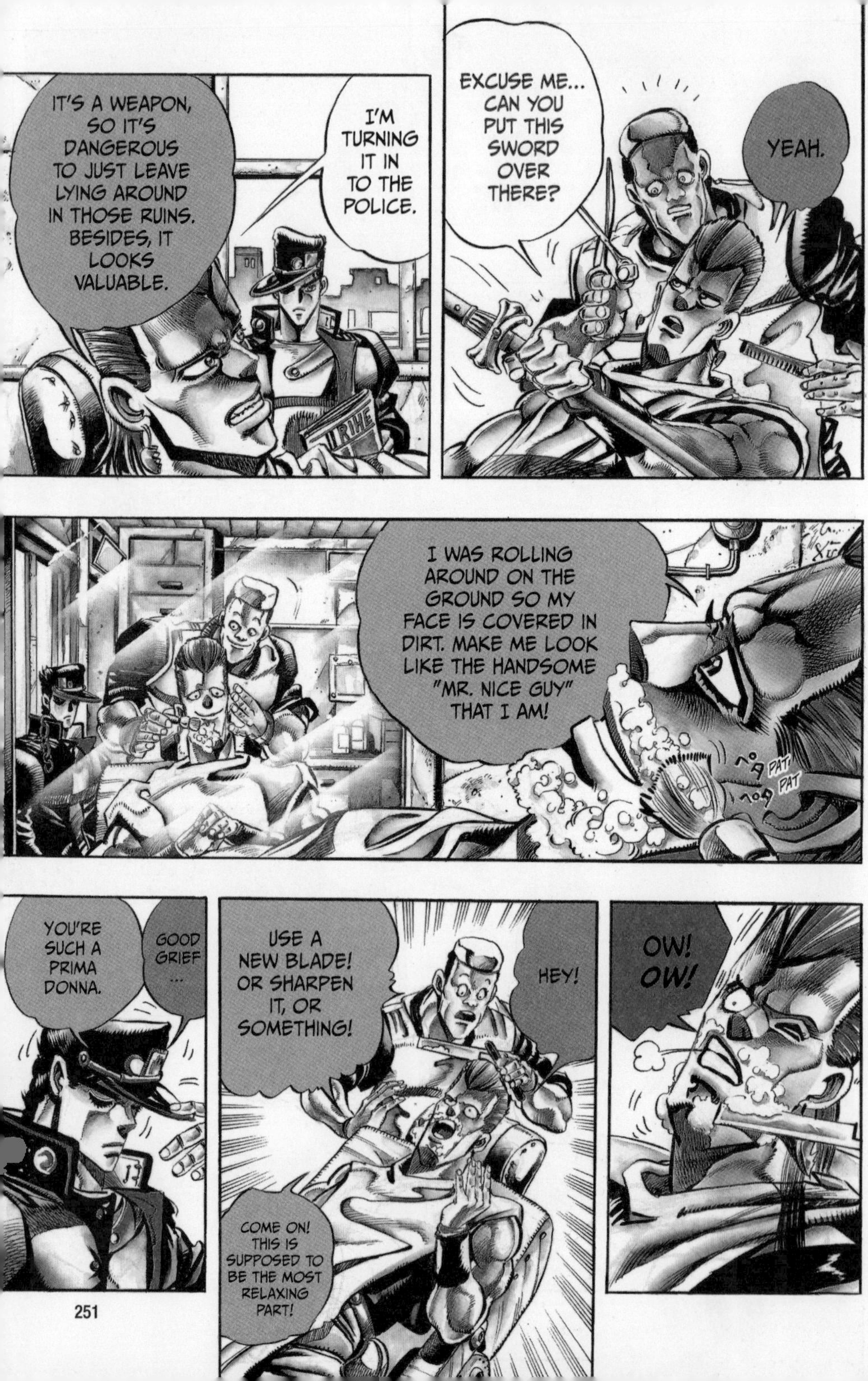
EXCUSE ME... CAN YOU PUT THIS SWORD OVER THERE?
YEAH.
I'M TURNING IT IN TO THE POLICE.
IT'S A WEAPON, SO IT'S DANGEROUS TO JUST LEAVE LYING AROUND IN THOSE RUINS. BESIDES, IT LOOKS VALUABLE.
I WAS ROLLING AROUND ON THE GROUND SO MY FACE IS COVERED IN DIRT. MAKE ME LOOK LIKE THE HANDSOME "MR. NICE GUY" THAT I AM!
ペタ PAT
ペタ PAT
OW! OW!
HEY!
USE A NEW BLADE! OR SHARPEN IT, OR SOMETHING!
COME ON! THIS IS SUPPOSED TO BE THE MOST RELAXING PART!
GOOD GRIEF ...
YOU'RE SUCH A PRIMA DONNA.

NOT SHARP? SO SORRY.
STROP
STROP
STROP
NOD
NOD
STROP
STROP
STROP
STROP
STROP
STROP
SPLSH
SPLSH
SPLSH
SPLSH
SPLSH
SPLSH
SPLSH
PAT
PAT

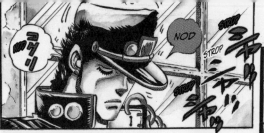

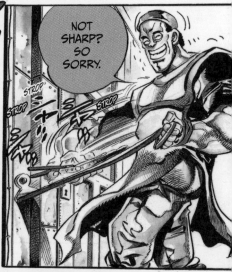

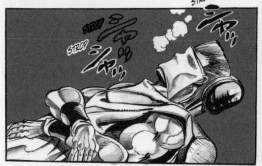

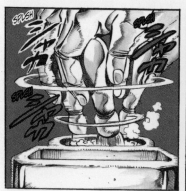

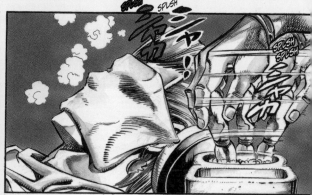

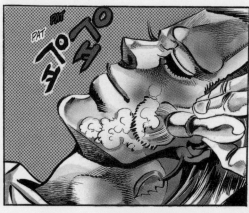

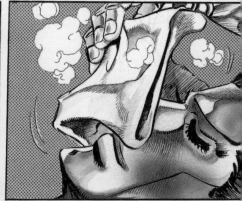

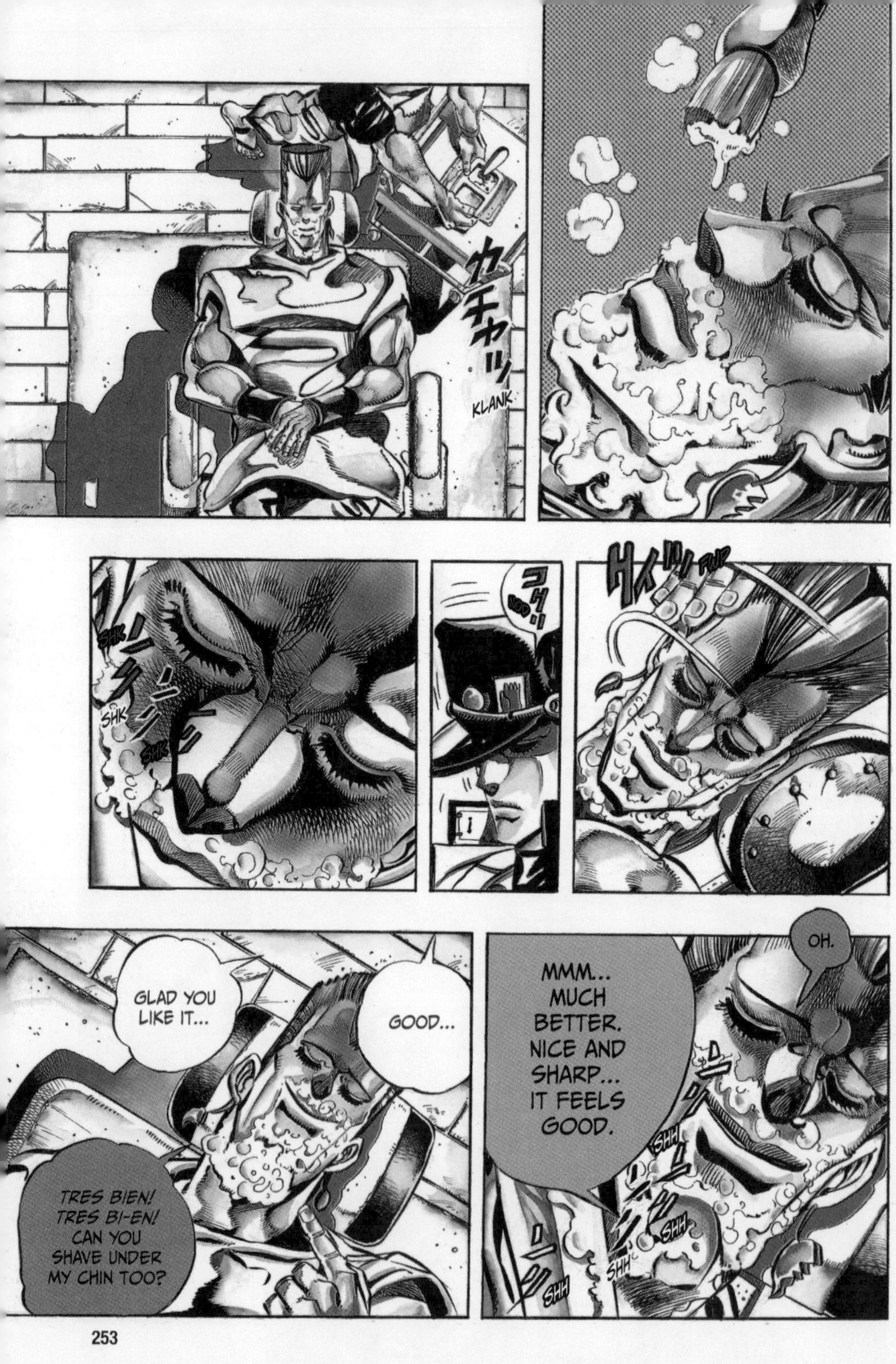
KLANK
FUP
NOD
SHK
SHK
SHK
OH.
MMM... MUCH BETTER. NICE AND SHARP... IT FEELS GOOD.
SHH
SHH
SHH
SHH
GOOD...
GLAD YOU LIKE IT...
TRES BIEN! TRES BI-EN! CAN YOU SHAVE UNDER MY CHIN TOO?

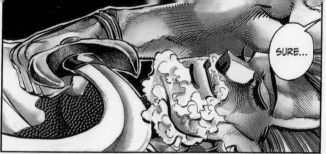

SURE...

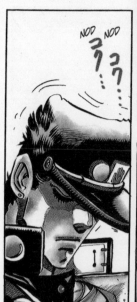

NOD NOD
コク...コク...

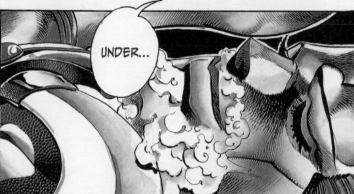

UNDER...

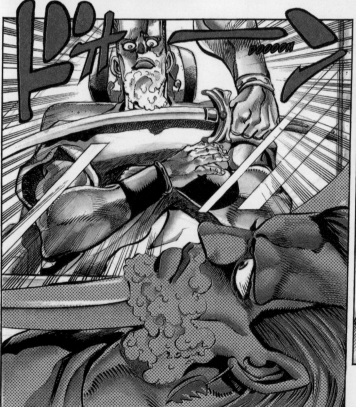

ドゴォーン
DOOOON

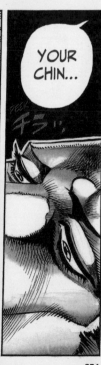

YOUR CHIN...

PEEK
チラッ

254

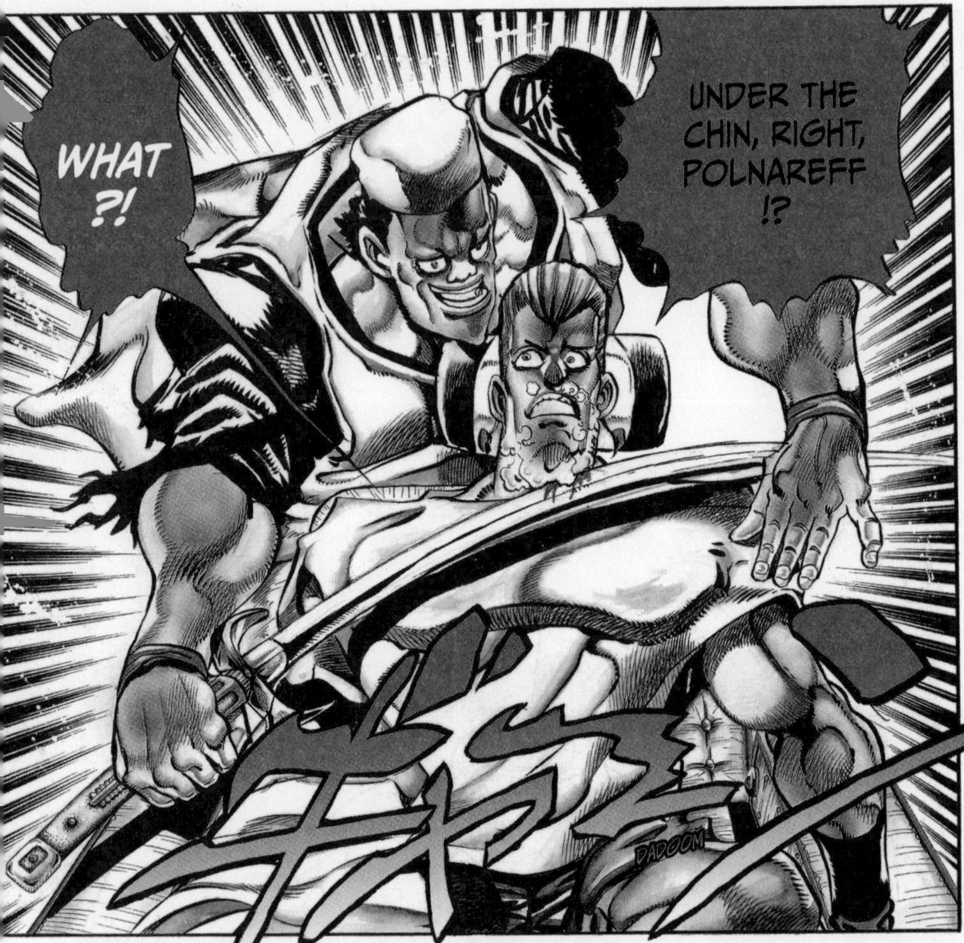
UNDER THE CHIN, RIGHT, POLNAREFF !?
WHAT ?!
DADOOM

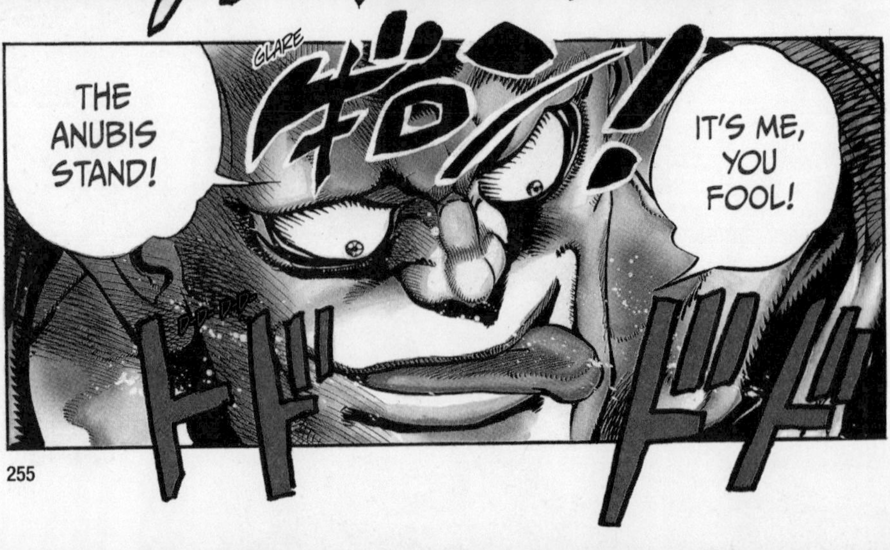
GLARE
IT'S ME, YOU FOOL!
THE ANUBIS STAND!

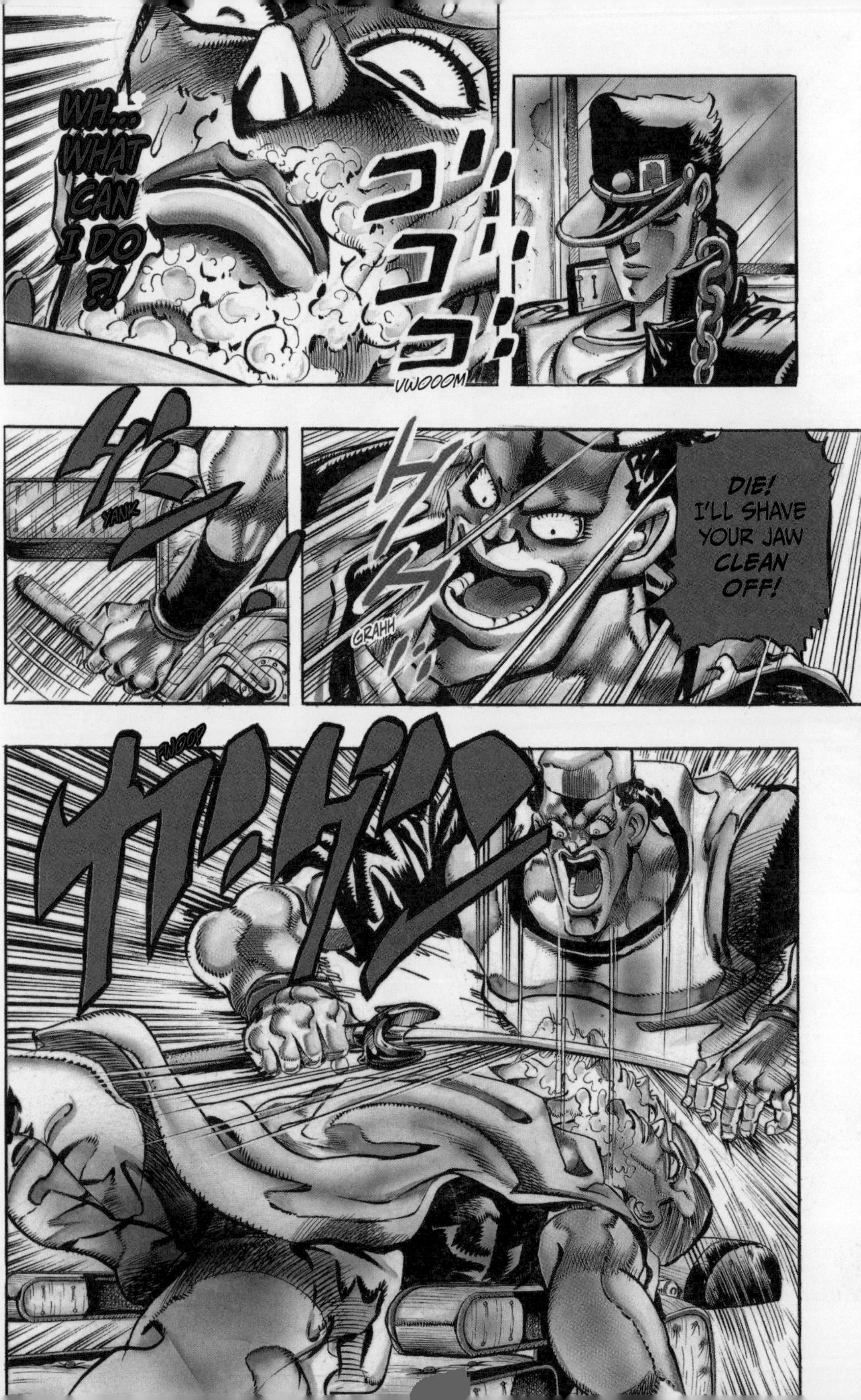
WH... WHAT CAN I DO ?!
VWOOOM
GRAHH
DIE! I'LL SHAVE YOUR JAW CLEAN OFF!
YANK
FWOOP

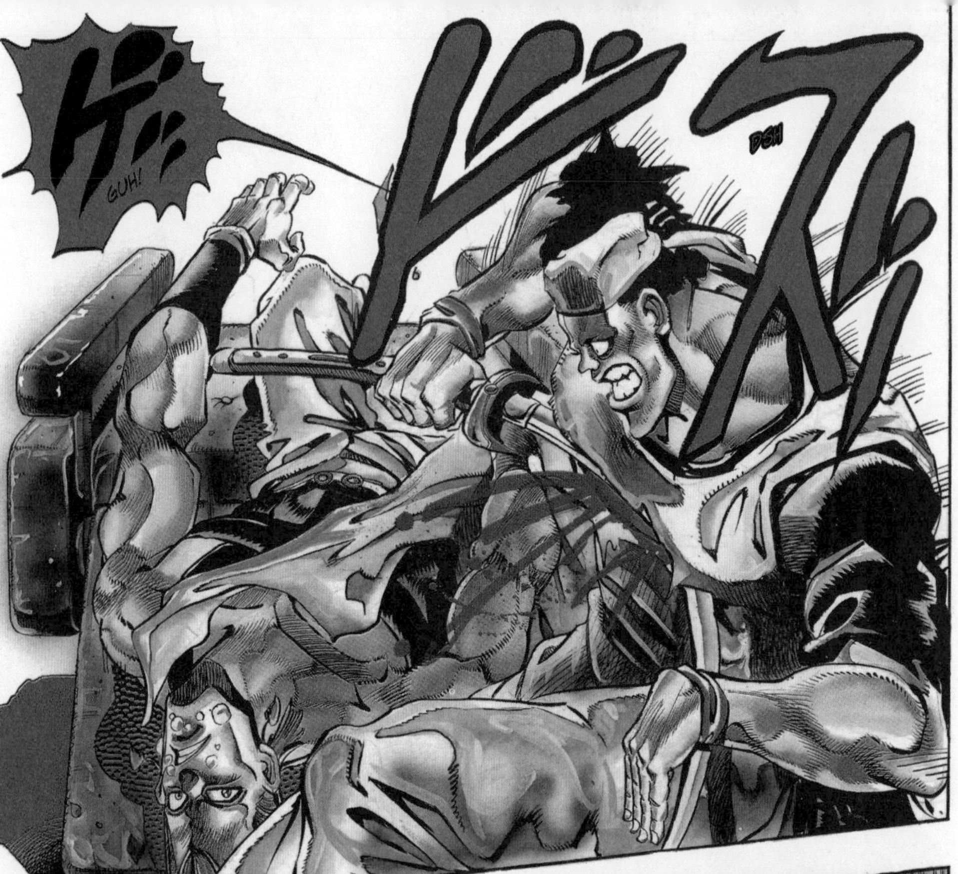
GUH!
DSH

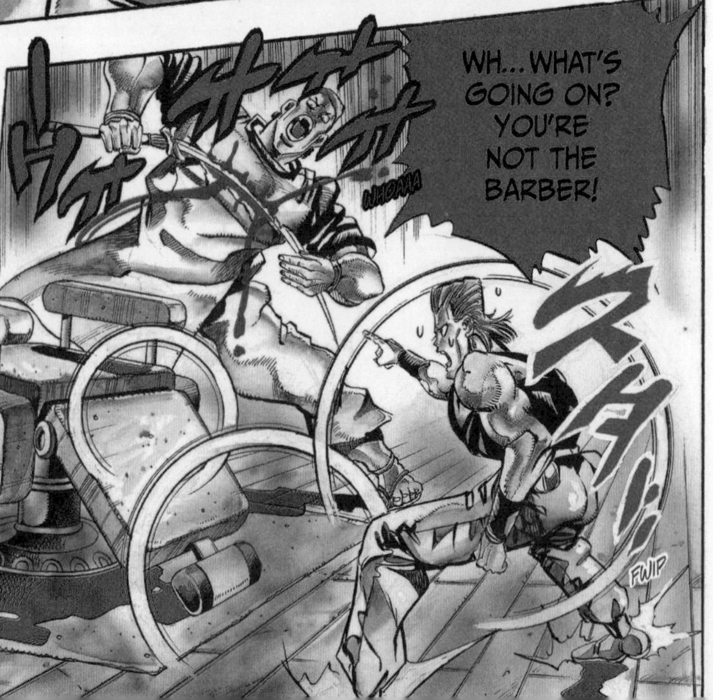
WHOAAA
WH...WHAT'S GOING ON? YOU'RE NOT THE BARBER!
FWIP

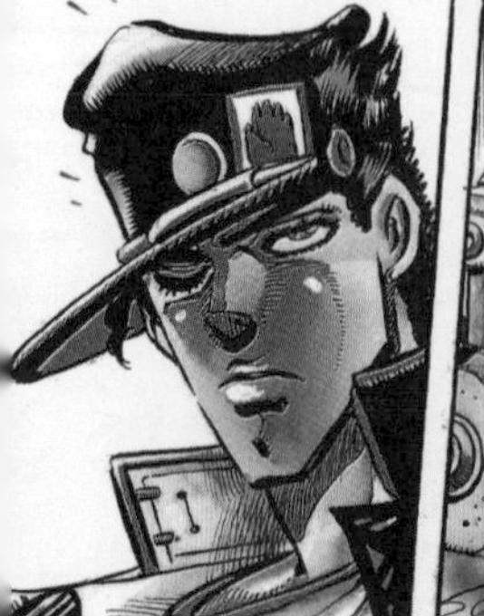

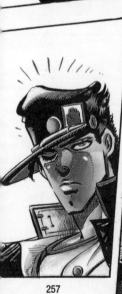

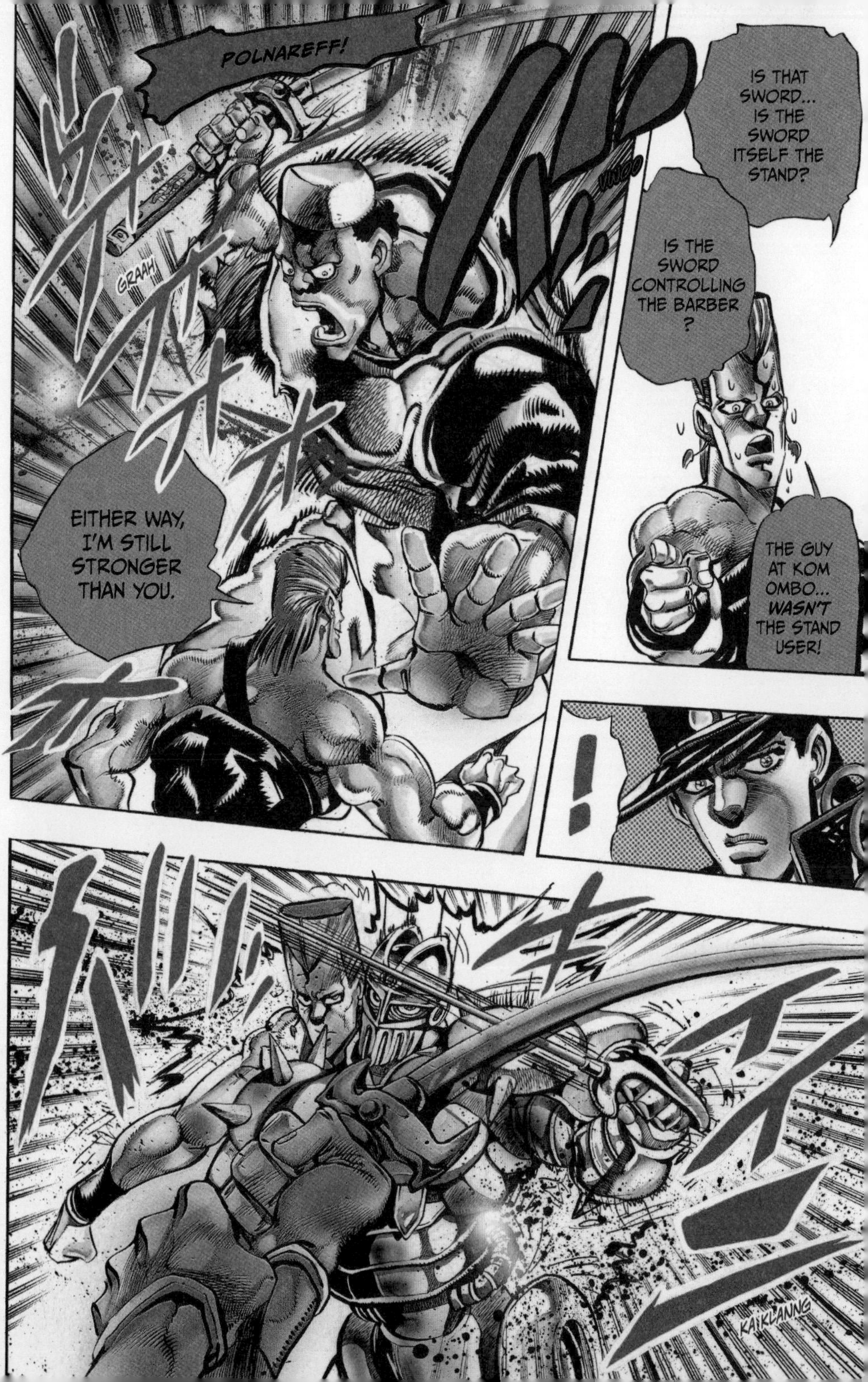
IS THAT SWORD... IS THE SWORD ITSELF THE STAND?
IS THE SWORD CONTROLLING THE BARBER?
THE GUY AT KOM OMBO... *WASN'T* THE STAND USER!
!
POLNAREFF!
VUUOO
GRAAH
EITHER WAY, I'M STILL STRONGER THAN YOU.
KAIKLANNG

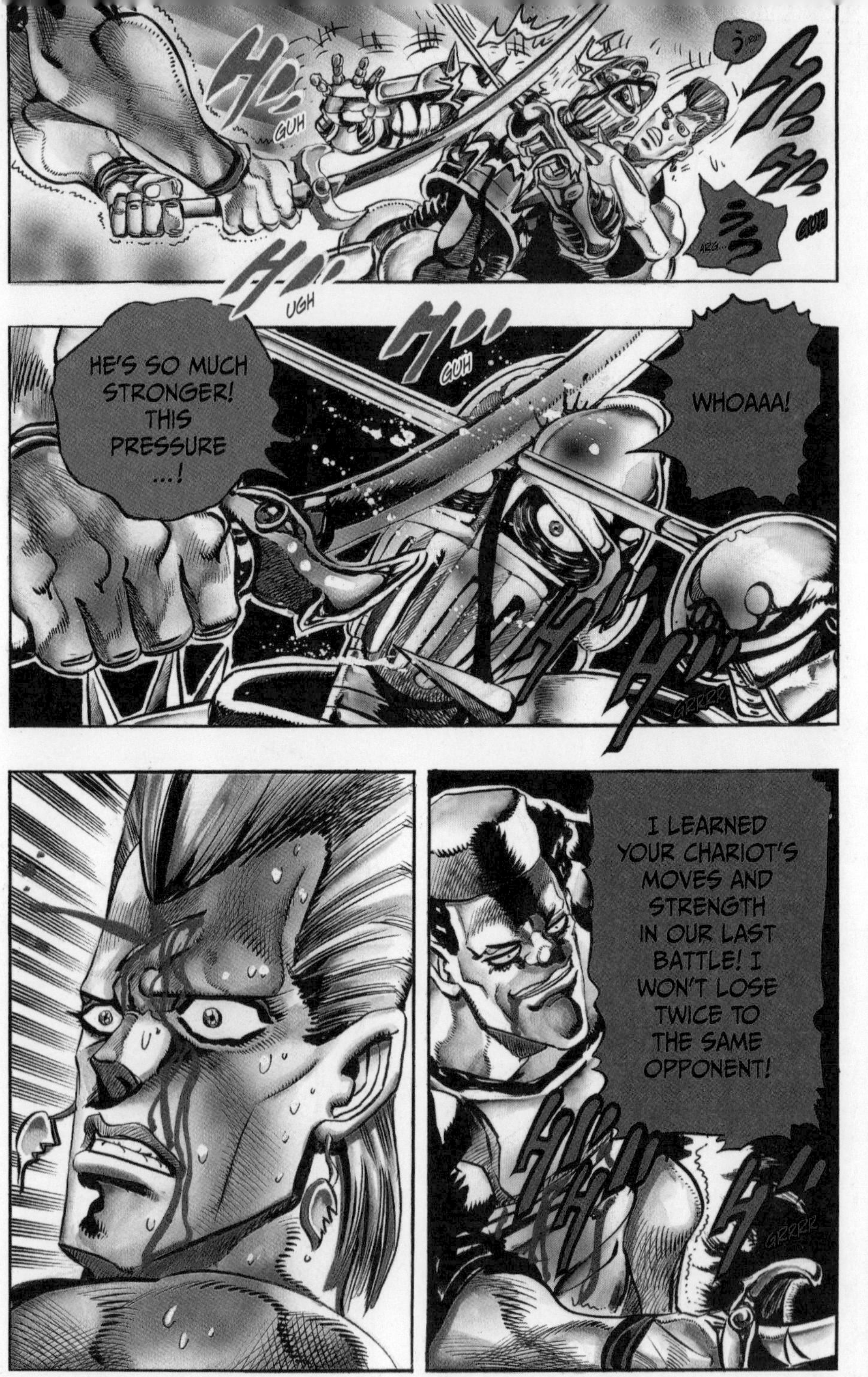
GUH
ARG...
GUH
UGH
WHOAAA!
HE'S SO MUCH STRONGER! THIS PRESSURE ...!
GUH
GRRRR
I LEARNED YOUR CHARIOT'S MOVES AND STRENGTH IN OUR LAST BATTLE! I WON'T LOSE TWICE TO THE SAME OPPONENT!
GRRRR

LUCKY LAND

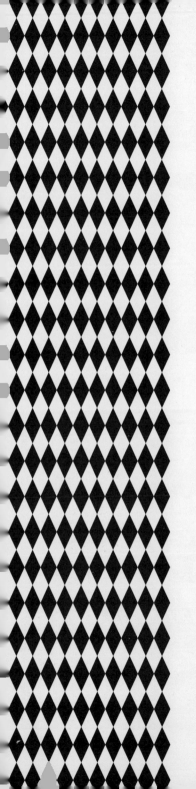

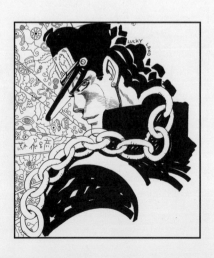

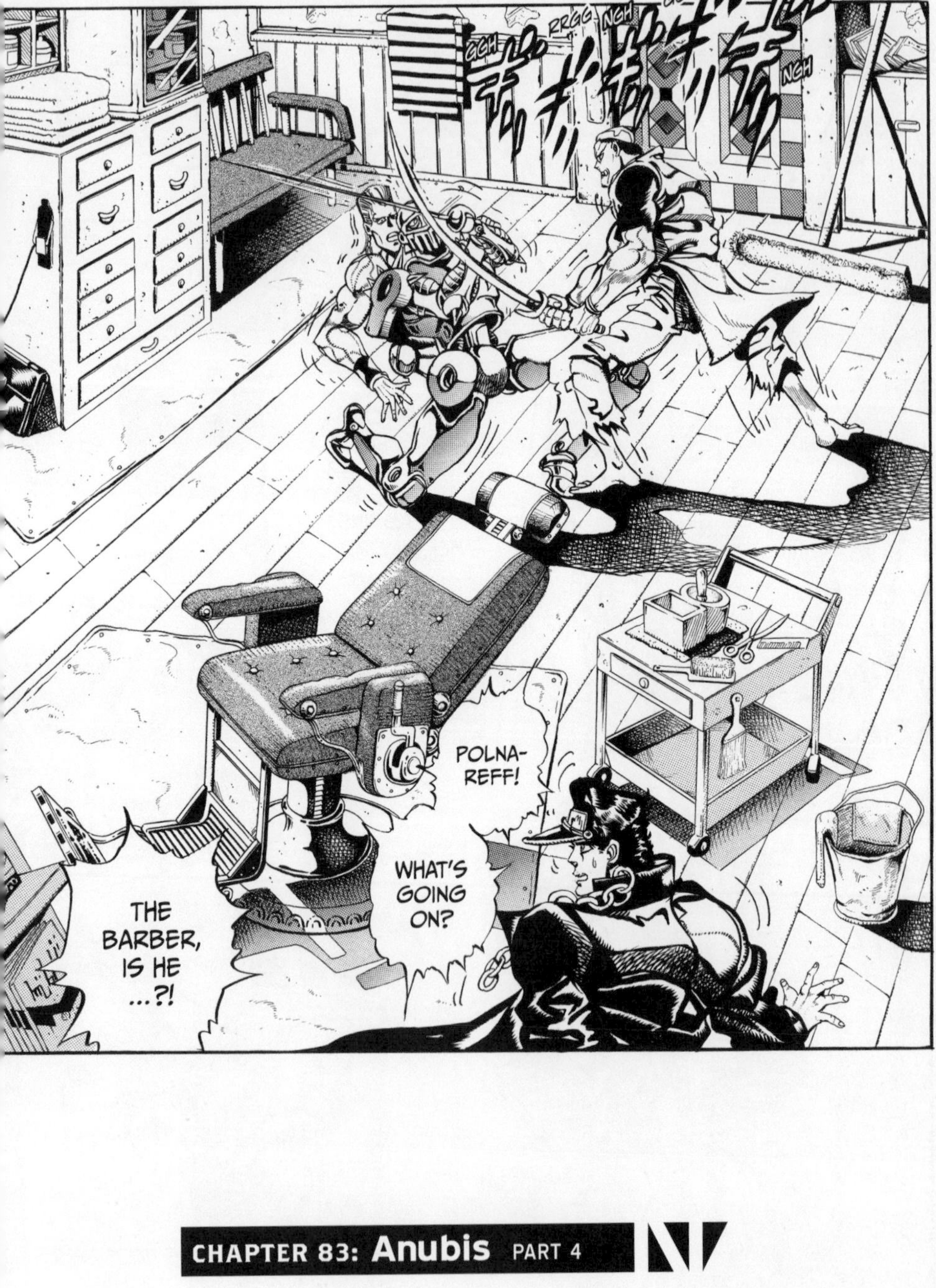
GGH
NGH
GGH
RRGG
NGH
GGH
POLNA-
REFF!
WHAT'S
GOING
ON?
THE
BARBER,
IS HE
...?!

CHAPTER 83: Anubis PART 4

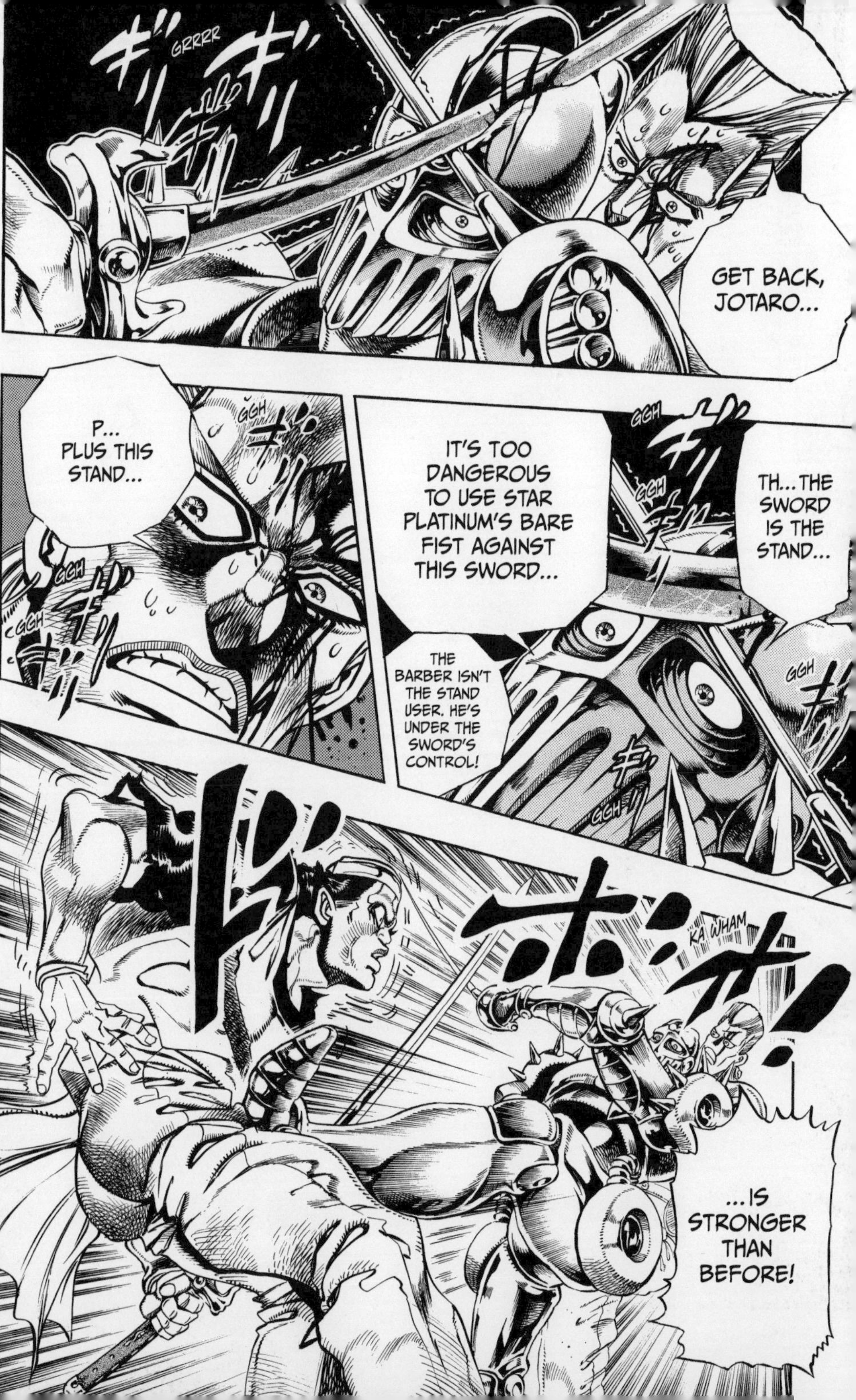
GET BACK, JOTARO...
GRRRR
TH... THE SWORD IS THE STAND...
GGH
GGH
IT'S TOO DANGEROUS TO USE STAR PLATINUM'S BARE FIST AGAINST THIS SWORD...
GGH
THE BARBER ISN'T THE STAND USER. HE'S UNDER THE SWORD'S CONTROL!
GGH
P... PLUS THIS STAND...
GGH
GGH
GGH
KA WHAM
...IS STRONGER THAN BEFORE!

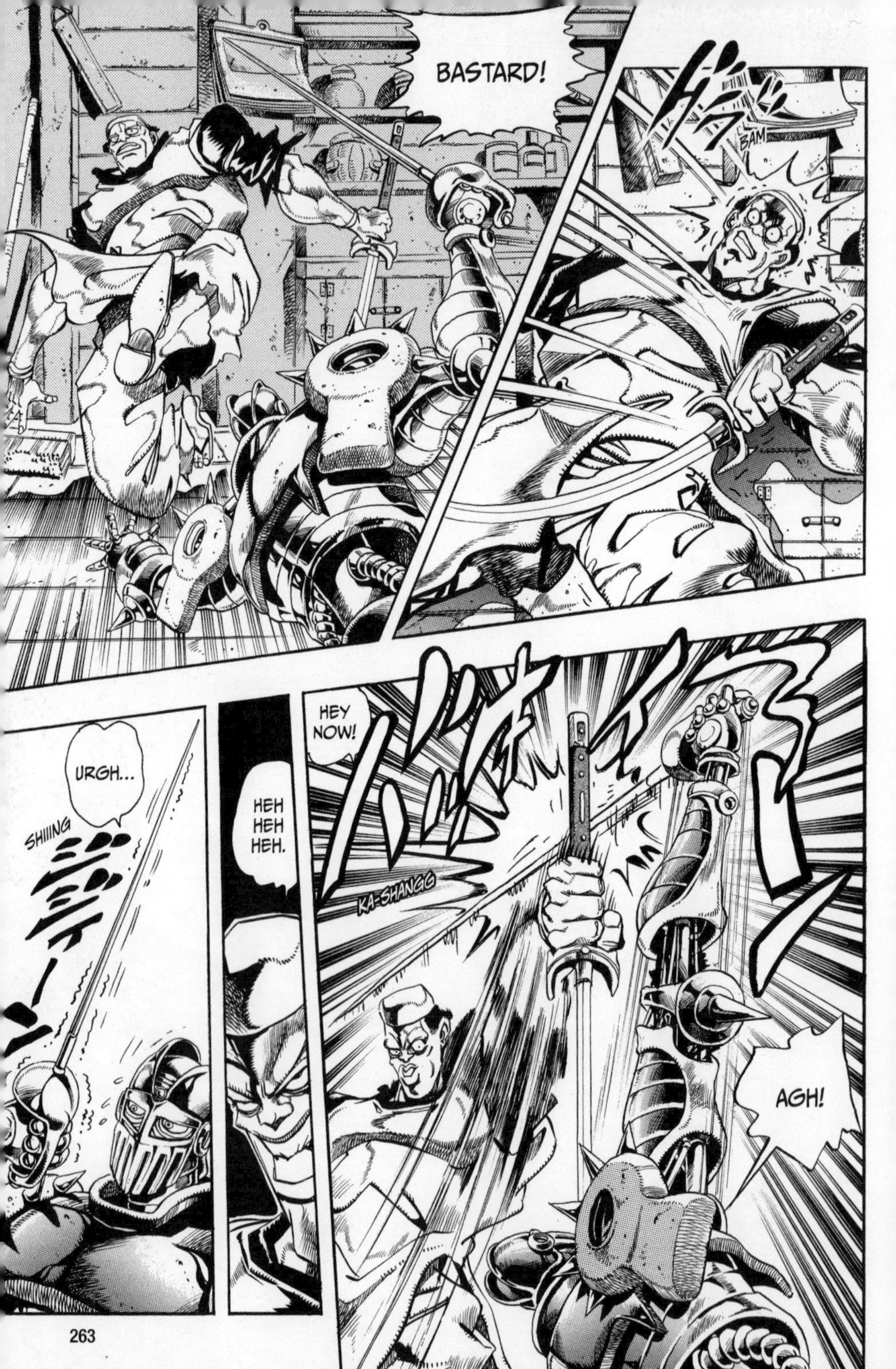
BAM
BASTARD!
HEY NOW!
KA-SHANGG
AGH!
HEH HEH HEH.
URGH...
SHIIING

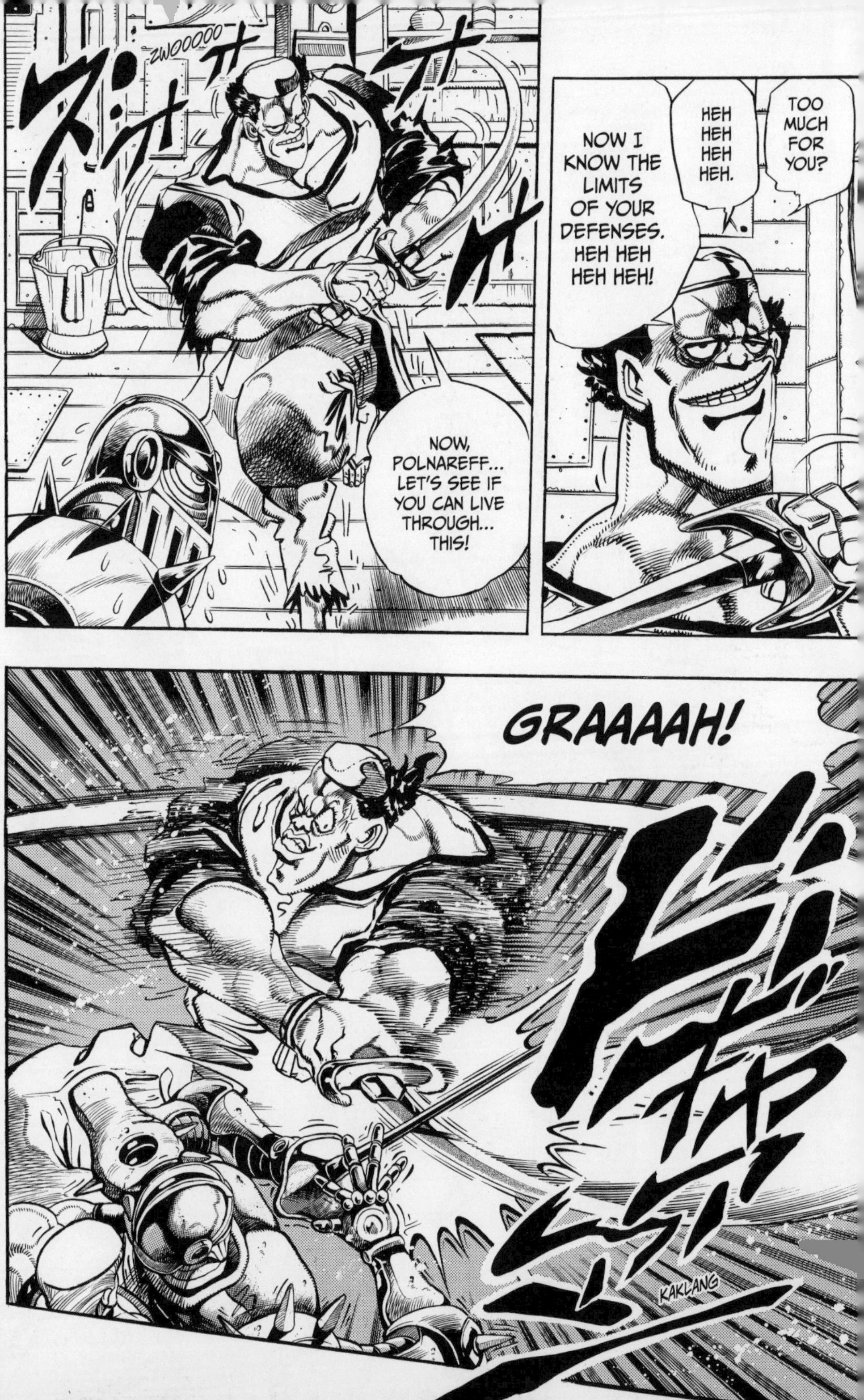
TOO MUCH FOR YOU?
HEH HEH HEH HEH.
NOW I KNOW THE LIMITS OF YOUR DEFENSES. HEH HEH HEH HEH!
ZWOOOOO
NOW, POLNAREFF... LET'S SEE IF YOU CAN LIVE THROUGH... THIS!
GRAAAAH!
KAKLANG

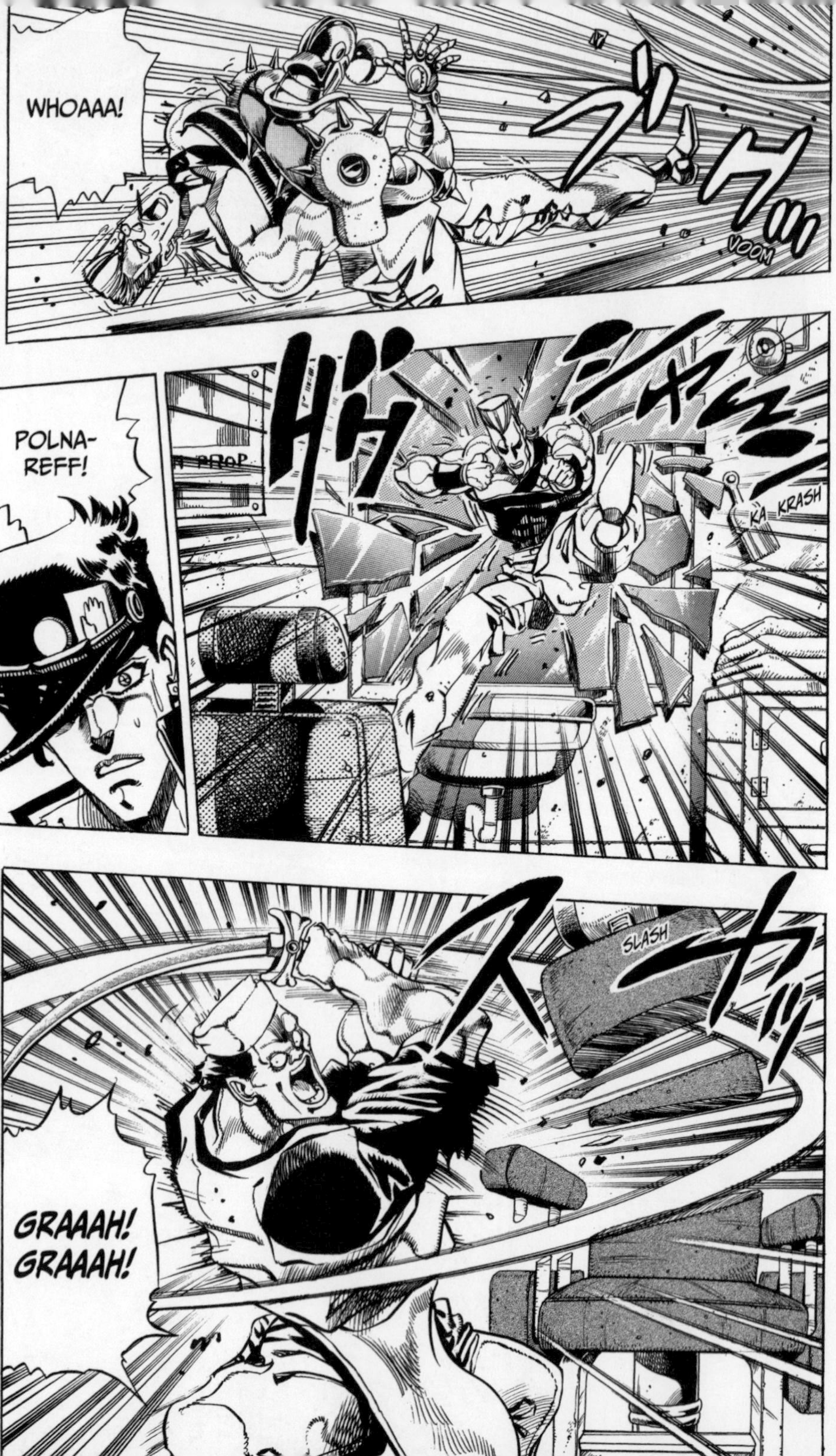
WHOAAA!
VOOM
KA KRASH
POLNA-REFF!
SLASH
GRAAAH! GRAAAH!

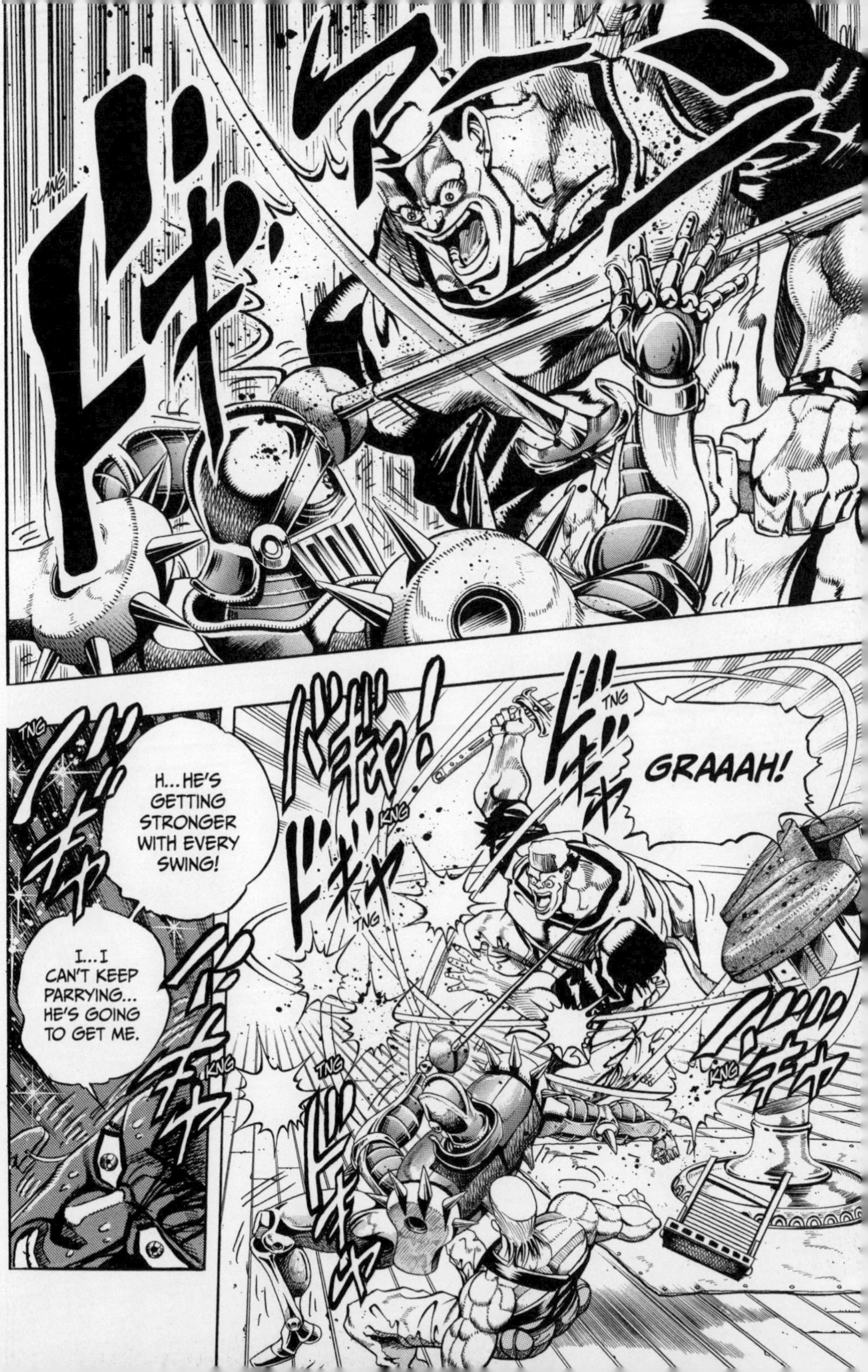
KLANG
TNG
GRAAAH!
KNG
KNG
TNG
TNG
H...HE'S GETTING STRONGER WITH EVERY SWING!
I...I CAN'T KEEP PARRYING... HE'S GOING TO GET ME.
TNG
KNG

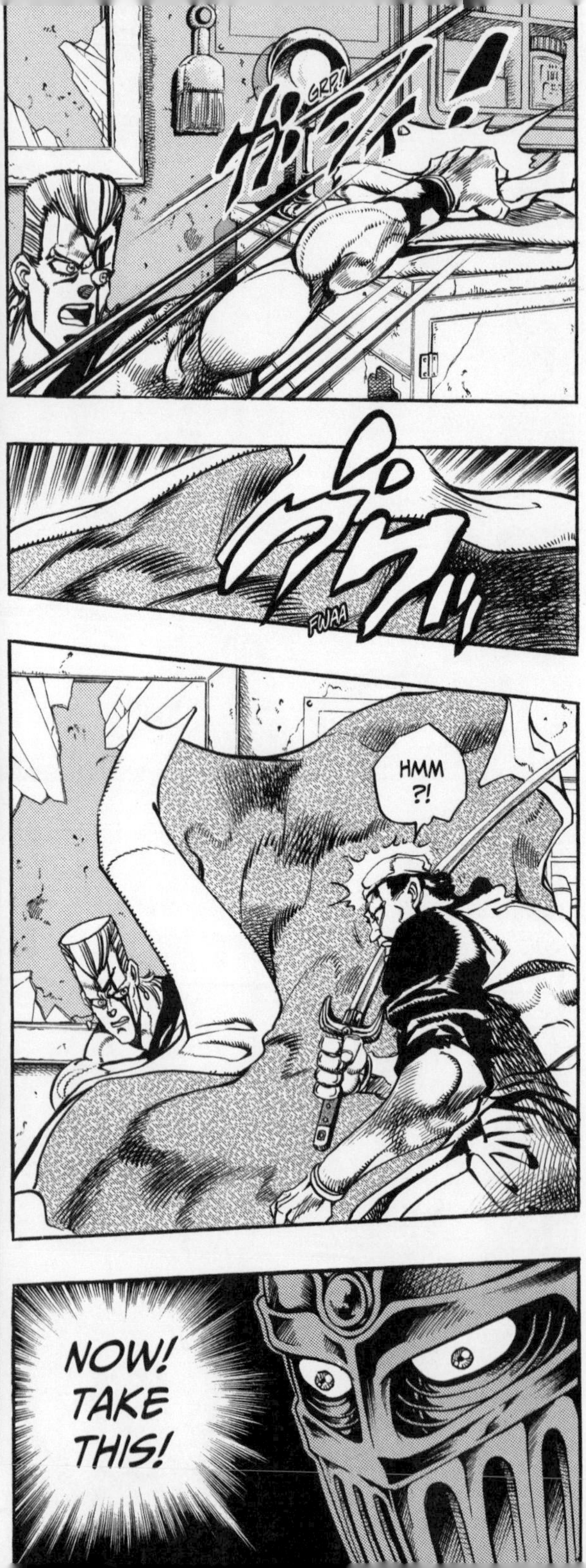
GRP!
FWAA
HMM ?!
NOW! TAKE THIS!
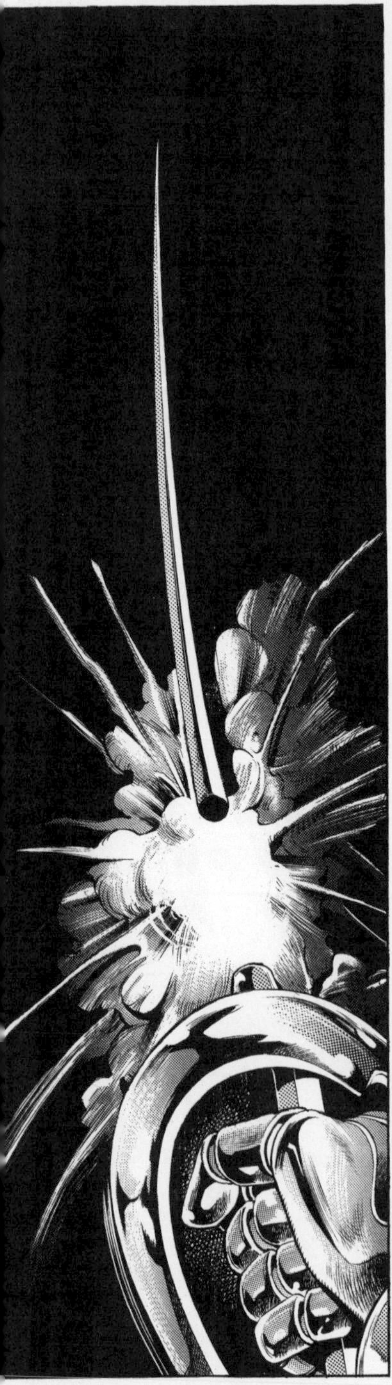

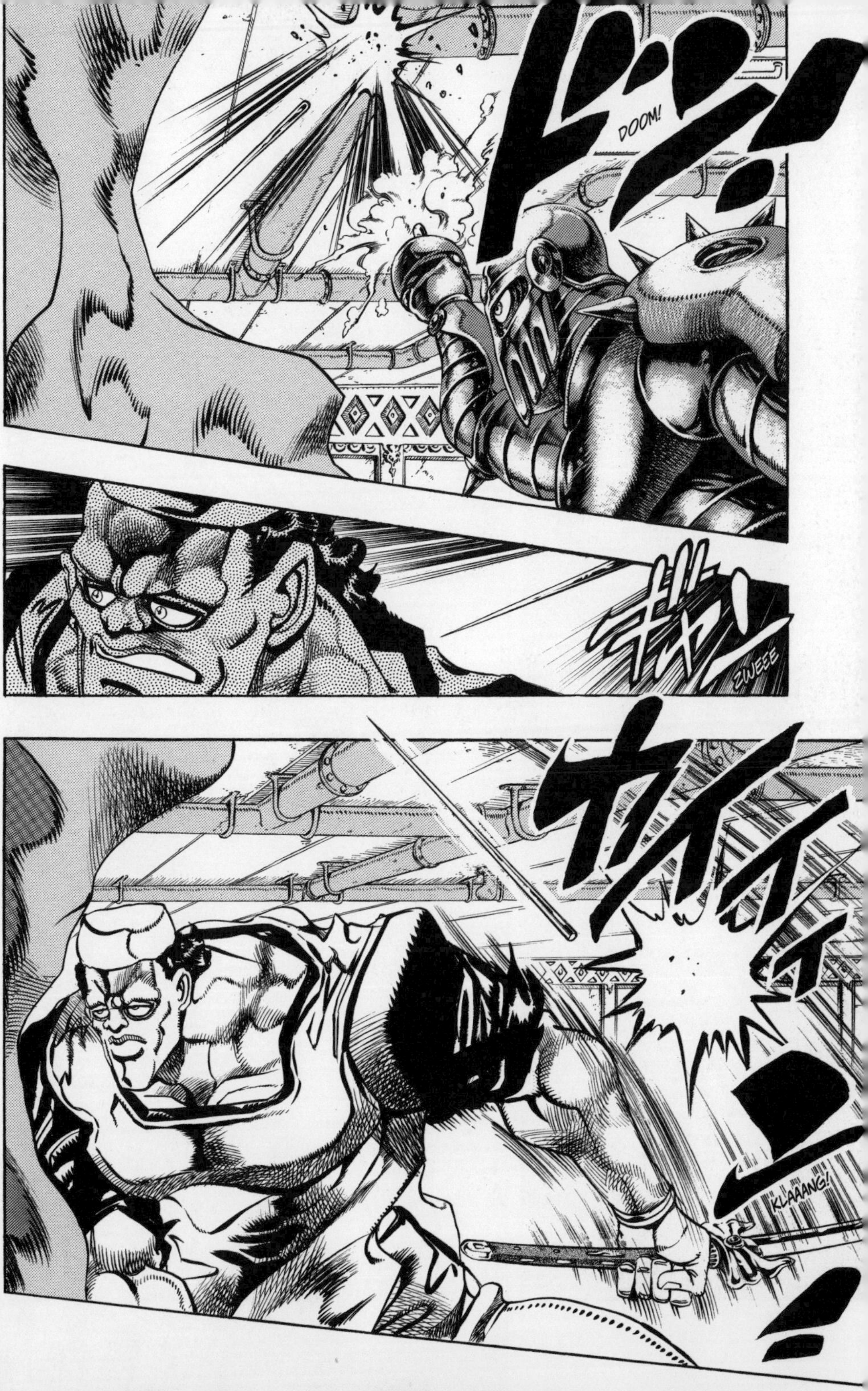
DOOM!
ZWEEE
KLAAANG!

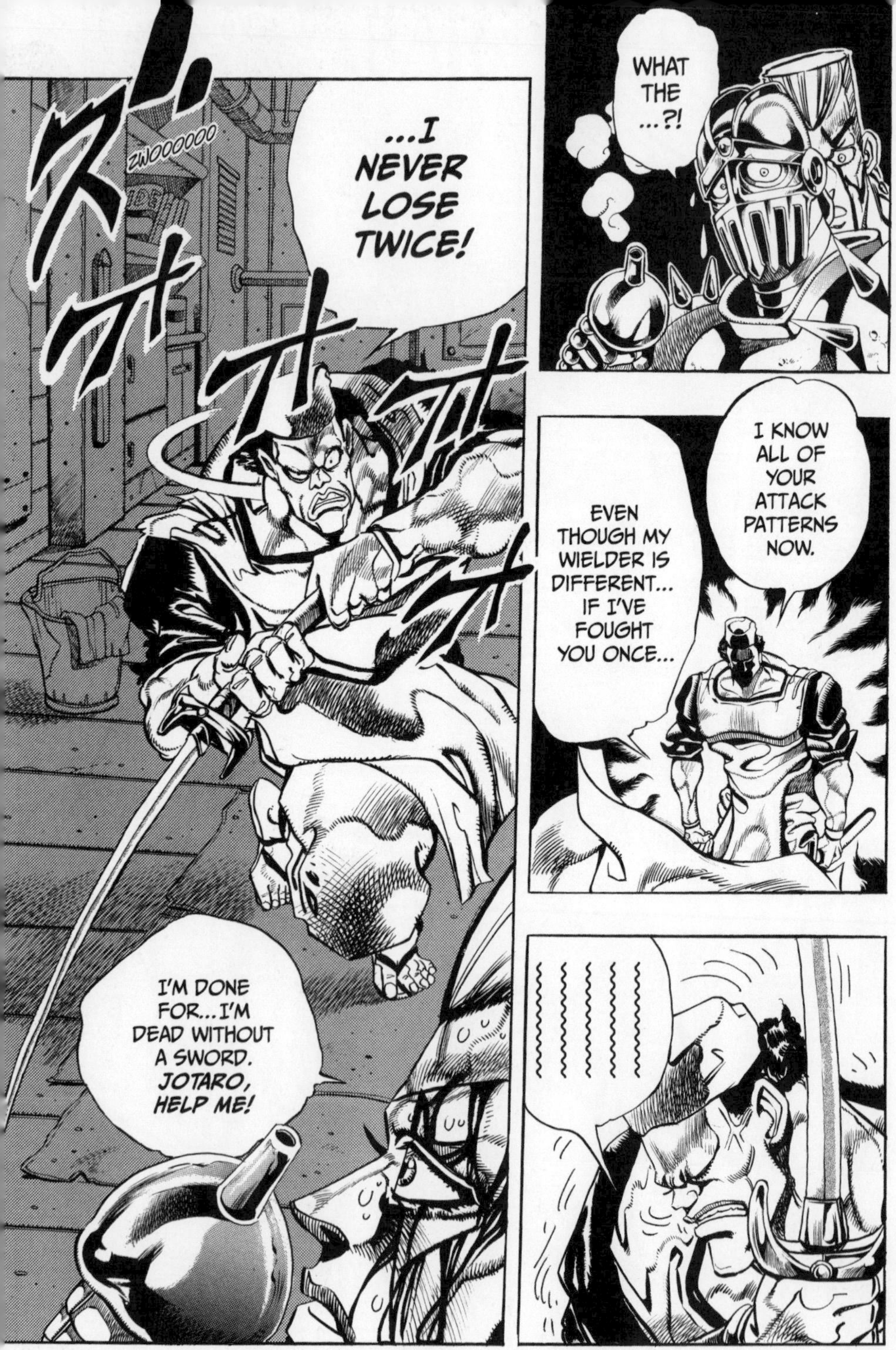
WHAT THE ...?!
I KNOW ALL OF YOUR ATTACK PATTERNS NOW.
EVEN THOUGH MY WIELDER IS DIFFERENT... IF I'VE FOUGHT YOU ONCE...
...I NEVER LOSE TWICE!
ZWOOOOOO
I'M DONE FOR...I'M DEAD WITHOUT A SWORD. JOTARO, HELP ME!

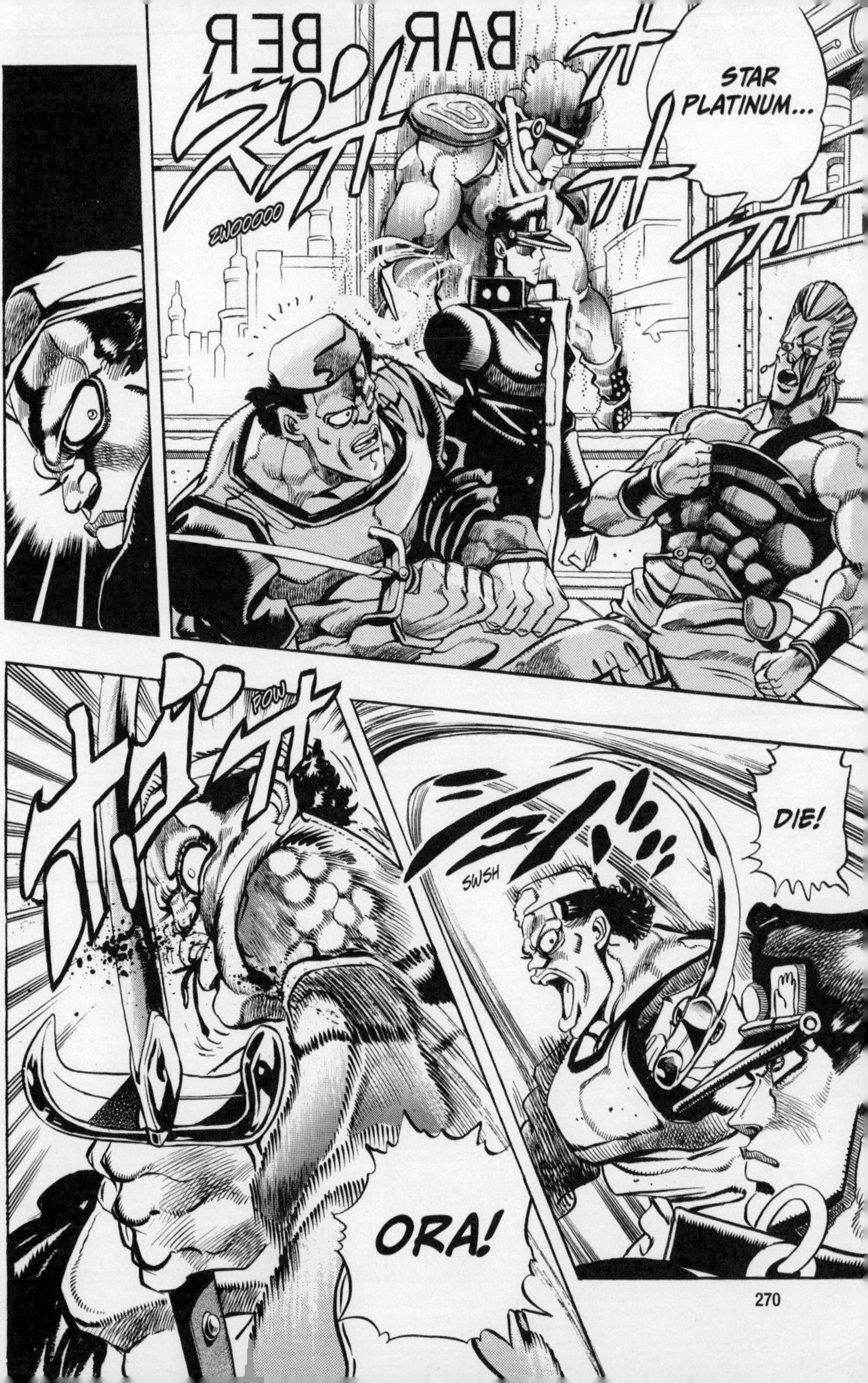
STAR PLATINUM...
BAR
BER
ZWOOOOO
DIE!
SWSH
POW
ORA!

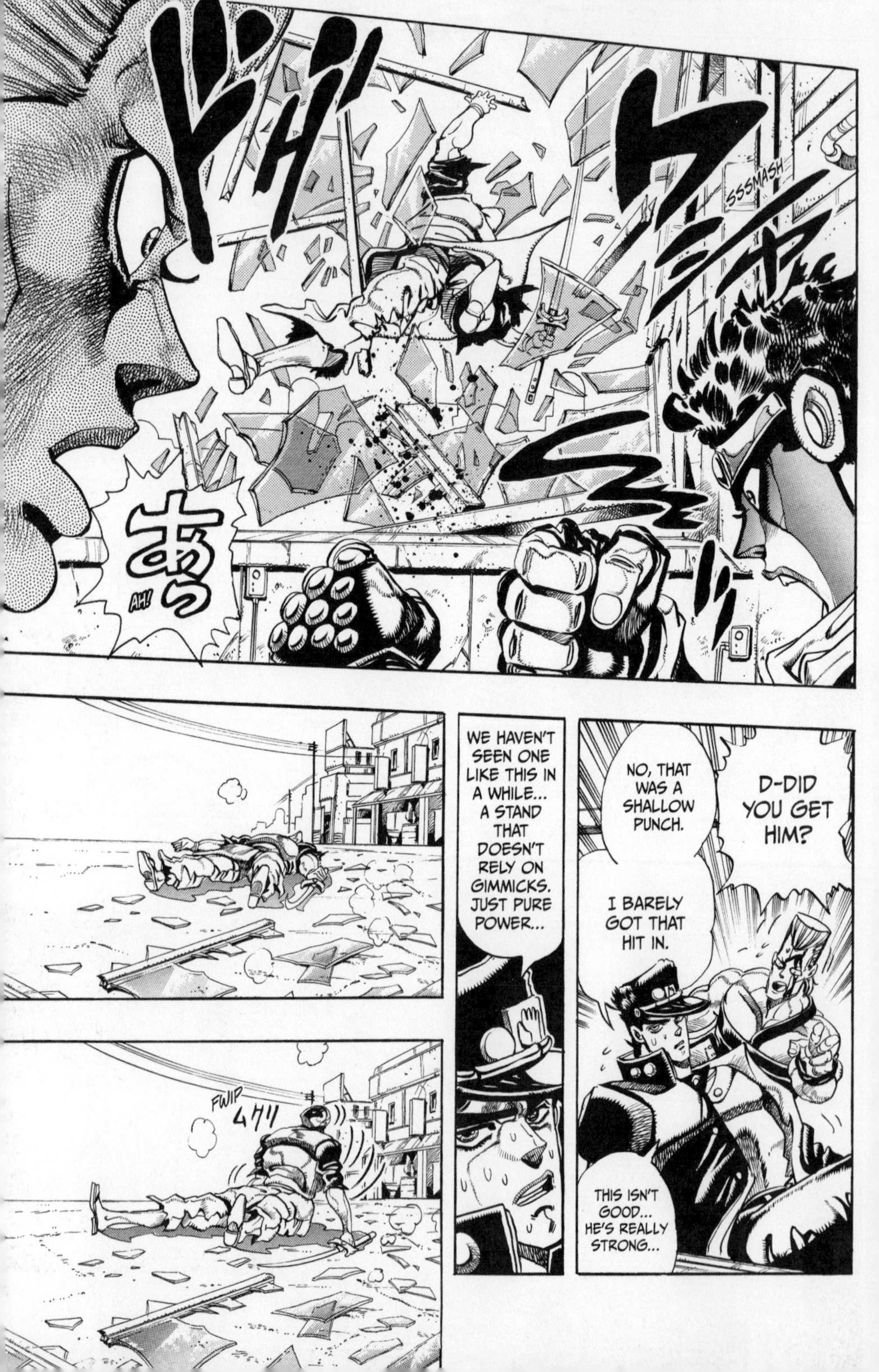
SSSMASH
あっ
AH!
D-DID YOU GET HIM?
NO, THAT WAS A SHALLOW PUNCH.
I BARELY GOT THAT HIT IN.
THIS ISN'T GOOD... HE'S REALLY STRONG...
WE HAVEN'T SEEN ONE LIKE THIS IN A WHILE... A STAND THAT DOESN'T RELY ON GIMMICKS. JUST PURE POWER...
FWIP
ムクリ

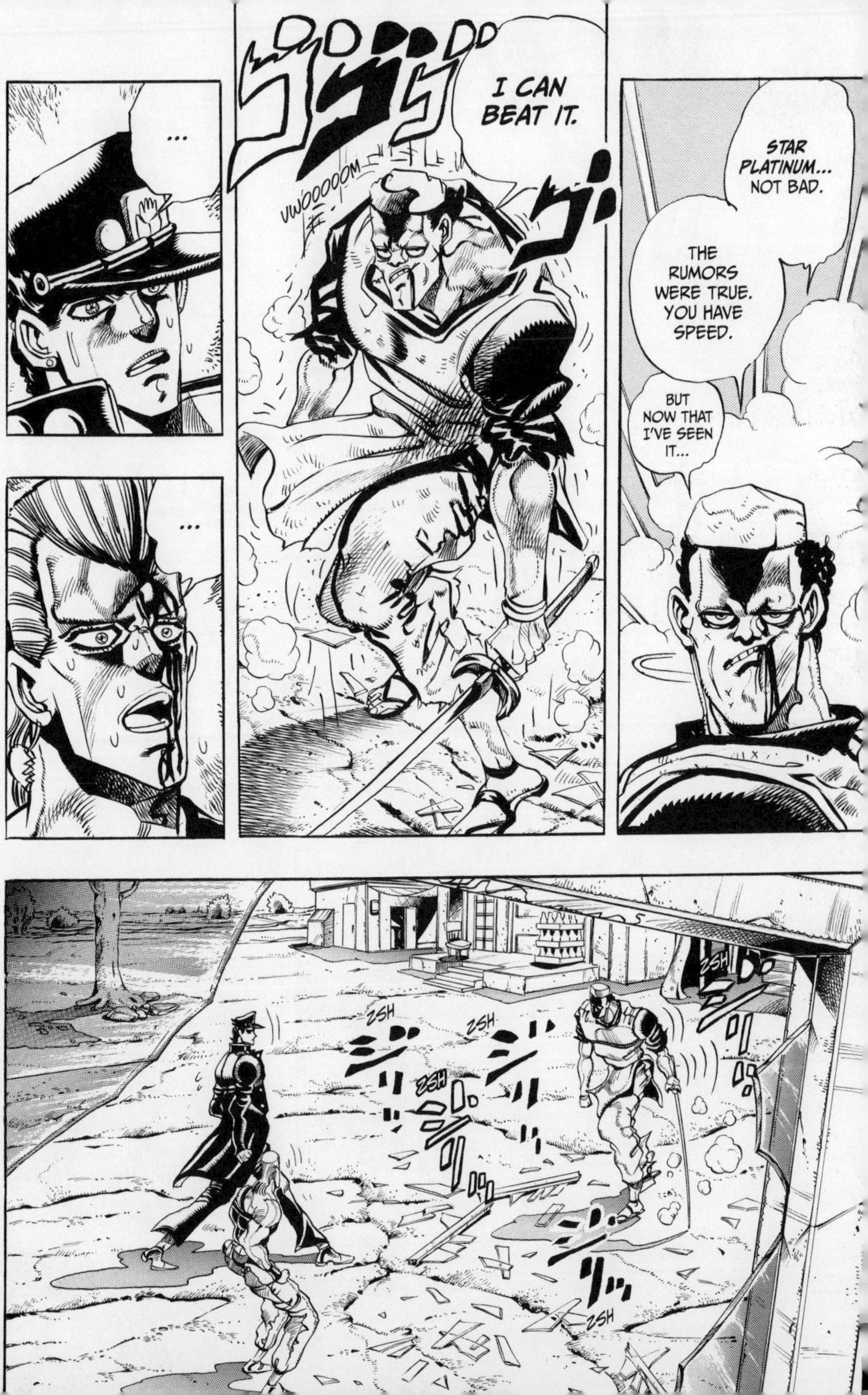
STAR PLATINUM... NOT BAD.
THE RUMORS WERE TRUE. YOU HAVE SPEED.
BUT NOW THAT I'VE SEEN IT...
I CAN BEAT IT.
VWOOOOOM
...
...
ZSH
ZSH
ZSH
ZSH
ZSH

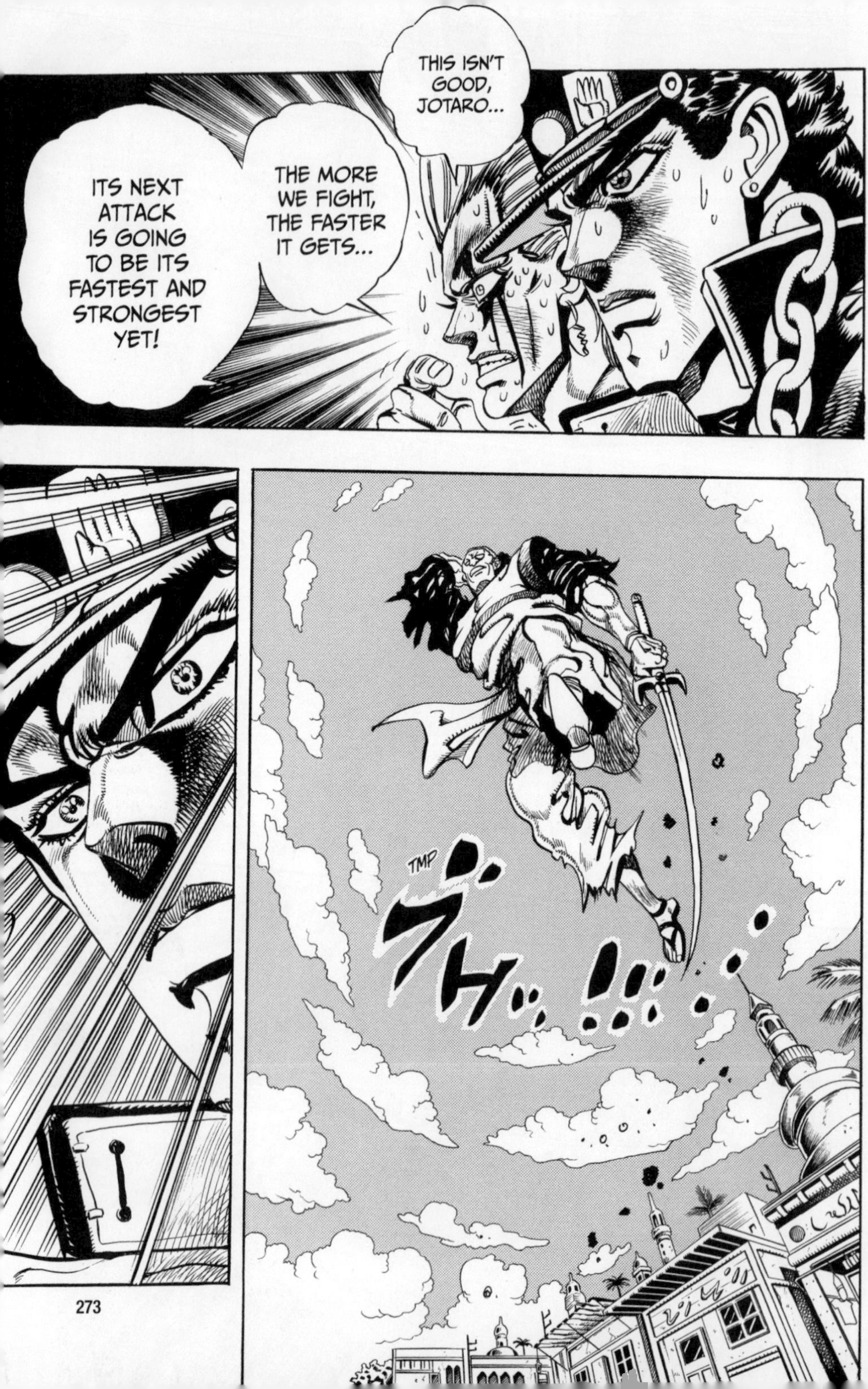
THIS ISN'T GOOD, JOTARO...
THE MORE WE FIGHT, THE FASTER IT GETS...
ITS NEXT ATTACK IS GOING TO BE ITS FASTEST AND STRONGEST YET!
TMP

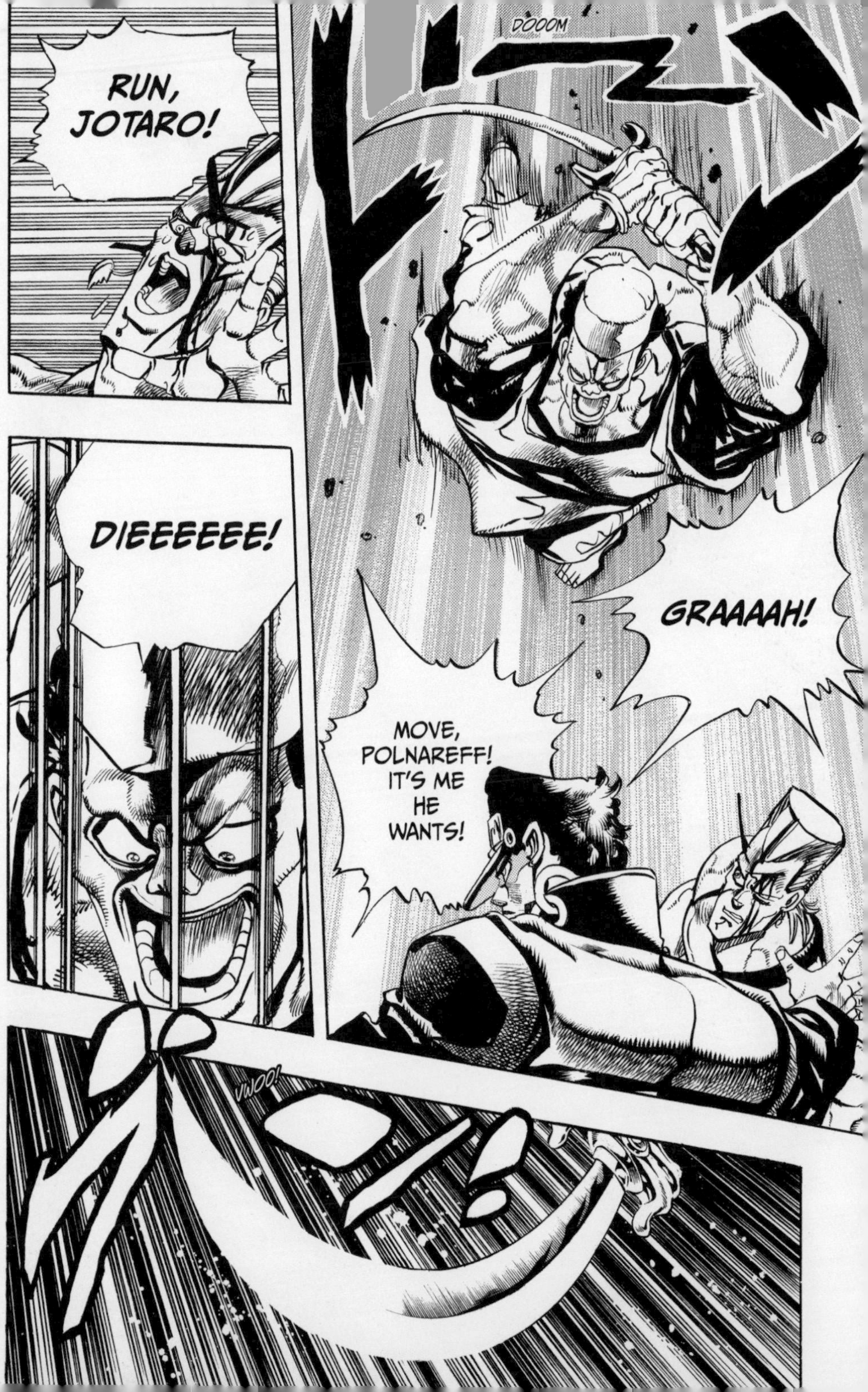
DOOOM
GRAAAAH!
MOVE, POLNAREFF! IT'S ME HE WANTS!
RUN, JOTARO!
DIEEEEEEE!
VWOO!

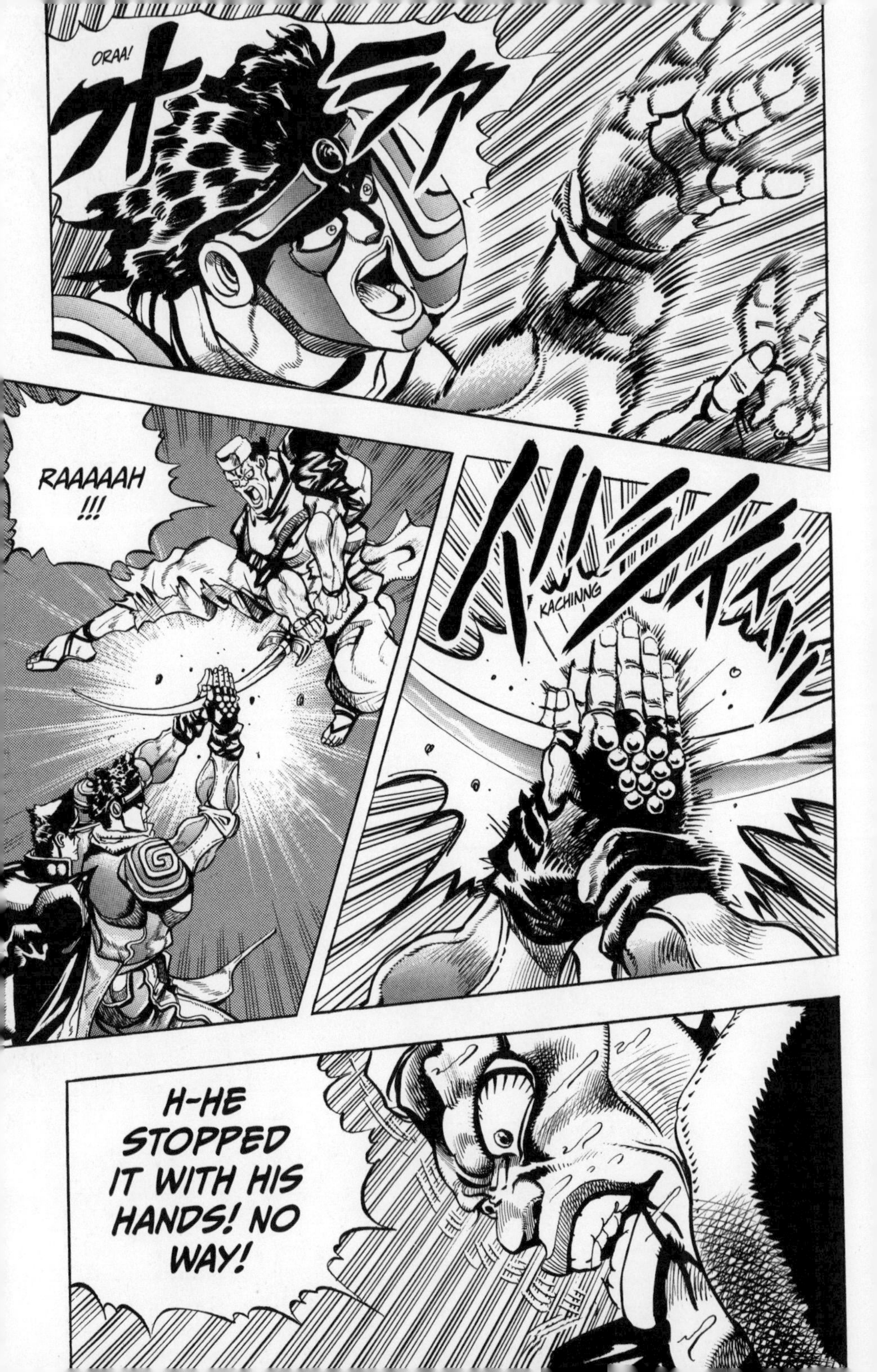
ORAA!
KACHINNG
RAAAAAH!!!
H-HE STOPPED IT WITH HIS HANDS! NO WAY!

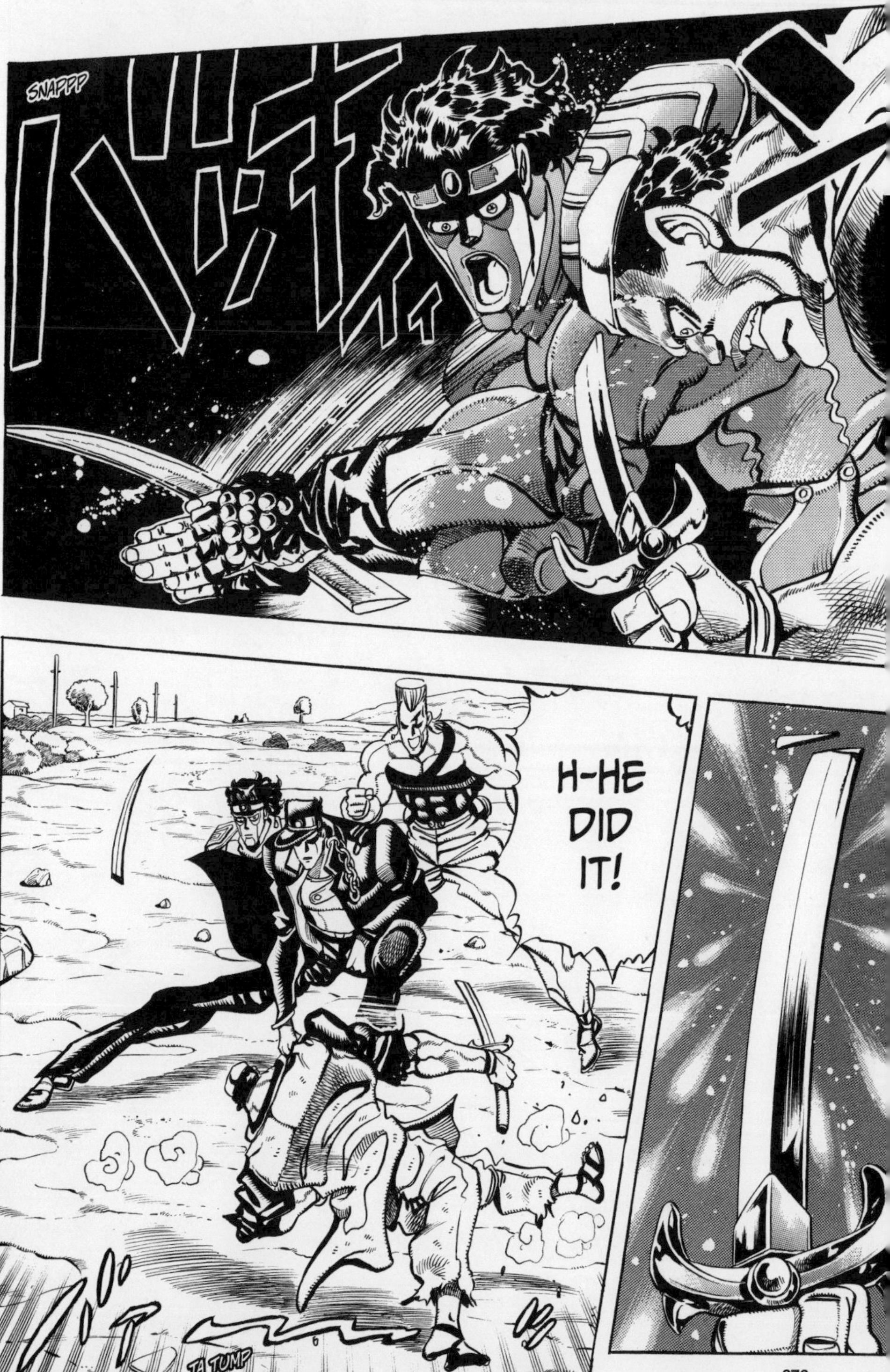
SNAPPP
H-HE
DID
IT!
TA TUMP

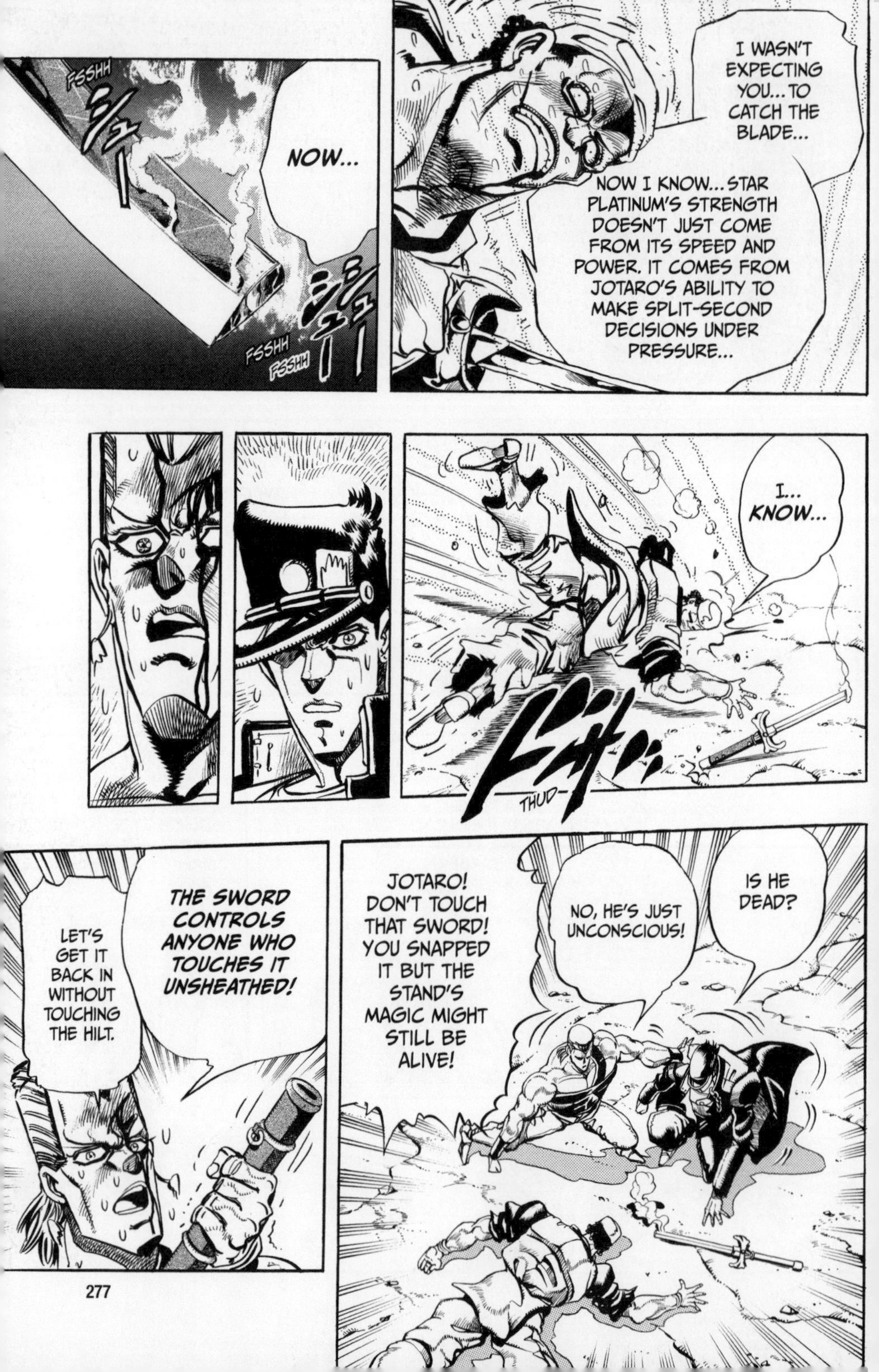
I WASN'T EXPECTING YOU... TO CATCH THE BLADE...
NOW I KNOW... STAR PLATINUM'S STRENGTH DOESN'T JUST COME FROM ITS SPEED AND POWER. IT COMES FROM JOTARO'S ABILITY TO MAKE SPLIT-SECOND DECISIONS UNDER PRESSURE...
NOW...
FSSHH
FSSHH
FSSHH
I... KNOW...
THUD-
IS HE DEAD?
NO, HE'S JUST UNCONSCIOUS!
JOTARO! DON'T TOUCH THAT SWORD! YOU SNAPPED IT BUT THE STAND'S MAGIC MIGHT STILL BE ALIVE!
THE SWORD CONTROLS ANYONE WHO TOUCHES IT UNSHEATHED!
LET'S GET IT BACK IN WITHOUT TOUCHING THE HILT.

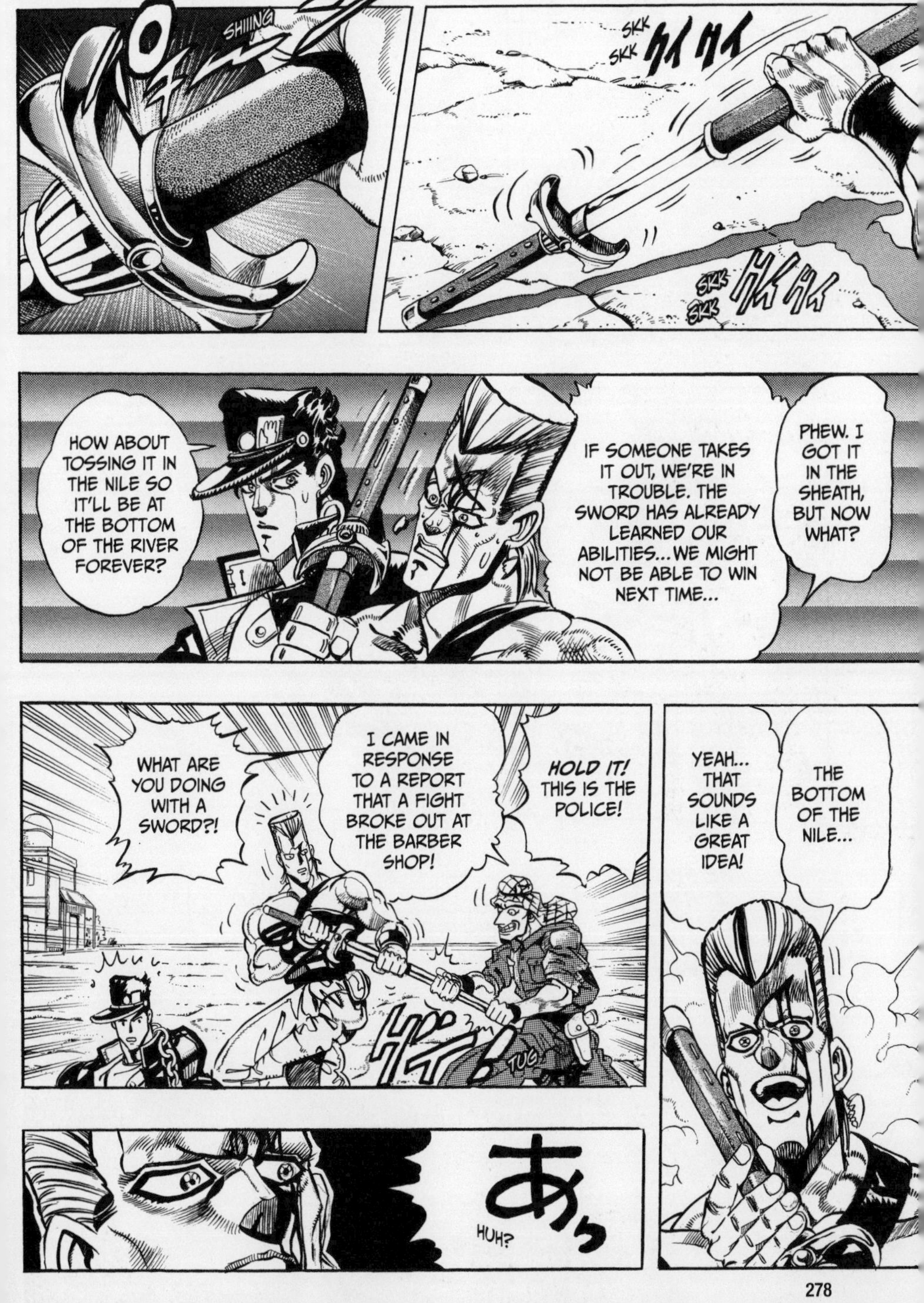
SKK SKK
SKK SKK
SHIIING
PHEW. I GOT IT IN THE SHEATH, BUT NOW WHAT?
IF SOMEONE TAKES IT OUT, WE'RE IN TROUBLE. THE SWORD HAS ALREADY LEARNED OUR ABILITIES...WE MIGHT NOT BE ABLE TO WIN NEXT TIME...
HOW ABOUT TOSSING IT IN THE NILE SO IT'LL BE AT THE BOTTOM OF THE RIVER FOREVER?
THE BOTTOM OF THE NILE...
YEAH... THAT SOUNDS LIKE A GREAT IDEA!
HOLD IT! THIS IS THE POLICE!
I CAME IN RESPONSE TO A REPORT THAT A FIGHT BROKE OUT AT THE BARBER SHOP!
WHAT ARE YOU DOING WITH A SWORD?!
TUG
あっ
HUH?

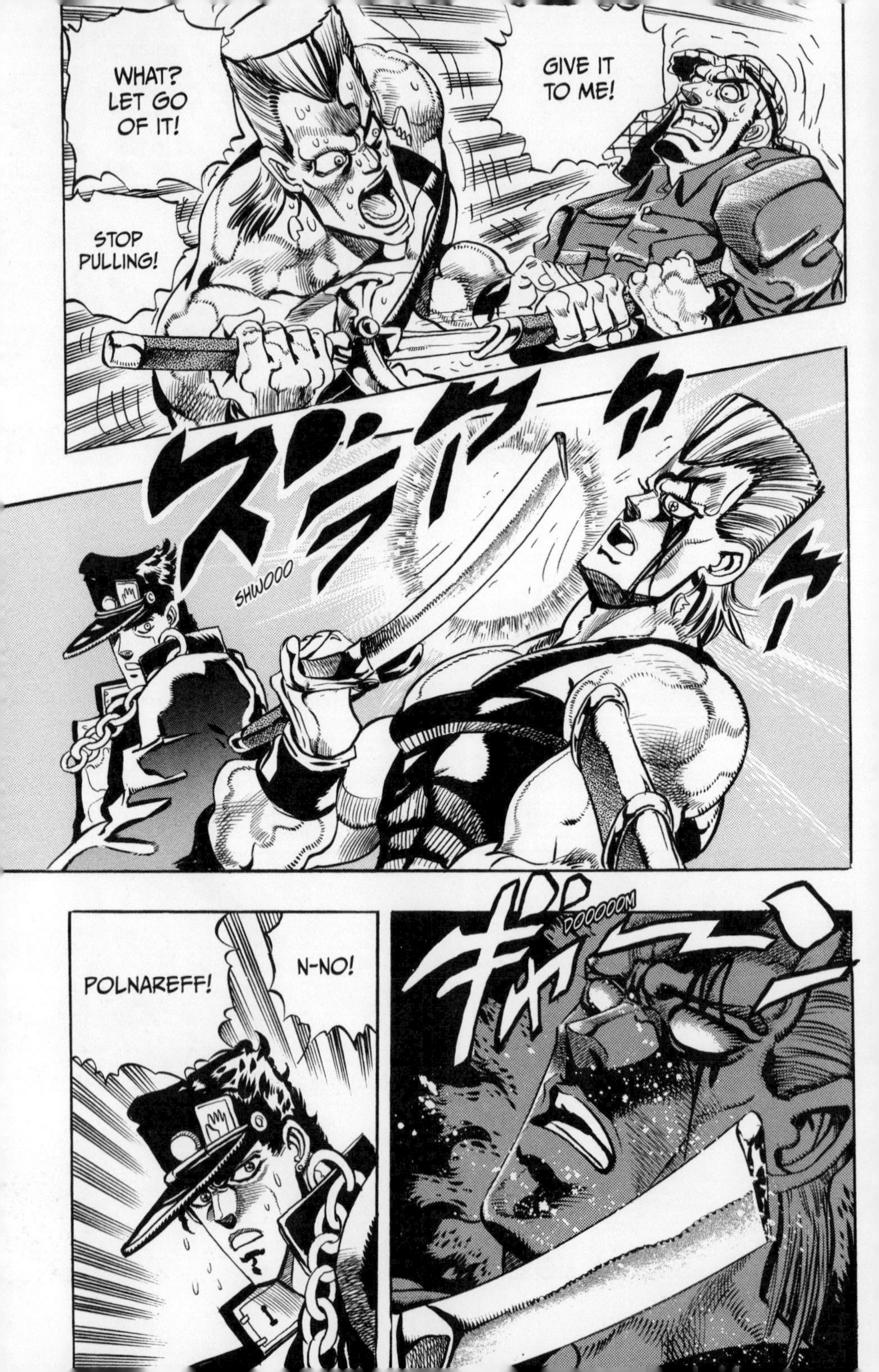
GIVE IT TO ME!
WHAT? LET GO OF IT!
STOP PULLING!
SHWOOO
DOOOOOM
N-NO!
POLNAREFF!

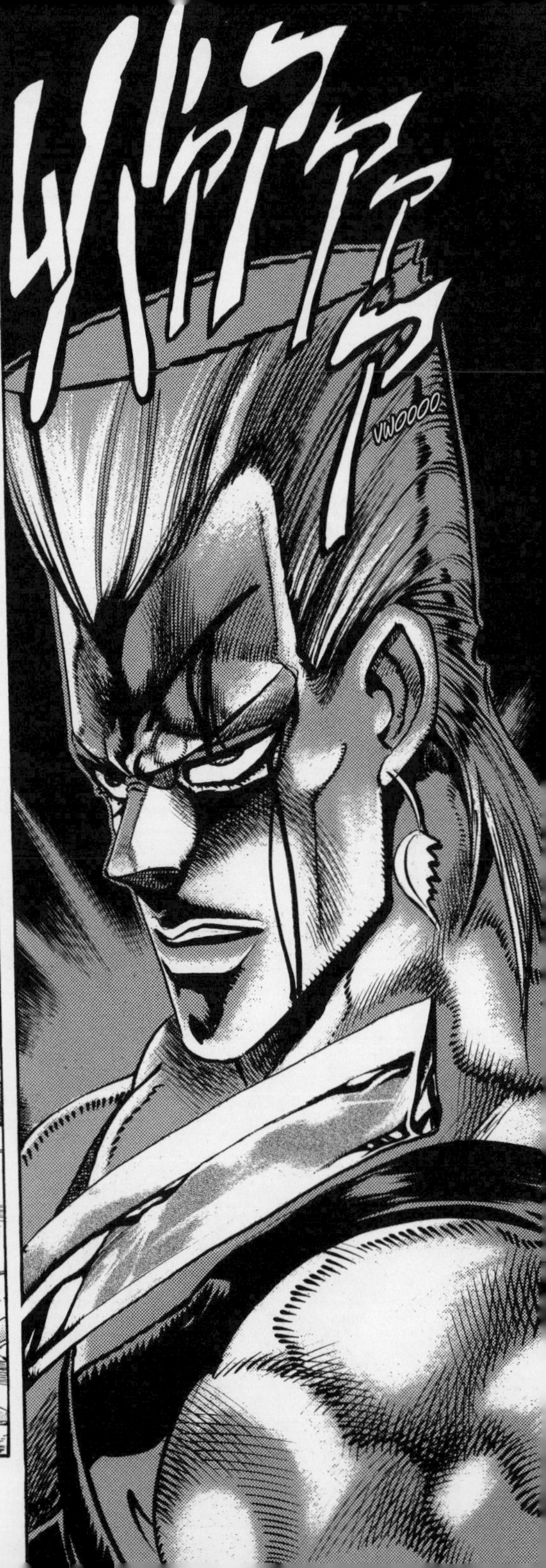
VWOOOO
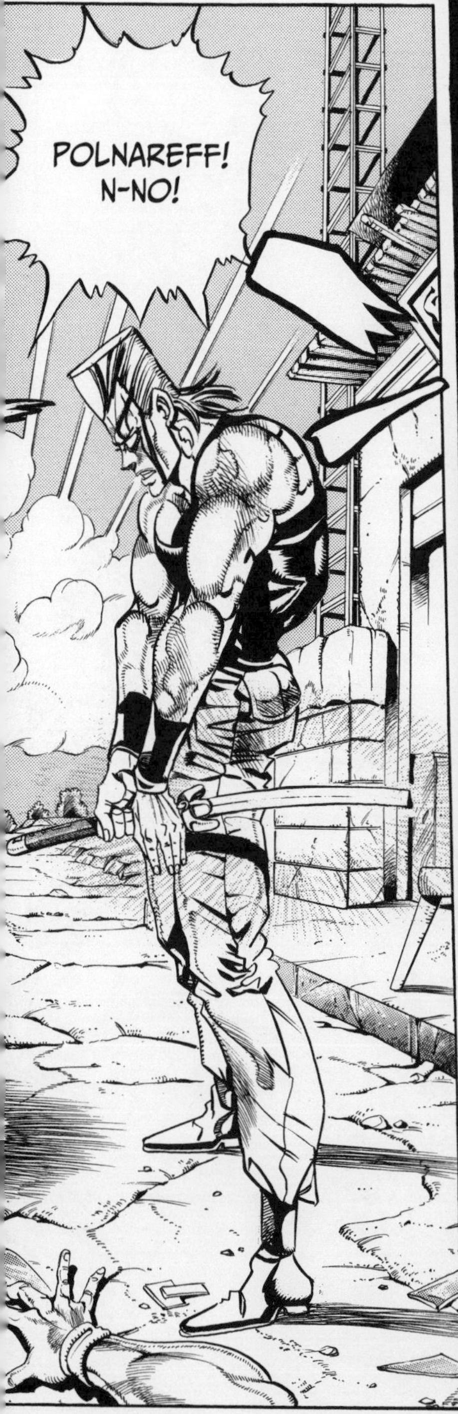
POLNAREFF!
N-NO!

CHAPTER 84: Anubis PART 5

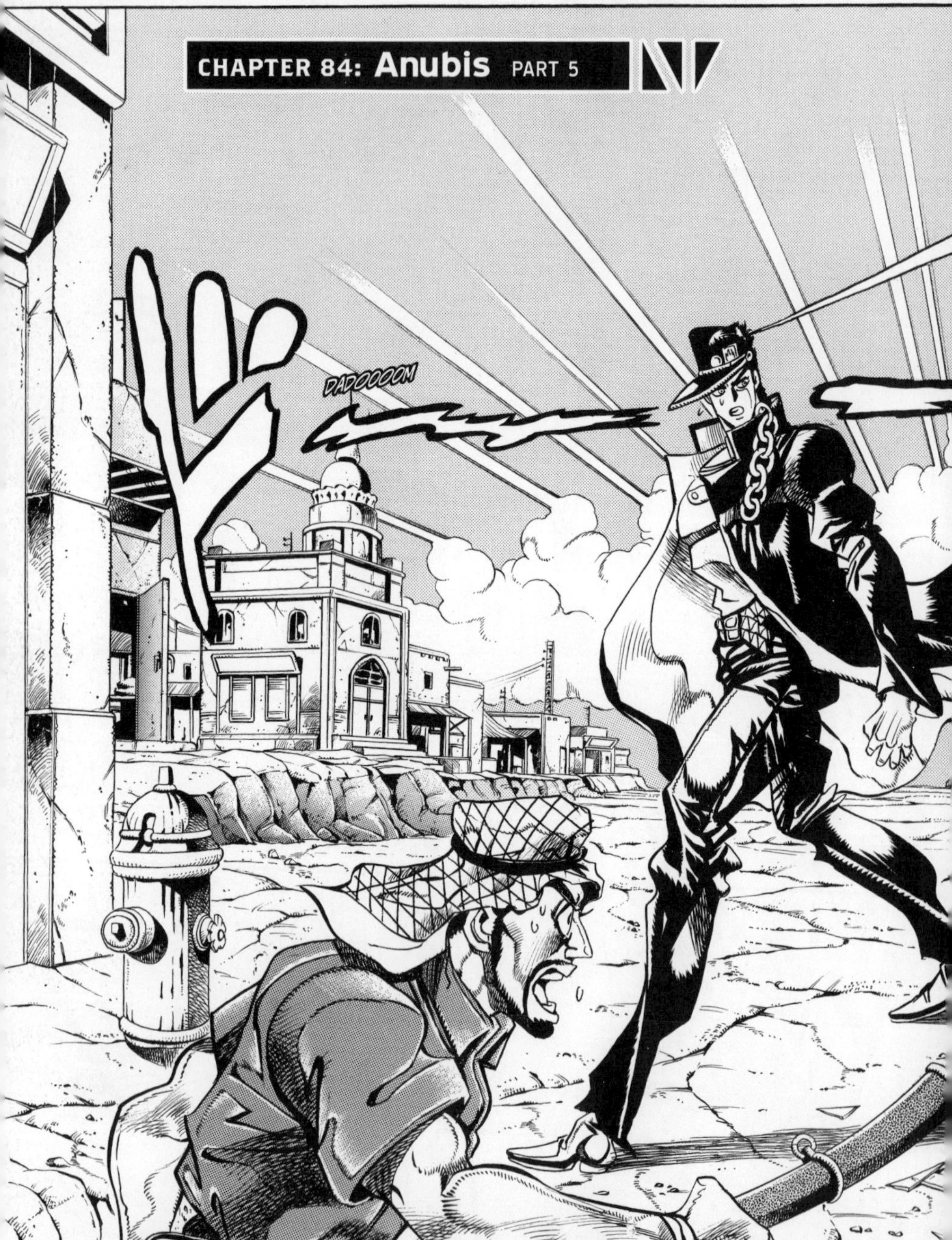
DADOOOOM

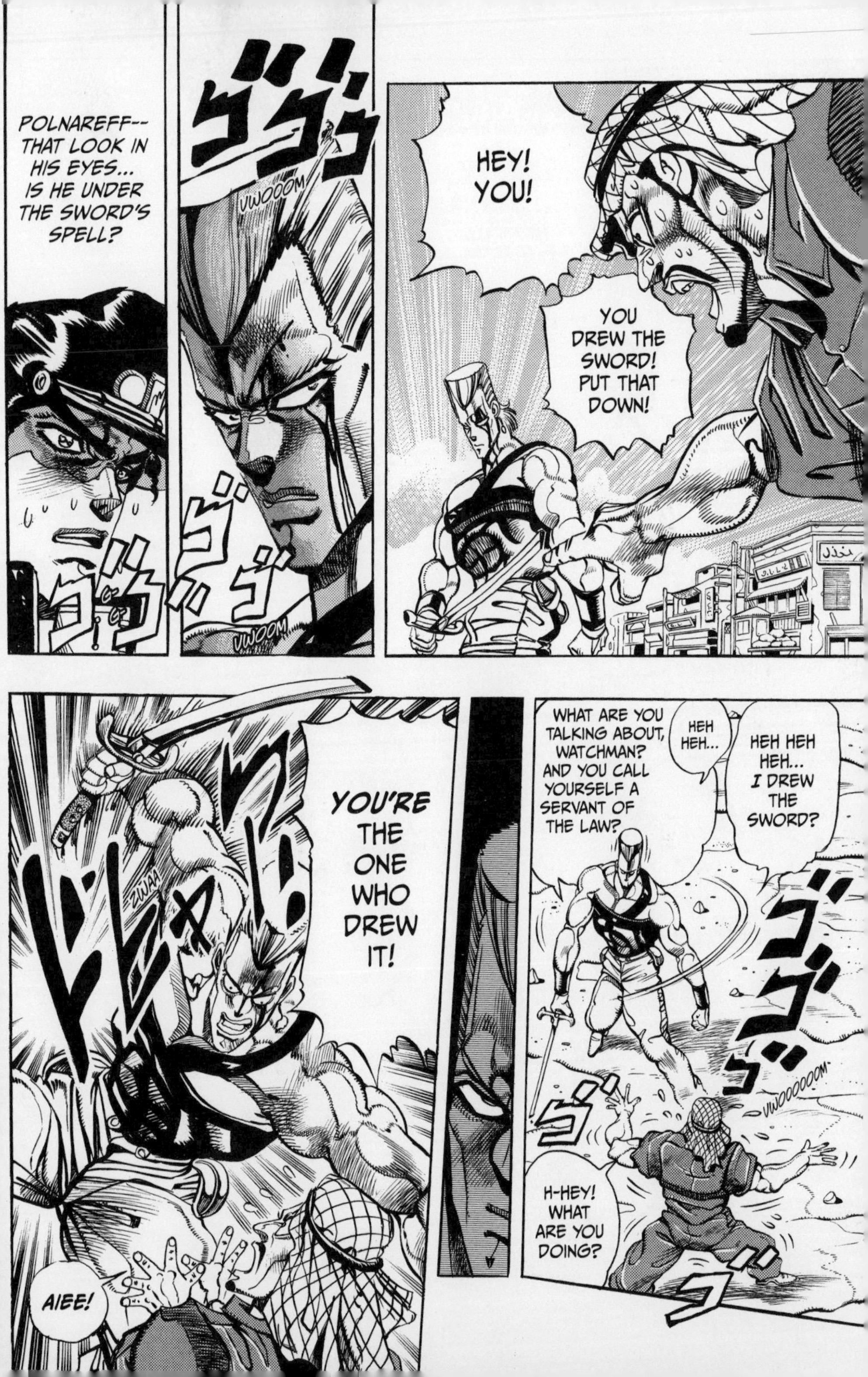
HEY! YOU!
YOU DREW THE SWORD! PUT THAT DOWN!
UWOOOM
UWOOM
POLNAREFF-- THAT LOOK IN HIS EYES... IS HE UNDER THE SWORD'S SPELL?
HEH HEH HEH... I DREW THE SWORD?
HEH HEH...
WHAT ARE YOU TALKING ABOUT, WATCHMAN? AND YOU CALL YOURSELF A SERVANT OF THE LAW?
UWOOOOOOM
H-HEY! WHAT ARE YOU DOING?
YOU'RE THE ONE WHO DREW IT!
ZWAA
AIEE!

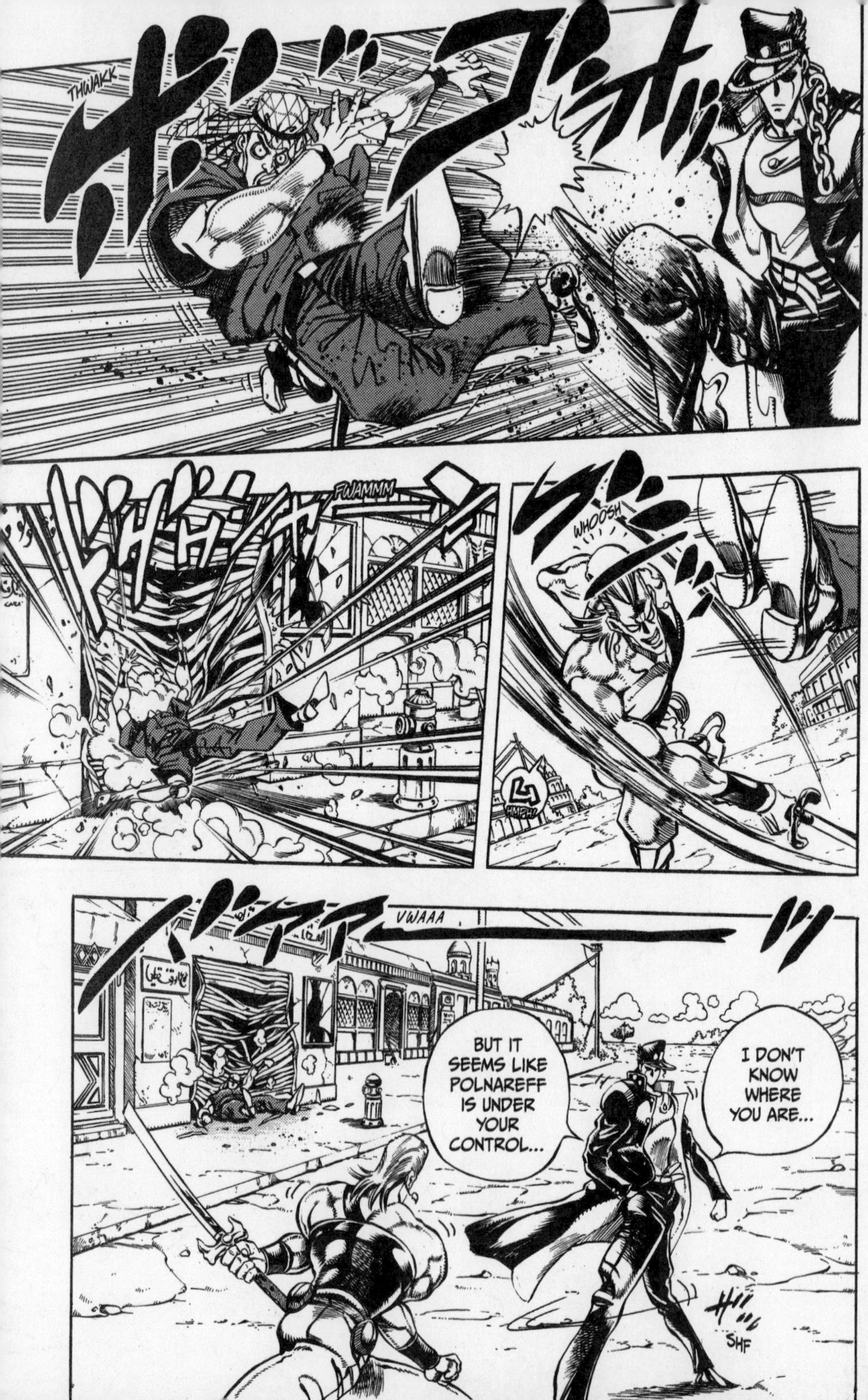
THWAKK
WHOOSH
HMPH
FWAMMM
VWAAA
I DON'T KNOW WHERE YOU ARE...
BUT IT SEEMS LIKE POLNAREFF IS UNDER YOUR CONTROL...
SHF

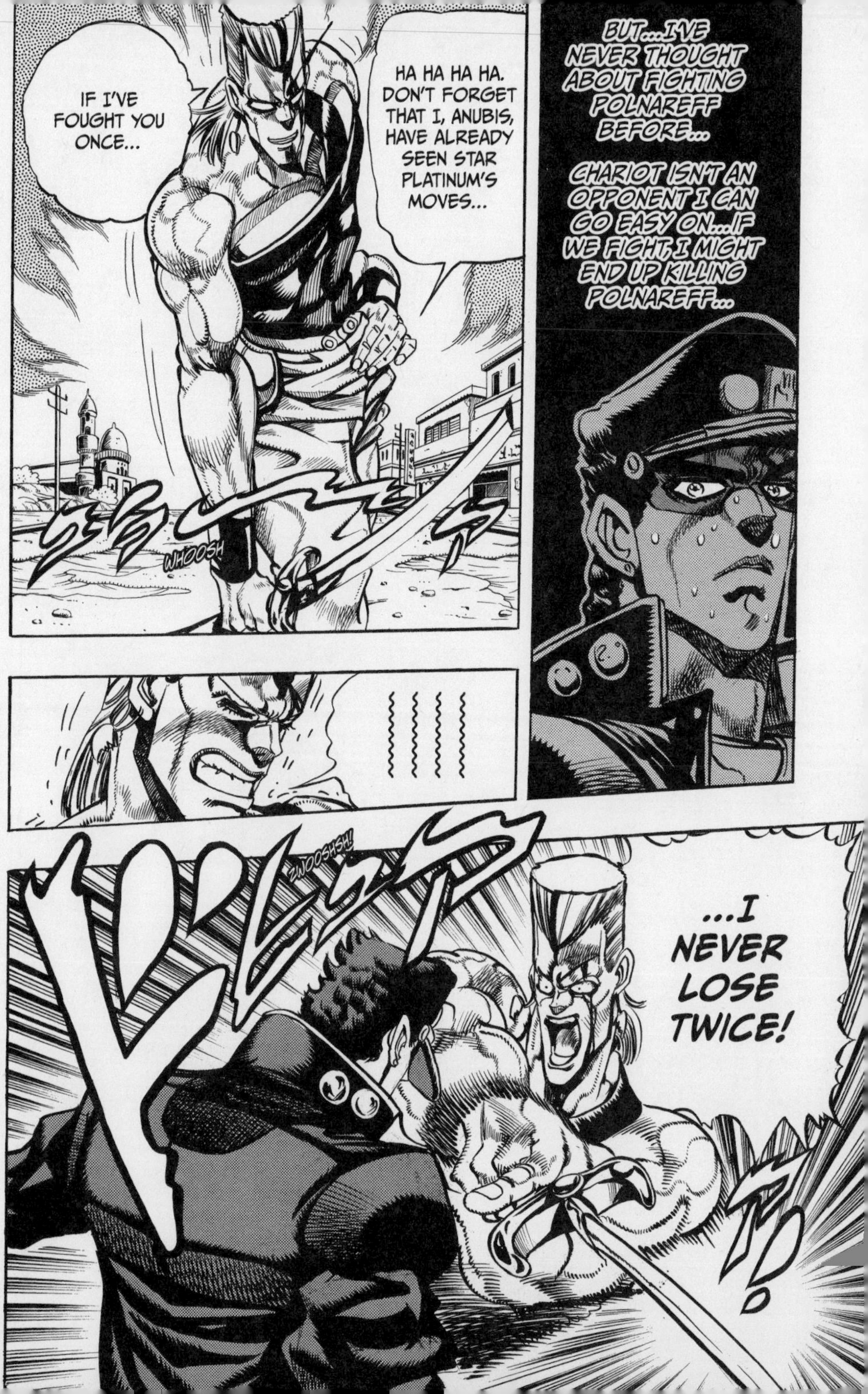
BUT...I'VE NEVER THOUGHT ABOUT FIGHTING POLNAREFF BEFORE...
CHARIOT ISN'T AN OPPONENT I CAN GO EASY ON...IF WE FIGHT, I MIGHT END UP KILLING POLNAREFF...
HA HA HA HA. DON'T FORGET THAT I, ANUBIS, HAVE ALREADY SEEN STAR PLATINUM'S MOVES...
IF I'VE FOUGHT YOU ONCE...
WHOOSH
ZWOOSHSH!
...I NEVER LOSE TWICE!

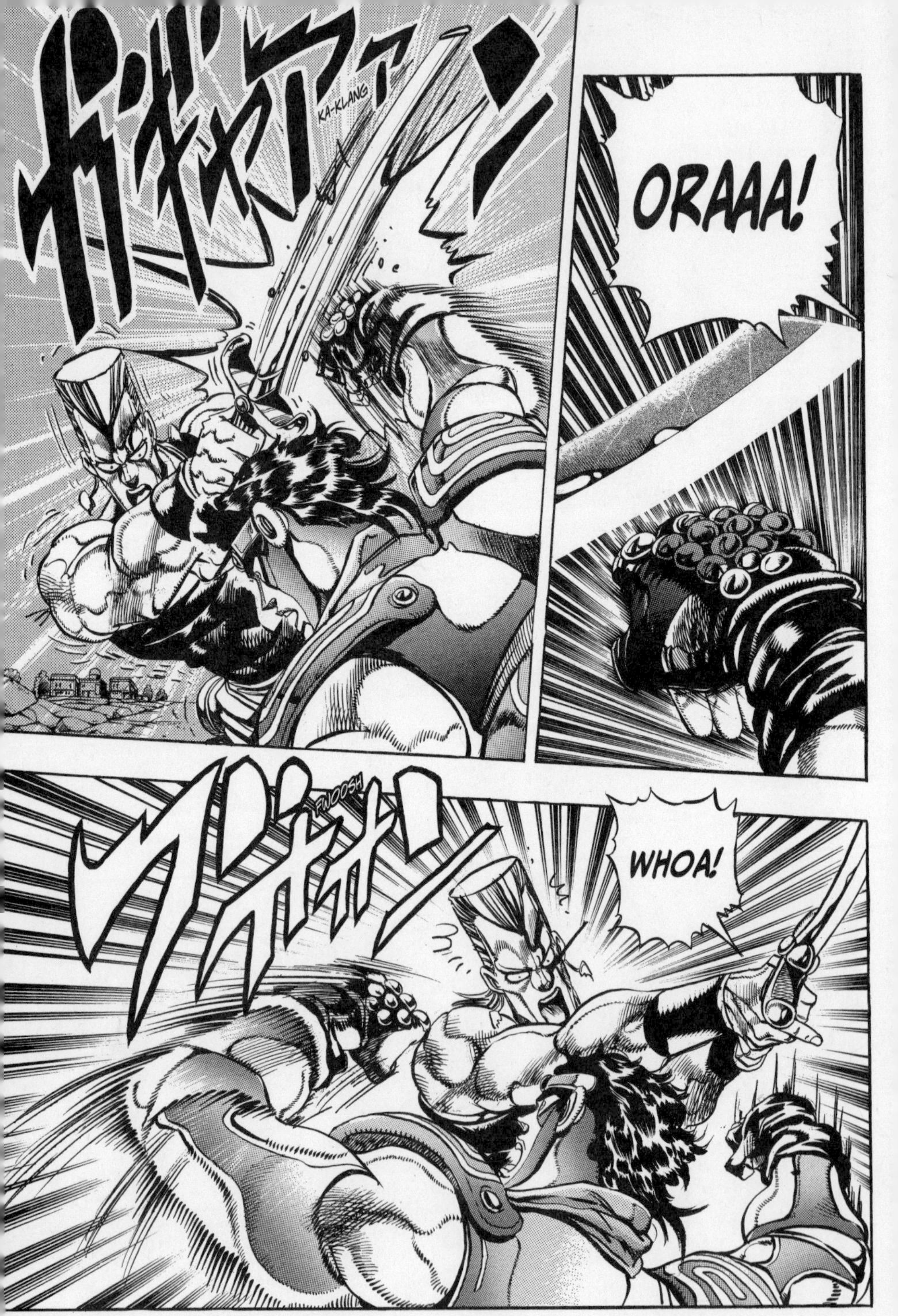
ORAAA!
KA-KLANG
WHOA!
FWOOSH

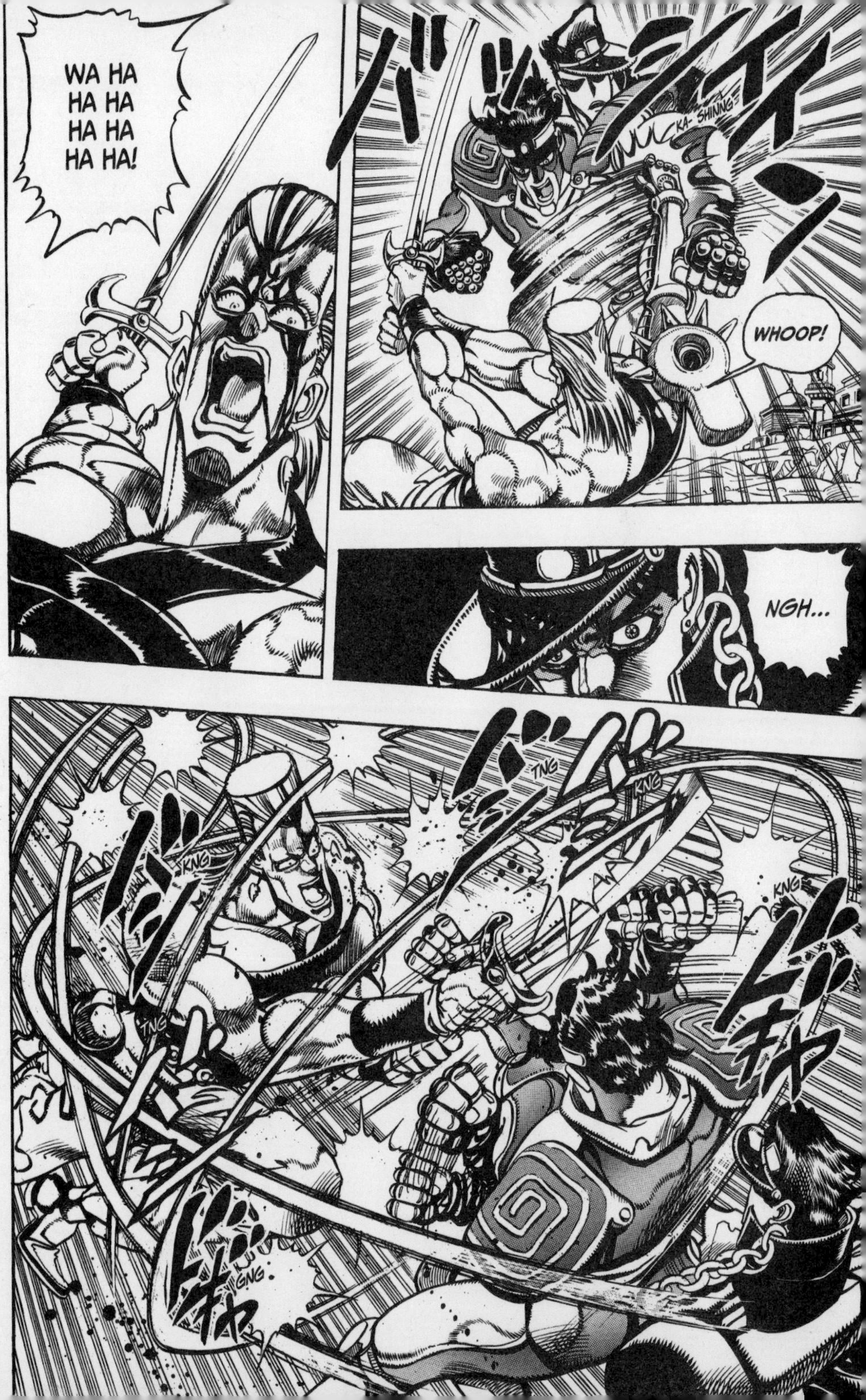
KA-SHINNG
WHOOP!
NGH...
WA HA
HA HA
HA HA
HA HA!
KNG
KNG
TNG
KNG
TNG
GNG

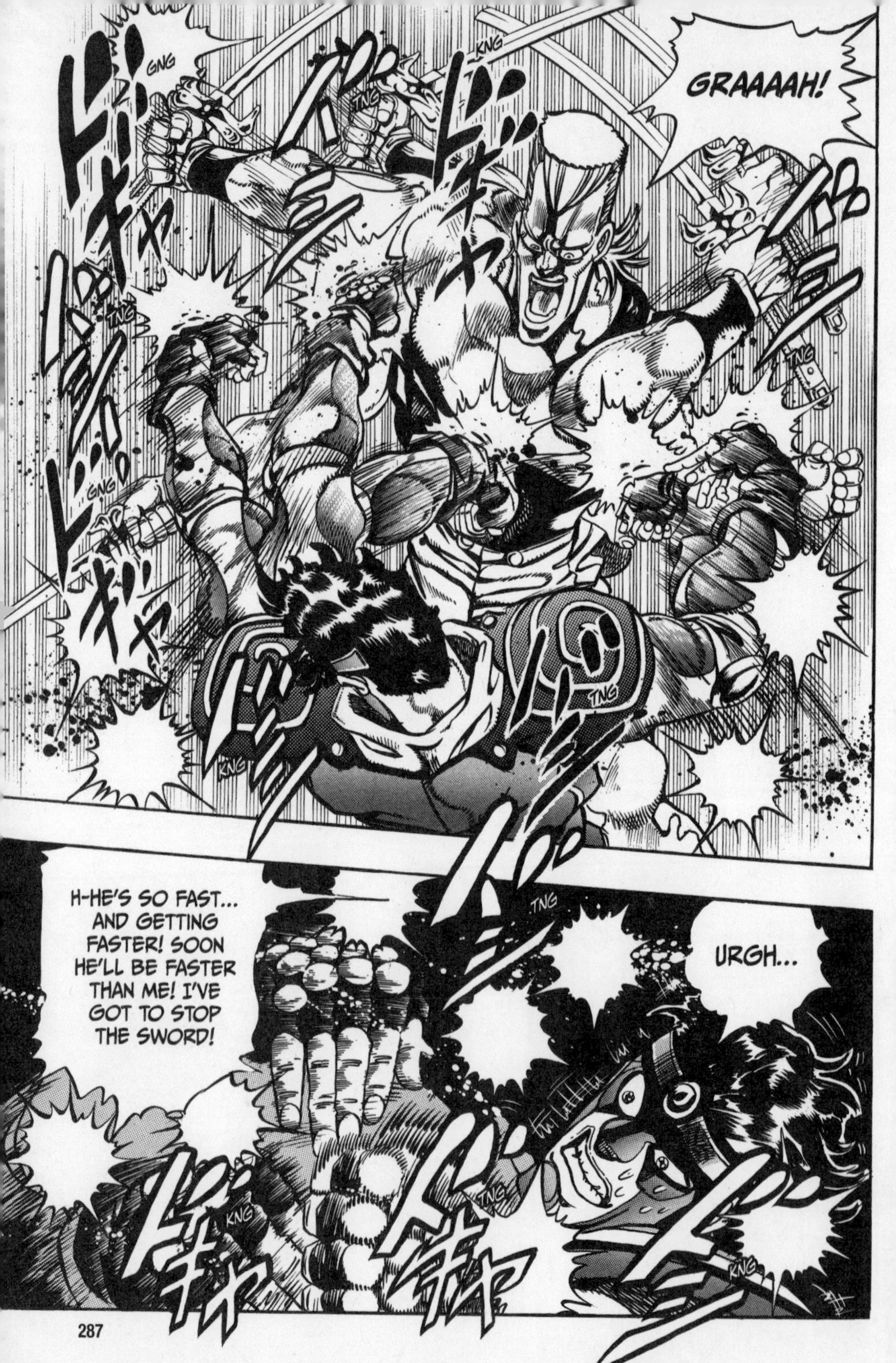
GRAAAAH!
KNG
TNG
GNG
TNG
GNG
TNG
KNG
URGH...
H-HE'S SO FAST... AND GETTING FASTER! SOON HE'LL BE FASTER THAN ME! I'VE GOT TO STOP THE SWORD!
TNG
KNG
TNG
KNG

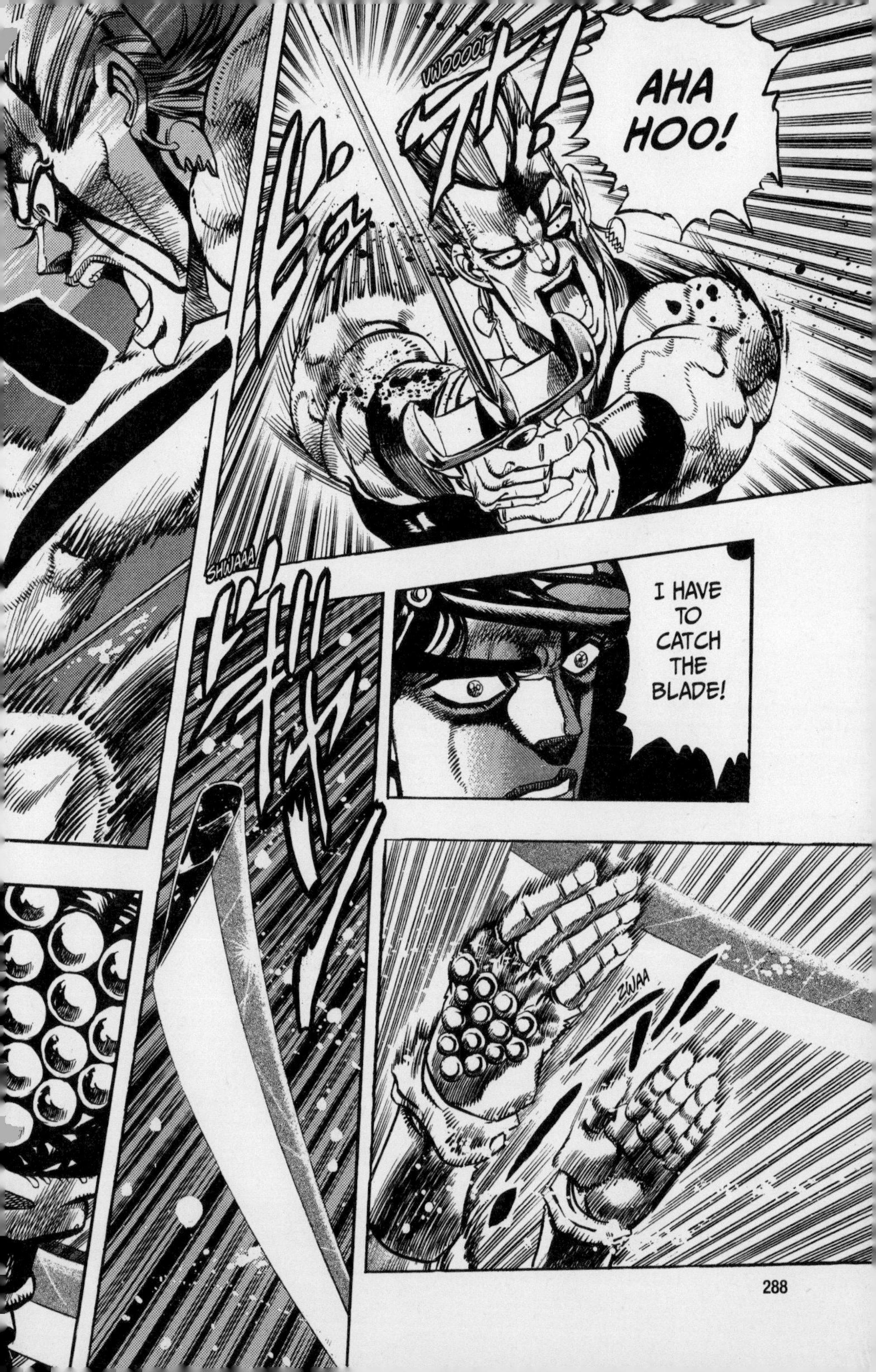

AHA HOO!
VWOOOO!
I HAVE TO CATCH THE BLADE!
SHWAAA
ZWAA

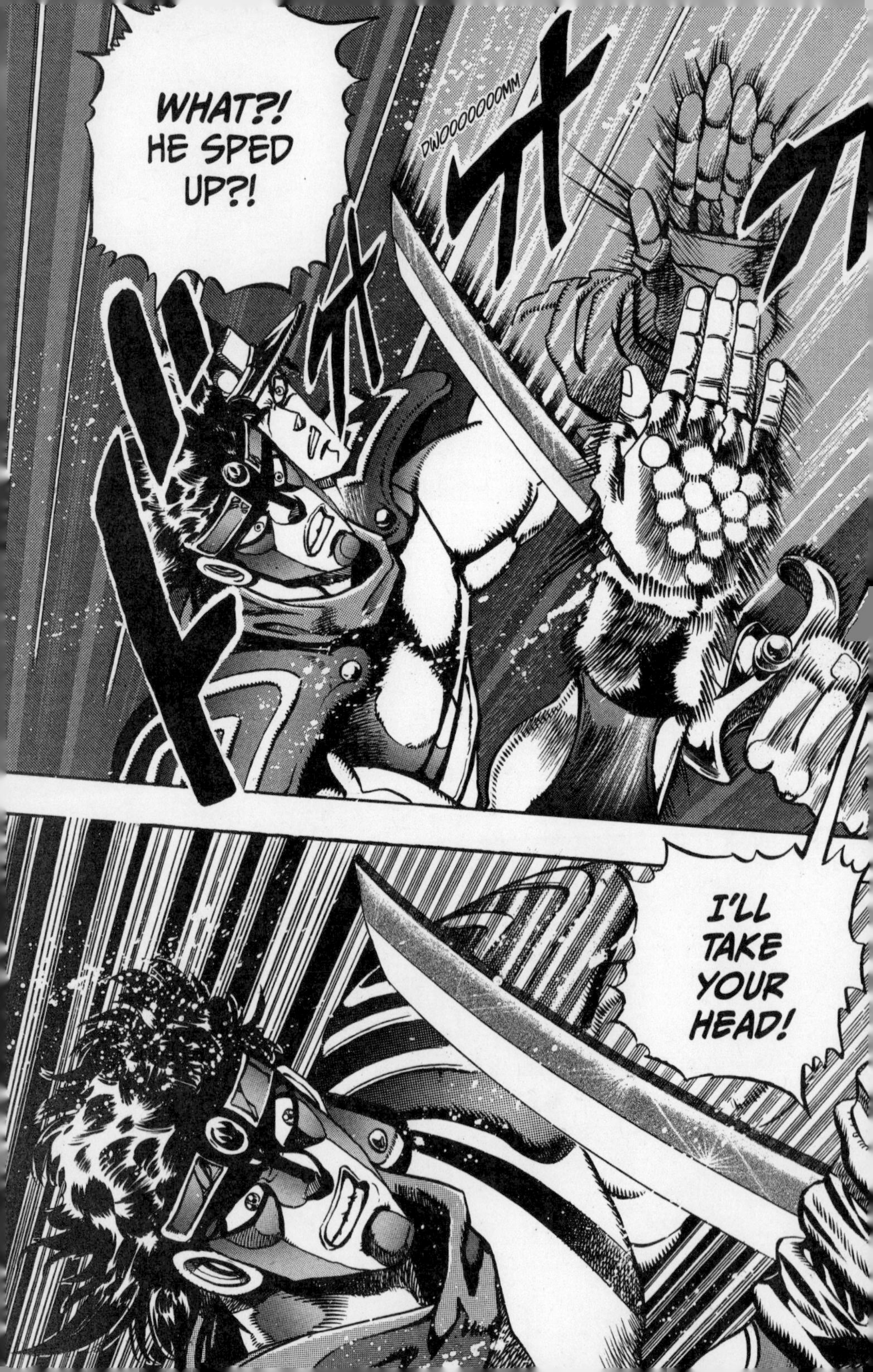
DWOOOOOOOOMM
WHAT?! HE SPED UP?!
I'LL TAKE YOUR HEAD!

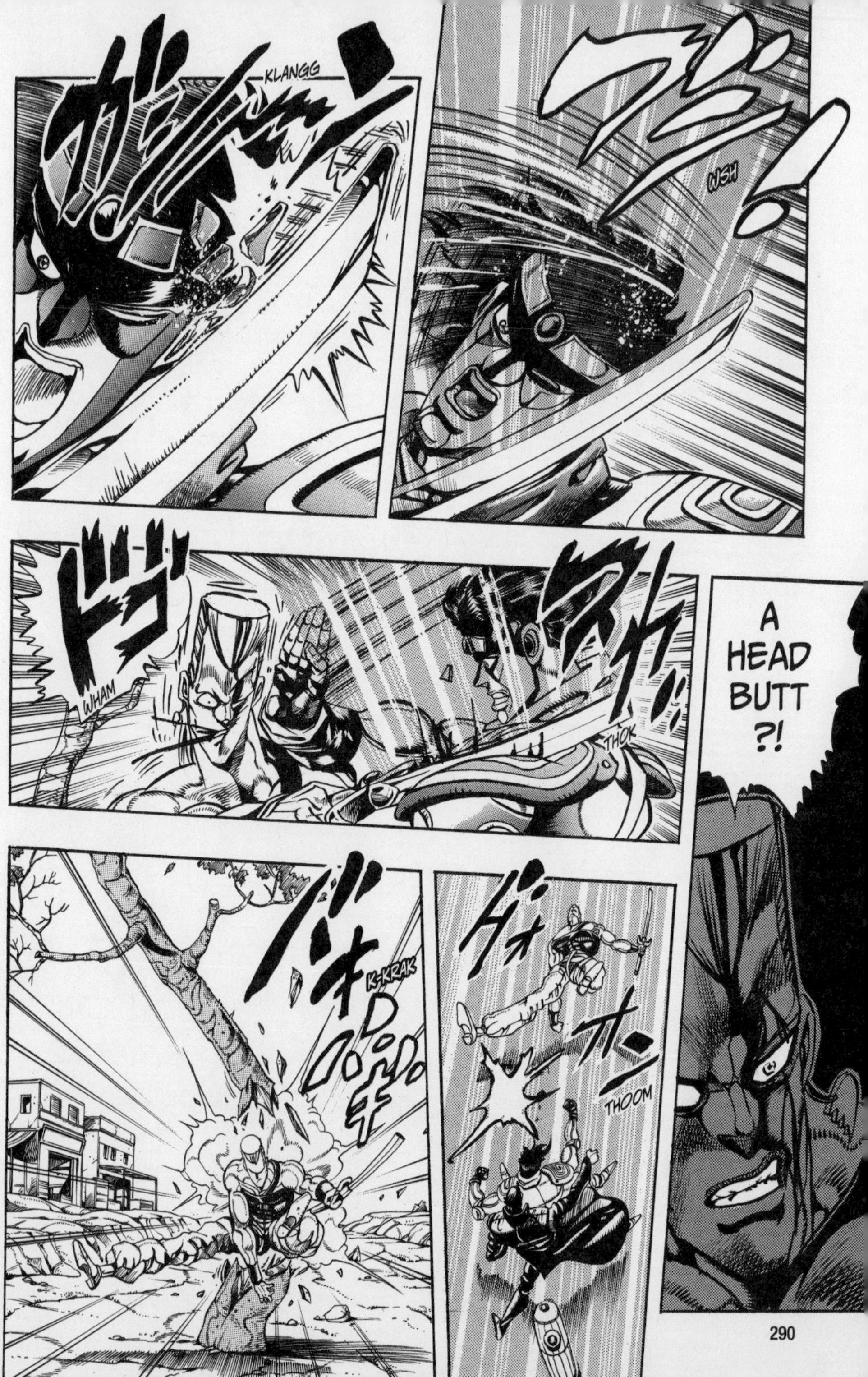
WSH
KLANGG
A HEAD BUTT ?!
THOK
WHAM
THOOM
K-KRAK

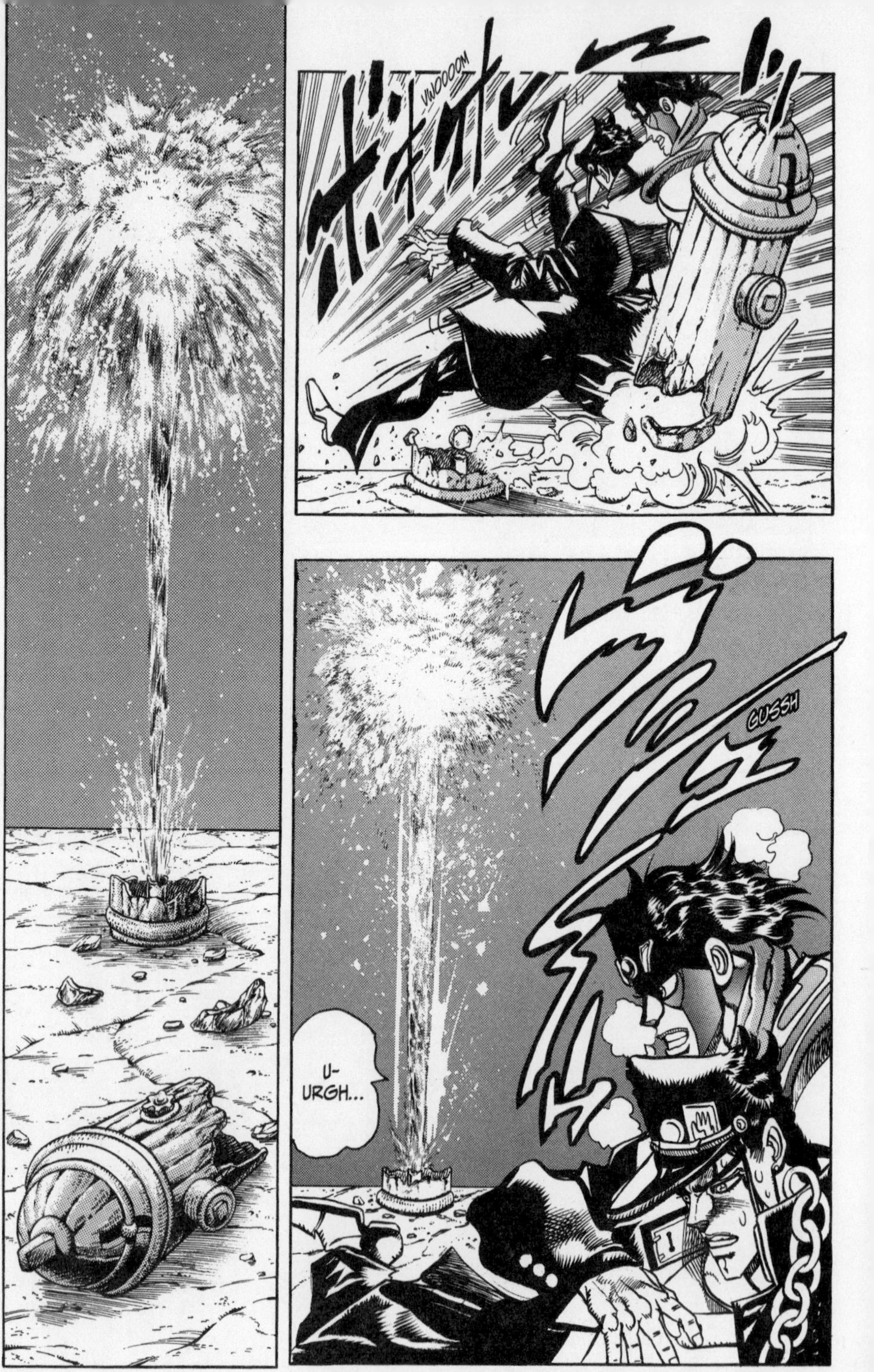
VWOOOOM
GUSSH
U-
URGH...

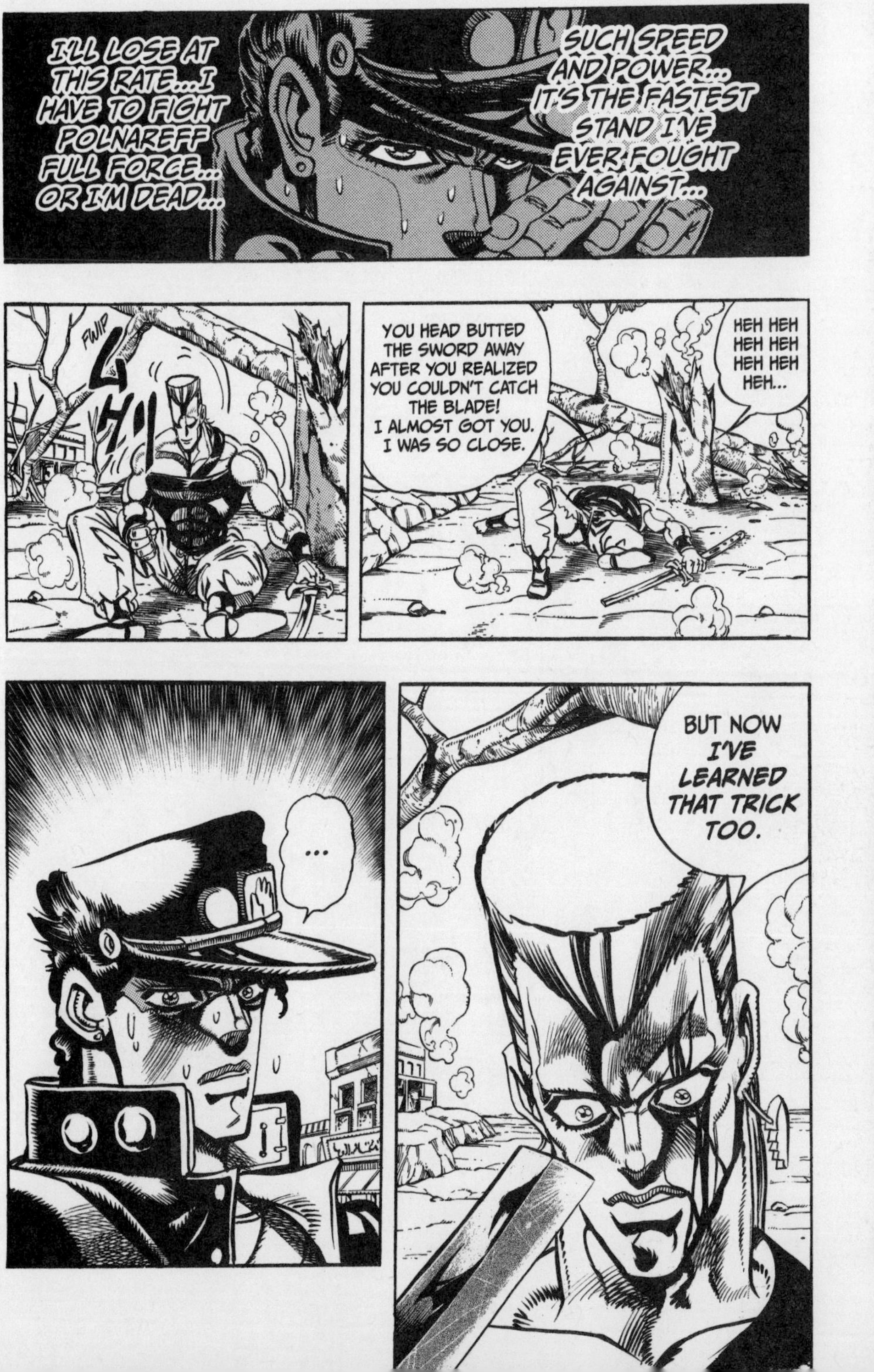
SUCH SPEED AND POWER... IT'S THE FASTEST STAND I'VE EVER FOUGHT AGAINST...
I'LL LOSE AT THIS RATE... I HAVE TO FIGHT POLNAREFF FULL FORCE... OR I'M DEAD...
HEH HEH HEH HEH HEH HEH HEH...
YOU HEAD BUTTED THE SWORD AWAY AFTER YOU REALIZED YOU COULDN'T CATCH THE BLADE! I ALMOST GOT YOU. I WAS SO CLOSE.
FWIP
BUT NOW I'VE LEARNED THAT TRICK TOO.
...

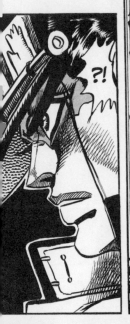

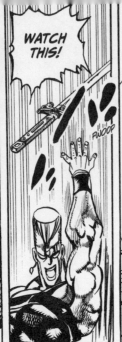

HEH HEH HEH HEH, JOTARO...
"I'VE GOT TO KILL POLNAREFF OR I'M GOING TO LOSE."
LET ME GUESS...
IS THAT WHAT YOU'RE THINKING? HA HA HA...
BUT YOU'RE WRONG. YOU'RE SO WRONG.
BECAUSE... MY NEXT MOVE WILL END THIS.
WATCH THIS!
FWOOP
?!
WHIP
WHIP
WHIP
DO YOU STILL THINK YOU CAN WIN?!
WELL, JO-TARO ?!
GRP
GLEAM
GLEAM

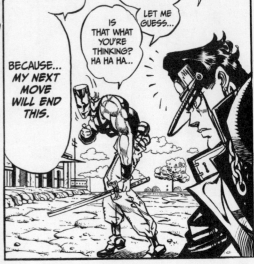

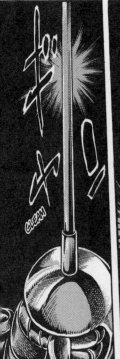

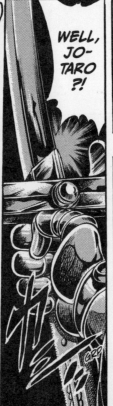

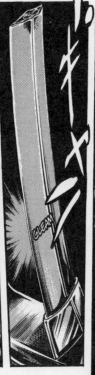

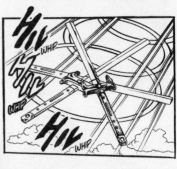

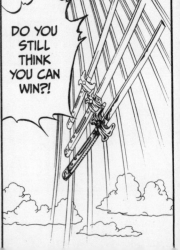

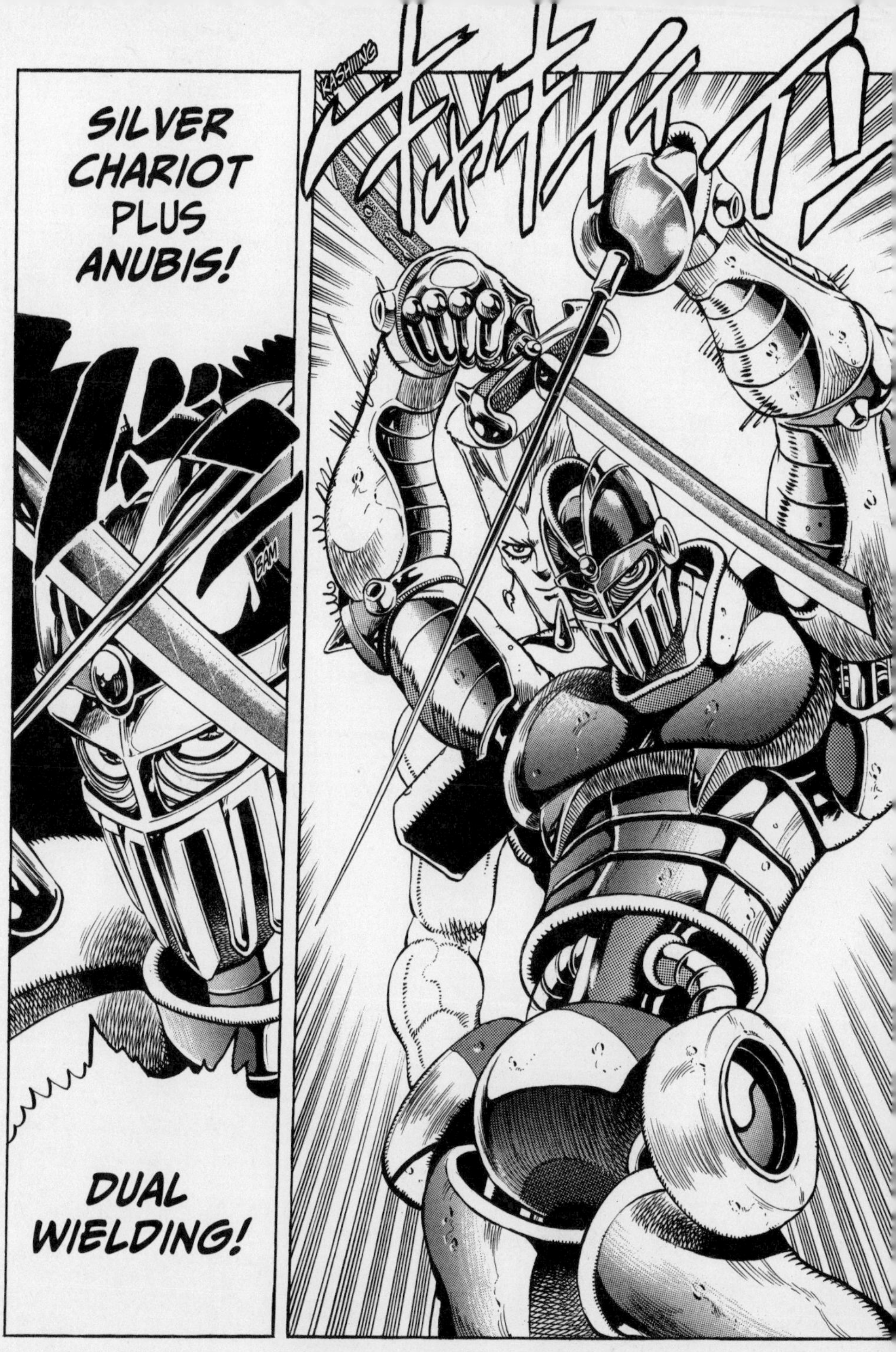
KASHING
SILVER CHARIOT PLUS ANUBIS!
BAM
DUAL WIELDING!

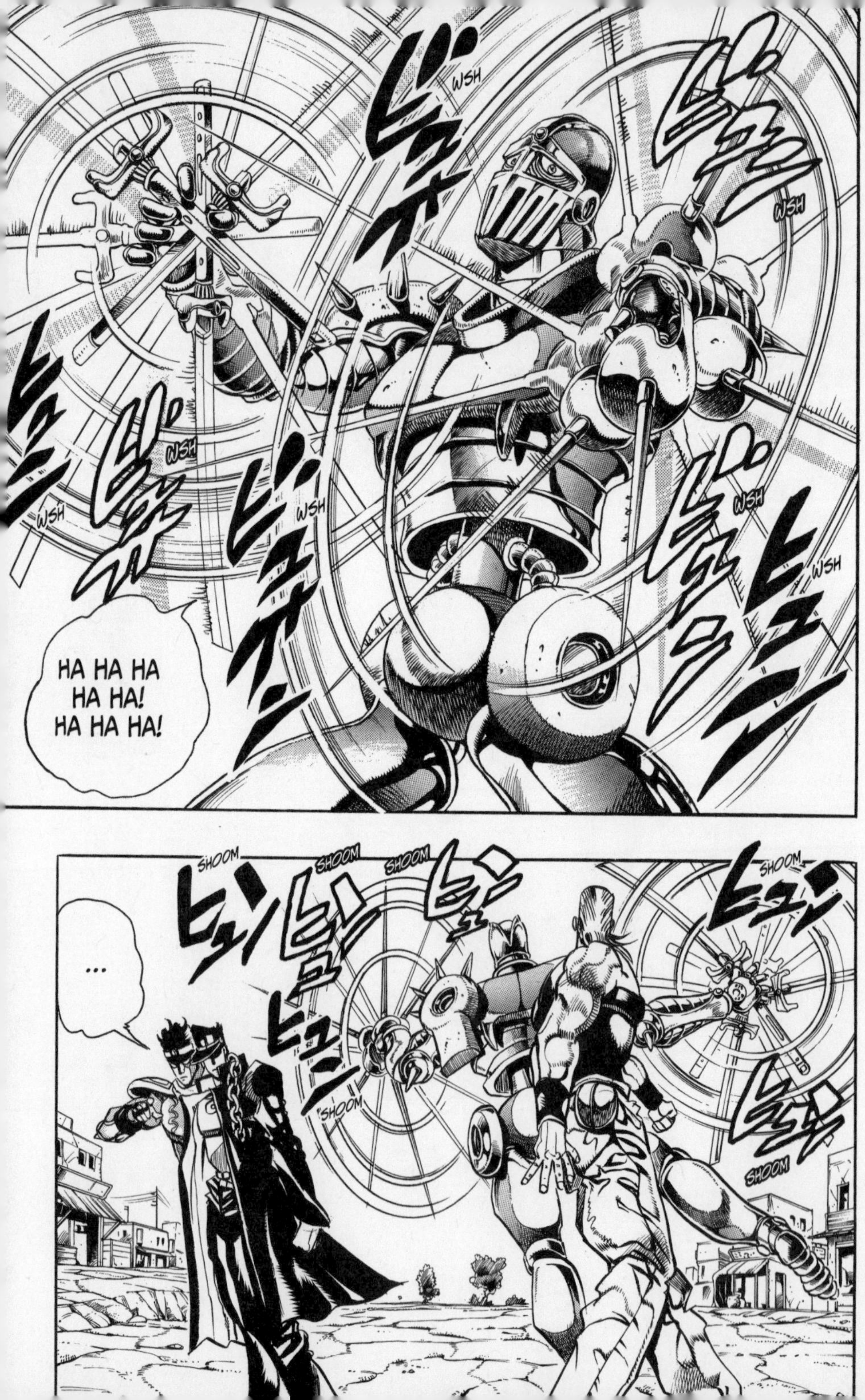
WSH
WSH
WSH
WSH
WSH
WSH
WSH
HA HA HA
HA HA!
HA HA HA!
SHOOM
SHOOM
SHOOM
SHOOM
SHOOM
SHOOM
...

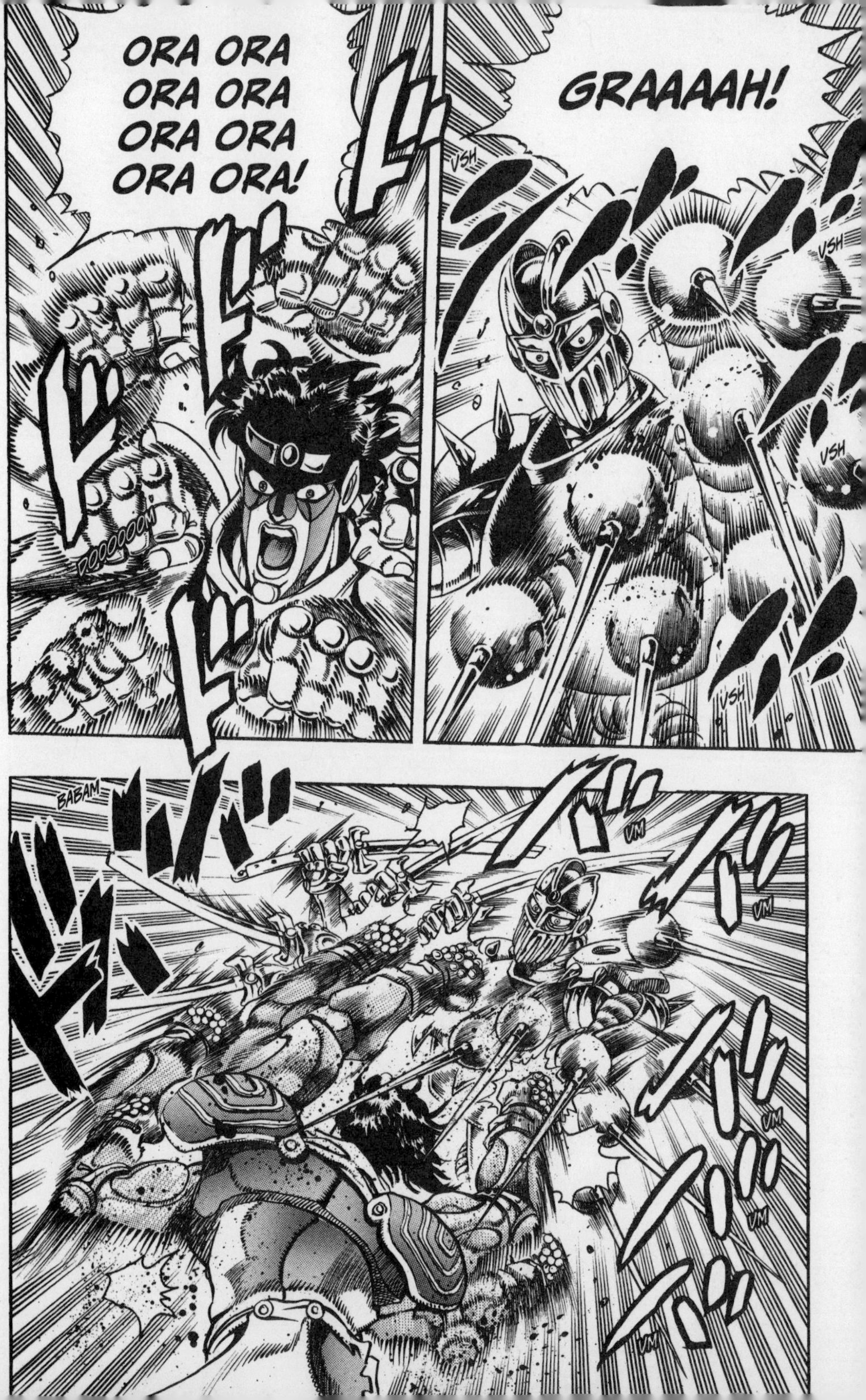
GRAAAAH!
VSH
VSH
VSH
VSH
ORA ORA ORA ORA ORA ORA ORA ORA!
VM
DOOOOOOM
BABAM
VM
VM
VM
VM

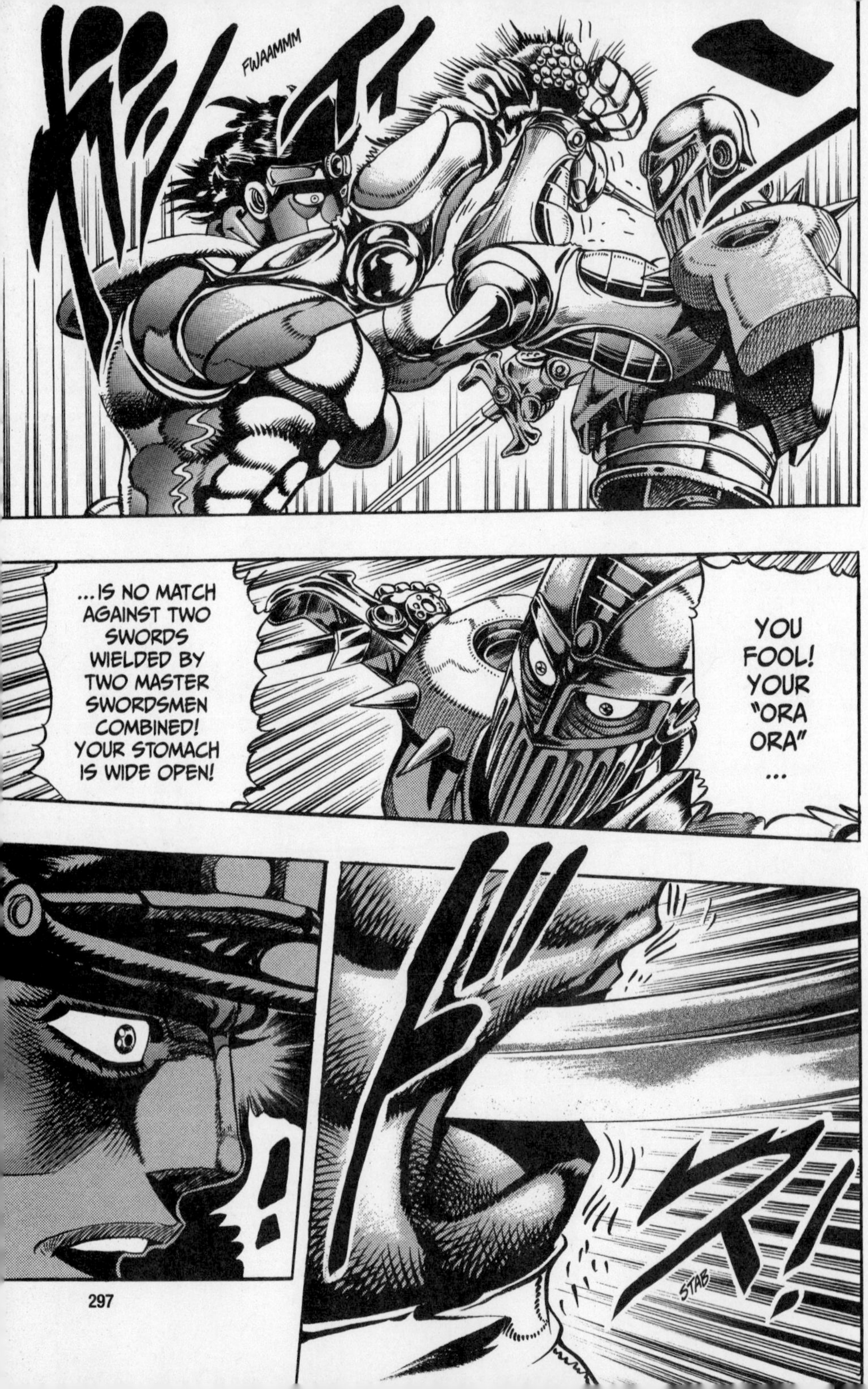

FWAAMMM
YOU FOOL! YOUR "ORA ORA" ...
...IS NO MATCH AGAINST TWO SWORDS WIELDED BY TWO MASTER SWORDSMEN COMBINED! YOUR STOMACH IS WIDE OPEN!
STAB

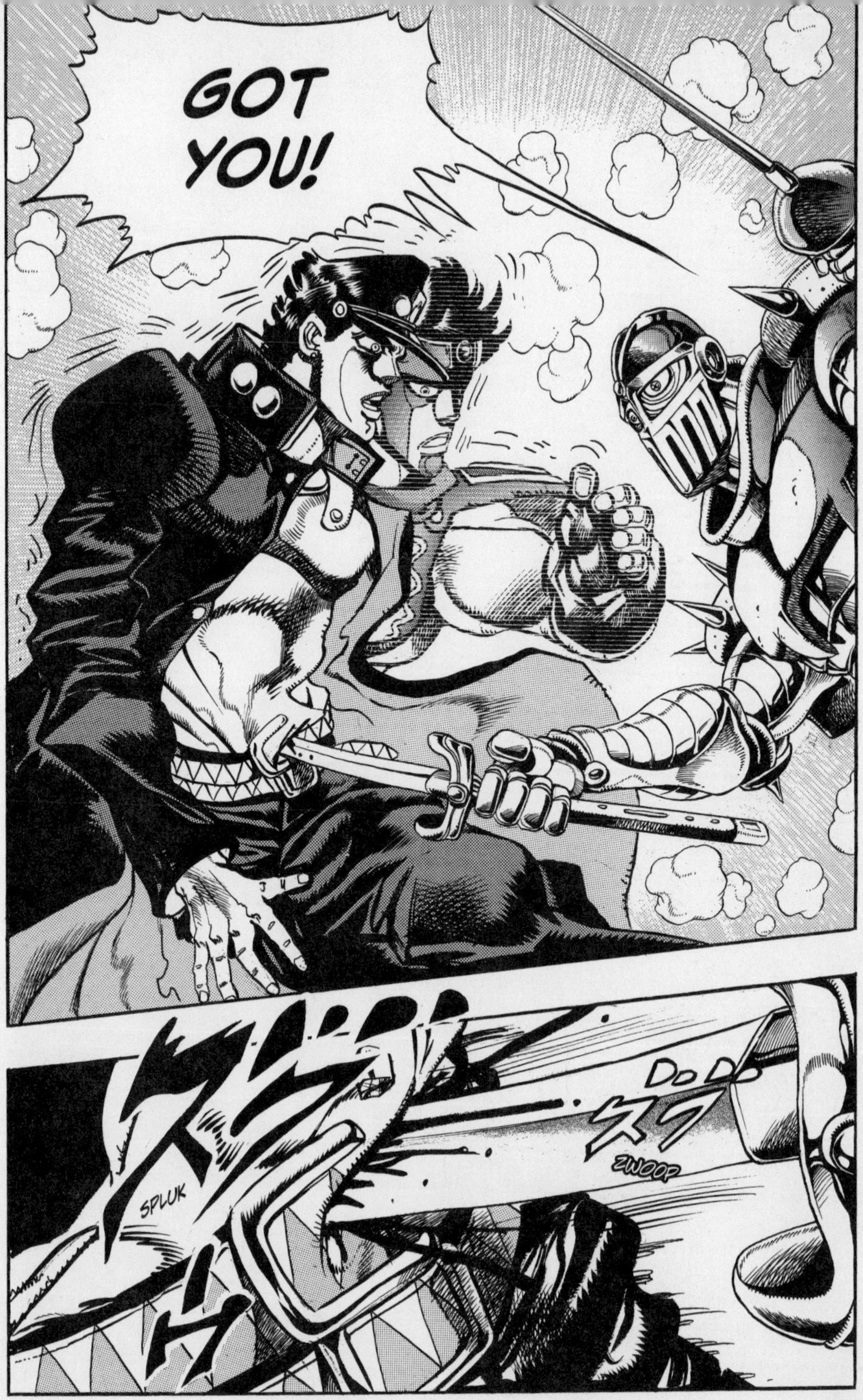
GOT YOU!
DO DO
ZWOOP
SPLUK

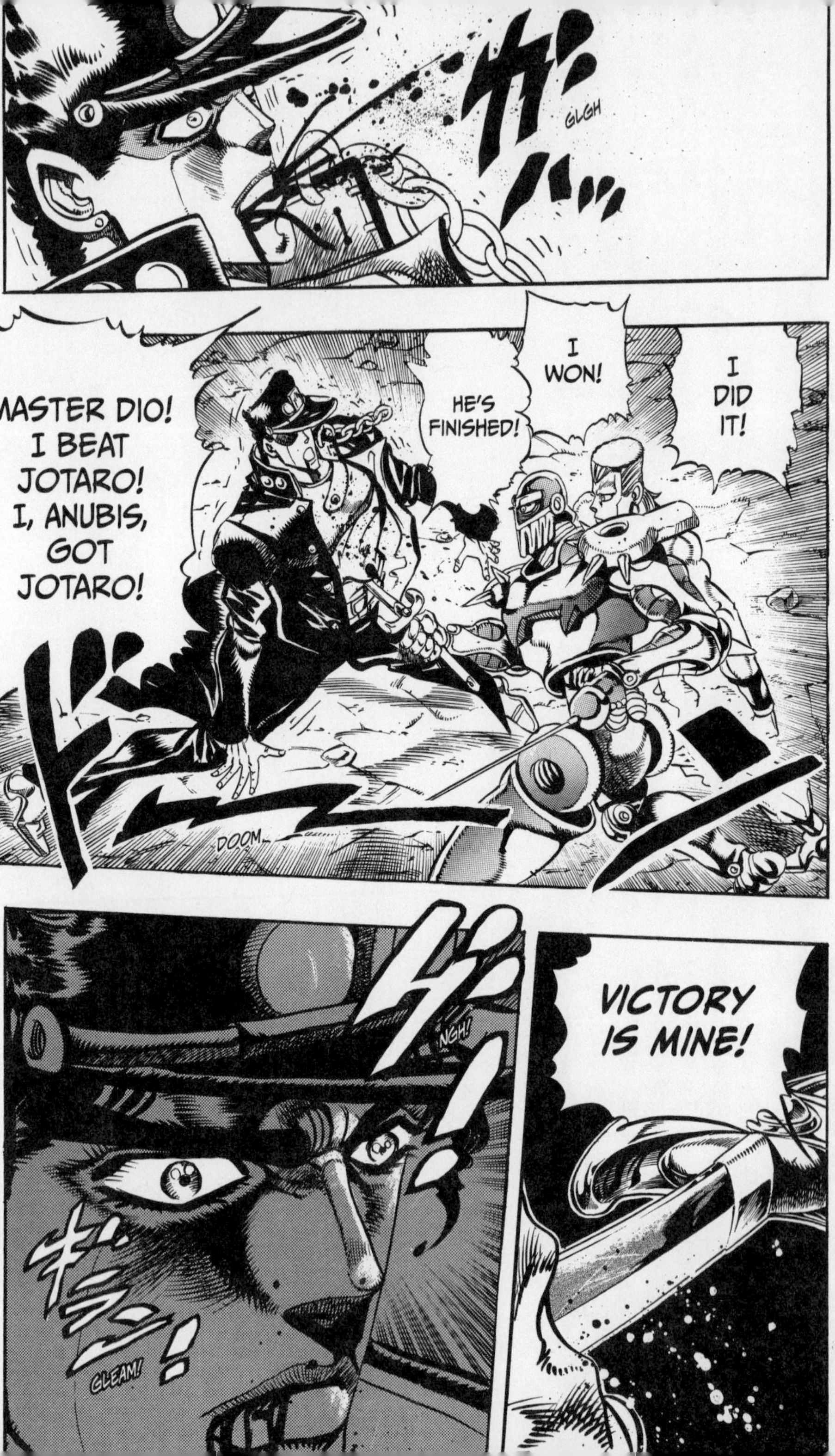
GLGH
I DID IT!
I WON!
HE'S FINISHED!
MASTER DIO! I BEAT JOTARO! I, ANUBIS, GOT JOTARO!
DOOM
VICTORY IS MINE!
NGH!
GLEAM!

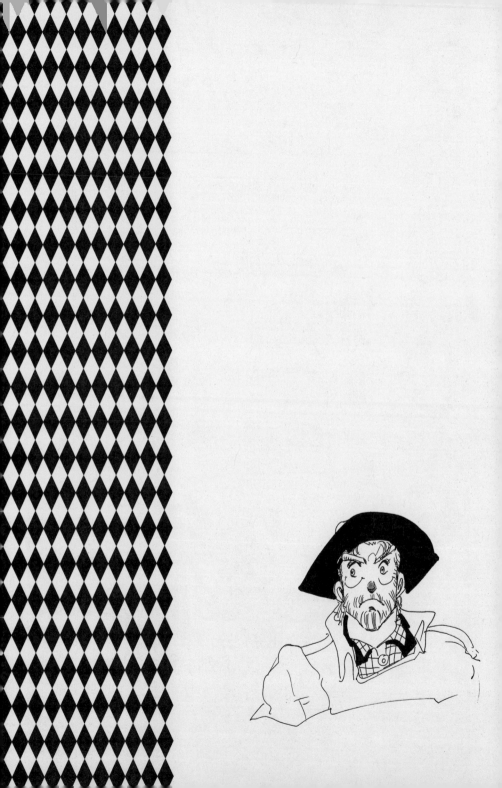

CHAPTER 85: Anubis PART 6

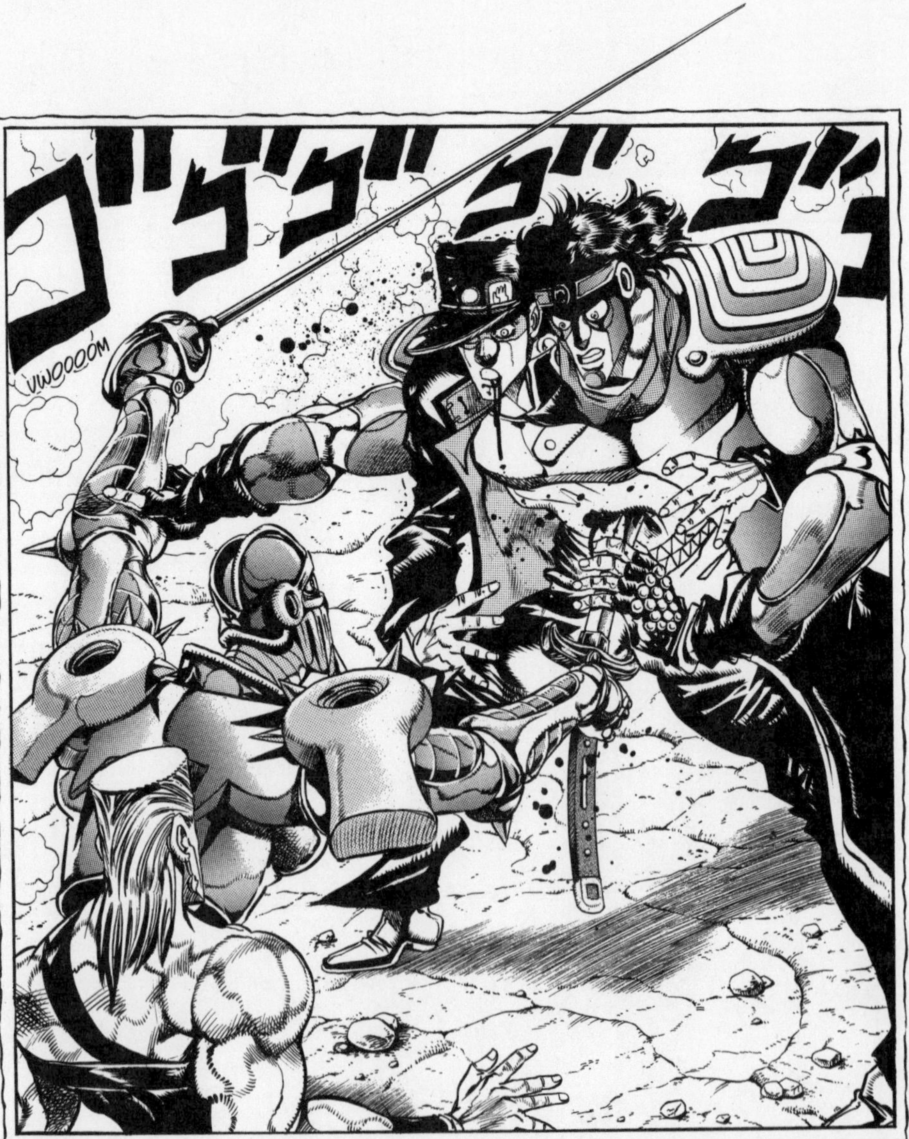
VWOOOOM

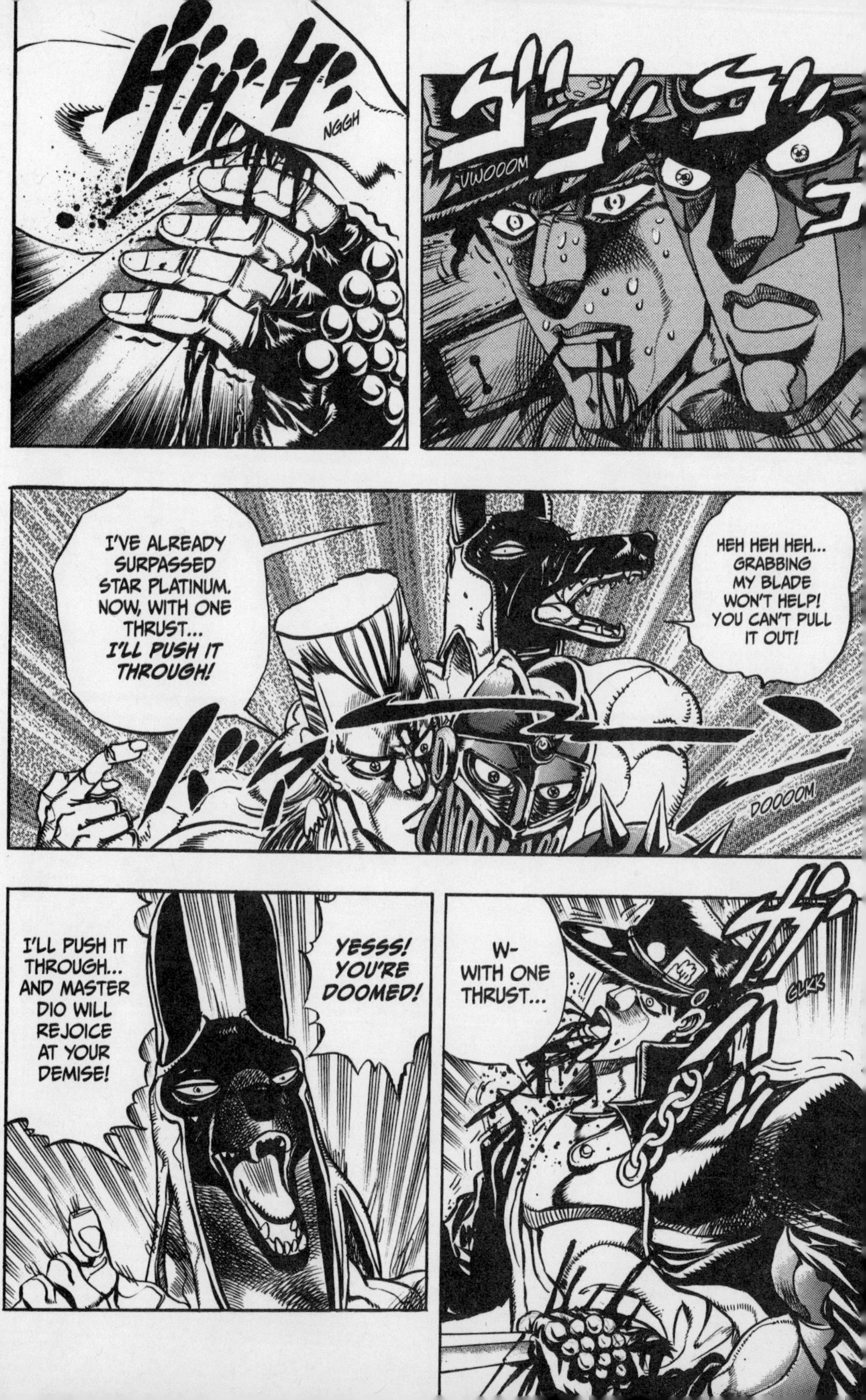
VWOOOM
NGGH
HEH HEH HEH... GRABBING MY BLADE WON'T HELP! YOU CAN'T PULL IT OUT!
I'VE ALREADY SURPASSED STAR PLATINUM. NOW, WITH ONE THRUST... I'LL PUSH IT THROUGH!
DOOOOM
W- WITH ONE THRUST...
CLKK
YESSS! YOU'RE DOOMED!
I'LL PUSH IT THROUGH... AND MASTER DIO WILL REJOICE AT YOUR DEMISE!

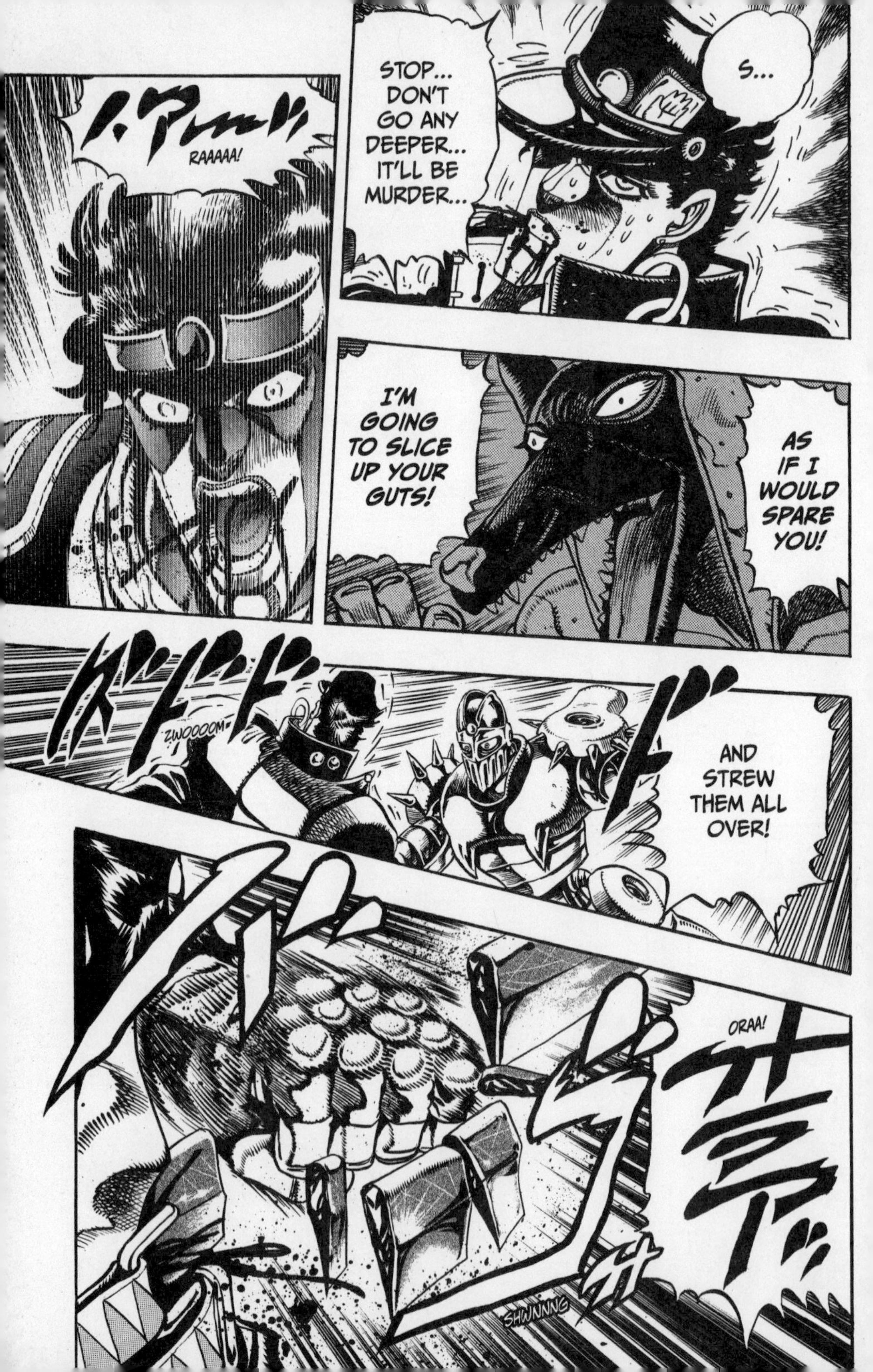
S...
STOP... DON'T GO ANY DEEPER... IT'LL BE MURDER...
AS IF I WOULD SPARE YOU!
I'M GOING TO SLICE UP YOUR GUTS!
RAAAAA!
AND STREW THEM ALL OVER!
ZWOOOOM
ORAA!
SHWNNNG

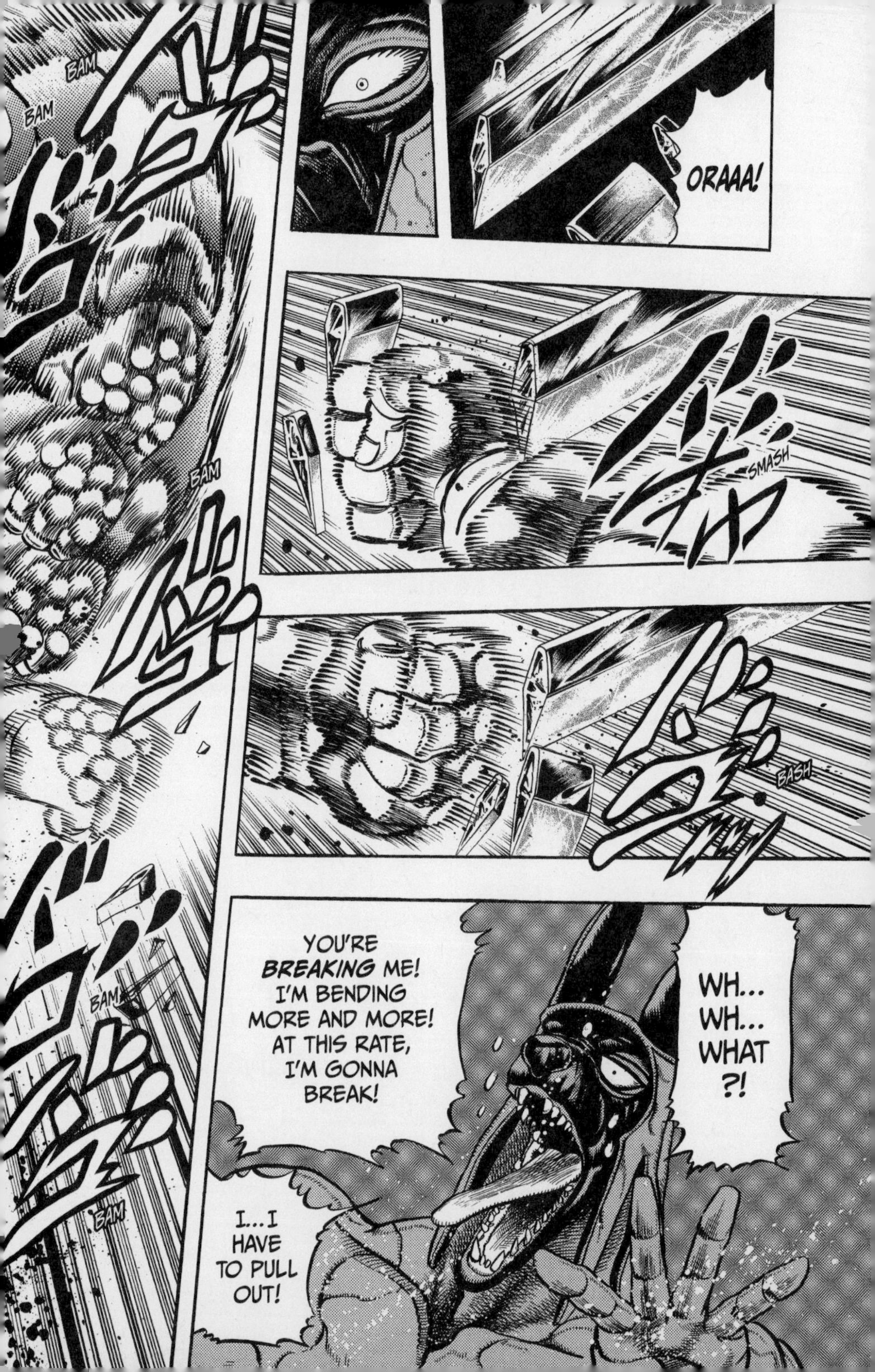
ORAAA!
SMASH
BASH
WH... WH... WHAT?!
YOU'RE *BREAKING* ME! I'M BENDING MORE AND MORE! AT THIS RATE, I'M GONNA BREAK!
I...I HAVE TO PULL OUT!
BAM
BAM
BAM
BAM
BAM

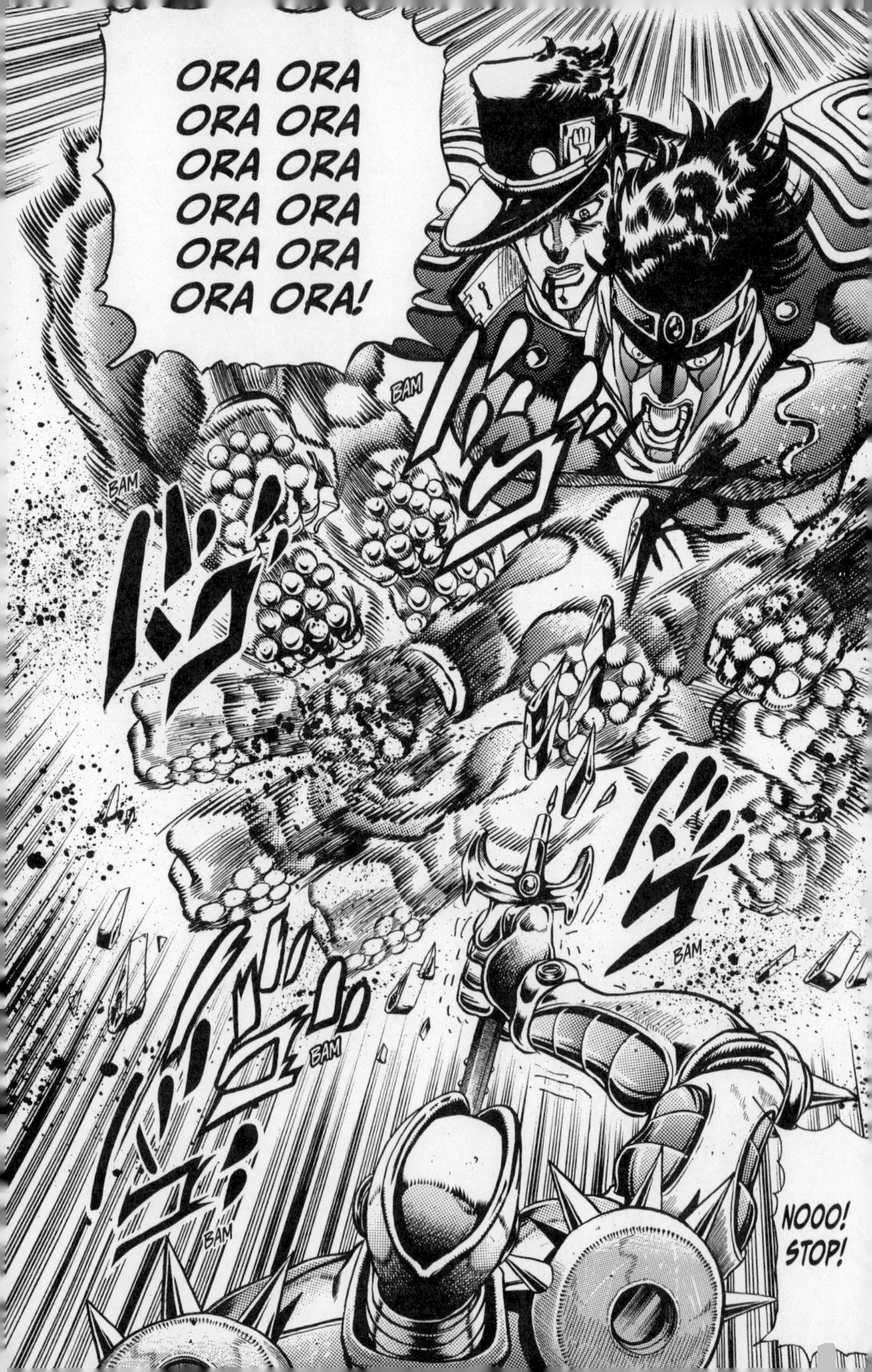
ORA ORA ORA ORA ORA ORA ORA ORA ORA ORA ORA ORA ORA ORA ORA ORA ORA ORA ORA ORA ORA ORA ORA ORA ORA ORA ORA ORA ORA ORA ORA ORA ORA ORA ORA ORA ORA ORA ORA ORA ORA ORA ORA ORA ORA ORA ORA ORA ORA ORA ORA ORA ORA ORA ORA ORA ORA ORA ORA ORA ORA ORA!
BAM
BAM
BAM
BAM
NOOO! STOP!
BAM

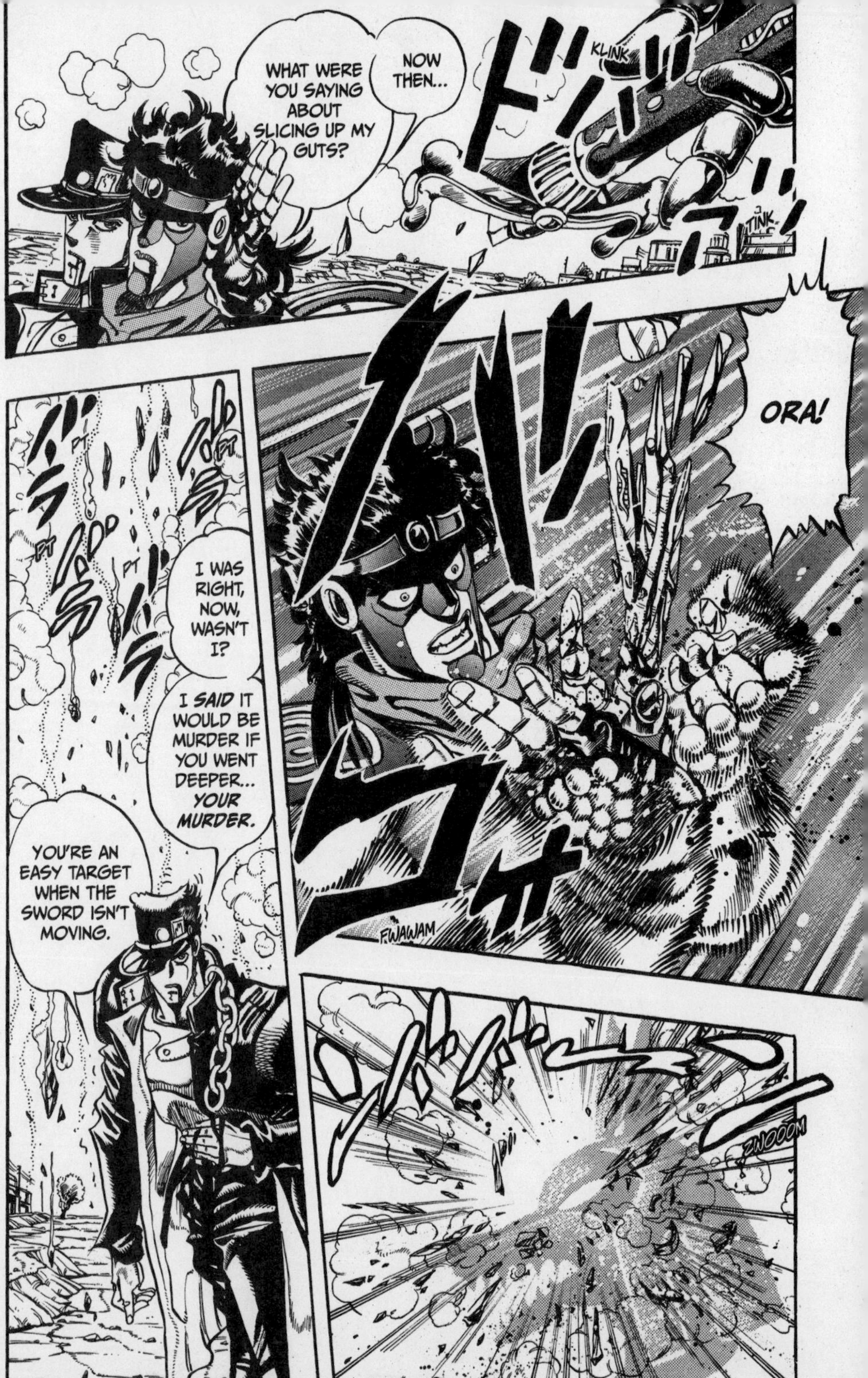
KLINK
NOW THEN...
WHAT WERE YOU SAYING ABOUT SLICING UP MY GUTS?
TINK
ORA!
FWAWAM
ZWOOOM
PT
PT
PT
PT
I WAS RIGHT, NOW, WASN'T I?
I *SAID* IT WOULD BE MURDER IF YOU WENT DEEPER... ***YOUR MURDER.***
YOU'RE AN EASY TARGET WHEN THE SWORD ISN'T MOVING.

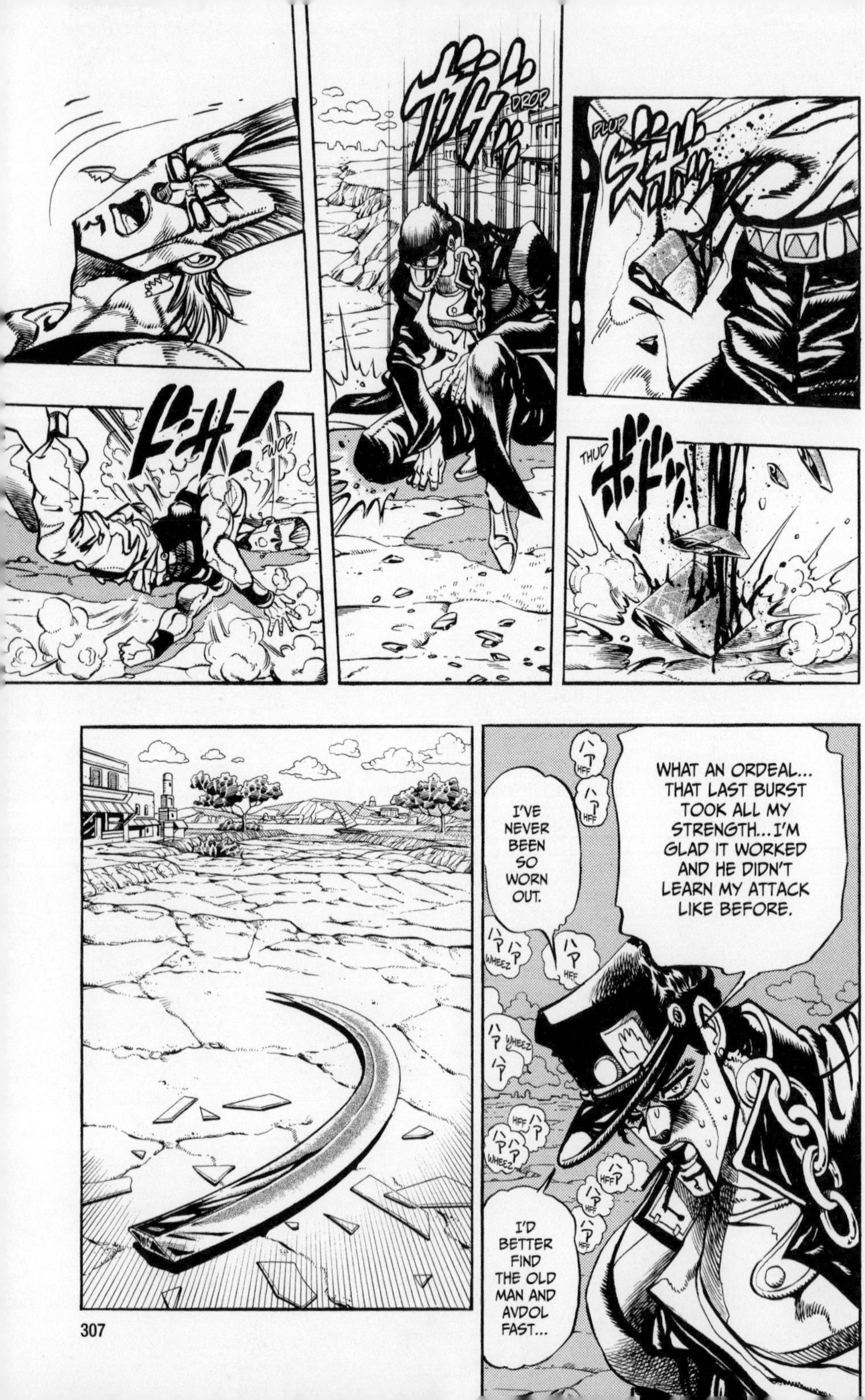
PLUP
THUD
DROP
FWOP!
WHAT AN ORDEAL... THAT LAST BURST TOOK ALL MY STRENGTH...I'M GLAD IT WORKED AND HE DIDN'T LEARN MY ATTACK LIKE BEFORE.
I'VE NEVER BEEN SO WORN OUT.
HFF
WHEEZ
I'D BETTER FIND THE OLD MAN AND AVDOL FAST...

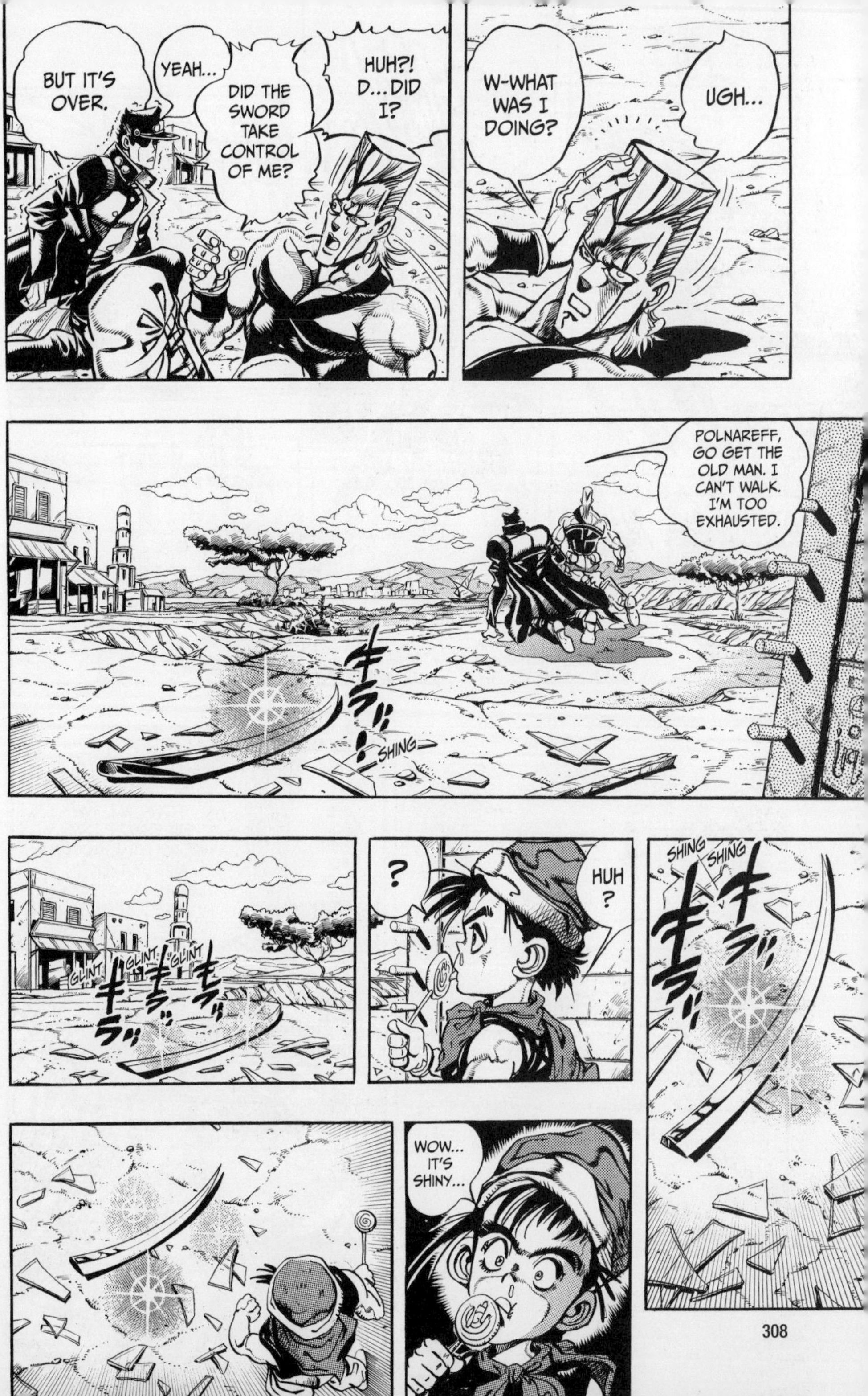
UGH...
W-WHAT WAS I DOING?
HUH?! D...DID I?
DID THE SWORD TAKE CONTROL OF ME?
YEAH...
BUT IT'S OVER.
POLNAREFF, GO GET THE OLD MAN. I CAN'T WALK. I'M TOO EXHAUSTED.
SHING
SHING
SHING
HUH ?
?
GLINT
GLINT
GLINT
WOW... IT'S SHINY...

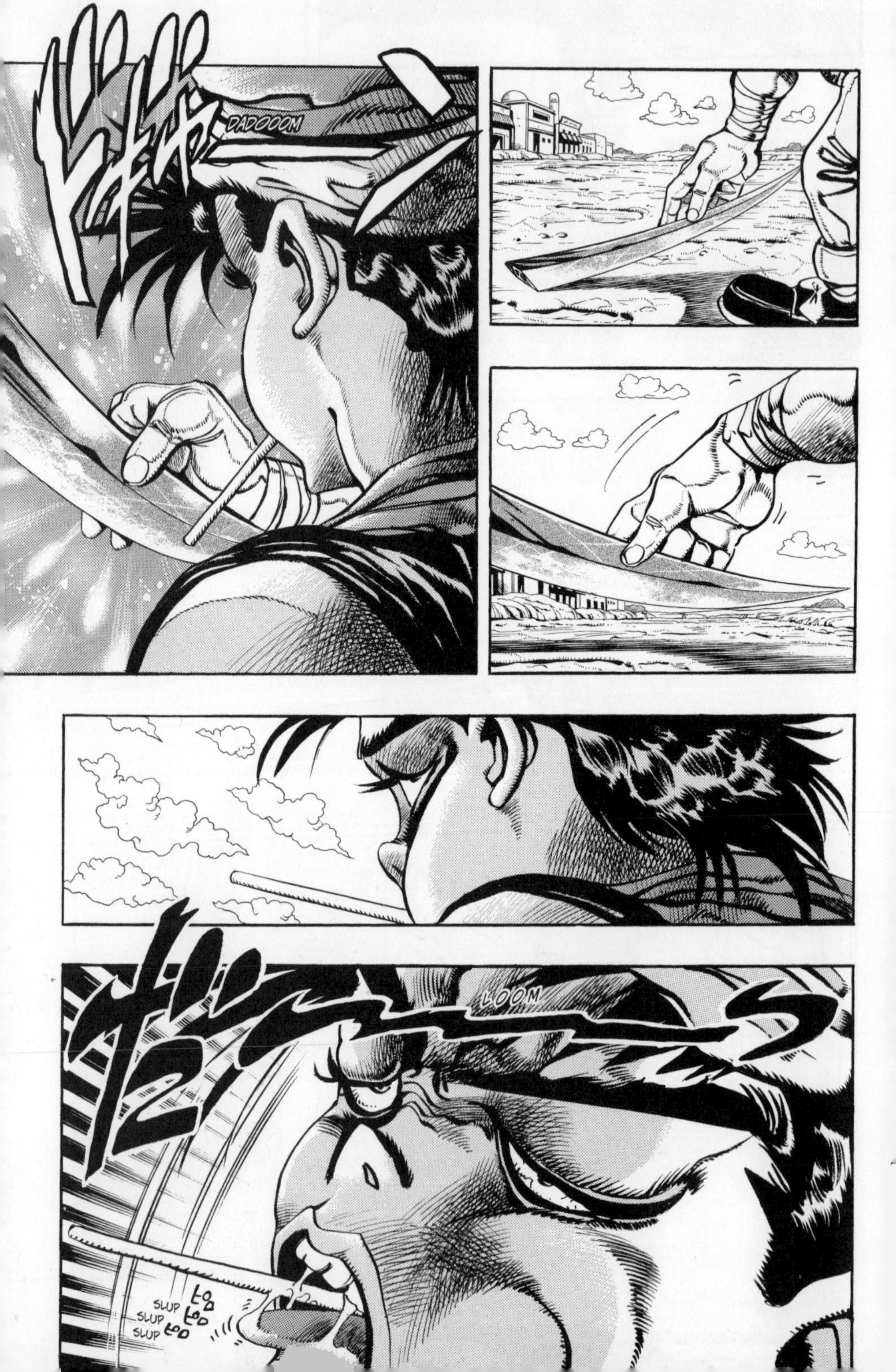
DADOOOM
LOOM
SLUP
SLUP
SLUP

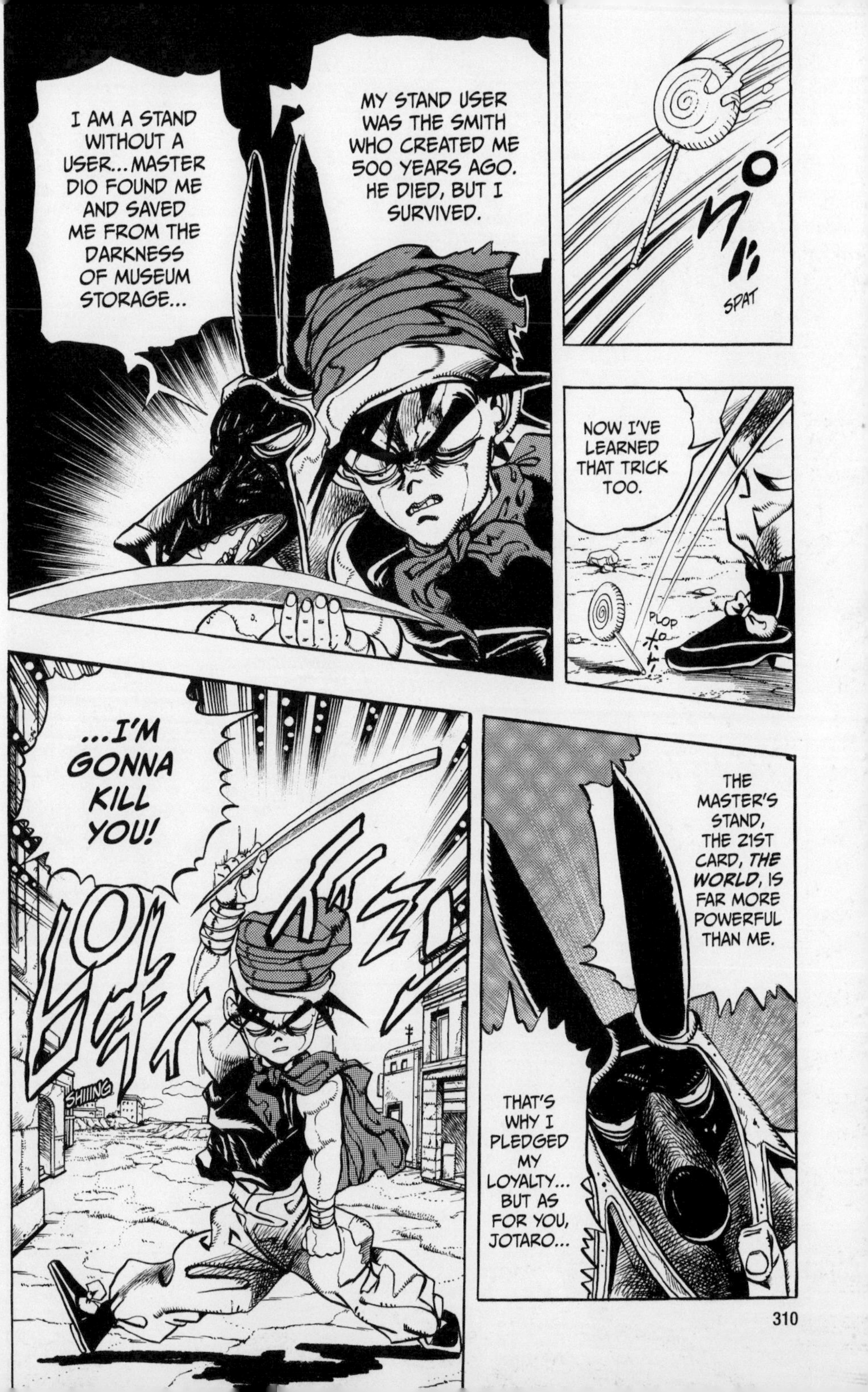
SPAT
NOW I'VE LEARNED THAT TRICK TOO.
PLOP
MY STAND USER WAS THE SMITH WHO CREATED ME 500 YEARS AGO. HE DIED, BUT I SURVIVED.
I AM A STAND WITHOUT A USER...MASTER DIO FOUND ME AND SAVED ME FROM THE DARKNESS OF MUSEUM STORAGE...
THE MASTER'S STAND, THE 21ST CARD, *THE WORLD*, IS FAR MORE POWERFUL THAN ME.
THAT'S WHY I PLEDGED MY LOYALTY... BUT AS FOR YOU, JOTARO...
...I'M GONNA KILL YOU!
SHIIING

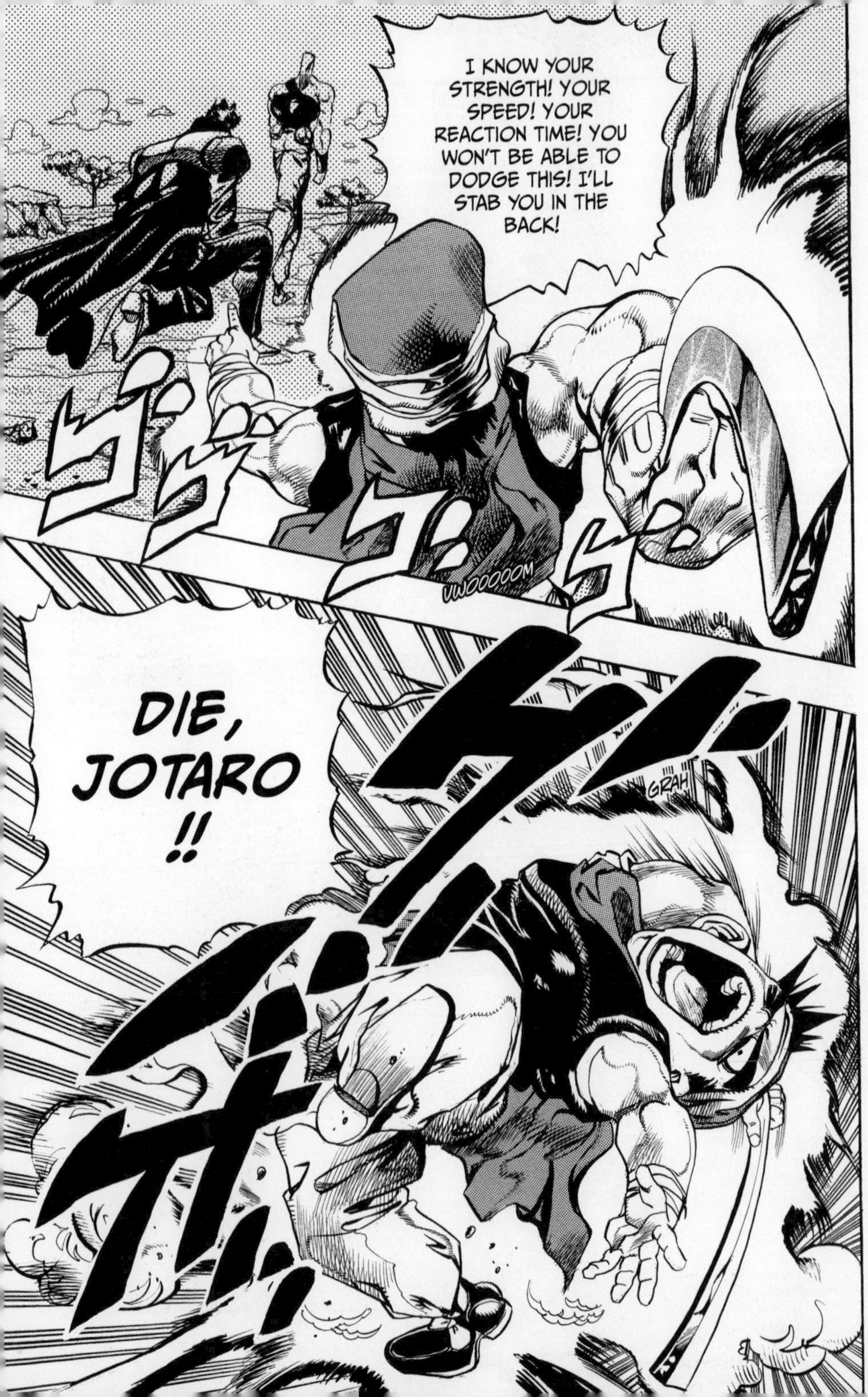
I KNOW YOUR STRENGTH! YOUR SPEED! YOUR REACTION TIME! YOU WON'T BE ABLE TO DODGE THIS! I'LL STAB YOU IN THE BACK!
UWOOOOOM
DIE, JOTARO !!
GRAH

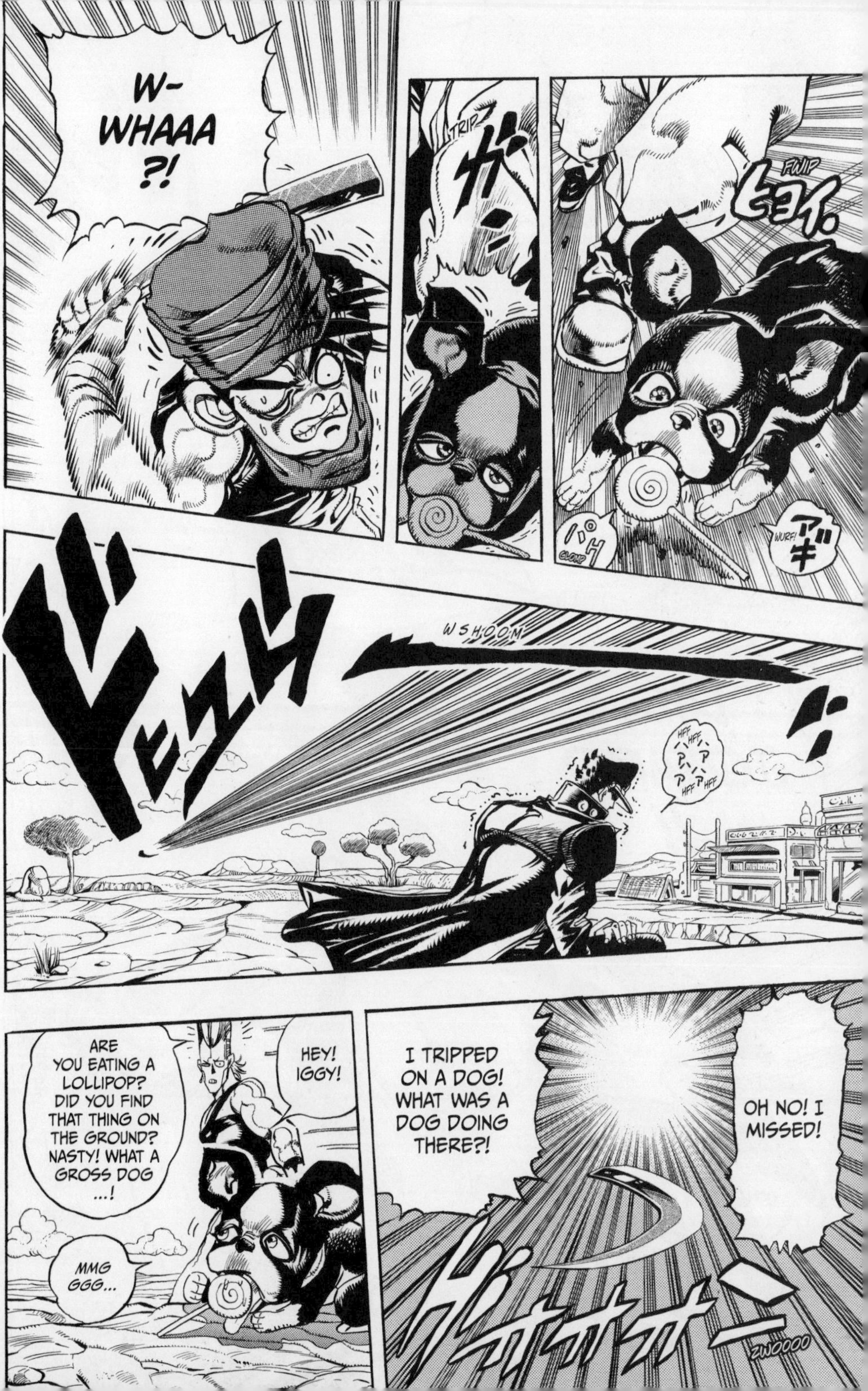
FWIP
WURF!
TRIP
CLOMP
W-WHAAA?!
WSHOOM
HFF HFF HFF HFF
OH NO! I MISSED!
I TRIPPED ON A DOG! WHAT WAS A DOG DOING THERE?!
ZWOOOO
HEY! IGGY!
ARE YOU EATING A LOLLIPOP? DID YOU FIND THAT THING ON THE GROUND? NASTY! WHAT A GROSS DOG ...!
MMG GGG...

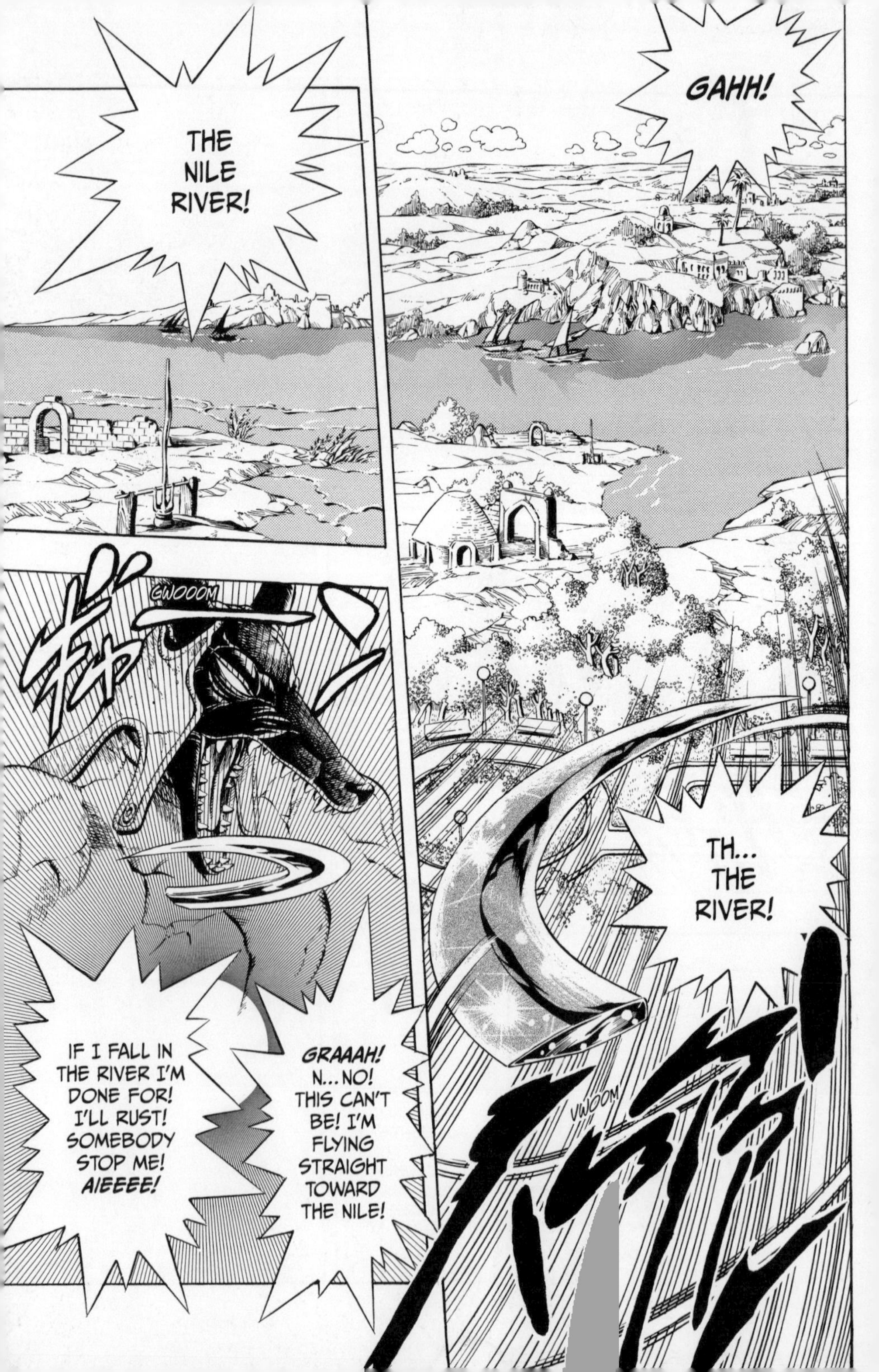
GAHH!
TH... THE RIVER!
VWOOM
THE NILE RIVER!
GWOOOM
GRAAAH! N...NO! THIS CAN'T BE! I'M FLYING STRAIGHT TOWARD THE NILE!
IF I FALL IN THE RIVER I'M DONE FOR! I'LL RUST! SOMEBODY STOP ME! AIEEEE!

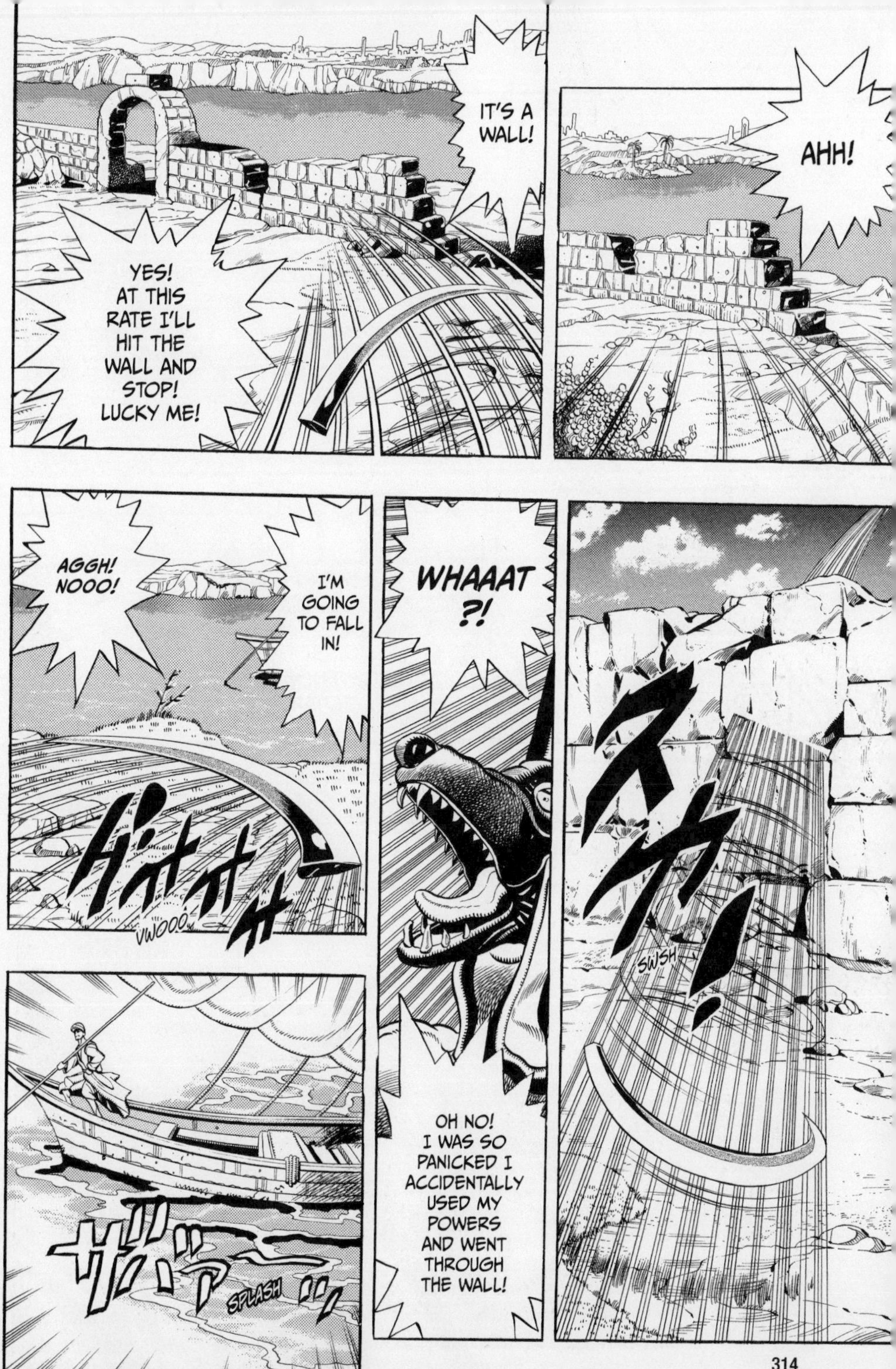
AHH!
IT'S A WALL!
YES! AT THIS RATE I'LL HIT THE WALL AND STOP! LUCKY ME!
SWSH
WHAAAT ?!
OH NO! I WAS SO PANICKED I ACCIDENTALLY USED MY POWERS AND WENT THROUGH THE WALL!
I'M GOING TO FALL IN!
AGGH! NOOO!
VWOOO
SPLASH

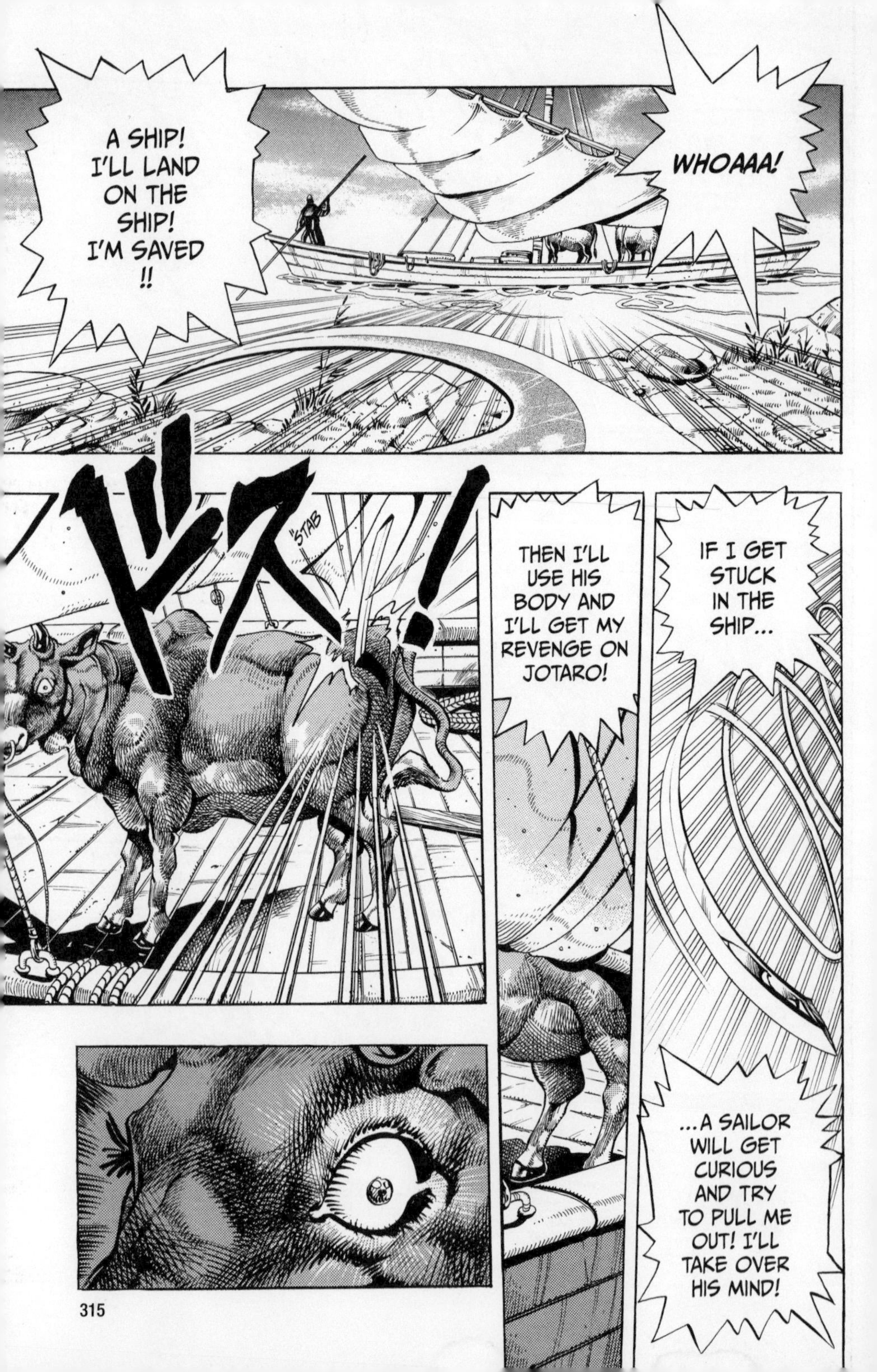
WHOAAA!
A SHIP! I'LL LAND ON THE SHIP! I'M SAVED !!
IF I GET STUCK IN THE SHIP...
...A SAILOR WILL GET CURIOUS AND TRY TO PULL ME OUT! I'LL TAKE OVER HIS MIND!
THEN I'LL USE HIS BODY AND I'LL GET MY REVENGE ON JOTARO!
STAB

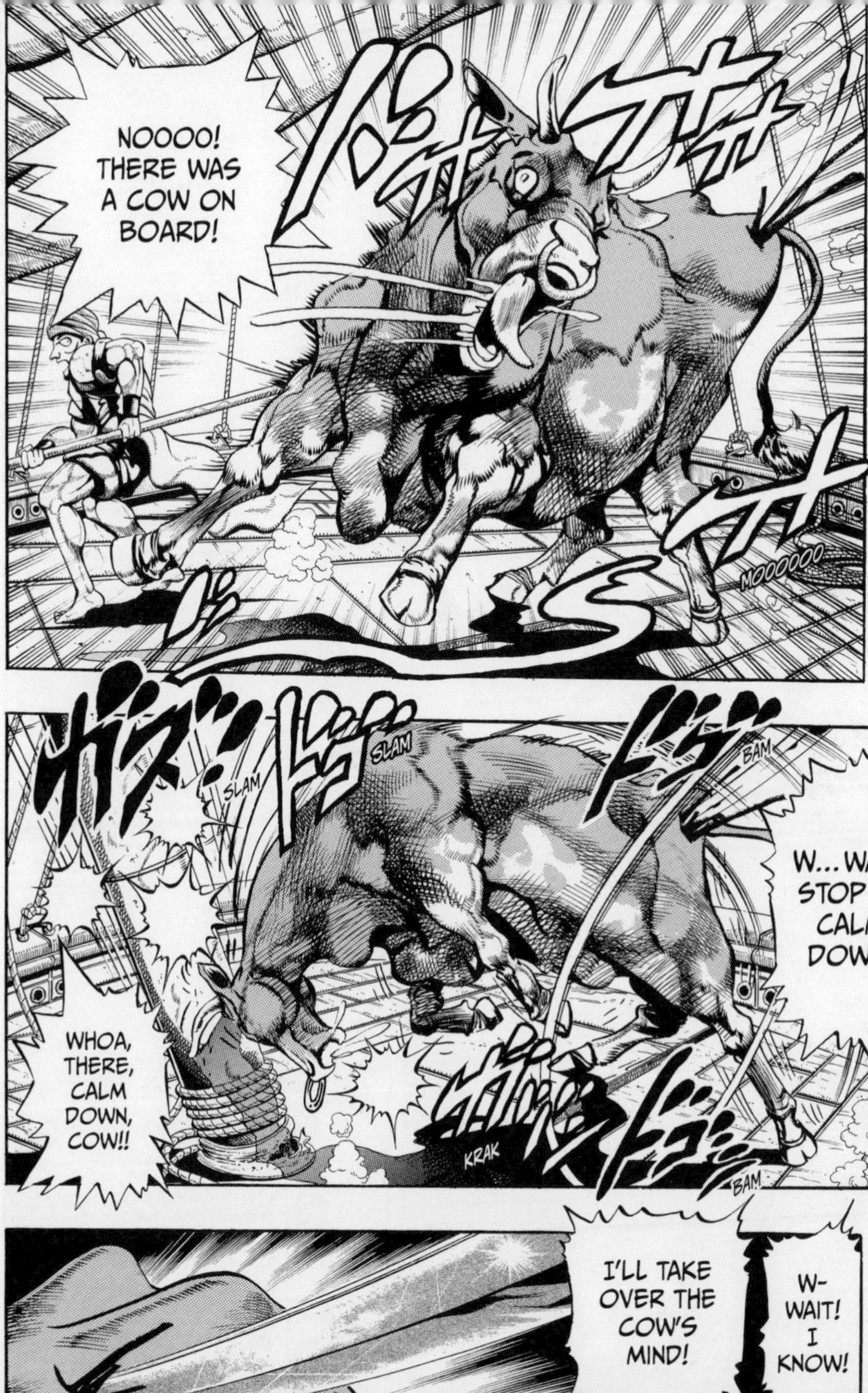
NOOOO! THERE WAS A COW ON BOARD!
MOOOOOO
BAM
SLAM
SLAM
W...WAIT! STOP IT! CALM DOWN!
WHOA, THERE, CALM DOWN, COW!!
KRAK
BAM
W-WAIT! I KNOW!
I'LL TAKE OVER THE COW'S MIND!

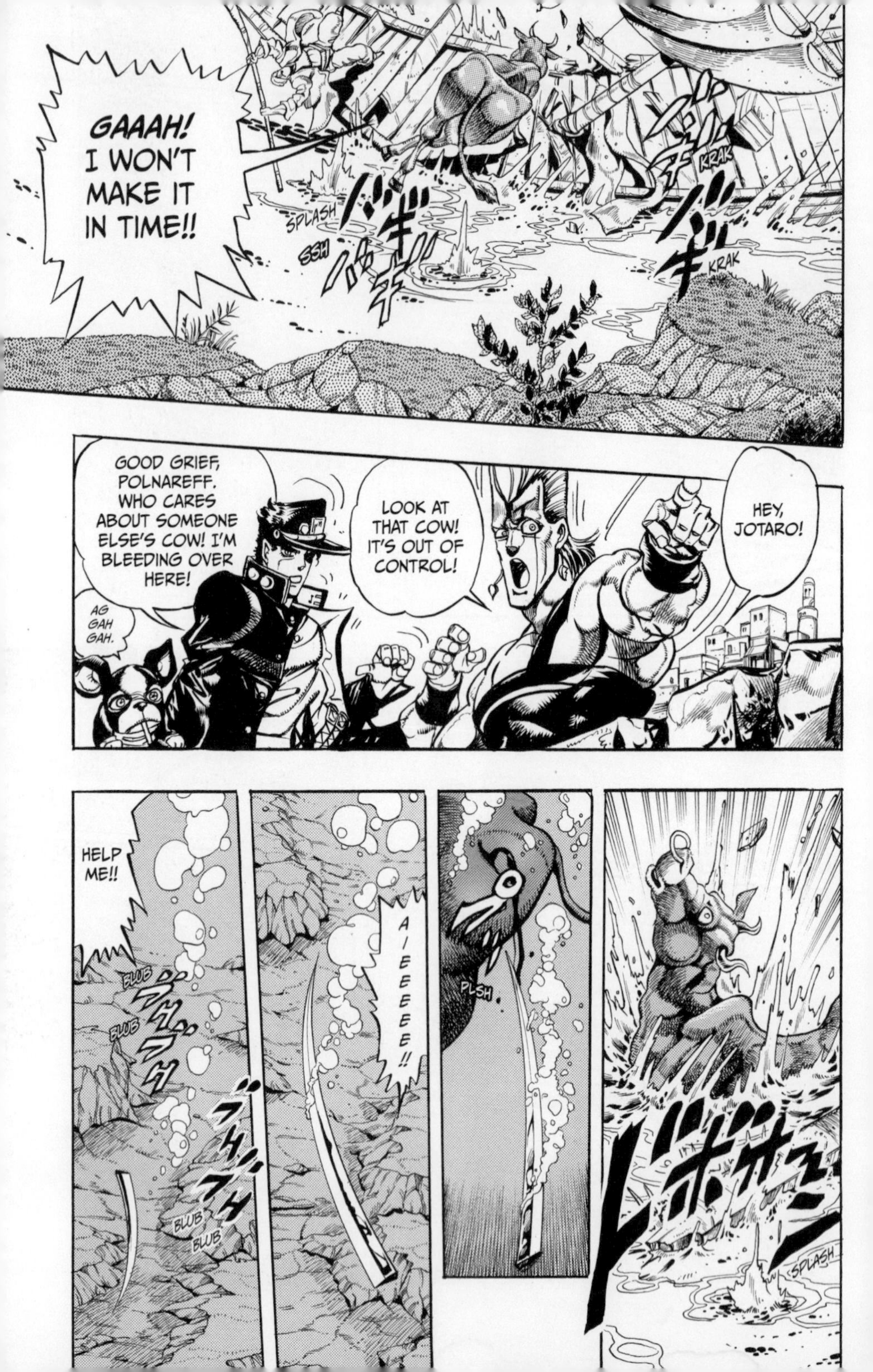
KRAK
KRAK
GAAAH! I WON'T MAKE IT IN TIME!!
SPLASH
SSH
HEY, JOTARO!
LOOK AT THAT COW! IT'S OUT OF CONTROL!
GOOD GRIEF, POLNAREFF. WHO CARES ABOUT SOMEONE ELSE'S COW! I'M BLEEDING OVER HERE!
AG GAH GAH.
SPLASH
PLSH
AIEEEEE!!
HELP ME!!
BLUB
BLUB
BLUB
BLUB

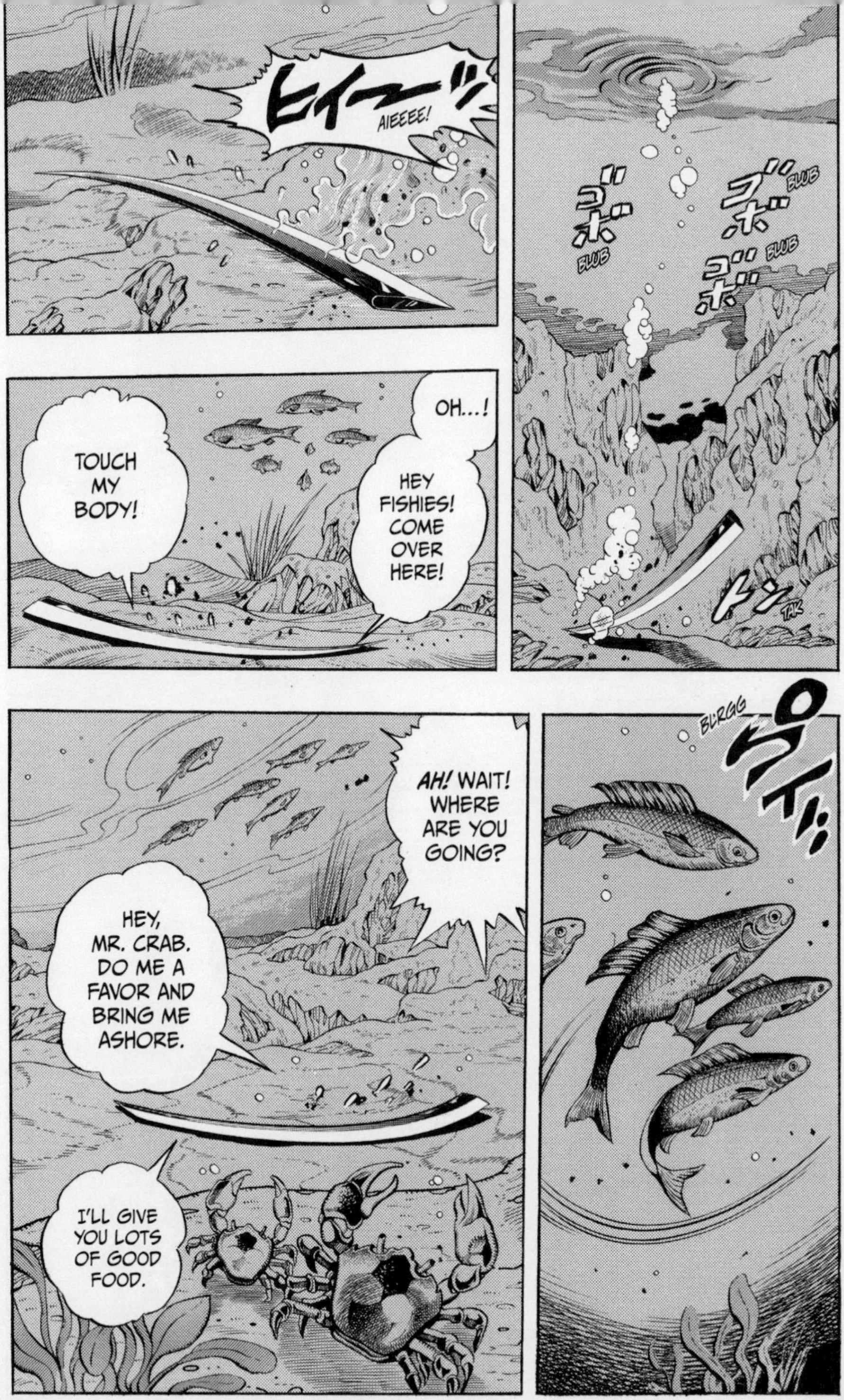
ゴボ
BLUB
ゴボ
BLUB
ゴボ
BLUB
トン
TAK
ヒイーッ
AIEEEE!
OH...!
HEY FISHIES! COME OVER HERE!
TOUCH MY BODY!
BURGG
AH! WAIT! WHERE ARE YOU GOING?
HEY, MR. CRAB. DO ME A FAVOR AND BRING ME ASHORE.
I'LL GIVE YOU LOTS OF GOOD FOOD.

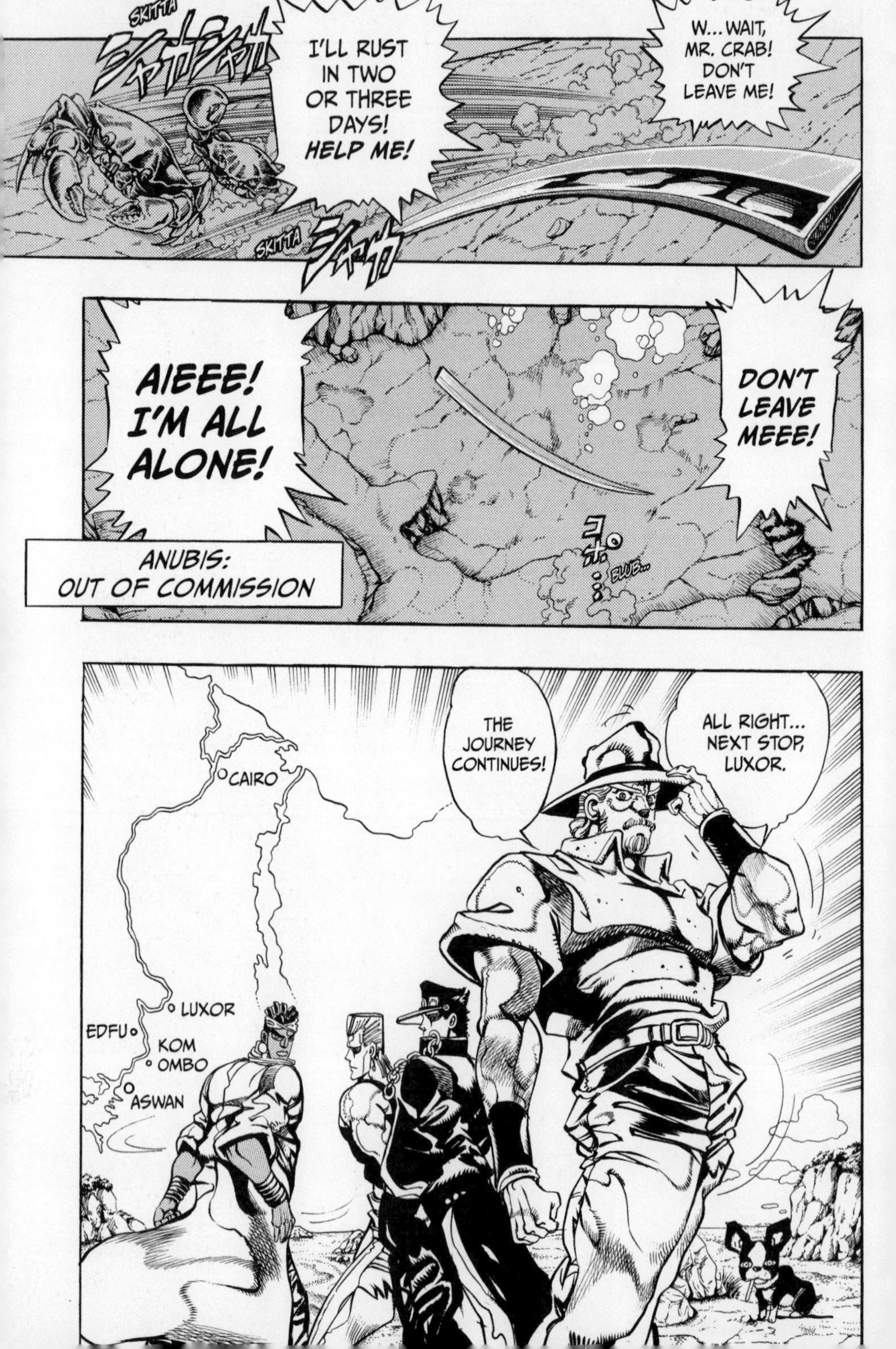
W... WAIT, MR. CRAB! DON'T LEAVE ME!
I'LL RUST IN TWO OR THREE DAYS! HELP ME!
SKITTA
SKITTA
DON'T LEAVE MEEE!
AIEEE! I'M ALL ALONE!
BLUB...
ANUBIS: OUT OF COMMISSION
ALL RIGHT... NEXT STOP, LUXOR.
THE JOURNEY CONTINUES!
CAIRO
LUXOR
EDFU
KOM OMBO
ASWAN

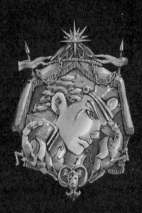

JoJo's
BIZARRE ADVENTURE

06
END

← To Be Continued

JoJo's BIZARRE ADVENTURE

06

AV

荒木飛呂彦が語るキャラクター誕生秘話

Hirohiko Araki talks about character creation!

JoJo's BIZARRE ADVENTURE
PART 3
STARDUST CRUSADERS

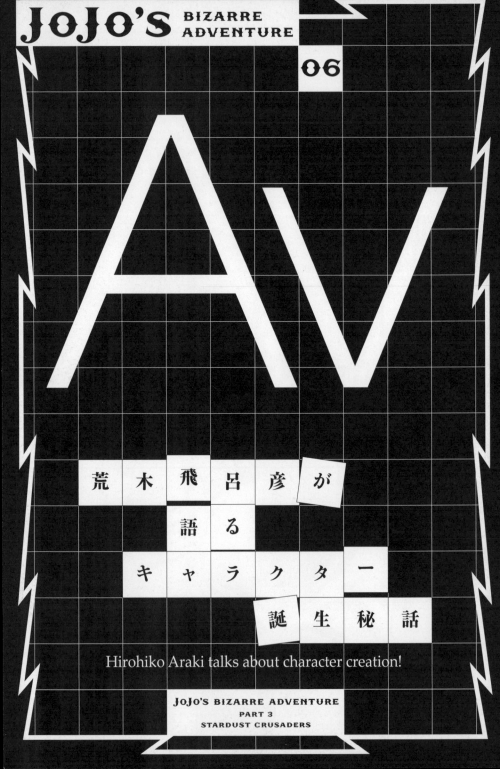

Avdol

06

"MAGICIAN'S RED WAS TOO STRONG FOR ENEMIES, AND THE CREATOR (LAUGHS)"

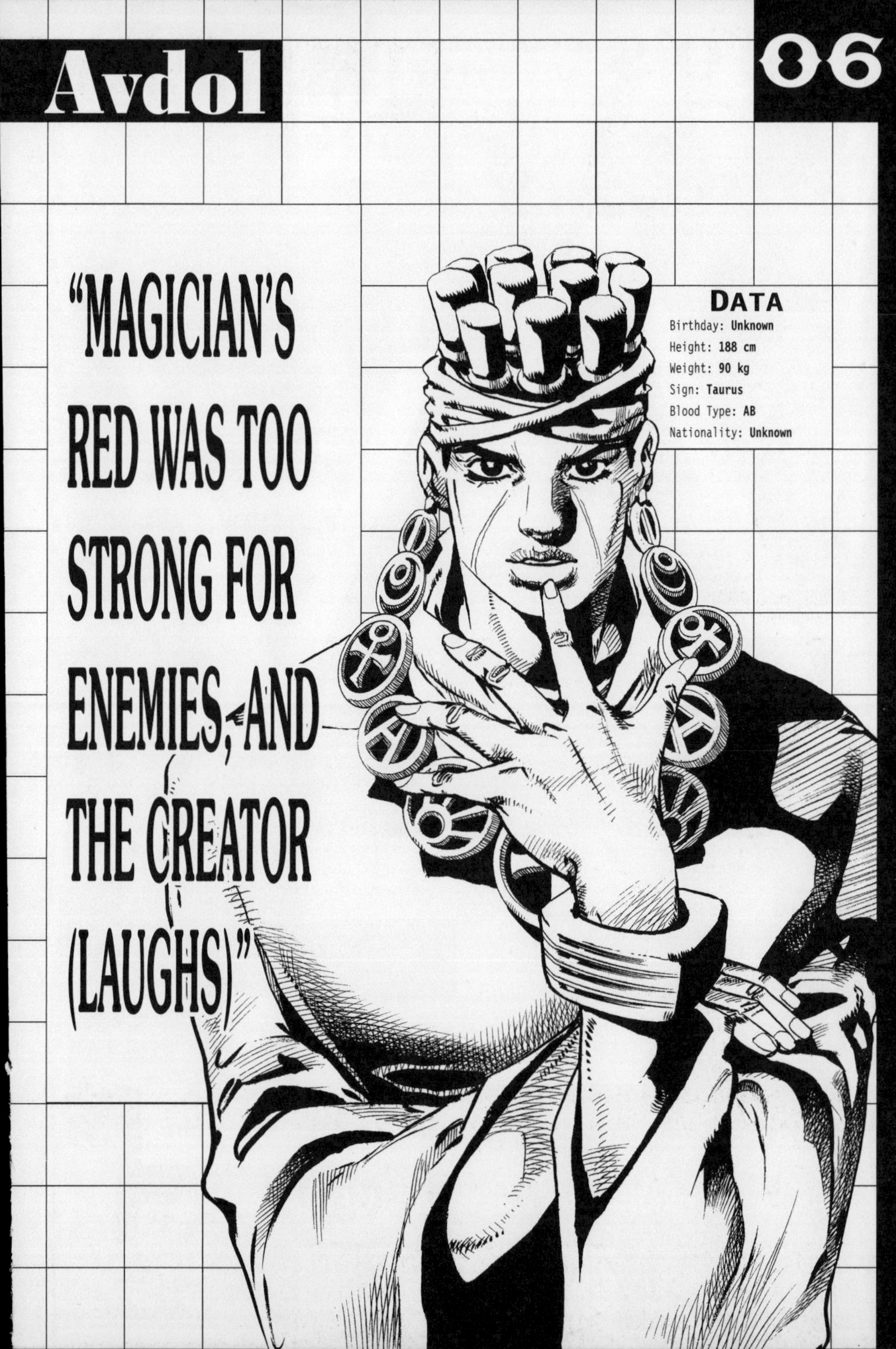

DATA

Birthday: **Unknown**
Height: **188 cm**
Weight: **90 kg**
Sign: **Taurus**
Blood Type: **AB**
Nationality: **Unknown**

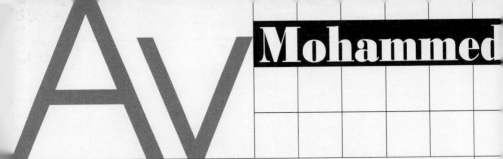

AV

Mohammed

Mohammed Avdol…If I had to nail down what role I was giving him as a member of the Joestar party, he would be the "subleader." Not only does he function as the navigator brought in by Joseph, the second JoJo, but given his steadfast determination--which is able to bring such a unique group together--and his unyielding sense of duty, I wanted him to be that member of the group who everyone could rely on. Within the story, he is also able to back up Joseph's story about DIO's revival when he tells it to Jotaro. I wanted to give him some sort of connection to Egypt, where DIO was in hiding, so I gave him his "ethnic" design. When Part 3 was originally being serialized, I, as well as the readership at large, had a strong interest in areas you could label the "birthplaces of civilization," so you could say that Avdol's design was a product of the times.

I put him out of commission for a while when the party was in India. I did that because I never want readers to get bored or complacent with the events taking place, so I wanted to inject a little reality in there with having someone get sacrificed every once in a while. I also was enamored with writing chapters where an ally is lost. But in the end, as you know, I wasn't planning on keeping him gone for long… The thing is, I thought it was kind of lame to have someone who died just come back to life immediately, so I wanted to come up with a good reason, as well as an appropriate setting to reintroduce him. When I'm working on *JoJo*, I try not to sweat the small things. In the end, I brought him back just before the party got to Egypt, but at the time, I didn't have any specific plans as to when I would bring him back. I just wrote what felt natural to me at the time.

Looking back on it now, I probably should have given Avdol a section where he played more of a primary role in the story, especially given the fact that I took him out of commission for a while. Of course, this is all in hindsight after having finished the story. At the time Part 3 was in serialization, it might have been quite an "adventure" to have the story focus on Avdol (laughs wryly). If we had a character popularity poll at the time, I doubt he would have ranked at the top. All the readership wanted was more battles featuring Jotaro. On top of that, his Stand, Magician's Red, was difficult to draw. The ability to control fire is a pretty common thing in manga, as well as movies, but in the end, they just burn things up and that's about it. If you play it too loose, as an ability, it can break the power balance. After writing *JoJo*, I think "fire" and "poison" are two abilities that I'm okay with putting behind lock and key.

If I were to write a portion of the story centering on Avdol, I think it would have been an origin story featuring his family--in particular, his relationship with his father. It might end up being a bit too mature of a story for *Weekly Shonen Jump* (laughs).

The story behind the new illustration for JoJo Part 3 06!

Q. Did Avdol get younger?!

Hirohiko Araki

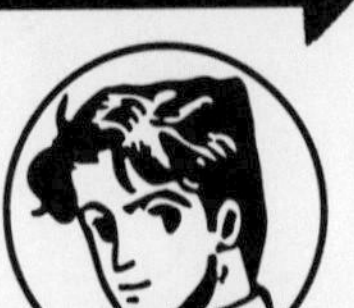

A. He's actually supposed to be in his late twenties.

He's younger than you might expect! He may look as if he's older than that, but if you ask someone who's been in the army their age, it always surprises you

06

JoJo's Bizarre Adventure

PART 3 STARDUST CRUSADERS

BY

HIROHIKO ARAKI

SHONEN JUMP ADVANCED EDITION
Translation ☆ Mayumi Kobayashi
Editor ☆ Jason Thompson

DELUXE HARDCOVER EDITION
Translation ☆ Evan Galloway
Touch-Up Art & Lettering ☆ Mark McMurray
Design ☆ Izumi Evers
Editor ☆ Urian Brown

Original Japanese cover design by
MITSURU KOBAYASHI (GENI A LÒIDE)

The stories, characters and incidents mentioned
in this publication are entirely fictional.

Printed in the U.S.A.

Published by VIZ Media, LLC
P.O. Box 77010
San Francisco, CA 94107

10 9 8 7 6 5 4 3 2 1
First printing, February 2018

PARENTAL ADVISORY
JOJO'S BIZARRE ADVENTURE PART THREE STARDUST CRUSADERS
is rated T+ for Older Teen and is recommended for ages 16 and up.
This volume contains graphic violence and some mature themes.

www.viz.com

SHONEN JUMP
ADVANCED
www.shonenjump.com

JoJo's Bizarre Adventure
PART 3 STARDUST CRUSADERS

OH! GOD!

OH! GOD!

JO

THIS IS THE LAST PAGE

ドドド

JoJo's Bizarre Adventure
has been printed in the original
Japanese format in order to
preserve the orientation of the
original artwork.

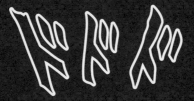